THE ORIGINS OF THE SOUTH AFRICAN WAR

ORIGINS OF MODERN WARS
General editor: *Harry Hearder*

THE ORIGINS OF THE SOUTH AFRICAN WAR, 1899–1902

Iain R. Smith

LONGMAN
London and New York

Longman Group Limited,
Longman House, Burnt Mill,
Harlow, Essex CM20 2JE, England
and Associated Companies throughout the world.

*Published in the United States of America
by Longman Publishing, New York*

First published 1996

ISBN 0 582 27777 9 CSD
ISBN 0 582 49520 2 PPR

British Library Cataloguing-in-Publication Data

A catalogue record for this book is
available from the British Library

Library of Congress Cataloging-in-Publication Data

Smith, Iain R.
   The origins of the South African War, 1899-1902 / Iain R. Smith.
      p.   cm. -- (Origins of modern wars)
   Includes bibliographical references and index.
   ISBN 0-582-27777-9. -- ISBN 0-582-49520-2 (pbk.)
   1. South African War, 1899-1902--Causes I. Title. II Series.
DT1894.S65   1996
968.04′81--dc20   95-15709
                                                                 CIP

Set by 7A in 10/12 Bembo
Produced by Longman Singapore Publishers (Pte) Ltd.
Printed in Singapore

Contents

Contents

Editor's Foreword

A study of a war in the age of imperialism introduces a new element in this series. Dr Iain Smith's masterly work, bringing a new interpretation and the results of fresh research in South African archives, is the thirteenth in the series, and the fifth in which Britain played a central role.

Whereas the great European powers partitioned Africa from 1880 to 1914 without going to war with each other, two peoples of European extraction, the British and the Boers, fought a bitter war over a country of great wealth, wealth which had been discovered in comparatively recent times. Africa, by its very size, had been able sufficiently to satisfy the appetites of the European great powers, without those countries going to war. But in South Africa the two Boer republics drew on different traditions to the two British colonies. Few societies could have been more different from each other than that of *fin de siècle* Britain and that of the Boers in the Transvaal.

Equally, the contrasting nature of the Transvaal Boers and the Uitlanders, so vividly described in this book, tempts one to say that conflict between them was inevitable. But Dr Smith shows that the presence of the Uitlanders was in itself less a cause of war than a justification used by the British to assert their control over the Transvaal. No single factor made war inevitable, and this series, by making detailed studies of crises leading to wars, is increasingly suggesting that war is never inevitable.

But unscrupulous men sometimes use arguments which may not seem to be contributing to a *casus belli,* but are couched in such terms that they have that effect. Thus Dr Smith shows that Milner, in December 1897, did not believe that the monopoly for the manufacture of dynamite granted to the Anglo-German Nobel Trust by Kruger's government was an issue with which governments should be concerned, but in January 1899 Milner believed that if the issue were 'judiciously worked into a general row, it would help not hurt us'. A 'row' is the kind of euphemism used by the ruling classes in the nineteenth century to make war seem like a quarrel in a prep school dormitory.

While no government can foresee the nature of the war on which they are embarking, and may even believe that 'it will be all over by Christmas', it is yet true that in crises leading to war there is almost always someone who believes that war would be a disaster. Thus Dr Smith records that the Permanent Under-Secretary at the Colonial Office, Sir Robert Meade, wrote in July 1894, 'Every nerve should be strained to prevent such a disgrace as another South African war'. And Sir Hercules Robinson, British High Commissioner in South Africa, threatened to resign after the Jameson Raid, in Dr Smith's words, 'if Britain persisted in a policy likely to lead to war'. In 1897 Robinson was simply replaced.

Dr Smith's Conclusion to this work gives a carefully argued answer to the question: 'Why did war come in 1899?' It is an answer which historians are unlikely easily to refute.

Harry Hearder

Preface

The South African War of 1899–1902 has attracted more attention than any other event in South African history. Recent writing about it, however, has seemed more at ease in dealing with the war itself than with its origins. This is perhaps a result of the transformation which has occurred in the study and writing of South African history during the past twenty-five years, when whole aspects of the area's past, which were previously neglected or ignored, have been opened up and many old topics have been re-cast within new frameworks of reference. A historiographical revolution took place ahead of the political transformation which has occurred during the 1990s. It was characterized by the coming into its own of the history of the African people, who form the overwhelming majority of the population of what has been, until very recently, a white-ruled land. Recent historians of South Africa have been primarily concerned to elucidate the complex economic and social history of the area, and they have moved away from political history (narrowly defined), and especially from the issues of *white* political history which so largely preoccupied earlier generations of South African historians. Like historians elsewhere, they have explored the history of ordinary people, as well as that of elites and policy-makers, and the result has been enormously enriching. What has been achieved in South African historiography has in turn been part of the wider process by which our knowledge of the history of the African continent has been transformed since the 1960s.

As many volumes in this series testify, the investigation into the *origins* of wars leads, sooner rather than later, to the study of elites and decision-makers. Situations of conflict may exist between peoples, but wars are declared by governments. In October 1899, war was resorted to by the British and Transvaal governments. Relations, and the reasons for the eventual breakdown of relations between these two governments must therefore form the core of this study. The South African War is a classic case of a war as Clausewitz defined it: for limited ends which could not be achieved by diplomacy. But the arcane world of diplomacy does not take place in a vacuum and it has been my purpose in this book to set the origins of this war in the growing conflict of interest between Britain and the British Empire, on the one hand, and the Boer elite ruling the Transvaal republic, under President Paul Kruger, on the other.[1] This war has also to be set in the context of the high noon of European imperialism on a global scale and the European scramble for Africa.

Controversy about the origins of this war has existed ever since it was fought and I hope that I have dealt clearly, in my Conclusion, with what that controversy has been about. Historians, however, have been in surprisingly broad agreement that Britain provoked the war and that the responsibility for bringing it about lies more with the British government than with that of the Transvaal. The government of President Paul Kruger was subjected to steadily increasing British pressure, intervention, demands and threats. It finally refused to capitulate, issued an ultimatum demanding an end to the build-up of British troops on the Transvaal's borders, and went to war essentially for reasons of self-defence. Afrikaner historians, such as J. H. Breytenbach and G. D. Scholtz have largely agreed, in this regard, with historians writing in English.[2] This consensus explains why historians have tended to concentrate on the British side in their analyses of the origins of this war. There is also the fact that the records on the British side are so much richer and more extensive, and in English.

The dominant tradition of writing about the origins of this war was first established by Leo Amery in 1900.[3] Here, the origins of the war were firmly located in a *political* conflict between the British and Transvaal *governments*. A separate but parallel body of writing developed out of the seminal work of J. A. Hobson, who also wrote a book about the origins of this war, published in 1900.[4] Where Amery provided a political explanation, Hobson propounded an *economic* explanation which, despite repeated attempts to rebut it, has exercised immense influence. During the 1950s, new government sources from both British and South African archives became available to historians and in 1961, J. S. Marais and R. Robinson and J. A. Gallagher published two classic works of historical scholarship which have been a challenge and an inspiration to all who have since followed in their footsteps, including myself.[5] Their findings have since been further explored, extended and qualified, but their approach, of looking at the war through the eyes and records of government officials and decision-makers – 'the official mind' – has remained essentially the same.[6]

Since 1961, the opening of the archives of some of the key institutions with an economic stake in South Africa in the 1890s – including those of the most important gold-mining companies, the Chamber of Mines, the Standard Bank, and the Bank of England – and the use of British Treasury and War Office records by a number of British historians and Ph.D. students, have subjected previously neglected or inaccessible sources for the subject to professional scrutiny. When I embarked upon this book, my objective was to provide a clear and dispassionate synthesis out of the vast amount of work, old and new, which has already been done by other people. That, I knew, was what would be of most value to the countless students who grapple with this fascinating but complicated subject. Very soon, however, I realized the necessity for very considerable primary research by myself in the relevant British and South African archives. This has delayed the completion of the book but it has, I believe, made it a much better one. The result is therefore a synthesis which embodies a very great deal of original research and utilizes new material as well as old in what I hope is a clear and accessible way.

NOTES

1. The official name of the state (1852–77 and 1884–1900) was the South African Republic, but it was frequently referred to as 'the Transvaal' or 'the Transvaal republic' so, throughout this book, I have used all three of these terms interchangeably.

2. J. H. Breytenbach, *Die geskiedenis van die Tweede Vryheidsoorlog in Suid–Afrika, 1899–1902.* 5 vols, Pretoria 1969–83; G. D. Scholtz, *Die oorsake van die Tweede Vryheidsoorlog, 1899–1902.* 2 vols, Johannesburg 1948–50.

3. L. S. Amery, *The Times History of the War in South Africa.* 7 vols, London 1900–1909, especially vol. 1.

4. J. A. Hobson, *The War in South Africa: Its Causes and Effects.* London 1900.

5. J. S. Marais, *The Fall of Kruger's Republic.* Oxford 1961; R. Robinson & J. A. Gallagher, *Africa and the Victorians: the Official Mind of Imperialism.* London 1961/1981.

6. G. H. Le May, *British Supremacy in South Africa 1899–1907.* Oxford 1965; L. Thompson, 'Great Britain and the Afrikaner Republics' in

L. Thompson & M. Wilson, eds, *The Oxford History of South Africa*. 2 vols, Oxford 1969/1971, 2, Chapter vi; A. N. Porter, *The Origins of the South African War, Joseph Chamberlain and the Diplomacy of Imperialism 1895–99*. Manchester 1980.

Acknowledgements

This book has been long in the making. The seed for it was sown in the late 1960s when I was one of the 'kindergarten' of post-graduate students who learned much from Jack Gallagher during his sojourn at Oxford as the Beit Professor. Christopher Saunders and Deryck Schreuder were also there at that time and our lively discussions spilled over from the Friday afternoon seminars to which Jack Gallagher brought his animating presence and sceptical eye. There, we pitted our wits against and subjected our research papers to the steely intellect of David Fieldhouse and the probing questions of Colin Newbury and were occasionally visited and challenged by Margery Perham and W. M. Macmillan – who appeared to some of us as living embodiments of the history which we were seeking to understand through books and documents.

At that time I was preoccupied with another part of Africa, where I had lived and worked for two years during that heady period just after independence. I had, however, spent a month in South Africa in 1964 and begun to read about its past. For a decade and a half thereafter my attention was elsewhere. During the 1980s, however, I returned to South African history, which had meanwhile undergone a transformation. I owe a great deal to four institutions which then nourished my interest. First, the University of Warwick, for its generous leave provisions and for the many students who chose to take my final-year Special Subject on South African history and challenged and stimulated me in our weekly classes for the best part of a decade. Then the Institute of Commonwealth Studies in London, where I spent a term as a Visiting Research Associate in 1987 and where, for over twenty years, the seminar in the history of southern Africa organized by Professor Shula Marks has been of seminal importance in the education of so many of us with regard to that part of the world. The History Departments at two South African universities also contributed enormously to my progress during three visits to South Africa between 1987 and 1993. In 1989 I spent a term as a Visiting Lecturer at the University of Cape Town and learned a great deal from the staff and students there. In 1993, I spent several weeks as a member of the History Department at the University of Pretoria, at the invitation of Professor Fransjohan Pretorius. There too I benefited greatly from discussion with Professor Johan Bergh and his colleagues and students, and from the opportunity to complete my research in the Government Archives for this book and begin it on the joint project on which Fransjohan Pretorius and I are now working together. I also made a Warwick History Video about this war with assistance from Fransjohan Pretorius and Thomas Pakenham. My research in South Africa was made possible by two awards from the British Academy and one from the South African Human Sciences Research Council. During these visits, I gained much from discussions growing out of guest lectures not only at Cape Town and Pretoria but also at Stellenbosch, Rhodes and the Rand Afrikaans Universities and at the University of South Africa. In England, seminars at Oxford, Cambridge, Bristol, Warwick and London proved similarly fruitful.

I owe a great debt to the many archivists and librarians who assisted me in my work, amongst whom I would like especially to mention Maryna Fraser (Barlow Rand Archives), Barbara Conradie (Standard Bank of South Africa Archives), Mary-Lynn Suttie (University of South Africa Library), Henry Gillett (Bank of England Archives) and the staff at the South African Library, Cape Town; the Government Archives, Pretoria; the Public Record Office, Kew; the Bodleian and Rhodes House Libraries, Oxford; and Birmingham University Library. Many other individuals have contributed most generously in discussion and in comments on various parts of the book as it emerged, and I would particularly like to acknowledge here Rodney Davenport, Burridge Spies, Greg Cuthbertson, G. H. Le May, Richard Mendelsohn, Mottie Tamarkin, Marc Yakutiel, Tony Hopkins and Peter Cain. To two people, especially, I wish to express my thanks for the encouragement and unstinting assistance which they have given me at every stage. Christopher Saunders, a fine and dedicated historian as well as a friend, did for me what he has done for a legion of other historians of South Africa: he cast his critical eye over every chapter of the book and thereby saved me from many errors and infelicities. Fransjohan Pretorius, whose careful scholarship and sound judgement make his own book on the war a model of its kind, sat in our attic for days on end going through my manuscript and then continued to fine-tooth comb the final version from Pretoria. I am immensely indebted to them both. Finally, to my immediate and extended family I owe all that we all owe to those who cushion our progress through life and bring to it not only their support and encouragement but their timely reminders that a preoccupation with the past is no substitute for living in the present.

Iain R. Smith
University of Warwick

Abbreviations

PRIVATE PAPERS

BRA HE	Barlow Rand Archives, Wernher, Beit/H. Eckstein Papers
FP	Sir Percy FitzPatrick Papers
GP	Philip Gell Papers
HP	Jan Hofmeyr Papers
JC	Joseph Chamberlain Papers
MP	Sir Alfred Milner Papers
MoP	Percy Alport Molteno Papers
RIP	Sir James Rose Innes Papers
RP	Ripon Papers
ScP	W. P. Schreiner Papers
SeP	Lord Selborne Papers
SmP	J. C. Smuts Papers
deVP	Sir Henry de Villiers Papers

PUBLISHED JOURNALS

BIHR	*Bulletin of the Institute of Historical Research*
CJH	*Canadian Journal of History*
CSSH	*Comparative Studies in Society and History*
Econ. Hist. Rev.	*Economic History Review*
EHR	*English Historical Review*
HJ	*Historical Journal*

JAH	*Journal of African History*
JBS	*Journal of British Studies*
JDS	*Journal of Development Studies*
JEH	*Journal of Economic History*
JICH	*Journal of Imperial and Commonwealth History*
JMH	*Journal of Modern History*
JSAS	*Journal of Southern African Studies*
PP	*Past and Present*
SAHJ	*South African Historical Journal*
SAJE	*South African Journal of Economics*

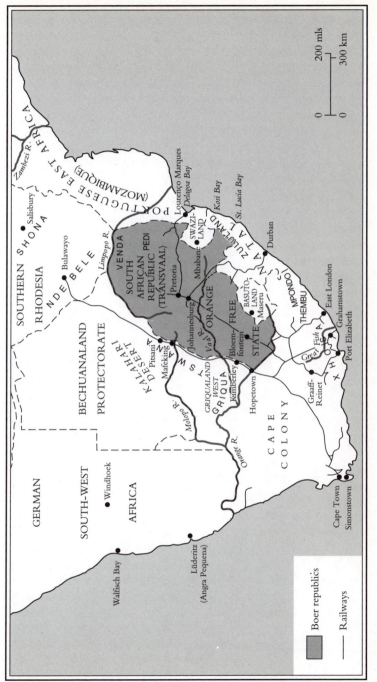

South Africa 1899

Introduction

NOT JUST 'A SMALL WAR'

The South African War of 1899–1902 was the most extensive, costly and humiliating war fought by Britain between the defeat of Napoleon in 1815 and the outbreak of the First World War in 1914. It involved over four times as many troops as the Crimean War and cost more than three times as much in money. It was a colonial war, by far the largest and most taxing such war fought by Britain during the century of her imperial pre-eminence, and the greatest of the wars which accompanied the European scramble for Africa. The British government resorted to war in 1899 to end a situation of Boer–British rivalry over the Transvaal, where political power was concentrated in Boer hands; to advance the cause of South African unification; and to establish British power and supremacy in southern Africa on a firmer basis. The two Boer republics (the Orange Free State, which was fully independent, and the Transvaal, or South African Republic, which was independent but not fully sovereign) fought for their independence in an anti-colonial war against full incorporation into the British Empire. The combined Afrikaner population, of what were then two of the world's smallest states, amounted to less than 250,000. By March 1990, some 200,000 British and Empire troops were involved in a war in South Africa with Boer forces fielding less than 45,000.

At the outset of the conflict, in October 1899, the Boer leaders hoped that if their commandos could advance deep into Natal and the Cape Colony, inflict a few decisive defeats on the 20,000 or so British forces already in South Africa, and bring about a Boer rebellion against British rule in the Cape Colony (where the Boers outnumbered the

1

British population by 3:2), the British government would choose to negotiate a settlement rather than despatch a massive expeditionary force – with all the costs and complications this might entail for Britain's position elsewhere in the Empire and the world. The Boers therefore hoped for a short war and a rapid peace settlement – as had happened in 1880–81 with the Transvaal War, when, after their defeat at Majuba Hill, the British had restored the Transvaal's independence by the Convention of Pretoria. But in 1899, the British Conservative government was in no mood to follow in Gladstone's liberal footsteps, did not believe that the problem of the Afrikaners could be 'killed with kindness', and was determined, as the Prime Minister, Lord Salisbury, put it, that 'the real point to be made good to South Africa is that we, not the Dutch are Boss'.[1] The possibility of using military force had long been faced but, until the very eve of the outbreak of war, it was widely believed that Kruger's government would 'bluff up to the cannon's mouth' and then capitulate to British demands. Only very belatedly, therefore, were the British garrisons in South Africa reinforced and did the War Office begin to grapple with the implications of mounting a major expeditionary force. On the eve of the war, the British government estimated that a war in South Africa might cost £10 million, require a maximum of 75,000 troops, result in – at worst – a few hundred casualties, and be over within three or four months. In the event, the war cost some £230 million, involved a total of 450,000 British and Empire troops, and resulted in the deaths of almost 22,000 combatants on the British side, something like 34,000 Boer civilians and combatants, and an unknown number of the African and Coloured population which has been estimated at not less than 15,000. A war which had been expected to last for three of four months lasted for two years and eight months.

These figures reveal the stark contrast between the war that was envisaged and the war which took place, but they look modest by twentieth-century standards. One of the reasons why the South African War tends to be regarded as 'a small war' is that we look back at it over the far vaster conflagrations of our present century. Like the Spanish–American and Russo-Japanese wars, the South African War took place away from Europe on the periphery of the world and this too has perhaps contributed to our Euro-centric tendency to underrate it. By nineteenth-century standards (which was how people received them then) the figures for what had been rather lightly embarked upon as 'another colonial war' were deeply shocking. When Sir George Colley had faced the Transvaal Boers in the war of 1880–81 he had only 1,500 men and his defeat at Majuba Hill had involved only 650.[2] Yet this defeat had been received in Britain as a major disaster. Lord Wolseley's Egyptian campaign in 1882 had involved 40,000 soldiers; Kitchener's Sudan campaign in 1898 had involved about 20,000 British and Egyptian troops. But the set-piece battle against the Mahdists at Omdurman was little different, in form, from the battles of the Napoleonic wars. What had changed was the military technology, and this was revealed in the grotesque casualty figures. No Mahdist got within 800 yards of the British lines, and, after five hours of fighting, 11,000 Mahdists had been killed and the British and Egyptian losses were 48.[3]

Mahdist, Zulu, Ashanti and Afghan wars had led the British, by the late nineteenth century, to think of colonial wars as small under-takings, in distant places, against exotic, non-European opponents who were poorly equipped and easily defeated. Such wars were no preparation at all for the sort of opponent and the sort of war the British found themselves fighting in South Africa. The Boers were the first well-equipped, European opponents the British army had faced since 1856 – the skirmishes over three months during 1880–81 bearing no comparison with the full-scale war of 1899–1902. The Boers were mobile, resourceful, crack shots, used to life in the saddle and with an intimate knowledge of the country. The latest artillery, much ammunition and large numbers of Mauser rifles had been imported from Germany between 1896 and 1899 and the Boer forces were able to inflict heavy reverses on the British during the first three months of the war, culminating in 'Black Week' in December 1899. This forced the British to develop a military operation of quite new and unanticipated dimensions. Under the fresh command of Lord Roberts, this British military 'steam-roller' then advanced and occupied the two republics during the first half of 1900. By September, both the Orange Free State and the Transvaal had been annexed as colonies of the British Crown.

But the war did not then come to an end. It simply took another form and continued as the first of the twentieth century's anti-colonial, guerrilla wars. This bitter conflict involved the British army in a scorched-earth policy which resulted in the wholesale destruction of farms and livestock (some 30,000 farms were burnt down), the savage treatment of the civilian population and other features with which we are today all too familiar. It also revealed the difficulty and cost to a Great Power of bringing such a war to an end despite its possession of an army ten times the size of the commandos it was fighting. Only with the development, after March 1901, of Kitchener's gigantic grid of some 8,000 blockhouses and 3,700 miles of wire-mesh, guarded by over 50,000 troops, were the Boer forces gradually squeezed into increasingly restricted areas. By 1902, this war was costing the British government £1.5 million a week. The Boers certainly proved very expensive to conquer and incorporate within the British Empire. It has been calculated that, at the end of the nineteenth century, Britain picked up new African subjects for her Empire at a cost of about 15 pence each; the Boers cost the British £1,000 a head to subdue.[4] And it was not a surrender but a negotiated peace which eventually brought the war to an end in May 1902.

The importance of the war, in revealing the scandalous state of unpreparedness of the British armed forces and the stimulus which it gave to the Esher and Haldane army reforms after 1902, has long been recognized. As Corelli Barnett has put it, in South Africa 'almost all aspects of the British military system had been found wanting in a war against the part-time commandos of 50,000 farmers'.[5] The demands which the war made on Britain were far greater than those of 'a small war' and the British government was forced to resort to measures which were unprecedented and a forewarning of things to come.[6] Yet some of the difficulties which Britain encountered in the South African War had been faced by other European powers elsewhere earlier in the nineteenth century. It had taken France seventeen years to conquer Algeria, after 1830, where, as in South Africa, vast areas of sparsely inhabited and inhospitable terrain similarly favoured the defenders, especially when they were mounted on horseback. The French in Mexico (1862–76) and the Spanish in Cuba (1868–78 and 1895–8) had also found themselves embroiled in protracted guerrilla wars. Their response had likewise been to send more troops, which had proved both costly and slow to take effect.

The military history of the South African War, which has been so vividly portrayed by Thomas Pakenham,[7] is not the subject of this book. Yet in its military aspect, as in so many other respects, this war spanned the nineteenth and twentieth centuries. The British government had to equip, transport and supply the largest army it had ever sent overseas and then sustain it for well over two years in a war 6,000 miles away. Both sides utilized the latest long-range, high-velocity, small-bore repeating rifles and machine-guns which were the product of late nineteenth-century advances in military technology. Yet horses played a far more important part than was to be the case in the wars of the twentieth century and Britain had to scour the world for the 400,346 horses, mules and donkeys that it 'expended'. Railways, steamships and the telegraph were also crucial. Steam-engines as well as oxen were used to haul wagons and gun-carriages over the dusty veld. The absence of the aeroplane certainly prolonged the war but air balloons were used by the British for reconnaissance purposes and bicycles were used by messengers. Signalling was done by semaphore, heliograph and early field telephones. Heavy artillery and trenches were features of the first phase of the war, and photographs of the British dead in their trench at Spion Kop convey a startling portent of the First World War. The advent of the cheap, portable Kodak camera meant that thousands of photographs were taken during the course of the war. With the onset of the guerrilla phase in the war, Boer women and children — whom the commandos were unable to look after — were herded into camps, hurriedly erected by the British authorities, where overcrowding, negligence, unsanitary conditions, and sheer ignorance resulted in devastating epidemics in which it has been estimated that between 25,000 and 28,000 died. The fact that these civilian deaths greatly outnumbered those combatants killed *on both sides* during the war and amounted to about 10 per cent of the Boer population of the two republics was to cast a long shadow over Boer–British relations after the war was over. The practice of 'concentrating' the civilian population in guarded camps during a guerrilla war, so that they could not assist those still fighting, was not new. It had been practised by the Spanish, during the Spanish–Cuban War, when it had also resulted in an appalling death rate. But it was the concentration camps established by the British during the South African War which first gave the term its notoriety. It was to be left to Hitler to give the term a quite new twist, during the Second World War, to denote camps in which death was deliberately intended.

In one particular respect, the South African War certainly belonged to the nineteenth century. Three-quarters of the British soldiers who died in it did so from infectious diseases, many of them in the typhoid epidemic after the British occupation of Bloemfontein in 1900. Infected wounds also claimed many lives. Field hospitals were rudimentary affairs in makeshift buildings or tents. Operations were often carried out in the open air. There were no antibiotics and an anaesthetic usually meant chloroform dripped on to a pad on the patient's face. This war took place on the hinge between the nineteenth and twentieth centuries but, in all sorts of ways — not least in the literature and poetry which it inspired — it was a harbinger of the twentieth century, and of the many anti-colonial wars which Britain and other European colonial powers were then to find themselves fighting elsewhere.[8]

NOT JUST 'A WHITE MAN'S WAR'

To the British, the war of 1899–1902 is known as 'The Boer War' or, more precisely, as 'The Second Anglo-Boer War' (to distinguish it from 'The First Anglo-Boer War' of 1880–81). To the Boers (or Afrikaners, since most of them are not now farmers) it is known as 'The English War' (*die Engelse oorlog*) or 'The Second War of Freedom' (*die Tweede Vryheidsoorlog*). These titles acknowledge who were the two main protagonists and correctly identify the war as occupying a crucial place in the development of Afrikaner nationalism and its bid for dominance and independence in a white-governed South Africa. But they are partisan. They also imply that only British and Boers fought in the war, and always on different sides. Recent work has demonstrated what a gross simplification it is to view this war as a struggle between two monolithic populations: Boer versus British. Neither the Boer nor the British populations in South Africa at this time were monolithic; and this was no clear-cut 'war between the races', much as nationalistic interpreters then and since have sought to claim it as such. The direct intervention of the British government and British troops in South African affairs, once again, aroused strong feelings of anti-imperialism and resentment at 'Downing Street meddling' amongst some of the English-speaking population in the self-governing colonies of the Cape and Natal. Olive Schreiner (the author of *The Story of an African Farm* and the sister of the Cape Prime Minister) and John X. Merriman (a leading Cape politician and future Prime Minister) were only the most prominent amongst a significant minority who regarded the war as a disaster for South Africa which had been deliberately provoked by the confrontationist policies of the British government. Merriman, who was decidedly more anti-imperialist than he was pro-Boer, felt that British politicians had become 'drunk with imperialism'. 'Our troubles always come from Downing Street', he observed, as a result of pushful Colonial Secretaries seeking to drive a wedge between the Boer and British populations in South Africa. To a Canadian friend, he wrote:

> I told you before and I tell you again – South Africa is lost to England if this policy is persisted in. . . . They [the Boers] will fight as long as they have a cartridge, and then they will set to work to plot and struggle to throw off the yoke if it takes 25 years.[9]

On the Boer side, the 'Second War of Freedom' has been a comfortable way in which to regard the war for Afrikaner nationalists, because it suggests a valiant Transvaal burgher population, united in their determination to defend their peace-loving republic against purely external attack. Assisted by their loyal kinsfolk in the Orange Free State, they have often been portrayed as fighting honourably, against hopeless odds, to defend their independence against the predatory designs of the then world's greatest power, backed up by 'the forces of Capitalism'. *Die Tweede Vryheidsoorlog* has tended to be cast in such a heroic mould that it has been difficult to admit that the war had its less heroic side. All wars do. Despite the direct and painful testimony of Boer generals and participants on commando, the rifts and divisions on the Boer side tended to be glossed over. An Afrikaner nation did not exist in 1899 and Afrikaners in different parts of South Africa had been moulded in different contexts and states by very different experiences during the course of the nineteenth century. There were more 'Boers' in the Cape Colony than in the two Boer republics put together and although, at the outset of the war, some thousands went over to the republican cause in the Cape frontier districts, repeated attempts to raise a Cape rebellion failed and the majority of Cape Afrikaners were content to remain British subjects.[10]

Amongst the Boers of the republics, there were divisions of class and outlook which the war opened up. The fissiparous tendencies which have always been such a feature of Afrikanerdom soon manifested themselves. When the British forces advanced into the two republics between March and June 1900, General Roberts issued proclamations assuring those burghers who were prepared to take an oath of neutrality and abstain from further participation in the war, that they would be allowed to return to their farms and their property would be respected. General Christian de Wet later described these proclamations as 'deadly lyddite bombs which . . . shattered Afrikanerdom'.[11] Some 13,900 of the Boer commandos voluntarily surrendered their arms by July 1900, this figure representing 26 per cent of those liable for military service in the two republics, or about 40 per cent of the number originally mobilized on the outbreak of war. Although many of these *hendsoppers* ('Handsuppers') were later forcibly re-commandeered, a fair number went on to assist the British as spies, scouts and go-betweens. The diaries of men like P. J. du Toit and R.W. Schikkerling provide graphic evidence of how some came to believe that they should assist the British, for not altogether dishonourable reasons, and of the hatred and bitterness felt by those who remained on commando against such 'traitors' – who were shot, if caught.[12] Some of those who defected were *bywoners* – members of a landless, underprivileged class within Afrikaner society who had been labour-tenants on richer Afrikaners' farms. When war began, they had to serve on commando with their own equipment and without pay. As the war dragged on, the numbers of 'Handsuppers' and 'Joiners' increased. By the end of the war, a fifth of the Boers still fighting were fighting on the British side.[13] But the 'Handsuppers' and 'Joiners' had no representation at the final peace negotiations and were ostracized by both church and kinsfolk after the war. Eugene Marais, editor of the Dutch newspaper *Land en Volk*, expressed the feelings of the majority of *bittereinders* ('Bitter-enders' or die-hards) when he wrote in October 1902:

> The feelings of hate . . . are deep as the ocean and wide as God's earth. . . . We hate these people from the depth of our hearts because they besmirched our honourable name. It is not possible to forgive and even less to forget.[14]

Not the least of the problems facing the Afrikaner leadership during the post-war period of reconstruction was the difficult task of healing the torn fabric of Afrikaner society.

The war of 1899–1902 was of a totally different order to the war of 1880–81. It was fought across the length and breadth of South Africa and it did not just involve Boers and British but virtually the whole population in one way or another. This needs to be acknowledged. This war may have had its origins in a struggle for supremacy between two rival white factions in the region, in which the British government intervened in an attempt to assist the forces of colonialism to overcome those of republicanism; but it was also a conflict in which many other struggles were also going on. The recent work of historians suggest than when one moves away from the main battlefields and examines the war in the countryside, what emerges is a *civil* war which took on widely varying and often specifically local forms and meanings.[15] Many wars take their titles not from the protagonists who initiated them but from the places where they were fought, e.g. the Crimean War, the Peninsula War, the Korean War, the Vietnam War. The war of 1899–1902 may have been declared and peace eventually signed between Britain and the two Boer republics. But it involved the whole of South Africa and profoundly affected all the inhabitants of the country. It is therefore both more accurate as well as more inclusive to describe it as the South African War – which is how it was widely referred to at the time, as is indicated on many of the war memorials dedicated to it in British towns and cities.

Historical research has also demolished the myth that this was purely a 'white man's war', fought in a region where the combined

Boer and British populations (then just under one million) were only about a fifth of the total.[16] Until recently, most books about the war presented it in terms of a conflict from which the majority African and Coloured populations of South Africa were excluded. Rayne Kruger's celebrated account, *Goodbye Dolly Gray*, is typical in describing it as 'a war fought across the breadth of a vast region, the majority of whose inhabitants were mere spectators'.[17] It is now clear not only that both sides in the conflict depended upon the African and Coloured populations of the area to a very great extent, but also that many of these people actively participated in the war on their own account. Over 100,000 Africans and Coloureds are known to have acted as scouts, spies, armed guards, patrols, transport drivers, servants, messengers and labourers on the British side alone. Despite British protestations to the contrary, they were often armed. Lord Kitchener (Commander-in-Chief of the British forces 1900–1902) himself admitted arming over 10,000 and the figure was probably closer to the 30,000 which Lloyd George estimated at the time.

On the Boer side also, something like 10,000 Africans and Coloureds were similarly involved, although only exceptionally were they armed. On specific occasions, as at the siege of Mafeking, Africans did fight alongside Europeans. There were probably four times as many Africans as Europeans in Mafeking during the famous siege, and they played a crucial and unacknowledged part not only in fortifying and defending the town but in rustling cattle to supply it with food and acting as spies and messengers – as is revealed in a number of diaries kept during the siege, including one by an educated African which was only discovered and published in 1973.[18] Whilst the Europeans were never really short of food, hundreds of Africans died from starvation as a direct result of the grossly unequal distribution of food during the siege.

Africans also died in large numbers in the separate 'concentration' and labour camps established for them by the British during the course of the war. Whereas the conditions and high death rates in the Boer camps were widely publicized at the time by Emily Hobhouse and others, the deaths of an estimated 15,000 Africans amongst those kept in separate but parallel camps, under even worse conditions, have been much less widely acknowledged and may well underestimate the total numbers involved.

For many Africans in Natal and in the Cape Colony the war meant a boom in employment opportunities, with better pay and better prices paid for agricultural produce, cattle, horses and services of all kinds by the huge British army at a time when recent drought and rinderpest (cattle disease), together with the cessation of work in the Rand mines, had seriously affected the rural areas. For the rulers of some of the African societies so recently incorporated within the four white-settler states, or dependent on them, the war provided an opportunity for them to secure or improve their positions through collaboration with the British. Khama (in Bechuanaland), Loratholi (in Basutoland), Dinizulu (in Zululand), and the Dlamini ruling elite (in Swaziland) all improved and consolidated their positions during the war in this way. In several areas of South Africa, Africans were armed by the British and effectively turned their territories into 'no go' areas as far as the Boer commandos were concerned.[19]

Whilst the Boers faced mounting hostility from the African population – whose livestock they seized and whose labour they sought to commandeer – the British enjoyed widespread support and assistance from African and Coloured people during the war, many of whom not only benefited from the increased opportunities for employment but also looked to the defeat of the Boers for a new and better future when British rule was established throughout the region. These hopes were not without some foundation. As late as March 1901, the British Colonial Secretary, Joseph Chamberlain, declared:

> We cannot consent to purchase a *shameful peace* by leaving the coloured population in the position in which they stood before the war, with not even the ordinary civil rights which the Government of the Cape Colony has long conceded to them.[20]

Yet peace between Boers and British in South Africa was to require a British abdication on this issue. The exclusion of Africans and Coloureds from any political rights (outside the Cape Colony, where they had long benefited, in a very limited way, from its colour-blind franchise) was specifically built in to every attempt at peace negotiations during the war and formed Article 8 of the final Vereeniging Peace Settlement in May 1902. It was also an integral part of the Act of Union in 1910. It was thus a direct product of the period of British ascendancy and overrule in South Africa.

Like the American Civil War (1861–5), the South African War marks a watershed in its country's history. It was as important in the making of modern South Africa as the American Civil War was in the history of the United States.[21] What began as a Boer–British conflict over the Transvaal republic soon developed into a full-scale war which profoundly affected the whole population and the future of the entire region. Despite obvious differences, comparisons between the American Civil War and the South African War are instructive.[22] Both wars played a crucial part in the establishment of the reconstructed, modern states which exist today; and both contributed to the advance of capitalistic modes of social and economic organization within these states. Neither in the United States nor in South Africa, however, were those whites who fought for freedom from what they regarded as 'alien' rule inclined to extend the kind of liberty they demanded for themselves to the non-whites over whom they ruled. The Transvaal Boers refused to treat even European immigrants (Uitlanders) on an equal basis. In the United States, the victory of the North over the South carried with it the seeds from which black civil and political rights could grow in the future, even if these were prevented from coming into effect immediately. In South Africa, no basic changes in the relations between whites and blacks resulted from the British victory over the Boers. In both cases, white supremacy took precedence over any ideas of a non-racial citizenship.

Nor was the South African War just a colonial war. Out of the war between Britain and the two Boer republics there developed a regional war with civil war dimensions to it. Between 1899 and 1902 war went on at many different levels in South Africa and there were other battlefields apart from those which have so preoccupied military historians. Many of the conflicts when then erupted into open warfare were home-grown, internally generated out of the recent South African past. The arrival of the British army did not create these conflicts. What happened was that the outbreak of war created a situation in which some of the conflicts endemic within South Africa flared up into open warfare and became part of the Boer–British struggle.[23] In its origins, however, the South African War was the product of a Boer–British conflict which had deep roots going back into the pattern of European settlement, expansion, conquest and overrule which had developed during the course of the nineteenth century. Any account of the origins of this war, therefore, requires that we begin in South Africa. For it was there, in the Transvaal – which had been the poorest and weakest of South Africa's four major states – that one of the most rapid and astonishing economic transformations in world history took place during the last two decades of the nineteenth century.

NOTES

1. Selborne to Milner, 27 July 1899, in D. G. Boyce, ed., *The Crisis of British Power: the Imperial and Naval Papers of the Second Earl of Selborne, 1895–1910* (London, 1990), p. 92.

2. J. Lehmann, *The First Anglo-Boer War* (London, 1985), p. 260.

3. L. James, *The Savage Wars: British Campaigns in Africa 1870–1920* (London, 1985), p. 108.

4. J. Lonsdale, 'The European scramble and conquest in African history', *Cambridge History of Africa* (Cambridge, 1985), 6, p. 718.

5. Corelli Barnett, *Britain and Her Army 1509–1920* (London, 1970), p. 344.

6. See C. Trebilcock, 'War and the failure of industrial mobilisation: 1899 and 1914', in J. M. Winter, ed., *War and Economic Development* (London, 1975); M. Yakutiel, 'The British Treasury and the South African War 1899–1905', Oxford D.Phil. thesis, 1989.

7. T. Pakenham, *The Boer War* (London, 1979).

8. For the poetry of the war see M. van Wyk Smith, *Drummer Hodge: the Poetry of the Anglo-Boer War 1899–1902* (Oxford, 1978).

9. J. X. Merriman to Professor Goldwin Smith, 6 February and 5 November 1900, in P. Lewsen, ed., *Selections from the Correspondence of John X. Merriman* 4 vols (Cape Town, 1966), 3, pp. 155–6, 237.

10. For the Boer side in the war see J. H. Breytenbach, *Die geskiedenis van die Tweede Vryheidsoorlog in Suid-Afrika, 1899–1902* 5 vols (Pretoria, 1969–83); also F. Pretorius, *Kommandolewe tydens die Anglo-Boereoorlog 1899–1902* (Cape Town and Johannesburg, 1991).

11. See A. Grundlingh, 'Collaborators in Boer Society', in P. Warwick, ed., *The South African War* (Harlow, 1980), p. 259.

12. P. J. du Toit, *Diary of a National Scout*, ed. J. P. Brits (Pretoria, 1974); R.W Schikkerling, *Commando Courageous: a Boer's Diary* (Johannesburg, 1966).

13. A. Grundlingh, *Die 'hendsoppers' en 'joiners': Die rasionaal en verkynsel van verraad* (Pretoria, 1979); also 'Collaborators', in Warwick, ed., *The South African War*.

14. A. Grundlingh, 'Collaborators', p. 276.

15. Bill Nasson, *Abraham Esau's War: a Black South African War in the Cape 1899–1902* (Cambridge, 1991); Jeremy Krikler, *Revolution from Above, Rebellion from Below: the Agrarian Transvaal at the Turn of the Century* (Oxford, 1993).

16. See especially P. Warwick, *Black People and the South African War 1899–1902* (Cambridge, 1983).

17. Rayne Kruger, *Goodbye Dolly Gray* (London, 1959), p. 421.

18. See B. Willan, 'The siege of Mafeking', in Warwick, ed., *The South African War*; also J. Comaroff, ed., *The Boer War Diary of Sol. T. Plaatje* (London, 1973).

19. See Warwick, *Black People*, and J. Krikler, *Revolution*, for further details.

20. Chamberlain to Milner, 6 March 1901, in Pakenham, *The Boer War*, p. 491.

21. As Leo Amery was the first to emphasize. See L. S. Amery, ed., *The Times History of the War in South Africa* 7 vols (London, 1900–1909), 1, p. 3.
22. See G. M. Fredrickson, *White Supremacy: a comparative study in American and South African history* (Oxford, 1981).
23. See Warwick, *Black People*; Krikler, *Revolution*; Nasson, *Abraham Esau's War*.

CHAPTER ONE

The Roots of Conflict

THE EXPANSION OF EUROPEAN SETTLEMENT

Until the end of the nineteenth century, South Africa was little more than a geographical expression for an area characterized by immense human and regional diversity. African societies, Afrikaner republics, and British colonies and protectorates – all of them multi-ethnic and multi-lingual – co-existed and competed for control over the limited well-watered land and few resources of what was a poor and peripheral region. Until the discovery of diamonds and gold, South Africa's only importance, for the rest of the world, lay in its strategic position at the tip of a large continent on the sea-route to India. The opening up of this sea-route by the Portuguese at the end of the fifteenth century changed the course not just of South African history but of world history. Throughout the sixteenth century, annual fleets were despatched round the Cape of Good Hope to the Indies. There were shipwrecks and temporary landings on the South African coast to obtain fresh water and food from the local Khoikhoi (Hottentot) population, but the Portuguese occupied no territory south of Angola and Mozambique.

During the seventeenth century, the Dutch replaced the Portuguese in the Indian Ocean and in 1652 Jan van Riebeeck arrived at Table Bay with 80 employees of the Dutch East India Company to establish a fort and supply station for the ships plying between Europe and the centre of the Dutch East India Company's activities in the Indies at Batavia (Java). Almost immediately, however, the port and supply station at Cape Town became the centre for an ever-widening area of European settlement by ex-Company employees and free burghers of Dutch, French Huguenot and German extraction. By 1707, the

European population at the Cape numbered about 2,000 and this grew to 13,830 by 1793. Following the practice in Dutch East India Company settlements elsewhere, slaves were introduced from Indonesia, India, Ceylon, Mozambique and Madagascar and throughout the eighteenth century the Cape was a slave-holding society in which the slaves outnumbered the European free burghers and the Europeans gradually appropriated land and cattle from the Khoikhoi, who were decimated by disease and reduced to a servile status.

By the eighteenth century, the British had established their maritime supremacy over the Dutch and in 1795, after the French invasion of the Netherlands, the British captured Cape Town to prevent it falling into French hands. Although the Dutch regained possession under the Treaty of Amiens (1803), this was short-lived and the Cape Colony again came under British control in 1806. British sovereignty over the area was confirmed in 1814 as part of the settlement after the Napoleonic wars.

For the British, as for the Dutch before them, it was primarily the strategic importance of Cape Town and the Cape peninsula as 'a stepping-stone to Asia' which attracted them. But attached to this strategic prize, by the nineteenth century, there was now a complex, slave-based, African colony of mixed European settlement spread over a vast hinterland.[1] The commercial potential of the Cape was not ignored but it was exaggerated. In 1800, Sir George Yonge had observed that 'the importance of the Cape grows in Its every Hour. It is and will become the Centre of Commerce with India, America and Europe'.[2] Yet until the discovery of diamonds and gold later in the nineteenth century, South African trade remained unimportant. The area produced some poor quality wine and wool but little of real significance for the British economy. It attracted far fewer immigrants and less foreign investment than most other areas of European settlement overseas. Nonetheless, the frontier of European settlement expanded rapidly and forcefully into the South African hinterland during the nineteenth century, as the European population grew and African societies were conquered or incorporated and their land expropriated.

The growth in the European population was assisted, under British rule, by government-initiated schemes, such as that of 1820, when some 5,000 British settlers were established on African land in the eastern Cape in an attempt to relieve unemployment and social unrest in industrial Britain. These nineteenth-century British immigrants, however, did not assimilate into the Afrikaner population as earlier

French Huguenot and German arrivals had done. They came from an urbanized, industrializing society in Britain and in South Africa they tended to settle in the towns, the larger of which therefore became predominantly English-speaking. They looked to Britain as their mother-country and were proud to be part of the British Empire and of a colony which achieved representative government in 1853 and became fully self-governing in 1872.

The Afrikaners, meanwhile, were descendants of a much earlier pattern of emigration from Europe. Many of their ancestors had arrived in South Africa as refugees from Europe determined to make a new life for themselves in a country which some regarded as destined by God to be their Chosen Land. They read the Bible in Dutch but in daily life they spoke the *taal* (Afrikaans). They were mostly farmers (Boers) who relied upon tied African labour. The richer wheat and wine farmers of the western Cape tended to own the largest numbers of slaves. Elsewhere, the *trekboers* were essentially pastoral farmers, raising cattle on generally poor land with the help of a handful of slaves and often seeming to European observers to resemble their African neighbours in their way of life – which was closer to subsistence than to capitalist production for a distant market.[3] Anti-Afrikaner attitudes and a conviction of English superiority were the norm rather than the exception amongst the English-speaking population in South Africa. There was little social mixing or intermarriage between the two groups except amongst the Cape Town elite. The European population in South Africa thus became ethnically divided between Afrikaners and British during the nineteenth century, rather as had happened between French and British in Canada. But whereas in Canada, the British settlers soon outnumbered the French, in South Africa the Afrikaners always predominated. Despite steadily increasing British immigration throughout the nineteenth century, the Afrikaner population in the Cape Colony still outnumbered the British by about 3:2 at the end of the century.[4]

Slavery was abolished throughout the British Empire in 1833 (but only took effect in South Africa after 1838) and by 1840, the European population at the Cape numbered 70,775. The population of ex-slaves, free blacks and Coloureds was 79,480.[5] Already, however, the European settlers were coming up against the dense Xhosa populations in the east of the Cape Colony, around the Great Fish River, where most of the well-watered land was already occupied. A century of frontier warfare was well under way for possession of this land, in which government troops repeatedly played a crucial role in supporting European settlers who were unable on their own to displace African farmers from the disputed areas.

THE FORMATION OF THE REPUBLICS

Between 1834 and 1844, in a movement which came to be known as the Great Trek, some 6,000 Afrikaner *Voortrekkers* and their families emigrated from the Cape Colony. This exodus involved about a quarter of the settler population of the eastern Cape Colony. The reasons for the Great Trek have been debated by historians ever since. Political and ideological objections to British rule were certainly articulated at the time but economic motives were also involved.[6] A voracious appetite for land, and access to new sources of African labour with which to farm it, probably featured as large in the considerations of these pastoral farmers as their growing discontent with the 'alien' British administration in Cape Town, which they experienced as more intrusive and efficient than had been the case with the Dutch before 1806. But their determination to move beyond British rule and govern themselves according to the 'old Burgher regulations and duties' and 'preserve the proper relations between master and servant' was certainly encouraged by Ordinance 50 of 1828 (which made 'Hottentots and other free people of colour' equal with whites before the law) and the emancipation of the slaves on whose labour European farming in the Cape had hitherto depended. These measures presented a direct economic threat to pre-capitalist, subsistence white farmers who were used to barter and tied labour rather than a cash economy and wages. They also offended their ideas about the right ordering of Boer society in a black continent. One of the *Voortrekkers*, Karel Tregardt, declared that the main objection of the emigrant Afrikaners 'to the coming order of things was the equalisation of the coloureds with the whites', a situation which Piet Retief's niece, Anna Steenkamp, felt was 'contrary to the laws of God and the natural distinction of race and religion'.[7] The Great Trek, therefore, was a response to what were regarded as deteriorating conditions in the Cape Colony. But it was also a political act: a determination to be free and independent of British rule. In his Manifesto of 1837, Piet Retief declared: 'We quit this colony under the full assurance that the English Government has nothing more to require of us, and will allow us to govern ourselves without its interference in future.'[8]

After enduring great hardships and attempting an initial settlement in Natal (which the British then annexed as a colony in 1843), the *Voortrekkers* moved on into the interior. There, amidst recurrent fighting with the African peoples whom they displaced, and a short-lived attempt to extend British authority over them in the Orange River Sovereignty (1848–54), they eventually established two states: the South African Republic (Transvaal) and the Orange Free State. The independence of these two Boer republics was recognized by the British government by the Sand River (1852) and Bloemfontein (1854) Conventions. This European expansion was, of course, part of that great movement of European migration, settlement, and dominance on a world-wide scale which began with the voyages of discovery and peaked at the end of the nineteenth century. In South Africa, the area under European settlement and control doubled within the short space of twenty years. From the 1850s, this settlement was divided between two Afrikaner republics in the interior and two British colonies dominating the coastline.

In both the republics non-whites were excluded from the franchise and their access to the ownership of land was progressively restricted. It was written into the constitution of the South African Republic that 'the people desire to permit no equality between coloured people and the white inhabitants either in church or state'.[9] This explicit political exclusion of non-whites was at variance with the colour-blind franchise in the Cape Colony (where repeated resort to property and other franchise qualifications meant that non-whites never accounted for more than 15 per cent of the electorate and never produced a member of parliament). But it was unremarkable for its time and reflected the minority position of thinly scattered Afrikaner farmers attempting to rule over large territories in which at any one time the African population outnumbered them by more than 2:1. Initially, it was a natural precaution to ensure group survival. Later, the limitation on the extension of the franchise even to other Europeans was used to ensure Afrikaner dominance.

The Great Trek was not a single event but part of a whole series of major population movements in South Africa during the first half of the nineteenth century which resulted in the formation of new states and societies. By far the most extensive of these movements took place amongst the African population as a result of the upheavals known as the *Mfecane* (Crushing), out of which the Zulu nation emerged as South Africa's largest single ethnic group.[10] The disruption of African societies which accompanied this outburst of conquest and empire-building made the Afrikaner expansion into the interior easier than it might otherwise have been.[11] Even so, the weakness of their position forced the Afrikaners into alliances with various African societies and factions. Relations between Europeans and Africans were far more fluid in nineteenth-century South Africa than they became in the twentieth century and it is a distortion of the evidence to see Africans at this time as all aligned together on one side of a frontier, with all the Europeans on the other. Cross-frontier and cross-racial alliances – in which whites formed alliances with blacks against common adversaries, white or black, and *vice versa* – were a feature of the situation right down to the 1880s. In almost every war that white people fought against black people in southern Africa, they had other blacks fighting on their side and this was often crucial to the outcome.[12] Relatively small numbers of scattered Boer frontiersmen had little hope of decisively defeating Xhosa, Zulu or Pedi chiefdoms. In each case, it was the later intrusion of British armies, with their superior weapons and military organization but backed up by large numbers of African auxiliaries, which resulted in the decisive defeats of the Xhosa, Zulu and Pedi.

The frontier of European settlement continued to advance throughout the century and in the process African land was appropriated, African labour was acquired, and African societies were steadily conquered and incorporated within white-ruled states. Some African societies successfully sought the protection of the British government and thereby preserved most of their land from conquest and incorporation within neighbouring white-settler states. Basutoland, Swaziland and Bechuanaland, for example, became British High Commission territories and later emerged as the independent African states of Lesotho, Swaziland and Botswana in the 1960s. Others, such as the Mpondo, Xhosa and Thembu, were absorbed wholesale or piecemeal into the Cape Colony. The powerful Zulu state survived the overthrow of Dingane (1838–40) and preserved a military system strong enough to defeat a British army at Isandhlwana before going down to defeat at Ulundi (1879) and eventual dismemberment and incorporation into Natal. The Pedi in the Transvaal, and the Ndebele across the Limpopo, long resisted the spread of white settlement but finally succumbed to conquest. The last of South Africa's independent African chiefdoms, the Venda, were only finally conquered and incorporated into the Transvaal republic in 1898. The great divisions between and fragmentation within African societies meant that there was never a concerted African resistance to white expansion in South Africa. Well-armed British colonists and Boer republicans were thus able to divide, conquer and incorporate African societies within white-ruled states – a process involving continuous violence and considerable loss of life.

The Europeans too were divided on ethnic, class and regional lines. In the Cape Colony, eastern separatism remained a divisive force in Cape politics to the 1870s, whilst for the two Afrikaner republics, precariously established in the interior, their boundaries and continued existence remained uncertain right down to the 1880s. Like the African societies with which they were in perpetual conflict over land and cattle, the Afrikaner republics eked out a pre-capitalist existence from near-subsistence and mainly pastoral farming. They initially lacked an effective state administration and their burghers exhibited strong personal and regional loyalties and an aversion to taxation and central government. Unsuccessful attempts at fusion, the short-lived establishment of further small breakaway republics, and endemic fissiparousness in church and state were features which persisted into the 1880s. Only gradually did the emergence of strong Presidencies in the two republics lead to a shift in power from the localities to central government in Bloemfontein and Pretoria. Throughout this period, therefore, the Afrikaner population in South Africa as a whole remained divided. Far more Afrikaners remained in the Cape Colony than trekked into the two republics and, over the next two generations, Afrikaners lived under different political systems and acquired different loyalties. In the Cape Colony and Natal (both of which became self-governing), where Afrikaners enjoyed equal rights with the English settlers, most of them became loyal subjects of Queen Victoria and appreciated the benefits of being part of the British Empire. Many tended to look down on their more backward republican kinsfolk. In the Orange Free State and in the Transvaal, however, different economic interests and the development of separate identities kept the two republics apart. Despite clear elements of white, male egalitarianism and individualism, Afrikaner republican society did not develop any strong tradition of individual rights and, as might be expected from the isolated and insecure position of white minorities in the interior of the African continent, ideas about democracy were essentially to do with the self-determination and domination of the group.[13]

Yet Britain remained the dominant power on the South African scene. The British navy controlled the seas. Nearly all the external trade was carried in British ships to and from the British colonial ports of Cape Town, Port Elizabeth and Durban. British traders and British missionaries, British goods and British influence predominated over the region as a whole. So long as Britain remained the only great power with an interest in the area, and so long as the various territories of South Africa remained poor, undeveloped and controllable by informal means, British governments saw little need for any further expansion of formal empire there, with all its costs and liabilities. During the 1870s, however, both the internal and external configurations began to change.

THE DISCOVERY OF DIAMONDS

In 1867 diamonds were discovered near Hopetown and subsequently in much greater abundance at what became Kimberley, in the triangle of land between the Orange and Vaal rivers which came to be called Griqualand West. At once a scramble took place for this already disputed territory. After a complicated wrangle between the rulers of the local Griqua and Tlhaping, the Orange Free State, the Transvaal, and the British and Cape governments, the matter was finally settled in Britain's favour by the Keate Award (1871). Griqualand West was annexed as a British Crown Colony until, in 1880, Britain succeeded in passing it on to be incorporated within the Cape Colony. The local inhabitants, in a pattern which was repeated in many other parts of South Africa, were soon persuaded to sell their land to white people, and by the end of the century they had been dispersed as labourers and had ceased to exist as an organized community. The Orange Free State retained a strong sense of grievance at the way in which it had been outmanoeuvred by Britain. The British government, however, had succeeded in achieving all its objectives in the area: the south-westward expansion of the Afrikaner republics had been checked; the way north for future Cape expansion, British missionaries and trade had been kept open; and the most important diamond fields in the world had been brought within the British Empire and would underpin economically the full self-government granted to the Cape Colony in 1872.[14]

Diamond mining transformed the economy of the Cape Colony and quickened that of the adjoining Orange Free State. It also brought into being South Africa's first industrial community and, with it, the key issues of capital and migrant labour which have been so important to the region's economic life ever since.[15] By 1871, Kimberley had become the largest centre of white settlement outside Cape Town, with some 10,000 white diggers assisted by about 30,000 black labourers — many of them from Basutoland and the north-eastern

Transvaal. By 1875, some 50,000 African migrant labourers were coming to work in the diamond mines each year and a steady process of amalgamation had begun by which 'organized capital' came to replace the small, individual claims at the diamond fields. By 1890, this process was complete and, largely through its greater efficiency and the efforts of Cecil Rhodes, backed up by powerful financiers in Britain and Europe, De Beers Consolidated Mines had established monopoly control.[16] With consolidation went economy, efficiency and a reduction in mining costs, above all in labour costs. The diamond-mining industry pointed where gold was to follow: towards the mobilization of South Africa's other vital resource – an abundant supply of cheap, African labour. As C. W. de Kiewiet acutely observed long ago, here lies the reason why South Africa consistently failed to attract European immigration on the scale of Canada or Australia. 'The truth is that she did receive a very considerable immigration. It was an immigration from within. Her immigrants were black.'[17]

The strategic importance of Cape Town, in an era of sea-borne trade and empire, was certainly not diminished by the opening of the Suez Canal (1869) and the development of the short sea-route to India. British governments continued to place the Cape alongside Malta, Gibraltar and Aden as a vital strategic interest for Britain and her Empire. Meanwhile, Cape Town's importance as a commercial port began to grow rapidly. Imports more than doubled between 1871 and 1875 in the wake of the diamond industry. Capital investment flowed into the country, enabling the Cape Colony to spend £14 million on the construction of 1,000 miles of railways between the coastal ports and the interior by 1886. Sir Donald Currie's Castle Line joined the older Union Line in 1872 to provide a weekly steamship service to England. European (mainly British) immigrant workers arrived in the colony in unprecedented numbers: 23,000 came in the single decade 1873–83. White and black farmers began to respond to the market demand for a rapid increase in produce by developing a more capitalist agriculture. Diamond mining stimulated a general quickening in the economy.

POLITICAL DEVELOPMENTS AND THE FAILED ATTEMPT AT FEDERATION

Economic growth also encouraged political development. The Cape Colony became self-governing in 1872 under a colour-blind franchise which ensured an overwhelmingly European electorate in which there was always a substantial Afrikaner majority. In 1878, under-capitalized Afrikaner farmers in the Cape Colony formed a *Boeren Beschermings Vereeniging* (Farmers' Protection Union) as a political pressure group to work on their behalf. In 1880 the Afrikaner Bond was founded and, by 1883, this had absorbed the *BBV* and emerged, under the leadership of Jan Hofmeyr, as the first organized political party in the Cape, able to make or break governments through the giving or withholding of its support. In 1889, Hofmeyr pledged the support of the Afrikaner Bond to Cecil Rhodes, whose political career had begun in 1881 when he was returned as one of the first representatives for the diamond fields in the Cape Assembly. Winning the support of Hofmeyr and the Afrikaner Bond, Rhodes was able to emerge as Prime Minister of the Cape Colony (1890–95).

The Cape was not only the oldest, largest and richest of the four white-settler states, it was also the most populated – with a white population of some 237,000 by the 1870s (compared with a total of less than 100,000 elsewhere in South Africa) and an African population of about half a million.[18] Much of the rest of South Africa was dependent upon Cape ports, the growth of Cape railways, and the Cape commercial economy, and this was especially true of the Orange Free State. Its President at this time, J. H. Brand (1864–89), was Anglophile and more eager to nurture closer relations with the Cape Colony than was President Burgers of the Transvaal (1872–7). The expectation that the rest of South Africa would gradually be drawn within the orbit of the Cape Colony remained a dominant assumption right down to the 1890s. After 1872, successive British governments looked to the Cape Colony to take the lead in initiating a movement towards closer cooperation between the two colonies and the two republics which might eventually unify the area into a South African federation on the Canadian model. To both Liberal and Conservative British governments the advantages of a federation seemed self-evident. A united, self-governing South Africa within the British Empire was seen as the cheapest and most effective way of securing both British predominance and South African progress. A unified economy and communications system would encourage foreign investment and development, facilitate the flow of African labour across state boundaries, and help to resolve many local conflicts of interest. An altogether more viable and effective dominion would result which would be an asset rather than a perpetual liability to the British Empire.[19]

In 1874, Lord Carnarvon became the British Colonial Secretary in

Disraeli's second ministry. More forceful than his Liberal predecessor, Lord Kimberley, and deeply influenced by the successful achievement of Canadian confederation when he had been Colonial Secretary in 1867, Carnarvon was determined to bring about the unification of South Africa, if necessary through the external intervention of the British government. He was encouraged in his policy by the new emphasis on the importance of the Empire, and the need to transform it into a more coherent edifice to buttress Britain's position in the world, which were characteristic of these years.[20] In South Africa, he was assisted in his task by a group of pushful subordinates in the form of J. A. Froude (historian and adviser on South Africa 1874–5), Sir Theophilus Shepstone (Native Administrator in Natal), Sir Garnet Wolseley (Special Commissioner in Natal), and Sir Bartle Frere (British High Commissioner at Cape Town 1877–80).

In May 1875, Carnarvon suggested that a conference of delegates from the South African colonies and republics should meet in Cape Town to consider 'the all-important question of a possible union of South Africa in some form of confederation'.[21] When this proposal met with no enthusiasm from any of the governments concerned, Carnarvon repeated it but this time switched the venue to London in August 1876. Meanwhile, he sought to conciliate the Orange Free State by the payment of £90,000 as compensation for Britain's overriding of its claims to the diamond fields – a modest sum to pay, considering the value of the territory. President Brand went to London, accepted the payment, but refused to discuss federation. Neither President Burgers of the Transvaal nor Prime Minister Molteno of the Cape Colony (both of whom were in Europe at the time) agreed to attend the conference, which was therefore a failure. Molteno – who was head of the Cape's first ministry under self-government – resented what he perceived as imperial interference and insisted that, when the time was ripe, any initiative involving the closer union of the Cape Colony with the other territories should be taken not by the British government but by the government in Cape Town. Undeterred, Carnarvon persisted. Convinced that it would promote the federation he desired, in September 1876 he decided to annex the Transvaal to the British Crown.

While the other three South African states had prospered after the discovery of diamonds, the Transvaal (or South African Republic, as it was officially called) had not. Despite the attempts of President Burgers to draw the republic out of its economic and political backwardness, it remained poor and divided, with a sparsely scattered European population of probably no more than 30,000 at this time. It did not have the prosperous sheep-farming of the Orange Free State, and its government was weaker and less efficient and not only failed to extract regular taxation but made extravagant grants of land. This created a shortage of free land, an abundance of under-utilized land, and a perpetual search for new sources of land which brought the Transvaal into perpetual conflict with African societies both within and beyond its ill-defined borders. The development of modest gold-diggings in the Lydenburg district in the early 1870s failed to make much impact on the economy, and the presence of mainly English people there added to the divisions within Transvaal society.

In July 1875, the rival claims of Britain and Portugal to the east coast port of Delagoa Bay (Lourenco Marques, later Maputo) were finally settled in favour of Portugal by the MacMahon Award. The Transvaal's dream of a port outside the sphere of British control, and closer than any of the existing colonial ports, became a reality. President Burgers tried to raise money in Europe for the building of a railway from the Transvaal to Delagoa Bay. Commercial interests in the Cape and Natal feared the growing competition (trade between Delagoa Bay and Natal had already more than tripled between 1872 and 1875). The British government regarded access by the Transvaal to an independent outlet to the sea as likely to weaken Britain's hold over her and to hinder rather than help the cause of South African unification. Carnarvon determined to act whilst the Transvaal was still weak and, by bringing it within the British Empire, both to strengthen British paramountcy over the whole region and to promote South African federation. Having failed to persuade either the Cape or the Orange Free State, Carnarvon now prepared to coerce the Transvaal. After discussions with Sir Garnet Wolseley, whose actions had already ensured a pliable Natal, Carnarvon authorized Sir Theophilus Shepstone to go to the Transvaal and annex the republic providing 'the inhabitants thereof, or a sufficient number of them, or the Legislature thereof, desire to become our subjects'.

When Shepstone entered the Transvaal in January 1877, he found the republican government in disarray. President Burgers had failed to secure adequate loans for the railway to Delagoa Bay and had lost the support of many of his burghers. A recent inconclusive war against the Pedi had bankrupted the Treasury, and the administration was on the verge of collapse. Shepstone settled down in Pretoria and for three months played a waiting game. He interviewed leading Transvalers, exploited their divisions and dislike of President Burgers, and heightened their fear of the Zulu. In March, Shepstone predicted that the Transvaal could be 'overrun and annihilated as a state' by African onslaughts within six months unless British imperial support were assured.[22] He demanded financial and administrative reforms from the Volksraad which it was incapable of carrying out. The Volksraad instructed President Burgers and the Executive Council to negotiate with Shepstone 'with the object of maintaining the independence of the State'. It then adjourned, and it was found that there was not even enough money in the Treasury to pay the travelling expenses of its members.[23]

The opposition of the President and leading Transvalers to annexation was ineffective, but it remained nonetheless. Paul Kruger, Shepstone noted, 'positively declined to enter upon the discussion of any subject that might involve in any way the independence of the State as a Republic'.[24] Kruger had left the Cape Colony, as a boy of ten, on the Great Trek and had early demonstrated the leadership qualities which were to make him the Transvaal republic's longest-serving and most popular President. Deeply religious (he belonged to the 'Doppers', the most uncompromising of the Dutch Reformed Churches), fiercely anti-British, socially conservative and politically astute, he was well-suited to lead the Transvaal Boers in their struggle against British imperialism. His uncomely appearance went with a determined character and a populist touch which made him both revered and feared. He was a skilled practitioner of the art of politics in a weak state where personal contact and influence counted for more than an effective bureaucracy. He was to be elected four times in succession as President and his determination to recover and then maintain the independence of the Transvaal from British rule was to be the dominating purpose of his life.

In 1877, however, the weakness and divisions within the Transvaal enabled Shepstone to annex it to the British Crown by a Proclamation issued on 12 April. This action had momentous consequences, but at the time it was met with sullen resentment rather than open resistance. The readiness of the British government to intervene and annex the Transvaal in 1877 has to be set against a background of widespread British annexations elsewhere at this time – in Fiji, Malaya, and the Gold Coast of West Africa – in areas where indigenous governments had broken down. It was the act of an impatient British government making little progress in its attempts to unify South Africa, and it came after almost a decade of renewed British intervention in the South African interior which had begun with the annexation of Basutoland in 1868 and of Griqualand West in 1871. The result was that in 1877 the Transvaal republic lost the independence which Britain had recognized in the Sand River Convention of 1852; this it was never fully to regain. Direct rule as a British colony, however, was to be short-lived. The imposition of an insensitive, authoritarian and unpopular British administration on the Transvaal after 1877 led directly to the first Anglo–Boer war in 1880–81 (more accurately described by its original British title as the Transvaal War) and had repercussions which have a direct bearing on the second resort to war between Britain and the Transvaal in 1899.

The annexation of the Transvaal was accompanied by the passing of a 'Permissive Act' by the British Parliament (a measure to provide for a South African federation which became a dead letter) and the arrival of Sir Bartle Frere as the new British High Commissioner in Cape Town in March 1877. Frere was an imperialist of the kind which was to reach full fruition when Sir Alfred Milner was appointed to the same post twenty years later. For both men, what they perceived as the interests of the British Empire were paramount; neither showed any understanding of Afrikaner society or the force of colonial nationalism; each sought quick results and was prepared to use force to achieve them. Frere's actions during the next three years obstructed the achievement of his objectives, led to his recall in 1880, and resulted in the forced march towards South African federation – which Carnarvon had initiated – ending in failure.

The British annexation of the Transvaal meant that the military resources of that state – which had proved insufficient to defeat the Pedi, let alone the Zulu – were now reinforced by the British army. Shepstone and Frere believed that it was now in British, as well as Afrikaner, interests for the power of the Pedi and the Zulu to be broken. Frere was an ambitious man, eager to crown his career by bringing into being a South African Confederation and convinced that the removal of the Zulu 'menace' (which he deliberately exaggerated) would facilitate this. He also wished to circumvent the recommendations, in the Zulu's favour, of a recent boundary commission. As the man on the spot, Frere was able to take advantage of the succession of a new Colonial Secretary in 1878, Sir Michael Hicks Beach, to press ahead with a confrontation with the Zulu, whom he represented as the most serious menace to peace and stability in both the Transvaal and Natal. After carefully organizing an invasion plan with Lord Chelmsford, Frere presented the Zulu ruler Cetshwayo with an ultimatum demanding that the Zulu army should be disbanded. Had Cetshwayo complied with this demand he would certainly have been overthrown and replaced by his own people; when he failed to do so, Chelmsford invaded the country with a substantial army in January 1879. The ensuing destruction of a British regiment at Isandhlwana – where the British army lost 1,600 men in its greatest disaster since the Crimean War – and the desperate defensive action at Rorke's Drift, demonstrated the truth of Paul Kruger's warning that the Zulu were a formidable force and exposed the ineptness of the British military. But with the despatch of British reinforcements, with far superior fire-power, the war drew to a close; the Zulu capital of Ulundi was destroyed and by the end of August Cetshwayo was a prisoner despatched to Cape Town, the Zulu army had ceased to exist, and Sir Garnet Wolseley set about dividing Zululand into thirteen separate chiefdoms.[25]

In September, Wolseley led a force of over 14,000 men against the Pedi and, after heavy fighting, succeeded also in defeating them. Their leader, Sekhukhune, was sent as a prisoner to Pretoria and Pedi power was finally broken.[26] Thus, British power succeeded in achieving for the Transvaal state what the Afrikaners had been too weak to achieve for themselves. British annexation may have removed their 'sacred independence' but by the end of 1879 it had also secured the Transvaal against its most powerful African neighbours. This crucial development freed the Afrikaners to make a bid to regain their independence during the following year.

The British defeat of the Zulu in 1879 was only the most dramatic of a series of African defeats at this time. Together with the final conclusion of the century-long war in the eastern Cape against the Xhosa, and a number of smaller conflicts elsewhere, these African defeats mark the virtual end of effective resistance to European rule in the nineteenth century.[27] Although further annexations of African land continued into the 1890s, something of a watershed in South African history had been reached by 1880 with the establishment of untrammelled European supremacy. During the last twenty years of the nineteenth century it was to be the intensification of the conflict between Boers and British which was to dominate the political scene.

THE TRANSVAAL WAR (1880–81)

In the Transvaal annexation proclamation of April 1877, Shepstone had promised that 'the Transvaal will remain a separate Government, with its own laws and legislature'.[28] Thereafter, the territory was ruled directly, as a Crown Colony, in a tactless, authoritarian way with a quite inadequate grant-in-aid of £100,000. The result was that the Afrikaner burghers were rapidly alienated. When Paul Kruger, who had emerged as their new leader and the chief contender against Burgers for the presidency, went to London in July 1877 on a mission authorized by the Volksraad before it was disbanded, he asked for a Transvaal plebiscite to test support for the British annexation. Carnarvon refused. On Kruger's return, signed petitions were collected which showed that 6,591 Transvaal burghers (out of a possible total white electorate of 8,000) opposed the annexation and only 587 were in favour of it. When these petitions were presented to the new Colonial Secretary, Hicks Beach, on a second visit to London in 1878, he refused to re-open the matter. He told Kruger and P. J. Joubert, who had accompanied him, that it was the British government's unalterable intention that the Transvaal should become 'an integral and separate State' within a South African confederation, 'possessing a Constitution securing, to the utmost practical extent, its individuality and powers of self-government under the sovereignty of the Queen'. Kruger and Joubert replied that, without independence, the Transvaal would never voluntarily enter any confederation. Kruger told Shepstone that Britain's annexation of the Transvaal had provoked protest from the burghers and 'a breach of so serious a nature, that for many years to come no friendly co-operation can be thought of'.[29]

By 1879, the British government of the Transvaal had become a 'timorous despotism', remote from the people, obsessed with making ends meet, and dependent on an inadequate military garrison. In June 1878, Frere had told the Boer leaders: 'Under the British flag you will have everything you desire but that the [British] flag will continue to fly over the land.' Joubert had replied: 'Over the land, possibly; over the people – never.'[30] In January 1879, a resolution was passed at a public meeting of Transvalers to work for independence and when Kruger met Frere, in April, he told him that he did not know how much longer he could restrain his burghers from active resistance against an annexation 'brought about by perjury and deceit'. In December, British sovereignty over the Transvaal was publicly denounced but open revolt was postponed pending the result of the forthcoming British general election.

In his Midlothian speeches, Gladstone denounced Disraeli's South African policy as against the wishes of the people concerned and as a product of a Conservative Party which was 'drunk with imperialism'. In the Transvaal, declared Gladstone, 'we have chosen most unwisely, I am tempted to say insanely, to place ourselves in the strange predicament of the free subjects of a monarchy going to coerce the free subjects of a republic and to compel them to accept a citizenship which they refuse'.[31] Meanwhile, Kruger and his burghers waited expectantly for Gladstone's return to power and the retrocession of the republic. When Gladstone won the elections, Kruger wrote to him, in May 1880, reminding him of his promise 'to rescind the annexation of our poor country and to reinstate in its full vigour the Treaty of Sand River'.[32] Two of the members of Gladstone's Cabinet in 1880, who were to occupy key positions in Salisbury's Cabinet in 1899 – Hicks Beach and Joseph Chamberlain - felt afterwards that Gladstone's government had been wrong in the way it handled the Transvaal in 1880. Chamberlain had actually pressed for Frere's recall and a reconsideration of the Transvaal annexation at the time.[33] Frere was recalled in August; but Disraeli's failure to achieve a federation in South Africa only made Gladstone more determined to succeed. His Colonial Secretary, Lord Kimberley, was also eager to try again where he had failed previously. Finally, Wolseley, after warning the government that 'we are hated by nine out of ten of the Boers with an intense hatred', nonetheless wrote a memorandum, in November 1879, which was persuasive in its argument that confederation in South Africa would never be achieved if Britain abandoned the Transvaal. Having rescued it from a corrupt and hopeless government, Wolseley urged that Britain should lead the Transvaal into a future in which 'the time must eventually arrive when the Boers will be in a small minority'.[34] Despite warnings from President Brand of the growing feeling in the Transvaal, and the rejection by the Cape parliament of a motion proposing federation, Gladstone insisted on Britain's retention of Transvaal sovereignty and thereby provoked the *coup de grace* to the achievement of federation under British rule. In December 1880, the seizure of a Boer wagon because its owner had refused to pay tax led to violence at Potchefstroom, 5,000 Transvaal burghers gathered at Paardekraal, the Transvaal again proclaimed itself a republic, and the Volksraad reconvened and gave executive powers to a triumvirate consisting of Paul Kruger, Piet Joubert and ex-President M. W. Pretorius. A British Cabinet preoccupied with the Irish question failed to realize that a Boer revolt against British rule was underway in the Transvaal.

The Transvaal War, which lasted for barely three months, was blundered into by a badly informed British government with its attention elsewhere. The Transvaal Boers rebelled against a British occupation and rule of the Transvaal which was unpopular and considered unjust.[35] Although some Boers from the Orange Free State came to the Transvaal's assistance, it was essentially a Transvaal war. A series of skirmishes on the Drakensberg escarpment never developed into a full-scale war because the numbers involved in these encounters were small and because both sides to the conflict were, almost from the outset, looking for a way out of it through a negotiated settlement. The events of 1880–81 bear no comparison with the second, far more resolute resort to arms in 1899–1902. The outcome of the first encounter, however, certainly influenced the second – not least because some of the same leading political figures were involved in both conflicts: Kruger and Joubert on the Boer side, for example, and Chamberlain and Hicks Beach on the British.

In 1880–81, Gladstone's government at once tried to extricate itself from a situation which it had provoked. A political settlement of the conflict was soon sought through negotiations which were actively assisted by President Brand (of the Orange Free State), Sir Henry de Villiers (Chief Justice of the Cape Colony), and Sir Hercules Robinson (who had replaced Frere as British High Commissioner in South Africa). Brand warned the British government of the growing inclination of his burghers to go to the assistance of the Transvaal and urged it to make a peace proposal at once. Robinson said that the loyalty of the Cape Afrikaners was being strained to the limit and that a British victory would only increase their sympathy for the Transvalers. Sir Henry de Villiers believed that the British government would only hold on to the Transvaal 'by means of a large force' and asked 'is it worth having on such terms?'[36] Lord Kimberley feared that the Transvaal Boers 'evidently aim at raising the whole Dutch population of S. Africa against us'. To a House of Lords which had begun to wonder whether Britain was creating another Irish question in South Africa, he admitted that 'These emigrant farmers left our territory [in the Great Trek] because they did not acquiesce in our rule. We have not succeeded in conciliating them . . . their hostility has culminated in the insurrection now going on.' Peace was vital, he declared, not only for the Transvaal 'but also for the peace and tranquillity of our own colonies' in South Africa.[37] All this was agreed and peace negotiations were already underway when the self-willed Sir George Colley, acting against the spirit of his instructions and ignoring a message from Joubert indicating a readiness to negotiate, made a series of military blunders which culminated in a British defeat at Majuba Hill on 27 February 1881.

This battle, in which only a few hundred troops were engaged and where British losses, including the death of Colley himself, accounted for about a third of the total for the whole war, soon acquired great symbolic importance.[38] Like the failure to relieve General Gordon at Khartoum, it came to be regarded in Britain as a blot upon the national honour which Conservatives pointed to as an example of

Liberal mismanagement. 'Remember Majuba' became the rallying cry with which many British soldiers were to go into action in 1899. On the Boer side it also took on a special significance. Kruger, in his *Memoirs*, put 'revenge for Majuba Hill' as the second most important cause of the war of 1899–1902 and observed that, but for the mistaken British annexation and retention of the Transvaal between 1877 and 1881, there would have been no Majuba Hill and no revenge would therefore have been necessary.[39]

Yet, at the time, this humiliating British defeat made no difference to the policy of a negotiated peace on which Gladstone's government was already set. On 5 March, John Bright noted in his journal: 'Cabinet at 2 o'clock . . . On Transvaal affair, no member of the Government urging war for sake of recovering the reputation of English arms – terms of pacification the same as before the conflict of Majuba Hill.'[40] On 6 March 1881, an armistice was declared and, after protracted negotiations, peace terms were agreed by the Convention of Pretoria (1881). Both Queen Victoria and the *Daily Telegraph* thought that these represented a British capitulation. Hicks Beach considered that such a British surrender, after defeat, would result in 'infinitely worse trouble' in the future. Sir Evelyn Wood, who played a central role in the peace negotiations, observed that 'within a few years . . . we shall have to take over the country'.[41] The concessions, granted by the British government after defeat in battle, filled many Afrikaners with contempt for Britain and were felt by many British subjects in South Africa to be deeply humiliating. The forward movement towards a British-led federation in South Africa came to a halt. Occupation and coercion of the Transvaal were now replaced by withdrawal and conciliation. Britain had alienated the Transvaal Boers at the same time as she had strengthened the Transvaal as a white-settler state, and she was to spend the rest of the century attempting to restore her dwindling hold over the area.

FROM THE PRETORIA CONVENTION TO THE LONDON CONVENTION (1881–4)

This 'second yielding' by the British government to Boer separatism did not, however, mean that there was any return to the independence of the Transvaal as embodied in the Sand River Convention of 1852. Self-government under British suzerainty, a British Resident in Pretoria, British rights over foreign relations and the conduct of 'native affairs', and the 33 articles of the Pretoria Convention, did not amount to the restoration of full independence. This was clearly recognized at the first meeting of the reconstituted Transvaal Volksraad when the Pretoria Convention was described as 'a cup of milk with 33 flies in it'.[42] The Pretoria Convention – which was not subjected to British parliamentary scrutiny but simply issued as an Order in Council – was not a treaty between equals but a prerogative act by the British government which conferred rights and freedoms on the Transvalers. Unlike the Orange Free State, which remained fully independent under the terms of the Bloemfontein Convention (1854), the Transvaal after 1881 was never a fully sovereign and independent state – much though the Transvaal government was to challenge and deny this. The Sand River Convention had ceased to operate when Britain had annexed the Transvaal in 1877. Now, the new state was established in an atmosphere of recrimination and mutual distrust between the British and Transvaal governments. The title of the 'Transvaal State' was introduced by the British to indicate that fully independent republican status had not been restored. But it so offended Kruger and his burghers – who considered that the old republic had never ceased to exist but had just been temporarily in abeyance between 1877 and 1881 – that they simply continued to use the old title of 'The South African Republic'. This state was guaranteed 'complete self-government subject to the suzerainty of Her Majesty', suzerainty being a vague term which was to cause serious trouble later.[43] No specific provision was made for the political representation of non-Afrikaner Europeans but, in discussion, Kruger promised that British subjects would enjoy the same privileges as Boers 'so far as burgher rights are concerned'.[44] The new state had a debt of half a million pounds and other financial obligations imposed upon it which the British Colonial Office later admitted 'were hardly regarded as workable from the first'.[45] Within a year there were defaults, expansion beyond the agreed borders, and other signs that the Transvaal burghers did not consider themselves to be bound by a Convention which they felt had been imposed upon them and which, in Britain itself, was considered by some as 'rapidly becoming a dead letter'.[46]

The rise of Kruger's republic had, in fact, already begun and with it a new focus on the Transvaal in Afrikaner consciousness. It was in connection with the Transvaal rebellion of 1880–81 that the call of 'Africa for the Africander' was first raised. The Transvaal victory over the British at Majuba Hill, and the re-establishment of the South African Republic by 1884, helped to stimulate a new national feeling amongst the disunited Afrikaner population within and beyond its borders. The Transvaal became the rallying point for the vision of a united Afrikaner nation, with a shared sentiment and a common destiny. An Afrikaner cultural and linguistic revival had already been under way in the Cape during the 1870s, but the war injected a new republican spirit and a new political focus into the early development of Afrikaner nationalism. Some leading members of Cape Afrikaner society began to look to, and move to, the Transvaal. S. J. du Toit, for example, who had been co-founder of the Afrikaner Bond and a leading figure in the establishment of Afrikaans newspapers in the Cape, became Kruger's Minister of Education in the Transvaal republic. The strong, anti-English feeling and the belief in the need to develop a pan-Afrikaner sentiment throughout South Africa, which were characteristic of his outlook, intensified under the external pressure and threat from Britain which was so striking a feature of these years. A new sense of Afrikaner unity in South Africa was encouraged by the Transvaal War and its aftermath, and during the following decade the Transvaal became 'the inheritance of young South Africa' for many able young Afrikaners born and brought up elsewhere in South Africa. Afrikaner nationalist aspirations began to stir, although it was not until the turn of the century that these took on a coherent form.[47]

In November 1883, after his election for the first of four successive terms of office as President of the Transvaal, Kruger again returned to London, this time with a delegation determined to revise the terms of the Pretoria Convention. Gladstone's government, preoccupied with the Mahdist revolt in the Sudan, was prepared to be conciliatory in the hope of establishing a more constructive basis for Anglo-Transvaal relations. Britain's main concern was to control the foreign relations of the Transvaal as a means of isolating what was still regarded as a poor, land-locked, ramshackle state in the South African interior.[48] So, the Pretoria Convention was replaced by the London Convention on the third anniversary of Majuba Hill on 27 February 1884.

By the terms of this new Convention, the name of the South African Republic was restored, no reference was made to British suzerainty, the debt was reduced to £250,000, the role of the British Resident in Pretoria was reduced to that of a Consular Officer and, apart from a prohibition against slavery, an end was made to any British attempt to control the Transvaal's treatment of its African population. The Transvaal, however, was not allowed to conclude treaties with any foreign state (other than the Orange Free State) without British approval and was denied the right to expand beyond its defined boundaries to the east and west (the northern boundary remained open). Overall, the new Convention represented an attempt by Britain to conciliate the Transvaal and return to a policy of minimal control. Kruger and his burghers regarded it as a victory for their efforts to remove the shackles which had been imposed upon them by the Pretoria Convention in 1881. Notwithstanding the later attempts of Joseph Chamberlain and others to resurrect it, by specious reasoning, British suzerainty over the Transvaal had, in fact, been abolished in 1884. Two years before the world's richest deposits of gold were discovered in the Transvaal, Gladstone's government had ensured that the future preservation of British supremacy over the area rested 'on the slender pillars of informal paramountcy and conciliation'.[49]

The London Convention formed the basis for the conduct of relations between Britain and the Transvaal republic right through to the outbreak of war in 1899. It was to be a perpetual point of reference and conflict between the two governments during the next fifteen years. It is therefore difficult to exaggerate its importance. Yet it was negotiated when Britain was still the only Great Power on the South African scene and when the Transvaal was still the poorest and weakest of the white-settler states in South Africa. The framework for Anglo-Transvaal relations to the end of the century was established just before gold changed everything.

In 1885, one of the most perceptive of British Colonial Office officials, Edward Fairfield, stated the British problem in relation to the Transvaal in the following terms:

> The policy embodied in the Sand River Convention gave us 25 years of peace and freedom from anxiety. We abandoned it, and we have been ever since in a horrid mess. We shall no doubt revert to it again some day, and be once more at rest. We are very far from being at rest now.[50]

The Sand River and Bloemfontein Conventions had represented a mid-nineteenth-century British policy of abandoning the Boer republics to their own devices in the interior and maintaining British supremacy over them, and over South Africa as a whole, by limiting their possibilities for territorial expansion and the acquisition of an independent access to the sea, and relying on their dependence upon the ports, trade, and communications of the Cape Colony and Natal to result in the dominance of English colonialism over Boer republicanism in South Africa overall. Yet already by 1884, events in South Africa itself had drawn Britain into ever increasing intervention in the area. Britain had not hesitated to intervene where necessary – to save diamond fields or Basuto territory from the Orange Free State, to defeat Zulu or Pedi, to annex more territory for the Cape or Natal, to occupy a bankrupt Transvaal. The forces at work which brought about this intervention were only to intensify during the remaining years of the nineteenth century. Fairfield's hope for an end, once more, to Britain's involvement in the affairs of the republics was a pipe-dream by the 1880s, but it was passionately shared by Kruger and his burghers in the Transvaal. As Sir Hercules Robinson, the British High Commissioner, had warned the British government in 1883:

> The object of the Boers is, of course, to break down and get rid of the [Pretoria] Convention. They want to shake off the suzerainty and the debt, to be free from all restrictions as to interfering with the Natives, within or without the State, and to conduct their foreign relations as they choose; to be fully inscribed on the roll of nations as they pompously say.[51]

Others, with much experience of South Africa, such as John Mackenzie (missionary and later Deputy Commissioner in Bechuanaland) wondered whether the Transvaal's ambitions were limited to becoming free of British restraint or rather that Kruger's republic aimed 'to become the paramount South African state'. 'What they want', he wrote in November 1883, 'is the supreme political position in South Africa; to become the empire state amongst its states.'[52]

The London Convention was negotiated by a British government on the rebound from the disastrous experience of annexing and attempting to govern the Transvaal directly between 1877 and 1881 and preoccupied with Egypt, the Sudan and Ireland. It was an attempt by Gladstone's government to limit British liabilities, and thereby the points of potential conflict between Britain and a small population of poor and recalcitrant farmers living in an area of the South African interior which at that time was of no apparent or necessary interest to Britain. Gladstone's government saw no reason therefore to withstand the demands of the Transvalers. For their part, the desire of the Transvaal Boers for the withdrawal of British government was not just a desire for political independence; it was also the protest of an economically backward and poorly organized people against the imposition and exactions of modern government.[53] In 1884, their way of life was still based on land and cattle, rather than cash and tax receipts. Yet the withdrawal of the British government did not bring an end to the steady penetration of Transvaal society by the forces of the modern world. With the discovery of gold, this was enormously accelerated. Within a decade of the signing of the London Convention, the Transvaal had become not the poorest but the richest part of South Africa. After the mutual suspicions and heightened sensitivities aroused by what had happened between 1877 and 1881, any attempt to turn the Transvaal Boers into willing collaborators in a future British South Africa was likely to evoke resistance. The transformation in the power and importance of the Transvaal, which followed the discovery of gold on the Witwatersrand in 1886, gave the Transvaal government the means to make its resistance formidable.

The end of British suzerainty over the Transvaal in 1884 did not mean that Britain had withdrawn from asserting her supremacy over South Africa as a whole. Precisely because the region was so disunited, Britain was drawn into exercising the role of a paramount power in order to keep other great powers out. The signing of the London Convention was followed by a sequence of events which relentlessly drew the British government into further commitments in the South African interior. Even before the discovery of gold, the European scramble for southern Africa had begun and a new Great Power had arrived on the scene.

THE GERMAN INCURSION

With no previous history of overseas colonial possessions, Germany under Bismarck embarked upon an outburst of colonial empire-building in 1884–5 during which all of Germany's African colonies were acquired in the space of eighteen months.[54] The reasons for this sudden venture have as much to do with German domestic political considerations as with the growing belief that, in an era of growing protectionism, colonies offered a potentially useful economic outlet and were an attribute of having arrived as a great power. Bismarck himself was unenthusiastic about African colonies but certain German shipping and trading interests became active pressure groups, and nationalistic organizations such as the Colonial and Navy Leagues fanned public opinion into an interest in acquiring 'a place in the sun'. 'This colonial business is all a swindle, but we will use it to win votes', Bismarck cynically observed during the run-up to the Reichstag elections of 1885.[55] Bismarck also appreciated the usefulness of having a stake in the colonial arena for the conduct of his relations with Britain and France; in 1884, he set out to challenge the 'sort of Munro [sic] doctrine' which Britain had assumed over South Africa.[56]

An initial expression of interest in establishing German 'protection' over the port established by a Bremen trader, Lüderitz, on the coast of South West Africa was treated in a desultory way by Britain and the matter was shuffled between the British and Cape governments for several months, without resolution, until Bismarck took pre-emptive action and annexed first Angra Pequena (Lüderitz) and then the whole of the coast of South West Africa, from the Orange River to the border with Angola, as a German Protectorate in August 1884. Competition had recently developed there between Cape and German merchants for access to the rich guano deposits and fishing of an area which the Cape had always regarded as its own preserve. Both sets of merchants had petitioned their governments to act on their behalf, but the reluctance of the Cape Colony to take on yet further territorial and financial commitments and the failure of Britain to act again as it had done over Walfisch Bay in 1878 (which was eventually incorporated in the Cape Colony in 1884) had left the way open to Germany.

By annexing South West Africa, Germany had broken the British monopoly of the South African coast and established the presence of a new Great Power in the area. The British government was first shocked by the German incursion and then fearful that it might be followed by further claims to undelimited areas of the east coast around St Lucia Bay and that these coastal possessions would then be used to establish claims to the hinterland behind them. A German presence on the coast was regarded as 'a dangerous complication' by the British Colonial Office, which perceived that 'a hostile cordon drawn around the Cape from Angra Pequena to Zululand would effectually cripple us'.[57] Even more threatening was the possibility that German projections into the hinterland could result in a conjunction with the Transvaal republic which would upset the whole balance of power in South Africa. Gladstone, who in 1883 had welcomed Germany as a colonizing power and 'our ally and partner in the execution of the great purposes of Providence for the advantage of mankind', was, by December 1884, alarmed to find 'that wherever there is a dark corner in South African politics there is a German spectre to be the tenant of it'. During 1885, he therefore set out to secure for Britain the remaining coastline of South Africa through the annexation of St Lucia Bay and the coastal region between the Cape and Natal.[58]

Bechuanaland also, which had been dismissed as worthless by the British government the year before, suddenly took on a new importance as the territorial wedge between the German hinterland in

South West Africa and the Transvaal republic. Tswana territory was already being competed for by the Cape Colony and the Transvaal. The Cape, urged on by Cecil Rhodes, wanted to preserve the fertile strip of land between the Transvaal's western border and the Kalahari desert as its 'road to the North' and the as yet unopened territory across the Limpopo. Transvaal *trekboers* had meanwhile 'drifted' over the frontier, in search of new land, and established the two small, new republics of Stellaland and Goshen. In September 1884, Kruger 'provisionally' annexed them to the Transvaal and only backed down when the British government insisted that this was a flagrant breach of the London Convention which had been signed in February. The potential German threat to the area finally stimulated the British government to intervene decisively, once more, in the interior. In January 1885, Sir Charles Warren was despatched with a strong force to establish British control over the region. The area to the south of the Molopo river was eventually incorporated within the Cape Colony, that to the north became part of the British Bechuanaland Protectorate. A possible conjunction between Transvaal westward expansion and German eastward expansion had been prevented.

The German arrival on the South African scene challenged Britain's complacent supremacy and introduced a new factor into South African affairs which remained important for the rest of the century. Even after Germany's acquisition of territory had been settled (the eastern boundary of South West Africa/Namibia was only settled in 1890), her role as a potential patron or ally of the Transvaal republic remained a source of concern to British governments during the 1890s. British fears were probably exaggerated. President Kruger attempted to play the German 'card' from time to time and granted the monopoly for the Transvaal railways to a German–Dutch syndicate; the Transvaal attracted some German immigrants and considerable German investment; and the German Kaiser sent the occasional timely telegram. But Kruger had no intention of putting his burghers under German colonial rule and Britain made it perfectly clear that she would not tolerate any challenge from Germany to her supremacy in a part of the world which she regarded as her 'sphere of influence'. Despite moments of anxiety for British governments, Germany came to accept this and, in August 1898, an Anglo-German Agreement was reached 'by which the German Government left to England the whole of South Africa'.[59]

NOTES

1. L. Thompson, *A History of South Africa* (Newhaven, 1990), pp. 52–3.
2. Sir George Yonge to Henry Dundas, 29 March 1800, cited in J. S. Galbraith, *Reluctant Empire: British Policy on the South African Frontier 1834–1854* (Los Angeles, 1963), p. 35.
3. A. Atmore and S. Marks, 'The imperial factor in South Africa in the nineteenth century: towards a reassessment', *Journal of Imperial and Commonwealth History* 111, 1 (October 1974), pp. 109–10.
4. Thompson, *A History of South Africa*, p. 56.
5. R. Elphick and H. Giliomee, *The Shaping of South African Society 1652–1840* (Cape Town and Harlow, 2nd edn, 1989), p. 524.
6. The best authority on the Great Trek is C. F. J. Muller, *Die oorsprong van die Groot Trek* (Cape Town, 1974), and *Die Britse owerheid en die Groot Trek* (Cape Town, 1976). A good short summary in English is given by J. T. du Bruyn in T. Cameron, ed., *An Illustrated History of South Africa* (Johannesburg, 1986), ch. 10. See also L. Thompson, *The Political Mythology of Apartheid* (Newhaven, 1985), ch. 2.
7. Elphick and Giliomee, *The Shaping of South African Society 1652–1840*, p. 507.
8. P. Retief, 'Manifesto of the emigrant farmers', 2 February 1837, printed in G. W. Eybers, ed., *Select Constitutional Documents Illustrating South African History 1795–1910* (New York, 1918), p. 145.
9. Grondwet of the South African Republic, February 1858, Article 9, printed in Eybers, ed., *Select Constitutional Documents*, p. 364.
10. On the *Mfecane* see: R. Edgecombe, 'The Mfecane or Difaqane', in Cameron, ed., *An Illustrated History*, ch. 9; J. D. Omer-Cooper, *The Zulu Aftermath* (Madison, Wisconsin, 1966), and 'Has the Mfecane a future?', *JSAS* 19, 2 (1993); E. Eldredge, 'Sources of conflict in southern Africa c.1800–1830: the Mfecane reconsidered', *JAH* 33, 1 (1992); J. Cobbing, 'The Mfecane as alibi', *JAH* 29, 3 (1988).
11. For a recent view see N. Etherington, 'The Great Trek in relation to the Mfecane: a re-assessment', *SAHJ* 25 (1991).
12. John Wright, 'Popularizing the pre-colonial past: politics and problems', unpublished paper, History Workshop, Witwatersrand University, February 1987.
13. H. Giliomee, *The History in our Politics* (Inaugural Lecture, Cape Town, 1986), p. 7. See also H. Giliomee and A. du Toit, *Afrikaner Political Thought 1780–1850* (Los Angeles, 1983), 1.
14. L. Thompson and M. Wilson, eds, *The Oxford History of South Africa* (Oxford, 1971), 2, pp. 253–7; R. Oliver and G. N. Sanderson, eds, *The Cambridge History of Africa* (Cambridge, 1985), 6, pp. 363–74.
15. On diamond mining and its effects see: W. H. Worger, *South Africa's City of Diamonds: Mine-workers and Monopoly Capitalism in Kimberley 1867–1895* (Newhaven and London, 1987); R. V. Turrell, *Capital and Labour on the Kimberley Diamond Fields 1871–1890* (Cambridge, 1987).

16. See Robert Rotberg, *The Founder: Cecil Rhodes and the Pursuit of Power* (Oxford, 1989), chs 6 and 9; Colin Newbury, *Diamond Ring: Business, Politics and Precious Stones in South Africa 1867–1947* (Oxford, 1990).

17. C. W. de Kiewiet, *A History of South Africa: Social and Economic* (Oxford, 1941), p. 87.

18. S. Marks in Oliver and Sanderson, eds, *The Cambridge History of Africa*, 6, p. 377. Population statistics for South Africa are notoriously unreliable before 1900, even for the Cape Colony.

19. For the attempt at federation in the 1870s see: L. Thompson in *The Oxford History of South Africa*, 2, pp. 289–300; S. Marks in *The Cambridge History of Africa*, 6, pp. 376–9; T. R. H. Davenport, *South Africa: a Modern History* (Basingstoke, 1987), pp. 193–8; C. F. Goodfellow, *Great Britain and South African Confederation* (Oxford, 1966). For the labour and economic aspects see N. Etherington, 'Labour supply and the genesis of South African Confederation in the 1870s', *JAH* 20 (1979), and R. L. Cope, 'Strategic and socio-economic explanations for Carnarvon's South African Confederation policy: the historiography and the evidence', *History in Africa* 13 (1986).

20. F. Harcourt, 'Disraeli's imperialism, 1868–1888: a question of timing', *HJ* 23, 1 (1980); ibid., 'Gladstone, monarchism and the new imperialism 1868–1874', *JICH* X1V, 1 (1974).

21. De Kiewiet, *A History of South Africa*, p. 101.

22. D. M. Schreuder, *The Scramble for Southern Africa* (Cambridge, 1980), p. 72.

23. C. W. de Kiewiet, *The Imperial Factor in South Africa* (Cambridge, 1937), p. 118.

24. C. J. Uys, 'Shepstone's letters and diary', *Natal Witness*, 10 July 1930.

25. Thompson, in *The Oxford History of South Africa*, 2, pp. 263–5. For a recent reappraisal of this much-mythologized war see: A. Duminy and C. Ballard, eds, *The Anglo-Zulu War: New Perspectives* (Pietermaritzburg, 1981).

26. P. Delius, *The Land Belongs to Us: the Pedi Polity, the Boers and the British in the Nineteenth Century Transvaal* (London, 1983).

27. See especially N. Mostert, *Frontiers: the Epic of South Africa's Creation and the Tragedy of the Xhosa People* (London, 1992); also J. B. Peires, *The House of Phalo* (Johannesburg, 1981), and *The Dead Will Arise* (Johannesburg, 1989).

28. Proclamation of the annexation of the South African Republic to the British Empire, 12 April 1877, printed in Eybers, *Select Constitutional Documents*, p. 452.

29. Published exchanges in CO 2220, Appendix 1, and C.2302. I owe these references to G. H. Le May, who gives an excellent, detailed account in ch. 4 of his forthcoming study of *The Afrikaners*.

30. D. M. Schreuder, *Gladstone and Kruger: Liberal Government and Colonial 'Home Rule' 1880–1885* (London, 1969), p. 88.

31. Ibid., p. 54.

32. Ibid., p. 58.

33. J. Chamberlain, *A Political Memoir*, ed. C. H. D. Howard (London, 1953), p. 14.

34. Schreuder, *Gladstone and Kruger*, p. 59; de Kiewiet, *The Imperial Factor*, pp. 249–51.

35. The political background to this war is best treated in D. M. Schreuder, *Gladstone and Kruger*, chs 1–3. The military campaigns are well covered by J. Lehmann, *The First Boer War* (London, 1972).

36. Schreuder, *Gladstone and Kruger*, pp. 128–30.

37. Lord Kimberley, Speech in the House of Lords, 21 February 1881, cited in ibid., p. 128.

38. Lehmann, *The First Boer War*, p. 260.

39. S. J. P. Kruger, *The Memoirs of Paul Kruger . . . told by himself* 2 vols (London, 1902), 1, p. 136.

40. G. M. Trevelyan, *Life of John Bright* (London, 1913), p. 431.

41. Schreuder, *Gladstone and Kruger*, p. 217.

42. De Kiewiet, *The Imperial Factor*, p. 286.

43. See Chapter 5 pp. 173–6.

44. E. Walker, *Cambridge History of the British Empire: South Africa* 8 vols, 2nd edn (Cambridge, 1963), p. 496.

45. De Kiewiet, *The Imperial Factor*, p. 294.

46. Ibid.

47. The phrase used by the young J. C. Smuts in his first published article in October 1895: see W. K. Hancock and J. van der Poel, eds, *Selections from the Smuts Papers* (Cambridge, 1966), 1, p. 79. For the emergence of Afrikaner nationalism, see H. Giliomee, 'The Beginnings of Afrikaner Nationalism, 1870–1915', *SAHJ* 19 (1987), and 'The beginnings of Afrikaner ethnic consciousness 1850–1915', in Leroy Vail, ed., *The Creation of Tribalism in Southern Africa* (London, 1989); also F. A. van Jaarsveld, *The Awakening of Afrikaner Nationalism 1868–1881* (Cape Town, 1961).

48. Schreuder, *Gladstone and Kruger*, p. 392. The following section is much indebted to this work's detailed account of the negotiations leading to the London Convention.

49. Ibid., p. 254.

50. Minute by Edward Fairfield, 27 July 1885, in de Kiewiet, *The Imperial Factor*, p. 327.

51. Report of a discussion between Sir Hercules Robinson and Lord Derby, 16 May 1883, in Schreuder, *Gladstone and Kruger*, p. 348.

52. J. Mackenzie to W. T. Stead, November 1883, cited in ibid., p. 376.

53. De Kiewiet, *A History of South Africa*, p. 107.

54. For the German role in South Africa see: J. Butler, 'The German factor in Anglo-Transvaal relations', and H. A. Turner, 'Bismarck's imperialist venture: anti-British in origin?', both in P. Gifford and W. R. Louis, eds, *Britain and Germany in Africa* (New Haven, 1967); H. Stoeckler, ed., *German Imperialism in Africa 1880–1945* (London, 1986); U. Kroll, *Die internationale Burenagitation 1899–1902* (Munster, 1973); H-U. Wehler, 'Bismarck's imperialism 1862–1890', *Past and Present* 48 (1970),

pp. 119–55; H. Pogge von Strandmann, 'Domestic origins of Germany's colonial expansion under Bismarck', *Past and Present* 42 (1969), pp. 140–59.

55. N. Rich and M. H. Fisher, eds, *The Holstein Papers*, vol. 2, Diaries (Cambridge, 1957), p. 161.

56. J. Butler, 'The German factor in Anglo-Transvaal relations', p. 185.

57. R. Hyam, *Britain's Imperial Century 1815–1914* (London, 1976), p. 283.

58. B. Porter, *The Lion's Share: a Short History of British Imperialism 1850–1980* (London, 1985), p. 102; Hyam, *Britain's Imperial Century*, p.284.

59. Balfour to Lascelles, 19 August 1898, reporting a conversation with the German ambassador, cited in Butler, 'The German factor', p. 205. See ch. 6 pp. 207–9 below.

CHAPTER TWO

Gold and Its Consequences

In 1886, gold was discovered on the Witwatersrand. This was not entirely fortuitous but the result of the intensified search for new sources of gold which accompanied the enormous expansion of world trade in the second half of the nineteenth century and the role of the Gold Standard in underpinning this expansion. There had already been gold-finds in the Transvaal, in the Lydenburg and Barberton areas, but these were soon dwarfed into insignificance by the scale of the Witwatersrand deposits. Within a decade, the country from which Gladstone had so lightly withdrawn had become 'the richest spot on earth'. Gold transformed not just the Transvaal but South Africa. From being 'an unprosperous State that had never known genuine solvency'[1], the Transvaal republic became the economic focus for the entire sub-continent. By 1898, the Transvaal was the largest single producer of gold in the world, accounting for 27 per cent of total world production; by 1913, this had risen to 40 per cent.[2] Within six years of the discovery of the Rand, gold had overtaken diamonds as South Africa's most important export. In the short space of twelve years (1883–95) the revenue of the South African Republic multiplied 25 times over. South Africa took on a quite new importance, in the eyes of the rest of the world, as her gold supplies contributed to the underpinning of currencies and international trade during the hey-day of the Gold Standard.

Capital investment poured into the Transvaal, some of it from the profits of the diamond-mining industry, much more of it from abroad; about three-quarters of the foreign investment in this period came from Britain. By 1899, a total of 75 million had been invested in the Transvaal gold-mines, and by 1914 this had increased to 125 million. The development of the Witwatersrand gold-fields was one of the most dramatic examples of late nineteenth-century capitalist enterprise in the world, involving far greater sums of capital investment than had been the case with the gold-mines of Australia or the United States.[3] Together with the simultaneous discovery of large coal deposits in the Transvaal and Natal, and the already established diamond-mining industry, the development of gold-mining constituted a 'mineral revolution' in South Africa at the end of the nineteenth century which changed the whole economic and political constellation of the region and led to the development of by far the most advanced industrialized economy on the African continent. Gold brought an end to Cape supremacy in South Africa. The centre of economic and political gravity for the region shifted north to the Transvaal. Gold became the hub round which the whole of South Africa's development since has revolved.

The nature of the gold deposits on the Witwatersrand exercised a crucial influence over the way the mining industry developed. Previously, most gold mined in the world had been alluvial gold, but the gold of the Rand could only be extracted with the power and inventions of the 'second industrial revolution' which had developed in Europe.[4] What the Rand contained was an abundant supply of low-grade ore from which about one ounce of gold could be extracted for every ton of ore milled. Initially, the gold was extracted from 'outcrops' where the gold-bearing reef surfaced. The reef extended for some 40 miles on an east–west axis but it was situated at such an angle in the ground that, once the outcrops were exhausted, ever deeper shafts had to be sunk to reach it. By the early 1890s, it was clear that the long-term future of the gold-mines lay in deep-level mining, with its enormous capital costs, although it was confidently predicted that, over the next half-century, production would reach 'upwards of £700 million in value, of which, in all probability, some £200 million will be clear profit'.[5] Considerable technical difficulties, however, had first to be overcome. There were the problems associated with mining at ever greater depths; and there was the pressing need – with poor quality ore, in which the gold particles were thinly dispersed – to maximize the degree of extraction. Initially, most mines extracted gold by the 'amalgamation process', whereby the ore was first crushed and then treated with mercury. But the ore that was brought from further beneath the surface was pyritic ore, mined with the use of Nobel's blasting gelatine (invented 1874), and this required the development of quite new extraction techniques, including the MacArthur-Forrest cyanide process (patented in 1887), which resulted in a recovery rate of about 90 per cent.

45

The early years of the Witwatersrand gold industry were marked by successive booms and slumps accentuated by waves of speculation in mining shares and land. Unlike the diamond-mining industry, in which consolidation under De Beers had gradually replaced the confusion of individual diggers and companies, in gold-mining oligopoly rather than monopoly developed. The immense capital costs involved meant that company mining was there from the outset; and the early slumps eliminated many of the smaller companies. By the 1890s, the requirements for developing the deep levels – which, needing extensive foreign capital investment, required access to the European money markets, and pooled technological and administrative resources – meant that the 'group system' soon developed, by which all of the mines on the Rand came to be part of one or other of nine mining finance 'houses' of which the two most important were Rhodes's Consolidated Goldfields and The Corner House (Wernher, Beit/H. Eckstein & Co.), both formed in 1892. Gold was never as central to Rhodes's fortune as diamonds had been, and Consolidated Goldfields took second place in importance to Wernher, Beit/H. Eckstein & Co. throughout this period. By 1899, this latter firm was responsible for about half of the total gold mined on the Rand. It also owned a number of other concerns and therefore had a major long-term interest in the development of the Transvaal. This brought the firm into regular contact with members of the government. When a Chamber of Mines was formed in 1889, this was the firm which provided it with a succession of chairmen right through to 1902.[6]

Immigration and urbanization followed rapidly in the wake of gold-mining. The extraction of South African gold has always depended upon huge numbers of African migrant labourers from elsewhere in southern Africa. By 1899 their numbers had reached 100,000 and rural African societies hundreds of miles beyond the Transvaal's borders were on the way to becoming dependent on the Transvaal and the wages earned there. During the 1890s, nearly half of the African migrant mine-workers on the Rand came from Mozambique. The fact that gold, unlike other commodities, had a fixed price, and that labour costs formed a high proportion of total costs in the mining industry, meant that from the outset reductions in the cost of African labour were eagerly sought. Recruited from far away, African mine-workers were housed and worked under extremely harsh conditions, for low pay and with a very high death rate during these early years. The emergence of such a widespread system of migrant labour profoundly affected African rural societies and represents a decisive move towards the creation of the detribalized and landless African urban proletariat of twentieth-century South Africa's industrial cities.[7]

THE UITLANDER INFLUX

The gold-mines also brought a massive influx into the Transvaal of European immigrants, known as Uitlanders. A decade after its foundation, Johannesburg had grown into one of the commercial capitals of the world as the original mining camp of about 3,000 diggers developed into a city of 100,000 people; by 1914, Johannesburg had over 250,000 inhabitants.[8] In 1870, the total European population of South Africa was still probably under a quarter of a million. By 1891, it had increased to over 600,000; by 1904 it was over one million. No census was ever made of the European population of the South African Republic and so the precise numbers of Uitlanders in relation to the Afrikaner burghers before 1899 is not known. By 1899, however, the total Afrikaner population (including women and children) certainly outnumbered the Uitlanders in the Transvaal, though there may have been more Uitlander than Boer male adults because these formed a larger proportion of the Uitlander population.[9]

The Uitlanders, however, were no monolithic body but a motley collection of individuals of diverse nationalities, divided by class and disunited. Many of them were birds of passage, drawn to the Transvaal for a few years to make money before returning home. Some came from other parts of South Africa, others from continental Europe and the United States; but the English element predominated. Between 1886 and 1899 some 75,000 people emigrated from Britain to South Africa, many of whom found their way to the Rand. They included skilled artisans, Cornish tin-miners, engineers, lawyers, and professional men. Some, like E. E. Kennedy, were fortune-seekers who came to 'make heaps of money' in 'the biggest boom the world has ever seen' and, having failed to do so, recorded their downward progress 'from confidence to hesitancy, from hesitancy to doubt, and from doubt to despair' and departure, all within a few months.[10] Others stayed longer, but only a minority envisaged settling there permanently. Few were eager to renounce their existing citizenship and take on that of the South African Republic. As Olive Schreiner pointed out, in 1899, the majority 'are *not* integral parts of the State, merely temporarily connected with it, have no interest in its remote future and only a commercial interest in its present'.[11] Most of them lived in Johannesburg which, as one of them put it, 'although a town in a foreign state, was enthusiastically British in its sentiments'.[12]

Whilst the Rand came into existence because of the gold-mines, by no means all of those who came to live and work there were directly involved in mining. About three-quarters of the African population living near the mines were mine-workers. Others, and many more of the Indian and Coloured population who were attracted there from other parts of South Africa, earned their living in the service industries which accompanied the development of a large urban area. Nearly a fifth of the total Johannesburg population were involved in trade, the majority being Europeans but a large minority being Indians who had moved there from Natal. About 6,000 people, mostly Africans and Coloureds, were employed in domestic service. There was a great demand for clerks and accountants, messengers and caretakers, drivers and construction workers, labourers and laundry men and all who provided food, lodging and entertainment for a rapidly growing urban community which had two striking features: most of its members were young and nearly 80 per cent of them were male. Two-thirds of the Uitlander population consisted of single men. Drinking, gambling and whoring became part of life on the Rand in the 1890s for thousands of Uitlanders, most of whom were there without families, whilst speculation and share-dealing formed a major preoccupation, especially during the early years. '*Everyone* speculates', observed one visitor, 'the place is a living hell'.[13] Eye-witnesses have left vivid accounts of life on the Rand during the 1880s and 1890s with the land values rocketing, the buildings going up, the bars, the dust, the high cost of living (everything had to be imported), the unreliable water supply, the high life and low life and worship of mammon. In a pattern which was typical of South Africa, the Uitlanders on the Rand moved in a different world from that of the African or Afrikaner populations living in the same area.

POLITICAL REPERCUSSIONS ON KRUGER'S REPUBLIC

The cultural gulf separating the urban, individualistic, materialistic Uitlanders from the poor, rural, God-fearing Afrikaner population of the Transvaal was immense. Kruger and his burghers were shocked by the behaviour of the Uitlanders and considered Johannesburg to be a

Sodom and Gomorrah in their midst. They regarded the gold-mining industry with mixed feelings, as both an asset and a liability. On the one hand, it rescued the Transvaal from its chronic poverty; on the other, the burgeoning industrial area and the sudden influx of so many 'aliens' into the Transvaal threatened their way of life and aroused their fears with regard to the future. Steps were soon taken to ensure that the Uitlanders would not be able to seize political control of the state. The period of residence in the republic required for naturalization and eligibility for the franchise was progressively extended from the two years required in 1881 until, in 1890, it was fixed at fourteen years. A Second Volksraad was established, for which naturalized citizens could vote two years after their arrival, but this body dealt mainly with local and secondary matters and its enactments could only become law with the approval of the First Volksraad, which remained the sovereign legislative body.[14] Uitlander grievances – over their exclusion from political power, the high cost of living, the private and state monopolies, the high rates of taxation, the poor provision of schools, the obstruction and corruption of the Transvaal government, which remained in the hands of Boer notables representing the landed and farming interest – were present from the beginning and never ceased to bedevil public life. As J. C. Smuts, a Cambridge-educated Cape Afrikaner who was to make his political career in the Transvaal, observed after a visit to the Transvaal in 1895:

> The most important and radical fact that one must take into account in studying Transvaal politics is simply this: the richest mineral-producing country in the world is inhabited by a small [Boer] population who are almost exclusively engaged in agriculture. . . . Then overwhelming numbers of foreigners come to work the mines of that country. Now of all the possible attitudes which the Transvaal Government could have taken to these Uitlanders, they have chosen one, which is to draw a sharp line between burgher and Uitlander and to do their best to keep the governing-power exclusively in the hands of the burghers. They long for the old pastoral conditions, which are already vanishing, and stubbornly resist the mining and industrial society which is developing with amazing speed. . . . Against that mining industry and its social consequences President Kruger fights with all his powers. . . . He fought for the freedom of his country because England threatened to interfere in the natural development of his pastoral people. Now he fights against industrial society in his country, because he sees that this is a still greater threat to its natural development. Indeed, the material development of Johannesburg, Barberton and Zoutspansberg is undermining, in a more dangerous way than English supremacy would ever have been able to do, the conditions under which the old farming and burgher community were able to count, and to maintain themselves over against other peoples.[15]

Not only did the large numbers of European immigrants to South Africa after 1886 make for the state where they could be least easily assimilated into the existing Boer population, but only a small amount of the wealth which was produced on the Rand found its way into Boer pockets.[16] Although some Boer farmers made large profits from the initial sale of land for mining purposes in the Rand area, this same land often then changed hands between foreigners, sometimes several times in the space of a few months, for many times the sum which had originally been paid. Land companies, as well as Uitlander individuals, began to buy up substantial amounts of land in the Transvaal where the supply of 'free' land had practically come to an end by 1890. A process of social differentiation amongst the Boer population of the Transvaal was thus accelerated by the economic transformations accompanying the gold-mining industry. An upper class of Boer notables, many of them holding office in the government, used their positions to acquire large amounts of land and some of them began to farm it in a capitalist way. Paul Kruger, Piet Joubert, Johannes Rissik, Lucas Meyer and Louis Botha are all examples.[17] Some lesser state officials were given land in lieu of salaries and came to perceive it as a marketable and appreciating asset. But this concentration of land in fewer hands was accompanied by the descent into landlessness of an increasing proportion of the Transvaal Boer population. In 1893, about a thousand Transvaal Boers emigrated to German South West Africa and Angola. Others became landless *bywoners*, working on other people's land in return for the use of a part of it. Some, having lost their land, began the 'second Great Trek' of the Afrikaner population into the cities, which was to become such a feature of the twentieth century. There were, however, no Afrikaner Randlords and very few Afrikaners were at first directly involved in the mining industry. The majority of the several thousand Afrikaner inhabitants of Johannesburg were landless and impoverished Boers who lacked both the capital and the skills to compete effectively with the Uitlanders, most of whom came from urban backgrounds. But they utilized their rural skills to establish themselves in such occupations as brick-making and transport-riding and they looked to the government to employ them in state enterprises, such as road-building and later the railways, and the government complied in order to reduce the scale of the growing 'poor white' problem.[18] With the onset of a series of natural disasters – drought, locusts and rinderpest – in the countryside during the later 1890s, their numbers and resentment increased rapidly.

The demands placed upon the Transvaal government by the burgeoning mining industry and population of the Johannesburg area were something which it was not well equipped to meet. Representing a Boer farming population, lacking sufficient skilled and educated personnel, and without an effective bureaucracy, Kruger's government came to rely first on imported Dutch advisers ('Hollanders'), some of whom, such as W. J. Leyds, came to occupy key positions of influence and to be regarded with suspicion by the English community.[19] Later, Cape Afrikaners (*Kapenaars*), such as J. G. Kotze, J. C. Smuts, Ewald Esselen, and Eugene Marais, came to occupy prominent posts. Many of the institutions of the state, however, pre-dated the industrial era and there was widespread bribery, corruption and inefficiency. The Volksraad consisted of 24–28 members, almost all of whom represented the farming interest. There was no adequate financial administration or control. The role of the President himself, both inside and outside the Volksraad, was crucial.

THE CONCESSIONS POLICY

Although large 'windfall profits' were initially made out of speculation in land and mining shares, the long-term profitability of the Rand depended on productive mining. Many of the legal and institutional frameworks established by the Transvaal government were, however, regarded by the mining industry as obstructing rather than encouraging its development. There was some truth in these claims, especially with regard to the concessions policy, but recent research has challenged the view that the overall attitude of Kruger's government towards the mining industry was one of 'neglect and obstruction' by an 'obdurate' old President and a Volksraad representing the 'pre-industrial' interests of Boer farmers.[20] Kruger's government sought, in various ways, to assist the gold-mining industry whilst at the same time exerting some control over its development so that it did not undermine the stability and Afrikaner dominance of the state. Some measures acted as a brake on development. The Gold Law, for example, encouraged the concentration of large tracts of land or 'claims' in the hands of a few large concerns with no necessary obligation to work them. This resulted in huge sums of capital being tied up in land and land-deals. Some of this land, called *Bewaarplaatsen*, was reserved for the dumping of mine spoil and the establishment of mine buildings and machinery without the right to mine underneath it being clearly established. This became a matter of growing importance as developments in mining technology made possible access to the reef at ever deeper levels and distances from it.

On some issues, such as the enforcement of the gold-theft clauses of the Gold Law, the state was simply unable to provide the effective policing required. On others, as over the passing of the 1895 Pass Law, Kruger's government actively assisted the mining industry in its perennial quest for a regular supply of cheap labour. Sometimes, as over the hurried imposition of a 5 per cent tax on mining profits in 1898, it was the way in which the government acted, rather than the measure itself, which aroused protest. Even so, leaders of the mining industry remained not altogether ill-disposed towards Kruger's government. As late as 1898, George Albu declared that 'this Government, though we are labouring under certain grievances, is not as black as it is painted', and Lord Harris, of Consolidated Goldfields, told Joseph Chamberlain in November 1898:

> I may say that we are by no means ill-disposed towards Kruger. We wish he could establish an honest executive, and then try [to] secure the observance of the provisions of the drink laws: but we don't think the principle of taxing declared net profits of mining Co.s unfair, or that we are working under a crushing tyranny.[21]

Shortly after the re-establishment of the republic, in 1881, the policy of granting concessions had been introduced by the Transvaal government. These concessions, or monopolies, were initially envisaged as a means of providing essential services and increasing much-needed state revenue in a pre-gold era and of promoting economic development by attracting to the republic individuals with the capital, technical and managerial skills which the state administration lacked. Prominent burghers, many of them members of the President's coterie (the so-called 'Third Volksraad'), were granted some of these concessions and many used them simply as a source of private profit. Since the government was unable to provide public amenities such as water, gas, electricity and tramways in the cities, it looked to private enterprise to supply them through concessions. In many cases government regulations and controls were inadequate to ensure that the public interest did not suffer in the pursuit of private profit. With the development of the Rand, accusations of over-charging, inefficiency and corruption were repeatedly made against the private monopolies which ran these public amenities. Three concessions, in particular, attracted heavy and persistent criticism from the mining industry. These were the concessions granted over alcohol, dynamite and railways.[22]

The original concession over the production of alcohol had been granted, in 1881, to A. H. Nellmapius in return for an annual payment to the government of £1,000. *De Eerste Fabrieken in de Zuid Afrikaansche Republiek* made a slow start but with the advent of a huge mining labour force, the profits to be made from alcohol sales were enormous, and a great stimulus was given to the farmers from whose fruit and grain the alcohol was produced. The traditional imported 'Cape Smoke' was soon overtaken by locally produced substitutes, some of which were so crude that they killed the African consumers for whom they were designed, and later still by sugar- and potato-derived spirits imported from Mozambique, Portugal and Germany. The number of licensed canteens on the Rand grew from 147 in 1888 to 552 in 1892, the year in which the liquor concession passed to a partnership led by Samuel Marks and Isaac Lewis in which several Rand mine-magnates had a substantial financial interest. This Hatherley Distillery yielded dividends of 16–20 per cent during the following three years.[23] Mine-magnates with a financial stake in it gained not only their dividends but also from the fact that mine-workers who spent their wages on liquor saved less and therefore signed on for longer periods of work at the mines than might otherwise have been the case. Large-scale alcohol consumption was recognized as a part of, even one of the attractions of, life on the Rand for African mine-workers; and many mine-managers operated the *tot* system, long-established on farms, whereby a daily measure of spirits formed part of the wages of the workers. The debilitating effects on the labour force of excessive alcohol consumption, however, soon became a matter for concern amongst mine-managers. In 1897, the Chamber of Mines estimated that 25–30 per cent of the African labour force was perpetually incapacitated through drink, and campaigned for the more effective enforcement of the liquor laws and an end to the huge rackets which had developed around the illicit sale of liquor to the African population. Throughout the 1890s, the Transvaal government was unable to act effectively against those who openly flouted the liquor laws because the police force was itself corrupt and involved in the rackets.

The dynamite concession was especially resented by the mining industry and formed one of its most consistent grievances against Kruger's government. With the development of gold-mining, South Africa became one of the most important markets for dynamite and blasting gelatine in the world.[24] Often referred to as a state monopoly, it was, in fact, an exclusive privilege or concession granted by the government in 1887 to E. A. Lippert, an enterprising German-Jewish financier who also acquired many other interests in the Transvaal. In 1894, the dynamite concession was taken over by the Anglo-German Nobel Trust which, in acquiring the Modderfontein factory of the South African Explosives Company, obtained a monopoly over the manufacture of dynamite, gunpowder, ammunition and explosives. Practically all of the eight tons of raw materials required to produce one ton of dynamite still had to be imported. Yet the result was that by 1899 the mining industry was paying over £600,000 per year more than it would have done if it had been allowed to purchase its explosives in a free market.[25] In 1897, the Transvaal government's own Industrial Commission pointed out that not only did the dynamite monopoly impose a heavy additional burden on the mining industry but the state revenue also derived very little benefit from it because the huge profits (about 100 per cent on each case) were going abroad into the pockets of the foreign investors. The dynamite industry had become not so much a state monopoly as a foreign monopoly aided and protected by the state. Despite repeated attempts by the mining companies, the Chamber of Mines, and the British government to get the Transvaal government to abolish the concession – including an offer from the mining houses to buy it out in 1899 for £600,000 – Kruger's government consistently refused. Indeed, it was the prospect of a renewal of the concession for a further fifteen years that finally persuaded the British government to challenge Kruger's government on the matter in January 1899.[26]

Why did Kruger's government refuse to modify its policy on dynamite when this brought it nothing but conflict with the Transvaal's key industry and the British government? There is no doubt that certain individuals gained financially, through shares and bribes, from upholding the concession even in the face of the attacks mounted against it by the more progressive members of the Transvaal Volksraad. But there were more important considerations at stake. To abolish the dynamite monopoly would have meant buying it out 'at a high price', so Kruger told President Steyn of the Orange Free State in 1899. Kruger also declared that 'we would cut our own throats by cancelling the contract . . . to talk of free trade in dynamite was to kill the factory. Within five years the company would be bankrupt', driven out of business by cheaper, more competitive imports.[27] Kruger himself repeatedly defended the monopoly on the grounds that it was 'the corner-stone of the independence of the republic'. By this, he meant his burghers to understand that the security of the state, and its ability to defend itself in time of war, depended on the ammunition factory which the dynamite company had to operate as part of its contract. This was in spite of the fact that the government actually purchased most of its ammunition abroad, and the company was dependent upon imported materials. Another consideration was the fact that the dynamite company and the Netherlands Railway Company were the only two major companies in the Transvaal which the government could and did turn to for financial assistance as 'capitalist' allies. They formed something of an economic counterpoise to the Rand mining capitalists, who were regarded as alien and pro-British and whose loyalty to the republic was suspect. They therefore had a vital political as well as economic role to play in the eyes of Kruger's government. This role increased in importance as pressure mounted, between 1895 and 1899, from Britain and the mining industry.

Perhaps the most important of all the concessions was that granted for the building of railways.[28] When gold was discovered in 1886, there were no railways in the Transvaal and therefore in the early years virtually everything to do with the gold-mining industry and the support of the large population attracted to the Rand had to be imported by ox-waggon at three times what it was to cost when railways were constructed. The 1880s constituted the hey-day of transport-riding, as vividly described in Percy FitzPatrick's *Jock of the Bushveld*. By 1890, however, railways were snaking their way from the coastal ports to the borders of the Orange Free State and the Transvaal and, thereafter, thousands of landless Afrikaners who had made a living out of transport-riding went out of business and formed one of the most conspicuous categories of the Witwatersrand's Afrikaner unemployed.[29]

Kruger at first hoped to prevent the railways from the British Cape and Natal ports entering the Transvaal until after the completion of a line from Delagoa Bay. In the Cape and Natal, railways were state enterprises, but in the Transvaal a concession was granted by the government in 1887 to the Netherlands South African Railway Company (NZASM), a Dutch concern financed mainly with German capital, giving it a monopoly over the establishment of railways in the Transvaal. The development of the mining industry clearly depended on the rapid building of railways. A short line connecting the coalfields around Boksburg with the Rand was opened in March 1890 but the first trunk-line tackled by the NZASM was to run from the frontier with Portuguese Mozambique to the Rand to connect with the railway being constructed from the coast at Delagoa Bay. Delays and financial difficulties in the construction of the Delagoa Bay line meant that Kruger was prevailed upon, by the Sivewright Agreement (December 1891), to allow the two lines from Cape Town and Port Elizabeth to be completed first and not to discriminate against goods imported into the Transvaal from the Cape Colony by these routes until after the agreement expired at the end of 1894. In effect this gave the Cape a virtual monopoly for a limited time. In return, the Cape government agreed to assist the Netherlands Railway Company with a substantial loan. This, together with a further loan negotiated through Rothschilds, enabled work to continue on the railway from the Cape to the Transvaal border and on the Delagoa Bay line, which eventually reached Pretoria in December 1894. A further line from Natal reached the Rand in 1895. Thereafter, the Cape's share of traffic to the Rand dropped rapidly as use of the shorter route from Delagoa Bay increased. A tariff war between the Cape, Natal and Delagoa Bay lines ensued which led to mounting friction between the governments of the various states involved as they competed with each other for the Rand trade on which a major part of their revenues depended. Only a unified railway system within a unified South Africa would eventually resolve the matter.[30]

RHODES, RHODESIA AND THE RESURGENCE OF THE IDEA OF UNIFICATION

From 1890, when he became Prime Minister of the Cape Colony, until January 1896, when he fell from office as a result of the Jameson Raid, political developments in southern Africa were profoundly influenced by the actions and ambitions of Cecil Rhodes. Rhodes is not only a remarkable example of the role and impact of an individual in history, he also embodies much of what we today associate with late nineteenth-century European imperialism in Africa in its most ruthless, land-grabbing and racist aspects. A self-made man who was a millionaire by the time he was 30, Rhodes used his wealth to gain political power and then used his political position to advance the cause of British imperialism in southern Africa. Rhodes was a convinced and determined imperialist who stopped at nothing in the pursuit of his goals. The charisma and charm masked a dominating ego, the ruthless exercise of power, and a certain emotional immaturity. Rhodes was essentially a loner who used other people. He acted on the principle that 'every man has his price' and can be 'squared'. A hard-headed realist, Rhodes was also something of a dreamer – 'the greatest dreamer of dreams in our country' was the opinion of J. C. Smuts.[31] His career was built upon perpetually taking risks. Having made his fortune in diamonds, he was slow to appreciate the even greater importance of the gold discoveries on the Witwatersrand, although he played an important role in the establishment of Consolidated Goldfields. Using his fortune to further his own political career in the Cape Colony, Rhodes won the support of the Afrikaner Bond, and by 1890 he was Prime Minister. From this political base, he devoted the rest of his life (he died in 1902) to furthering his two great objectives with regard to southern Africa: the opening up and establishment of European settlement in the country that was, for a while, to bear his name; and the unification of southern Africa under British leadership and within the British Empire – a process in which he always included Rhodesia/Zimbabwe.[32]

Rhodes believed that the future prosperity and development of South Africa depended upon its unification and that the first step towards the attainment of this goal was through the creation of a railway and customs union which would establish free trade between the various South African states and bring an end to their rivalry over railway and customs rates.[33] In the longer term, Rhodes looked towards a political federation of self-governing South African states (including Rhodesia) within the British Empire, in which he believed a British predominance would naturally occur. When he became Prime Minister of the Cape Colony in 1890, Rhodes knew that neither the British colonies nor the Boer republics were receptive to the idea of political unification. He therefore set out first to bring about economic unification by consent.[34]

The strongest opposition to economic or political unification came from the Transvaal republic. The natural economic ties of the Orange Free State were with the coastal British colonies of Natal and the Cape Colony. A Customs Convention between the Orange Free State and the Cape Colony was signed in 1889, and this paved the way for the extension of the Cape railway northwards first to Bloemfontein and then to the border of the Transvaal. The Cape government had failed to establish a customs agreement with the Transvaal when the opportunity arose in 1885, the year before gold was discovered on the Rand. Thereafter, Kruger's government resisted all further attempts to draw the Transvaal into such agreements and sought to acquire an independent access to the sea, outside the British sphere of control, on the east coast. Forestalled by the British annexations of St Lucia Bay (1884) and Kosi Bay (1894), Kruger looked to the development of the Delagoa Bay railway to take the major share of Transvaal trade after the Sivewright Agreement expired at the end of 1894. He also sought to forge closer links between the two republics. In 1889, the new President of the Orange Free State, F. W. Reitz, signed a mutual defence pact with the Transvaal government (which was renewed in 1897). Utilizing the new-found wealth of the Transvaal, Kruger sought to avoid economic dependence on British colonial ports and railways and to work towards the political goal of full and complete independence from Britain.

Rhodes, impatient with Kruger's obstruction, determined to press on with the building of a railway line from Cape Town to Central Africa which would bypass the Transvaal by running along its western border from Kimberley to Mafeking (in Bechuanaland) and then northwards to the Zambesi. This 'Suez Canal to the north' would, he believed, gradually attract all the trade of the region and bind the Cape Colony, the Orange Free State, Bechuanaland, and the 'Charterland' across the Zambesi (the future Rhodesia/Zimbabwe) into a powerful, British-dominated economic union which Natal and the Transvaal would eventually be compelled to join by their own interests. In 1889, Rhodes was granted a charter by the British government for his British South Africa Company which included the right to extend the railway and telegraph north to the Zambesi. Rhodes also tried, unsuccessfully, to buy the port of Delagoa Bay from the Portuguese government. As the full, long-term importance of the Rand gold deposits emerged during the 1890s, the resistance of the Transvaal government to economic federation and anything but complete political independence increased.[35]

The scramble for territory to the north, between the Limpopo and the Zambesi, was also well underway by 1890, and both of the chief contenders for control of the area were based in South Africa. The first was Kruger's republic and the second was Rhodes's British South Africa Company. Northward expansion into the lands of the Ndebele and Shona remained one of the few possibilities left open to the Transvaal republic and, in July 1887, Piet Grobler arrived at the court of Lobengula, ruler of the Ndebele (on the site of modern Bulawayo), to sign a treaty of friendship on behalf of Kruger's republic. Grobler's treaty was not properly witnessed and he himself died shortly afterwards, but his action alerted Rhodes and his close ally and supporter Sir Hercules Robinson (the British High Commissioner in Cape Town) to the danger of a Transvaal pre-emption in the area. On the dubious legal basis of the hurriedly obtained Moffat Treaty and the Rudd Concession (1888), Rhodes was granted a charter for his British South Africa Company in 1889 because the British government was eager to use the opportunity this provided to exclude the Transvaal from the area and secure it for British and Cape interests at Rhodes's expense.[36]

The Pioneer Column which set out from the Cape Colony to occupy what was to become Rhodesia in 1890 was a risky enterprise, poorly prepared and led but well-armed (with a Maxim gun and a steam-powered searchlight to ward off night attacks) and expecting to fight its way into the conquest of not only the country of the Ndebele but also of the Shona, to the north, who were beyond Lobengula's rule but conveniently assumed to be within the 'concession' which had been granted to the Chartered Company.[37] The Pioneer Column was, in fact, an invasion force of both British and Afrikaner adventurers – latter day *conquistadores* with few scruples in search of land and spoil. Rhodes had initially thought of infiltrating the Bechuanaland Protectorate with 500 armed and mounted men and using these to launch a *coup* against Lobengula's headquarters at Bulawayo, but this idea was abandoned when it was decided to adopt a route to Mashonaland which made unnecessary the immediate defeat of the Ndebele. The Jameson Raid was thus not the first occasion on which Rhodes contemplated an armed *coup*.[38]

For those who joined the Pioneer Column – and many of those who did so were men of small means who had already failed on the Rand, and some were Afrikaners – the lure was not primarily agricultural land and cattle but gold. Mashonaland was identified with the legendary land of Ophir, the Rudd Concession had granted to Rhodes and his agents 'the complete and exclusive charge over all metals and minerals' situated in Lobengula's dominions, and the Charter granted Rhodes's Company a virtual *carte blanche* to administer the area, issue shares, engage in mining, and redistribute land.[39] By 1890, any African society whose land was thought to contain gold was likely to become the target for European conquest. Joseph Chamberlain had put the matter bluntly, as far as the area occupied by the Ndebele and Shona was concerned, in 1888 when he observed:

> So far as the unoccupied territories between our present colonial possessions and the Zambezi are concerned, they are hardly practically to be said to be in the possession of any nation. The tribes and Chiefs that exercise domination in them cannot possibly occupy the land or develop its capacity, and it is as certain as destiny that, sooner or later, these countries will afford an outlet for European enterprise and European colonisation.[40]

Nonetheless, the violent and wholesale expropriation of land and cattle from the African population which accompanied the conquest of Rhodesia was extraordinary even by the standards of the rest of the scramble for Africa. It resulted in the Ndebele war of 1893–4 and then the Shona and Ndebele revolts of 1896–7, after which the Shona especially were put down with great severity. When Milner visited Rhodesia, in November 1897, even a tough-minded imperialist like him found it 'an eye-opener'. 'Between ourselves', he wrote to the Colonial Secretary, 'it is a bad story. On the one hand land alienated in the most reckless manner to Companies and individuals, on the other hand a lot of unfit people were allowed to exercise power, or at any rate did exercise it, especially with regard to the natives in a manner that cannot be defended'. In a remarkably shrewd assessment, he considered that Rhodesia was 'neither going to be a fiasco nor yet a rapid success' and although he saw 'no signs of an Eldorado' he thought that there would prove to be sufficient gold 'to give the country a start in the next two or three years, *if there is peace and decent government'*. His major concern was not to 'throw an impecunious, undeveloped country bigger than France' on to the British government and Treasury, which he believed 'would starve Rhodesia' of the sort of investment which was needed. Since this would be more forthcoming from the British South Africa Company 'as well as Rhodes's private purse', Milner concluded that these were still the best means available for 'the successful development of Rhodesia'. This, in turn, would enable Britain to 'win the South African game *all round'* since the British government would possess 'very great powers of control, the *maximum* of power indeed, which it can possibly have without itself taking over the whole government, and facing the enormous cost of it'.[41] In the longer term, Milner commented, Rhodes 'looks to making the territory of the British South Africa Company into a separate Colony ultimately self-governed (the Company keeping its mineral and other valuable rights, but giving up administration). The Colony . . . he means to unite with the Cape Colony and Natal, and then the three combined will bring *peaceful* pressure upon the Republics to drive them into a South African federation.'[42] Thus, Rhodesia would not only be included in a future unified South Africa but would play a crucial part in ensuring a British dominance of the whole.

When the British South Africa Company had first been granted its charter, in 1889, Milner had foreseen its usefulness for the broader British imperial purpose in South Africa:

> Whatever may be the personal sentiments of its managers, the force of circumstances will make the Company British. He must be a pessimist indeed who does not see but surely . . . [that] British influence is once more on the ascendant. . . . The Cape might be separatist, and South Africa by itself might be separatist, but a South Africa reaching up to the

Zambezi, marching into foreign spheres of influence, and needing the protecting arm of Great Britain against Portuguese or German interference with its own development will lean more and more on us.[43]

Rhodes himself had embarked on his Rhodesian venture with the hope that a 'second Rand' was waiting to be discovered which would pay for the administration of the area by the company and form the basis of an eventual fifth South African state of European settlement which would act as a vital 'counterpoise' to Kruger's Transvaal republic and tilt the balance of power away from Afrikaner republicanism and towards British predominance in a future South African federation within the British Empire. Rhodesia would thus provide the means to the larger political end of surrounding the Transvaal and binding it into a British South Africa.

In the event, Rhodes's great northern expansion consumed rather than added to his wealth. After 1890, almost all of his large investments were in companies related to his Rhodesian venture, and most of them did badly. The British South Africa Company was only saved from bankruptcy during the early 1890s by successive injections of capital by De Beers and by land speculation which was not backed up by profitable mining until the end of the century.[44] The gold and mineral potential of Rhodesia had, in fact, been exaggerated. In August 1894, the Hays Hammond Report finally ended any hopes that 'a second Rand' existed in Rhodesia. The future of gold-mining in South Africa now clearly lay in the 'deep levels' of the Witwatersrand. The Transvaal, therefore, became the key to the economic and political future of the region. This crucial fact underlay the considerations of Rhodes, and of the British government, thereafter, and must be constantly borne in mind in any consideration of their actions between 1894 and 1899.

Preoccupied as he was with Rhodesia, Rhodes was also Prime Minister of the Cape Colony from July 1890 to January 1896. He had achieved this office because he had won the admiration and support of the largest political party in the Cape parliament, the Afrikaner Bond, and the resulting Rhodes–Bond coalition provided the Cape with a strong government. The fact that Rhodes simultaneously occupied key positions in De Beers and Consolidated Goldfields, and was also the dominant influence behind the British South Africa Company's conquest of Rhodesia, was not considered a disadvantage, least of all by Rhodes himself. 'I have interfered in the interior because I wished the movement to the interior to be conducted as an expansion of the Cape Colony', he declared.[45] The alliance of Rhodes and the Bond was to their mutual advantage. Rhodes obtained a strong political base in the Cape parliament and the Cape farmers were well served by the energetic steps which he took with regard to their interests. Individual Bondsmen participated in the Pioneer Column and gained farms in Rhodesia; others obtained shares in the British South Africa Company. Yet the way in which Rhodes won the admiration and support of many Cape Afrikaners during these years cannot simply be explained in terms of their material interests. As J. C. Smuts, himself an ardent admirer of Rhodes before the Jameson Raid, later confessed:

> Some Dutch members of Parliament and some influential people may have materially benefited from Mr Rhodes's friendship; but a people cannot be bribed in the vulgar sense. It was hero-worship pure and simple. The Dutch set aside all considerations of blood and nationality and loved him and trusted him and served him because they believed that *he* was the man to carry out that great idea of an internally sovereign and united South Africa in which the white race would be supreme – which has been the cry of our forefathers even as it is our cry today. Here at last our Moses had appeared – and it made no difference that he was an Egyptian in blood and in occasional mode of expression. With the exception of a very small minority, the whole Dutch people in the Cape Colony shared this faith in and admiration for Mr Rhodes.[46]

In 1894, Rhodes won a general election and was returned for a further period as Prime Minister of the Cape Colony. The war with the Ndebele was brought to an end and the future of Company rule, over the country which was to bear his name from 1895, seemed assured. The railway from the Cape reached Mafeking. At this time, before the Delagoa Bay railway had been completed, the Cape Colony had captured 85 per cent of the Rand traffic and Kruger's republic was surrounded by British territory – 'hemmed in, as in a kraal'. This heightened fears amongst the Transvaal Boers that between the ambitions of Rhodes and the designs of the British government, even the qualified independence of their country under the London Convention was under threat.

THE DRIFTS CRISIS

In 1895 there occurred the first in what was to be a succession of confrontations between the British and Transvaal governments in which Britain threatened to use force if Kruger's government did not give way. Kruger complied and the crisis subsided. Yet the importance of this confrontation, both in relation to the Jameson Raid – which followed shortly afterwards – and to the expectations and illusions which it helped to foster in British government circles about how Kruger's government would react in future, has probably been understated.[47]

The Drifts Crisis grew out of the competition over railway rates which developed once the lines from Delagoa Bay and Natal reached the Rand and began to compete with the Cape route which had enjoyed a virtual monopoly during the previous two years covered by the Sivewright Agreement. Between 1892 and 1895, the value of Cape imports increased by more than 50 per cent as a result of the Transvaal trade, and railway and customs receipts formed a major part of Cape revenues. But the distance of Johannesburg from Cape Town was about twice the distance from Durban or Delagoa Bay and, when these routes became available, the Cape share of rail traffic to the Rand dropped sharply. At the end of 1894, the Sivewright Agreement lapsed and in February 1895, the Transvaal government concluded a railway convention with Natal which, in conjunction with the increased use of the Delagoa Bay railway, led to the promotion of traffic between the Transvaal and the ports of Durban and Delagoa Bay at the expense of that going to the ports in the Cape Colony. Both the Cape Colony and the Orange Free State, bound together in a Customs Agreement which reached to the border with the Transvaal, felt a deep sense of grievance at this 'unfriendly' act by the Transvaal. The Transvaal was not only the focus for the whole railway system in South Africa but the Netherlands Railway Company controlled the terminal sections of all the lines from the Transvaal's borders to the Rand. It could therefore vary the charges on these sections and, by imposing high rates on the 50-mile section from the Vaal river (where the Cape railway reached the border) to the Rand, and undercutting the Cape in the charges on the Delagoa Bay line, divert traffic away from the Cape lines and ports. The Transvaal government encouraged the Netherlands Railway Company to adopt just such a policy as from January 1895. It was also stipulated that no Cape locomotives were to run beyond the Vaal, where NZASM engines would take over the task of hauling Cape goods trains to Johannesburg. The rates fixed for this 50-mile section were to be increased from 2.4 pence per ton per mile to 8 pence. When Rhodes met Kruger, in October 1894, it would seem that he made clear that such a discriminatory policy would be challenged.[48]

As soon as the NZASM brought its exorbitant tariff into operation in 1895, Cape merchants stopped booking their freight through to

Johannesburg and instead booked it just to the border. There, it was off-loaded on to ox-waggons which crossed the river at the drifts (fords) and continued on to Johannesburg. This solution paid both the merchants and the Cape railways whose efficiency, combined with that of the Cape ports, seemed likely to ensure that they would retain a substantial share of the growing Rand traffic despite the greater distance. Kruger's government could not even complain that the decision to use the drifts was a hostile measure since it was taken by the Cape merchants and not by the Cape government. Nonetheless, both sides recognized that the use of the drifts was only a temporary expedient whilst the whole matter of railway rates was settled at a conference to be held in Cape Town in April 1895.

The conference, however, was a complete failure with Natal siding with the Transvaal in their joint interests, on the one side, and the Cape and the Orange Free State on the other. Determined to enforce his policy, Kruger then announced that as from 1 October the drifts would be closed as a point of entry for goods to the Transvaal. The Cape government responded by claiming that Kruger was breaking Article 13 of the London Convention (which forbade the Transvaal from discriminating against goods imported from any part of the British dominions) and appealed to the British government to intervene. The new British Conservative government of Lord Salisbury, which had come into office in June 1895 with Joseph Chamberlain as Colonial Secretary, acted promptly and firmly. In the temporary absence of Chamberlain abroad, Lord Salisbury himself took a direct interest in the matter and urged a tough response, observing that 'The Transvaal Government is unfriendly to us and it is a great mistake to run away from them. The Cape Government must be supported to the end in this matter.'[49] Chamberlain telegraphed equally emphatically on 17 October that Kruger's action was 'intolerable' and that 'they must give way'. Advised by its law officers that the London Convention was indeed being breached and that the Cape government had a strong case, the British government first tried to resolve the matter through diplomatic means. The Transvaal Consul-General in London, Montagu White, was informed in October that his government's action would not be tolerated. When Kruger failed to respond, the British government decided to threaten him with an ultimatum. First, however, it demanded and received an assurance from the Cape government that, if military measures were needed, it would itself send a contingent of troops, allow free use of its railways to any British troops involved, and bear half of the cost. Both the British government and Rhodes (as Prime Minister of the

Cape Colony) were convinced that, faced with such a combined response, Kruger would back down.[50] The British ultimatum was handed to Kruger on 4 November, the day before a further conference on railway rates was due to open in Pretoria. Kruger's government then backed down, the drifts were re-opened, and the immediate crisis was over. *De Volksstem* (the leading pro-government newspaper in Pretoria) protested at 'this hateful British intervention' and 'the meddlesomeness of England in matters of a purely local character'.[51]

The action of the British government had been important in strengthening the weak hand of Rhodes and the Cape government, who were averse to a settlement which would have reduced the Cape share of the Rand traffic from two-fifths to one-third. Yet the facts of the situation soon asserted themselves. With the opening of the Natal line, at the end of 1895, the diversion of trade away from the Cape line began in earnest and by 1897 the Delagoa Bay line was carrying 60 per cent more traffic than it had the previous year, the Natal line was up by 15 per cent, and the Cape share was down to 28.4 per cent of the total, i.e. less than the 33 per cent offered by Kruger in 1895. Cape railway profits dropped to a third of what they had been three years previously. If Kruger had simply ignored the Cape's boycott of the Vaal–Rand railway line, the other lines would have gradually driven the ox-waggon trade out of business, assisted, during 1896, by the rinderpest epidemic which decimated the oxen on which it depended. The fact was that the arrival of other railway routes to the Rand had ended the commercial hold which the Cape had previously possessed over the Transvaal.

Rhodes's role in the Drifts Crisis has to be set in the context of his already maturing plans for a *coup d'etat* against Kruger's government which were to result in the Jameson Raid at the end of December 1895. As Prime Minister of the Cape Colony, Rhodes succeeded in mobilizing both the support of the Bond and of the British government for a strong stand against Kruger's government during the Drifts Crisis of October–November, and Kruger backed down. The peaceful resolution of this crisis encouraged Rhodes, Chamberlain and the British government to believe that Kruger would always climb down if 'firmly summoned'. It also paved the way for the further cooperation between Rhodes and Chamberlain over Bechuanaland which followed during November 1895.

Certain other features of the challenge posed to Kruger's government over the Drifts Crisis are worth noting. The first is the isolation of the Transvaal government in 1895 when it failed to win the support of most Afrikaners either in the Orange Free State or the Cape Colony. Cape Afrikaners especially were critical of Transvaal policy and convinced that Kruger was in the wrong on this matter. The British government had been assured, by W. P. Schreiner and the Bond, that Rhodes's government would have the support of the Cape Afrikaner population if British military measures became necessary, before the ultimatum was delivered. The government of the Orange Free State had also refused to support the Transvaal. The situation was to be quite different in 1899.

The Drifts Crisis demonstrated the determination of the British government to uphold the London Convention, at the risk of war if necessary, and to utilize it to maintain British dominance over the Transvaal and to champion the claims of the Cape Colony, where these were well-founded. But the British Colonial Office was also concerned to avoid 'giving the Johannesburg people [i.e. the Uitlanders] the idea that Her Majesty's Government would back them up in every and any demand of theirs'.[52] This too was to change between 1895 and 1899.

The close cooperation between Rhodes and the British government during the Drifts Crisis also raises the question of the relationship of the Drifts Crisis to the Jameson Raid, which followed less than two months later. Throughout the Drifts Crisis Rhodes, Sir Hercules Robinson (British High Commissioner in South Africa) and Chamberlain were all convinced that military measures would not be necessary and that Kruger's government would back down. There is no evidence to suggest that 'for Chamberlain the Drifts Crisis was intended in effect to be the Jameson Raid', or that either Chamberlain or Rhodes expected it to provide an opportunity to topple Kruger's government.[53] In October 1895, Rhodes was already plotting for an Uitlander uprising on the Rand, but preparations for this were not yet far advanced. His plans for the establishment of a force of mounted police in the strip of territory on the Bechuanaland border (recently transferred to the British South Africa Company) had also still to be realized. Preparations for what became the Jameson Raid certainly overlapped with the events of the Drifts Crisis; but they began before the Drifts Crisis arose and they continued after it was over. It is probable, however, that the experience of the Drifts Crisis encouraged Rhodes to go ahead with the reckless gamble which was to ruin his career and set Britain and the Transvaal on a collision course; and Chamberlain did nothing to stop him.

NOTES

1. C. W. de Kiewiet, *A History of South Africa: Social and Economic* (Oxford, 1941), p. 123.
2. P. Richardson and J. J. Van Helten, 'The development of the South African gold-mining industry 1895–1918', *Econ. Hist. Rev.* XXXVII, 3 (August 1984), pp. 320–1.
3. Ibid. See also the same authors' chapter, 'The gold-mining industry in the Transvaal 1886–1899', in P. Warwick, ed., *The South African War* (London, 1980).
4. R. V. Kubicek, *Economic Imperialism in Theory and Practice: the Case of South African Gold-mining Finance 1886–1914* (Durham, NC, 1979), p. 51.
5. F. H. Hatch and J. A. Chalmers, *The Gold Mines of the Rand* (London, 1895), p. 291.
6. A. P. Cartwright, *The Corner House: the Early History of Johannesburg* (London, 1965); G. Wheatcroft, *The Randlords: the Men who made South Africa* (London, 1985).
7. W. Beinart, *Twentieth Century South Africa* (Oxford, 1994); Alan Jeeves, *Migrant Labour in South Africa's Mining Economy: the Struggle for the Gold Mines' Labour Supply 1890–1920* (Johannesburg, 1985).
8. Charles van Onselen, *Studies in the Social and Economic History of the Witwatersrand 1886–1914* 2 vols (Harlow, 1982), especially vol. 1, ch. 1; Richardson and Van Helten, 'The gold-mining industry in the Transvaal 1886–1899'.
9. J. S. Marais, *The Fall of Kruger's Republic* (Oxford, 1961), pp. 2–3.
10. E. E. Kennedy, *Waiting for the Boom* (London, 1890).
11. Olive Schreiner, *An English South African's View of the Situation* (London, 1899), p. 66.
12. Thomas Adlam, in M. Fraser, ed., *Johannesburg Pioneer Journals 1888–1909* (Cape Town, 1985), p. 58.
13. K. F. Bellairs, *The Witwatersrand Goldfields: a Trip to Johannesburg and Back* (London, 1889), p. 44.
14. L. Thompson, 'Great Britain and the Afrikaner Republics 1870–1899', in M. Wilson and L. Thompson, eds, *The Oxford History of South Africa* 2 vols (Oxford, 1969/1971), 1, p. 309.
15. J. C. Smuts, 'A Trip to the Transvaal', October 1895, printed in W. K. Hancock and J. van der Poel, eds, *Selections from the Smuts Papers* 7 vols (Cambridge, 1966), 1, pp. 76–7.
16. Marais, *The Fall of Kruger's Republic*, p. 4.
17. Stanley Trapido, 'Reflections on land, office and wealth in the South African Republic 1850–1900', in S. Marks and A. Atmore, eds, *Economy and Society in Pre-industrial South Africa* (London, 1980), p. 357.
18. See van Onselen, *Studies*, vol. 2, ch. 3.
19. P. J. van Winter, *Onder Krugers Hollanders* 2 vols (Amsterdam, 1937–8); L. E. Van Niekerk, *Kruger se regterhand: 'n Biografie van dr. W.J. Leyds* (Pretoria, 1985); W. J. Leyds, *Eenige Correspondentie uit 1899* (Dordrecht, 1938).

20. Patrick Harries, 'Capital, state, and labour on the 19th century Witwatersrand: a reassessment', *SAHJ* 18 (1986).
21. Marais, *The Fall of Kruger's Republic*, p. 228.
22. Ibid., ch. 2; Trapido, 'Reflections'; J. J. Van Helten, 'German capital, the Netherlands Railways Company and the political economy of the Transvaal 1886–1900', *JAH* 29 (1978); R. Mendelsohn, *Sammy Marks, 'The Uncrowned King of the Transvaal'* (Cape Town, 1991).
23. Mendelsohn, *Sammy Marks*, chs 2–3; van Onselen, *Studies*, vol. 2, ch. 3.
24. For dynamite I have used the Chamber of Mines Annual Reports and Letter Book for 1898–9; the Memorandum on the subject, written in 1898, in the Wernher, Beit/H. Eckstein Papers (Barlow Rand Archives HE 131); D. A. Etheredge, 'The early history of the Chamber of Mines, Johannesburg, 1887–1897', unpublished M. A. thesis, Witwatersrand University, 1949; J. J. Van Helten, 'British and European Economic Investment in the Transvaal with specific reference to the Witwatersrand Goldfields and District 1886–1910', unpublished Ph.D thesis, London University, 1981; and the accounts published in Marais, *The Fall of Kruger's Republic*, pp. 27–33; C. T. Gordon, *The Growth of Boer Opposition to Kruger 1890–1895* (Oxford, 1970), pp. 46–57; Kubicek, *Economic Imperialism*, pp. 46–52.
25. See Mine Managers to F. W. Reitz, 27 March 1899, printed in J. P. FitzPatrick, *The Transvaal from Within* (London, 1899), pp. 347–8.
26. See ch. 7 pp. 218–21 below.
27. Report of Volksraad debate on 18 August 1899, in *The Standard and Diggers News*, 19 August 1899.
28. Van Helten, 'German capital' and Jean van der Poel, *Railways and Customs Policies in South Africa 1885–1910* (London, 1933).
29. Van Onselen, *Studies*, vol. 2, pp. 121–2.
30. Van der Poel, *Railways and Customs Policies*; Kenneth E. Wilburn, 'The climax of railway competition in South Africa 1887–1899', D.Phil. thesis, Oxford, 1982.
31. Smuts speech, 22 March 1936, cited in P. B. Blanckenberg, *The Thoughts of General Smuts* (London, 1951), p. 85.
32. The most recent biography is Robert I. Rotberg, *The Founder: Cecil Rhodes and the Pursuit of Power* (Oxford, 1989); but see also J. Flint, *Cecil Rhodes* (London, 1976), and J. S. Galbraith, *Crown and Charter: the Early History of the British South Africa Company* (Berkeley, CA, 1974), and 'Cecil Rhodes and his "cosmic dreams": a reassessment', *JICH* 1, 3 (1974).
33. Van der Poel, *Railway and Customs Policies*, and *The Jameson Raid* (Oxford, 1951).
34. Van der Poel, *The Jameson Raid*, pp. 1–2.
35. Van der Poel, *Railways and Customs Policies,* chs 3 and 4; Marais, *The Fall of Kruger's Republic,* chs 2 and 3.
36. For the establishment of Rhodesia/Zimbabwe see Rotberg, *The Founder*, and Galbraith, *Crown and Charter;* also D. M. Schreuder, *The Scramble for Southern Africa* (Cambridge, 1980); I. Phimister, 'Rhodes, Rhodesia and

the Rand', *JSAS* 1, 1 (1974), and *An Economic and Social History of Zimbabwe 1890–1948* (Oxford, 1988); T. O. Ranger, *Revolution in Southern Rhodesia 1896–7* (London, 1967).

37. See Phimister, *An Economic and Social History of Zimbabwe*, ch. 1.

38. The plan, outlined in an agreement signed by Rhodes, Maurice Heany and Frank Johnson on 7 December 1889, is discussed in Rotberg, *The Founder*, pp. 294–6; also L. H. Gann, *A History of Southern Rhodesia* (London, 1965), pp. 88–9.

39. See Galbraith, *Crown and Charter*, and Phimister, *An Economic and Social History of Zimbabwe*, for full details, also Philip Mason, *The Birth of a Dilemma* (Oxford, 1958).

40. Galbraith, *Crown and Charter*, p. 25.

41. Milner to Chamberlain 1/12/1897, in C. Headlam, ed., *The Milner Papers* 2 vols (London, 1931), 1, pp. 139–46.

42. Milner to Selborne 2/6/1897, Headlam, ed., *The Milner Papers*, 1, pp. 105–6.

43. Milner to Mackenzie, n.d. 1889, cited in Schreuder, *Scramble for S.A.*, pp. 264–5.

44. Phimister, *An Economic and Social History of Zimbabwe*, ch. 1.

45. Rotberg, *The Founder*, p. 338; also Flint, *Cecil Rhodes*, p. 158.

46. J. C. Smuts, Article of 1897, printed in Hancock and van der Poel, eds, *Selections Smuts Papers*, 1, pp. 173–4. This section owes much to lively discussions with Professor Mordecai Tamarkin (University of Tel-Aviv) who is completing a study of Rhodes and the Afrikaners.

47. The most recent work is by Wilburn, 'The climax of railway competition', and Richard Mendelsohn, 'The Cape and the Drifts Crisis of 1895', unpublished B.A. Honours Essay, Cape Town, 1971. Older accounts are to be found in van der Poel, *Railways and Customs Policies*, ch. 5, and T. R. H. Davenport, *The Afrikaner Bond* (Oxford, 1966), pp. 160–2.

48. Van der Poel, *Railways and Customs Policies*, pp. 80–1.

49. Salisbury note on E. Fairfield to Lord Selborne, 15 October 1895, SeP MS 15.

50. R. H. Wilde, *Joseph Chamberlain and the South African Republic 1895–1899*, Archives Yearbook for South African History Part 1 (Pretoria, 1956), p. 12.

51. See Wilburn, 'The climax of railway competition', p. 205, and *De Volksstem*, 9 November 1895.

52. E. Fairfield to Lord Selborne, 15 October 1895, SeP MS 15.

53. This is suggested by Wilburn, 'The climax of railway competition', pp. 206–7.

CHAPTER THREE

The Jameson Raid

In 1895, Cecil Rhodes was 42 and at the zenith of his power and influence both in Britain and South Africa. He had recently been made a member of the Privy Council and had been well received by Queen Victoria. He had the ear of senior British government ministers. In February 1895, Lord Salisbury praised 'the foundation of a splendid empire' being laid by Rhodes in South Africa where 'even the Government of the Transvaal . . . is finding the pressure of English activity all round them so strong that they are slowly giving way . . . they will be compelled to fall into line and join the great unconscious federation that is growing up'.[1] In South Africa, Rhodes had won the support and admiration of not just the English but the Cape Afrikaner population to a degree never before attained by any political leader. The 'Charterland' carved out in the interior at his instigation had that year been officially named after him. Yet he knew that it would never provide an adequate counterpoise to the Transvaal and that no second Rand was waiting to be discovered there. The Hays Hammond report of 1894 made it certain that the economic centre of gravity for the future of South Africa lay in the Transvaal. And the Transvaal was under the political control of Paul Kruger, a man who could not be 'squared' and whose regime presented an implacable obstacle to the goal shared by Rhodes and the British government: the unification of South Africa under British auspices and British dominance and its firm anchorage within the British Empire.

Until 1895, successive British governments had looked to what they saw as the natural and inevitable working-out of local forces in South Africa to achieve a 'peaceful revolution' by which Kruger's exclusive oligarchy would be replaced by a 'progressive bloc' in Transvaal politics, made up of young Afrikaner reformers in alliance with

Uitlander leaders. Kruger was 70 years old in 1895 and his personal regime would not last for ever. It was anticipated that when a younger, better educated, and more progressive element in the Afrikaner elite came to power, they would collaborate in the larger design for a future South African federation in which the two republics would combine with the two self-governing British colonies of Natal and the Cape Colony, and possibly Rhodesia as well, to form a federation – on Canadian lines – in which the British element would predominate. The 'great unconscious federation' which Lord Salisbury saw emerging did not require that either the Transvaal or the Orange Free State be re-annexed as colonies of the British Crown. As Lord Ripon, the Colonial Secretary in the Liberal government had indicated in 1894:

> What I look to is a sort of federal Union of South Africa, of British territory, South African Republic and Orange Free State in which we, of course, should have the hegemony but no more. For my own part, I should not want more and I should care little whether the Transvaal became a British Colony or remained the South African Republic within such a federation.[2]

It was anticipated that the transformation of the Transvaal, in a direction favourable to British interests, would be assisted by the burgeoning numbers of Uitlanders arriving there and the political incorporation of those of them who decided to settle permanently through the acquisition of citizenship and the franchise in the South African Republic. British governments were aware of the growth of Boer opposition to Kruger's policies amongst young, well-educated Afrikaners in the Republic, some of whom were in close contact with the leaders amongst the Uitlanders. Lord Selborne noted:

> There must be rival candidates and rival sections competing for power among the Boers, and one day one of those candidates and one of those sections will seek for support among the Uitlanders. If this does not occur, it will be the only case in history in which it has not occurred.[3]

Until 1895, therefore, British governments believed that, with regard to Britain's long-term objectives for South Africa, time was on their side and no direct external intervention was necessary. As Lord Salisbury optimistically observed, on 30 December 1895:

> It is evident that sooner or later that State [Transvaal] must be mainly governed by Englishmen: though we cannot yet precisely discern what their relations to the British Crown or the Cape Colony will be . . . but

still it would be better if the revolution which transfers the Transvaal to British rulers were entirely the result of the action of internal forces, and not of Cecil Rhodes's intervention or of ours.[4]

Salisbury had become Prime Minister, in June 1895, at the head of one of the strongest Conservative governments in the nineteenth century. This was to be the government which took Britain into the war with the Transvaal republic four years later. Arguably the most powerful member of the government – after the Prime Minister – was the new Colonial Secretary, Joseph Chamberlain, whose energy and ambition transformed what had traditionally been a second-rank office into one of first-rank importance.[5]

Chamberlain already had a remarkable career behind him by 1895, both in Birmingham and in national politics.[6] Coming from a non-conformist background, he was a self-made man in a new mould. A successful businessman and social reformer, he was also a determined imperialist who had broken with Gladstone and split the Liberal Party over the question of Irish Home Rule in 1886. Thereafter, during a decade when he was out of office, he had articulated his deep commitment to the British Empire in a series of speeches which attracted much attention. 'I mean some day to be Colonial Minister', Chamberlain had written to his fiancée in 1888.[7] That is the post which he finally obtained as a member of Salisbury's government in 1895.

Chamberlain was an imperialist of a new and unusual type in British politics. The British Empire was not marginal but central to his thinking. He did not believe in the unlimited expansion of that Empire but in its strengthening and more effective organization. Like others of his outlook and generation, he had been deeply influenced by J. R. Seeley's *The Expansion of England*, a series of lectures given to undergraduates by the Regius Professor of History at Cambridge and first published as a book in 1883. Seeley, pointing to the indifference with which the British regarded the world-wide Empire which they seemed to have acquired 'in a fit of absence of mind', argued that Britain would be eclipsed as a great power, by the United States and Russia, unless this Empire was strengthened and consolidated as an imperial federation. Chamberlain became convinced that, in the twentieth century, the world would be dominated by large continental states which could command far greater populations and resources than those of the British Isles. The example of Germany's rapid development (via the establishment of a *Zollverein* and later unification), and the size and resources of the United States, seemed to him to point to a future in which Britain's power and position in the world would be displaced by new great powers unless the resources of the British Isles could be buttressed by those of the British Empire. He regarded Britain's tropical colonies as representing 'undeveloped estates', many of them recently acquired, which needed developing as more and more of Britian's rivals resorted to protectionist policies. As for her colonies of European settlement, like Seeley he considered that the political, economic and military strengthening of this Empire of kith and kin lay at the heart of all that was meant by imperial consolidation. 'Our patriotism is warped indeed if it does not embrace the greater Britain beyond the seas', he declared. Speaking in Toronto, in 1887, he had expressed the hope that Canadian Confederation (1867) 'might be the lamp to light our path to the confederation of the British Empire'.[8]

Like Cecil Rhodes, Chamberlain was convinced that the Empire 'was a bread and butter question'. 'Is there a man in his senses', he asked, in an address to the London Chamber of Commerce in 1888, 'who believes that the crowded population of these islands *could exist for a single day* if we were cut adrift from the great dependencies which now look to us for protection and which are the natural markets for our trade?'[9] Chamberlain had been President of the Board of Trade in Gladstone's government in the 1880s and the development of imperial trade became a growing preoccupation for him as Britain was overtaken by both the USA and Germany in key economic indicators during the course of the 1890s. During his first months as Colonial Secretary, Chamberlain, concerned by the fact that foreign goods now accounted for a third of the total of imports into British colonies, circularized all colonial governors stressing 'the extreme importance of securing as large a share as possible of [our] mutual trade . . . for British producers and manufacturers'.[10] Chamberlain was also an imperialist because he was a social reformer. He was convinced that the measures which he supported for social reform could only be paid for through the expansion of trade within the Empire, a development made all the more urgent as Britain began to feel the effects of foreign tariffs and competition. The expansion of imperial markets for British manufactured goods would provide employment for British workers as well as strengthening the bonds of Empire. Chamberlain's conversion to tariff reform and the creation of an imperial tariff union – the issue on which he was to leave the government and fail to convince the electorate after 1903 – was thus a product of both British and imperial considerations. 'I am a fiscal reformer mainly because I am an imperialist', he declared in 1904.[11]

In seeking to strengthen the British Empire, Chamberlain believed that the consolidation of regional groupings of British possessions, through local unions or federations, was likely to be a necessary preliminary to any scheme of imperial federation for the whole. The Canadian precedent of 1867 encouraged him as he worked towards the establishment of the Australian Commonwealth in 1901. South Africa remained as 'the last considerable portion' of the British Empire unfederated and disunited. There, Chamberlain was acutely aware that the secession of the American colonies represented not just a precedent but the logical alternative outcome if the republican tradition of the two Boer republics triumphed and held sway. Chamberlain was not the sort of imperialist to rely on the government of the Cape Colony for the preservation of British interests in the region. Writing of the problem facing Britain in South Africa, before he took office, Chamberlain had stated:

> I am inclined to advocate a bold policy, fully recognising Imperial responsibilities and duty, but then I intend that it should be the policy of the Imperial and not of the Cape Government, and should be carried out by officials taking their instructions from the former.[12]

From 1895 to 1903, therefore, the British government had a Colonial Secretary who was a pushful and committed imperialist in a new mould. Joseph Chamberlain was not only determined to strengthen the British Empire but to educate the British public about its importance for the future. Amongst the imperial problems facing the British government, it was those to do with South Africa which were to predominate during Chamberlain's tenure of the Colonial Office. During these years, South Africa came to be regarded in British ruling circles as something of a test-case for the future of the British Empire – rather as the American colonies had been in the 1770s, Canada had been between 1839 and 1867, and India was to be in the 1940s.

Chamberlain was no newcomer to South African affairs. As a member of Gladstone's government at the time of the Transvaal War in 1880–81, he had been amongst the most prominent of those urging the recall of the then British High Commissioner, Sir Bartle Frere, for his role in bringing on the war. At that time, Chamberlain believed that the British annexation of the Transvaal in 1877 had been a mistake. In July 1881, he spoke in support of a British withdrawal from the Transvaal, despite the British defeat at Majuba Hill, and declared 'that it would have been wiser and better to have evacuated the country when we first came into office'.[13] By 1884, however, a certain hardening had occurred in Chamberlain's attitude towards the

Transvaal. Two developments probably contributed to this. The first was the rapidity with which Kruger's government infringed the terms of the London Convention. Chamberlain's more resolute stand first surfaced in connection with the 'drifting' of Boer settlers over the Bechuanaland frontier within months of the signing of the Convention. Chamberlain urged that the British and Cape governments should be firm and send an expedition to evict the 'Boer marauders' and hold the Transvaal government to strict observance of the terms of the Convention. He also argued that the British garrison in South Africa should be strengthened. The second development was the arrival of Germany on the South African scene, the declaration of a German protectorate over South West Africa, and the British government's persistent fears that this might lead to further German territorial ambitions elsewhere in the region and a possible new great-power ally for the Transvaal which would be against British interests. Chamberlain was therefore a strong advocate behind the despatch of the Warren expedition in 1885 and the subsequent division of Bechuanaland into a Crown Colony (subsequently absorbed into the Cape Colony) and a Protectorate, north of the Molopo river, which by 1895 seemed destined to come under the control of Rhodes's British South Africa Company.

THE SUB-IMPERIALISM OF THE CAPE COLONY

Between 1885 and 1895, as gold transformed the power and importance of the Transvaal, the chief means by which successive British governments sought to preserve British interests in southern Africa and curtail the ambitions of Kruger's Transvaal republic were centred on the Cape Colony. Strict adherence to the terms of the London Convention might be insisted upon; foreign powers such as Germany might be warned off a region which Britain considered as her 'sphere of influence'; Britain herself might intervene directly and annex territory to prevent the expansion of the Transvaal into Bechuanaland or towards the sea. But it was from the Cape Colony that, aided and abetted by the British government, a series of moves were made to counter and curb the expansionist tendencies of the Transvaal republic. The Cape Colony thus came to act as the major British imperial proxy-agent in the politics of South Africa.[14] And the crucial link-man between the Cape Colony and the British government during this period was Cecil Rhodes.

Rhodes was the driving-force behind the British South Africa Company's expansion into the interior which blocked off Kruger's republic to the north and west. The British government had granted a Royal Charter to his British South Africa Company in 1889 because its activities in the interior closely served the interests of the British government whilst not being at the expense of the British tax-payer. Rhodes not only succeeded in harnessing Cape expansionism in the service of British interests through the British South Africa Company; he also mastered Cape politics, as Prime Minister between 1890 and 1895, through his alliance with Hofmeyr's Afrikaner Bond. This gave him the strongest political base imaginable amongst the European population, as the Drifts Crisis of 1895 demonstrated.[15]

Until 1894, Rhodes had worked for the peaceful incorporation of the Transvaal into a future South African federation by surrounding it with British territory on whose railways and ports the Transvaal depended. Like the British government, he looked to the eventual predominance of the Uitlanders over the Boers in the Transvaal itself. Towards the end of 1894, however, Rhodes became impatient and prepared to use force to achieve the end which both he and the British government shared with regard to the incorporation of the Transvaal in a future South African federation. Time, it appeared to him, was actually strengthening the ability of the Transvaal government to withstand British predominance. Gold had transformed the poorest of the South African states into the richest. The extent of the deep-level deposits now revealed on the Rand made it certain that here lay the key to the future economic development of the whole of South Africa. Yet Kruger and his ruling Afrikaner oligarchy presented a major obstacle to the achievement of a British-led federation of South Africa. In June 1894, the British government made it clear to Rhodes that Germany's opposition meant the end to any hope of either Britain or Rhodes himself acquiring Delagoa Bay. This meant that, as soon as the railway from Delagoa Bay to the Rand was completed, the Transvaal would have access to an independent port, outside the sphere of British influence, on the east coast. This would soon result in the diversion of trade away from the Cape and Natal routes (with the loss of considerable revenue to these states). The economic independence of the Transvaal would be increased and this would enable it to avoid any customs union with the other South African states. At the same time, it was feared that Germany would seek to extend her patronage towards the Transvaal republic, a fear reinforced by the friendly reception accorded to Dr Leyds, Kruger's State Secretary, when he visited Berlin. As the Liberal Colonial

Secretary, Lord Ripon, noted in November 1894, 'the German inclination to take the Transvaal under their protection is a very serious thing. To have them meddling at Pretoria and Johannesburg would be fatal to our position and our influence in South Africa'. He was therefore in favour of making it clear to Germany 'that the Transvaal is within our sphere of influence, and that they must *keep their hands off*'.[16]

In October 1894, on his way back from the mineral survey of Rhodesia, Rhodes met President Kruger in Pretoria. We do not know precisely what passed at this meeting but it is probable that Kruger's intransigent stand with regard to railway rates led Rhodes to warn him that his isolationist policy would result in the rest of South Africa combining against him. Certainly, the encounter did nothing to diminish the mutual suspicion and dislike of the two men. When they parted, Kruger was observed to shake his fist at Rhodes. Finding that Kruger could not be 'squared', Rhodes turned to a conspiracy to overthrow him. By December 1894, a plan was already being hatched for an Uitlander uprising on the Rand assisted by what, a year later, became the Jameson Raid from the Bechuanaland border.

THE BACKGROUND TO THE JAMESON RAID

The origins of this notorious fiasco lie in a proposal first put forward not by Rhodes but by the British High Commissioner in South Africa, Sir Henry Loch.[17] In 1894, Loch had made a visit to Pretoria, accompanied by his Imperial Secretary, Sir Graham Bower, to negotiate with Kruger's government the exemption of British subjects, resident in the Transvaal, from being obliged to serve on commando and also to settle details of an agreement about Swaziland. In Pretoria, he had been greeted by a cheering mob of Uitlanders waving Union Jacks, singing English patriotic songs and insisting on presenting him with a petition about their grievances against the Transvaal government. Loch, after reminding them that he was there as the guest of President Kruger, had nevertheless agreed to receive a deputation of Uitlanders who assured him that there were plenty of rifles in Uitlander hands in Johannesburg and that a visit from him would lead to a demand for a British annexation. Bower, observing that Loch 'believed he could make the Transvaal a British colony by raising a hand and said so', dissuaded him from visiting Johannesburg as he was convinced such a visit would lead to a riot.[18]

Whilst in Pretoria, Loch had two private interviews with Lionel Phillips, who was not only a senior manager of Wernher, Beit/H. Eckstein & Co. but also President of the Chamber of Mines at this time. At these meetings, Phillips reported, 'Sir Henry Loch . . . asked me some very pointed questions, such as what arms we had in Johannesburg, whether the population could hold the place for six days until help arrived, etc. etc.'. Phillips emerged convinced that if, in future, a well-prepared Uitlander uprising took place in Johannesburg, the British government would be prepared to intervene on the Uitlanders' behalf.[19] In a secret despatch to the Colonial Office about the Transvaal on 18 July 1894, Loch stated his own disposition:

> to force matters with a high hand on the ground . . . that the Uitlanders were bound to win in their struggle with the Boers, and that if they won without British help, they would probably maintain the independence of the Republic and pursue a policy hostile to federation.

He also commented that 'the extension of the railway to Mafeking in British Bechuanaland renders the approach to Johannesburg easy of accomplishment'.[20]

Loch's 'extremely dangerous proposal' was at once rejected by the British Colonial Office, whose Permanent Under-Secretary, Sir Robert Meade, declared that it would simply encourage the Uitlanders 'to make excessive demands and the Boers will understand that we deliberately mean to force things to an issue and bloodshed will be the inevitable result'. 'Every nerve should be strained to prevent such a disgrace as another South African war', he concluded.[21] Having sown the seeds of an idea for external armed intervention in support of an Uitlander revolt on the Rand which would result in the annexation of the Transvaal as a British colony, Loch was recalled from his post by a British government alarmed by his 'extraordinarily injudicious manner in coquetting with the would be Rebels as almost to lead to an insurrection'.[22]

Nonetheless, before that Liberal government fell from office in the summer of 1895, plans for an Uitlander uprising at Johannesburg were already underway and Rhodes had taken over the Loch plan and adapted it in a way which was far more likely to win the connivance of the British government. His proposal was that the external armed intervention from the Bechuanaland border should not be by British troops operating from British territory but by border police, in the employment of his British South Africa Company, operating from the strip of territory along the Transvaal border which the British government had already agreed to transfer to the Company for the purpose of extending the railway north from Mafeking to Bulawayo. Despite opposition within the British Cabinet, Rhodes also secured the appointment of his nominee, Sir Hercules Robinson, as Loch's replacement as British High Commissioner in South Africa, despite Robinson's age, poor health and past record of being almost literally in Rhodes's pocket. Further, Sir Graham Bower was prevailed upon to forego the governorship of Newfoundland – for which he had been recommended – and return to South Africa to assist Robinson. Bower had advised the Colonial Office that an Uitlander rising was probable and that, if it took place, the British High Commissioner should intervene to prevent the declaration of 'a plutocrats' republic'.[23]

Joseph Chamberlain had no sooner taken up office as Colonial Secretary in the new government of Lord Salisbury, when Rhodes wrote to him requesting the immediate transfer of the Bechuanaland Protectorate to the British South Africa Company and promising to begin the building of the railway north from Mafeking to Bulawayo a month after the transfer had taken place. Some of Chamberlain's advisers in the Colonial Office were eager to shed the responsibility and annual expense (£100,000 per year) which Bechuanaland represented to the British government and saw the future development of the territory as more likely to result from the railway and injections of Rhodes's private capital than from meagre grants wrung from the British Treasury. The transfer of the southern part of Bechuanaland, south of the Molopo river, to the Cape Colony had already been approved by the previous government. The transfer of the much larger northern section (the Bechuanaland Protectorate) to the Chartered Company had also been agreed in principle.[24] Chamberlain, however, distrusted Rhodes and at first prevaricated. Meanwhile, a deputation of Tswana chiefs arrived in London to protest against the transfer of their land to Rhodes's company, whose real intention, they declared, was less to govern them than to seize their land, as had already happened in Rhodesia with the Ndebele, and 'impoverish us so that hunger may drive us to become the white man's servants who dig in his mines and gather his wealth'.[25]

Their appeal to the British Colonial Office for protection enabled Chamberlain to achieve a compromise, on 6 November 1895, by which the chiefs secured considerable reserves of land and continued British protection and Rhodes's British South Africa Company obtained the promise of some 100,000 square miles of territory, including the much sought-after border strip for the railway. Rhodes was furious at this compromise and found it 'humiliating to be utterly beaten by these niggers . . . simply to please the temperance and the missionary section of the English people'.[26] A striking feature of the settlement is that Rhodes did not get all that he wanted from Chamberlain. For successive British governments, Rhodes had his uses, but Chamberlain was never an unqualified supporter of Rhodes and his ventures. Not the least of the results of the failure of the Jameson Raid was to be that the Bechuanaland Protectorate was never transferred to the British South Africa Company but remained under the British government, as the Tswana wished, until it became the independent country of Botswana in 1966.[27] Nonetheless, Chamberlain had agreed to transfer the strip of territory along the Transvaal border, and he had ensured that this was done by the date of 7 November which Rhodes had stipulated. This was the day after Kruger re-opened the drifts over the Vaal river. The final preparations for what became the Jameson Raid were thus set in train, with the assistance of the British government, hard on the heels of the resolution of the Drifts Crisis.

The question of Chamberlain's complicity in the preparations for the Jameson Raid has never ceased to fascinate historians. After almost a century of detective work, there now seems little reason to doubt that when Chamberlain agreed to the transfer of the border strip he did so knowing that it was needed by Rhodes not just for the building of the railway but as a springboard for the armed force which Jameson was already assembling at Pitsani.[28] Further, the evidence suggests that not only Chamberlain but at least two other senior members of the British Colonial Office (Lord Selborne and Edward Fairfield) and the British High Commissioner in South Africa and his assistant (Sir Hercules Robinson and Sir Graham Bower) also knew of Rhodes's plan to station Jameson with a force under the British South Africa Company on the Bechuanaland border for the purpose of assisting an Uitlander uprising on the Rand.[29] Chamberlain connived at this because he never envisaged that there would be a raid from the border without a rising at Johannesburg to justify it. If an Uitlander uprising did occur on the Rand, and an armed force were to go to its assistance from the border, it would be much better, from the British government's point of view, if that force was not in government employment or operating from British territory. Chamberlain and the Colonial Office might connive at the existence of this force, but the entire responsibility for it and its actions must rest with Rhodes and his Company.[30] On 7 November, Chamberlain authorized the British High Commissioner in South Africa, Sir Hercules Robinson, to release the Bechuanaland border police and allow them to transfer their services to the British South Africa Company. Many of them did so and, together with the men who had been brought with Jameson from Rhodesia, formed the force established at Pitsani which set out on the Jameson Raid at the end of December.

THE ABORTIVE UITLANDER UPRISING

Chamberlain never had to deny that he expected an Uitlander uprising to take place on the Rand because it was common knowledge, towards the end of 1895, that an Uitlander revolt was being planned in Johannesburg. 'Never before was there so open a conspiracy', observed James Bryce, who visited the Transvaal at this time, although he omitted to mention that he was told the full details by Lionel Phillips himself when he stayed with him in December.[31] Captain Francis Younghusband, who had been sent by Moberly Bell of *The Times* to act as a 'messenger' and contact man with the conspirators on the Rand, arrived in Johannesburg in mid-December to find that everywhere there was 'the vague apprehension that trouble was brewing'. The great majority of the Uitlanders were not involved in political activity, he reported, they were too busy making money. Amongst those who were involved, 'none of them want to see the British flag hoisted here', he reported, or 'the present Republic done away with' and the Transvaal made into a British colony instead. What they wanted was for 'the present oligarchy' to be replaced 'by a Republic in the true sense of the term' in which Uitlanders could apply for citizenship and the franchise and be treated on an equal basis with the Boers – as was already the case in the Cape Colony.[32] Such sentiments were widely and publicly expressed in Britain, where *The Times*, reflecting that belief in the irresistible force of progress which was such a feature of late nineteenth-century Britain, declared on 16 December 1895 that 'The time is past, even in South Africa, when a helot system of administration, organized for the exclusive advantage of a privileged minority, can long resist the force of enlightened opinion.'

The grievances of the Uitlander population against the Transvaal government were no new issue in 1895 and were a direct product of the situation which had developed in the Transvaal over the previous decade. When a census was taken in 1896 of the European population living within a three-mile radius of the centre of Johannesburg, it was found that of a total European population of 50,907, only 6,205 were Boers, the rest were 'aliens', the majority of them British.[33] As Bryce observed:

> Hearing nothing but English spoken, seeing nothing all round them that was not substantially English . . . it was natural that the bulk of the Uitlanders should deem themselves to be in a country which had become virtually English, and should see something unreasonable and even grotesque in the control of a small body of persons whom they deemed in every way their inferiors.[34]

Most of the Uitlanders in the Transvaal were concentrated in and around Johannesburg and came from urban backgrounds – though a substantial number came from the Cape Colony. The majority were transients there to make money, and very few of them could speak Dutch. There was therefore little social contact, let alone assimilation, between them and the scattered rural Boer population amongst whom they had arrived so suddenly and in such large numbers. Johannesburg and Pretoria, although only 40 miles apart, represented different worlds.

Amongst the Uitlander population, anti-Boer attitudes and grievances against the Transvaal government had manifested themselves from the beginning. As early as March 1890, when President Kruger paid one of his rare visits to the Rand, the flag of the republic had been cut into ribbons and sold off 'at from two to five shillings per strip' by angry Uitlanders determined to demonstrate 'that the inhabitants of Johannesburg felt their grievances to be serious and would insist on having them redressed'. There were also rumours on that occasion about a secret Political Reform Association preparing for an Uitlander revolt and a *coup de force*, assisted by arms brought in from Mafeking, in which the President and other senior state officials would be seized and held as hostages until a 'Republic of the People' had been established under a progressive triumvirate consisting of General Joubert, Ewald Esselen and J. W. Leonard. An eye-witness recorded that 'some big men had offered to back any properly conducted revolutionary movement with money'.[35] Further demonstrations had occurred in 1893 and 1894, at the time of Loch's visit, and Uitlander petitions to the Volksraad had become a regular event. In May 1894, a petition for the franchise was submitted with 13,000 signatures. In August 1895, a further franchise petition supported by 32,000 signatures was submitted to and rejected by the Volksraad.

The grievances of the Uitlander population in general need to be distinguished from the particular grievances of the mining industry. Whereas the mine-magnates were concerned with the additional and unnecessary costs which the government's policies imposed upon their industry, the Uitlander population was initially more preoccupied with such matters as the high cost of housing, living and taxation, the poor educational provision, the inadequate policing, and the refusal of the government to grant official status to the English language, than with the granting of a franchise which few Uitlanders would have been prepared to give up their existing citizenship to obtain. As the leading Uitlander newspaper on the Rand, *The Star*, declared, the majority of the Uitlanders cared little whether Queen Victoria or President Kruger ruled over them 'so long as they have good laws, so long as these laws are justly administered, so long as they are allowed to pursue their vocations in peace, and so long as equality in the incidence of taxation and equality in the state is permitted to be enjoyed by all alike'.[36] The problem was that the essentially tribal politics of Kruger's republic did not result in these things. The Transvaal became a state in which those who felt that they contributed most to the wealth and revenue of the country were effectively discriminated against and excluded from citizenship and political power. Changes to the franchise laws deliberately created new obstacles in the way of access to citizenship. By 1894, applicants had to be European, over 40 years of age and to have had fourteen years of residence in the Transvaal. Since full burgher rights were only obtainable twelve years after naturalization, and naturalization required the forswearing of any previous citizenship, Uitlander applicants were faced with the prospect of a twelve-year period during which they would be without the rights of citizenship in any country. All these requirements contrasted most unfavourably with those prevailing elsewhere in South Africa and in the countries from which the Uitlanders came.

The political problem facing Kruger's government was a real one. Seldom, if ever, has any country been faced with immigration of such a kind and scale and in so short a time as was the Transvaal after 1886. These immigrants were skilled and vociferous and many of them were British citizens and thus could appeal to the British government, the 'paramount power' over the area, for support. They were also concentrated in the industry which provided nine-tenths of the country's revenue, an industry in which few of the Transvaal burghers were directly involved. By 1895, Kruger believed that the Uitlanders outnumbered his Boer burghers and were in danger of swamping them with their 'alien' traditions and way of life. Further, the experience of granting Uitlanders a more ready access to citizenship and the franchise in the recent past had not been encouraging. They had welcomed the annexation of the country by Britain between 1877 and 1881 and had never ceased to criticize the partial restoration of its independence thereafter. Kruger's attitude towards them was therefore understandably wary and suspicious. Those who wanted to come and mine the gold were free to do so; the revenue from their taxes and from the mining industry strengthened the Transvaal's economy and independence. Few of them really wanted to settle permanently and most of them, Kruger believed, should be encouraged to depart when they had made their pile. They were Uitlanders and transients, not Boers, and they were not in the Transvaal on the same basis as his burghers 'who had fought for and won the country with their blood'. Therefore they had no real claim to equal political rights and Kruger was determined not to risk the possibility that the future control of the state might pass, via the ballot box, out of Boer hands.

The 1890s thus constituted a decade of genuine and mounting grievances amongst some sections of the Uitlander population who formed a political movement which was, for the most part, poorly organized and led. Successive appeals to the Transvaal government, by letter and petition, proved ineffective. This encouraged the growing politicization of what had initially been mainly practical grievances. The achievement of political representation came to be seen as the only means by which these could be alleviated. The franchise thus became the pivot of reform. As early as 1890 a Political Reform Association had been formed and this was followed, in 1892, by the establishment of the Transvaal National Union, an organization dedicated to 'the maintenance of the independence of the South African Republic' and to 'the redress of all grievances' and the achievement of equal rights for all citizens of the republic by constitutional means.[37] At the end of 1894, Charles Leonard, a well-known lawyer, became its Chairman. One of the reasons why this had been a rather ineffective body up to this time was because, as he noted, the mining magnates had 'stood aloof from the National Union and its work' and 'were in fact abused roundly for leaving the professional and commercial classes and the working men to fight for liberty'.[38]

During 1895, the Uitlander political movement on the Rand was transformed. Cecil Rhodes set out to organize and subsidize an Uitlander revolt, utilizing Charles Leonard and the National Union to assist in this; and he succeeded in persuading some of the leading mine-magnates to join him. Their leadership and resources gave the Uitlander reform movement a new impetus. But Rhodes intended to use this movement for his own purposes, which were essentially political. He sought to guide and, if need be, deceive the Uitlander reformers so that they neither settled for a compromise with the Transvaal government nor aimed to establish in its place a 'cosmopolitan republic' which might be as hostile to incorporation in a British-dominated federation as was Kruger's Boer republic.

Rhodes was at the heart of the plan for an Uitlander uprising which was developed during 1895 alongside the stationing of Jameson with a force on the Transvaal border.[39] Uitlander grievances certainly existed, but Rhodes took them up and exploited them as a means to a larger end. They presented the best means and justification for an external intervention in the internal affairs of the Transvaal and the overthrow of Kruger's government. This external intervention would not, as in the Loch plan, come directly from the British government, but from Rhodes and his agents. Rhodes organized the financing of the conspiracy through Consolidated Goldfields and the British South Africa Company.[40] A Reform Committee was established made up of Rhodes's friends and supporters. By mid-1895, Rhodes had persuaded his long-standing friend and collaborator, Alfred Beit, to join the plot, forestalling Beit's advice to wait with: 'You might say Oh yes wait but, as you know, we will wait too long and, with its marvellous wealth, Johannesburg will make South Africa an independent Republic, which you and I do not want.'[41]

All those who took a leading part in the conspiracy in South Africa (apart from British government officials) were satellites of either Rhodes or Beit. Rhodes's motives are well documented and they were essentially political. When, on the eve of the Jameson Raid, one of those involved in the plot for an Uitlander uprising asked him what his motives were for seeking to bring about a revolution in the Transvaal, Rhodes replied:

> You may well ask. Here am I, with all the money a man could possibly want, Prime Minister of the Cape, a Privy Councillor – why should I run all these risks? Well . . . I don't want to annex the Transvaal, but I want to see it a friendly member of a Community of South African States. I want equal rights for the English language, a Customs Union, a common Railway policy, a common native policy, a central South African Court of Appeal, British coast protection. I have tried to do a deal with old man Kruger and I have failed. I never shall bring him into line. . . . What I want to do is to lay the foundations of a united South Africa. I want men to associate my name with it after I have gone, and I know that I haven't much time.[42]

Beit's motives for joining in the plot are less clear and are poorly documented.[43] His long-standing admiration for Rhodes was certainly of great importance, but Beit was a German who was less preoccupied than Rhodes was with politics and with the cause of advancing the British Empire in southern Africa. Beit had been a close economic adviser of Rhodes ever since they had joined forces on the Kimberley diamond fields in the 1870s. It is therefore unlikely that economic considerations did not form at least a part of his decision to join Rhodes's conspiracy in 1895. Beit was Rhodes's partner in De Beers and in the British South Africa Company. But on the Rand his importance came less from his associations with Rhodes than from his position as a senior partner in Wernher, Beit/H. Eckstein & Co. By 1895, this firm had outstripped Consolidated Goldfields to become the premier mining company on the Rand, ahead of all others in its development of the 'deep levels' which required large-scale and long-term investment. By no means all of the mining companies on the Rand took part in Rhodes's conspiracy. Apart from Consolidated Goldfields and Wernher, Beit/H. Eckstein & Co., only the Anglo-French Company, represented in the conspiracy by George Farrar, was actively involved. Many of the smaller mining firms, such as those of Albu, Goerz, Barnato and J. B. Robinson, remained aloof. It is therefore incorrect to generalize and assume a general 'capitalist conspiracy' behind Rhodes's plot in the way so persuasively popularized by J. A. Hobson.[44] Senior representatives of the two largest mining companies on the Rand, Consolidated Goldfields and Wernher, Beit/H. Eckstein & Co., were, however, deeply involved – even if other senior personnel in both of these companies remained largely unaware of what was going on.[45] The chief difference between those firms which joined Rhodes's conspiracy and those which did not was that the former were, by 1895, all committed to long-term mining developments. This meant that they had most to gain from the replacement of the corrupt, inefficient and obstructive government of 'Kruger and his grafters' – with its dynamite and other monopolies, which unnecessarily increased mining costs – by one more sympathetic to the needs of the mining industry.[46] Economic considerations, therefore, certainly existed alongside more specifically political ones amongst those who took part in the conspiracy.

Lionel Phillips, a senior manager of Wernher, Beit/H. Eckstein & Co., who was still President of the Chamber of Mines at this time, was recruited by Beit and also came to play a leading part in the conspiracy. Phillips, like Beit, had known Rhodes since Kimberley days and until 1894 had avoided any direct role in Uitlander politics, although he had been active behind the scenes and his firm had contributed substantial sums in support of progressive candidates for the Transvaal Volksraad. At the time of the Uitlander demonstrations accompanying Sir Henry Loch's visit to Pretoria in June 1894, Phillips had told Beit of his mounting impatience with Kruger's government and asked his advice about consulting Rhodes, although he himself considered that an Uitlander rebellion was unlikely – 'anyhow, not for a couple of years'. On that occasion, Phillips had candidly admitted that he 'had no desire for political rights and believe as a whole the [Uitlander] community is not ambitious in this respect and only wants good government'.[47] Phillips had originally hoped that 'gradually a better and more enlightened policy would prevail' and that progressive elements amongst the Boers and Uitlanders in the Transvaal would join hands and form 'a strong Republic' which would bring an end to the domination of Kruger and his Hollander cronies. In the interim, he began to support the National Union financially and to tire of the endless need to bribe government officials. 'If the spending of money does not bring reform, the only alternative is force, and that will come in time', he commented.[48]

Later, a further member of this firm, Percy FitzPatrick, also joined and became the Secretary of the Reform Committee. Thus, representatives of the two largest and most powerful mining companies on the Rand played a central part in the organization of the plot for an Uitlander uprising, details of which were discussed at a meeting of the key conspirators with Rhodes at Cape Town in October 1895. At this meeting, Lionel Phillips, Charles Leonard, and John Hays Hammond and Frank Rhodes (both employed by Consolidated Goldfields) were present alongside Cecil Rhodes himself. Frank Rhodes was given a temporary appointment with Consolidated Goldfields in Johannesburg by his brother, but his real task was to assist with the arrangements for the uprising. By this time the British High Commissioner, Sir Hercules Robinson, had also been told informally of the plan.[49] Charles Leonard had, with some difficulty, been persuaded to join the conspiracy so that the National Union could be used to widen support for the plot amongst the Uitlander population on the Rand. Leonard himself drew up the 'Manifesto of Uitlander grievances' which was eventually published in December. It was arranged, via De Beers in Kimberley, that arms and ammunition would be smuggled into Johannesburg, where these would be hidden in disused mine-shafts. When all was ready, the idea was for the Reform Committee to issue arms and ammunition to a body of Uitlanders who would then take over the city. There was also a plan to seize the arsenal in Pretoria. Jameson, equipped by the Reform Committee with a letter urgently asking for his assistance on behalf of 'thousands of unarmed men, women and children . . . at the mercy of well-armed Boers', would ride with his force from the border to join the rebel Uitlanders in Johannesburg. The date of 28 December 1895 was set for the Uitlander uprising on the Rand.

It was not envisaged that Kruger's government would collapse in the face of these events, merely that a situation of deadlock would develop which would enable the British High Commissioner, as the representative of the 'paramount power', to intervene 'to avoid bloodshed'. Arriving from Cape Town by special train, he would 'issue a Proclamation directing both parties to . . . submit to his arbitration'. He would then order the election of a Constituent Assembly, 'to be elected by every adult white male in the country', the majority of whom were believed to be Uitlanders.[50] Meanwhile, the British government would support these measures by announcing that a substantial force was being held in readiness to proceed to South Africa. Many of those taking part in the plot believed, like the British High Commissioner, 'that a revolution might take place without the loss of a life and even without firing a shot' and that the threat of revolt backed up by the intervention of the British government would be sufficient to bring about the replacement of Kruger's Boer oligarchy by 'an Anglicised and liberalised republic'.[51] But Chamberlain believed that 'an entirely independent Republic, governed by or for the capitalists of the Rand, would be very much worse both for British interests in the Transvaal itself and for British influence in South Africa'.[52] He therefore wanted the British High Commissioner to annex the Transvaal as a British colony, as Shepstone had done in 1877. In November, Rhodes was specifically challenged about the flag under which the revolt was to take place. 'I of course would not risk everything as I am doing excepting for British flag', he telegraphed in reply.[53] Rhodes, like Chamberlain, was not working to establish a 'true republic' which might be controlled by the mining industry. His aim was to establish the Transvaal as an anglicized state which could then play its crucial part in the larger South African federation within the British Empire which it had become his overriding purpose to establish. 'You may be sure', Rhodes remarked shortly afterwards, 'that I was not going to risk my position to change President Kruger for President J. B. Robinson'.[54]

This extraordinarily risky conspiracy required detailed and synchronized planning, close contact and coordination between diverse circles of people in Johannesburg, Cape Town and Pitsani, and the active cooperation not only of the British High Commissioner in South Africa but of the British Colonial Office in London. The whole venture was no sudden act of opportunism but was long premeditated and actively organized during the last five months of 1895. The extent to which Chamberlain and the British High Commissioner in South Africa, Sir Hercules Robinson, aided and abetted Rhodes's plan was almost certainly hidden from the British Cabinet at the time. Chamberlain himself, it would seem, found it convenient to make a distinction between his 'official' ignorance and his 'private' knowledge of what was going on. He did, however, have some idea of the risks he was taking. On 6 December, he telegraphed to Sir Hercules Robinson approving the proposed action of the High Commissioner in the likely event of an Uitlander uprising in the Transvaal. 'I take for granted that no movement will take place unless success is certain', Chamberlain warned, 'a fiasco would be most disastrous'.[55] Yet the question of the complicity of Joseph Chamberlain and the British government in what then occurred in the Transvaal has tended to divert attention away from the central fact that behind both the Jameson Raid and the planned Uitlander uprising on the Rand at the end of 1895 lay 'the forcing hand of Rhodes and his associates'.[56]

Despite the later protestations to the contrary of some of their leaders, the mining companies on the Rand were no newcomers to political activity in 1895. Directly and indirectly these companies always exercised considerable influence with the Transvaal government as key employers and patrons and sources of state revenue. The ramifications of their influence grew as they diversified into secondary industries and became large-scale land and property owners. They were in regular contact with senior government officials. They even had their spies, one of whom, Matt Spence, had access to the deliberations of the Transvaal's Executive Council.[57] They utilized substantial slush funds to support sympathetic candidates in the Volksraad, to bribe the corrupt state bureaucracy, and to support rival candidates to Paul Kruger in presidential elections.

The political activities of the mining industry were, however, uncoordinated and fragmented. A Chamber of Mines had been formed as early as 1887 (and re-formed in 1889 on a more substantial basis) to represent and promote mining interests, but this was initially a remarkably ineffective body, weakened by divisions amongst its members and largely unsuccessful in its attempts to extract better terms and conditions for the mining industry from Kruger's government.[58] It tended to be dominated by Wernher, Beit/H. Eckstein & Co., whose senior officials provided the Chamber with a succession of Presidents. The Chamber of Mines comprised so many conflicting elements, however, that it was not a useful instrument for conspiracy and historians have concluded that the Chamber of Mines itself, as opposed to the individual exploits of some of its members, was not involved in the plot.

Nonetheless, it was at the opening of the Chamber's grand new building in Johannesburg, on 20 November 1895, that Lionel Phillips, as its President, made a challenging speech in which he threw down the gauntlet to Kruger's government, demanding for the Uitlander community an uncorrupt Transvaal administration and 'an equitable share and voice in its affairs'. The government's 'present policy will not do', he declared, and if it were not soon changed it would result in an 'upheaval' which might well involve bloodshed. Speaking not just for the mining industry but for the Uitlanders as a whole, he warned that 'it is a mistake to imagine that this much maligned community . . . will consent indefinitely to remain subordinate to the minority in this country and that they will for ever allow their lives, their property, and their liberty to be subject to its arbitrary will'.[59] This speech caused a sensation when it was published in the newspapers and contributed a great deal to the general expectation that an Uitlander revolt was imminent.

FIASCO

In fact, the Uitlander population on the Rand was ill-prepared for a rebellion during the boom months of 1895. As Captain Younghusband, who was not only privy to the plot but supported it, observed: 'The old saying that Englishmen are never so peacefully employed as when they are engaged in making money is fully borne out here at the present time. . . . Rebellion and money-making do not go together.'[60] Privately, he wrote that the uprising was likely 'to fizzle' and that this might turn the whole venture 'into not only a fiasco but a disaster'.[61]

Fewer Uitlanders rallied to the cause than the members of the Reform Committee had expected and, amongst the conspirators themselves, the lack of effective leadership and the conflicts of opinion, which were eventually to wreck the movement, soon manifested themselves. Both Lionel Phillips and Charles Leonard began to suspect that they were being used by Rhodes for his own purposes and these suspicions were intensified when two reliable informants arrived from Cape Town in December and reported that Rhodes was seeking the outright annexation of the Transvaal as a British colony and the Uitlander uprising was therefore expected to take place under the Union Jack. Since the preservation of the independence of the republic had been a vital consideration for some of the conspirators, it had always been understood that the uprising would take place under the flag of the republic, the Vierkleur. Captain Younghusband was therefore despatched by the Rand conspirators on 20 December to clarify the matter with Rhodes in Cape Town. There, he told Rhodes that those involved in the planned Uitlander uprising on the Rand were beginning 'to quaver' and 'wanted Jameson stopped'.[62] When, on his return to Johannesburg on 25 December, he confirmed that the uprising was indeed expected to take place under the Union Jack, several participants in the conspiracy refused to have anything further to do with it. Charles Leonard, who had only reluctantly become involved in October on the express condition that the independence of the republic would be maintained, felt that Rhodes had deceived him and rushed off to Cape Town to confront him personally. John Hays Hammond (an American) spoke for many others who were not British subjects (and some who were) when he declared 'we won't stand for having a British flag hoisted over Johannesburg' and reported that, when the Reform Committee met, on 31 December, every member of it 'swore allegiance to the flag of the South African Republic and bound themselves to uphold its independence'.[63] The whole plot began to fall apart. Lionel Phillips warned Beit that if an immediate uprising were insisted upon it would end in complete failure.[64]

The flag question was only one of many manifestations of disarray amongst the members of the reform movement in Johannesburg. Insufficient guns and ammunition, the abandonment of the plan to seize the Pretoria arsenal, the news that Jameson's force on the border was far smaller than had been envisaged, the absence of Beit in the Cape, and the fact that it was Christmas and large numbers of Boers were gathering in Pretoria to celebrate communion and so would be at hand to assist Kruger's government, all contributed to the realization that any uprising would have to be delayed. Meanwhile, it was decided to publish Charles Leonard's Uitlander Manifesto on 26 December, in his absence and with an additional list of ten objectives amongst which were demands for 'a true Republic', a new constitution, and 'an equitable franchise law and fair representation'.[65] It was decided to seek a meeting with President Kruger, on 6 January 1896, at which these demands could be discussed.

Action was also taken to alert Jameson and prevent him setting off with his force from the border into the Transvaal. Frank Rhodes informed his brother in Cape Town that it was absolutely necessary to postpone the 'flotation'. Telegrams were sent directly to Jameson ordering him not to move; and two men were despatched by different routes to explain the changed situation to him at Pitsani, where they both arrived on 28–29 December. Jameson, however, was getting impatient and was determined to stick to the original plan. After hearing their news, Jameson, 'cocksure of success and convinced that he had only to succeed to be forgiven', decided to stimulate the Johannesburgers into an uprising by leaving at once. On 29 December, he telegraphed to Rhodes: 'Shall leave tonight for the Transvaal . . .'[66]

Jameson himself was therefore responsible for the final decision to launch the Raid into the Transvaal in the hope of forcing an Uitlander uprising in Johannesburg. Rhodes had already received some intimation that this might happen and failed to act decisively to prevent it. Why? It has been suggested that he deliberately took a gamble and did not himself send a categorical order to Jameson not to move because he hoped that somehow Jameson might still succeed in sparking off an Uitlander revolt which Rhodes knew would not otherwise occur. The week-end closure of the telegraph lines and the Cape Town telegraphic office (even to the Prime Minister?) have also been blamed for the fact that no clear order from Rhodes reached Jameson in time. On Saturday 28 December, when he knew that an Uitlander uprising on the Rand was not going to take place, Rhodes delegated to Rutherfoord Harris the task of sending the crucial telegram to Jameson. Harris avoided sending a 'peremptory prohibition' in Rhodes's name, telling Jameson instead that 'you and we must judge regarding flotation', i.e. leaving it up to Jameson to decide.[67] One of Rhodes's biographers concludes that 'Rhodes could have stopped Jameson and did not do so'.[68] Another argues that although the Jameson Raid was designed and prepared by Rhodes, 'he lost control at the end' and placed an impatient and headstrong Jameson in a position where he could and did act on his own initiative.[69] This, it would seem, is exactly what happened.[70]

Throughout the autumn of 1895, Chamberlain had not been just an interested spectator of the mounting Uitlander unrest on the Rand. On the contrary, he had given detailed instructions to the British High Commissioner about his role if an Uitlander revolt occurred. He had also twice intervened: first, to ensure that the revolt would take place under the British flag, and secondly with regard to its timing. On 17 December, President Cleveland, in a message to the United States Congress, threatened Britain with war over the disputed border between Venezuela and British Guiana. Although Chamberlain believed that the matter was unlikely to become serious for some time, this development led him to the conclusion that, if there was to be trouble in the Transvaal, 'either it should come *at once* or be postponed for a year or two at least'. Chamberlain's view was conveyed to Rhodes via the Colonial Office and Rhodes's agents in London through a 'hurry up' telegram which later went missing.[71] Chamberlain thus not only knew about the planned Uitlander revolt but took a significant part in trying to ensure that it would serve British interests. On 26 December, he informed the Prime Minister that 'a rising in Johannesburg is imminent and will probably take place in the course of the next few days'. After outlining the actions he had taken in sending secret instructions to Robinson about 'how to act in an emergency' and arranging for two British regiments to call at the Cape in January, Chamberlain concluded by observing that 'If the rising is successful it ought to turn to our advantage'.[72]

The news that the Uitlander uprising on the Rand was unlikely to come off reached London the following day. Edward Fairfield (from the Colonial Office) heard from Bouchier Hawksley (Rhodes's solicitor) 'that he and his friends were being much chaffed in the City about the "fizzle" of their revolution'. Hawksley also spoke of the possibility that Rhodes 'might be driven into an attitude of frenzy and unreason and order Dr. Jameson to "go in" from Gaberones with the Company's police and manipulate a revolution'. In passing on this information to Chamberlain (who was in Birmingham) Fairfield commented: 'Were the Company's police to go in filibustering it would be a breach of their Charter.'[73] Chamberlain at once notified the Prime Minister that 'the Transvaal business is going to fizzle out. Rhodes has miscalculated the feeling of the Johannesburg capitalists', but said nothing about the possibility of Jameson acting on his own to try and force an Uitlander rising. At the same time, he warned Robinson (who would in turn warn Rhodes) that any attempt 'to force matters at Johannesburg to a head by someone in the service of the Company advancing from the Bechuanaland Protectorate with police' might lead to a revocation of the Company's charter. This warning arrived too late. Jameson had already left. When Chamberlain heard this, he at once repudiated Jameson's action in a telegram to Robinson which reveals the difference between what Chamberlain had expected to happen and what had now occurred. 'If the Govt. of the S.A.R. had been overthrown, or there had been anarchy at Jo'burg, there might have been some shadow of an excuse for this unprecedented act', Chamberlain observed. As things had turned out, Jameson had committed 'an act of war, or rather of filibustering'.[74] To the Prime Minister, Chamberlain described Jameson's action as 'a flagrant piece of filibustering, for which there is no justification that I can see in the present state of things in the Transvaal'. Salisbury simply commented cynically, 'If filibustering fails it is always disreputable'.[75]

In Cape Town, Rhodes was told on 28 December, by Charles Leonard and F. H. Hamilton (the editor of the Rand newspaper *The Star*) who had been sent from Johannesburg to tell him, that, as he put it to Bower, the plans for an Uitlander uprising on the Rand had 'fizzled out like a damp squib'. Bower then informed Robinson of this and Robinson duly telegraphed the news to Chamberlain.[76] Only on Sunday evening, 29 December, does Rhodes seem to have realized that Jameson's Raid was also likely to result in a fiasco. Shortly before midnight, Bower was summoned to Rhodes's bedroom at Groot Schuur where an ashen-faced Rhodes told him that Jameson had taken the bit between his teeth and gone into the Transvaal.[77] Next day, W. P. Schreiner found Rhodes 'absolutely broken down in spirit, ruined'. 'It is true', Rhodes declared, 'Old Jameson has upset my apple-cart . . . twenty years we have been friends and now he goes and ruins me.'[78]

Jameson and his raiders reached Doornkop, fourteen miles from Johannesburg, before the Transvaal commandos – who had been shadowing them – finally surrounded and forced them to surrender on 2 January 1896 after skirmishes in which seventeen of Jameson's men were killed and 55 were wounded. In a speech towards the end of December, Kruger had said that he was aware of rumours about threatened risings or revolts but his view was to 'wait until the time comes. Take a tortoise, if you want to kill it, you must wait until it puts out its head, then you cut it off'.[79] Kruger had known about what he described as 'an incursion of British troops from Mafeking' since 30 December. The leaders of the Uitlander reform movement on the Rand, however, were totally unprepared and had not known that Jameson was coming until he was well on his way. Arms were hurriedly distributed and Johannesburg took on the appearance of a town in revolt as the Uitlanders prepared to give Jameson a hero's welcome. Kruger's government ordered the Johannesburg police to withdraw to their barracks in the gaol to avoid clashes with the Uitlanders who, by 31 December, were in control of the town. It then issued an invitation to the Uitlanders to send a deputation to Pretoria to lay the issue of Uitlander grievances before a government commission. Lionel Phillips left for Pretoria at the head of this deputation on 1 January.

Meanwhile, a number of concessions to the Uitlanders were offered by Kruger's Executive Council on 30 December – the day it became known in Pretoria that Jameson had crossed the border. It agreed to recommend to the Volksraad that special duties on foodstuffs should be abolished, that English-language schools should have equal access to the state subsidy, and that the Netherlands Railway Company would be approached to see if transport costs to and from the mines could be reduced. Kruger also declared that the franchise should be granted 'to those who were really worthy of it – those for instance who rallied round the Government in this crisis and took no part in the mischievous agitation and clamouring for so-called reforms'.[80] When a deputation of Americans from Johannesburg came to see him, Kruger asked them: 'If a crisis should occur, on which side shall I find the Americans?' When they answered: 'On the side of liberty and good government', Kruger replied: 'You are all alike, tarred with the same brush; you are British in your hearts.'[81]

Whilst he was in Pretoria, Lionel Phillips heard the news of Jameson's arrest and learned that Kruger's government had accepted the offer of the British High Commissioner in Cape Town to come to the Transvaal and use his good offices to seek a peaceful settlement. When he arrived, Sir Hercules Robinson met Kruger's Executive Council on 6 January and was told that the Uitlanders must surrender Johannesburg unconditionally within 24 hours. This he persuaded them to do as the precondition for negotiations and as the best safeguard for the captured Jameson and his raiders. Kruger then granted an amnesty to the Uitlander rebels, except for the members of the Reform Committee, and issued a Proclamation in which he offered to put a proposal for the granting of an elected municipal council for Johannesburg before the Transvaal Volksraad. Meanwhile, the members of the Uitlander Reform Committee – whose names and correspondence were found in the saddlebag of one of Jameson's raiders – were gradually rounded up and imprisoned in Pretoria gaol, there to await trial on the charge of plotting the overthrow of the government.[82]

Kruger handled the subsequent situation with considerable skill and forbearance. Jameson and his raiders were soon released into British custody to be subject to British legal processes of investigation. The leaders of the Uitlander Reform Committee were tried and sentenced under Transvaal law, three of them (including Lionel Phillips) receiving death sentences for treason. These sentences were then commuted and within six months most of those involved had had their fines paid for them by Rhodes (the total cost to Rhodes being some £400,000[83]) and were able to leave the country after promising to abstain from political activity for the next three years. The subsequent enquiries into the Jameson Raid, in Cape Town and in London during 1896–7, established that Rhodes was at the centre of the conspiracy but that Jameson had acted on his own initiative in riding into the Transvaal with his force in defiance of orders to wait. These enquiries, however, became a by-word for exercises in damage-limitation by those involved, and most especially by Joseph Chamberlain and the British government. Chamberlain emerged from what W. T. Stead called the 'lying in state at Westminster' officially cleared of being implicated in 'Rhodes's plot'. In fact, it would seem that immediately after Rhodes arrived in England, in February 1896, he and Chamberlain met and came to an agreement whereby, when he faced the Official Enquiry, Rhodes would accept full responsibility for the events surrounding the Jameson Raid and avoid implicating Chamberlain, the British government and its representatives. In return, Chamberlain undertook to see that the Charter of the British South Africa Company was preserved.[84]

As a result of these events, Rhodes was forced to resign as Prime Minister of the Cape Colony and as a Director of the British South Africa Company (the majority of whose Board of Directors were ignorant of what he had been up to). The capture of Jameson's force (which had been largely formed out of Rhodesian police) helped to trigger a revolt in 1896 by the Ndebele in Rhodesia against the rapacious actions of the British South Africa Company. During the following two years, Rhodes was therefore preoccupied with Rhodesia. He then re-emerged as a potent influence behind the pro-British party in Cape politics in the run-up to the 1898 elections there. By 1898 he was also back on the board of the British South Africa Company, which not only retained its Charter but never paid the compensation claimed against it by the Transvaal government. Meanwhile, Jameson, who had soon been released 'into British custody', was greeted as a popular hero when he arrived in England for a trial which resulted in a verdict of guilty and a modest prison sentence from which he was released after four months. As Kruger wryly noted in his memoirs: 'Dr. Jameson was released from prison on account of illness and recovered his health immediately afterwards.'[85] Jameson then returned to South Africa and went on to a successful career in Cape politics, becoming Prime Minister (1904–10) and, after his retirement in England, President of the British South Africa Company (1913–17).

This rapid rehabilitation of those whom Kruger never ceased to regard as 'enemies of the republic', who had plotted to overthrow its independence, confirmed his deep suspicions that behind those who had engineered and participated in the Jameson Raid stood the British government and Joseph Chamberlain. From 1896, therefore, Kruger and his government expected and began to prepare for further assaults on the independence of the Transvaal from this alliance of British interests both within and without the republic.

THE SIGNIFICANCE OF THE JAMESON RAID

After the Jameson Raid and the abortive Uitlander uprising, relations between the Transvaal republic and the British government could never be the same again. These events therefore helped to set South Africa on the course which led to war in October 1899. The British and Boer populations throughout South Africa were polarized by what had occurred. The worst suspicions of many Afrikaners were confirmed and those outside the Transvaal felt a surge of sympathy towards their threatened kinsfolk within it. A powerful charge was given to the development of Afrikaner nationalism and republicanism throughout the region. Most of those Cape Afrikaners who had supported Rhodes felt bitterly betrayed. As one of their most eloquent spokesmen declared, Rhodes had acted as 'a sort of dividing wall between the Colonial Afrikaners and their brothers in the Republics'; his 'dagger-thrust' had sent 'an electric shock to the heart of Afrikanerdom' and aroused in it a new nationalist awareness and solidarity fired by the threat of British dominance and imperialism.[86] The alliance which Rhodes had constructed with Hofmeyr's Afrikaner Bond was shattered. Henceforth, white politics in South Africa divided on ethnic lines.

In the Jameson Raid and the planned Uitlander uprising on the Rand, Rhodes and Chamberlain had risked war. Rhodes may have been at the centre of the conspiracy, but both Chamberlain and the British High Commissioner in South Africa were deeply implicated in what was, in effect, a plot to overthrow Kruger's government by a *coup d'état* the result of which was expected to be the imposition, by the British High Commissioner, of a political settlement on the Transvaal which would make it British. The planned Uitlander uprising was thus little more than an excuse for the intervention of the British government as an arbiter in the internal affairs of the Transvaal. Without this intervention, and without the promise of armed assistance from Jameson and his force from the border, the plan for an Uitlander uprising would never have developed even as far as it did. The role of the British government was therefore not marginal but vital to the whole conspiracy.

Chamberlain was probably unaware of the extent to which the

Uitlander agitation during the last months of 1895 was being artificially stimulated by Rhodes and his agents. Without this external assistance and encouragement it is clear, from the events of December 1895, that the Uitlanders were not yet capable of mobilizing and sustaining an effective political movement in the Transvaal – let alone of mounting a *coup* against Kruger's government. Uitlander grievances certainly existed, but their significance in 1895 is that, led by the new Colonial Secretary, the British government took them up. Hitherto, British governments had been reluctant to intervene on behalf of the Uitlanders, whose grievances had been regarded sceptically as 'fictitious to a great extent'.[87] With the arrival of Chamberlain at the Colonial Office, however, Uitlander grievances began to be taken much more seriously by the British government – which came to believe that they were genuine and well-founded and offered the best justification for British intervention in what was essentially an internal matter for the Transvaal government. The fact that in Rhodes's conspiracy, Uitlander grievances had been used as a front for the achievement of other purposes seems not to have shaken the widespread popular belief in Britain that these grievances were real and demanded redress. Since it was the British government which had intervened, via the British High Commissioner, to persuade the Uitlanders to surrender to Kruger's forces in January 1896, it was now widely felt that it was up to the British government to do something to rectify their grievances. *The Times* argued this point strongly, in a leader on 16 January 1896. The response of the British government to the Uitlander agitation on the Rand at the time of the Jameson Raid thus marks an important watershed in the development of British policy towards the Transvaal republic.[88] Henceforth, 'Uitlander grievances' join 'the strict observance of the terms of the London Convention of 1884' as the basis on which the British government now asserted its right to intervene in the Transvaal.

The *means* by which these Uitlander grievances were to be rectified was also clearly established at this time, and agreed by Chamberlain and the British High Commissioner, Sir Hercules Robinson, in their exchanges of November–December 1895. What they hoped to do was to impose a constitution on the Transvaal which would enable a 'peaceful revolution' to occur through the ballot box. Control of the Transvaal would be taken away from the Boers and given to the Uitlanders through the establishment of an 'equal franchise' for the European population, as existed in the Cape Colony, at a time when both Robinson and Chamberlain believed that the adult male Uitlanders exceeded the adult male Boers in numbers and would continue to do so by a steadily increasing margin. Once they had the franchise, the Uitlanders would be in a position to rectify their own grievances without the need for further direct intervention by the British government in the future. Chamberlain was later to claim that a five-year franchise for the Uitlanders 'was the remedy which we borrowed from our predecessors in office'.[89] But it was after his accession to office, and at the time of the Jameson Raid, that this *mechanism* for the transformation of the situation in the Transvaal, and the establishment of British supremacy there, becomes clearly articulated as the policy of the British government. This was a development of great significance for the future.

It occurred at a time when Chamberlain's survival as British Colonial Secretary was in question. Chamberlain's success in veiling from public view the extent of his complicity in the events surrounding the Jameson Raid and the abortive Uitlander uprising on the Rand may not have silenced the rumours, but it enabled him to remain in office. Had he failed in his efforts to muzzle Rhodes and limit the investigations of the Official Committee of Enquiry during 1896–7, Chamberlain would almost certainly have had to resign from the government. But he made sure that he was himself a member of the Enquiry, and he was greatly assisted by the failure of the Liberal Party to act as an effective Opposition.[90] Had Chamberlain resigned, and a less powerful and confrontationist Colonial Secretary occupied that important office during the following crucial years, Britain's relations with the Transvaal republic might have followed a different course. As Jean van der Poel has so persuasively argued, 'the shielding of Chamberlain had much to do with the coming of war'.[91]

Kruger and the Transvaal Boers never doubted that the British government, and Chamberlain in particular, had been behind the plot to overthrow their independence. This conviction meant that thereafter relations between the British and Transvaal governments were characterized by a deep mutual suspicion which vitiated all attempts to resolve peacefully their mounting differences and conflicts of interest. This is a point which has to be constantly borne in mind. After 1896, Kruger's government expected war and began to prepare for it. The Uitlanders had proved that they were not to be trusted and so political control of the Transvaal state had to be kept out of their hands. The weakness and vulnerability of the Transvaal's defences, and the limited number of outdated weapons in the possession of the Boer commandos, had been revealed. A massive programme of defence works and arms importation was therefore embarked upon during the next three years. By the time that war broke out, in October 1899,

Boer commandos were well-equipped with the latest Mauser and Martini-Henry rifles imported from Europe.[92]

NOTES

1. Speech in the House of Lords, 14 February 1895, cited in D. M. Schreuder, *The Scramble for Southern Africa* (Cambridge, 1980), p. 264.
2. Lord Ripon to Lord Rosebery, 5 September 1894, RP 43516.
3. Selborne to Milner, 28 June 1898, printed in D. G. Boyce, ed., *The Crisis of British Power: The Imperial and Naval Papers of the Second Earl of Selborne, 1895–1910* (London, 1990), p. 64.
4. Salisbury to Chamberlain, 30 December 1895, JC 5/67/35.
5. See R. V. Kubicek, *The Administration of Imperialism: Joseph Chamberlain at the Colonial Office* (Durham, NC, 1969).
6. For this brief summary, I have drawn on J. L. Garvin and J. Amery, *Life of Joseph Chamberlain* 6 vols (London, 1932–69), 3 (1934); P. Fraser, *Joseph Chamberlain: Radicalism and the Empire* (London, 1966); R. Quinault, 'Joseph Chamberlain: a reassessment', in T. R. Gourvish and A. O'Day, eds, *Later Victorian Britain* (London, 1988); and J. S. Marais's model of succinct exposition in *The Fall of Kruger's Republic* (Oxford, 1961), pp. 64–70.
7. Garvin, *Life of Chamberlain*, 2, p. 347.
8. Quinault, 'Joseph Chamberlain', in Gourvish and O'Day, eds, *Later Victorian Britain*, p. 85.
9. Address to the London Chamber of Commerce, 14 May 1888, in C. Boyd, ed., *Mr Chamberlain's Speeches* 2 vols (London, 1914), 1, pp. 191–202.
10. 'Trade of the British Empire and Foreign Competition: Despatch from Mr Chamberlain', 28 November 1895, quoted in A. J. Friedberg, *The Weary Titan: Britain and the Experience of Relative Decline 1895–1905* (London, 1988), p. 47.
11. Quinault, 'Joseph Chamberlain', in Gourvish and O'Day, eds, *Later Victorian Britian*, p. 88.
12. Robert Rhodes James, *The British Revolution: British Politics 1880–1939* 2 vols (London, 1976), 1, p. 167.
13. Speech in the House of Commons, 25 July 1881. Full account in C. H. D. Howard, ed., *Joseph Chamberlain: A Political Memoir 1880–1892* (London, 1953), p. 14.
14. I am much indebted in this section to Schreuder, *Scramble for S.A.,* especially chs 6–8.
15. See ch. 2, pp. 62–6 above.
16. Ripon to Kimberley, 25 November 1894, in Schreuder, *Scramble for S.A.*, p. 295.
17. For the Jameson Raid, see especially Jean van der Poel, *The Jameson Raid* (Oxford, 1951); Elizabeth Longford, *Jameson's Raid* (London, 1982 edn);

Marais, *The Fall of Kruger's Republic*; Denys Rhoodie, *Conspirators in Conflict* (Cape Town, 1967); Robert I. Rotberg, *The Founder: Cecil Rhodes and the Pursuit of Power* (Oxford, 1988). See also the evidence in E. Drus, 'A report on the papers of Joseph Chamberlain relating to the Jameson Raid and the Inquiry', *BIHR* XXV (1952), and 'The question of imperial complicity in the Jameson Raid', *EHR* LXVIII (1953).

18. Van der Poel, *The Jameson Raid*, p. 15, citing material from the Bower Papers.

19. Ibid., p. 16. See also M. Fraser and A. Jeeves, eds, *All That Glittered: Selected Correspondence of Lionel Phillips 1890–1924* (Cape Town, 1977), pp. 78–83.

20. Van der Poel, *The Jameson Raid*, pp. 16–17.

21. R. H. Wilde, *Joseph Chamberlain and the South African Republic 1895–1899*, Archives Yearbook for South African History Part 1 (Johannesburg, 1956), p. 7, citing CO 537/128, 16.

22. E. Fairfield to J. Chamberlain, 5 January 1896, in Drus, 'A report', p. 42.

23. Van der Poel, *The Jameson Raid*, pp. 23–4.

24. Wilde, *Joseph Chamberlain*, pp. 9–10.

25. Paul Maylam, *Rhodes, the Tswana and the British: Collaboration and Conflict in the Bechuanaland Protectorate 1885–1899* (London, 1980), p. 167, citing a statement from the Tswana chiefs to the Colonial Office on 4 November 1895.

26. Ibid., p. 168.

27. R. Hyam, *The Failure of South African Expansion 1908–1948* (London, 1972).

28. In addition to the evidence long ago advanced by E. Drus and Jean van der Poel, the letter from Bouchier F. Hawksley (Rhodes's solicitor) to Rhodes of 22 May 1897, now in Rhodes House Library, Oxford, reinforces this conclusion. In it, Hawksley criticizes Chamberlain for not having 'had the courage to admit that he allowed the troops to be put on the border in connection with the anticipated rising in Johannesburg'. He also accuses him of acting without the full knowledge of the Cabinet. See R. Blake, 'The Jameson Raid and the "Missing Telegrams" ', in H. Lloyd-Jones *et al.*, eds, *History and Imagination: Essays in Honour of H.R. Trevor-Roper* (Oxford, 1981).

29. The evidence from the Grey and Bower Papers needs to be added to that provided in the articles of Drus already cited. See J. S. Galbraith, 'The British South Africa Company and the Jameson Raid', *JBS*, November 1970, and van der Poel, *The Jameson Raid*. The two key letters from Grey to Chamberlain of 17 November 1895 and 10 December 1896 are in the Chamberlain Papers, JC 10/6/1/9.

30. See Marais, *The Fall of Kruger's Republic*, pp. 84–5, and the letter from Fairfield to Chamberlain, 4 November 1895, cited there.

31. James Bryce, *Impressions of South Africa* 3rd edn (London, 1900), p. 438; Lionel Phillips, *Some Reminiscences* (London, 1924), pp. 149–50.

32. F. Younghusband, *South Africa Today* (London, 1898), pp. 60–9; for Younghusband's role see Patrick French, *Younghusband: the Last Great Imperial Adventurer* (London, 1994), ch. 9.

33. Marais, *The Fall of Kruger's Republic*, p. 1.
34. Bryce, *Impressions*, p. 424.
35. See Rhoodie, *Conspirators in Conflict*, pp. 24–6, who uses a memorandum from the W. J. Leyds Papers in the Government Archives, Pretoria. The eye-witness account is by E. E. Kennedy, *Waiting for the Boom* (Cape Town, 1985), written in 1890, pp. 52–4. The flag incident in 1890 is also mentioned in Percy FitzPatrick, *The Transvaal from Within* (London, 1899), pp. 80–1.
36. See A. Mawby, 'The political behaviour of the British population of the Transvaal 1902–1907', Ph.D. thesis, Witwatersrand University, 1969, p. 18. I am much indebted to this work in this section.
37. The Constitution of the Transvaal National Union, published in *The Star*, 22 August 1892.
38. Charles Leonard Papers cited in Rhoodie, *Conspirators in Conflict*, p. 21.
39. For succinct summaries of the details of the plot see Marais, *The Fall of Kruger's Republic*, chs 3–4, and Rotberg, *The Founder*, ch. 19. For a more extensive treatment see van der Poel, *The Jameson Raid*, and Rhoodie, *Conspirators in Conflict*.
40. £61,500 was provided by the Chartered Company and £120,000 came from a body called the Development Syndicate (which was almost certainly utilizing money from Consolidated Goldfields). See J. Flint, *Cecil Rhodes* (London, 1976), p. 188.
41. Rhodes to Beit, n.d. August 1895, Ms. 114, Brenthurst Library, Johannesburg, quoted in Rotberg, *The Founder*, p. 518.
42. Sir Frederick Hamilton to Howell Wright, 27 September 1937, Wright Papers, Yale University Library, quoted in V. Harlow, 'Sir Frederic Hamilton's narrative of events relative to the Jameson Raid', *EHR* LXXII (1957), p. 299.
43. See R. Mendelsohn, 'Blainey and the Jameson Raid: the debate renewed', *JSAS* 6, 2 (1980), pp. 166–7, to which I am much indebted here; also R. V. Kubicek, 'The Randlords in 1895: a reassessment', *JBS* Xl, 2 (1972), pp. 98–9.
44. J. A. Hobson, *The War in South Africa: its Causes and Effects* (London, 1900).
45. See Kubicek, 'The Randlords in 1895'; Galbraith, 'The British South Africa Company and the Jameson Raid', *JBS* X, 1 (1970); Rotberg, *The Founder*, ch. 19. I have also used the correspondence between G. Rouliot and J. Wernher in the archives of H. Eckstein & Co.(now in the Barlow Rand Archives, Johannesburg).
46. Mendelsohn, 'Blainey and the Jameson Raid', p. 170; the phrase describing Kruger's government comes from one of the conspirators, John Hays Hammond, *Autobiography* 2 vols (New York, 1935), 1, p. 343.
47. Phillips to Beit, 16 June 1894, printed in Fraser and Jeeves, eds, *All That Glittered*, pp. 78–9.
48. Phillips to Beit, 12 August 1894, in ibid., p. 81.
49. Rhoodie, *Conspirators in Conflict*, p. 32.
50. See Sir Hercules Robinson's private letter to J. Chamberlain, 4

November 1895, and Chamberlain's response, printed in Garvin, *Life of Chamberlain*, 3, pp. 59–63.

51. Ibid., p. 61. See also FitzPatrick, *The Transvaal from Within*, p. 131.

52. J. Chamberlain memorandum, June 1896, quoted in Garvin and Amery, *Life of Chamberlain*, 3, p. 74.

53. Ibid., p. 75, quoting telegram from Rhodes of 6 November 1895.

54. Rotberg, *The Founder*, p. 525. J. B. Robinson was an independent mine-magnate who did not take part in the conspiracy.

55. Garvin, *Life of Chamberlain*, 3, p. 63. About the disappearance of this letter, see Drus, 'A report', p. 36.

56. This was, of course, the essential conclusion of the Enquiry into the Jameson Raid in 1897 which was otherwise, in most respects, a travesty of what it should have been. It is also the conclusion (and apt phrase) of Rhodes's biographer, Robert I. Rotberg: see *The Founder*, p. 506.

57. See J. J. Van Helten, 'British and European economic investment in the Transvaal: with specific reference to the Witwatersrand gold fields and district 1886–1910', Ph.D. thesis, London University, 1981, pp. 165–6.

58. The archives of the Chamber of Mines in Johannesburg contain very little material before 1900 but, for this section, I have drawn on the annual reports; the unpublished M.A. thesis of D. A. Etheredge, 'The early history of the Chamber of Mines, Johannesburg 1887–1897', Witwatersrand University, 1949; and J. Lang, *Bullion Johannesburg* (Johannesburg, 1986).

59. Lionel Phillips speech of 20 November 1895, reported in *The Star*, 21 November 1895.

60. Younghusband, *South Africa Today*, p. 91; Rhoodie, *Conspirators in Conflict*, p. 52.

61. French, *Younghusband*, p. 127.

62. Ibid.

63. John Hays Hammond, *Autobiography*, 1, pp. 342–3; see also E. Garrett and E. J. Edwards, *The Story of an African Crisis* (London, 1897), p. 288.

64. Van der Poel, *The Jameson Raid*, p. 78.

65. Details in Rhoodie, *Conspirators in Conflict*, p. 53.

66. Van der Poel, *The Jameson Raid*, p. 88.

67. V. Harlow, 'Sir Frederick Hamilton's narrative of events relative to the Jameson Raid', *EHR* LXXII (1957), p. 298 fn. 1.

68. Flint, *Cecil Rhodes*, p. 132.

69. Rotberg, *The Founder*, p. 529.

70. The evidence is most fully considered in van der Poel, *The Jameson Raid*, pp. 88–98, and Rotberg, *The Founder*, pp. 524–32.

71. See van der Poel, *The Jameson Raid*, pp. 42, 49–50, 221–2.

72. Chamberlain to Salisbury, 26 December 1895, printed in Garvin, *Life of Chamberlain*, 3, pp. 76–8.

73. Edward Fairfield to J. Chamberlain, 27 December 1895, quoted in van der Poel, *The Jameson Raid*, pp. 80–1.

74. Chamberlain to Robinson, 31 December 1895, printed as No. 11 in C.7933.

75. Chamberlain to Salisbury, 29 December 1895, in Garvin, *Life of Chamberlain*, 3, p. 90; Salisbury to Chamberlain, 31 December 1895, printed in Drus, 'A report', p. 37.
76. Van der Poel, *The Jameson Raid*, pp. 85–6.
77. Rotberg, *The Founder*, p. 531.
78. See Eric Walker, *W.P. Schreiner, a South African* (Oxford, 1937), p. 71.
79. Speech reported on 27 December 1895 in C.7933, p. 64.
80. FitzPatrick, *The Transvaal from Within*, p. 136; Marais, *The Fall of Kruger's Republic*, p. 102.
81. FitzPatrick, *The Transvaal from Within*, p. 135.
82. See A. H. Duminy and W. R. Guest, eds, *FitzPatrick: South African politician, selected papers 1888–1906* (Johannesburg, 1976), pp. 24–45; also van der Poel, *The Jameson Raid*, pp. 138–43.
83. Rotberg, *The Founder*, p. 535.
84. Van der Poel, *The Jameson Raid*, pp. 157–9.
85. S. J. P. Kruger, *The Memoirs of Paul Kruger . . . as told by himself* 2 vols (London, 1902), 2, p. 279.
86. The phrases are those of J. C. Smuts: see W. K. Hancock and J. van der Poel, eds, *Selections from the Smuts Papers* 7 vols (Cambridge, 1966–73), l, pp. 103–15.
87. E. Fairfield to J. Chamberlain, 5 January 1896, in Drus, 'A report', p. 42.
88. A. N. Porter, *The Origins of the South African War, Joseph Chamberlain and the Diplomacy of Imperialism 1895–1899* (Manchester, 1980), pp. 88–90.
89. Speech in the House of Commons, 5 February 1900, in C. Boyd, ed., *Mr Chamberlain's Speeches* 2 vols (London, 1914), p. 57.
90. J. Butler, *The Liberal Party and the Jameson Raid* (Oxford, 1968).
91. Van der Poel, *The Jameson Raid*, p. 262.
92. F. Pretorius, *Kommandolewe tydens die Anglo-Boereoorlog 1899–1902* (Johannesburg and Cape Town, 1991), pp. 26–7.

CHAPTER FOUR
Aftermath (1896–7)

The Jameson Raid embarrassed Joseph Chamberlain and the British government and poisoned Anglo-Transvaal relations. The fact that Chamberlain remained in office, and that neither Rhodes nor Jameson were eliminated from the political scene thereafter, convinced Kruger and his burghers that further attacks upon the independence of their republic were likely to be made in the future. In the successive crises and confrontations which were to follow, between 1896 and 1899, Kruger's government had to deal with a British Colonial Secretary whom it had every reason to regard with profound distrust. The Raid served to strengthen Kruger's position amongst his own burghers and to weaken those amongst them who might, in other circumstances, have emerged to form a progressive bloc in Transvaal politics committed to reform and to tackling the problem of Uitlander grievances. The treasonable tendencies exhibited by so many of the leading Uitlanders in the Transvaal at the time of the Raid also stiffened Kruger's attitude towards them. As in 1880–81, they had proved themselves to be utterly unreliable and ever ready to make common cause with 'British interests'. They had collaborated with 'enemies of the republic' in an attempt to overthrow its elected government. They were essentially aliens, who were present in the Transvaal on a quite different basis to his burghers. They had now revealed themselves to be a potential Trojan Horse within the country in league with its enemies without.

The Jameson Raid polarized opinion not just in the Transvaal but throughout South Africa. The Orange Free State, whose government had sent a commando to the Vaal river border at the time of the Raid, now drew closer to the Transvaal republic. Whilst maintaining his country's interest in the established customs union with the Cape

Colony, her new President, M. T. Steyn, took the management of the country's railways out of Cape hands and arranged for cooperation with the Netherlands Railway Company in the event of war. In March 1897, the two republics renewed a treaty for mutual support and defence 'when the independence of one of the two States may be threatened or attacked', which had been made in 1889, and added a clause proclaiming the goal of a federal union between them. Steyn declared himself to be 'strongly in favour of a closer union with our sister republic. We have the same people, the same history, the same language, and the same form of government.'[1]

In the Cape Colony, the division within the European population meant that many Cape Afrikaners, who were British subjects, had been alienated. In April 1896, the British High Commissioner warned Chamberlain that:

> the feeling of the Dutch African inhabitants of the Cape Colony has undergone a complete change since Jameson's raid and they would now neither sympathize with nor support any forcible measures undertaken by Imperial Government to secure redress of Uitlanders' grievances. . . . I think it my duty to point out that in event of hostilities growing out of the Jameson raid the South African Republic will be openly assisted by the Orange Free State and, at all events covertly, by a large number of Dutch both in the Cape Colony and in Natal.[2]

A surge of sympathy towards their kinsfolk in the Transvaal marked a shift in the attitude of many Afrikaners outside the republic from that which they had exhibited at the time of the Drifts Crisis two months previously. Kruger's position was thus greatly strengthened as a result of the Jameson Raid, not only within the Transvaal but amongst the Afrikaner population of South Africa generally. This, in addition to his adroit handling of Jameson and his accomplices after their arrest, meant that in the immediate aftermath of the Raid Kruger's bargaining position in relation to the British government was much improved.

THE GERMAN FACTOR

Events were further complicated by the intervention of the German government. On 3 January 1896 – the day after the surrender of Jameson and his raiders – the Kaiser despatched the famous telegram congratulating Kruger on his success 'without calling on the aid of friendly Powers . . . in re-establishing peace and defending the independence of the country against attacks from without'.[3] This provocative telegram contained two innuendos which were calculated to infuriate the British government. The first was the reference to 'the independence' of the Transvaal – which ignored the limitations on the Transvaal's autonomy imposed by the London Convention and reflected the German government's view that the British claim to 'suzerainty' had lapsed when the Pretoria Convention had been replaced by the London Convention in 1884. The second was the reference to 'the aid of friendly powers' in which that of Germany was implied.[4] When the text of this telegram was published in *The Times* on 4 January, it aroused a wave of anti-German feeling in Britain which diverted attention away from Jameson's fiasco.

Chamberlain, who saw that much was to be gained from taking advantage of this popular outburst, promptly urged the Prime Minister to make 'an Act of Vigour . . . to soothe the wounded vanity of the nation. It does not much matter which of our numerous foes we defy, but we ought to defy someone'.[5] He suggested that a strongly worded despatch should be sent to Germany (and also published) declaring that Britain would not tolerate any interference with the London Convention and would treat as an act of war any attempt to impair Article IV of that Convention to her disadvantage. He also urged the commissioning of more warships and 'the immediate preparation of a force of troops for Cape Town, sufficient to make us masters of the situation in South Africa'.

It is tempting to regard Chamberlain's response as a diversionary tactic adopted by a Colonial Secretary caught wrong-footed over the failed attempt by a group of British subjects to stage a *coup d'état* against a neighbouring 'friendly' government in an area of the world in which Britain was recognized as the paramount power. But it must also be set in the context of the British government's anxiety about the growing *rapprochement* between Germany and Kruger's government which had developed since 1894. In Germany, Kruger's government sought a Great Power ally as a counterpoise to Britain and the pressure which Britain and British interests were able to exercise, politically and economically, on the Transvaal. In a speech on the German Kaiser's birthday, a year previously, Kruger had praised not only the Kaiser but also the loyalty to the Transvaal of German subjects amongst the Uitlander population there:

> All my subjects are not so minded . . . the English, for instance,
> although they behave themselves properly and are loyal to the state,
> always fall back upon England when it suits their purpose. Therefore I
> shall ever promote the interests of Germany, though it be but with the

resources of a child, such as my land is considered. This child is now being trodden upon by a great Power, and the natural consequence is that it seeks protection from another. The time has come to knit ties of the closest friendship between Germany and the South African Republic – ties such as are natural between father and child.[6]

The unease of the British government was increased by the growing numbers of Germans in the Transvaal, the amount of German capital behind the Netherlands Railway Company and the mining industry, and the suspicions surrounding the diplomatic missions of Kruger's State Secretary, Dr Leyds, to Lisbon and Berlin during 1895. The German government had stiffened the resistance of the Portuguese to the sale of the port at Delagoa Bay to Cecil Rhodes and had made it clear to Britain that Germany would oppose any attempt to change the *status quo* either at Delagoa Bay or in the Transvaal republic – to the disadvantage of the Boers, their government, or their outlet to the sea outside British territory via the Delagoa Bay railway, which had opened in January 1895. In diplomatic exchanges during 1895, the British government had warned Germany that encouraging Kruger to rely on the 'unconditional support' of Germany might encourage the Transvaal government to adopt policies which were 'incompatible with the Republic's international position'. The German government had replied that it was only seeking to maintain the *status quo* in the area and that it was the activities of Cecil Rhodes which seemed both to threaten this and to encourage the hostility of the Transvaal Boers towards Britain.[7]

The German economic stake in the Transvaal had also increased with the development of deep-level mining on the Rand. When the British Prime Minister asked the German ambassador in London, Hatzfeldt, early in January 1896, what Germany's interests were in the Transvaal, he replied: 'over 500 million marks of German capital and . . . about 15,000 Germans'.[8] Four years later, a confidential analysis of the relative stake of British and foreign shareholders in the Transvaal mining companies revealed that 81 per cent were British and only 19 per cent were 'continental European'. Only in two of the smaller mining companies, A. Goerz & Co. and G. & L. Albu, did the non-British shareholding amount to more than 23 per cent of the total.[9] These figures were reassuring to a British government which had been fed inflammatory rumours, emanating from Rhodes and his allies, about the scale of the German stake on the Rand and the intrigues of 'the German–Hollander clique'. When, in 1897, he faced the Official Enquiry into the Jameson Raid, Rhodes attempted to justify himself by claiming that he had been 'greatly influenced' by the pro-German policy of Kruger's government and its attempts 'to introduce the influence of another foreign power into the already complicated system of South Africa, and thereby render more difficult in the future the closer union of the different states'.[10]

When Kruger had first heard of Jameson's Raid, he had sought the assistance of Herff, the German consul in Pretoria. Herff had persuaded the German government to authorize a small landing-party from a German cruiser in Delagoa Bay 'to protect German interests in the republic', but this idea had to be abandoned when the Portuguese government refused permission for them to land and Kruger decided that he did not want them to cross the border into the Transvaal 'so as not to complicate the situation'.[11] Meanwhile, the German Foreign Minister, Marschall, warned the British government that the independence of the Transvaal, as defined in the London Convention, must be maintained; and Hatzfeldt was ordered to ask the British Prime Minister, Lord Salisbury, if the British government approved of the Raid and to demand his passports if the answer was in the affirmative. Hatzfeldt at once assured Berlin that the British government were doing everything possible to stop the Raid. At the same time, Marschall approached the French ambassador with the suggestion of joint action on the matter and urged Kruger, through Herff and Dr Leyds (who was in Berlin at this time), to stand firm and concede nothing to the Uitlanders. On 2 January, Hatzfeldt prepared an unfriendly note to the British government which implied some doubt about the sincerity of the British condemnation of the Raid and reiterated Germany's insistence that the *status quo* in the Transvaal must be maintained; but the news of Jameson's arrest, and Salisbury's fortuitous absence, enabled Hatzfeldt to retrieve this note before it was opened.[12]

The German background to the despatch of the 'Kruger Telegram' on 3 January is vividly summarized in Marschall's diary:

> January 3, 1896. At 10 o'clock Conference with His Majesty, at which Reichskanzler, Hollmann, Knorr and Senden also present. His Majesty develops rather amazing plans. Protectorate over the Transvaal, from which I dissuade him straight away. Mobilisation of the marines. Dispatch of troops to the Transvaal. On the Chancellor's objection that this would mean war with England, His Majesty said, 'Yes, but only on land'. In the end His Majesty, on my proposal, addresses a telegram of congratulation to President Kruger. Joy over the defeat of the Englishmen is universal.[13]

The despatch of the 'Kruger Telegram' evoked fervent popular support in Germany. This, like the outburst of strong anti-German feeling which was aroused in Britain, reflects the mounting Anglo-German antagonism which, already apparent during the 1890s, was to continue through to 1914. Hatzfeldt wrote that if the British government had wanted to declare war on Germany at that time, the British people would have stood enthusiastically behind it.[14] But the despatch of the telegram was more a product of the posturing of the impetuous Kaiser than a reflection of the policy of the ministers who surrounded him and strove to curb his often capricious behaviour. The long-term aim of the German government at this time was to obstruct Britain, in the colonial arena and elsewhere, as a means of challenging her 'splendid isolation' from the two continental European blocs and attracting her into the orbit of the Triple Alliance.[15] The assertion of *Weltpolitik* and the advancement of a cause dear to the hearts of the Kaiser, Admiral Tirpitz, and the German people – the expansion of the German navy – are also present in the background. But the German government would never jeopardize its relations with Britain over the Transvaal and had no real intention of seeking to establish any sort of German protectorate over Kruger's republic or of encouraging it into a confrontation with Britain. Kruger himself did not consider that Germany was a dependable ally and warned Leyds in Berlin to be very sure of material assistance from Germany before embarking on a course which might well result in the Transvaal being left in the lurch by Germany and the other European powers and give Britain an excuse for tightening rather than loosening the hold which she had over the Transvaal by the London Convention.[16]

Germany encountered no positive response to her efforts to persuade France and Russia to make a common cause with her against Britain over the Transvaal. The French contented themselves with an outburst of sympathy for the Transvalers in the popular press and the despatch of a ceremonial sword (depicting a Boer strangling a crowned lion!) to General Cronje in recognition of 'Boer valour'. The Russians sent a large fraternity cup.[17] When the German government offered to support the convening of a conference of the Powers to guarantee the future integrity of the Transvaal – a proposal which there is every reason to believe the British government would have challenged – Kruger and his Executive Council replied that they preferred 'to act without the Powers and finish the matter alone'. Surprised by the furore which the 'Kruger Telegram' had raised in Britain, the German government beat a hasty retreat.

The correspondence between Pretoria and Leyds (in Berlin) is revealing in terms of the objectives of Kruger's government at this time.[18] First and foremost was the replacement of the London

Convention of 1884 by a treaty in which the full independence of the Transvaal republic was recognized. Next, there was the need for guarantees against future aggression. Finally, there was the question of compensation for the damage done by the Raid – a matter which dragged on and on, with the British government successfully procrastinating and never reaching a settlement. The achievement of full, independent statehood for the republic remains a central preoccupation of Kruger's government right through to 1899, as does the determination of the British government to prevent it. This objective was relentlessly and continuously pursued at every turn during the remaining years of the republic, with the British and Transvaal governments straining to interpret in precisely opposite directions the meaning of the Articles of the London Convention (especially Article IV) which had been agreed to when the South African Republic had been poor and weak and Gladstone had hoped to kill Afrikaner republicanism with kindness. But, even in January 1896, Kruger found that his country had no reliable allies amongst the European Powers. Leyds reported that neither France nor Russia was interested in an international conference and that none of the Powers would act alone in support of the Transvaal. The German government advised Kruger not to insist on the termination of the London Convention. Kruger's republic was left on its own to make such terms as it could in direct negotiations with Britain.

THE BRITISH GOVERNMENT TAKES UP UITLANDER GRIEVANCES

Having once taken up the question of Uitlander grievances, Chamberlain and the British government never thereafter let them go. Even amidst the failure of the uprising on the Rand and the fiasco of Jameson's Raid – when the British High Commissioner, having rushed up to Pretoria, was desperately seeking to bring about the surrender of Johannesburg and the Uitlander leaders to Kruger's forces as a condition for securing the safety of Jameson and his raiders and the prevention of civil war – Chamberlain returned to the question of the redress of Uitlander grievances in two trenchant telegrams to Robinson on 4 and 15 January 1896. In astonishingly truculent mood, Chamberlain urged Robinson 'to use firm language and to tell the President that neglect to meet the admitted grievances of the Uitlanders by promising definite concessions would have a disastrous effect upon the prospects of a lasting and satisfactory settlement'. Uitlander eligibility for the franchise after five years' residence, tax reductions, a better provision of English-medium schools, and full municipal rights for Johannesburg, were all specifically mentioned by Chamberlain as what he meant by 'reasonable concessions'. To obtain them, Chamberlain was prepared to threaten Kruger's government by sending a flying squadron of warships to South Africa and persuading the War Office to order the commander of the Cape garrison to send troops to Mafeking.[19] Chamberlain seems to have believed that 'facing the risk of war would remove it' and that the recent Drifts Crisis had demonstrated that 'Kruger when firmly summoned would always climb down'.[20]

Robinson thought that Chamberlain was completely misjudging the extremely tense and delicate situation in the Transvaal. He therefore concentrated on bringing about the disarmament of Johannesburg and the surrender of the Uitlander leaders as a condition for the release of Jameson into British custody. Then, on the train back to Cape Town, he sent a telegram telling Chamberlain why he considered the action which Chamberlain had urged to be 'inopportune'. Pointing out that nearly all the Uitlander leaders were now in gaol, charged with treason and with conspiring 'to seize the government of the country on the plea of denial of political privileges, and to incorporate the country with that of the British South Africa Company' (*sic*), Robinson observed that 'meanwhile to urge claim for extended political privileges for the very men so charged would be ineffectual and impolitic'. Whilst admitting that in his talks with President Kruger 'the question of concessions to Uitlanders has never been discussed between us', he promised to raise the matter 'at the first moment I think it can be done with advantage'. His opinion was that 'any attempt to dictate in regard to the internal affairs of South African Republic at this moment would be resisted by all parties in South Africa, and would do great harm'.[21]

Uitlander grievances presented Chamberlain with an issue on which he could be confident of winning the support both of his Cabinet colleagues and of the British public for an increasingly trenchant policy with regard to Kruger's governmment. They also seemed to offer some justification for what had taken place in the Transvaal at the time of Jameson's Raid. Defending the rights of Britons, in a country over which Chamberlain was to insist Britain had suzerainty, combined principle with popular appeal and encouraged the assumption that Britain had the right to intervene in the Transvaal to secure them.[22] Out of the high risk and failure of the Jameson Raid, it was no small achievement of Chamberlain's to have moved the British government and public towards the acceptance of this view.

The taking up of their grievances by the British government also encouraged the Uitlander community in the Transvaal to unite behind this issue and to look, in future, to the British government and its representatives in South Africa to press their case for them with the Transvaal government. Until 1895, the Uitlanders had been left to prosecute their demands against Kruger's government on their own and their weakness, divisions and poor organization had rendered them an ineffective body. After 1896, however, this civil conflict within Transvaal society takes on new and ominous implications as the Uitlanders acquire the backing of a Great Power. Once the British government commits itself to achieving a redress of Uitlander grievances, what had hitherto been a purely internal matter in the Transvaal becomes a point of conflict between governments.

As Lord Selborne soon pointed out, however, the British government was in something of a cleft stick on this issue. The Uitlanders:

> clamour for our interference in the internal affairs of the South African Republic ignoring the fact that we have no legal right and no moral justification for so interfering, and that any such interference would be violently resented by the Dutch subjects (the majority) of the Queen in South Africa. . . . What we have to aim at is clear: we have to retain in loyal and confident attachment to our policy the Dutch subjects of the Queen, and at the same time not to alienate from us her English subjects. We have indeed to do more than this. We have to confirm the Dutch in their sense of our justice, and to so attract the English to us as to make those in the Transvaal anxious to increase British influence and to cement the British connection if they are ever in a position to shape their own fortune. The worst thing that could happen to us and to South Africa would be for the English whether in the Transvaal or in the Queen's dominions [i.e. the Cape Colony and Natal] to come definitely to the conclusion that the Imperial government had no sympathy for their aspirations and to decide that the Imperial connexion was a barrier to their legitimate hopes. The next worse thing for us would be to unite all the Dutch in South Africa in determined hostility to British rule and the British flag.[23]

Selborne went on to suggest that Kruger should be invited to come to London 'to discuss matters fully and frankly' and that if he refused to come 'a full despatch should be drawn up as an indication of our policy'. This despatch should emphasize that whilst the British government was determined to maintain its rights under the London

Convention of 1884 (especially Article IV), it was 'equally determined to respect the independence of the South African Republic'; and was 'quite willing, as part of a general arrangement, to guarantee its independence against any external attack etc'. It should also be stated that whilst the British government recognized that it had no right of interference in the internal affairs of the South African Republic, it did have the right to make 'friendly representations and of warning the President of the dangers' which lay ahead. Britain had this right both as 'the paramount power in South Africa' and as the representative of British subjects 'who are suffering under real grievances'. Selborne believed that such a policy would both reassure Afrikaner opinion in the Cape Colony and give a sense of sympathy and support to the Uitlanders in the Transvaal. It would also enable Britain to continue putting pressure on Kruger and his government 'at one time on behalf of the Uitlanders, at another in connection with our own grievances or Kruger's infringements of the [London] Convention'.

Chamberlain was very receptive to the idea of inviting Kruger to a conference in London because he had also been approached with this suggestion by Isaac Lewis and Sammy Marks – who had business interests in the Transvaal, who had not taken part in the Uitlander conspiracy, and the latter of whom had the ear of Kruger himself – and Sir James Sivewright, a member of the Cape government. After making it clear that there could be no discussion of Article IV of the London Convention, Chamberlain obtained reassurances, via these intermediaries, that Kruger would accept an invitation to come to London. The invitation was therefore issued on behalf of the British government on 27 January.[24] Chamberlain saw this as an opportunity to win back the initiative in Anglo-Transvaal relations, and initially he was quite optimistic: 'I am hoping to make a great coup and get Kruger over here', he wrote to his wife, 'if he will walk into my parlour it will be very nice of him'.[25] There then ensued many weeks of haggling over the agenda, with Kruger determined to use the occasion to renegotiate the terms of the London Convention and to free the Transvaal from the remaining limitations this imposed on its independence, and Chamberlain refusing any discussion of, or change to Article IV, and insisting that at any conference the question of Uitlander grievances must be addressed. Kruger refused to accept this on the grounds that it represented an outright intrusion by the British government into the internal affairs of the republic which would establish a dangerous precedent for the future.

Matters were made worse by Chamberlain's publication of the important despatch of 4 February when only a telegraphic summary of it had been conveyed to Kruger's government. This was both a blunder and a breach of diplomatic etiquette which was received as a deliberate slight in Pretoria. In this despatch, Chamberlain surveyed the situation of the Uitlanders in the Transvaal and described their list of grievances as 'formidable in length and serious in quality'. Their position, Chamberlain declared, had become anomalous. In numbers, he believed that they now exceeded Kruger's burghers and they were responsible for something like nineteen-twentieths of the revenue of the state. Many of them had been used to exercising political rights in their country of origin. Most countries had a generous provision for immigrants desirous of naturalization and admission to citizenship. In the Transvaal, however, Uitlanders encountered obstacles which had been progressively increased. Chamberlain stated that he recognized Kruger's difficulties and anxiety 'that if he were to meet the wishes of the Uitlanders, he might indirectly be the cause of subordinating the interests of the burghers and of the pastoral population to the interests of the Rand'. The aim was therefore to meet Uitlander grievances 'without in any way endangering the stability of the institutions of the republic'. Chamberlain therefore proposed a scheme whereby 'home rule' or local autonomy might be established for the Rand district:

> Those living in, and there enjoying a share in the government of the autonomous district would not, in my view, be entitled to a voice in the general Legislature or the Central Executive, or the Presidential election. The burghers would thus be relieved of what is evidently a haunting fear to many of them – although I believe an unfounded one – that the first use which the enfranchised newcomers would make of their privileges would be to upset the republican form of government.[26]

In a private letter to the British High Commissioner on 17 March, however, Chamberlain bluntly stated that no lasting settlement could be reached with Kruger's government 'unless the President will frankly recognise the superior interests of the Paramount Power in the welfare of South Africa'. As part of a settlement, Chamberlain continued, 'H.M. Government could no doubt guarantee the safety of the Republic against the result of all intrigues or attacks from without . . . We, on our part, have no desire to destroy the independence of the Republic provided that our position as Paramount Power is fully acknowledged, and that the Republic no longer gives cause for disturbance of the peace in South Africa by its treatment of British subjects.' Chamberlain concluded by saying that he considered the situation to be 'urgent and serious' and that Kruger should be warned 'of the complications that will certainly arise if an early attempt is not made to come to an agreement with Her Majesty's Government'.[27] When, in a speech in the House of Commons, Chamberlain combined threatening language to Kruger's government with praise for Cecil Rhodes 'for the great services he has rendered', and went on to assert his belief that Rhodes 'is capable of great service still', Kruger's worst suspicions were confirmed.[28] Amidst mounting recriminations, Kruger finally made it clear during March that he would not come to London for a conference on the terms laid down by the Colonial Secretary. Selborne felt that Kruger's refusal presaged ever more strained and even broken relations between the British and Transvaal governments in the future. 'I don't break my heart over that', he commented to the Prime Minister, 'but there is no denying that it will be a biggish business'.[29]

This second failure within three months to get Kruger to respond on the question of Uitlander grievances represents a notable set-back for Chamberlain. It occurred at a time when some of the government's own back-bench MPs, together with an influential section of the British press, led by *The Times* and fed pro-Rhodes material by South African newspapers, were waging a campaign of increasing bellicosity against Kruger's government and demanding the despatch of troops to South Africa to force Kruger's hand on the grounds that the Transvaal was arming rapidly. Chamberlain took advantage of this to press for the strengthening of the British garrison at the Cape. The outbreak of the Ndebele rebellion in Rhodesia, he suggested to Sir Hercules Robinson, presented an excellent excuse. Robinson was horrified and replied that any increase in British troops at present would be 'most impolitic'.

> Such a transparent excuse as the Matabeleland rising would only confirm the burghers in their belief that we have designs on their independence and in the present suspicious temper, the increase might precipitate action on their part which would involve us in a war. . . . To deal effectively with the Transvaal and Orange Free State aided as they would be by the Boers of Cape Colony and Natal would require force of at least thirty thousand men.[30]

During March and April 1896, the implications of a resort to war as the ultimate solution to Britain's problems with Kruger's government were certainly discussed, both inside and outside the Colonial Office. But the Cabinet, having just committed itself to the military reconquest of the Sudan from the Mahdists, would certainly have resisted a simultaneous military engagement in South Africa, and Chamberlain eventually decided against it.[31] Some of Chamberlain's senior advisers at the Colonial Office, Lord Selborne and G.V. Fiddes – who were to play important background roles during the next few years – prepared important memoranda assessing the situation facing the British government in South Africa.[32] Others, including Edward Fairfield – who was the Colonial Office specialist on South Africa – were worried that Chamberlain might succumb to the clamour of 'the extreme war party' at this time. The British High Commissioner in South Africa, Sir Hercules Robinson, who feared that Chamberlain was embarking on a policy which would precipitate war, warned him that it was too soon after the Jameson Raid for Britain to demand reforms and threaten dire consequences if these were not forthcoming. If it came to war, Robinson predicted that the conquest of the Transvaal might require 'the whole strength of the Empire' to reach a successful conclusion. 'Any repetition of the peace under defeat policy of 1881 would result in the loss of our colonies in South Africa', he warned. Even after a victory, 'there will remain the question of government of a people embittered by race hatred and torn asunder by internal dissensions which will for generations require the maintenance of a large permanent garrison' by Britain. He therefore urged Chamberlain 'to sit still and wait patiently'.[33] He also despatched his Imperial Secretary, Sir Graham Bower, to London to warn Chamberlain that the High Commissioner would resign if Britain persisted in a policy likely to result in war. The Governor of Natal and the Prime Minister of the Cape Colony, Sir Gordon Sprigg, joined in the warnings, the latter stating bluntly that 'this is not the time for an Ultimatum and troops, the resources of diplomacy are not yet exhausted'.[34]

Others, with a particular interest in South Africa, voiced their alarm at the deterioration in Anglo-Transvaal relations. P.A. Molteno, the son of the Cape's first Prime Minister after self-government, arranged an interview with Chamberlain at the end of March at which he warned him about the 'strong and close analogy between what was being done now and what was done by Lord Carnarvon' in the 1870s, when he had 'forced his views on South Africa and led to all our trouble there and to the present feeling, which was a relic of that time'. He accused Chamberlain of 'pressing for changes which could only come gradually and would only be retarded by premature pressure'. British interference in the Transvaal, Chamberlain was told, would only weaken those internal forces amongst the Boers themselves which were in favour of progress and it was only through 'these local influences that any real valuable reform would come'. Jameson's interference had had a thoroughly regressive result. What was needed now was patience, moderation and a recognition that 'the unfettered working of Responsible Government' was the only solution for South African troubles.[35]

President Steyn of the Orange Free State, who declared that he was doing his 'utmost to bring about the co-operation of all in South Africa and to restore the confidence which was grievously shaken by Jameson's Raid', warned that:

> We must live together, do what we like. A war would only make the breach wider and would make it still more difficult for Dutch and English to live together. No one here thinks of such a thing. If Imperial interference can be prevented, and if the Imperial Government will only exercise patience and not push matters, things in the Transvaal will come right. Neither the Transvaal nor the Free State wishes for war because we know what it means, but should it be forced on us then of course we will have to fight.[36]

Chamberlain was irritated by what he privately noted as Robinson's 'prejudiced view of the details as well as the facts' of the South African situation and his reluctance, as in January, to follow Chamberlain's own lead in taking a firm stand and threatening Kruger. He therefore determined to replace him as British High Commissioner as soon as this could conveniently be arranged. He also suspected that Edward Fairfield and some of the other Colonial Office advisers he had inherited from the previous government were unreconstructed Gladstonian liberals.[37] Chamberlain's mood of frustration and exasperation at this time is well caught in the 'Statement of Policy in 1896' which he drafted for his immediate advisers on 5 April. In it, however, he showed that the warnings he had received had not been without their effect. He began by recollecting the considerations which he and other members of Gladstone's government had had in mind when making the Pretoria Convention in 1881, when

> we all believed that the Transvaal was absolutely in our hands. We were influenced by moral considerations i.e. we thought the Boers had been badly treated and were true patriots . . . that we were bound as a great and powerful Christian nation to be magnanimous etc. It was really a chivalrous piece of business – and it certainly has not brought any reward in this world. The Boers (and Mr Fairfield) believe that we gave way because we were afraid of them and they (the Boers – not Mr Fairfield) have been intolerable ever since.

Chamberlain then revealed that he had recently consulted General Sir Evelyn Wood who had said 'that he did not believe that the conquest of the Transvaal would be a very difficult thing *now*. Of course it would mean an army, but Wood thought that if the campaign were perfectly conducted the Boers would not show much fight.' Chamberlain noted that in the Transvaal 'the best information available gives a maximum of 25,000 male Boers and a minimum of 50,000 Uitlanders of whom three-quarters are British'. But these estimates were wrong and were to persist, right through to 1899, in turning the calculations of the British government into miscalculations as far as the relative numbers of Boers and Uitlanders in the Transvaal were concerned.[38]

Chamberlain declared that he could not feel 'the least sympathy' for either Kruger or the Uitlanders. 'The former is an ignorant, dirty, cunning and obstinate man who has known how to feather his own nest and to enrich all his family and dependents. The latter are a lot of cowardly, selfish, blatant speculators who would sell their souls to have the power of rigging the market.' Nonetheless, he concluded, 'our business is to bring about a fair settlement. . . . I do not believe that there will be war – but Kruger will not be wise if he dismisses that possibility altogether from his calculations – or assumes that if it comes the result will be favourable to him. . . . I shall never go into such a war with a light heart, and at the present time we have no reason – either of right or of interest – which would justify the enterprise.'[39] Three days later, after he had read Fairfield's comments on this statement, Chamberlain noted:

I entirely agree that we have no '*casus belli*' at present and shall not have even if Kruger definitely refuses our invitations and declines to make any changes in his precious Constitution. I do not think it wise however to explain this to the housetops and I do not mind the noisy exaltation of the Jingo party, since it does not commit me and *may* put some pressure on the people in the Transvaal who are afraid of war. I should like to infuse a little more spirit into Sir H. Robinson and I wish he would show his teeth to Kruger occasionally. But for all that I am not at all anxious for war – and do not believe it will come.[40]

Chamberlain was also sensitive to the fact that, in South Africa, he was widely believed to be under the influence of the 'Burlington House party', i.e. Rhodes and those who had been discredited by the Jameson Raid. In an important speech in the House of Commons on 8 May, Chamberlain retreated from a warlike policy and made a public statement of the British government's objectives with regard to South Africa. 'Our first object', Chamberlain declared, 'is to preserve our position as the paramount State. It matters not whether we call ourselves suzerain or paramount, but it is an essential feature in our policy that the authority and influence of this country should be predominant in South Africa'. Secondly, in order to bring about better relations between Boers and British there, the admitted grievances of the Uitlanders against the Transvaal government would have to be remedied. Chamberlain then stated that 'in some quarters the idea is put forward that the Government ought to have issued an ultimatum to President Kruger, an ultimatum . . . which must have led to war'. Chamberlain replied:

> I do not propose to discuss such a contingency as that. A war in South Africa would be one of the most serious wars that could possibly be waged. It would be in the nature of a Civil War. It would be a long war, a bitter war, and a costly war; and as I have pointed out already, it would leave behind it the embers of a strife which I believe generations would hardly be long enough to extinguish. Of course there might be contingencies in which a great Power has to face even such an alternative as this . . . but to go to war with President Kruger in order to force upon him reforms in the internal affairs of his State, with which successive Secretaries of State, standing in this place, have repudiated all right of interference, that would have been a course of action as immoral as it would have been unwise.[41]

Chamberlain also used this speech, as he had done his speech in February, to praise Cecil Rhodes – 'without whom our English history would be much poorer and our British dominions much smaller'. This was a deliberate riposte to the Liberal leader, Sir William Harcourt, who had described the government's support for Rhodes and the British South Africa Company as 'imperialism on the cheap' which had recently turned into 'privateering degenerating into piracy'.[42] In the light of what had been revealed about the Jameson Raid during recent months, Kruger had also been pressing the British government to cancel the Charter of the British South Africa Company and to bring Rhodes, Beit and Harris (Rhodes's London agent) to trial. On 5 May, however, Chamberlain had received legal opinion that there was not sufficient evidence to justify criminal proceedings and he used this to repudiate the demands of the Transvaal government. Later, when in the official enquiries both Cape Town and London had exposed and condemned Rhodes for his key role in the Jameson Raid, he was still never brought to trial. The British government's refusal to press charges against Rhodes undoubtedly owed something to his popularity in Britain, but a greater consideration would seem to have been the fear of what might be revealed in a full, judicial investigation. It was widely rumoured that Rhodes's London solicitor, Bouchier Hawksley, had documents about the background to the Jameson Raid (including the 'missing telegrams') which proved that Chamberlain had been 'in it up to his neck'. The Colonial Office called upon Hawksley to produce the documents and, after he had done so, Lord Selborne wrote a secret memorandum about them in which, after repudiating the claim that they implicated Chamberlain (and himself) in the plot, he concluded:

> I never had the least idea from anything that was said, either that the Johannesburg revolution was being wirepulled from Cape Town or Matabeleland; or that any kind of assistance to it by an organised force was contemplated; or that Mr Rhodes was thinking of any organised action, previously to, or subsequently to, a revolution at Johannesburg independently of the High Commissioner; and I am sure that Dr. Jameson's name was never mentioned, much less his plans.[43]

After Chamberlain had read the documents, he also wrote a long memorandum, which he sent to the Prime Minister, in which he too asserted that:

> my action both immediately before and after the Raid, and my endeavours by every means in my power to stop it is a clear and convincing proof that I never directly or indirectly, publicly or privately, gave the slightest approval or encouragement to such an undertaking; and I may say at once that it never entered into my head, then or at any subsequent time, until the suggestion was made to me while I was at Birmingham in the last days of December, that any entry into the Transvaal by an organised armed force could possibly be contemplated by Mr Rhodes, unless under circumstances of immediate danger to life, and then only with the sanction of Her Majesty's Representative, the High Commissioner.[44]

Chamberlain sensed that the documents might be used by Rhodes's agents in an attempt to blackmail the government. He therefore offered to resign. Lord Salisbury refused to accept his resignation but ruled against publication of the memorandum. Chamberlain continued to fume about 'blackguards' and 'blackmail' in private and, ever after, to assert 'that while I knew all about the revolution I knew nothing of anything so mad as Jameson's Raid'.[45] A raid from outside the Transvaal, without the excuse of an Uitlander uprising already taking place within it, had, of course, never been envisaged by Chamberlain or anyone else. As Earl Grey, who was both a director of the British South Africa Company and the man who had acted as an intermediary between Rhodes's agents in London and the Colonial Office during 1895, revealed in a letter to Chamberlain a year afterwards:

Our whole object was to place Jameson in a position which would enable him to *assist* a Revolution at the right *moment* – That he should attempt to *initiate* a Revolution in time of peace never so much as entered into my imagination.[46]

THE SELBORNE MEMORANDUM

Anglo-Transvaal relations remained tense throughout 1896. In March, the long-term problem facing the British government in South Africa was analysed by Lord Selborne in an incisive Memorandum.[47] Selborne was not only Parliamentary Under-Secretary at the Colonial Office, he was also the Prime Minister's son-in-law. In a letter accompanying the copy of this Memorandum which he sent to Lord Salisbury, Selborne implied that he had set down his views on the South African situation because of recent differences of opinion between the two of them on this subject. At the heart of the matter was the question of whether South Africa was going to develop into another United States, outside the British Empire, or into another Canada within it. In a challenging exposition of what present trends were likely to lead to in the future, the man who was to play an important role in the creation of a Union of South Africa within the British Empire between 1907 and 1910 began by posing the fundamental question:

Are the British Possessions in South Africa more likely to become separated from the British Empire,
1. If they become confederated with the two Republics under the British flag as a British African Dominion, or
2. If they remain as now separate units under various forms of Government and continue to have as their neighbours two independent Republics?

In his answer to this question, Selborne began from an assumption, which he already took to be a fact, that 'the key to the future of South Africa is in the Transvaal'. Not only was it already 'the richest spot on earth' because of its known gold deposits; it was also rapidly outstripping all other parts of South Africa in terms of its population growth. In combination, these two factors meant that in the future, the Transvaal 'is going to be the natural capital state and centre of South African commercial, social and political life'. Commercially, the Transvaal would become 'the market for South Africa' and 'the commercial interest of the closest connexion with the Transvaal will outweigh all other considerations' as far as the British territories of the Cape, Natal and Rhodesia are concerned. They will therefore pursue close commercial union with the Transvaal. 'But if the Cape Colony and Natal remain separate self-governing Colonies; if Rhodesia develops into a third self-governing Colony, and if the Transvaal and the Orange Free State remain independent Republics, what then? I think nothing can prevent the establishment of a United States of South Africa.' Since the Transvaal had 'no intention of becoming British', such a commercially-driven amalgamation was likely to result in 'a United Republic of South Africa' outside the British Empire. This stark and unacceptable prospect was mitigated, for Selborne, by his belief that 'the Transvaal cannot permanently remain a Dutch Republic'.

> There has never been a census; but the best information obtainable gives a maximum of 25,000 male Boers and a minimum of 50,000 Uitlanders, of whom 3/4 are British. Before Jameson's criminal blunder the Uitlanders were said to be pouring into the Transvaal at the rate of 500 males a week. Just think what would be the result of 10 or of 20 years of an immigration maintained at one fifth or even one tenth of this rate! Therefore, according to the experience of history, this country, so powerful in its future wealth and population, must be a British Republic if it is not a British Colony; and I cannot myself see room for doubt but that a British Republic of such great wealth and of so large a population, situated at the geographical centre of political South Africa would assuredly attract to itself all British Colonies in South Africa.

Selborne's conclusion was that the achievement of Britain's long-desired objective – the unification of South Africa under British auspices – had now become an urgent matter since, 'if we can succeed in uniting all South Africa into a Confederacy on the model of the Dominion of Canada and under the British Flag, the probability is that that confederacy will not become a United States of South Africa'. He also considered it 'a matter of vital importance to us to prevent the Delagoa Bay Railway passing into the control of any power whatever except the Portuguese or British Governments' since 'powerful use could be made of this instrument in squeezing the British South African Colonies into joining in a United South African Republic'.

In October 1896, Selborne restated, in more succinct form, the views of his March Memorandum and his conviction that 'South African politics must revolve round the Transvaal' and that 'a Union of the South African states with it will be absolutely necessary for their prosperous existence. The only question in my opinion is whether that

Union will be inside or outside the British Empire'.[48] At the same time, he commented on the 'indictment of the South African Republic' which G.V. Fiddes had produced in his survey of past relations between Britain and the Transvaal. 'It is a story of broken pledges and unfriendly action on the part of the Republic; of weakness and slackness on our part', Selborne observed.

> We sat down meekly under many misdoings of the Boers because we had no force in South Africa with which to assert ourselves and because the sending out of an expedition from home seemed to us too big an action for the occasion. The Boers quickly appreciated this fact. The average Boer knows nothing of the real strength of the British Empire nor of its predominant strength for action in South Africa.[49]

This led Selborne to join Chamberlain in calling for a strengthening of the British garrison in South Africa. He also felt that 'the British in South Africa need to be clearly shown that we have not abandoned them in the South African Republic' and that 'both Dutch and British need to be shown that in its internal affairs a self-governing colony is as absolutely independent as a Republic. They do not seem to see this, but keep on talking about "emancipation from Downing Street", a phrase which has no applicability to a self-governing colony'. Finally, he thought that those who believed that a future United States of South Africa which was outside the British Empire would still be able to rely on British naval power for defence should have such a delusion dispelled.

Selborne's reflections on the situation facing Britain in South Africa are important because there is no doubt that the questions which he raised form vital background considerations in the policy-making of the Colonial Office and Lord Salisbury's government between 1896 and the resort to war in October 1899. This policy-making was influenced by a growing awareness that the old assumptions, on which British policy towards South Africa had hitherto been based, no longer held. The discovery of gold, and the rise to power and prominence of the Transvaal republic since the 1880s, had resulted in an irreversible shift in the centre of gravity of South Africa away from the Cape Colony, with its strong British connections, towards Kruger's Afrikaner-dominated republic.

The old British 'imperial paramountcy of influence' over South Africa could no longer be taken for granted.[50] For the past half-century, this paramountcy had essentially meant two things: the exclusion of other European powers from the area and the recognition by them that South Africa was a British sphere of influence; and the ability of British governments to guide the development of the region towards a loyal, imperial confederation on the Canadian model. Hitherto, successive British governments had looked to the Cape Colony as the foundation-stone from which this confederation would be constructed. Cape expansionism – whether with direct encouragement from Britain, as in the case of Basutoland, or indirectly, through the energy and enterprise of Cecil Rhodes and the counterpoise which he had established in Rhodesia – had therefore had a significant part to play towards the achievement of this goal. The loyalty and self-government of the Cape where, under equal rights, the Afrikaner population outnumbered the British by 3:2; the readiness with which these Afrikaner subjects of the Queen seemed to recognize the advantages of maintaining the imperial connection; the great preponderance of the Cape in terms of its share of the total European population in South Africa; its control – together with loyal and 'very English' Natal – of the ports and sea-board of South Africa and all but one of its key railways – all of these considerations had underpinned British hopes for a Cape predominance in South Africa. By 1896, British policy-makers knew that their Cape-based plans were finished. The future lay with the Transvaal, an Afrikaner-dominated republic under an unfriendly government determined to minimize and, if possible, to sever the British connection; and likely, with its burgeoning wealth and importance, to draw after it all the other parts of South Africa, which would come to orbit as satellites around it. The acquisition of a railway outside British control to the sea at Delagoa Bay, and the long-term future which had now been revealed for gold-mining through the development of the 'deep levels', meant that time was now on the side of the Transvaal and was likely to work ever more favourably towards the development of an Afrikaner-dominated and republican future for South Africa. By 1896, the prospect facing the British government was that South Africa was drifting out of British 'guidance' and out of the Empire.[51]

If informal British paramountcy was failing; if the Cape Colony was no longer an effective means to the achievement of the larger British ends in South Africa; if everything now rested on the future of the Transvaal; then the incorporation of this state – not just economically but politically – into a confederation or union of South African states, under British auspices, became a matter of urgency. British governments could no longer rely on intermediaries or the workings of time to swing things in their favour; now, they might have to intervene directly. 'Pushful Joe' Chamberlain had come into office at precisely the moment when what seemed to be required from a strong British government was a reassertion of what Rhodes had called 'the Imperial factor' in South Africa if British interests there were to be safeguarded. The likes of President Kruger (Chamberlain was not alone in his derogatory remarks about him) with his hostile, inefficient, backward-looking, corrupt, and essentially tribal, government could not be allowed to obstruct the 'forces of progress' and the unification of South Africa into a new British dominion which had an important role to play in the future of the British Empire.

It must never be forgotten that Chamberlain approached the problem posed by the Transvaal to the future of South Africa with the larger issues of the Empire and the future of Britain in the coming century ever in mind. Without this Empire, Britain, in his view, would cease to be a great power. As Colonial Secretary, he saw it as his larger task to strengthen and consolidate the Empire as a network of trade, influence, and the provision of defence without which Britain could not hope to compete with Germany or the United States. Imperial consolidation meant imperial federation and the way to that lay first through the sort of regional consolidations which had already taken place in Canada (1867) and was soon to be achieved in Australia (1901). South Africa was vital for imperial defence, communications and security and also for imperial trade. Since the Mediterranean route to the East via the Suez Canal could not be guaranteed in time of war, the Cape route remained of great strategic importance; and the docking facilities at Cape Town and the British naval base on the Cape peninsula at Simonstown were used more and more intensively as the century wore on. The development of gold-mining in the Transvaal beckoned towards a future in which this could be used to benefit and bring progress to the whole region, and to Britain as the financial capital of the world in the hey-day of the Gold Standard. At the end of a century during which British governments had repeatedly used Britain's naval superiority and military might to acquire and retain imperial possessions, and to challenge and defeat colonial rivals, Lord Salisbury's government was not going to surrender the Transvaal to the sort of future dreamed of by Paul Kruger and his burghers. A British government which, between 1896 and 1898, committed itself to the massive military operation and huge expenditure involved in the reconquest of the Sudan from the Mahdists, and which was prepared to confront and face down the French at Fashoda, was not going to give up its increasingly tenuous hold on the Transvaal without a fight. On the contrary, the determination of this government was to strengthen

Britain's position in South Africa, to unite the region under British auspices, and to see that British supremacy there was established on a firmer basis.

At heart, both Chamberlain and Lord Salisbury regarded the semi-independence of the Transvaal republic as a temporary expedient. Like the full and complete independence of the Orange Free State, it was the product of a past situation which had now changed. It was tolerable only so long as it did not obstruct the achievement of the wider goal of the creation of a new British Dominion in South Africa which had a vital part to play in the future of the British Empire and of Britain as a world power. Like Lord Selborne, Chamberlain and Lord Salisbury assumed that, sooner or later, Uitlander immigration would make the Transvaal British. By 1896, they believed that the Uitlanders already formed a majority in the state and were responsible for nine-tenths of its revenue. The enfranchisement of the Uitlanders would thus enable a peaceful take-over to occur. It presented the best means by which the British government could hope to obtain its ends without a resort to war. It also appeared to be the best basis on which to win the support of the British public. It therefore becomes the new, key objective of British policy towards the Transvaal from 1896. Preoccupied as it was with the reconquest of the Sudan and the uneasy situation in Europe, Salisbury's government would not have welcomed a resort to war in South Africa between 1896 and 1898. The situation there was still unfolding, Kruger was an old man who was not expected to last long, and there was still some hope that after he had gone a more progressive coalition of forces might come into power and preside over a peaceful transition to a reformed administration and the rectification of Uitlander grievances. In the meantime, the steady application of political pressure to Kruger's government seemed likely to result in its capitulation over minor matters. The granting of an Uitlander franchise remained, repeatedly stated but not yet demanded from the barrel of a gun. In comparison to what the achievement of the franchise would secure, ensuring that the Transvaal government was kept to a strict observance of the terms of the London Convention was a mere holding operation.

THE SOUTH AFRICAN LEAGUE

The Uitlanders of the Transvaal thus became the new allies of the British government, the latest in a series of intermediaries through whom British governments had sought to work to achieve their objectives in South Africa. Yet the Uitlanders were an amorphous and unreliable lot, whom Chamberlain disliked and distrusted; and in 1896 the Rand was a place where, as the new British Agent there, Conyngham Greene, observed, 'nobody cares a fig for politics if only he can fill his pockets'.[52] In the disunity and disorganization which had marked their abortive uprising on the Rand at the time of the Jameson Raid, the Uitlanders had also revealed their fickleness with regard to the British flag and the preference of many of them for an independent *true* republic, in which Uitlanders would replace Kruger's Afrikaner burghers as the predominating element in a self-governing state which would remain outside direct control from Downing Street. As Chamberlain himself noted in June 1896:

> I have never at any time concealed my opinion that, whatever defects may exist in the present form of the Government of the Transvaal, the substitution of an entirely independent Republic, governed by or for the capitalists of the Rand, would be very much worse both for British interests in the Transvaal itself and for British influence in South Africa.[53]

The aim of the British government was therefore to guide and influence Uitlander politics towards the achievement of objectives which harmonized with those of the British government. To do this it was necessary to convince the Uitlanders that the British government would keep faith with them and not abandon them as the Uitlanders felt had been the case after the British defeat in 1881. Holding the Uitlanders together and persuading them that the British government was their best champion in their struggle to extract reforms from Kruger's government was therefore the tricky task of the British government's representatives in South Africa between 1896 and 1899. Since the British High Commissioner resided in Cape Town, the brunt of this task was borne by the British Agent in the Transvaal, Conyngham Greene.

In the aftermath of the Jameson Raid, the shaky Uitlander political movement in the Transvaal had disintegrated. Most of its chief spokesmen, who had given it leadership and direction through the National Union and the formation of the Reform Committee in 1895, had been arrested in January 1896. After being tried, fined and released, many of them had either left the country or had been allowed to remain there only on condition that they refrained from political activity for the next three years. Meanwhile, in the Cape Colony, the polarization of politics had resulted in the Afrikaner Bond emerging purified and strengthened after the break with Rhodes, while the 'British party' there was left disorganized and discomfited. During the early months of 1896, this situation in the Cape led to the formation of a new political association there, dedicated to strengthening and upholding British interests. By March this had developed into a 'loyal colonial league' which soon established branches throughout the Cape Colony and then in the Transvaal and Natal as well. In May, it took the name of the South African League. The aims of this League were to work for the strengthening of British interests and British supremacy in South Africa and the creation of a federation there under the British flag.

In the Cape Colony, where this movement started, the Sprigg government was widely regarded with dismay as an opportunistic ministry of all opinions and no clear programme. The South African League therefore campaigned to get candidates with 'progressive' and 'pro-British' views elected to the Cape Assembly through ensuring that thousands of its supporters got themselves registered on the electoral role. By the end of 1897, some 12,000 new voters had been added.[54] Here, the object was to create and sustain a 'British party' which could challenge the Afrikaner Bond. Since the Bond was committed to friendly relations with Kruger's government in the Transvaal, the South African League favoured a 'strong policy' of the kind adopted by Joseph Chamberlain. But the South African League was also dedicated to the wider task of educating public opinion, both in Britain and South Africa, about South African issues. A South African Association was formed in London, affiliated to the League, and by 1897 this had developed into a very effective propaganda organization, mounting an active campaign in the press and holding public meetings all over Britain which were addressed by ardent supporters of the League such as George Wyndham, H.M. Stanley, and Rider Haggard. The purpose of all this activity was to strengthen the hand of the British government in its dealings with Kruger's government. As George Wyndham put it, in a speech in June 1896:

> It was not the intention of the Association to conduct the policy of the Government, but they hoped to reinforce the hands of the Government to steer the ship of State, but if they would all cooperate with the Association, they would raise a wind to fill their sails.[55]

Between 1896 and 1899, the South African League became a force in South African politics. Its 'good work' was praised by Chamberlain, who recognized its usefulness as a means through which his policies were both justified and supported.

In the Transvaal, meanwhile, the collapse of the Reform movement and the National Union left the Uitlanders disillusioned, leaderless, helpless, hopeless and divided.[56] A political vacuum opened up which was soon filled by the South African League (SAL). This became 'the organised vanguard of the determined Uitlander movement'.[57] Only a minority of Uitlanders ever became members, but the ideas of the South African League were widely propagated via the English-language press in the Transvaal and especially by *The Star* and later by *The Transvaal Leader*. It is no exaggeration to say that through these media, the ideas and attitudes of the South African League became a pervading influence on Uitlander opinion. Kruger's government feared that the League had simply replaced the National Union and the Reform Committee. There were, however, ominous and significant differences. The first lay in the fact that, unlike previous Uitlander organizations in the Transvaal, the League was part of a much wider movement both in South Africa and in Britain. Secondly, there was a pronounced shift in emphasis. Whereas the National Union had declared its loyalty to the republic and had sought the redress of Uitlander grievances through an appeal to Kruger's government, the South African League proclaimed its loyalty to the Queen and appealed directly to the British government, as the paramount power, to act on behalf of the Uitlanders to secure from Kruger's government a redress of their grievances. It also openly proclaimed its goal of 'uniting the Transvaal in a federation of the States of South Africa under the British flag'.[58]

Meetings of the League in the Transvaal were stridently British and jingoistic in tone, with fervent expressions of loyalty to the British monarch and much singing of 'Rule Britannia' and 'God Save the Queen'. Although some non-British Uitlanders joined, they formed a small minority amongst a membership which was notable not just for its 'Britishness' but also for its broadly representative nature of the Uitlander working population – much of it drawn from the commercial and non-mining sector. Although skilled and semi-skilled European mine-workers were well represented, senior mine-managers were noticeably absent and so were the 'capitalists' who had emerged to play such a prominent part in Uitlander politics in 1895 and were to emerge again in 1899. Meanwhile, the President of the SAL in the Transvaal, W. Wybergh, who was a mining engineer, was sacked by Consolidated Goldfields when he became too involved in politics for their liking. The Secretary, Thomas Dodd, was a colliery engineer who was described as being 'a man of lower class and rougher fibre than Wybergh, but an enthusiast and . . . the best type of radical reformer of the first half of this century'. The League membership consisted of 'small professional men, tradesmen and miners', most of whom had been members of Trade Unions in England. By April 1899, they numbered 'between 1,000 and 2,000' but formed 'the only organised body among the Uitlanders'.[59]

This last point requires further comment if the role and influence of the SAL in the Transvaal is to be understood. Uitlander political activity in the Transvaal was always difficult to organize and sustain and, so long as it was both sporadic and disorganized, Kruger's government did not have to take it very seriously. Most of the Uitlander population were transients who had come to the Rand not to campaign for the franchise but to make money. When the economic situation there was good they tended to forget about politics and concentrate on making money. When there was an economic down-turn (as was the case in 1897–8) protests and political agitation increased. But the record since 1890 suggested that Uitlander politics had little staying power. As the British Agent, Conyngham Greene, observed in 1897, 'Johannesburg is a revolving light, and one which it is very difficult to steer by'. Again, a few months later, he commented: 'I have . . . so little confidence in the "thoroughness" of Johannesburg that I hesitate to admit that any reliance whatever can be placed on its attitude past, present or to come.'[60] What the SAL achieved in the Transvaal, between 1896 and 1899, was the creation of a modest but critical mass of Uitlander support for a political purpose. At the heart of that purpose was the involvement of the British government in extracting reforms and the franchise for the Uitlanders from Kruger's reluctant government.

This political purpose was a two-way stretch. The Uitlanders wanted to involve the British government because they were now convinced that their own direct appeals to the Transvaal government were useless and would never, of themselves, achieve their object. The representatives of the British government in South Africa, for their part, came to look to the SAL to organize the Uitlanders into a useful instrument for the advancement and justification of British policy in the Transvaal. There are parallels between the roles played by the National Union and the Reform Committee in 1895 and that of the SAL between 1896 and 1899; but the parallels are not exact. Rhodes used the former as a front for a conspiracy to overthrow Kruger's government; the SAL, on the other hand, was never simply the creature of the British government or of its agents in South Africa. From 1897 onwards, the leaders of the SAL in the Transvaal kept in close touch with the British Agent there and he sought to influence the League's activities through the advice which he gave. He also encouraged them to look to the British government in their pursuit of reform in the Transvaal and the redress of Uitlander grievances. But it is not true to say that the League was controlled by him. As Conyngham Greene wrote to the British High Commissioner in Cape Town:

> In dealing with the South African League, I am placed in a very delicate position. The League is . . . the only body in Johannesburg that has a spark of real Imperial feeling, or a particle of any higher ambition than the worship of mammon. . . . It therefore, in a certain sense, deserves sympathy, and looks to me for encouragement. On the other hand . . . it requires careful and constant watching. Up till now I have managed to keep some sort of control over the Executive, notwithstanding that they are, of course, being continually pressed by the mass of the League to resort to more vigorous action.[61]

In other words, the members of the South African League had minds and wills of their own, they were not just puppets brought into being and manipulated at will by representatives of the British government in South Africa. Indeed, the British Agent soon found himself attempting to temper and curb the increasingly shrill and excessive demands of SAL members, not always successfully.

In 1897 and again in 1898, representatives of the SAL in the Transvaal approached Conyngham Greene with proposals to hold public meetings at which the extent of Uitlander opinion against Kruger's regime could be demonstrated with the purpose of strengthening the hand of the British government in its dealings with the Transvaal. On both occasions, Conyngham Greene urged them not to pursue the matter as this would only complicate the situation. The SAL also protested at some of the legislation passed by the Transvaal government during these years, claiming that it represented 'a blow aimed at the rights and liberties of British subjects in the Transvaal'. The SAL therefore called for the intervention of Her Majesty's Government.[62]

THE ALIENS LEGISLATION AND THE CRISIS OF APRIL 1897

The matter of the British government's rights with regard to legislation passed by the Transvaal government was governed by Articles IV and XIV of the London Convention, but these had been drafted somewhat carelessly with regard to the point at which the legislation should be submitted for British approval. This purely procedural matter was finally settled towards the end of 1898 when Chamberlain insisted that such legislation could only come into force when it had been submitted to the Queen and approved. More momentous was the head-on confrontation between the two governments during 1897 over the substantive issues involved in legislation which Kruger's government sought to enact to deal with the immigration and expulsion of aliens, and control over the press.

This confrontation stemmed directly from Chamberlain's determination to seek out and make the most of any possible infringement by the Transvaal government of the terms of the London Convention in order to emphasize and, where possible, extend Britain's rights as the 'suzerain' power. As he stated quite candidly to his Colonial Office staff:

> If we were dealing with the S.A.R. *after* a settlement which had placed our relations on a permanent and friendly basis, I should not be disposed to take any technical objections. But the situation is exceptional and indeterminate and I think our policy should be to press the Convention Article IV for all it is worth. Kruger tells us in offensive language that we have no right to meddle in his internal affairs. This is substantially true, but if he rejects our friendly suggestions in these matters we must show him that we have rights under the Convention which may be used to annoy and embarrass him if he takes up the position of an enemy.[63]

Chamberlain emphasized that, as a matter of policy, he was determined 'to maintain the most stringent possible interpretation of the [London] Convention and of all that remains to us of our suzerainty over the Transvaal'. Since 1881, British influence over the republic had been steadily 'whittled away', he observed, and 'we ought to keep our hands clenched on what remains, and if possible magnify it by any plausible interpretation of the Convention'.[64] Chamberlain denied that the relations between Britain and the Transvaal were comparable to those existing between independent states. On the contrary, he argued, because the London Convention was established when the Transvaal was a dependent state under the suzerainty of the Queen, Britain had rights of intervention over the legislation of the Transvaal government which were greater than would normally be the case. During 1896–7, the British government acted on this assumption to challenge Kruger's government over a series of legislative measures and forced it to withdraw them.

At the time of the Jameson Raid, a substantial number of Transvaal burghers had petitioned the government to enact a bill dealing with people who were 'a danger to the internal peace of the state'. Kruger's government therefore introduced into the Volksraad an Aliens Expulsion Bill authorizing the expulsion from the Transvaal republic of any 'alien' who was considered by the President and Executive Council to be 'a danger to the public peace and order'. Secondly, an Aliens Immigration Act was brought into effect, on 1 January 1897, the purpose of which was to check the influx into the Transvaal of 'undesirable foreigners' and to secure the registration of such foreigners as were already there. All prospective immigrants had to prove their ability to support themselves financially and all resident 'aliens' had to register and renew their passports each year. These laws gave Kruger no powers not already possessed in Britain by the Home Secretary, but they were greatly resented by the Uitlanders. Chamberlain protested to the Transvaal government that these measures also infringed Article XIV of the London Convention which stated that all persons, other than natives, who conformed to the laws of the South African Republic, had the right to enter the Transvaal and reside there. Thirdly, in response to the appearance in the English-language press of articles and cartoons which not only criticized but lampooned President Kruger, the Volksraad passed a Press Law empowering the government to suppress any printed paper or publication which was 'in conflict with public morals or dangerous to the order and peace of the republic'. This was then used, in December 1896, to suspend the Johannesburg weekly, *The Critic*, for six months. The owner promptly renamed his journal *The Transvaal Critic*, continued publication, and appealed to the British government for redress. In March 1897, the leading English-language newspaper in the Transvaal, *The Star*, was also suppressed on the same grounds and re-appeared as *The Comet*, but under a new editor. In London, it was agreed that the articles and cartoons in question were 'coarsely offensive' but not 'dangerous to the order and peace of the republic'. After taking advice from the law officers of the Crown, the Colonial Office protested, and the proprietors appealed to the Transvaal High Court. This ruled that the suppression was illegal. The proprietors then claimed compensation.[65]

On the Aliens legislation, the British government was determined to take a resolute stand. On 15 February 1897, Kruger's government replied to the challenge which the British government had sent about this legislation by rejecting any suggestion that it breached the London Convention. Chamberlain then decided 'that we must put our foot down if we are to keep our ground in this matter' and set about formulating two strong despatches, finally dated 6 March 1897, one summarizing the British case against the republic on the grounds of its breaches of the London Convention, the other demanding the immediate repeal of the immigration law.[66] In a speech which angered President Kruger a good deal, Chamberlain accused him of making promises with regard to the Uitlanders which he then failed to keep.[67] Chamberlain also wanted to back up the sending of the despatches by a show of force.

Chamberlain's proposed course of action met with some misgivings amongst his advisers and within the Cabinet. Selborne warned Chamberlain that unless the Cabinet was prepared to go to war if Kruger's government refused to withdraw the legislation, then the despatches should not be sent. Writing to Lansdowne, at the War Office, Chamberlain admitted that although he hoped and believed that war would be avoided, 'it could not be denied that an appeal to arms was within the scope of practical politics'.[68] The time had therefore arrived for strengthening the British forces in South Africa. This was a matter which Chamberlain had twice raised during 1896, without success. A combination of circumstances in March–April 1897 made this a propitious moment for Chamberlain to try again. The sending of the despatches was to be accompanied by a Cabinet decision to strengthen the British military presence in South Africa and by a naval demonstration at Delagoa Bay.

Since early in 1896, British military intelligence work had been increased in South Africa. Spies had been sent into both the South African Republic and the Orange Free State and they had gathered information about the Transvaal's armaments, forts, railways, bridges and the numbers of burghers available for commando. They sketched maps, tried to estimate the number of rifles in the possession of the Uitlanders, and reported on what the likely response of Afrikaners in the Cape and Natal would be in the event of war. One member of the Colonial Office staff kept a continuous account of the state of armaments in the Transvaal republic, a task in which he was greatly assisted by the management of the Maxim-Nordenfelt company which was supplying them.[69] The rapid and continuing programme of rearming his country, which Kruger had embarked upon after the Jameson Raid, was well known. The Colonial Defence Committee was concerned that the garrison at Cape Town might now be inadequate to defend the Cape peninsula, including the important naval base at Simonstown. In November 1896, Chamberlain had used this information in a bid to get the Cabinet to agree to reinforce the British garrisons in South Africa 'until they amount to at least 10,000 men, including a large proportion of cavalry and artillery'. This, he argued, would 'be a visible demonstration of the determination of the Imperial Government to maintain the *status quo*, and to insist on the observance of the Convention'. It would also 'strengthen the loyalty of all the English in South Africa – greatly shaken by successive defeats and humiliation – and give them confidence in the Imperial factor, which there is now too much readiness to "eliminate" at short notice'. Finally, it would 'prevent the Boers from putting forward impossible claims and from taking aggressive action and will greatly strengthen the hands of our representatives in the communications which they may have to make to the Transvaal Government in the next few months'.[70]

At that time (the largest military operation hitherto undertaken by Britain in Africa was already underway in the Sudan) the War Office, backed up by the Treasury, had opposed Chamberlain's bid, declaring that not even 5,000 additional men could readily be found to send to South Africa. Chamberlain decided not to press the matter for the moment.

In December 1896, however, the Prime Minister, in conjunction with the Treasury and the Admiralty, had toyed with the idea of a naval demonstration at Delagoa Bay, both as a warning to Britain's European rivals (especially Germany) about Britain's position as the paramount power in the area and as an exercise in sabre-rattling with regard to the Transvaal government. The Cabinet returned to this idea in March 1897 – the month during which the two republics renewed their mutual alliance for both offensive and defensive purposes – and it was decided to send a naval force to Delagoa Bay to accompany the delivery of the despatches. As Chamberlain wrote candidly to Conyngham Greene:

> I have been considering how it might be possible to demonstrate to the Transvaal authorities our determination to maintain our rights in their integrity. I am unwilling, as at present advised, to send out reinforcements of troops because such might have a provocative effect, while, at the same time, we could hardly send a sufficient number to put our army in S. Africa on a war footing. In view of possible action by the Orange Free State and by some of the Dutch in our own colonies, a very large force would be necessary if hostilities broke out. This could be sent at very short notice, and we are fully prepared for such an emergency; but to send five or even 10,000 troops, would bring about the collision which we desire if possible to avoid. Accordingly, the Government have decided as an alternative, which it hopes will have equal significance – although it will not be so provocative – to arrange for a considerable force of ships to rendezvous . . . at Delagoa Bay. . . . The presentation of the despatches will therefore be made almost simultaneously with the

appearance of the fleet, and I hope the Transvaal Government will draw the proper conclusion and will understand that while we desire above all things friendly relations with them, we will not suffer our rights to be impaired. I repeat that our object is to maintain the peace, if that is possible consistently with the rigid adherence to the terms of the Convention. If however, the Boers are bound on desperate courses, it is desirable that they should openly show their hands before we make a definite move.[71]

Chamberlain considered that although the action of Kruger's government was 'most objectionable, it hardly gives us, up to the present time, such a strong position as to justify extreme measures'.[72] He wanted, however, to take advantage of the moment to obtain Cabinet approval for the increase in the British military presence in South Africa which he had long been seeking. On 5 April, he wrote to the War Office that 'adequate military measures of precaution' had now become 'a matter of pressing importance'. Once again, Lansdowne (the War Office Minister) disagreed. This reinforced Chamberlain's accumulating impatience with the War Office and his determination to override what he regarded as its obstruction and inefficiency. At a meeting of key ministers on 8 April, whilst Salisbury was away and Balfour was presiding in his place, Chamberlain returned to the issue. He presented incontrovertible evidence that the Transvaal 'has armed and is persistently arming, until now it has a stock of artillery, rifles and ammunition of all sorts, enough to furnish a European army. . . . Meanwhile, we have only one battery at the Cape; and the War Office agreed that in the event of war being declared, they could not defend the Cape Colony'. Lansdowne's reluctance to do anything was overruled by Balfour, Goschen (Treasury), and Hicks Beach (Chancellor of the Exchequer) – the latter of whom believed that additional forces should be sent 'chiefly for political reasons'. It was therefore agreed that about 3,500 additional troops (mainly cavalry and artillery) should be sent out after Easter. Writing to ask Salisbury's assent to this decision, Chamberlain stated his conviction that, as over the Drifts Crisis, Kruger and his Boers would not fight: 'if they see we are in earnest, I believe they will give way, as they have always done'.[73] Balfour wrote separately but to the same effect, adding a perceptive comment about Chamberlain's methods and the likely reaction to them:

His favourite mode of dealing with the South African sore is the free application of irritants; and though it does not easily commend itself to me, this method may possibly be the best. In any case, however, I cannot think it wise to allow him to goad on the Boers in his speeches, and

refuse him the means of repelling Boer attacks, when, as responsible
Minister, he earnestly and persistently presses for them. My own view is
that a Boer attack is exceedingly improbable, and that it will only take
place if the Boers come to the conclusion that we are fixed in the
determination to attack them, and that what must come had better come
soon.[74]

In the end, only 1,500 troops were quietly sent out to South Africa
and these included no cavalry. The government was reluctant to excite
either the Boers or the Liberal Party and therefore decided to avoid
having to ask Parliament for a supplementary grant. This modest
reinforcement brought the total British forces in South Africa to about
8,000 men and 24 field guns.[75]

The two despatches were finally delivered to Kruger in person by
Conyngham Greene on 15 April at a meeting at which Joubert, the
Commandant-General, was also present. As instructed, Greene also
informed Kruger about the accompanying naval demonstration and
reported that when Kruger heard about this, he 'started up and got
very excited. . . . He declared that I was holding a knife to his
throat'.[76] During the following days, the British government was
closely informed, through its intelligence network, of the reactions in
the Transvaal as Kruger consulted his advisers. When it seemed likely
that, having been encouraged 'to temporize' by the government of the
Orange Free State, he would simply procrastinate about the challenge
to the Aliens legislation contained in the despatches, the Colonial
Office staff were dismayed. The fleet could not remain at Delagoa Bay
indefinitely. An immediate reply would have to be insisted upon but
the difficulty was how to do this without issuing an ultimatum which
might 'drive Kruger into a corner'. On 26 April, having obtained
Cabinet approval, Chamberlain further instructed Greene to inform
Kruger that Britain expected early action on her despatch about the
Aliens legislation and a strict observance of the London Convention
but that she had no desire to interfere with the internal independence
of the Transvaal. He was also to tell Kruger that the British
government had kept a careful record of the growing armaments in
the republic and, 'for purely defensive purposes', had decided to
increase her forces in South Africa; a considerable force, including
artillery, had already been 'told off' for that purpose, although its exact
destination had not yet been decided.[77] Meanwhile, the Cape House
of Assembly, having debated British policy towards the Transvaal,
resolved that Britain's best course was to be moderate and to be
prepared to accept arbitration over the disputed legislation.

This exercise in brinkmanship by the British government paid off.

On 5 May, the news arrived that Kruger's Executive Council had decided to ask the Volksraad to 'temporarily suspend' the Aliens legislation, just as the Drifts Crisis had been brought to an end by the 'temporary' suspension of the order closing the drifts. In May, the Aliens Immigration Law was repealed and in July the Expulsion Law was revised to take account of Britain's objections. Meanwhile, the British intelligence network revealed that the Volksraad had been told, in secret session, that Kruger thought it unwise to provoke war. The staff at the Colonial Office were relieved. One of its members observed that, as in the cases of the Warren expedition (1885) and the Drifts Crisis (1895), Kruger had bluffed to the last but then climbed down when he was sure that Britain was in earnest. Another commented that it was not the reasons Kruger gave but Chamberlain's despatch, the fleet, and the troops which had done it. Chamberlain himself was gratified. Calling Kruger's bluff had worked, once again, and tension had been relaxed as a result. 'We have scored a point', he observed.[78]

The crisis of April 1897, and the way in which it was resolved, strengthened Chamberlain's hand in the British Cabinet and restored his stature amongst the British public, both in Britain and in South Africa, after the corrosive effects of the Jameson Raid and the long-drawn-out Enquiry during 1896–7. It also encouraged those in British ruling circles to assume that in dealing with Kruger a firm, even confrontationist policy brought the best results; that he would always climb down if his bluff was called. The Colonial Office documents reveal a new note of impatience and a growing animosity towards Kruger's government by Chamberlain and his officials during 1897. Every act of the Transvaal government was scrutinized to see if it gave the slightest grounds for a challenge. A long catalogue of that government's alleged sins of commission and omission was assembled under the heading 'The Case against the South Africa Republic'.[79] The *bona fides* of Kruger's government came to be regarded as always suspect. Information about what transpired in secret meetings of the Transvaal Volksraad and Executive Council was obtained from a spy within Kruger's immediate circle. The Transvaal came to be regarded as in the hands of an unfriendly and corrupt oligarchy under the thumb of an uncouth, obstinate old man assisted by his 'Hollander advisers'.[80] Chamberlain might still claim that he hoped it would be possible 'to maintain the peace until time and the increase of the British [Uitlander] population gradually bring about a solution', but the evidence is that he was less and less inclined to believe that time, by itself, would solve anything. What Chamberlain believed to be 'of the greatest importance' was that Kruger's government should put itself completely in the wrong.[81] Then, and only then, would the British government be able to act.

This 'new' policy, initiated and sustained at Chamberlain's insistence, was opposed by some of his most experienced advisers in the Colonial Office, especially Meade (the Permanent Under-Secretary) and Fairfield (the expert on South African affairs). Towards the end of 1896, however, illness and then retirement removed both of them from Chamberlain's entourage and they were followed in 1897 by the retirement of Sir Hercules Robinson, as British High Commissioner, and Sir Graham Bower, as his Secretary. Since the Jameson Raid, these four had favoured 'a rest cure for South Africa with a minimum of imperial intervention'.[82] They had acted as something of a check on Chamberlain's tendency towards challenge and confrontation. Their replacements were men of a rather different stamp. At the Colonial Office, Fred Graham replaced Fairfield as head of the South African section, and Edward Wingfield succeeded Meade as Permanent Under-Secretary. Meanwhile, H. Lambert studied Dutch and took on the new task of translating summaries for Colonial Office use of the Dutch-language South African newspapers such as *De Volksstem, Land en Volk*, and the *Staats Courant*. In Pretoria, where Conyngham Greene had succeeded Sir Jacobus de Wet as British Agent towards the end of 1896, he did so equipped with an authorization to send and receive despatches under flying seal, a provision which would enable him to bypass the British High Commissioner and allow the Colonial Office to communicate with him directly. Chamberlain also picked out George Fiddes, the young man on the Colonial Office staff who had compiled 'The Case against the South African Republic', and saw that he was appointed as Secretary to the new British High Commissioner who was to succeed Robinson in Cape Town. Fiddes was a staunch imperialist who saw 'no prospect whatever' of a satisfactory solution to Britain's problem in the Transvaal 'save by an appeal to arms, and the longer it is delayed the greater the difficulties we shall have to face ultimately'.[83] Both Chamberlain and Selborne regarded the new High Commissioner as their greatest *coup*: a dazzling appointment for a most difficult job. In April 1897, Sir Alfred Milner sailed for South Africa as the new British High Commissioner there.

NOTES

1. Speech by President Steyn reported in *The Cape Argus*, 21 December 1895. The best source for the Orange Free State in this period is S. F. Malan, *Politieke Strominge onder die Afrikaners van die Vrystaatse Republiek* (Durban, 1982), especially ch. 8.
2. Robinson to Chamberlain, 27 April 1896, CO 537/130.
3. J. L. Garvin and J. Amery, *Life of Joseph Chamberlain* 6 vols (London, 1932–69), 3, p. 92.
4. Jean van der Poel, *The Jameson Raid* (Oxford, 1951), p. 135.
5. Ibid., p. 95.
6. Percy FitzPatrick, *The Transvaal from Within* (London, 1899), p. 106.
7. J. S. Marais, *The Fall of Kruger's Republic* (Oxford, 1961), pp. 47–9.
8. Hatzfeldt to Holstein, 4 January 1896, in *Die Grosse Politik der Europaischen Machte 1871–1914*, ed. J. Lepsius *et al.* (Berlin, 1922–7), XI, p. 33.
9. Table compiled by Samuel Evans of Wernher, Beit/H. Eckstein & Co. and enclosed in Milner to Chamberlain, 18 April 1900, FO 244/588.
10. Rhodes's evidence before the Select Committee appointed to enquire into the Jameson Raid (1897), HC 311.
11. Marais, *The Fall of Kruger's Republic*, p. 98.
12. Van der Poel, *The Jameson Raid*, pp. 133–6.
13. Garvin, *Life of Chamberlain*, 3, p. 93.
14. E. T. S. Dugdale, ed., *German Diplomatic Documents (1871–1914)* 4 vols (London, 1930), 3, pp. 303–4.
15. Van der Poel, *The Jameson Raid*, pp. 132–3. For further elaboration see Paul Kennedy, *The Rise of the Anglo-German Antagonism 1860–1914* (London, 1980).
16. Van der Poel, *The Jameson Raid*, pp. 136–7.
17. Ibid., p. 136.
18. Ibid., pp. 136–7, for a summary from the papers of W. J. Leyds.
19. Chamberlain to Robinson, 15 January 1896, printed in C.7933; also Marais, *The Fall of Kruger's Republic*, pp. 105–6.
20. Garvin, *Life of Chamberlain*, 3, pp. 251–2.
21. Robinson to Chamberlain, 15 January 1896, printed in C.7933.
22. A. N. Porter, *The Origins of the South African War: Joseph Chamberlain and the Diplomacy of Imperialism 1895–1899* (Manchester, 1980), pp. 88–94.
23. Draft memorandum by Lord Selborne, n.d. (? January 1896), printed in D. G. Boyce, ed., *The Crisis of British Power: the Imperial and Naval Papers of the Second Earl of Selborne 1895–1910* (London, 1990), pp. 30–2.
24. R. Mendelsohn, *Sammy Marks, 'The Uncrowned King of the Transvaal'* (Cape Town, 1991), pp. 66–7; Marais, *The Fall of Kruger's Republic*, pp. 108–10.
25. Chamberlain to his wife, 23 January 1896, cited in Garvin, *Life of Chamberlain*, 3, p. 127.
26. Chamberlain's despatch of 4 February 1896, printed as No. 220 in C.7933.

27. Chamberlain to Sir Hercules Robinson, 17 March 1896, CO 417/180, 4510. See also R. H. Wilde, *Joseph Chamberlain and the South African Republic 1895–1899*, Archives Yearbook for South African History 1956 Part 1 (Pretoria, 1956), p. 33.

28. Speech on 13 February 1896, *Hansard*, Fourth Series, vol. xxxvii, cols 308–32.

29. Selborne to Salisbury, 24 March 1896, in Boyce, ed., *Crisis of British Power*, p. 32.

30. Chamberlain to Robinson, 31 March 1896, and Robinson to Chamberlain, 1 April 1896, CO 537/130, printed in E. Drus, 'Select documents from the Chamberlain Papers concerning Anglo-Transvaal relations 1896–1899', *BIHR* 27 (1954), p. 158.

31. See Drus, 'Select documents', to which I am much indebted.

32. Lord Selborne's Memorandum of 26 March 1896 is discussed below. The memorandum by G. V. Fiddes, entitled 'The Case against the South African Republic', was eventually printed in July as a White Paper for Colonial Office use, CO 417/180 (1896).

33. Robinson to Chamberlain, 27 April 1896, CO 537/130, cited in Drus, 'Selected documents', p. 158.

34. CO 537/130, Cape/145 Secret, 7 April 1896, printed in ibid., p. 159.

35. P. A. Molteno to J. C. Molteno, 1 April 1896, reporting an interview with Chamberlain, in V. Solomon, ed., *Selections from the Correspondence of P. A. Molteno* (Cape Town, 1981), p. 17.

36. President Steyn to P. A. Molteno, 4 May 1896, printed in ibid., pp. 26–7.

37. Wilde, *Joseph Chamberlain*, pp. 38–40.

38. John Benyon, *Proconsul and Paramountcy in South Africa* (Pietermaritzburg, 1980), p. 261, citing Chamberlain to Salisbury, 18 March 1896.

39. 'A Statement of Policy in 1896', enclosed in Chamberlain to Fairfield, 5 April 1896, and printed in Drus, 'Select documents', pp. 160–1.

40. Chamberlain to Fairfield, 8 April 1896, printed in ibid., pp. 161–2.

41. Speech to the House of Commons, 8 May 1896, *Hansard*, Fourth Series, vol. xl, cols 914–15.

42. Ibid., cols 884–905.

43. Memorandum by Lord Selborne, 6 June 1896, printed in Boyce, ed., *Crisis of British Power*, pp. 37–40.

44. Memorandum by Chamberlain, 12 June 1896, printed in E. Drus, 'A report on the papers of Joseph Chamberlain relating to the Jameson Raid and the Enquiry', *BIHR* XXV (1952), pp. 46–50.

45. Chamberlain to Sir Robert Meade, 24 October 1896, in Garvin, *Life of Chamberlain*, 3, p. 115.

46. Earl Grey to Chamberlain, 10 December 1896, printed in J. S. Galbraith, 'The British South Africa Company and the Jameson Raid', *JBS* X, 1 (November 1970), p. 149.

47. Copies of this Memorandum exist in both SeP and the Salisbury Papers and it is printed in full in Boyce, ed., *Crisis of British Power*, pp. 34–7 (from the former) and R. Robinson and J. A. Gallagher, *Africa and the Victorians* 2nd edn (London, 1979), pp. 434–7 (from the latter).

48. Selborne to Chamberlain, 18 October 1896, printed in Boyce, ed., *Crisis of British Power*, pp. 42–4.

49. Selborne to Chamberlain, 6 October 1896, printed in ibid., pp. 40–2.

50. Robinson and Gallagher, *Africa and the Victorians*, pp. 434–46, to which, like all who have written on this subject since, I am deeply indebted.

51. Ibid., pp. 437–8.

52. Conyngham Greene to Selborne, 20 December 1896, SeP MS 14.

53. Chamberlain Memorandum of 12 June 1896, printed in Drus, 'A report', p. 49.

54. See letter to Percy FitzPatrick of 8 October 1897 printed in A. H. Duminy and W. R. Guest, eds, *FitzPatrick, South African Politician, Selected Papers 1888–1906* (Johannesburg, 1976), p. 121.

55. M. F. Bitensky, 'The South African League 1896–1899', M.A. thesis, Witwatersrand University (1950), p. 39, to which I am much indebted.

56. FitzPatrick, *The Transvaal from Within*, p. 285.

57. Bitensky, 'The South African League', p. 43.

58. Marais, *The Fall of Kruger's Republic*, p. 163, citing a petition of May 1897 from the SAL to the British Agent in Pretoria.

59. G. V. Fiddes to Lord Selborne, 3 April 1899, printed in Boyce, ed., *Crisis of British Power*, pp. 72–3.

60. Conyngham Greene to Milner, 7 July and 24 October 1897, cited in Bitensky, 'The South African League', pp. 45–6.

61. Conyngham Greene to the British High Commissioner, 24 March 1898, in Marais, *The Fall of Kruger's Republic*, p. 164.

62. Bitensky, 'The South African League', p. 142, quoting SAL to British High Commissioner, 16/3/1897.

63. Minute by Chamberlain, 26 February 1896, CO 417/189, quoted in Wilde, *Joseph Chamberlain*, p. 48.

64. Chamberlain, Minute of 5 March 1896, CO 417/189, quoted in Marais, *The Fall of Kruger's Republic*, p. 125.

65. See accounts in Wilde, *Joseph Chamberlain*, p. 46; Marais, *The Fall of Kruger's Republic*, pp. 127–32.

66. Marais, *The Fall of Kruger's Republic*, pp. 148–9; Wilde, *Joseph Chamberlain*, pp. 55–8.

67. Speech in the House of Commons, 29 January 1897, *Hansard*, Fourth Series, vol. xlv, cols 803–8.

68. Wilde, *Joseph Chamberlain*, p. 53.

69. Ibid., p. 53.

70. Memorandum for the Cabinet, 10 November 1896, cited in Garvin, *Life of Chamberlain*, p. 139; Marais, *The Fall of Kruger's Republic*, p. 158.

71. Chamberlain to Conyngham Greene, 18 March 1897, printed in Wilde, *Joseph Chamberlain*, pp. 56–7.

72. Ibid.

73. Chamberlain to Salisbury, 8 April 1897, printed in Garvin, *Life of Chamberlain*, pp. 140–1.

74. B. E. C. Dugdale, *Arthur James Balfour* 2 vols (London, 1936), l, pp. 247–8.

75. Marais, *The Fall of Kruger's Republic*, pp. 156–7.

76. Conyngham Greene's report in Rosemead to Chamberlain, 18 April 1897, CO 537/131.
77. Wilde, *Joseph Chamberlain*, p. 58.
78. Ibid., pp. 59–60.
79. Printed for Colonial Office use as a White Paper in July 1896, CO 417/180.
80. Wilde, *Joseph Chamberlain*, pp. 50–1.
81. Quotations from Chamberlain's instructions to Conyngham Greene, 18 March 1897, CO 537/133, cited in ibid., p. 56.
82. Marais, *The Fall of Kruger's Republic*, p. 136.
83. Minute by G. V. Fiddes on High Commissioner to Chamberlain, 31 March 1897, CO 537/131.

CHAPTER FIVE

The Parting of the Ways (1897–8)

THE NEW BRITISH HIGH COMMISSIONER

The appointment of Milner as the British High Commissioner to South Africa was a fateful development with regard to the future. He was a man of different calibre to any of his immediate predecessors, with an acute intelligence, an able pen, a forceful personality and an immense capacity for hard work. In him, Chamberlain found a collaborator of similar outlook for whom the strengthening of the British Empire was a central preoccupation. At a time when South Africa appeared to be the test case with regard to the future of the British Empire, the presence of Milner in South Africa and Joseph Chamberlain at the Colonial Office resulted in a formidable combination of two powerful individuals in key positions of influence as far as British policy-making was concerned.

Milner's appointment to what was acknowledged to be the most difficult but important post in the Empire was widely welcomed by Liberals and Conservatives alike.[1] Milner was no career diplomat, he was a political appointment of the first rank. Like Chamberlain, he was a self-made man. The only child of his mother's second marriage (she was over 40 when he was born and died when he was fifteen), he grew up in straitened, middle-class circumstances with little experience of human warmth or family support. After winning a scholarship to Balliol College, Oxford, he became a legend in his own time there for his brilliant academic progress, his string of prizes, his position as first Treasurer and then President of the Oxford Union, and the award in 1877 of a Fellowship to New College. Whilst at Oxford, he came under the influence of two people, neither of whom was his equal intellectually but both of whose ideas were to make a profound impression on him. The first was Arnold Toynbee, with whom Milner and a small circle of earnest young men discussed social questions and in whose memory Toynbee Hall was founded as a university settlement amongst the working classes in the East End of London. From him, Milner acquired an interest in socialism, social reform, and a more interventionist role for the state in rectifying the harsh excesses of *laissez faire* capitalism. Although Milner read and rejected Marx, he admired the sort of state socialism practised in Bismarck's Germany and retained a lifelong commitment to social reform and the role of government in what we today would call social engineering.

Imperialism and social reform were ideas which went easily together for many of Milner's generation and Milner's ideas about the British Empire were deeply affected by a second contemporary at Oxford, the Canadian, George Parkin. Parkin was an Empire patriot in the fullest sense of the term. He became a key figure in the movement for imperial federation and was later Secretary of the Rhodes Trust. He and Milner formed a lifelong friendship and, at Oxford, he certainly helped to focus Milner's interest on the Empire and to make this the central preoccupation of his political life. Parkin, Milner and Cecil Rhodes were all at Oxford during the 1870s (although Rhodes and Milner did not meet), in what was a heady decade there for those of an imperialist persuasion. In 1869, Charles Dilke had published his *Greater Britain*, in which he had championed the idea of an Anglo-Saxon world hegemony based on racial superiority. The following year, John Ruskin had used his inaugural lecture (as the Slade Professor of Art) to issue a clarion call to the 'youth of England' to rise to their Anglo-Saxon destiny and 'advance the power of England by land and sea', seizing waste land and making it fruitful, founding colonies as fast and as far as possible. This, he declared, 'is what England must do or perish'.

The idea of a Greater Britain, made up of English-speaking people in the colonies of settlement as well as in Britain itself, and bound together in some form of closer union or imperial federation, was developed during the 1870s and widely popularized by Sir John Seeley's lectures and book on *The Expansion of England* during the 1880s. A product of social Darwinist thinking, it was unashamedly based on the assumption of Anglo-Saxon racial superiority. Its protagonists always set the white settlement colonies at the heart of things and remained rather vague about the future of India and what was known as 'the Dependent Empire'. The idea of self-government for 'natives' was regarded with derision at a time when the concept of 'trusteeship' was being developed to meet the objections of

Gladstonian Liberals to the forcible subjection to European rule of those whom Kipling was to describe as 'lesser breeds without the law'. Milner, like Chamberlain, came from a Liberal background but was attracted to both Conservatism and Socialism because the former put more emphasis on the Empire and the latter on social reform; and both were ready to extend the role of government to get things done.[2] Milner was later to describe himself as a British Race Patriot and there is no doubt about the centrality of racial concepts in his thinking, as in the thought of most Europeans at that time. 'My patriotism knows no geographical but only racial limits', he declared in the statement which he called his 'Credo'. 'I am an Imperialist and not a Little Englander, because I am a British Race Patriot'. He himself emphasized 'the importance of the racial bond' in many of his writings, and admitted that 'from my point of view this is fundamental. It is the British race which built the Empire, and it is the undivided British race which can alone uphold it. Not that I underestimate the importance of community of material interests in binding the different parts of the Empire together. . . . But deeper, stronger, more primordial than those material ties is the bond of common blood, a common language, common history and traditions'.[3]

Like Chamberlain, Milner was an imperialist of an unusually thoroughgoing kind.[4] The Empire came first in his thinking and he told Chamberlain that he had always 'had the desire to devote the best years of my life to the Imperial interests of my country'.[5] Milner had also come from a Liberal past to serve a Unionist government in the 1890s by way of Ireland. In his only foray into parliamentary politics, in 1885, Milner had fought and lost the Harrow constituency as a Liberal candidate. Thereafter, he repudiated party politics and sought non-elected posts for the public work which he craved. In the autumn of 1886, he visited Ireland and there expressed himself as 'profoundly thankful that, by the goodness of Providence . . . I was saved from taking the Gladstonian side in the late struggle. All my natural leanings were to Home Rule, and in the far future, I still think it may be the best, or only, constitution for Ireland. But, under present circumstances, I am sure that it would have meant a most fearful disaster. . . . I have no hesitation in saying, that I am for all practical purposes, a Tory'.[6] Milner was more of a British race patriot than Chamberlain was but both, by the 1890s, were consolidationists rather than expansionists as far as the British Empire was concerned. In 1884, Milner had declared:

> I am not anxious to extend the bounds of an Empire already vast or to increase responsibilities already onerous. But if I desire to limit the sphere of our actions abroad, it is in order that within this limited sphere we may be more and not less vigorous, resolute and courageous.[7]

What both of them sought was not further annexations but the strengthening of the British Empire through the consolidation of its various parts and the establishment of a closer union or imperial federation amongst its self-governing dominions. Milner was not alone in considering South Africa to be 'just now the weakest link in the Imperial chain', and he felt that it was his great task 'to try to prevent it from snapping'.[8] Beyond that, his objective was to succeed where his predecessors had repeatedly failed in uniting South Africa's various parts into an effective whole within the British Empire, under white minority rule and British dominance. Milner's actions in South Africa were therefore framed in terms of a deeply-held, long-term objective. The traditional pragmatism and empiricism of British policy were dismissed by him as 'drift'. He was convinced that the power of government could and should be used to 'shape the future' and that 'an act of political will' was probably necessary before 'natural forces' could be brought into play to underpin what had been achieved through political action. The South African issue was crucial because failure to unite the country and achieve a 'British' self-governing dominion would, he believed, open the way for the victory of Afrikaner nationalism and republicanism. Further, it would powerfully assist the centrifugal forces at work elsewhere in the world which were tending to dissolve the British Empire into separate nation states and thus to undermine the basis of Britain's position as a world power.[9]

On the eve of his departure for South Africa, Milner stated his conviction that 'the growth of the colonies into self-governing communities was no reason why they should drop away from the Mother Country, or from one another'; that no political objective could compare in importance with that of preventing a repetition of such a dire disaster as the loss of the American colonies; that 'there is one question upon which I have never been able to see the other side, and that is precisely this question of Imperial union. My mind is not so constructed that I am capable of understanding the arguments of those who question its desirability or possibility'.[10] With Milner, a certain inflexibility of mind went along with an authoritarian temperament. He did not believe in compromise. He was a leader who attracted disciples and set out to crush opposition. When it came to means, he was a hard-headed and calculating tactician; but when it came to ends, he often exhibited a closed mind. John Buchan, who later worked with him in South Africa and was his lifelong admirer, commented on 'a certain rigidity' which Milner brought to his 'set purpose':

> When he had satisfied himself about a particular course – and he took long to satisfy – his mind seemed to lock down on it, and after that there was no going back. Doubts were done with, faced and resolved; he moved with the confident freedom of a force of nature.[11]

What Milner lacked was imagination. He found it impossible to understand men like Paul Kruger or movements like Afrikaner nationalism. He never liked South Africa. He was impatient with all opposition. He did not suffer fools gladly (and most South African politicians he considered fools or worse). He lacked the common touch. He was a workaholic and a bachelor who had long ago decided that for someone from his background to get on in life some sacrifices were necessary: 'One cannot have everything. I am a poor man and must choose between public usefulness and private happiness. I choose the former, or rather I choose to strive for it.'[12]

Milner had already proved his usefulness as a first-rate administrator, able to cope with immense amounts of work with great efficiency and clarity of mind. He had been Goschen's Private Secretary at the Treasury; later, as Chairman of the Board of Inland Revenue between 1892 and 1897, he had won the esteem of both Sir William Harcourt (now Leader of the Liberal Party) and 'Black Michael' (Sir Michael Hicks Beach, who was now Chancellor of the Exchequer). In between, he had spent nearly three years in Egypt on the staff of Sir Evelyn Baring (Lord Cromer) and had helped to turn the British occupation there into something of a showpiece of imperial administration.[13] This had been a formative experience which has a direct bearing upon the task which Milner was to undertake in South Africa between 1897 and 1905. In Egypt, Milner had been one of the half-dozen men who ran the country and, six months after he left, he published a book, *England in Egypt* (1892), which went through five editions in eighteen months and deserves to be regarded as a classic text of the New Imperialism. In it, Milner sought to show how a British occupation and administration had rescued a weak, corrupt and bankrupt country and reconstructed it on sound financial and administrative foundations. He also asserted the case for continued British control there both in terms of British imperial and strategic interests and for the benefit of the Egyptians. Any attempt to fix a time for a British withdrawal, he argued, would be 'the greatest possible disaster'. Where Ireland had turned Milner into a Tory, Egypt intensified his imperialism. Writing to Goschen from Egypt in 1890, Milner referred to 'my strong and ever-increasing jingoism' and defined a jingo as someone who 'is for limited expansion but unlimited tenacity'. The more he saw of Britain's work in Egypt, declared Milner, 'the more proud and convinced I become of the great service which jingoism has rendered to humanity in these regions and I touch my hat with confirmed reverence to the Union Jack'.[14]

Milner had also worked with W. T. Stead on *The Pall Mall Gazette* for a couple of years in the 1880s. Stead too was an imperialist and a social reformer and he pioneered a new form of popular journalism – involving 'stunts' and 'sensational disclosures' – which was later to be further developed by Northcliffe. This experience as a journalist gave Milner an acute awareness of the importance of the press in the formation, even manipulation, of public opinion – a consideration which he was never to lose sight of with regard to the conduct of British policy towards South Africa during the period before war broke out in 1899.[15]

The man who was to have such an important influence on South Africa was nearly 43 years old, and therefore already fully-formed in his outlook and opinions, before he arrived there. He said that he was going to South Africa 'as a civilian soldier of the Empire' in the service of a cause in which he believed absolutely. Fulsome tributes were paid to him by leading members of both the Liberal and Conservative parties before he left Britain, but his old boss and future critic, the Liberal Sir William Harcourt, told Chamberlain that he regarded Milner's ideas 'with a good deal of disquietude' since he was one of 'the pattern Jingoes of these times . . . he is not by nature a *safe* man'.[16] At a farewell banquet, Chamberlain made what Milner described as 'a very political and rather bellicose speech', in which he outlined 'the most difficult task' which faced Britain in South Africa.[17] This was to solve there a problem which had already been satisfactorily solved in Canada and elsewhere, namely 'to reconcile and to persuade to live together in peace and goodwill, two races whose common interests are immeasurably greater' than their differences. For this to happen, however, the Transvaal government had to fulfil its obligations under the London Convention and 'extend the hand of fellowship to the large numbers of foreigners who have contributed so largely to the success and prosperity of the State'. Britain, meanwhile, in her colonies in the Cape and Natal, had shown her readiness 'to extend to our Dutch fellow-subjects, with open hands, all the privileges which we enjoy ourselves' and had 'no intention and no desire to interfere with the independence of neighbouring States'. She was, however, determined to maintain 'in their integrity, the rights which we have under the [London] Convention, and our position as the paramount power in South Africa'. If there were 'eminent persons in South Africa who have aspirations for an independent federation of States in which Dutch influence would be predominant, and which would look for sympathy and support rather to the Continent of Europe than to this country', then this was 'incompatible with the highest British interests . . . and until it is frankly abandoned there cannot be a final and satisfactory settlement'.

This speech was made when the April crisis over the Aliens legislation was approaching its peak. Yet, as we have seen, whilst Chamberlain was prepared to risk war, he did not think that war with the Transvaal was at all likely at this time. Milner had been consulted during the drafting of the despatches and had expressed the firm opinion that Britain should not threaten war unless she was prepared to fight. Whilst he too considered it 'very improbable' that Kruger's government would fight rather than back down on the issue of the legislation, he believed that 'We should continue to press our point firmly, but in a very temperate and unmenacing tone for the present. We can always stiffen up later, even on this particular question, if we think it desirable'.[18]

Before Milner left England, he and Chamberlain had agreed that 'the waiting game was the best for this country as time must be on our side'. They felt that 'the irritation' caused by the Jameson Raid had placed Britain 'in a false position' and that this should be allowed to 'pass away before we resume any pressure upon the Transvaal in regard to its internal policy'. Afrikaner opinion throughout South Africa had been alienated. A war with the Transvaal would arouse the antagonism of the Cape Afrikaners and present Britain with a situation of civil war amongst her own subjects there. 'If a struggle was to come, it was most important that the Transvaal should be the aggressor, and that the Imperial Government should have the active sympathy of at all events a considerable section of the Dutch in the [Cape] Colony.' 'A war with the Transvaal, unless upon the utmost and clearest provocation would be extremely unpopular' in Britain, 'would involve the despatch of a very large force and the expenditure of many millions', and 'would leave behind it the most serious difficulties in the way of South African union'. Kruger's 'misgovernment' was likely to produce opposition from within the Transvaal itself and his rule was in any case likely to come to an end before long (he was over 70); thereafter, Britain 'might confidently look for an improvement in the position'.[19]

Before Milner arrived in South Africa, therefore, the possibility of a resort to war with the Transvaal had been considered in the context of the April crisis of 1897. This was the third occasion within eighteen months when Chamberlain had contemplated war (November 1895, over the Drifts Crisis, and March–April 1896 had been the others). Each time the implications had been more fully examined than previously, and each time Chamberlain had not expected war to result. As the possibility of war repeatedly loomed, was faced, and avoided, a certain confidence is detectable in Chamberlain's papers that war would not occur unless it was deliberately provoked, and that the British government held most of the initiative in this vital matter, whilst Kruger's government maintained a defensive stance. When Milner set out for South Africa, he saw clearly that war was a possibility; but he and Chamberlain were of the firm opinion that, in this year of Queen Victoria's Jubilee, a major war in South Africa was not desirable and should, if possible, be avoided. Sir Michael Hicks Beach too urged patience, at least for the present, emphasizing that

> Impatience has been at the root of our difficulties – the premature annexation of the Transvaal – the Zulu war – the abandonment of the Transvaal – the Jameson Raid – all were due to it. If Kruger's Govt. really mean to fight, the utmost patience on our part is absolutely necessary, in order to make them put themselves clearly in the wrong: for otherwise we should not get on our side such an amount of public opinion, both in the Cape Colony and here, as is essential to a successful issue. If they do not really mean to fight, the natural increase of the Rand population will in time secure all that is necessary, as, but for Rhodes' folly, it would probably have done by this time. But, if the stories one hears about Boer insolence are true, they will put themselves in the wrong before long – and then Majuba Hill will be wiped out.[20]

Lord Selborne also, in a letter outlining British policy to Conyngham Greene, emphasized that although 'we will be courteous and patient . . . our firmness must bring Kruger to a point one day when he will have to decide between giving way and fighting'.[21]

Milner at once set about doing something to see that the British military forces in South Africa were strengthened so that they would be in a position to cope, if and when war came. This he made into a priority, fighting a running battle with the War Office and the Treasury to get what he wanted. Before leaving England, he had been appalled at the way vital considerations of policy had 'had to give way to economy' in his discussions with the War Office about reinforcements. Chamberlain felt that 'to ask the House of Commons for £500,000 would be tantamount to a declaration of war and could not be done, not yet at any rate'.[22] Milner had therefore been reduced to asking how the £200,000, which was the maximum sum available, could most effectively be spent and eventually settling for three battalions of field artillery and one of infantry, most of this to be concentrated on the Natal frontier with the Transvaal. As a result, British military strength in South Africa was increased from 5,400 men and six field guns to 8,000 men and 24 field guns during 1897. Milner thought that this was inadequate and that the number of men should be increased to 10,000. This he considered to be an absolute minimum if Britain was to be in a position 'to hold our own, in case of war, till the necessary force for assuming the offensive could be sent out'.[23] Meanwhile, the Transvaal, as a result of its steady rearmament programme, was able to field twice this number of men; and British Intelligence reported that it had imported 50 field guns, 26 Maxim guns, and some 45,000 rifles of the latest German make, together with a massive stockpile of ammunition.[24] On the voyage out to South Africa, Milner wrote to his close ally in the Colonial Office, Lord Selborne, begging him 'to hang on like grim death to the decision to send reinforcements and not to let the Government slip out of it on any account. . . . I desire peace – honestly – and I hope to maintain it. But we cannot answer for the other side, and I shall never rest as long as we are in such a position that a sudden move on their part would involve us in a discreditable disaster'.[25]

Milner's honesty in desiring peace at this juncture has, I think, to be accepted. Certainly, he was greatly relieved to find that the April crisis was over by the time he arrived in Cape Town. This point has to be emphasized because it has sometimes been assumed that, from the time of his appointment in 1897, Milner and Chamberlain set out to conquer and annex the Transvaal as a British colony and to use force to attain this end. The historical evidence simply does not support this view. Milner, Chamberlain and the British government neither planned nor wanted a war with the Transvaal in 1897, but neither were they dedicated to peace at any price. War was always a possibility, from the Drifts Crisis of 1895 onwards, if Kruger's government failed to observe the limits which the British government had set according to a strict observance of the London Convention. First Chamberlain and then Milner had therefore pressed, and continued to press, for a marked strengthening of the British military forces in South Africa. By 1897, they accepted that 'no doubt the sending of troops will cause some commotion' but, given the rapid expansion of expenditure on armaments by the Transvaal government, it had to be done. The detailed evidence of what kind of troops and equipment were to be sent out from Britain to South Africa, and where they were to be placed, suggests essentially defensive purposes – Milner wrote of the 'danger of a Boer incursion into Cape Colony . . . and, as things stand, we might be turned out of Natal tomorrow'. He also pointed out that 'the force we are sending is too small for any aggressive purpose' – which was certainly true – and that it was important to make it perfectly clear that 'we have not the slightest intention of attacking anybody'.[26] Britain wanted to ensure that the British military presence in the Cape Colony and Natal was strong enough to defend these territories if they were attacked by Boer forces from the Transvaal republic. But in 1897, Britain had no plans for an offensive action by her forces against the Transvaal and it was accepted that if this were ever to be contemplated, it would require the despatch of a separate major expeditionary force from Britain. Militarily, therefore, Britain was in a defensive, not an offensive, position at this time, and a military conquest of the Transvaal was not envisaged.

This was because – as Salisbury, Chamberlain, Milner and Hicks Beach each makes clear – the British government still believed that 'patience' and 'the waiting game' might still, 'in time, secure all that is necessary'. Relentless pressure on Kruger's government might still secure sufficient concessions to enable a peaceful resolution of the situation in the Transvaal to occur. The annexation, and nothing but the annexation, of the Transvaal republic was not the objective. Yet, as Milner wrote to Chamberlain shortly after his arrival in Cape Town:

> The only thing which interests anybody is the question of Peace or War. Everybody recoils with real abhorrence from the latter alternative, but while some think to avert it by 'conciliation' others, with more wisdom as I think, believe that a firm policy on the part of the Imperial Government is the likeliest means of maintaining peace. . . . It will seem incredible to you, after all that has been said, but the mass of the Dutch do still firmly believe that we mean to 'jump' the Transvaal. If it could only be gotten into their heads that while we mean to be masters and to exclude foreign interference, we have not the least wish to take away their local independence.[27]

Chamberlain, too, assured the Prime Minister 'that we have no desire to attack or intention of attacking the independence of the Transvaal but that we do intend to maintain our rights in their integrity'.[28] Nor was the British government yet prepared to fight for the establishment of an equal Uitlander franchise (i.e. equal for all Europeans, as in the

Cape Colony, where there was a clear Afrikaner majority). It felt that it would be on dubious ground if it took a stand on this essentially 'internal matter' in the Transvaal. But steady pressure did seem to bring some results.

Even in the aftermath of the Jameson Raid, Kruger had proved not totally obdurate. Reforms had been made. On 17 August 1896, the Volksraad had passed a resolution giving effect to the promise, made by Kruger's government on 30 December 1895 amidst the Jameson Raid, to enfranchise those Uitlanders who had shown themselves loyal to the republic and ready to defend it. Despite delays, occasioned by charges that some Uitlanders had succeeded in making fraudulent claims, this resulted in a considerable number of Uitlanders being enfranchised by May 1899. Schalk Burger, a member of Kruger's Executive Council, put the number at 3,437; the British Agent in Pretoria put it at 1,800; but both acknowledged that an increase in the enfranchisement of Uitlanders had occurred. During 1896, the Volksraad had also passed an Education Act, the effect of which was that the Uitlander complaint about the discrimination against English-medium schools with regard to state subsidy had largely been met by 1898.

Changes had also been made in the administration of Johannesburg. In January 1896, Kruger had declared his intention to convert the sanitary board of the town into a municipal council. A bill to do this was published later in 1896 and became law in 1897. A City Council (*stadsraad*) was established, to consist of not more than 24 members, half of them to be elected by the small number of born or naturalized resident burghers. The government appointed the burgomaster (who was also the Chairman of the Council and its chief executive officer) but, by 1899, the Council had obtained the right to levy its own local taxes.[29]

All these measures represented modest but positive advances. Far more striking and dramatic was the way in which Kruger's government had backed down over the Aliens legislation. For the British government, a policy of strict adherence to the terms of the London Convention and no compromise over essentials, coupled with the application of steady pressure over Uitlander grievances, still had everything to recommend it. The new High Commissioner needed time to spy out the lie of the land in South Africa and he sought to avoid 'causes of offence' with Kruger's government whilst he did so. Meanwhile, with the assistance of the new British Agent in Pretoria, Conyngham Greene, Milner 'happily disposed of a whole lot of minor questions' by informal negotiations with the Transvaal government and thus prevented 'each one becoming the subject of irritating controversy' between London and Pretoria.[30] After the resolution of the April crisis, the rest of 1897 passed relatively peacefully.

In South Africa, Milner spent many weeks on a tour of the country, first through the Cape Colony, then north to the Bechuanaland Protectorate and Rhodesia. In London, Chamberlain was preoccupied with the Colonial Conference and the festivities to mark Queen Victoria's Diamond Jubilee. But in May, he and Selborne met Leyds, Kruger's State Secretary, whom they found in a conciliatory mood. Chamberlain warned him that the dynamite monopoly was likely to be challenged by Britain as being in breach of the London Convention and that any suggestion of referring points at issue to foreign arbitration was unacceptable to the British government. Leyds declared that he, personally, opposed the dynamite monopoly and would like to see it changed. Chamberlain also expressed the hope that if the grievances of the Uitlanders could be discussed 'in a friendly and confidential way . . . they might be dealt with without injury to the Transvaal'.[31] Meanwhile, the British government heard from its embassies in Paris and Berlin that the French and German governments had advised Leyds to urge Kruger to make reforms and come to terms with the British government as they would certainly not quarrel with Britain for the sake of the Transvaal. These governments were, in fact, receiving pleas from Uitlanders of their own nationalities demanding that Kruger should concede reforms.[32] Leyds later blamed his lack of success in Berlin, Paris and Lisbon on British pressure behind the scenes and never returned to negotiate again with Chamberlain or the British government. The withdrawal of the Aliens legislation by Kruger's government was followed by the withdrawal of the British fleet from the vicinity of Delagoa Bay on 20 May. Chamberlain noted: 'The Transvaal Government are stewing in their own juice and our policy is to watch and wait.'[33] In the meantime, however, he and his staff put together, in leisurely manner, two despatches – one on the dynamite monopoly, the other on the question of Britain's suzerainty over the Transvaal – which were to pose fundamental challenges to Kruger's government in the future.

A VIEW FROM THE TRANSVAAL

Viewed from London, the peaceful resolution of the April crisis of 1897 and the appointment of an energetic new British High

Commissioner to South Africa might appear to have inaugurated a period of relative calm. But at precisely this time, the most penetrating and wide-ranging assessment of the situation was being made in South Africa by the man who was shortly to become Kruger's State Attorney and was to play a key role in the negotiations between Britain and the Transvaal government during the remaining two years of peace. A Cape Afrikaner, 'with not a drop of English blood in his veins', Jan Christian Smuts already had a double First in Law from Cambridge and had returned to Cape Town in 1895. In 1897, he married and moved north to the Transvaal, where he practised as a lawyer in Johannesburg. By June 1898, he was the Transvaal government's State Attorney. This was a legal and administrative rather than a political post. Smuts was not a member of either the Executive Council or the Volksraad, but he attended both when needed. His outstanding ability was soon recognized and, by 1899, he was widely acknowledged as a key figure in Kruger's government. In a long and distinguished career, he was to become the most famous statesman of the British Empire before Nehru and the only South African political figure to occupy the world stage before Nelson Mandela. But he was to begin that career by fighting Britain and everything that British imperialism stood for in the era of Chamberlain and Milner.[34]

Some time between March and June 1897, Smuts wrote an unpublished article of over 30 pages on 'The British position in South Africa'.[35] With his usual acute intelligence, Smuts probed beneath the surface events and pointed to the 'far deeper and more momentous issue . . . which ought to overshadow every other . . . : the parting of the ways in the South African policy of Great Britain'. The question posed by Smuts was: 'Is England going to revert from the traditions of her greatest colonial statesmen and is she trying now to reintroduce into South Africa that element of material force which has been gradually receding from her colonial Empire?' At a time when 'the ties binding the British Empire together are not those of material force but the ties of a community of ideas and sympathies', Smuts observed, Britain was increasing her armaments in South Africa and threatening to use force.

> When I saw how Mr Chamberlain – in those leading questions and that spirit of partisan animosity which have been deeply pondered by every thinking man in South Africa – continually referred to the maintenance of England's rights in South Africa *even by force*, I thought of the same phrase as it was bandied about the floor of the Houses of Parliament in the years immediately preceding the War with the American Colonies.

'The British Empire cannot be kept together by force and armaments', Smuts warned, and a 'vigorous policy' pursued with regard to the South African Republic would have repercussions on Britain's position throughout the length and breadth of South Africa and affect the Empire as a whole. The 'new policy' emanating from the British Colonial Office towards South Africa was, Smuts asserted, a force making for republicanism there. Already, the sense of 'a common danger' was drawing the two republics together 'on the road to a great federal republic'. Republicanism was a grand cause all over the world and 'nowhere in the world has it such a chance as in South Africa . . . its day is coming and may be nearer than many think. . . . The old ship of state is at last leaving her moorings, but it is the wind of republicanism and not of imperialism that is speeding her along'. In observations which form a striking parallel to those of Lord Selborne, Smuts noted that:

> Already the political centre of gravity in South Africa has followed the commercial centre of gravity and shifted from Cape Town to the republican capital. The Colonies will gradually have to accustom their pride and readjust their economic and political relations so as to fall in with the new disposal of political forces in South Africa . . . . The Dutch and even the English in the Colonies will come to look more and more to the Transvaal for material help and support. The Union Jack – which has been in South Africa, not a symbol of peace and goodwill, but of blood, force and aggression – will more and more be relegated to that limbo of innocuous fads in which 'imperial federation' and similar entities and nonentities flourish.

Afrikaner loyalty to Britain, he emphasized, was a fragile thing which owed nothing to a 'blood-relationship nor to long political habits of thought and life nor to an overwhelming feeling of gratitude'. It rested upon the by no means unshakeable conviction that British rule was fair and just and a force for good. This could easily 'decay and shrivel up. Let England pursue for one decade a policy in South Africa which shocks the Dutch sense of what is fair and just . . . and this sentiment of loyalty will soon vanish into thin air'. Any shift in British policy 'intended to substitute for local self-government in South Africa an increased exercise of imperial authority from Downing Street is bound to miscarry fatally', he warned. 'War policies', 'vigorous policies' and 'Jingoistic movements' were only likely to stiffen resistance.

> It is simply the law of action and reaction: but who knows whether such insignificant Jingoistic matches, primarily intended to inflame Jingo minds,

may not set fire to the Imperial stack in South Africa? . . . To my mind, the die is already cast in the [Cape] Colony; the Dutch are absolutely committed to the support of the [Transvaal] Republic in South Africa, and should an ambitious Colonial Minister choose to bring his 'vigorous' policy into operation in South Africa the entire South Africa will be speedily involved in a final conflagration.

Some people already feared, observed Smuts, that in South Africa Britain faced a repetition of the secession from the British Empire of the United States; the danger was that, by their own policies, the British government would make of the situation there another Ireland. In particular, Smuts wanted to warn the British people against their new 'vigorous' Colonial Secretary, who had become 'a more serious obstruction to progress than any other force in South Africa'. That the Uitlanders on the Rand had grievances could be admitted, even if these grievances were exaggerated, but no redress could be expected so long as Chamberlain was 'flaunting war in the face of republican South Africa'. As for the political grievances of the Uitlanders, 'they are too absurd and dishonestly put forward to merit the least consideration. We have Mr. Lionel Phillips's private opinion that the English Uitlanders "don't care a fig for the franchise"; and I think that if the franchise were offered them tomorrow not ten per cent would accept it'.

Smuts also challenged as a fiction the British claim to be the paramount power in South Africa, stating that no such term was recognized in the vocabulary of international law and that 'the relation of sovereign to subject, or so-called semi-sovereign states, is exhausted by the terms: suzerainty, protectorate, confederation or federation'. As for British suzerainty over the Transvaal, this had ceased to exist with the replacement of the Pretoria Convention by the London Convention in 1884 and Chamberlain's purpose in attempting to resurrect it was simply in order to secure for England a *locus standi* in the Transvaal and thus be in a position to adopt 'menacing language to its Government even on the most indisputably domestic concerns'. The suzerainty being gone, 'the Transvaal is a sovereign state as much as Brazil and only hampered in respect of its treaty-making power. The utmost that Great Britain could claim in South Africa is (I don't say that it exists in fact) a sort of Monroe doctrine'. Bitterly condemning Chamberlain for a policy which had done more harm in two short years than that which had culminated in the first Anglo-Boer war of 1880–81, Smuts concluded by suggesting that South Africa had become 'the crucible in which crude schemes of imperial policy are continually being tried . . . the *corpus vile* on which great colonial ministers and proconsuls perform the experiments which have to make or mar reputations for so-called statesmanship'.

This powerful indictment of Chamberlain and of British policy towards South Africa was written before Milner had yet had time to have any effect on the situation. It was written by the man who, in 1900, was to make an even more searing attack on the 'Century of Wrong' which had, he believed, characterized Britain's relations with South Africa since her first arrival on the scene in 1795.[36] If he was later to become the great apologist for the British Empire, and a key architect of the British Commonwealth of nations, Smuts was to remain unrelenting in his condemnation of the imperial policy of Chamberlain and Milner. To the end of his long life, he believed that what happened in South Africa between 1895 and 1905 was a betrayal of all that was best in Britain's nineteenth-century tradition of liberal empire and the England of John Bright. When what he regarded as a disastrous decade was over, Smuts looked back on it, and the 'assertive imperialism' which had formed so striking a part of it, with revulsion and relief that it was now 'as extinct as the cognate mastodon'.[37] He was also convinced that in fighting it, in the greatest of all Britain's nineteenth-century colonial wars, South Africa had played a vital part in bringing about its extinction.

From the moment of his appointment as Kruger's State Attorney in June 1898, Smuts was a force for reform in the Transvaal government. He was only 28 years old and without parliamentary or governmental experience but he had soon made his mark in the Transvaal and Kruger recognized his formidable ability, describing him as a man of 'iron will' who was destined to play a great role in the history of South Africa.[38] Only sixteen months were to pass between Smuts's appointment and the resort to war in October 1899 but during this time Smuts was to play a key part in the deliberations of the Transvaal government and in its negotiations with Britain and with leading Uitlanders on the Rand. For most of this time Smuts is to be found working tirelessly to remove the causes of conflict in so far as these lay in the policies and administration of Kruger's government. He at once tackled bribery and corruption within the police force, illegal gold-buying and racketeering in liquor sales, prostitution, and counterfeit money. He was the legal adviser, not only to the Volksraad and the Executive Council, but to all the departments of government and thus became responsible for drafting virtually all new legislation.

The validity of much of the legislation passed by the Volksraad had been called into question by the Chief Justice of the Transvaal, Sir J.G. Kotze, by his judgement in the case of *Brown* v. *Leyds* in January

1897. The matter hinged on the difference between laws passed after due public notice (*wetten*) and those passed as resolutions without such notice (*besluiten*). Kotze's judgement brought into question the validity of legislation which had been enacted as *besluiten*. It also asserted the 'testing right' of the judiciary. An additional element of personal conflict was involved since Kotze was not only a judge but a man with political ambitions who had stood as a candidate against Kruger in the presidential election of 1893. He was described by Edward Fairfield, of the British Colonial Office, as 'an ambitious, intriguing man who wants to be President, or a K.C.M.G., or both'.[39] Kotze was a reformer, in favour of concessions to the Uitlanders and critical of Kruger's 'Hollander' advisers. Conyngham Greene believed that the 'progressive' element amongst Transvaal Afrikaners hoped to secure Kotze's appointment as State Secretary after Leyds's term of office expired in May 1897. Kotze seems to have hoped that his judgement in the *Brown* v. *Leyds* case would induce the Transvaal government to devise safeguards against hasty legislation. President Kruger and the Volksraad, however, treated the matter as an attack on the constitution (*Grondwet*) and promptly enacted a law which denied the competence of the judiciary to exercise the 'testing right' and empowered the President to dismiss from office any judge who persisted in claiming it. Kotze's four colleagues resolved to stand by him in defence of the independence of the judiciary. A prolonged conflict then ensued between the Transvaal government and the judiciary which the Chief Justice of the Cape Colony, Sir Henry de Villiers, attempted to resolve by acting as a mediator. In March 1897, he persuaded the judiciary not to exercise the 'testing right' for the present, whilst President Kruger undertook to introduce a Bill into the Volksraad which would establish the constitution (*Grondwet*) on a firmer basis so that it was safeguarded against sudden alteration by a simple resolution of the Volksraad.

Sir Henry de Villiers used the opportunity of his mediation in 'the judges case' to raise with President Kruger the grievances of other sections of the Transvaal population, urging him to do something to satisfy the legitimate demands of the Uitlanders and thus make them the friends rather than the enemies of the country. 'If redress is not granted', he emphasized, 'the danger will always exist that it may be sought elsewhere.'[40] Kruger responded by making a clear distinction between the grievances of those involved in the gold–mining industry and 'those of the discontented people [who] will not be satisfied until they have my country'. Kruger emphasized that he was 'responsible for the independence of the State and must take care that it is not lost' and urged de Villiers not to 'be under the delusion that any concessions I can make will ever satisfy the enemies of my country'. He made clear his conviction that the Uitlanders could not be trusted with the franchise – 'If I give them the franchise they may ask the Chartered people [i.e. Rhodes] to rule over them' – but expressed a readiness to redress their other grievances. As for the complaints of the mining companies, he intended to establish a full enquiry into them despite the fact that 'some of the Johannesburg people turn to others for support instead of to me, and they do not seem to be agreed among themselves as to what their grievances really are'.

THE MINING INDUSTRY AND THE TRANSVAAL INDUSTRIAL COMMISSION OF 1897

The result was the setting up of an Industrial Commission of Enquiry into the Mining Industry by Kruger's Executive Council at the end of March 1897. Its Chairman, Schalk Burger, was a progressive member of the Executive Council who was to stand against Kruger in the presidential election the following year. His appointment was widely welcomed by the mining magnates, as was the role played in the Commission's work by James Hay and George Albu, the Chairmen of the two bodies representing the mining industry. Such a Commission of Enquiry had long been sought by the mining companies and its establishment represents the first of two bold attempts by Kruger's government to come to terms with the mining industry. Neither this Commission nor the Great Deal negotiations of March 1899 were the result of any specific agitation, but both were initiatives taken by Kruger's government at times of acute difficulty.

A combination of natural disasters and a sharp fall in outside investment made 1897 a year of economic hardship in the Transvaal. The rinderpest epidemic, which had swept down through Africa, devastated the cattle stocks, which formed the only real wealth of much of the population, and it was accompanied by an invasion of locusts, drought, and famine. Measures taken in response to the rinderpest epidemic were not only costly but failed to stop the spread of the disease and antagonized the farming population.[41] In the Transvaal, the loss of their cattle accelerated the 'second Great Trek' of impoverished Boer farmers from the rural to the urban areas, where they found themselves poorly equipped to compete with newly-arrived Uitlanders for such jobs as were available.[42] The volume of Transvaal trade also began to shrink markedly during the first quarter of 1897, imports declined, and a wave of insolvencies in the second half of the year indicated that the economic depression had deepened.[43] On the Rand, although the output of gold continued to grow steadily throughout the 1890s, there was a slump in the 'Kaffir' shares market during 1896 which continued well into 1898. Many mining and finance companies were left with holdings of very doubtful value. The opportunity to make windfall profits at the expense of what one magnate called 'the poor share-holders of Europe' – which had been such a feature of the boom years of 1894–5 – disappeared. Profits now had to be made from actual mining rather than speculation in land and shares, and this focused attention on the need to reduce costs and increase efficiency. In particular, as the *South African Mining Journal* stated in a leader at the end of 1896: 'The most acute of the difficulties under which the mining industry struggles may be set down to unskilled government and unskilled labour.'[44]

Kruger's government also faced considerable domestic criticism from its own burghers at this time, in addition to the confrontation with the judiciary sparked off by the Kotze case. Throughout the 1890s, a progressive group in the two Volksraads, under the nominal leadership of General P. J. Joubert – who challenged Kruger in all four presidential elections and had only narrowly been defeated by him in that of 1893 – had criticized Kruger's government for its 'Hollander' advisers, corruption, and concessions policies, and had urged a more liberal treatment of the Uitlanders in order to make Transvaal patriots out of them.[45] Although these 'progressives' relied very little on support from either Uitlanders or the mining industry, the Jameson Raid had been an immense set-back to their efforts. In its wake, there had been a closing of the ranks amongst Transvaal Afrikaners although, at the end of August 1897, Milner was still hopeful that unless 'all this nascent opposition' in the Transvaal was stifled:

> by trotting out the old bugbear of 'our independence in danger', we shall surely see a strongish opposition spring up which will be bound to lean, timidly at first but with more and more openness as the fight thickens, upon Uitlander support. They will angle for it in the first instance by concessions to the Mining Industry, but sooner or later they must come to a gradual extension of the franchise, which some of them would propose tomorrow if they dared, because they will need *some* Uitlander votes to turn the scale in their own favour against the men in power.[46]

Poorly organized, and without a clear programme, the 'progressives' could muster 8–11 votes out of the total of 24 in the First Volksraad of 1893, and perhaps 10 out of the total of 27 as late as 1899.[47] In 1897, Kruger's government was therefore not without its difficulties at home. Abroad, Leyds's efforts to win political and financial support in Europe had met with complete failure. All of these factors contributed to Kruger's readiness to make some move towards tackling the grievances of the mining industry.

The mining industry was not only facing a down-turn in economic conditions, it was also undergoing a transformation as a result of the development of the deep-level mining which was now seen to hold the key to the future. At the end of 1895, only one 'deep-level' mine (the Geldenhuis Deep) had commenced operation, and it was working at a loss.[48] The capital costs of 'deep levels' were vastly greater than had been the case with the earlier 'out-crop' mining – an initial investment of £600,000 was required for the equipment and development of even a moderately deep-level mine at only 3,000 ft. The magnitude of the capital investment required and the length of time needed for the development of a deep-level mine before any gold could be extracted meant that many of the smaller mining houses were unable to compete and over half of the total number of working mines were operating at a loss. This intensified both competition and resentment at the burden of any unnecessary additional costs imposed on the industry by Kruger's administration.

Shortly after the Jameson Raid, a group of the mining companies which had not been involved in Rhodes's conspiracy broke away from the Chamber of Mines and formed a separate Association of Mines. Although the leaders of some of these firms – which included A. Goerz, George Albu, J.B. Robinson and Barney Barnato – were loud in their denunciation of those who had taken part in the plot, their motives were not just political. They resented the domination which the larger firms, and especially Wernher, Beit/H. Eckstein & Co., exercised in the Chamber of Mines through the appointment of their employees as office-holders.[49] They also hoped to win concessions from Kruger's government if they dissociated themselves from those companies which had been compromised by being associated with Rhodes's plot.[50] In this they were to be disappointed, their only notable achievement being that after Kruger had refused an invitation to be Honorary President of the Chamber, he was persuaded to accept the same position in the Association. Apart from this, the really important concessions were all won through joint action by the two bodies, the first being the agreement of October 1896 which produced the first significant reduction in the wages of African mine-workers. This was accompanied by the establishment of the Witwatersrand

Native Labour Association to coordinate the recruitment of African migrant labour in the interests of the mining industry. The devastating effects of the rinderpest epidemic on African farmers eased the shortage of African mine labour and enabled the industry to impose a further 30 per cent reduction in African wages in 1897. This was a major achievement from the point of view of the mining companies, since it was not until 50 years later that African mine-workers' wages were to rise, in cash terms, above the 1897 level. In addition, Kruger's government assisted the mining industry by enacting labour legislation (including the Pass Law) and negotiating an agreement with the Mozambique government to facilitate a plentiful supply of cheap, immigrant labour for the Rand. The cooperation between Kruger's government and the mining industry at this time marks a vital stage in the development of South Africa's cheap, migrant labour system which has been crucial to the viability of gold-mining there.[51]

Meanwhile, there was no corresponding cut in European wages, the one short-lived attempt at this (by J. B. Robinson) having resulted in strike action and a move towards the sort of union organization which the mining companies wished to avoid.[52] These early attempts by the mining companies to cooperate rather than compete with each other over labour practices were only partly effective but they resulted in the single most important cost-reduction achieved by the mining industry in this period. They also encouraged further joint action in what was a far from monolithic, and still very divided, industry. By 1897, the point had been reached when the need for the reunification of the Chamber and the Association was being discussed. The establishment of the Industrial Commission, and the appointment as members of it of the chairmen of both bodies representing the mining industry, gave an additional powerful impulse in this direction.

All sectors of the mining industry recognized the need to present a united front to the Industrial Commission if they were to make an effective case for reform and extract from Kruger's government some of the other concessions which they had long been seeking. There was also the well-founded suspicion that Kruger intended to use the Commission to expose to the world the malpractices which had long been a feature of the mining industry on the Rand. In particular, it was widely acknowledged that the collapse in the share market since 1895 was the direct result of the gross over-speculation and dubious dealing of the mining and finance houses during the boom years.[53] The Commission's task was to 'institute a thorough and searching inquiry into the alleged grievances of the Mining Industry'. It sat from April to June 1897 and it is clear that, led by Wernher, Beit/H.

Eckstein & Co., the mining industry went to great lengths to amass evidence and see that it was cogently presented by those who appeared before the Commission.[54]

When the Commission's Report appeared, in July 1897, it surprised everyone. Even Milner considered it to be 'a startler. It never occurred to me as at all probable that the Commission would give a verdict which is practically one of "Proven" to all the main charges of the Mining Industry', he commented.[55] Conyngham Greene, who was closer to what had been going on, was less surprised since he felt that the Report was largely the work of the mining industry itself, which had worked hard 'to secure a good report' and had largely succeeded in using the Commission for its own purposes.[56]

The Report revealed that about half of the mines in production on the Rand were being worked at a loss and others had not yet come into production at all. Of the 79 gold-mines which were in production in 1896, only 25 had declared dividends. It praised the 'honest administration' of the mining companies and their introduction of 'the most up-to-date machinery' and it urged the Transvaal government to 'take an active part' in cooperating with an industry which was 'the financial basis, support and mainstay of the State'. It declared that it 'entirely disapproved of concessions, through which the industrial prosperity of the country is hampered' by impositions which were not only unnecessary but 'irksome and injurious to the industry and . . . will always remain a source of great irritation and dissatisfaction'. It recommended that the cost of living on the Rand should be reduced, through the abolition of all duties on foodstuffs (many were imported), and that a Local Board should be established in Johannesburg on which government nominees should sit alongside representatives from mining and commerce to see that the laws affecting their businesses – e.g. the Pass laws, the Liquor Law and the Gold Law with regard to thefts, which were estimated at 10 per cent of production (£750,000p.a.) – were properly administered. The reasons for the collapse of the share market and the loss of confidence and reduction in external investment in the mining industry were not examined.

Kruger's government was even more startled than Milner by a Report so favourable to the long-standing complaints of the mining industry and so critical of the record of the Transvaal government. The dynamite concession (which had been granted to the South African Explosives Company) and the railway rates (charged by the Netherlands Railway Company) came in for particularly damning criticism. The Commission pointed out that the railway rates operating in the Transvaal were far higher than anywhere else in South Africa and urged their considerable reduction, but it did not recommend that the Netherlands Railway Company should be expropriated. Dynamite was a different matter. At this time, the Transvaal was the largest single consumer of dynamite and blasting gelatine in the world. The Commission, after strongly criticizing the Explosives Company for failing to give any detailed evidence, estimated that, if there were a free market, both of these substances could be imported for 40–45 shillings per case less than the Company was charging. Of this 'mark-up', only 5 shillings was benefiting the state revenue, the remainder being pure profit for the private monopolists running the company. Further, this private monopoly had been granted by the state on the basis that local materials were to be used. Yet it was found that 'none of the raw material used is found in this country, or in such small quantities as to make it practically valueless' and that almost everything was imported (chiefly from Germany). The quality of the explosives finally produced was so poor that they were dangerous and unreliable and serious accidents had resulted. The Commission concluded that as a result of the dynamite monopoly, the mining industry was bearing sizeable additional costs which were quite unnecessary, did not benefit the state, and simply served 'to enrich individuals for the most part resident in Europe'. The dynamite concession had not only failed to meet the original objective, the company operating it had also failed to abide by the conditions of their contract. It was therefore recommended that the government should take legal advice to see if the contract could be cancelled and, if this was possible, then a free trade in explosives should at once be established, subject only to a modest duty payable to the government.

A Commission of Inquiry, and its damning Report, was one thing, however; effective action in response to it by Kruger's government was another. After the Commission's chairman, Schalk Burger, had been accused in the Transvaal Volksraad of being a traitor to his country for putting his name to such a report, delaying tactics were applied and a Volksraad committee was appointed to discuss the Report with the Executive Council and make recommendations. When these were finally made in mid-October 1897, they were received with dismay by the mining companies, their European investors, the bulk of the Uitlander population, and a fair number of Kruger's own burghers. Modest reductions in railway rates and import duties on certain foodstuffs were approved, but other duties were increased to compensate. The establishment of a Local Board to supervise the more effective implementation of the law was rejected outright as the formation of 'a government within the government'. The way was left open for the granting of further monopolies – and concessions for the manufacture of paper, matches, woollen goods, starch, chocolate, soap and oils were all granted during the following two years.[57] Most devious of all was the treatment of the dynamite issue. After nine days of debate in the Volksraad, in which Kruger himself intervened several times with his usual assertion that 'the Dynamite Factory is the cornerstone of our independence and those who cannot see this are blind', the matter was referred to the Executive Council by a majority of one vote – apparently cast in error.[58] The Executive Council then passed on the matter to the State Attorney (Smuts had not yet been appointed) and he set up a further committee of enquiry. The end result was a modest reduction of 10 shillings per case; but the monopoly remained in place. The mining industry regarded the reduction as quite inadequate and bitterly resented the additional and unnecessary cost to its operations of an estimated £600,000 per annum, which the continuation of the monopoly represented. Kruger's government continued to import all its arms and ammunition from Europe.[59]

The result of the Industrial Commission was a severe set-back to any hopes held by those in the mining industry that Kruger's government would ever act to rectify their grievances. The government stood condemned of failing to implement the recommendations of its own Commission. Percy FitzPatrick, the representative of Wernher, Beit/H. Eckstein & Co., who had worked as hard as anyone to use the Commission to educate the government, as well as some sections of the mining industry, about the scale of the unnecessary costs borne by the mining companies as a direct result of Kruger's policies, was confirmed in his pessimistic view that 'if the signs are worth anything, there is no hope of substantive redress'. 'If Schalk Burger's report carries no weight with the Raad, our protests will carry none', he commented.[60] To Otto Beit, he expressed his own conviction 'that Paul Kruger is as tough as the best or worst of them and is not going to cut any Gordian knots just yet'.[61]

By failing to grant major reforms at this critical juncture to this key sector in the Transvaal, Kruger's government contributed to the emergence of a reunited, more formidable, and more hostile Chamber of Mines. By the end of 1897, the two bodies representing the industry had reunited in a new Chamber of Mines with Georges Rouliot (of Wernher Beit/H. Eckstein & Co.) as its president. Where previously, Kruger had been able to play upon the weaknesses and divisions within the industry, and favour some sections at the expense of others, he now faced a much more effective and fully representative organization. Erstwhile 'friends' of Kruger's government amongst the mining magnates, who had stayed aloof from Rhodes's conspiracy and Jameson's Raid in 1895–6, now changed sides and joined its critics. J. B. Robinson, for example, who had been closely associated with Kruger, not only broke with him but wanted to lead a new reform movement and initiate a campaign against 'Kruger and Krugerism' which would aim to secure his removal from office. The newspapers owned by Robinson, the Johannesburg *Times* and the Pretoria *Press*, joined those owned by the Argus Company (a subsidiary of Wernher Beit/H. Eckstein & Co.), especially *The Star*, in becoming openly critical of the government. Even businessmen beneficiaries of Kruger's regime, like Sammy Marks – who distrusted, and was mistrusted by, the mining magnates, and had done well out of a pliable administration favourably disposed towards non-gold-mining ventures – began to call for thoroughgoing reforms and was heard to declare that he would give £100,000 to have the British flag flying over his money.[62] The mine-magnates also determined to find and support the campaign of an opposition candidate to Kruger in the presidential elections at the beginning of 1898.[63]

In addition to the alienation of the mining industry, Kruger's government also faced mounting criticism from the Chamber of Commerce and from foreign investors. Dismayed at the failure of the government to do anything to restore business confidence, the Chamber of Commerce not only itself protested but urged foreign consuls in Pretoria to urge their governments to make representations to Kruger that reforms were essential if external loans and investment were to be forthcoming. Although British capital amounted to between a half and three-quarters of the total foreign investment in the Transvaal at this time, there was also sizeable German and French participation. During 1898–9, Kruger's government became increasingly isolated, with the representatives of European governments in the Transvaal joining its critics and insisting on reform. Those mining companies with prominent German connections, for example, such as Goerz and Albu, were amongst those most firmly opposed to the dynamite monopoly because they represented poorer mines, which used more dynamite per ounce of gold extracted than the average, and so felt that they suffered most from the excessive charges imposed by the dynamite monopoly. Whatever the view of German public opinion generally about the Transvaal, it is clear that German investors and German policy-makers not only wanted major reforms by Kruger's government but moved towards tacitly supporting the British government's determination to extract them. A similar attitude came to prevail in the United States.[64]

The failure of the Industrial Commission therefore isolated Kruger's government and cast serious doubt on its ability to reform either itself or the situation of conflict in the Transvaal over which it presided. It also suggested that the development of the mining industry was outrunning the rudimentary administrative structures of the Transvaal state and threatening its stability.[65] Kruger's government was not totally unresponsive to the needs of the mining industry, and on many aspects, e.g. labour recruitment, railway-building, Pass laws, Liquor laws, the Gold Law, etc. it had acted to assist in its operations. The trouble was that it lacked the ability to enforce even the legislation which it had passed. The administration had been designed for a thinly-populated republic of poor farmers, not for a flood of urbanized Uitlanders and the needs of the most technologically-sophisticated, capital-intensive gold-mining industry in the world. It lacked both sufficiently educated, honest and experienced personnel and adequate administrative structures.

There was also a shrewd element of calculation, and not just maladministration and muddle, behind the policies of the government which hampered the growth of the mining industry. It was not Kruger's intention to provide conditions which would promote the unrestricted expansion of the gold-mines and encourage a further influx of Uitlanders. He was quite prepared to impose additional costs and taxes on the mines, particularly if something of strategic importance to the republic – such as the possession of its own ammunition and explosives factory – was at stake. He sought, at every turn, to balance the over-mighty Randlords with capital and capitalist enterprises which were 'friendly' to his government, the coal-mining and other businesses developed by Sammy Marks and Isaac Lewis in the Transvaal during these years benefiting from this policy as well as the more obvious, large-scale concessions such as the Netherlands Railway Company.[66]

The British Colonial Secretary – a businessman himself – was not averse to discussing with his contacts amongst the Randlords, when they were in London, how they might possibly bring additional pressure to bear on Kruger's government. As the fall in gold-mining shares continued during 1896–7, Johannesburg was full of rumours about a plan to shut down some of the mines in order to persuade the Transvaal government to modify its economic policies. One correspondent, whose letter reached Chamberlain in London, suggested that the slump had been deliberately brought about by the larger mining houses as a means to compel the Transvaal government to do something to reduce mining costs. The writer was almost certainly wrong in his suggestion of a 'conspiracy plot,' but Chamberlain immediately shared the idea with Lionel Phillips to whom he wrote asking:

> Is it probable that any considerable number of mines will be shut down? What effect would this have on the labour market, and what would be the general result on the population of Johannesburg if want of employment made itself felt? Would not any serious depression in the mining industry affect the Revenues of the Transvaal Government? If so, would this not be a legitimate means of bringing pressure to bear to secure the reasonable reforms which are required in order to maintain the prosperity of the Rand? It has been represented to me that the mining magnates of Johannesburg could, if they chose, bring matters to a satisfactory issue by closing the mines, and that in this case the Transvaal Government would be obliged to make concessions in order to secure their revenues.[67]

We do not have Phillips's considered reply but we do know that further possibilities of applying pressure to Kruger's government by concerting action to block its access to loans were explored. In March 1898, Milner urged Chamberlain to do something 'through [the] international influence of big financial houses in London to make difficulties for the Transvaal government borrowing money'.[68] Lord Selborne, after consulting both Alfred Beit and Lord Rothschild, minuted that 'any loans can be stopped, and would be, in London and possibly in Paris, but we cannot influence the market in Holland or Germany'.[69] But both the German and Dutch governments were receiving increasing representations from their own subjects with economic interests in the Transvaal, urging them to throw their weight behind the efforts of the British government to extract reforms from Kruger. By 1898, Kruger's government found itself unable to obtain the £2 million loan which it was seeking in Europe and was eventually compelled to resort to the Netherlands Railway Company for the money.

CHAMBERLAIN TAKES UP THE DYNAMITE MONOPOLY AND THE SUZERAINTY CLAIM

Meanwhile, Chamberlain determined to challenge Kruger's government on the dynamite monopoly. He had had this in mind earlier in

1897, and Kruger's retreat in April over the Aliens legislation, and then the recommendation of the Industrial Commission on the dynamite issue, certainly encouraged him to bring it forward. The Colonial Office, after taking legal advice, was convinced that, unlike other breaches of the London Convention, the ban on importing dynamite directly affected British interests and firms, some of which had protested to the British government about their exclusion. In July, a draft despatch was prepared and sent to Milner. Milner, however, argued strongly that it should not yet be presented to Kruger's government. Whilst the verdict of the Industrial Commission on the dynamite monopoly was, he felt, '*absolutely crushing*', he argued that 'their dealing with this question is doing the S.A.R. Govt. the greatest possible harm with their own friends, and that to give them such a splendid red herring as "British interference with a purely domestic question" would simply be to help them out of an awful fix'.[70] Some representatives of the mining industry on the Rand believed that the dynamite monopoly was doomed if Kruger was not able to raise the bogy of 'imperial meddling'. Milner clearly recognized the gravity of the British government taking up the matter. 'Our doing so would attract tremendous attention, and we should be obliged to see the thing through. Yet, unpopular as the monopoly is, I don't think it is quite the question on which the world at large, and public opinion at home, would approve our going to war.'[71] Milner drew a clear distinction between making requests or suggestions to Kruger's government and making '*a claim of right*', on the basis of the London Convention. The former, Kruger's government could disregard or refuse, but if the British government made a claim on the Convention

> We are no longer neighbours asking for a favour but over-lords
> demanding our dues, and we must get them or look fools. Therefore I say
> broadly I should never mention the Convention, unless I was prepared to
> fight, if any demand based upon it was not conceded. But I should be
> very sorry to fight about the Dynamite Monopoly – a capitalist's question
> pure and simple . . . [72]

Chamberlain was persuaded by Milner's argument and by the fact that Britain had nothing to lose by waiting. He therefore minuted for the benefit of his Colonial Office staff:

> The worst thing that can be done in diplomacy or politics is to 'wobble'.
> For good and sufficient reasons, after the fullest consideration, I decided
> that our policy for the present was to let the Boers 'stew in their own
> juice', fight out their internal quarrels and not be able to raise prejudice

and confuse the issues by pointing to external interference as the danger to be faced. The decision may be right or wrong, but I intend that it shall have a fair trial. I am therefore prepared to support Sir A. Milner in withholding the despatch.[73]

Any arguments for not pressing the dynamite issue were, however, set aside when it came to answering the case put forward by Kruger's government that the differences between itself and the British government should be put to foreign arbitration. This had been proposed by the Transvaal government in the same despatch in which it had 'climbed down' over the aliens legislation in April 1897. Milner had at once dismissed this as 'a try-on' which Kruger's own government did not really expect to see accepted. To agree to arbitration in any form would be a serious error, he argued, for it would undermine Britain's prestige and position in South Africa. It should be rejected straight away.[74] Chamberlain agreed and, with the strong support of the government, determined to use the opportunity this provided to put together a major despatch in which the British claim to suzerainty over the Transvaal republic was argued and asserted.[75] This claim raised a fundamental issue between Britain and the Transvaal, over which the relations between their two governments were finally to founder in August 1899. The background to Britain's claim of suzerainty over the Transvaal therefore merits attention.

Suzerainty was a vague term with no clear legal standing. Essentially a political concept, denoting a form of overlordship by a superior power over an inferior one, it was derived from Britain's experience in India and had only come into use with regard to the Transvaal in 1881. Before Chamberlain had addressed the issue, Smuts had already dismissed the British claim. Whilst acknowledging that Britain had exercised suzerainty over the Transvaal by the terms of the Pretoria Convention of 1881, he had denied that this continued in existence after the London Convention of 1884, had deliberately excised the passage dealing with the matter and replaced it by the reference to Britain's 'control of the relations of the Transvaal with other powers' as stated in Article IV. Thus, after 1884, Britain was no longer the 'suzerain power' over the Transvaal and had no *locus standi* with regard to its internal affairs.[76] This was the vital issue. Kruger clearly believed, when he returned from negotiating the London Convention in 1884, that the suzerainty had been abolished and stated this in the Volksraad shortly afterwards.[77] The British Colonial Secretary, Lord Derby, with whom Kruger and the Transvaal representatives had negotiated the terms of the Convention, also believed that the articles of the London Convention had replaced those of the Pretoria Convention and that the latter were 'no longer in force' thereafter.[78] Nonetheless, a month after the conclusion of the London Convention, Derby was still using the word 'suzerainty' to describe the 'certain controlling power' which Britain had retained over the Transvaal through its 'right to veto any negotiations into which the dependent State may enter with foreign powers'.[79] By 1889, however, the view within the Colonial Office was that 'it is more than doubtful whether the suzerainty still exists'.[80]

For a decade after 1884, successive British governments were sparing in their use of the term 'suzerainty' when discussing their relations with the Transvaal republic. In 1894, however, when Lord Rosebery's Liberal government was in office, Sydney Buxton (who was the Under-Secretary for the Colonies) gave a fresh twist to the justification for using the term 'suzerainty', which Salisbury and Chamberlain were later to follow. Comparing the two Conventions, of 1881 and 1884, Buxton declared: 'that of 1884 affects the Articles of the Convention of 1881, but does not touch the preamble, and it is the preamble that has reference to the question of suzerainty'.[81] Lord Ripon, the British Colonial Secretary, had meanwhile referred the question of 'suzerainty' to the Law Officers of the Crown and they had concluded, after three pages of closely reasoned argument, that the suzerainty had been abandoned as a result of the negotiations which preceded the signing of the London Convention. According to them, Britain's 'right of interference' in the affairs of the Transvaal was now restricted to the terms set out in Article IV of the London Convention, which governed the ratification of agreements with foreign powers.[82] In a House of Commons debate on the Transvaal, on 2 July 1894, it was clearly acknowledged that the London Convention of 1884 'contains no express reservation of the Queen's right of suzerainty . . . it is a cardinal principle of that settlement that the internal government and legislation of the South African Republic shall not be interfered with'.[83] On the eve of Chamberlain's arrival at the Colonial Office, the agreed view was that British suzerainty over the Transvaal no longer existed.

It was not Joseph Chamberlain but the Prime Minister, Lord Salisbury, who first reasserted the 'suzerainty' claim in January 1896. This he did by following the specious reasoning first adopted by Sydney Buxton, declaring 'that in our view, the preamble to the Treaty of 1881, by which the suzerainty was reserved, had not been extinguished, and that the suzerainty consequently still existed'.[84] Thereafter, Chamberlain simply followed where Buxton and Salisbury had led. At a time when the British government wished to maximize the hold which it claimed over the Transvaal, against the efforts of

Kruger's government to minimize it, a reassertion of the British claim to suzerainty had obvious uses. Lord Derby had described suzerainty 'as a vague word, not capable of any precise legal definition'.[85] But its very vagueness had its attractions to Salisbury and Chamberlain. Salisbury was able to claim that a Convention between a suzerain and a dependent Power was not of the same kind or standing as a treaty between two independent Powers.[86] Chamberlain now felt able to use the suzerainty claim as the reason why the arbitration proposal put forward by Kruger's government in 1897 was not, and never could be, acceptable to the British government.[87] The despatch, asserting Britain's claim to suzerainty over the Transvaal, was finally sent by Chamberlain on 16 October. Selborne thought that it 'will give the old man a fit at Pretoria, but it will be of great value as asserting our position before all the world'.[88] Milner agreed; he had already warned Chamberlain that 'the mention of the word "suzerainty" or "paramountcy" exercises a curiously maddening effect on the Boers. I don't suppose the word matters much to us, so long as we have got the substance', he added.[89]

In the despatch, which was finally delivered to Pretoria in December 1897, Chamberlain rejected the Transvaal's claim that the London Convention should be 'interpreted according to the generally accepted principles of the law of nations'. This was because he did not accept that the Transvaal republic was a fully sovereign state but was 'subordinate' to the sovereign power of Britain with regard to its external relations.[90] In this, Chamberlain was undoubtedly correct. But he went on to argue that since the London Convention had been concluded at a time when the Transvaal was a dependent state, under the suzerainty of the Queen, the relations of Britain towards the Transvaal republic were those 'of a Suzerain who has accorded to the people of that Republic self-government upon certain conditions'. It would therefore be 'incompatible' with Britain's position, as the suzerain power, 'to submit to arbitration the construction of the conditions on which she accorded self-government to the Republic'.[91] Chamberlain also maintained that the Preamble to the Pretoria Convention had never been revoked and that therefore the suzerainty of the Queen remained. In this, Chamberlain was following the specious reasoning first outlined by Buxton. It was specious because the London Convention had its own preamble and was, in fact, a new convention which replaced the Pretoria Convention entirely.

When Leyds, on behalf of the Transvaal government, eventually replied to this despatch, on 16 April 1898, he rejected the suzerainty claim outright.[92] Chamberlain refused to withdraw the claim and continued to reassert it, adding the further argument that if the Preamble to the Pretoria Convention had ceased to have legal validity then not only Britain's suzerainty but the Transvaal's right to internal self-government had also ceased because both owed their existence to that Preamble.[93] Milner seems to have been well aware of the shaky ground on which Chamberlain was basing his arguments and told him that the London Convention 'is *such a wretched instrument*, that even an impartial Court would be likely to give such an interpretation to it as would render it perfectly worthless'.[94] What Chamberlain, Selborne and Milner all agreed was that the conflict over terminology mattered little so long as the substance of the Transvaal's 'subordination' to Britain was maintained.[95] A protracted diplomatic correspondence on the subject ended in an impasse in July 1899 when Chamberlain simply declared: 'Her Majesty's Government . . . have no intention of continuing to discuss this question with the Government of the Republic, whose contention that the South African Republic is a sovereign international State is not, in their opinion, warranted either by law or history, and is wholly inadmissible.'[96]

Kruger's government rightly regarded Britain's suzerainty claim as bogus, as an insidious attack on the status of the Transvaal republic, and as an attempt by Britain to establish a basis which would give her the right to intervene in the internal affairs of the Transvaal. Kruger's government therefore not only continued to repudiate it but was to make the agreement of the British government to cease asserting it a first condition, in the final negotiations of August 1899, for the peaceful resolution of a conflict which then looked set on war. The fact was that Kruger had long since regarded the terms of the London Convention as 'injurious to the dignity of an independent Republic' and had sought consistently to have them superseded by a new agreement between two independent states. He also quite rightly saw that 'the continual arguments on the question of suzerainty' (which he denied had existed since 1884) were being used as a pretext for the reassertion of the British imperial factor generally in the affairs of the Transvaal.[97] By the late 1890s, British paramountcy or supremacy in South Africa – which the British government was determined not just to assert but to establish on a firmer basis – was not compatible with the full and sovereign independence which the Transvaal had enjoyed after 1852, lost in 1877, and which Kruger's republic had never thereafter regained, despite determined efforts to do so. By 1899, a head-on conflict over this issue by the British and Transvaal governments was probably beyond peaceful resolution. Kruger's burghers were convinced that they would have to fight for their independence. The British government would certainly fight to prevent them achieving it. It would also take advantage of the opportunity, which a resort to war presented, to annex the Transvaal and incorporate it fully within the British Empire. Without a resort to war, this would have been difficult. Once war began, it became an inevitable result of a British victory.

THE ELECTIONS OF 1898

The delivery of Chamberlain's 'Suzerainty Despatch' shortly before a presidential election was due in the Transvaal enabled Kruger to use it, in his campaign for re-election, as evidence that the independence of the republic was in danger. In addition to Kruger, P. J. Joubert and Schalk Burger also presented themselves as candidates. This was Joubert's fourth contest but, unlike in 1893, this time he failed to attract the support of any key sector of the electorate. Schalk Burger was a more formidable candidate. His patriotic credentials were beyond doubt and he could attract the support of the progressive vote amongst burghers and Uitlanders alike. But there were rather few Uitlander voters and their support, together with that of the mining industry, may well have alienated some of the burghers. Schalk Burger campaigned on a platform of modest reform: for the implementation of the recommendations of the Industrial Commission, of which he had been the chairman; for the modernization of the constitution; for the securing of the independence of the judiciary; and for a very modest extension of the franchise.[98]

The mining industry gave considerable financial support to Schalk Burger's election campaign and attempted to persuade Joubert to withdraw in his favour, with the aid of a financial pay-off. In this, they failed. Percy FitzPatrick warned Julius Wernher:

> You can be sure of this: if there be any sign of movement or restlessness on the part of the Uitlanders, or a disposition on England's part to meddle, there will be only one man in the hunt. Kruger is hunting about for evidence to show that Rhodes or Chamberlain or Johannesburg is at the bottom of the opposition to him. His organ, the *Volksstem*, has gone to the length of stating that we have put up £50,000 to secure Burger's election. He will go *any* length.[99]

But FitzPatrick was sure that Schalk Burger would not win, that Kruger would be returned, that he would not make any major concessions or reforms. He even wondered whether 'it would be better to let Kruger go on and "end it" ' rather than putting vain hopes and some effort into a campaign to enable Schalk Burger to 'come in and "mend it" '.[100] Certainly, many supporters of the South African League, reported Conyngham Greene, 'hope that Mr Kruger, if re-elected and elated by success, will be encouraged to persevere in his present policy, and thus precipitate a crisis'.[101]

What surprised everybody, when the results were announced in February, was not Kruger's victory, but the scale of it. Kruger won 12,764 votes as against Burger's 3,716 and Joubert's 1,943. Not only in the rural areas, but in the towns – and in Johannesburg as well as in Pretoria – Kruger was returned by a large majority of an electorate which amounted to about 10 per cent of the total Transvaal European population.

The re-election of Kruger and the entrenchment of his government in the Transvaal was followed, later in 1898, by the fall of the Sprigg ministry in the Cape Colony and the most bitterly contested general election in the Cape's history. Sprigg and the Progressives had been supported by Rhodes and the South African League and had themselves supported the British imperial cause in South Africa. Rhodes now poured money into their election campaign, which was also assisted by the South African League. The Transvaal government was accused of using secret funds to support the campaign of the Afrikaner Bond but there is no firm evidence to support this. Although the situation in the Transvaal figured in the Cape election campaign, it was by no means the dominant issue. Rhodes and the Progressives openly claimed that in fighting the Afrikaner Bond in the Cape they were fighting 'Krugerism'. W.P. Schreiner, who led the opposition South African Party, and who was not himself a member of the Bond, denied that his party was either republican or Krugerite but simply working for friendly relations with all the neighbouring states, including the South African Republic. There is no doubt that the prominence of Rhodes, and the men and money at his disposal, was a deeply divisive factor in the elections. Even Milner conceded that Schreiner and his party were moderate and not hostile either to the British Empire or to British interests 'but only to the personal domination of Mr Rhodes, to "the Chartered clique" and their corrupt methods of government, "the influence of Mammon in politics" '.[102] The activities of the South African League undoubtedly exacerbated the situation. 'There is too much flag-wagging going on', observed James Rose Innes, 'one would think the British Empire is in danger here'.[103]

When the results of the Cape elections were declared in September, Schreiner's South African Party held a majority of two and, after carrying a vote of no confidence in Sprigg's ministry, Schreiner formed a moderate government, supported by the Afrikaner Bond, in which there were only two members of the Bond in the Cabinet. Milner conceded that it was a government of 'compromise and conciliation', consisting of individuals of ability and integrity who were neither reactionary nor anti-British.[104] It promptly passed a long-pending redistribution measure, which added eighteen new seats to the Cape Assembly. This might have been expected to favour the opposition, but the government did so well in the elections to fill them that it substantially increased its majority. Henceforth, the Schreiner ministry in the Cape Colony was secure, and Milner would have to work with it. This was a prospect which he did not relish and came to regard with mounting irritation. Schreiner, like the majority of Cape Afrikaners, regarded himself as 'a loyal colonist' and subject of Queen Victoria, but he was also determined to 'respect and maintain the right of the free republics to work out their own destiny' and would oppose any resort to war by Britain against them.[105] He regarded his ministry as 'truly South African' and was to work actively but ultimately unsuccessfully as a conciliator in the mounting conflict between Britain and the Transvaal government during 1898–9.[106]

NOTES

1. See Sir Edward Grey to Milner, 9 April 1897, in C. Headlam, ed., *The Milner Papers* 2 vols (London 1931/1933), 1, p. 32.
2. J. Marlowe, *Milner* (London, 1976), p. 8.
3. Milner, *The Nation and the Empire* (London, 1913), Introduction; see also Marlowe, *Milner*, pp. 4–8.
4. E. Stokes, 'Milnerism', *HJ* V, 1 (1962), p. 48.
5. Milner to Chamberlain, 3 February 1897, JC 10/9/1.
6. Marlowe, *Milner*, p. 15.
7. Ibid., p. 49.
8. Milner to Sir George Parkin, 28 April 1897, in Headlam, ed., *The Milner Papers*, 1, p. 42.
9. Ibid., p. 52.
10. Milner's speech at the Cafe Monico, 27 March 1897, in ibid., p. 35.
11. J. Buchan, *Memory Hold the Door* (London,1940), pp. 102, 105.
12. Milner Diary, 16 December 1881, cited in Marlowe, *Milner*, p. 10.
13. Marlowe, *Milner*, ch. 1.
14. Ibid., p. 18.

15. A. N. Porter, 'Sir Alfred Milner and the Press, 1897–1899', *HJ* 16, 2 (1973), pp. 323–39.

16. Harcourt to Chamberlain, 29 August 1897, cited in H. W. McCready, 'Sir Alfred Milner, the Liberal Party and the Boer War', *CJH* 11, 1 (March 1967), p. 15.

17. 'Our Rights and Obligations in South Africa', speech at the Cafe Monico, 27 March 1897, printed in C. Boyd, ed., *Mr. Chamberlain's Speeches* 2 vols (London, 1914), 2, pp. 220–5.

18. Milner to Selborne, 20 March 1897, in Headlam, ed., *The Milner Papers*, 1, p. 38.

19. Chamberlain to Milner, 16 March 1898, summarizing the position when Milner had left England for South Africa, in ibid., p. 227.

20. Sir Michael Hicks Beach to Milner, 22 March 1897, in ibid., p. 33.

21. Selborne to Conyngham Greene, 9 April 1897, in D. G. Boyce, ed., *The Crisis of British Power: The Imperial and Naval Papers of the Second Earl of Selborne, 1895–1910* (London, 1990), p. 48.

22. Selborne to Milner, 29 April 1897, in ibid., p. 50.

23. Milner to Selborne, 2 August 1897, SeP MS 11.

24. British Cabinet Memorandum of 10 November, 1896, cited in J. L. Garvin and J. Amery, *Life of Joseph Chamberlain* 6 vols (London 1932–69), 3, p. 139.

25. Milner to Selborne, 20 April 1897, in Headlam, ed., *The Milner Papers*, 1, pp. 40–1.

26. Ibid., p. 41.

27. Milner to Chamberlain, 11 May 1897, in Garvin, *Life of Chamberlain,* 3, p. 350.

28. Chamberlain to Salisbury, 19 April 1897, JC 11/30/78.

29. J. S. Marais, *The Fall of Kruger's Republic* (Oxford, 1961), pp. 134–5.

30. Milner to Selborne, 16 June 1897, in Headlam, ed., *The Milner Papers*, 1, p. 70; Milner to Chamberlain, 5 October 1897, p. 121.

31. Chamberlain's report on the meeting, 15 May 1897, CO 537/133, in R. H. Wilde, *Joseph Chamberlain and the South African Republic 1895–1899.* Archives Yearbook for South African History 1956 Part 1 (Pretoria, 1956), p. 67.

32. Ibid., p. 68.

33. Note by Chamberlain in CO 537/132 No. 323, in ibid., p. 69.

34. For Smuts see W. K. Hancock, *Smuts* 2 vols (Cambridge, 1962, 1968); K. Ingham, *Jan Christian Smuts* (London, 1986).

35. Printed in full in W. K. Hancock and J. van der Poel, eds, *Selections from the Smuts Papers* 7 vols (Cambridge, 1966–73), 1, pp. 155–85.

36. See n.17, p. 424 below.

37. Smuts Papers. Unpublished notes for a speech, October 1946.

38. S. J. P. Kruger, *The Memoirs of Paul Kruger as told by himself* 2 vols (London, 1902), 2, p. 299.

39. Marais, *The Fall of Kruger's Republic*, p. 140, citing a Memorandum of 11 February 1896.

40. A full transcription of Sir Henry de Villiers's notes of the meeting in

March 1897 was later published in *The Cape Times*, 12 February 1898, from which all quotations are taken.

41. C. van Onselen, 'Reactions to Rinderpest in South Africa 1896–7', *JAH* XIII, 3 (1972), p. 474.

42. C. van Onselen, *Studies in the Social and Economic History of the Witwatersrand 1886–1914* 2 vols (Harlow, 1982), 2, ch. 3.

43. Marais, *The Fall of Kruger's Republic*, pp. 136–7.

44. Alan Jeeves, 'Aftermath of rebellion – the Randlords and Kruger's republic after the Jameson Raid', *SAHJ* 10 (1978), p. 103.

45. C. T. Gordon, *The Growth of Boer Opposition to Kruger 1890–1895* (Oxford, 1970), ch. 9.

46. Milner to Chamberlain, 29 August 1897, in Headlam, ed., *The Milner Papers*, 1, p. 89.

47. T. R. H. Davenport, *South Africa: a Modern History* (London, 1991), p. 85.

48. Jeeves, 'Aftermath of rebellion', p. 104.

49. D. A. Etheredge, 'The early history of the Chamber of Mines, Johannesburg, 1887–1897', unpublished M.A. thesis, University of the Witwatersrand, 1949, ch. 7.

50. A. Jeeves, 'The Rand Capitalists and the Coming of the South African War 1896–1899', *Canadian Historical Association Papers*, 1973, p. 71.

51. Patrick Harries, 'Capital, state, and labour on the 19th century Witwatersrand: a reassessment', *SAHJ* 18 (1986), pp. 42–5.

52. Alan Jeeves, *Migrant Labour in South Africa's Mining Economy 1890–1920* (Johannesburg, 1985), Part 1.

53. Jeeves, 'Aftermath of rebellion', p. 106.

54. Evidence from the Barlow Rand Archives (H. Eckstein & Co. Papers), BRA HE. See also Jeeves, 'Aftermath of rebellion', pp. 110–12 and, more fully, Part 2 of his Ph.D. thesis, 'The Rand Capitalists and Transvaal Politics 1892–1899', Queens University, Kingston, Ontario, Canada, 1971; P. FitzPatrick, *The Transvaal from Within* (London, 1899), pp. 303–12; A. H. Duminy and W. R. Guest, eds, *FitzPatrick: South African Politician: Selected Papers 1888–1906* (Johannesburg, 1976), pp. 99–111. The Witwatersrand Chamber of Mines published the *Evidence and Report of the Industrial Commission of Enquiry* in English (1897) and all quotations etc. are from this version.

55. Milner to Conyngham Greene, 12 August 1897, in Headlam, ed., *The Milner Papers*, 1, p. 82.

56. P. FitzPatrick to J. Wernher, 7 June 1897, in Duminy and Guest, eds, *FitzPatrick*, p. 107.

57. Gordon, *Growth of Boer Opposition*, p. 46.

58. Ibid., p. 56.

59. FitzPatrick, *The Transvaal from Within*, p. 325; see also Duminy and Guest, eds, *FitzPatrick*, pp. 116–20.

60. P. FitzPatrick to Julius Wernher, 21 June and 23 October 1897, BRA HE 140.

61. P. FitzPatrick to O. Beit, 23 August 1897, in Duminy and Guest, eds, *FitzPatrick* p. 110.

62. Richard Mendelsohn, *Sammy Marks, 'The Uncrowned King of the Transvaal'* (Cape Town, 1991), pp. 98–9.
63. Jeeves, 'Aftermath of rebellion', pp. 113–14.
64. Harald Rosenbach, *Das Deutsche Reich, Grossbritannien und der Transvaal (1896–1902)* (Göttingen, 1993); T. J. Noer, *Briton, Boer and Yankee: the U.S.A. and South Africa 1870–1914* (Kent State University Press, 1978).
65. Jeeves, 'Aftermath of rebellion', p. 112; this important point is further developed in the same author's unpublished Ph.D. thesis, 'The Rand capitalists', especially Part 2.
66. See Mendelsohn, *Sammy Marks*.
67. J. Chamberlain to Lionel Phillips, 1 January 1897, printed in E. Drus, 'Select documents from the Chamberlain Papers concerning Anglo-Transvaal relations 1896–1899', *BIHR* 27 (1954), p. 165.
68. Milner to Chamberlain, 9 March 1898, CO 537/134.
69. Minute by Selborne on ibid. See also J. J. Van Helten, 'German capital, the Netherlands Railway Company and the political economy of the Transvaal 1886–1900', *JAH* XIX, 3 (1978), pp. 384–7.
70. Milner to Selborne, 29 December 1897, in Headlam, ed., *The Milner Papers*, 1, p. 138.
71. Milner to G. Fiddes, 2 November 1897, in ibid., p. 129.
72. Milner to Selborne, 29 December 1897, in ibid., p.138.
73. Wilde, *Joseph Chamberlain*, p. 73.
74. Milner to Chamberlain, 15 May 1897, in Headlam, ed., *The Milner Papers*, 1, p. 68.
75. See C.9507, 'Correspondence regarding the status of the South African Republic', August 1899; I have also used material in the Transvaal Archives, Pretoria, British Agent's file BA 14, in this section.
76. J. C. Smuts, article published in *Ons Land*, 19 March 1896, and reprinted in Hancock and van der Poel, eds, *Selections Smuts Papers*, 1, pp. 109–12.
77. deVP, File 7, Box R, 'Memoirs'; also his letter to Milner of 6 October 1899, printed in E. Walker, *Lord de Villiers and his Times* (London, 1925), p. 361, and fn. 3 on p. 180.
78. Lord Derby to Messrs Kruger, Du Toit and Smit, 15 February 1884, reprinted in D. M. Schreuder, *Gladstone and Kruger* (London, 1969), App. 2.
79. Speech by Lord Derby, *Hansard*, House of Lords, Third Series, vol. cclxxxvi, col. 7, 18 March 1884.
80. Note by E. Fairfield, 30 December 1889, CO 417/35.
81. Buxton, Speech in the House of Commons, *Hansard*, Fourth Series, vol. xxvi, col. 686.
82. Enclosure (3 July 1894) in British High Commissioner to British Agent in Pretoria, 9 August 1894, Transvaal Government Archives, BA 14.
83. *Hansard*, Fourth Series, vol. xxvi, col. 685, 2 July 1894.
84. A. N. Porter, *The Origins of the South African War, Joseph Chamberlain and the Diplomacy of Imperialism 1895–1899* (Manchester, 1980), p.86, citing Salisbury to Lascelles, 7 January 1896.

85. Speech in the House of Lords, 17 March 1884, *Hansard,* House of Lords, Third Series, vol. cclxxxvi, col. 7.
86. Porter, *Origins*, p. 125.
87. Chamberlain, Minute, 9 January 1897, CO 417/185.
88. Selborne to Milner, 11 November 1897, in Headlam, ed., *The Milner Papers*, 1, p. 123.
89. Milner to Chamberlain, 29 August 1897, in ibid., p. 88.
90. The term 'subordinate state' was used by the Lord Chancellor, Lord Halsbury, in a Memorandum on the legal aspect to Chamberlain on 22 May 1897. See Garvin, *Life of Chamberlain*, 3, p. 352.
91. The full text of the 'suzerainty despatch' was printed as a Blue Book and presented to the British parliament on 8 February 1898 in C.8721, pp. 18–22. There is a discussion of the issues in Marais, *The Fall of Kruger's Republic*, pp. 197–200.
92. Leyds to Milner, 16 April 1898, CO 417/244.
93. Chamberlain to Acting High Commissioner, 15 December 1898, in C.9507 (1899).
94. Milner to Chamberlain, 11 May 1897, JC 10/9/3.
95. See Chamberlain to Milner, 16 March 1898; Selborne to Milner, 22 March 1898; Milner to Selborne, 9 May 1898, all in ibid., 1, pp. 227–32.
96. Chamberlain to Milner, 13 July 1899, in C.9507.
97. State President to the British High Commissioner, 25 February 1896, C.8063, pp. 12–14.
98. Marais, *The Fall of Kruger's Republic*, pp. 200–1.
99. P. FitzPatrick to J. Wernher, 8 November 1897, printed in Duminy and Guest, eds, *FitzPatrick* p. 133.
100. P. FitzPatrick to J. Wernher, 13 December 1897, in ibid., p. 138.
101. Greene to Milner, 10 December 1897, in Marais, *The Fall of Kruger's Republic*, p. 201.
102. Milner to Chamberlain, 19 October 1898, in Headlam, ed., *The Milner Papers*, 1, p. 282.
103. J. Rose Innes, *Autobiography*, ed. B. A. Tindall (Cape Town, 1949), p. 170.
104. Milner to Chamberlain, 19 October 1898, in Headlam, ed., *The Milner Papers*, 1, p. 282.
105. W. P. Schreiner to Mrs Hogewoning (Pretoria), 9 December 1898, ScP, Cape Town, MS 27, Letter Book for 1898.
106. See E. van Heyningen, *The Relations between Sir Alfred Milner and W. P. Schreiner's Ministry 1898–1900*, M.A. thesis, University of Cape Town, 1971, published in Archives Yearbook for South African History (Pretoria, 1976); also T. R. H. Davenport, *The Afrikaner Bond* (Oxford, 1966), ch. 10.

CHAPTER SIX

Working up to a Crisis (1898–9)

MILNER'S IMPATIENCE

The re-election of Paul Kruger as President of the South African Republic for a fourth term, in February 1898, had a pronounced effect on Milner's thinking with regard to the future. For the first nine months after his arrival in South Africa, he had been content to play 'the waiting game' which had been agreed between himself and Chamberlain before he left England.[1] Now, Milner became convinced that Kruger was entrenched; that hopes for the emergence of a 'progressive bloc' in Transvaal politics, led by 'liberal' Afrikaners and supported by commercial interests and the mining industry, were illusory. Both Joubert and Schalk Burger had proved to be broken reeds. The mining industry, disillusioned by the failure of Kruger's government to implement the recommendations of its own Industrial Commission in 1897, felt that Kruger was becoming 'more and more absolute' and was getting what he wanted through 'a subservient Volksraad' and uniting his Afrikaner electorate behind him on the claim that the independence of the state was in danger.[2] A new note of impatience enters Milner's correspondence in February 1898. He told Conyngham Greene that the perpetual 'snarling' he was obliged to do at Kruger's government 'bores me fearfully. It is perfectly useless and undignified. . . . But while I do as little as possible of this useless protesting, complaining, reminding business, I still try to do that minimum as well as ever I can, and to take the farce as seriously as I can – not with any immediate hope of results – but with a view to the great day of reckoning'.[3] On 23 February, Milner sent a long despatch to Chamberlain – which he thought, 'if things get worse, it may be useful some day to publish'.[4] At the same time, he sent a private letter in which he warned Chamberlain that 'after a few months' respite, we are once more on the verge of serious trouble with the Boers' and declared that his purpose in writing was 'simply to put before you, with the greatest frankness, the situation as I now see it'. Milner began by asserting that:

> There is no way out of the political troubles of S. Africa except reform in the Transvaal or war. And at present the chances of reform in the Transvaal are worse than ever. The Boers quarrel bitterly amongst themselves, but it is about jobs and contracts, not politics! In their determination to keep all power in their own hands and to use it with a total disregard of the interests of the unenfranchised, as well as their own hatred and suspicion of Great Britain, the vast majority of them are firmly united. . . . Kruger has returned to power, more autocratic and more reactionary than ever. . . . He has immense resources of money and any amount of ammunitions of war, to which he is constantly adding. Politically, he has strengthened his hold on the Orange Free State, and the Colonial Afrikanders continue to do obeisance before him. . . .
> *Looking at the question from a purely S. African point of view*, I should be inclined to work up to a crisis, not indeed by looking about for causes of complaint or making a fuss about trifles, but by steadily and inflexibly pressing for the redress of substantial wrongs and injustices. It would not be difficult thus to work up an extremely strong *cumulative case*. But the drawback to this policy is that it puts the choice of the time, when we may be forced to take strong aggressive action, out of our hands. As long as we remonstrate about this, that, or the other in a perfunctory sort of way, we can, if we get unsatisfactory answers, or no answers, afford to assume a manner of indifference. But if we are going to remonstrate incisively, to insist on being answered promptly and unevasively – in short to show that we mean business – then we cannot disregard either a persistent silence or a flat refusal. It means that we shall have to fight, and to fight *more or less* at a moment chosen by the other side, who very likely may not realize what they are doing. The question which line to take cannot therefore be settled exclusively with reference to S. Africa. *It depends on the Imperial outlook as a whole*. It is that which must determine, whether we are to be passive here . . . or whether we are to pursue an active policy, never aggressive indeed, but vigilant and insistent on all our rights, not only treaty rights but the inherent rights of every nation to protect its subjects against injury by foreigners. The latter policy may, *and probably will*, require a much larger army, and will require it at a time which can only be approximately foreseen.[5]

Milner went on to question the policy which had been adopted hitherto, that of dealing with 'single questions singly' and of being prepared to 'put up with anything that is not a breach of the [London] Convention'. Since this offered a prospect of endless wrangling between the British and Transvaal governments about their different interpretations of the Conventions between them, and since Britain refused to accept arbitration about this, then, if Britain was determined to get her interpretation accepted, this 'in itself involves an active policy'.

> As, therefore, it will be necessary to take a strong line with them, if we determine even to make the Conventions respected, I see less objection to taking up in addition strong popular points, not falling under the Conventions, such as the independence of the Bench, or the expulsion of Aliens on frivolous pretexts, more particularly as the points which arise under the Conventions are very apt to be thin and technical. If, on the other hand, the more passive policy appears *for the present* the right one, then, of course, there is no use embarrassing ourselves by taking up anything, which we are not actually driven to.

Milner was growing impatient with the policy of perpetual appeal to the Articles of 'that wretched old instrument', the London Convention, and doubted whether this would ever provide an adequate or popular basis for challenging Kruger's government and extracting reforms. After nine months in South Africa, he was now convinced that Kruger would only bow to force and that this would require a more active policy from Britain backed up by a readiness to threaten war. Milner had consistently argued that Britain should not make demands on the Transvaal government which it was not prepared to extract, if necessary, by force. The possibility that, sooner or later, this might result in war had therefore always been acknowledged. But Kruger's actions in the sequence of crises since the Drifts Crisis of 1895 encouraged the belief that, faced with a resolute British government, he would capitulate and back down. Like Conyngham Greene, Milner believed that the strengthening of the British military and naval presence in South Africa had had a direct bearing on Kruger's 'climb down' during the April crisis of 1897 and that the presence of British troops remained 'our best guarantee against having to use them. The Boers are accustomed to deal forcibly with those whom they know to be weaker than themselves, and this is the line of treatment which they can best understand'.[6]

By early 1898, therefore, Milner had shifted away from conciliation towards a policy of confrontation. As he wrote to his close friend, Philip Gell, 'I *will* have submission or a fight – no compromise this time – although I know they will damn me at home for not muddling on in an indecisive fashion. But the general state of things here doesn't permit of a Fabian policy in this case. We must assert ourselves'.[7] If confronted, did Milner believe that Kruger's government would capitulate or fight? Certainly, he believed that the best chance for capitulation lay in the clear readiness of Britain to go to war if her demands were not met. But it is doubtful if Milner now felt confident that capitulation would result. At times, when writing to correspondents whom he knew hoped that war could be avoided, he would emphasize the likelihood that a last-minute capitulation would result from a policy of confrontation. From 1898 onwards, however, he accepted that war was likely if Britain did adopt a more 'active policy' towards the Transvaal and at no time is he to be found expressing the view that a war should be avoided. Since he mistakenly believed that if it came to war this would be a short affair, resulting in a rapid British victory and the annexation of the Transvaal as a British colony, Milner came to regard a resort to war as an acceptable and probably inevitable means by which Britain would be able to achieve her larger ends in South Africa.[8]

One of Kruger's first acts after his re-election was to dismiss the Chief Justice of the Transvaal, Kotze. Kotze himself had provoked this by writing to the President to say that, as the draft of the promised revision of the Constitution had not been published, he was going to reassert the testing right. Kruger refused to accept this new and far-reaching claim for the judiciary and exercised the right which had been granted to him by the Volksraad in February 1897, to dismiss anyone who claimed it. Milner promptly announced in a despatch to Chamberlain, that a fatal blow had been struck at the independence of the Transvaal judiciary and that Kruger's action was an 'evil augury' for the peaceful settlement of the points at issue between the British and Transvaal governments. Certainly, the judiciary was weakened by the clash between Kotze and Kruger, but some of Kotze's fellow-judges felt that his action had been deliberately provocative and fuelled by personal motives. Although the Johannesburg Bar did protest, Kotze then alienated even some of those who had initially supported him by declaring that he would appeal 'to the Suzerain Power', i.e. the British government.

Milner, who declared that his sympathy for Kotze was 'absolute', thought that the reaction to Kotze's dismissal 'has been disappointing. I thought it would have attracted more attention and excited more indignation throughout South Africa'. But he doubted whether Chamberlain would take up the case and felt that he could not advise him to do so because 'our *rushing in*' might give the impression that Kotze's action had been 'a put-up job'.[9] Nonetheless, Milner made the most of the matter, receiving and advising Kotze when he came to

Cape Town, and encouraging Percy FitzPatrick – whom he now met for the first time – to engineer a public demonstration in support of Kotze amongst Uitlanders on the Rand.[10] Although he doubted whether Britain had any clear entitlement to intervene in the matter, Milner suggested to Chamberlain that 'the immense British interests in the Transvaal and our responsibility for South Africa generally would justify our intervention to prevent acts of flagrant injustice and tyranny' by Kruger's 'despotic oligarchy'.[11]

Milner's wish for a more 'active policy' towards the Transvaal and his championship of Chief Justice Kotze's case as part of that drew a firm and immediate riposte from Chamberlain, who telegraphed:

> The principal object of H.M. Government in S. Africa at present is peace. Nothing but a most flagrant offence would justify the use of force. I do not believe that Kotze can properly claim redress under Convention and, if not, his arrest, however arbitrary, would not be sufficient ground for intervention as he is not a British subject.[12]

A fuller and more telling letter followed from Lord Selborne, the Under-Secretary of State at the Colonial Office, who saw it as his task to set out before Milner 'in the clearest manner, the lines on which we should go' with regard to British policy towards the Transvaal.[13] Selborne began by repeating that

> Peace is undoubtedly the first interest to South Africa, but not peace at any price. Our object is the future combination of South Africa under the aegis of the Union Jack, and I think we all feel that, if by the evolution of events this combination can be achieved without a rupture, or war, of any sort between the two white races in South Africa, it will have a more durable and valuable result than it would have if the same result were achieved by means of war. At the same time it is clear that if we refused war under certain conditions we should invariably forfeit the result altogether, and whether there will be war or not depends much more on the Government of the South African Republic than upon us. . . . [War is to be avoided if] it can be done safely, but if war is to come what are the conditions under which we must manoeuvre for it to come. It must command the practically unanimous consent of the British in South Africa – it must conquer the moral assent of as large a proportion as possible of our own Dutch in South Africa, and the action must be endorsed by the practically unanimous assent of public opinion at home.

Selborne went on to make a clear distinction between words and deeds. 'Short of a formal and definite denunciation of the Conventions by the South African Republic, we must not mind what they say. Doubtless they will say some very insolent and irritating things, but we must ignore them. . . . Any action in clear contravention of the Conventions which on our request they refuse to annul or to redress', however, must 'be treated as a *casus belli*'. Selborne then made three acute predictions. The first was that, unless Britain became engaged in a war with one of the great powers which presented the Transvaal with an opportunity to declare her independence, 'Messrs Kruger and Company will confine themselves strictly to irritating language'. The second was that 'this may include a repudiation of our assertion that the suzerainty of Her Majesty still exists'. In this case, Selborne's inclination would be 'to tell them that words are of no consequence; if they transform their words into acts the consequences will be immediate'. His third prediction concerned the likely outcome of the Kotze case. In this, Selborne declared that he differed sharply from Milner. He considered that Kotze had mismanaged his case and that the British government had nothing to do with the matter: 'Kotze is not a British subject; he is a Boer burgher pure and simple. Under what conceivable interpretation of the Convention have we the right or the duty to protect a burgher of the South African Republic from an injustice of his own Government?' Further, Kotze had not yet appealed to the British government, he had simply announced his intention of doing so. The unanimous disapproval which this had incurred amongst his compatriots would persuade him to drop the idea. Kruger was therefore unlikely to arrest him and, even if he did so and Kotze then did appeal to the British government, as the suzerain power, Britain would gain a great deal of approval from her Afrikaner subjects in the Cape and elsewhere if she showed the impartiality with which she interpreted the London Convention by declaring that this was an internal matter for the Transvaal government. Selborne concluded by reminding Milner that, in its policy towards the Transvaal, what Britain was engaged in was 'a waiting game', which required 'immense self-control', and that nothing had yet occurred to change this.

Chamberlain too followed up his telegram with a confidential letter in which he explained why he saw no reason to alter the policy which had been agreed before Milner left England a year previously. The same considerations still held and he felt that 'we must endure a great deal rather than provoke a conflict'. Imperial intervention would be greatly resented by many British subjects in the Cape Colony, as well as in Britain itself, who did not consider the grievances at issue 'sufficient to constitute a *casus belli*'. Kruger's government 'must be clearly in the wrong on some serious question before we can interfere'. Chamberlain was prepared 'to take scant notice' of differences over the interpretation of suzerainty, though he would maintain his own interpretation. On other issues, so long as the Articles of the London Convention were not infringed, he was against making representations 'too categorically' and thought these might be better done verbally, via Conyngham Greene, than formally in despatches. These issues aroused little general support either in Britain or South Africa and could 'be made emphatic at a later time if we desire it and included in an ultimatum summing up all our case; but for the present we must "suffer fools gladly" '. In terms of 'the general Imperial outlook', Chamberlain told Milner that there were very strong additional reasons 'in favour of a policy of reserve and delay':

> We have on hand difficulties of the most serious character with France, Russia, and Germany. We are engaged in an important expedition in the Soudan, and it is uncertain as yet whether the war on the north-west frontier of India has been finally concluded. We may emerge from all these troubles without a war, but I cannot conceal from myself that the prospect is more gloomy than it has ever been in my recollection.

Should Britain become embroiled in a war elsewhere, Chamberlain acknowledged that the Boers might take advantage of this to declare their independence, but he did not fear this. 'It would be a small addition to more serious troubles, and would give us an opportunity to settle the South African question once for all.' For the present, Chamberlain wished to emphasize the fact that 'our greatest interest in South Africa is peace, and that all our policy must be directed to this object'.[14]

Milner had no choice but to obey orders. He therefore replied:

> You may rely on me not to do anything to render the situation more acute. It is exceedingly difficult in view of the aggressive and insolent temper of the Transvaal to pass the time without a quarrel and yet without too conspicuously eating humble pie. Still, I hope we may manage, by a judicious combination of caution and bluff, to worry on without discredit until we are in a better position to "round" upon them. . . . When we are once more in quieter waters it will be for Her Majesty's Government to consider whether we ought to acquiesce permanently in the situation of having a strong and bitter enemy for ever seated on our flank, only waiting for the occasion of our being definitely involved elsewhere in order to fly at our throats. For the present time there is no more to be said on that subject. I know where I am and shall act accordingly.[15]

These exchanges of February–March 1898 reveal that a gap had opened up between Milner and the Colonial Office over British policy towards the Transvaal. Since this was to remain a feature of the situation right through to the outbreak of war, eighteen months later, it requires further examination at this time during 1898 when it first appeared. The matter was addressed in a further exchange of letters between Milner and Selborne, his closest confidant in the Colonial Office.

Milner acknowledged to Selborne that they were not quite in accord on the Kotze case, but then focused his attention on the larger issue of the general policy to be followed towards Kruger's government.[16] Here, Milner expressed his impatience with the policy of perpetual pin-pricks over 'the technicalities of these wretched treaties' and his concern that the Colonial Office was in danger of 'losing sight of the essentials of South African policy'. Rather, argued Milner, 'in our dealings with the South African Republic I say let us look to the big facts, all of them internal Transvaal questions, with which *in theory* we have nothing to do, and do not think we can disregard them because they may not be "breaches of the Convention". . . . What I am driving at', Milner continued, 'is our concern with the Transvaal apart from all Conventions, which is far more important than our rights under these miserable documents'. Milner saw little likelihood of any open denunciation by Kruger of a Convention 'when it is so easy to interpret it away and then tell us, if we don't like the interpretation, to call in an arbitrator'. He also considered that a 'breach of the Convention is, as likely as not, to be some trumpery thing which nobody cares about, and which would excite absolutely no sympathy either in S. Africa or elsewhere'. Worse, he feared that the British government's concentration on its rights – 'mostly worthless' – under the Conventions was 'becoming a hindrance' and 'precluding us from that interest – and in the last resort – interference in the internal affairs of the Transvaal which by the nature of things every state has in the internal affairs of its neighbours, when they directly and vitally affect its own internal affairs'. Warming to his theme, Milner focused on the key role played by the Transvaal in the situation in South Africa:

All its political troubles, which are of serious moment – yes, *all* have their origin in the state of affairs in the South African Republic. That the South African Republic should call the Queen 'suzerain' is a small matter. That it should treat its Uitlander population with justice, its natives with humanity, that its administration should be decently honest, its Courts decently competent and independent – these things are essential to the peace of British South Africa. Unless things improve in these respects –

and at present the tendency is not to improvement, but the other way – the bitterness of feeling between different sections of our own subjects, *for which there is no local cause*, will not abate, nor will the relations of the [Cape] Colony to the Mother Country or its position in the Empire be less critical and unsatisfactory, and less a cause of weakness than they are today.

Finally, the issues raised by the Kotze case, Milner argued, were big issues – which did not just concern 'capitalists' and in which all parts of the population had an equal interest since they involved the independence of the courts from the caprice of the government. If Britain had taken up the matter it would have had 'as much S. African sympathy, and I believe as much European sympathy, as we are ever likely to get'. Whilst he accepted that there were 'good and sufficient reasons' why the British government could not act at present, this was the sort of big issue – 'a thing worth fighting for' – over which, Britain might some day take a stand. 'You will see from all this that my opinions have been somewhat modified by a year of S. Africa', Milner told Selborne.

While I still, by personal temperament, sympathize with, and fully appreciate the arguments for a policy of patience, and while, such being my orders, I shall loyally carry it out, I am less hopeful than I was of an ultimate solution on these lines. Two wholly antagonistic systems – a mediaeval race oligarchy, and a modern industrial state, recognizing no difference of status between various white races – cannot permanently live side by side in what is after all *one country*. The race-oligarchy has got to go, and I see no signs of its removing itself. . . . The whole political power in the Transvaal is in the hands of the Boer oligarchy – armed to the teeth. And there is no *reform party* among that oligarchy. The delusion, under which most of us, including myself, laboured on that point, has been finally dispelled by the election and by the desertion of Kotze by even the most progressive of his fellow-burghers. The Boers may quarrel bitterly among themselves, but it only needs the mention of any genuine reform, the suggestion that they should share their profitable monopoly of power with any others, to unite them against such a dangerous innovation. And in that attitude they are upheld, both by the O[range] F[ree] S[tate] and by the whole force of the Dutch party in the [Cape] Colony. . . . To hope that we shall ever have the sympathy of any considerable number of our Dutch subjects in removing it [Kruger's race-oligarchy] – a Dutch monopoly – by force, seems to me idle. The Dutch may become as loyal as French Canadians – but *after*, not *before* the principle of equality is established all round. In the fight for its establishment, if it comes to a fight, we shall have to rely on British forces alone. And whether we shall have the whole of British S. Africa enthusiastically on our side, depends, as it seems to me, on our previous policy being a sufficiently broad one, and on letting everybody understand that, whatever the immediate occasion of the quarrel, our real cause is not a phrase, or a technicality, but the establishment of a good system of government – pure justice and equal citizenship – in the Transvaal.[17]

Selborne pondered the contents of Milner's 'most interesting and important letter' and left behind, in his papers, a series of notes, dated June 1898, which he seems to have jotted down as an *aide-memoire* before composing his reply.[18] In these notes, Selborne gave a number of reasons why, unlike Milner, he still considered that time was likely to work in Britain's favour in South Africa. Included in the list were the continuing growth of Uitlander immigration into the Transvaal; the increasing political representation of the towns in the Cape Colony – which 'will soon put power in the hands of the English rather than the Dutch party'; the hope that the influence of the Orange Free State government would strengthen 'moderate Hollander' opinion in the Transvaal; and the probability that Kruger's death 'will make a great difference'. Selborne also noted why, in his view, it would 'not be a good thing for the Imperial Government to force the pace' and included here 'Lord Rosemead's [i.e. Sir Hercules Robinson's] opinion that if we attack the S.A.R. and O.F.S. they will, after being defeated, have to be held down for a generation'; and the fact that Milner 'has a jingo bias'. Selborne also discussed the matter 'several times' with Chamberlain.

In his reply to Milner, on 28 June, Selborne acknowledged that 'a divergence' seemed to exist between Milner's views and those of the Colonial Office, but he sought to diminish it by contrasting a close agreement on the general principles outlined by Milner with a difference of opinion about 'an immediate application of those principles, in which we hesitate to follow you'. In particular, the Colonial Office did not agree with Milner that the Kotze case presented the British government with an 'opportunity' to intervene in a situation which was 'already ripe for interference'. On Milner's general propositions, however, Selborne recorded close agreement. It was true that the Conventions 'are by no means of great value, that the cases likely to arise under them are niggling ones, bad points d'appui for a popular war'. It was also true that the existence of the Conventions 'cannot deprive us of grounds of interference which exist in the nature of things and arise from our paramount interests in South Africa; that on that broader basis we are more likely to find strong and valid grounds of interference than on the narrow basis of the Conventions; and that there is a danger that by fixing its eyes too rigidly on the Conventions the Colonial Office may lose sight of bigger questions and broader issues'. Again, it was probably true 'that Dutch opinion will be against us; and that British public opinion in South Africa will enthusiastically follow if we lead, unless we make it lose faith in our power to lead by persistently refusing to lead'. But, noted Selborne, 'we could not interfere in the Transvaal except where, under exactly similar circumstances, we should interfere in the OFS or in Portuguese South East Africa' without leaving 'a vast body of public opinion here in the U.K. unconvinced of the justice of our cause. . . . Above and before and beyond all other considerations', emphasized Selborne, 'we must carry with us the force of an almost unanimous public opinion at home in our dealings with the Transvaal; and no such force or anything like it would be at our backs now in support of the general case against the South African Republic, as it stands at present'.[19]

Milner had pressed for a shift from a 'passive' to a more 'active' policy towards the Transvaal, and he had been rebuffed. He had also failed, as he had half-expected, to get Kotze's case taken up by the British government. He had no option but to accept the line of policy laid down by Chamberlain, and he understood the wider considerations which had to be taken into account by the Colonial Office. But this exchange of views reveals the shift which had taken place with regard to Milner's assessment of the situation since August 1897.[20] This change was marked by a greater readiness on Milner's part to resort to a policy of confrontation with Kruger's government which could be expected to result either in a capitulation or a resort to war. Milner undoubtedly felt that the Kotze case marked the overthrow of the independence of the judiciary in Kruger's republic; but it also presented itself as a possible opportunity for 'working up to a crisis' on a general issue which he mistakenly anticipated would attract widespread support both in Britain and South Africa. In the event, Milner was proved wrong, Kruger did not arrest Kotze, and Kotze did not carry out his threat to appeal to 'the suzerain power'. Selborne was proved right in his predictions and Chamberlain and Selborne had firmly applied the brake to Milner's tendency to run ahead of the Colonial Office in his determination to challenge Kruger's government. 'It is provoking to think how easily everything might be put straight if the authorities at Pretoria would behave with a . . . "sweet reasonableness"', Chamberlain commented 'Nothing, as you know, is further from our wishes than any further conflict, and the changes that would satisfy us absolutely are not such as to involve any sacrifice on the part of the South African Republic.'[21]

A MANIFESTO AT GRAAFF–REINET

Meanwhile, at the historic town of Graaff-Reinet, a centre of Cape Afrikaner settlement in the Eastern Cape, Milner made a resounding speech, on 3 March 1898, which was received throughout South Africa as a personal manifesto. He went there to open a new branch-line of the railway and, upon arrival, he was unexpectedly presented with an address by the local branch of the Afrikaner Bond in which they protested their loyalty and attachment to the British Empire and indignantly rejected the doubts which had recently been cast upon this by the South African League. This address was delivered (in Dutch) when Milner arrived at the station in the morning and it was not part of the official programme. In brief interludes during a busy day, Milner composed a reply which he then gave as a speech at the banquet in the Market Hall that evening. This was no hurried response, however, but what Milner himself described as 'a very deliberate utterance on my part' which he had been waiting for some weeks for an opportunity to deliver.[22]

In the Cape Colony, the Afrikaner Bond had always showed respect for the British monarch and expressed gratitude for British naval protection as 'the first line of defence' in South Africa; and it had never given any encouragement to Germany or any other foreign power to take an interest in the region. It therefore bitterly resented the allegations of disloyalty which had been made against it. It had, however, sent a telegram congratulating President Kruger on his re-election (but so had the Prime Minister of 'very English' Natal). It had also been not uncritical of the British government's handling of relations with Kruger's republic. This had convinced Milner, and some members of the Colonial Office, that its sympathies were Afrikaner and republican and that it was an organization to be regarded with deep suspicion and distrust. This distorted British view undermined the potential role of the Bond as an intermediary between the British and Transvaal governments and as a force for peace in 1898–9.[23]

In February 1898, Milner had written to the Governor of Natal:

> There has got to be a separation of the sheep from the goats in this sub-continent, by which I don't mean the English and the Dutch, but those who disapprove and are not afraid to show their disapproval of the present dishonest despotism at Pretoria, and those who either admire or truckle to it. There has been a great deal too much secret truckling and the time has come when we should, I think, quietly but firmly force the wobblers to show their colours and not expect us to recognize them as loyal citizens of a free British Community, as long as they give any

countenance to men who trample on freedom and on everything British in a neighbouring state.[24]

In his speech at Graaff-Reinet a fortnight later, Milner told a predominantly Cape Afrikaner audience that he was glad to be assured of their loyalty, but he would have preferred to be able to take that for granted. After outlining the great advances which had been made in the Cape Colony under British rule and the protection of the British navy, and the 'other blessings' which as British citizens they enjoyed under a free system of government, a secure and independent judiciary, and equality of rights and citizenship with other Europeans, Milner declared: 'of course you are loyal. It would be monstrous if you were not'. He then went on to say that, nonetheless, he could not shut his eyes 'to unpleasant facts'. Whilst he believed that 'the great bulk of the population of the [Cape] Colony, Dutch as well as English' were thoroughly loyal, some allowed their sympathy for the Transvaal to lead them to think 'that if they can only impress upon the British Government that in the case of war with the Transvaal it would have a great number of its own subjects at least in sympathy against it, that is the way to prevent such a calamity'. In this, declared Milner, they were totally wrong, for this view rested on the assumption that Britain had 'some occult design on the independence of the Transvaal . . . and that it is seeking causes of quarrel in order to take that independence away'. That assumption, Milner claimed, was 'the exact opposite of the truth'. It was not the aggressiveness of the British government but the 'unprogressiveness, I will not say the retrogressiveness, of the Government of the Transvaal' which kept up 'the spirit of unrest in South Africa'. So great was the suspicion of that government about the intentions of Britain, that it devoted its attention 'to imaginary external dangers, when every impartial observer can see perfectly well that the real dangers which threaten it are internal'. Milner said that he accepted that this suspicion, although 'absolutely groundless', was not unnatural 'after all that has happened'. But it was here that those who wished 'to preserve the South African Republic and to promote good relations between it and the British colonies and Government' had an important role to play in using their influence 'not in confirming the Transvaal in unjustified suspicions, not in encouraging its Government in resistance to all reform, but in inducing it gradually to assimilate its institutions and, what is even more important than institutions, the temper and spirit of its administration to those of the free communities of South Africa, such as this [Cape] Colony or the Orange Free State. That is the direction in which a peaceful way out of these inveterate troubles, which have now plagued this country for more than 30 years, is to be found'.[25]

Milner made this speech with the clear and premeditated intention of giving a warning to those members of the Afrikaner Bond who, whilst enjoying the advantages of British citizenship as Afrikaners in the Cape Colony, were, he claimed, 'for ever adulating the Transvaal, while casting suspicion on the actions and intentions of Her Majesty's Government'. The effect of this was 'to encourage the Transvaal oligarchy in their present policy till it becomes intolerable and ends in war'. Milner felt that there were many Cape Afrikaners, including members of the Bond, who 'though they do not speak out very boldly, are thoroughly disgusted with the recent proceedings of the Transvaal Government, are anxious to live on good and friendly terms with their British neighbours, and deplore the course pursued by the leaders of the Bond. It was to encourage and help these people, even more than to warn the extremists, whom I regard as hopeless, that I spoke as I did'.[26] But the effect of the speech was to antagonize many Cape Afrikaners, who were outraged by the doubts cast on their loyalty, and to provide emotive material which both the South African League and the jingoistic section of the English-language press did not hesitate to exploit. A further attack on the Bond by Rhodes, in an interview in *The Cape Times* on 8 March, added further fuel to the flames. As John X. Merriman remarked, of the outbursts of Milner and Rhodes, 'through both these runs the note of thinly veiled hostility to the Transvaal and the uneasy menace of trouble ahead', and he urged President Steyn, of the Orange Free State, to persevere in his efforts to persuade Kruger to make reforms as 'such a state of affairs cannot last . . . and it will be well if the fall does not sweep away the freedom of all of us'.[27]

Milner's speech at Graaff-Reinet exuded menace and was the first time that the representative of the British government had publicly pointed to the possibility of war with the Transvaal. It had an electrifying effect. The British High Commissioner had come down off the fence and revealed himself in his true colours. Many regarded it as a challenge to all South Africans to choose their side in a forthcoming struggle between Boers and British for supremacy. Kruger told his Executive Council that Milner's attitude reminded him of Sir Bartle Frere and the result of that had been the war of 1880–81.[28] In the Cape Colony, Milner's speech, combined with the re-emergence of Rhodes as the effective force behind the pro-British Progressive Party in the Cape election campaign, intensified the divisions between Boers and British which had opened up in the wake of the Jameson

Raid. Throughout South Africa, the effect of the Graaff-Reinet speech was that Milner came to be regarded as 'the commander-in-chief' of the 'pro-British party'. In the Transvaal, he had presented himself as the natural focus and intermediary for the revived Uitlander political movement in its efforts to involve the British government on its behalf.[29] When forwarding a copy of his Graaff-Reinet speech to the Colonial Office, Milner openly admitted that one of his intentions with regard to 'the British section of the community' had been to give them 'something to cheer them up' whilst, at the same time, he hoped to divide the extremists from the moderates in the Afrikaner Bond.[30]

THE NEW LINK-MAN IN JOHANNESBURG

In February 1898, an important first meeting had also occurred between Milner and Percy FitzPatrick. Although debarred from political activity for three years for his part as Secretary of the Reform Committee at the time of the Jameson Raid, FitzPatrick had been one of very few from that circle to resume his career in Johannesburg. He had taken over Lionel Phillips's old job in charge of intelligence at Wernher, Beit/H. Eckstein & Co. and he had continued working behind the scenes for reforms despite the pessimistic conclusions which he had formed out of his experience with the 1897 Industrial Commission. Whilst on holiday near Cape Town, in February 1898, he cycled over to Milner's residence at Newlands with the object of making contact with the High Commissioner. He was warmly received by Milner who, though committed to a formal dinner engagement, insisted that FitzPatrick remain until they could resume their exchange of views. This they did 'under the oaks' on a warm summer's evening and their talk went on well into the night.

Ever afterwards, FitzPatrick looked back on this meeting as one of the most formative of his life, not just because it marked the beginning of a long friendship but also because he believed that the future of South Africa was affected by what came out of it. The relationship between Milner and FitzPatrick was not between equals. Milner was the charismatic leader-figure, FitzPatrick was the devotee. FitzPatrick was ten years younger and no match for Milner intellectually, but the two men shared closely similar views about South Africa and their projections into the long-term future proved similarly unsound. Both were redoubtable fighters for the lost cause of British supremacy in a South Africa united and transformed into a loyal dominion of the

British Empire. Born and bred in South Africa, FitzPatrick already had a colourful life behind him out of which he had a gift for spinning engaging tales with a fluent pen. His career might be with a major mining company but his preoccupation was with politics, by which he meant white, South African politics.[31] Between 1897 and the outbreak of war in 1899, Percy FitzPatrick was to play a major part in negotiations between the mining industry on the Rand and the Transvaal government. He was also to regard Milner as something of a political mentor. As the vital link-man between the mine-magnates, the Transvaal government, the Uitlanders, and Milner during this period, FitzPatrick's role was to be of considerable importance. No one realized this more than FitzPatrick himself – who left behind him a mass of letters, books, papers and reminiscences which have served to draw attention to himself and to intrigue and confuse historians.

FitzPatrick was something of a maverick figure on the South African scene, a loner in politics who, although an employee of the major mining company on the Rand, cannot just be regarded as the slavish advocate of the interests of a far from monolithic industry. In his political views, he was more influenced by the British imperial ideology which he and Milner shared than by his involvement in gold-mining. The archives of Wernher, Beit/H. Eckstein & Co. reveal that considerable differences of opinion existed amongst the senior management of FitzPatrick's own firm as the political crisis mounted in the Transvaal during 1898–9. The political views of FitzPatrick should not therefore be equated with those of the firm which employed him, let alone with those of the mining industry or the capitalists on the Rand generally. In the historiography of the origins of this war, FitzPatrick's activities and papers have been too readily used as a basis upon which grand, Hobsonian hypotheses have been constructed about the role of 'the mining industry' and 'the capitalists' in the resort to war. There has been a slipshod tendency to generalize from the particular.[32]

FitzPatrick's first meeting with Milner, in February 1898, occurred at a crucial time when, as we have seen, Milner's views with regard to the situation in the Transvaal were undergoing a marked change. FitzPatrick made extensive notes of their conversation immediately afterwards, and these were later used in three different accounts by him of what they discussed, the first of which was sent as a letter a week later.[33] FitzPatrick reported that Milner 'wanted to know *everything* and he was very frank in return'.[34] FitzPatrick told him that unless the British government was 'determined to see the *whole* thing settled', it was better to wait until they were prepared to do so 'in full from A to Z: the status of the Courts, the native policy, the franchise, redistribution of seats, language, customs, Railways, Court of Appeal etc., settled once and forever'. Milner 'ticked off each item with a nod' and agreed that what he was to describe as 'a cumulative case' should be built up to be presented to Kruger's government when a suitable opportunity arose. At one point, according to FitzPatrick's account, Milner said: 'There is only one possible settlement – war! It has got to come. . . . The difficulty is in the occasion and not in the job itself, that is very easily done and I think nothing of the bogies and difficulties of settling South Africa afterwards. You will find a very different tone and temper when the centre of unrest is dealt with.'[35] FitzPatrick then suggested that 'immigration, properly regulated and effected, would in a couple of years settle the question of parties in South Africa'.

During this meeting, FitzPatrick made clear the circumscribed nature of his own position with regard to political activity, and the fact that his employers had warned him to be careful and stick to business. 'Eckstein's are not political agents but a business firm desirous only of pursuing their business in a legitimate and unhampered fashion and politics only concern us where they touch our business', he commented. Milner accepted this and told FitzPatrick that he would only be able to support him if he was careful to see that he was absolutely in the right and justified whatever he did in terms of the pursuit of his business interests. Their discussion then moved on to the Kotze case and Milner suggested that, when he returned to Johannesburg, FitzPatrick should engineer a public petition in support of Kotze, but FitzPatrick felt that this would expose him to possible expulsion from the Transvaal for breaking his pledge concerning political activity.

Milner then turned to the key question of franchise reform. FitzPatrick stated his view that it was highly unlikely that this would ever be given on generous terms to the Uitlanders and that, even if it were offered, few would accept it if they had to forfeit their 'status and rights as British subjects' and face the possibility of being drawn into 'hostility to and probably war against their own people and their own Flag'. Milner responded to this by arguing that 'if in the terms of settlement the franchise should be conceded on reasonable terms, he expected that we would avail ourselves of it. Having asked for it, we must in good faith take it when offered. He would not be party to a sham and would far rather wash his hands of the whole business'. Milner even extracted a promise from FitzPatrick that, if the franchise were conceded on reasonable terms, he would be the first 'to go forward and claim the franchise and sign the oath of allegiance'.

FitzPatrick took advantage of the opportunity provided by this meeting to convey to Milner the deeply-rooted suspicion of many Uitlanders that, after being encouraged to work towards a situation in which a settlement could be imposed by the British government, they would once again be left in the lurch, as many felt they had been in the past. (It is unclear whether FitzPatrick had 1881 or January 1896 primarily in mind at this point.) Milner gave the firm assurance that this time this would not occur and FitzPatrick reported that 'putting together Chamberlain's speech, Selborne's speech, Milner's speech and what we observe here, it is clear that Joe [Chamberlain] has got his teeth in and does not mean to let go'.[36]

After his meeting with Milner, FitzPatrick returned to the Transvaal at the end of February and there had a further frank exchange of views with the British Agent, Conyngham Greene, after which he felt that he had a good idea of 'what is running in the minds of Greene, Milner and (I presume) Chamberlain'. FitzPatrick asked Greene who he had in mind to run the Transvaal's 'future administration in the event of a row'. Greene at once declared 'We shall make a clean sweep. . . . We see no difficulty about the future! When the Tommies get scattered about and the military bands play, they will soon get to like it. As for those who won't like it – well, they will be taught that it is not so necessary for a Boer to be a good marksman and a citizen soldier as it is to be a good farmer.' When FitzPatrick asked how long 'the piling up of the account against Kruger' would 'drag on', Greene replied:

My dear fellow, in my opinion it is time to act *now*. The account is so colossal that there is no sense in piling it up further. Some of the things we have against them would make your hair stand on end. Now is the time to act while they are floundering in the mud. This is the very time to jump on them. You must remember that Kruger has a bit of luck at times and may just happen to flounder onto his feet instead of getting deeper in the mire! Kotze should appeal now. . . . The people of the Rand should appeal to us *now*. It all makes action easier and more justifiable.

When FitzPatrick told him 'that he must not look to us to take risks to suit the book of the British Government as we are not political agents but business people only anxious for decent conditions', Conyngham Greene laughed and said: 'I see your distinction, but tell me, if things come right, who will make the millions? It seems to me you can regard it as very good business.'[37]

FitzPatrick's excitement at gaining an insight into the thinking of the British High Commissioner and Agent in South Africa at this time is understandable. 'The elaborate structure of our imaginings [regarding the weakness of the imperial factor] had been brushed aside like a house of cards, the very bedrock of things had been exposed', he recalled later.[38] On a personal level, FitzPatrick had found in Milner a mentor for the rest of his life. On a political level, a crucial link had been established, through FitzPatrick, between Milner and the Uitlanders and the mining industry on the Rand. Further, a strategy had been outlined which was to be developed with great effect during the next eighteen months, namely the encouragement and utilization of Uitlander agitation to bring about the intervention of the British government in the internal affairs of the Transvaal and thereby to impose a settlement.[39] External pressure would henceforth be allied with internal unrest in that most potent of all combinations in a situation of conflict between two states.

The delivery of the suzerainty despatch, Kruger's re-election, the dismissal of Chief Justice Kotze, Milner's growing impatience and the alarm signals sent by the speech at Graaff-Reinet all combined to make something of another 'Spring crisis' in 1898 in which Milner had taken on the role of chief engineer. But even chief engineers have to obey orders and Chamberlain had curtly told Milner in March that he was not to escalate the situation, that the primary objective for the British government at present was peace, and that they therefore favoured 'a policy of reserve and delay'. The despatch which Milner had hoped might be published as part of 'working up to a crisis' was suppressed by Chamberlain because it 'would only stir up Jingo feeling here at a time when we want to keep things quiet'.[40] Milner had no option but to pass on the appropriate signal to Conyngham Greene in Pretoria – who had just seen FitzPatrick and was reporting that 'the Uitlanders . . . are very generally clamouring, as openly as they dare, for interference by Her Majesty's Government. There is more . . . now in this [imperial] sentiment than at any previous time'. The Uitlanders wanted good government 'if need be under the British flag, established in the place'.[41] Now, Milner warned him, 'I have reason to believe that H.M.'s Government are not at all anxious to bring matters to a head. We must keep up our wickets but not attempt to force the game'.[42]

The establishment of Percy FitzPatrick's important role as a link-man in 1898 was not limited to his contact with Milner. In June of that year, Smuts took up his appointment as the new Attorney-General in Kruger's government and FitzPatrick soon established contact also with him. The failure of the Transvaal government to implement the recommendations of its own Industrial Commission in

1897 did not mark the end of the attempts of the mining industry to win the cooperation of Kruger's government in the enactment of reforms from which both would benefit. On the contrary, considerable progress continued to be made on a whole range of issues and this background of mutual cooperation has to be kept in mind if the 'Great Deal' negotiations of early 1899 are to be understood. During the course of 1898, discussions took place on the sale of the *bewaarplaatsen*, on the government's proposal to introduce a 5 per cent tax on mining profits, on measures to improve mine-labour recruitment, and on the readiness of the mining industry to underwrite a loan of £2,500,000 to the Transvaal government in return for the cancellation of the dynamite monopoly. Percy FitzPatrick took a major part in most of these discussions and this brought him into regular contact with Smuts, whom he found 'very fair, when he has the facts, very willing and very bright, but he has a heart-breaking task'.[43] 'Our hope is Smuts', he told Julius Wernher in London, 'but we cannot rush him and must gain his confidence first by working with him in a way which will show that we are sincere and single-minded in our offers of cooperation'.[44]

Relations between the two men got off to a good start with Smuts urging FitzPatrick not to 'nurse grudges' but to dispense with intermediaries and come to him directly. This FitzPatrick proceeded to do when it was learned that the Transvaal government was proposing to introduce a 5 per cent tax on mining profits. First, however, he discussed with Friedrich Eckstein (the head of his firm) an ambitious scheme which would settle all the grievances of the mining industry: the sale by valuation of mining rights to the *bewaarplaatsen*, the cancellation of the dynamite, railway and liquor monopolies and their replacement by a sales tax and a compensation payment together with a loan to the Transvaal government which the mining industry would underwrite. FitzPatrick's hope was that if these reforms were achieved 'and all friction on material points removed' then it might be possible to reach agreement also on political issues. He envisaged 'a kind of three-cornered, round-table talk', which a representative of the British government would attend, at which issues such as the suzerainty question and the Uitlander franchise would also be discussed with the hope that a final package-deal would result.[45]

With Eckstein's approval, FitzPatrick then outlined the proposal to Smuts – whom he regarded as the best hope for progress and reform and with whom he had made a habit of discussing wider issues. Smuts, whilst acknowledging that this was the first genuine effort to bring about a real settlement, soon poured cold water on FitzPatrick's hopes and told him that whilst he personally was in favour of some such settlement of the *bewaarplaatsen* issue and the ending of the dynamite monopoly, he was not optimistic about the cancellation of any of the other concessions – in some of which the mining companies themselves were involved. Wernher, Beit/H. Eckstein & Co. included concessions over cement and the supply of water to Pretoria amongst their holdings. Smuts told FitzPatrick that Kruger's mind was 'poisoned by the hangers-on who abuse the capitalists' and 'the dynamite people were far too strong' for their influence to be overcome. Far from making concessions to the mining industry, Kruger presented a proposal to the Volksraad whereby the dynamite monopoly would be renewed for a further fifteen years. FitzPatrick's initial hopes in Smuts waned and he began to feel that all their joint efforts really counted for very little since Smuts would either 'succumb to the old man's influence, or he will bump up against the local "Wall of China" and smash himself'.[46]

As FitzPatrick became increasingly disillusioned, so he became more and more convinced that the grievances of the mining industry would never be settled if they were separated from the wider political issues. What was needed was a political breakthrough to achieve a general settlement of all outstanding grievances and this would require the participation of the British High Commissioner. When he shared this view with Smuts, FitzPatrick was treated to an insight into the thinking of Kruger's government which was as revealing as the discussion with Milner had been under the oaks at Newlands. Smuts at once dismissed any involvement of a representative of the British government in discussion of the Transvaal's internal affairs as 'inconsistent with the dignity of an independent state'. FitzPatrick thereupon 'let himself go'. 'Do you realise what it's leading to?' he asked, 'and what must inevitably happen if we don't make a supreme effort to get a settlement; do you realise that it means war?' Smuts calmly replied that he knew what it meant and, when FitzPatrick incredulously enquired whether he seriously contemplated a war with the British Empire which would mean the end of the Transvaal's independence within six months, Smuts replied:

> Not in six months . . . not in six years. You may take the cities and the mines, for we would not meet you there, but for six or seven years we shall be able to hold out in the mountains . . . and long before that there will be a change of opinion in England. Other things will crop up, they will become tired and lose interest; there will be another general election and the Liberals will come into power. . . . And this time we shall get all that we want.[47]

FitzPatrick later wrote that this exchange put 'a devastating end to my fine dreams' and convinced him that war had become a 'dismal certainty'.[48]

The hardening in Smuts's attitude which FitzPatrick detected was almost certainly affected by an extraordinary conversation which Smuts had recently had with the Acting British Agent in Pretoria, Edmund Fraser, with whom he was 'on a very confidential footing'. Fraser was acting in place of Conyngham Greene whilst the latter was on leave in England and, though an able man, who claimed to be 'very well acquainted with "the mind of the Colonial Office" ', he was 'inclined to be more than is discreet for his superiors'.[49] On 22 December 1898, Fraser came to see Smuts about the alleged ill-treatment of Cape Coloured residents in the Transvaal (who were British citizens) and various other matters. After they had concluded their business, Smuts reported:

> Fraser began to talk to me in a most unexpected way. He said that the British Government had now sat still for two years because its own officials had put it in a false position in the Jameson Raid. The time had now, however, come for her to take action. I asked him what he meant. He said that Gladstone had made a great mistake in giving the country back after Majuba before having defeated the Boers. The Boers throughout South Africa had a vague aspiration for a great republic throughout South Africa and Gladstone had by his action encouraged this aspiration in them. The British Government knew of this but had always remained sitting still, but in his opinion the time had now come to make an end of this by 'striking a blow'. When he left London he was instructed that England would be satisfied if the South African Republic should become a richer Orange Free State; but that was not the intention of the South African Republic, to play a humble role. She would have nothing to do with the paramount influence of England but had always tried to play a role among the nations and had, with a view to that, always coquetted with the European powers. In his opinion the time had come to make an end of all this by showing the Boers that England was master in South Africa. I asked him what would give occasion for this. He said that England was very dissatisfied about the maladministration and especially about the ill-treatment of her subjects which was worse here than elsewhere. On this point England would take action. He knew well that England would not go fighting about abstract subjects, such as suzerainty, which are not understood by the English people and the man in the street. She would fight about things that everyone could understand.[50]

'You can imagine with what ears I listened to all this', Smuts wrote later, adding that Fraser had said that 'the position and the influence of the South African Republic . . . had filled all Dutchmen with the idea that a great Afrikaner republic would be established in South Africa. The longer England waited, the stronger would this separationist aspiration become and the weaker her own position; and it was now a question whether she would sit still any longer'.[51] Clearly shaken by this outburst, Smuts at once wrote down an account of it for the Transvaal government. He also made a connection between what Fraser had said and 'the rumours in the newspapers that England is strengthening her forces in South Africa and that she is going to make serious representations to this Government'.[52]

THE ANGLO-PORTUGUESE NEGOTIATIONS AND ANGLO-GERMAN AGREEMENT (1898)

Viewed from London rather than the Transvaal, 1898 was not a year for a forcing policy which might result in a war in South Africa. As both Chamberlain and Selborne had indicated to Milner in March, the British government already had its hands full elsewhere. The military reconquest of the Sudan was underway, culminating in the defeat of the Mahdists at Omdurman in September and the Fashoda crisis with France, which was only resolved at the beginning of November. In the Far East, the German seizure of Kiaowchow and the Russian occupation of Port Arthur threatened a scramble for territory in China which Lord Salisbury feared would seriously threaten the traditionally predominant British interests there. Meanwhile, the American victory in the Spanish–American War marked not just the end of the Spanish colonial empire but the arrival of the United States as a new imperial power on the world scene. It also prompted Salisbury to make a famous speech in which he applied social Darwinist ideas to international relations:

> We know that we shall maintain against all comers that which we possess, and we know, in spite of the jargon about isolation, that we are amply competent to do so. But that will not secure the peace of the world. You may roughly divide the nations of the world as the living and the dying . . . the weak States are becoming weaker and the strong States are becoming stronger . . . the living nations will gradually encroach on the territory of the dying, and the seeds and causes of conflict amongst civilised nations will speedily appear.[53]

If a defeated and deeply humiliated Spain was widely considered to be amongst the 'dying nations', what about Portugal and her colonies in Africa and Asia? In May 1898, the Anglo-Portuguese negotiations about Delagoa Bay – which had been broken off the previous year – were resumed. A weak Portuguese government, heading towards insolvency, was desperate to secure a foreign loan but feared being threatened with international control of its domestic finances, as Egypt had been during the 1870s, and was reluctant to use her colonial possessions as collateral. Although the Portuguese claim to Delagoa Bay had been confirmed by the MacMahon Award (1875), Britain wished to make sure of not only a pre-emptive claim to the area, if Portugal were ever to relinquish it, but to acquire immediate control over the harbour and the stretch of railway to the Transvaal border if at all possible. 'I look on possession of Delagoa Bay as the best chance we have of winning the great game between ourselves and the Transvaal for mastery in South Africa without a war', Milner wrote to Chamberlain in July 1898, adding, 'I am not indeed sure that we shall ever be masters without a war. The more I see of S.A. the more I doubt it. . . . I fear that the overwhelming preponderance in wealth and opportunity on the side of the Transvaal may turn the scale against us, unless we have some means to bring very effective pressure to bear upon that country. There is none that I can see except the command of all its trade routes, of which I need not tell you that Delagoa Bay is the most important'.[54]

The Anglo-Portuguese discussions collapsed, in July 1898, when the German government intervened and made it clear that German interests would have to be considered in any settlement between Portugal and Britain. The Portuguese government took fright, abandoned the idea of using colonial possessions as security, and determined to seek the loan it needed elsewhere. Chamberlain resented Germany's 'preposterous' claim to have an interest in the matter and regarded her demand for 'compensation' as blackmail. 'The only advantage to us is the assurance of Germany's abstention from further interference in Delagoa Bay and the Transvaal', he observed, 'in other words, we pay Blackmail to Germany to induce her not to interfere where she has no right of interference. Well! it is worth while to pay Blackmail sometimes . . . '[55]

Chamberlain shrewdly perceived that Germany's real purpose was to use her leverage over South Africa to obtain colonial compensation elsewhere, most obviously in West Africa and Samoa. An Anglo-German colonial agreement at this juncture, however, had a particular part to play in the British government's determination to strengthen her position in South Africa and ensure German neutrality in the event of a war with the Transvaal. It also has to be viewed against the background of Chamberlain's shift away from a belief in the advantages to Britain of a policy of 'splendid isolation' and his determined but unsuccessful pursuit of a wider Anglo-German alliance during 1898.[56]

For its part, the German government was now quite prepared to abandon any claims to Portuguese territory south of the Zambesi to Britain in the event of a redistribution of Portuguese colonies, provided she obtained adequate compensation elsewhere. As for the Transvaal, it was clear by 1898 that the German intervention via the 'Kruger Telegram' in January 1896 had marked the high-water mark of Germany's support for Kruger's republic. Thereafter, the sceptical views of Baron Fritz von Holstein prevailed over those of the impulsive Kaiser in German government circles as far as South African questions were concerned. It was Holstein's:

> firm conviction that we must get out of the position in which the Kruger Telegram placed us. For what practical results can we expect from the Kruger Telegram policy? No sensible person can expect Germany to establish herself at Delagoa Bay or its vicinity . . . [and] if we don't want that, what business have we to be there at all? We can't burden ourselves with the luxury of England's antipathy simply for the sake of the Boers.

With the clear perception of Germany's broader interests in mind, he worked to extricate Germany from 'the South African blind alley' into which the Kaiser's headstrong action had led the government and to work instead for an understanding with Britain based upon 'the idea of compensating us if we agree not to place further obstacles in England's way in South Africa'.[57] This had already formed the basis for inconclusive discussions in 1897 and was now to come to fruition in the Anglo-German Agreement of 30 August 1898. The full terms of this agreement were kept secret until after the First World War but they provided for the future partition of the Portuguese territories in Africa between Britain and Germany if Portugal defaulted on the loans which Britain and Germany were to make to her. Britain was careful to ensure that her portion included Delagoa Bay, the railway to the Transvaal border, and the whole of the southern half of Mozambique up to the Zambesi and beyond.[58] The agreement remained a dead letter because of Portugal's success in obtaining from France the loan she desperately needed. But through it Britain extracted from the German government the two vital concessions which she sought: the withdrawal of Germany from any say in the future of the Delagoa Bay area, and the elimination of Germany as a political ally of the

Transvaal. Henceforth, Kruger's government obtained no encouragement or support from Germany in its mounting conflict with Britain. On the contrary, the German government consistently advised Kruger to grant the reforms which German traders and investors, as well as British Uitlanders, urged on the Transvaal government. It also warned him against risking war with Britain and made it clear that, if war came, Germany would not interfere.[59] By 1899, a leading German envoy was able to assure Chamberlain that 'all the sensible politicians in Germany as well as the capitalists look upon an absorption of the Transvaal by England as an historical and commercial necessity'.[60] Thus, from 1898 onwards, Kruger's government knew that it had no German ally, in fact no ally at all other than the Orange Free State. In its conflict with Britain, it was on its own.

NOTES

1. See Chapter 5, p. 151 above.
2. G. Rouliot (President of the Chamber of Mines) to J. Wernher, 21 August 1897, BRA, HE 175.
3. Milner to Conyngham Green, 11 February 1898, in C. Headlam, ed., *The Milner Papers* 2 vols (London, 1931/1933), 1, pp. 214–15.
4. Despatch from Milner to Chamberlain, 23 February 1898, printed in ibid., pp. 218–20.
5. Milner to Chamberlain, 23 February 1898, in ibid., pp. 220–4.
6. Conyngham Greene to Selborne, 18 June 1897, in D. G. Boyce, ed., *The Crisis of British Power: The Imperial and Naval Papers of the Second Earl of Selborne, 1895–1910* (London), 1990), p. 52.
7. Milner to Philip Gell, 11 January 1898, MP (P. Gell collection). N.B. A 'Fabian policy' denotes a cautious strategy, avoiding confrontation, to wear out an opponent.
8. For a variety of interpretations about Milner's expectations during 1898–9 see: T. Pakenham, *The Boer War* (London, 1979), Part 1; J. S. Marais, *The Fall of Kruger's Republic* (Oxford, 1961), chs Vll–X; G. H. Le May, *British Supremacy in South Africa 1899–1907* (Oxford, 1965), ch. 1; A. N. Porter, *The Origins of the South African War, Joseph Chamberlain and the Diplomacy of Imperialism 1895–1899* (Manchester, 1980), ch. V; J. Benyon, *Proconsul and Paramountcy in South Africa*, ch. 12; A. H. Duminy, *Sir Alfred Milner and the Outbreak of the Anglo-Boer War* (Durban, 1976).
9. Milner to Conyngham Greene, 18 February 1898, in Headlam, ed., *The Milner Papers,* 1, pp. 216–17.
10. A. Duminy and B. Guest, *Interfering in Politics: A Biography of Sir Percy FitzPatrick* (Johannesburg, 1987), p. 51.

11. Milner to Chamberlain, 15 March and 1 March 1898, in Headlam, ed., *The Milner Papers*, 1, p. 226.
12. Chamberlain to Milner, 19 March 1898, in ibid., p. 226.
13. Selborne to Milner, 22 March 1898, in Boyce, ed., *Crisis of British Power*, pp. 55–7.
14. Chamberlain to Milner, 16 March 1898, in Headlam, ed., *The Milner Papers*, 1, pp. 227–9.
15. Milner to Chamberlain, 22 March 1898, in J. L. Garvin and J. Amery, *Life of Joseph Chamberlain* 6 vols (London, 1932–69), 3, p. 370.
16. Milner to Selborne, 9 May 1898, in Boyce, *Crisis of British Power*, pp. 58–61. The version printed in Headlam, ed., *The Milner Papers*, 1, pp. 232–5, is incomplete.
17. All quotations in the above paragraphs are from this same letter of 9 May 1898 from Milner to Selborne.
18. SeP, MS 15 (1898).
19. Selborne to Milner, 28 June 1898, in Boyce, ed., *Crisis of British Power*, pp. 63–4.
20. See Milner to Chamberlain, 29 August 1897, in Headlam, ed., *The Milner Papers*, 1, pp. 88–90.
21. Chamberlain to Milner, 3 June 1898, JC 10/9/24.
22. Milner to Chamberlain, 9 March 1898, Confidential, Cape Archives GH 26/395 (1898).
23. T. R. H. Davenport, *The Afrikaner Bond (1880–1911)* (Oxford, 1966), pp. 177–9.
24. Milner to Sir W. Hely Hutchinson, 18 February 1898, in Headlam, ed., *The Milner Papers*, 1, p. 216.
25. Speech at Graaff-Reinet, 3 March 1898, in ibid., pp. 244–6.
26. Milner to Chamberlain, 9 March 1898, Cape Archives, GH 26/395.
27. John X. Merriman to President Steyn, 11 March 1898, in P. Lewsen, ed., *Selections from the Correspondence of John X. Merriman* 4 vols (Cape Town, 1960–8), 2, pp. 301–2.
28. Marais, *The Fall of Kruger's Republic*, p. 207.
29. Ibid. p. 208.
30. Milner to Chamberlain, 9 March 1898, Cape Archives GH 26/395 (1898).
31. This paragraph draws on FitzPatrick's books and letters and the excellent biography by Duminy and Guest, *Interfering in Politics*.
32. See Iain R. Smith, 'The origins of the South African War: a re-appraisal', *SAHJ* 22 (1990), especially pp. 30–8.
33. There is a useful discussion of these accounts, written between 1898 and 1925, in A. H. Duminy, 'The political career of Sir Percy FitzPatrick 1895–1906', Ph.D. thesis, University of Natal, 1973, pp. 109–14.
34. P. FitzPatrick to A. Beit, 4 March 1898, in A. H. Duminy and W. R. Guest, eds, *FitzPatrick, South African Politician: Selected Papers 1888–1906* (Johannesburg, 1976), pp. 143–7.
35. Ibid., p. 143.
36. Ibid., p. 145.
37. Ibid., pp. 146–7.

38. Sir Percy FitzPatrick, *Lord Milner and His Work* (London, 1925), p. 11.
39. A. Duminy and Bill Guest, *Interfering in Politics*, p. 52.
40. Chamberlain Minute on Milner to Chamberlain, 23 February 1898, CO 417/242, and Chamberlain's reply to this letter on 19 March 1898, in Headlam, ed., *The Milner Papers*, 1, p. 226.
41. Marais, *The Fall of Kruger's Republic*, p. 209.
42. Milner to Conyngham Greene, 21 March 1898, in Headlam, ed., *The Milner Papers*, 1, pp. 226–7.
43. FitzPatrick to A. Beit, 27 October 1898, in Duminy and Guest, eds, *FitzPatrick*, p. 164.
44. FitzPatrick to J. Wernher, 7 November 1898, in ibid., p. 165.
45. P. FitzPatrick, *South African Memories* (London, 1932), pp. 161–4; also Duminy and Guest, *Interfering in Politics*, p. 56.
46. Ibid., pp. 165–6; also FitzPatrick to Wernher, Beit & Co., 13 June 1898, FP Q2 A/LB XVIII.
47. P. FitzPatrick, *South African Memories*, pp. 167–8. The problems with this source, and with the precise dating of this exchange, are well treated by Andrew Duminy in his Ph.D. thesis, 'The political career of Sir Percy FitzPatrick', pp. 81–3. See also Deborah Lavin's Introduction to the new edition of FitzPatrick's *South African Memories: Scraps of History* (Johannesburg, 1977). Although he was a 'romancer', FitzPatrick's letters form a vital corroborating source for his discussions with Smuts at this time and this exchange has about it the ring of truth.
48. Ibid., pp. 168–9; also Duminy and Guest, *Interfering in Politics*, p. 58.
49. Smuts to J. H. Hofmeyr, 10 May 1899, in W. K. Hancock and J. van der Poel, eds, *Selections from the Smuts Papers* 7 vols (Cambridge, 1966–73), 1, p. 234.
50. Memorandum by Smuts, 22 December 1898, in ibid., pp. 212–13.
51. Smuts to J. H. Hofmeyr, 10 May 1899, in ibid., p. 234.
52. Memorandum by Smuts, 22 December 1898, in ibid., pp. 212–13.
53. Speech at the Albert Hall, 4 May 1898, in Garvin, *Life of Chamberlain*, 3, p. 281.
54. Milner to Chamberlain, 6 July 1898, in Headlam, ed., *The Milner Papers*, 1, pp. 267–8.
55. Chamberlain to Balfour, 19 August 1898, in Garvin, *Life of Chamberlain*, 3, p. 315.
56. See ibid., chs LVII–LXII; J. A. S. Grenville, *Lord Salisbury and Foreign Policy: the Close of the Nineteenth Century* (London, 1964), ch. VII; Paul Kennedy, *The Rise of the Anglo-German Antagonism 1860–1914* (London, 1980), ch. 13.
57. Holstein to Hatzfeldt, 12 April 1897, in N. Rich, ed., *The Holstein Papers* 2 vols (Cambridge, 1965), 2, pp. 21–5.
58. See map in W. L. Langer, *The Diplomacy of Imperialism 1890–1902* (New York, 1960), p. 525.
59. Marais, *The Fall of Kruger's Republic*, p. 216; Garvin, *Life of Chamberlain*, 3, p. 333.
60. Baron Eckhardstein to Chamberlain, 12 September 1899, in Garvin, *Life of Chamberlain*, 3, p. 334.

CHAPTER SEVEN

Getting Things 'Forrarder' in South Africa

MILNER'S VISIT TO ENGLAND

In November 1898 Milner left Cape Town for a visit to England. It was his first leave home, he needed to see an eye specialist, and he intended to use the visit for vital discussions with the Colonial Office about the future direction of British policy towards South Africa. He also planned to use his network of contacts in the press and amongst leading political figures in both parties to educate British public opinion and 'to stamp on rose-coloured illusions about S. Africa'.[1]

The British Agent in Pretoria, Conyngham Greene, had been in England since July and he had reported that the current attitude of Chamberlain and the Colonial Office was not to force the pace in South Africa since to do so would not command the support of either the Party or the Opposition. The government's policy therefore was to let things slide and not to act 'unless a distinct and serious breach of the Convention' occurred. Milner had replied that he was not discouraged by this and recognized that British public opinion could only think of one thing at a time and was preoccupied elsewhere. Nonetheless, he observed, 'the question is are we to have a S.A. Policy with a definite aim or intention? If we know what we are driving at, then I don't the least mind public attention being directed elsewhere during the slow operations of the siege. We can easily make noise enough to attract it when the time comes to storm'. As for the attitude of the Colonial Office, 'this again, can alter, as it has altered'.[2] Milner returned to England determined to prepare the British government and public opinion for the confrontation with Kruger's government which he was convinced must soon take place.

Milner's visit lasted from 18 November 1898 to 28 January 1899 and it was used by him for intense lobbying and activity. At the Colonial Office, he found that the 'no war' policy was still in favour and that the aim of the government was 'to keep the peace with Kruger unless he were very outrageous'.[3] He was also reassured that the Anglo-German agreement 'does formally and for ever eliminate Germany as a *political* influence in the Transvaal and the countries immediately surrounding it'.[4] Whilst in England, Milner engaged in a busy round of meetings and dinners and week-end house-parties where he met a wide cross-section of the political and opinion-forming elite. He met capitalists – amongst them Alfred Beit, Julius Wernher, the Rothschilds, and Cecil Rhodes – and military men, like Kitchener, as well as politicians from both the Liberal and Conservative parties. He visited the royal family at Sandringham, the Prime Minister at Hatfield, Lord Rosebery at Mentmore, and the Chamberlains at Highbury. He also found time to slip away for a cycling holiday with a lady-friend he had secretly set up in a house in Brixton.[5]

Milner went out of his way to meet and talk to leading members of the press about South Africa; and he played an important role in recruiting W. F. Monypenny of *The Times* as the new editor of *The Star* – the leading English newspaper on the Rand which was owned by The Argus Group belonging to Wernher, Beit/H. Eckstein & Co.[6] This was no run-of-the-mill appointment but a vital matter in which Milner took a personal interest. Milner had an acute awareness of the role of the press in forming public opinion, and a wide network of contacts stemming from his own earlier spell as a journalist with W. T. Stead on *The Pall Mall Gazette*. In South Africa he was in regular and close contact with the like-minded Edmund Garrett, who was editor of *The Cape Times* (which had the largest circulation of any newspaper in South Africa) and a forthright supporter of the Uitlander cause in the Transvaal and of British paramountcy in South Africa. In W. F. Monypenny, Milner sought someone who would undertake in the Transvaal the sort of role carried out by Garrett in the Cape Colony. The job description was set down with remarkable candour by one of the Argus directors in a letter to W. T. Stead:

> Do you know of another Garrett whom you can recommend? . . . The Proprietors of the STAR will not interfere with the editorial work provided the Editor is honest, capable and holds the right views. He must have faith in the English speaking race and be able and willing to render substantial aid to Sir Alfred Milner in forwarding the Imperial Policy in South Africa. . . . His mission would be to educate and unite men who read English on the Rand and who are for the most part today an incoherent and factious crowd.[7]

W. F. Monypenny was eventually appointed on terms which enabled him to combine the posts of Editor of *The Star* with that of being *The Times* correspondent in Johannesburg. He would therefore be in a position to influence public opinion in Britain as well. By March 1899, he was established in Johannesburg, where he remained in regular contact with both Milner and Conyngham Greene, the British Agent at Pretoria, to both of whom he looked for guidance. In March 1899, a new Uitlander newspaper, *The Transvaal Leader*, also came into existence under an editor of 'the right views', F. Pakeman. It was financed by Wernher, Beit/H. Eckstein & Co. and became notorious for its fervently pro-Uitlander and anti-Boer opinions. In September 1899, a month before war broke out, both Monypenny and Pakeman had to flee from the Transvaal to escape arrest.

Thus, from March 1899, there came into being a powerful, opinion-forming, Uitlander press on the Rand under the influence, even the guidance, of Milner and Conyngham Greene. In Wernher and Beit, Milner felt that he had found 'a new and astonishing kind of millionaire: men with some higher conception than the piling up of money' who were prepared to fund an English-language press in the Transvaal sympathetic to the British imperial cause.[8] Milner recognized the importance of this for his own purposes. Not only would it create a climate of opinion amongst the Uitlanders which would underpin his own diplomacy, it would also play a significant part in the heavily-biased flow of information about conditions in the Transvaal which reached London during the following months. This in turn would help to create a receptive environment there for the line of policy set out in Milner's own despatches.

Milner did not restrict his attentions to the South African press (The Argus Group included at least six regional newspapers). He also sought, wherever possible, to influence the press in England through what Monypenny referred to as 'the daily drip of discussion'. When Garrett had to go to England for health reasons in mid-1899, Milner encouraged him to 'keep alive' such papers as *The Daily News* and the *Westminster Gazette* to the situation in South Africa. He also urged his friend Philip Gell to tackle the *Manchester Guardian* and 'lose no opportunity of getting the liberal Press to appreciate his point of view'.[9] By mid-1899, Milner was so concerned about cultivating support for his policies, both in Britain and South Africa, that he tried to get Leo Maxse, the editor of the *National Review*, to come out to South Africa and stand in for Garrett at *The Cape Times*. In June, after he had read the manuscript of Percy FitzPatrick's *The Transvaal from Within*, Milner strongly encouraged him to go to England, bring his account of the Uitlander reform movement before and after the Jameson Raid up to date and publish it. FitzPatrick spent the weeks before war broke out finishing his book and having discussions in London with Alfred Harmsworth of the *Daily Mail*, E. T. Cook of the *Daily News*, and Moberly Bell of *The Times*. When the book appeared in October, it became a best-seller and was very influential in persuading British public opinion that a war with Kruger's republic was justified.[10]

The close relationship between Milner and the press is a striking feature of the situation in 1899. It was a deliberate involvement by Milner, who was a shrewd propagandist in his own cause, and it enabled him to exercise a remarkable degree of influence on the sources of information which reached England and helped to form opinion there. J. A. Hobson, who arrived in South Africa in mid-1899 as a correspondent for the *Manchester Guardian*, later pointed to the existence of what he called 'a kept press' which had played an important part in bringing about the war.[11] He revealed the close connections between the press and the mining industry (especially Wernher, Beit/H. Eckstein & Co.) – which he accused of conspiring to bring about the war – but he failed to discover the role played by Milner. Preoccupied with a plausible but mistaken explanation for the war, which put the mining magnates at the centre of the picture, Hobson wrongly assumed that Milner had simply allowed himself 'to become the instrument' of the mining industry. What Hobson rightly detected and emphasized was the role played by the press in the run-up to the war in South Africa and in what he later called the psychology of jingoism.[12] What he missed was that if anyone can be said to have sought to use the press to manipulate opinion in 1899 it was Milner.

There were, however, two sides to the press war which developed in South Africa during 1898–9. Historians, following in the wake of Hobson's analysis, have tended to concentrate on one side of the struggle: the emergence of an active Uitlander press on the Rand, fervently pro-British in tone, subsidized by the mining industry, and regarded by Milner as a useful auxiliary in mobilizing public opinion behind a policy of British intervention on behalf of the Uitlanders in their conflict with Kruger's government.[13] The appointment of W. F. Monypenny to revitalize *The Star* and F. Pakeman to initiate *The Transvaal Leader* were, however, moves to counter a militant campaign against the mining industry and the 'capitalists' which had already been initiated by Kruger's government through the daily columns of the English-language newspaper *The Standard and Diggers News*. The proprietor of this paper, Emanuel Mendelssohn, had originally offered Alfred Beit 12,000 shares in it by which he could buy influence over the paper's attitude towards the mining industry. But both Beit personally, and the firm of Wernher, Beit/H. Eckstein & Co., believed – on good grounds – that Mendelssohn was a thoroughly unscrupulous and untrustworthy character and so refused the offer. Mendelssohn had thereupon turned to Kruger's government and, in return for a subsidy (much of it in the form of government-sponsored advertising in his paper), had turned it into a stridently pro-government organ which never ceased to attack the mining industry and the 'capitalists' for being at the root of the difficulties in the Transvaal.[14]

During 1898, this newspaper repeatedly argued that, as at the time of the Jameson Raid, the issue of Uitlander grievances was now being deliberately exploited by the 'capitalists'. These were referred to as 'the puppets of Mr Rhodes', 'the capitalist wire-pullers in London', and the source of 'the unrest industry'.[15] In December 1898, Percy FitzPatrick had warned Wernher of 'the bitterness of feeling and the distrust of the capitalist' which was being fomented in the Transvaal by *The Standard and Diggers News*.[16] In January 1899, Rouliot (President of the Chamber of Mines and the senior manager of Wernher, Beit/H. Eckstein & Co. in Johannesburg) repeated the warning about the damage being done by this newspaper with its anti-capitalist campaign. Not only was it a well-written and widely read newspaper (it had a circulation of about 7,500–8,000 copies a day, compared with that of about 11,000 for *The Star*) but it sought to play upon divisions within the mining industry, blaming the 'capitalists' and seeking to woo the ordinary European mine-workers and 'small men' to the side of the Transvaal government and thus divide the Uitlanders.[17] Kruger was hailed as 'the grand old man of South Africa' and it was claimed that 'there is every disposition on the part of the President, the Executive, and the Volksraad to adopt the forward and progressive policy contemplated in 1895'.[18] Throughout the early months of 1899, *The Star* was described as 'an organ dictated to and controlled by a handful of capitalists' and *The Cape Times* was dismissed as one of 'the noisy organs of the unrest factory influenced by the financial groups'.[19]

By April, all the elements of what was later to become known as 'the Hobson thesis' about the causes of the South African War are to be found clearly articulated and wearisomely reiterated in the columns of *The Standard and Diggers News*. 'The capitalist press, in obedience to orders from London' was accused of 'endeavouring to bring about a condition of things closely resembling the crisis of three years ago'. The mining group leaders were 'goading the British government by every means, fair or foul, to coerce this state by forcible intervention. . .'[20] Their object was 'to enable them to obtain a controlling influence in the administration of this Republic'. Whereas, in 1895–6, 'it was Dr. Jameson's troopers and the people of Johannesburg who were sacrificed . . . it is now the British nation which is being urged to action to take the capitalist chestnuts out of the fire'.[21] When Hobson arrived in South Africa later in 1899, he picked up this ready-made conspiracy theory, manufactured out of what had already been revealed about the background to the Jameson Raid and the abortive Uitlander uprising of 1895–6, and integrated it with his own liberal anti-imperialism to provide an attractive but mistaken explanation of the causes of the South African War of 1899–1902 which has exercised immense influence ever since.[22]

Hobson was not an historian but a journalist with a particular axe to grind. What historical research has revealed is that, in the run-up to the war, there is no evidence that the British government was ever swayed in its policy-making and decisions with regard to South Africa by the 'capitalists' or 'the mining magnates' and their particular interests. Rather the contrary. Lord Salisbury, Joseph Chamberlain and the staff of the British Colonial Office distrusted the 'capitalists' and wished to avoid the replacement of Kruger's republic by 'a plutocrats' republic' – which is what they feared 'a true republic' would mean if it were not firmly under the control of the British government.[23] On certain occasions during 1899, as we shall see, leading figures in the mining industry would consult the British government and its representatives in South Africa; and Chamberlain and Milner were certainly not reluctant to give their advice. But it is a crude and determinist conception to imagine that when 'capitalists' consult governments it is always the 'capitalists' who call the tune. British policy towards the Transvaal in 1899 was made by the British government. War resulted from the eventual breakdown in relations between the British and Transvaal governments. On the way, both governments engaged in discussions with representatives of the mining industry and the Uitlander population. Given the situation of conflict and unrest in the Transvaal, this was only to be expected. But on neither side was government policy determined by them.

THE DYNAMITE MONOPOLY CHALLENGED

Whilst Milner was in England a number of significant moves were made on other issues which contributed towards the mounting confrontation with Kruger's government. The British reply to the Transvaal on the question of suzerainty was discussed and despatched and an impasse was reached on this issue which was to remain unresolved right through to the outbreak of war.[24] As Smuts was well aware, the British claim to suzerainty was not just an academic question since its effect was to rule out any possibility of arbitration by an outside power over the points at issue between the British and Transvaal governments.[25] Then, on 12 December 1898, it was learned that the Transvaal government proposed to ask the Volksraad to extend the dynamite monopoly for a further fifteen years.

Milner had previously regarded the dynamite issue as 'a capitalists' question, pure and simple' and certainly not a matter to fight over.[26] In 1897, as already mentioned, he had persuaded Chamberlain that a major despatch, which the British government had prepared on the matter, should not be delivered because he feared that this might leave the British government perilously exposed if Kruger refused to respond to what he was likely to regard as an unjustified external intervention on a purely internal matter. Now, however, Milner abandoned his reluctance to take up the dynamite issue and at once commented to the Colonial Office:

> I have hoped against hope that we should be able to keep out of this business. *I hate it*. But I really cannot see how some action on the part of Her Majesty's Government can *now* be avoided. . . . But we want – or rather we should be better for – some recent peg to hang our remonstrance on.

He suggested that attempts might be made 'to stir up' the Roburite Company – which had protested at the monopoly in 1897 – and wondered why the mining companies on the Rand had not immediately protested. His inclination was to hint to the Acting British Agent in Pretoria, Edmund Fraser, that he might 'pull their tails'. But he doubted if Chamberlain would agree to go as far as that.[27] Why had Milner changed his mind on the dynamite issue? Certainly, he had not altered his view that dynamite was a poor issue, by itself, on which to make a stand. As he wrote to Selborne: 'When you want to fight the Transvaal, I can pick you a dozen better causes of quarrel in half an hour.'[28] But if the British government took up the dynamite monopoly as part of a wider challenge to Kruger's government then, by the end of 1898, this fitted in nicely with Milner's policy of working towards a confrontation. 'Of course, if it were judiciously worked into a general row, it would help not hurt us', he commented.[29] So now it was.

In 1893, the then British government had been told by its own law officers that the Transvaal was entitled to operate a dynamite monopoly if it wished to do so and that this was not inconsistent with its treaty obligations to Britain.[30] During 1897, however, a number of British firms specializing in mining explosives (the Roburite Company included) had protested to the British government about the way their products – which were very favourably regarded by the mining industry on the Rand – had been systematically excluded by Kruger's government. They had also objected that the dynamite monopoly in the Transvaal was not a state monopoly (which would have safeguarded it from being in conflict with Article XIV of the London Convention) but an exclusive privilege, granted by the state to a private company, the huge profits of which went not to the state Treasury but to private individuals. Further, it had become a purely packaging and distributing concern of imported products. All of this meant that the basis on which the original concession had been granted had been so changed that the issue was now open to challenge.[31] The Colonial Office had replied that the matter was being investigated and Chamberlain had reasserted the British claim to interfere later, if it became necessary.[32]

Encouraged by Milner, this is what Chamberlain and the British government decided to do in January 1899. They thereby took up the cudgels in support of one of the mining industry's central grievances against Kruger's government. A formal despatch was sent to the Transvaal government, on 13 January, which extended the one prepared but not delivered in 1897. In it, the British government, after surveying the history of the dynamite monopoly, expressed its displeasure that the matter had not already been dealt with along the lines recommended by the Transvaal's own Industrial Commission. The prospect of an extension of the concession now compelled the British government to state that this was 'inconsistent with the [London] Convention'. Whilst Britain did not desire a public controversy about the matter, it would not admit 'either the legality of the concession or its extension'. In an accompanying letter to the Acting British High Commissioner, Chamberlain emphasized that the despatch was 'moderately worded and not intended, in any sense, as an ultimatum'. Nonetheless, he also wrote to suggest that Edmund Fraser (the Acting British Agent in Pretoria) might inform 'those with whom he is in communication' amongst the mining industry's representatives that the British government was now taking up the dynamite issue with Kruger's government and encourage them to do the same.[33] Fraser promptly did so and when the representatives of the mining industry said they were afraid of being accused of treason by Kruger's government if they protested and so would only do so if they had the assurance that the British government would back them up in the matter, Fraser showed them Chamberlain's telegram to reassure them.[34]

The President of the Chamber of Mines then made a 'strong speech' at the annual meeting of the Chamber on 2 February and a motion was passed condemning the dynamite monopoly and the proposal to extend it. Representatives of all the major mining houses put forward a proposal to Kruger's government to buy out the dynamite monopoly for the sum of £600,000 – which they would raise as a loan amongst themselves.[35] Fraser commented that this was the first time that the mining industry had ever offered direct financial assistance to Kruger's government.[36] Smuts warned Percy FitzPatrick that the offer was unlikely to be accepted; that the Volksraad was likely to postpone a decision on the prolongation of the concession; and that Kruger would resist all efforts to interfere with what he regarded as 'the cornerstone of the country's independence'.[37] When the British government's formal despatch, protesting about the dynamite monopoly, was delivered in February, Kruger was well aware that the offer from the mining industry of a loan with which to buy out the monopolists was not coincidental. He was also convinced that 'England will not fight about dynamite'.[38] The loan was refused and the official protest from the British government was rejected. Kruger's government, nonetheless, had a difficult task convincing its own Volksraad to support the proposal for an extension when the matter came up for debate in March. Despite the fact that several Volksraad members had a personal financial interest in preserving the monopoly, the proposal was rejected, by a vote of 15 to 13, and the matter was referred back to the government. When it was again brought before the Volksraad, in August 1899, it took all Kruger's persuasive powers – and almost certainly a resort to bribery – to push the proposal through, at a time when the independence of the country really was being threatened. The dynamite monopoly was finally to be abolished only as a result of the war and the overthrow of Kruger's government.[39] Thereafter, the local production of explosives grew to become South Africa's largest single manufacturing industry by 1914.

The decision by the British government to challenge Kruger's government on the dynamite monopoly in January 1899 has been much pondered by historians, not least because of the way in which the challenge was delivered in concert with the mining industry.[40] J. S. Marais has suggested that this marked the point at which Chamberlain entered into an understanding with the mining magnates.

> Henceforward their leading spirits acted in close concert with him and his representatives in South Africa. Milner and [Conyngham] Greene were thus able to reconstitute the reform movement of pre-raid days on the Rand with some of the magnates taking a share in public. Chamberlain had, in fact, stepped out along the road that led to vigorous intervention within the republic. His first attempt at intervention had been spoilt by the raid. This time he was to be more successful.[41]

This is, I believe, to imply too much. Whilst there is no doubt that the British government did act in concert with the mining industry to challenge Kruger's government over the dynamite issue in January 1899, this was not the first or the last or the most formidable of the issues over which Chamberlain had taken up the challenge since January 1896; and, like Milner, he certainly did not regard it as an issue to fight over. Nor was it the challenge over dynamite which brought into being either a wider public commitment to Uitlander political issues, by some of the mine-magnates, or a reconstituted reform movement on the Rand. The former only occurs in March 1899, during the Great Deal negotiations,[42] whilst the latter had already occurred, as a result of a quite separate sequence of events, in December 1898, whilst both Milner and Conyngham Greene were absent in England.

THE EDGAR INCIDENT AND THE FIRST UITLANDER PETITION TO THE QUEEN

On 18 December 1898, an Uitlander called Edgar, returning home after midnight, was involved in a drunken brawl with another Uitlander whom he knocked down unconscious. Fearing that the man was dead, some of his friends called the police. Four Afrikaner policemen arrived on the scene and followed Edgar to his house. When he refused to open the door, one of the policemen, called Jones, forced it open and entered the house without a warrant. When Edgar then hit him with a stick, Jones shot him dead. Jones was promptly arrested and charged with murder. The public prosecutor then reduced the charge to manslaughter and released Jones on the very modest bail of £200. When the Acting British Agent, Fraser, protested about this, Smuts (the State Attorney) had Jones re-arrested. At the trial in February, Jones was found not guilty by the jury and the judge (who was only 25) said that he hoped that the police would always know how to do their duty.[43]

The Edgar incident was not so extraordinary in a rough town like Johannesburg in the 1890s. But it occurred in the wake of a whole number of cases in which armed Transvaal police (known as Zarps) had acted in an arrogant and brutal manner towards British subjects (both white and coloured) on the Rand, raiding houses at night and making arrests without warrants. A situation of tension and hostility between Uitlanders and the police had built up. The shooting of Edgar, and then the light treatment and acquittal of the policeman who had killed him, brought about the second reform movement on the Rand.

The case was immediately made into a political issue by the efforts of the South African League (SAL), aided and abetted by the Uitlander press. Immediately after the shooting, an Edgar committee was formed consisting largely of prominent members of the SAL in the Transvaal. When Jones was released on bail, a massive public demonstration was organized in Johannesburg. Leaflets were distributed and notices were published in the newspapers calling on British subjects to assemble before the British consulate to sign and deliver a petition to the Queen. No permission was sought from the authorities for holding this meeting, although this was required by law. Feelings were running high when this gathering of 4–5,000 people assembled on 24 December, singing patriotic British songs, parading a signed petition to the Queen, and engaging in scuffles with the local police. The petition was then read out by Thomas Dodd (Secretary of the South African League in Johannesburg) and handed over to the inexperienced young British Vice-Consul, Evans, on the balcony of the Consulate. Evans undertook to deliver it to 'the proper quarters'. Clem Webb (another SAL official) addressed the crowd, which then gradually dispersed, although the newspapers reported that 'late into the night squabbles and street disturbances took place. It was a very lively Christmas Eve'.[44]

The grievances listed in this first Uitlander petition to the Queen focused on 'the innumerable acts of petty tyranny at the hands of the police' suffered by British subjects, both white and coloured, on the Rand. The Edgar case, which had been the immediate cause of the petition, was described as symptomatic of a wider malaise and it is clear that it was the actions of the public prosecutor and other officials afterwards, even more than the incident itself, which had caused the trouble. The petitioners declared that they had no voice in the government of the country, no longer felt that an independent judiciary existed to which they could appeal, were not allowed to arm and defend themselves, and so sought 'the extension of Your Majesty's protection to the lives, liberties, and property of your loyal subjects here, and such other steps as may be necessary to terminate the existing intolerable state of affairs'. They also demanded the proper trial and punishment of the policeman, Jones, and that provision be made for Edgar's widow and child.[45]

The petition was to be refused but the damage had already been done. From Pretoria, Fraser had urged Evans to 'avoid anything in the shape of a public meeting outside the Consulate' and considered he should never have allowed the petition to be read in public from its balcony.[46] He also made it clear to Wybergh (President of the SAL in the Transvaal) that life would be impossible for representatives of the British government if they allowed themselves to be associated with public criticism of the Transvaal administration.[47] Wybergh was promptly sacked by his employer, Consolidated Goldfields, who had been determined to distance themselves from overt political activity ever since the Jameson Raid and feared that Wybergh's prominent position in the SAL would rebound on them. The Transvaal government was so incensed by the way the British Vice-Consul had 'identified himself with a body which is inimical to this government' that it wanted Evans recalled, but was prevailed upon to drop this in return for an undertaking that any future complaints or petitions would only be accepted by the British Agent in Pretoria 'which had the additional advantage of being geographically removed from the Johannesburg crowd'.[48] Dodd and Wybergh had meanwhile been arrested for their part in the unauthorized meeting of 24 December; they were then released on bail set far higher than had been the case with Jones (£500 each). This in turn provoked protest meetings in various parts of South Africa calling the attention of the British government to the way British subjects were being treated in one of the Queen's suzerain states. In Johannesburg, a huge meeting organized at the amphitheatre by the SAL on 14 January ended in uproar and fighting when Boers present heckled the speakers and the police refused to intervene. The SAL subsequently collected 28 affidavits, alleging that the Transvaal government had itself organized the disturbances in the hall, but took no action in the courts on the grounds that it would not receive a fair hearing. This material was later used to swell the grievances against Kruger's republic published in a British government Blue Book.[49]

Meanwhile, the fate of the first Uitlander petition to the Queen was sealed by the refusal of the Acting British High Commissioner in South Africa to forward it. During Milner's absence in England, his place was occupied by Sir William Butler, who had been appointed as Commander-in-Chief of the British troops in South Africa at the end of November 1898. An Irish Catholic who had served twice in South Africa during the 1870s, Butler regarded the Uitlanders on the Rand as trouble-makers, the South African League as 'an agency of disquiet', and Rhodes as a menace to the peace of the country. Politically, he was convinced that what South Africa needed was not 'a surgical operation' but an effort at compromise and conciliation. In him, the new Schreiner ministry in the Cape found a sympathetic Acting High Commissioner after their own hearts. In him, Milner faced someone with diametrically opposed views to his own of the situation who was in a position to obstruct him. Sooner or later one of them would have to go.[50]

Butler regarded the whole agitation following the Edgar incident as 'a prepared business', got up by the South African League with the deliberate intention of creating a political crisis through which the British government could be drawn in by the Uitlanders to confront Kruger's government. He was outraged by the incendiary role played by the press, publishing the text of the petition and telegraphing this to England 'before it had even passed the meeting whose views it was supposed to represent' with the object of 'forcing our hands by newspaper publicity'.[51] Butler used the fact that the petition had been widely published in the press before it had been handed in to the representative of the British government as good grounds for refusing to accept and transmit it to London. Representatives of the SAL thereupon called on Fraser, in Pretoria, to ask his advice about how best to present petitions in future. His insistence that advance publicity had to be avoided at all costs was carefully observed next time.[52]

At the Colonial Office, Chamberlain, perhaps under the influence of Milner's presence in England, had initially felt that 'The Edgar affair may be very important and may give us the right of remonstrance and action – outside the [London] Convention – which we have not hitherto had.'[53] He was susceptible to the idea, put forward by Fraser and Conyngham Greene and encouraged by Milner, that the members of the South African League 'represent the democratic English opinion so to say – the opinion of the small people as opposed to the capitalists . . . they are probably the soundest element from the Imperial point of view in S.A.R.'.[54] Milner's private secretary, Walrond, also wrote from Johannesburg that 'the condition of things is fast becoming what it was in 1894 and 1895'. He reported that there was a great deal of discontent amongst the Uitlander population but they had 'no organization for united action, everything being done disjointedly on occasions when a particular section feels itself wronged. They have no cohesion and never will have until they are quite sure H.M.G. is with them'.[55] Nonetheless, a reconstitution of the Uitlander reform movement on the Rand certainly seemed to be occurring.

Milner acknowledged that the SAL was exploiting the situation but was furious that, in his absence, Butler had 'sat upon' the petition.[56] Henceforward, he regarded him as a 'Krugerite' and a thorn in his flesh.[57] Members of the Colonial Office staff, however, were relieved that by his action Butler had defused the situation, at least for the present. As H. W. Just (who had replaced Fiddes at the Colonial Office) minuted:

> The acceptance of this petition would . . . have constituted a new departure of a serious kind. . . . So long as the policy of simply keeping the S.A.R. to the Convention is pursued, petitions of this character can do no good and will only demonstrate the impotence of Her Majesty's Government. If friction is to be avoided, it would seem good policy to prevent further petitions, and Mr Greene will be able to manage this no doubt, as he has found the S. Af. League in the past very willing to defer to his advice on such matters.[58]

The nature of the South African League at the time of the agitation accompanying the Edgar incident and the first Uitlander petition to the Queen requires some further comment. It was not, at this stage, a movement which was supported by the mine-magnates or the 'capitalists', many of whom criticized and condemned it in no uncertain terms in public.[59] None of the mining companies were willing to be associated with an organization so blatantly hostile to Kruger's government; that is why Wybergh had been sacked by Consolidated Goldfields. The SAL was a volatile and disorganized body which, as Walrond reported, lacked stamina and cohesion. Its leaders were certainly not in the political service of the capitalists and had no large funds at their disposal; its membership consisted of no more than 5,000 Uitlanders, most of whom were ordinary working men, not all of them British. The mine-magnates kept apart from the second reform movement, initially, as they had done from the first such movement in 1895. Those who had played a leading role in the first Uitlander reform movement in 1895–6, like Percy FitzPatrick, were prevented from overt involvement with the second reform movement at this time because of their undertaking to refrain from political activity for three years as a condition of their release in 1896. This ban was only to elapse at the end of May 1899.[60]

The relationship of the SAL to the British government also needs to be understood. It had not been created by the British government, nor was it the creature of that government's representatives in South Africa. In January 1899, Fraser, the Acting British Agent in Pretoria, indignantly repudiated the claim that he was acting as 'the wire-puller of the South African League' and he had deliberately distanced himself and his colleagues from the League's activities.[61] Evans was reprimanded for his failure to do this sufficiently at the Johannesburg Consulate on 24 December. For their part, the leaders of the SAL recognized that, given their objective of involving the British government on the Uitlanders' behalf, they were dependent on the goodwill of that government's representatives in South Africa and consequently sought their advice and guidance. But this did not put them under their control.

THE SITUATION AT THE BEGINNING OF 1899

When Milner left England to return to South Africa in company with Conyngham Greene on 28 January 1899, he felt '*well-pleased* with the result' of his visit. As he intimated to his 'great stand-by', Selborne:

> *My views about the situation are absolutely unaltered*, but I have come to the conclusion that, having stated them, it is no use trying to force them upon others at this stage. If I can advance matters by my own actions, as I still hope I may be able to do, I believe that I shall have support when the time comes. And if I can't get things 'forrarder' locally, I should not get support whatever I said.[62]

By early 1899, the international situation had much improved, as far as Britain was concerned. Most of the preoccupations elsewhere in the world, which had weighed heavily on Chamberlain during 1898, had now been resolved. Kitchener had completed his conquest of the Sudan, the French had been outfaced at Fashoda, the Russians were negotiating an agreement with respect to China, and the Germans had been removed as a factor in the South African situation as a result of the Anglo-German agreement. Britain was now in a strong position with no serious international complications to fear. Yet neither the

British government nor Chamberlain himself expected that Britain would be at war with the Transvaal before the end of the year. The Cabinet had not discussed South Africa for almost a year and there were few questions and no debate about it when Parliament reassembled in the New Year.

The gap which had emerged a year previously between Milner and Chamberlain with regard to their different approaches to the South African problem remained. Milner wished to pursue an active policy and work towards a confrontation with Kruger's government which he recognized would result either in reform or war. Chamberlain agreed that the situation in the Transvaal might become untenable before long, but saw no reason for hastening a crash; and if the crash came he, like most of the Cabinet, expected that Kruger's government was at least as likely to capitulate to Britain's demands as to resort to war. War therefore remained a possibility. But if it came, Chamberlain remained as convinced in 1899 as he had been in 1897 – when Milner first went to South Africa – that three things were essential: Kruger's government must have put itself clearly in the wrong; Britain must have the support of a sizeable body of colonial opinion in South Africa (including that of the Cape Afrikaner population and the Cape and Natal governments); something greater than Uitlander grievances must be at stake since these were 'of a character which would not excite great sympathy in this country [Britain] and they would not be considered as sufficient to constitute a *casus belli*'.[63] Chamberlain and Selborne had originally believed that Kruger's maladministration was bound, sooner or later, to produce opposition *from within the Transvaal itself*, and that this was the best way in which change could be brought about. Kruger's re-election in 1898 may have shaken their expectation that he was likely to be replaced before long but, as Smuts shrewdly observed, Britain had no convincing case, at the beginning of 1899, to justify to the world an external attack on the Transvaal to overthrow him.[64]

Whilst the British Colonial Office therefore studiously avoided anything approaching the tone of an ultimatum in its weighty despatches on suzerainty or dynamite, and Butler refused to make an issue of the first Uitlander petition, Milner was forced to bide his time. The reconstitution of the reform movement on the Rand, in the wake of the Edgar incident, however, provided a movement of opposition to Kruger's government from within the Transvaal itself which Milner was certainly prepared to make the most of on his return. Here, perhaps, lay the key to the future. If the Uitlanders could organize themselves effectively in pursuit of their own interests, they might provide the means to work up to a crisis. At this stage, Milner would seem to have had more faith than Chamberlain did in the potential of Uitlander grievances to appeal to, and win the support of the British public. Milner, however, had to proceed cautiously. As he wrote, with exceptional frankness, to Fiddes, from London in January:

> Joe [Chamberlain] may be led but he can't be driven. I go on pegging mail after mail, month after month, and I think it tells; but if I were *once* to make him think that I am trying to rush him, he would see me to the devil and we might as well all shut up. I put everything in the way most likely to get him to take our view of *himself*. Whether he takes it, or rather when he takes it, depends on the amount of external pressure and excitement corresponding to our prodding of him from within. If only the Uitlanders stand firm on the formula 'no rest without reform' and can stand on it not 6 days, but 6 weeks, or six months, we shall do the trick yet my boy. And by the soul of St. Jingo they get a fair bucking up from us all one way and another.[65]

The revived Uitlander reform movement on the Rand, in the wake of the Edgar incident, placed the British government in an awkward position but it presented Milner with the means to 'get things "forrarder" locally'. Only if it signalled to these vital collaborators in the long-term British objective of British supremacy that it had not abandoned them and would continue to press their case with the Transvaal government, could the British government hope to retain some hold over the Uitlanders and provide the most effective channel for the rectification of their grievances. But, as Milner clearly foresaw, this was likely to encourage the Uitlanders to challenge Kruger's government and would draw in the British government in support of their cause. The Uitlander problem was at least a decade old by 1899 and was a product of South African, even specifically Transvaal, circumstances. It long pre-dated the arrival of either Chamberlain or Milner on the scene; and with each year that went by it became more intractable and disruptive.

What had been a civil conflict within the Transvaal European population, and essentially an *internal* matter for the Transvaal government, had remained just that until the Uitlander issue had been taken up by Chamberlain and the British government at the time of the Jameson Raid in January 1896. Once this happened, a civil conflict within Transvaal society was transformed into a deadly conflict between the British and Transvaal governments. During 1899, the issue of Uitlander grievances was to become the hub around which all else turned. The British government was to get itself into a position, on the Uitlander issue, from which it could not withdraw without unacceptable humiliation and loss of prestige at the hands of Kruger's government. Either Kruger's government would capitulate to British demands on this issue, or there would be a resort to war. Thus, the South African War was to begin out of a specific civil conflict in Transvaal society which became a conflict between governments when Britain intervened. The failure of Kruger's government to resolve the Uitlander problem in the Transvaal was to lead directly to the outbreak of war in October.

THE GREAT DEAL NEGOTIATIONS

By no means all of the initiatives taken with regard to the situation in the Transvaal were made by either the Uitlanders or the British government and its representatives in South Africa. Kruger's government also took deliberate steps to try to lessen the situation of mounting conflict which it faced with the mining industry, the Uitlanders, and the British government. In this it was consistently encouraged by the Afrikaner-led governments of the Orange Free State and the Cape Colony, whose conciliatory efforts were only fully revealed when the evidence for them was discovered after the British occupation of Bloemfontein in 1900. The British liked to portray Kruger's government as 'obdurate' and reactionary, corrupt, inefficient, opposed to all change and run by a small clique who were totally submissive to the will of Kruger himself. In fact, considering the range and magnitude of the problems it faced, the poor resources in skill and expertise of its administration, and the limited room for manoeuvre available to it in its resistance to the growing encroachments on its qualified independence, Kruger's government demonstrated a surprising degree of adaptability and readiness to embrace change. Much of this may have been reluctant, and the sum total certainly amounted to too little too late, but Kruger's government did move − and never more so than during 1899, as the crisis mounted. But there were clear limits. Kruger was unwilling to do anything which might undermine the foundations of both his government and the burgher republic. Above all, he would not allow political control of the state to fall into the 'alien' hands of Uitlanders, who had proved disloyal in the past and were clearly untrustworthy in the present.

By February 1899, an economic recovery had begun on the Rand − fuelled by the growing contribution of the 'deep levels' to the total gold output – which was to continue until the eve of the war in October. The share market was booming but the manager of the Standard Bank was one amongst many who feared that economic growth would be obstructed if Kruger's government failed to enact reforms because 'without reforms, the European money market is closed to the Republic'.[66] The recovery also stimulated renewed protest from the commercial sector at the restrictions imposed on it by the government – which continued to grant exclusive concessions for the manufacture of an ever wider range of products. On 1 February, after an angry debate, the Chamber of Commerce passed a resolution condemning the government for policies which resulted in the enrichment of certain private concessionaires at the expense of both the state and its inhabitants.[67] Kruger's government faced a formidable series of other challenges, from both within and without the Transvaal, at the same time. The British government's despatches on the dynamite and suzerainty questions had just been received. The second Uitlander reform movement on the Rand was gaining a much wider range of support than had been the case with the first. The mining industry had combined its offer of a loan with which to buy out the dynamite company with a stinging attack on the government, its repeated failure to address the grievances specific to the mining industry, and its anti-capitalist campaign. The President of the Chamber of Mines, speaking on behalf of the industry, had declared at the end of January:

> We carefully avoid anything that touches on high politics. The Chamber has never taken part in any political agitation, and has neither organised nor encouraged demonstrations of a political character. We take our stand on a purely economic platform, trying to obtain constitutionally relief from our burdens, offering our advice on questions interesting the State, as well as the industry, where our competency is undeniable. We do not ask for any concessions or monopolies; all that we ask for is good government and fair treatment for our industry and our shareholders.[68]

Discussions between the mining industry and representatives of Kruger's government had meanwhile been going on at an informal level – as they did most of the time. In particular, Percy FitzPatrick had discussed the *bewaarplaatsen* issue with Smuts during February; he had also proposed a round-table discussion to reach a settlement of grievances in which those of the Uitlander population generally would be included alongside those specific to the mining industry.[69] At the end of February 1899, Kruger's government approached the mining industry, through an intermediary, with a proposal for a general settlement of the matters at issue between them. What followed, during March, came to be called the Great Deal negotiations.

These important discussions have come to be regarded, with hindsight, as one of three particular occasions during 1899 when Kruger's government attempted to negotiate its way out of a situation of mounting conflict which looked likely to end in war. It has been argued that the Great Deal negotiations in March presented a better opportunity for the Transvaal government to extricate itself than either the Bloemfontein Conference, at the beginning of June, or the final franchise discussions in mid-August.[70] Yet the Great Deal negotiations were unlike the other two occasions in that the British government was not a direct party to them. This is not to say that it was not kept closely informed about their progress. The British Agent in Pretoria, Conyngham Greene, was kept fully informed by Percy FitzPatrick – a leading participant on the side of the mining industry – and he shared this information with both Milner, in Cape Town, and the Colonial Office in London, where Wernher, Beit and Lord Harris also consulted Selborne and Chamberlain. Those representing Kruger's government knew that these consultations were going on. But the Great Deal negotiations were initiated and conducted in the Transvaal (a proposal to transfer them to London was instantly quashed). They were not negotiations between governments but essentially an attempt by Kruger's government to reach a settlement with the mining industry and, with its support, to defuse the growing Uitlander conflict as well. The refusal of the mining industry to allow its specific grievances to be detached from those of the Uitlander population generally and to form the subject of a separate peace probably foredoomed these negotiations to failure. It also meant that Kruger's government faced a much more formidable opposition from within the Transvaal thereafter, as issues to do with the mining industry became combined with the 'political' issue of Uitlander enfranchisement. The discussions of March 1899 therefore form a watershed in the mounting conflict within the Transvaal.

But it is only after the Great Deal negotiations fail, and the British government commits itself to obtaining a redress from Kruger's government of the grievances embodied in the Second Uitlander Petition – by force if necessary – that the situation in the Transvaal becomes a conflict between governments and war-clouds form. The British government was not a direct party to the Great Deal negotiations, which were never discussed by the Cabinet. The Colonial Office was well-informed and consulted, its officials gave advice and recorded their opinions, but all this was at one remove from what was going on in the Transvaal. Milner exaggerated when he said that he was 'completely in the dark as to what is going on inside the inner ring in Pretoria' and he certainly found the role of being an observer and a passing-on station frustrating.[71] His scheming hand itched to steer the ship and he sought to make his influence felt by sounding-off his opinions in letters to all and sundry. But he was largely dependent for information on what Conyngham Greene (a thousand miles away in Pretoria) and the Colonial Office (in London) told him until, after the negotiations had ended in failure, FitzPatrick came down to Cape Town to tell him all about them.[72]

From beginning to end, the Great Deal negotiations were also profoundly affected by other developments going on at the same time. In particular, the difficulties Kruger's government encountered over the dynamite issue with its own Volksraad during March; the campaign organized by the South African League to present a Second Uitlander Petition to the Queen (which was delivered to Conyngham Greene on 24 March); public speeches outlining reforms by President Kruger at Heidelberg (17 March), Rustenburg (25 March) and Johannesburg (1 April); and a provocative speech by Chamberlain in the British House of Commons (on 20 March). All of these influenced the proceedings. The two parties to the negotiations also approached them with mutual distrust and very different expectations. Kruger's government considered that it was making 'very serious efforts . . . to bring about a reconciliation' with the mining industry, and expected something positive to result from its initiative. It was therefore very dashed when its 'earnest attempt to facilitate a lasting reconciliation' turned into 'a disastrous failure'.[73] The mining industry expected failure from the beginning.[74] Chamberlain initially hoped that some sort of a breakthrough might occur. Milner was convinced that 'the whole thing will fizzle' but that the exercise might have results which would be useful subsequently.[75]

The timing of the negotiations was prompted by the delivery of the British despatch challenging Kruger's government on the dynamite issue, coupled with the offer from the mining industry of a loan of £600,000 to buy out the dynamite company. These placed the Transvaal government in a quandary. Kruger was determined to hang on to the monopoly because, as he reaffirmed in March, the dynamite factory 'formed part of our independence'. 'The position today was such that if we required tomorrow 1,000,000 cartridges for Martini-Henry rifles we could get them', he observed. If the country found itself at war, and foreign countries refused to supply it with powder and ammunition, where would the government be then? So long as the factory existed, the Transvaal would have its own supplies.[76] But the retention of the dynamite monopoly would require other concessions to be made to the mining industry and perhaps some general concessions to the Uitlanders as well. If these could be successfully negotiated, this would not only ease the situation with the mining industry; it would also take the wind out of the sails of the campaign being waged by the South African League, in connection with a second Uitlander petition, to bring about British imperial intervention. The time was ripe for a bold stroke by the Transvaal government to initiate discussions to which the British government was not a party. Although these were supposed to be secret, it was accepted that the mining representatives would communicate the details to their headquarters in London and to the British government as well.

Accordingly, on 27 February – the anniversary of both Majuba and the signing of the London Convention – Eduard Lippert unexpectedly approached E. Birkenruth (the manager of Consolidated Goldfields, who had played no part in the reform agitation accompanying the Jameson Raid) with a proposal to discuss terms on which a general settlement could be made between the Transvaal government, the mining industry and 'the whole of the Uitlander population'. The mining companies were to acquiesce in the continuation of the dynamite monopoly (but with some reduction in prices) and support the Transvaal government in its efforts to secure a £2 million loan and settle the problems affecting Indian and Coloured immigrants into the Transvaal. The mining industry was also to discourage Uitlander and press agitation against the Transvaal government and dissociate itself from the South African League. In return, the government was prepared to settle the *bewaarplaatsen* issue, on terms favourable to the mining companies, and appoint a qualified financial adviser to the government to scrutinize all legislation on financial matters. In addition, it would recommend to the Volksraad that the Uitlanders should be offered the franchise after five years' residence – although Kruger had not yet accepted this, preferring nine years' residence for newcomers and seven for those who had already resided in the Transvaal for at least two years.[77]

These proposals had not yet been approved by the Executive Council and would seem to have originated with Smuts and Leyds who, together with F. W. Reitz (the State Secretary), took the leading part in the negotiations which followed. Birkenruth discussed the matter with A. Brakhan (the German manager of A. Goerz & Co.) and Georges Rouliot (the French senior partner in Wernher, Beit/H.

Eckstein & Co. who was also President of the Chamber of Mines). Rouliot at once communicated the proposals to Wernher, in London, and discussed them with Percy FitzPatrick. Since FitzPatrick was what Friedrich Eckstein called 'the political member of our firm' – and was in regular contact with Smuts – this was a perfectly reasonable thing to do.[78] FitzPatrick regarded the proposals as a device by Kruger's government to secure the dynamite monopoly by offering the mining industry something in return, and an attempt to divide the Uitlanders by winning the support of the mine-magnates and isolating the South African League. FitzPatrick then saw Smuts, who told him that the proposals were really the outcome of their own previous discussions and had the backing of Reitz, Leyds and the President, who believed he could carry the deal through the Volksraad. Smuts implored FitzPatrick 'to try and get it well received as the real settlement of all our troubles and removal of war cloud for ever'.[79] In reporting this conversation to Conyngham Greene, FitzPatrick said that, whilst he believed that Smuts's efforts to reach a settlement were genuine, he mistrusted the others and did not believe that the Volksraad would accept the proposals.

FitzPatrick felt that Kruger's government had made 'a fatal mistake' in using Lippert as their initial intermediary, since his personal stake in the dynamite monopoly made him 'the arch-enemy of the [mining] industry'. He thought that the involvement of Leyds did not augur well either and was 'an avowal of insincerity'.[80] It was known that Leyds had recently returned from Europe having failed everywhere to persuade financiers to grant the £2 million loan which the Transvaal government was urgently seeking. For their part, the representatives of Kruger's government regarded FitzPatrick himself with the deepest distrust, because of his arrest and conviction as Secretary of the first Uitlander reform movement in 1895–6 and his prominent place in the Uitlander community on the Rand. Since he was supposedly still under a ban prohibiting him from engaging in political activity (which only expired on 31 May 1899), FitzPatrick insisted on getting written authorization from the government before taking further part in the negotiations. Thereafter, he acted as a crucial link-man, representing the mining industry, informing both Conyngham Greene and the Uitlanders on the Rand about the progress of the negotiations, and writing long reports to Wernher in London. The insight which he had gained into Milner's thinking and the feedback which he regularly obtained from Conyngham Greene meant that, as he acknowledged later, during the Great Deal discussions 'everything was not guesswork or inspiration on my part'.[81] It was also FitzPatrick who persuaded his mining colleagues to insist that Uitlander representation at the negotiations should be widened. As a result, Smuts, Leyds and Reitz were forced to agree to the inclusion of H. F. E. Pistorius (Chairman of the Johannesburg Chamber of Commerce) and J. M. Pierce (Manager of Robinson's bank) and were warned that no final settlement could be reached until its terms had been discussed with a gathering representative of the wider Uitlander community. The outlook for the negotiations was not good from the outset because, as Rouliot observed to Wernher, 'the crux of the matter is that the government mistrusts us and we have no faith in them'.[82] Nonetheless, FitzPatrick considered it important to get the details of the Transvaal government's proposals in writing, even though he expected the negotiations themselves to fail. As he told Conyngham Greene, the 'attitude of the Rand representatives will be firm but reasonable, their object being to go on with the negotiations, no matter how sceptical, in order to secure for future use a number of witnesses and plenty of evidence to demonstrate that the Govt. admit impossibility of position and propose radical change'. Milner thought that this was 'thoroughly statesmanlike'.[83]

When Milner heard about the Great Deal proposals from Conyngham Greene, he feared that the senior partners of the mining companies might be encouraged by the Colonial Office to reach a separate agreement with Kruger's government. His own view, as he immediately made clear to Conyngham Greene, was:

> to keep in the closest possible touch with the Uitlanders. If they ask our advice, we ought not to refuse to give it. The more they rely on us the better, as, while they look to us, they will neither do anything rash, nor come to terms with the S.A.R. Government behind our backs, which, if we *disinterest ourselves*, is always a danger. . . . I am all for the Uitlanders negotiating and coming to terms *if they can*. But I think they can afford to be stiff in the bargain, for it is evident that . . . the S.A.R. Government begins to find its position intolerable. It has now not only England but all the great financial interests on the Continent against it.[84]

Chamberlain's response to the proposals was much more positive and reveals a good deal about his attitude towards the Transvaal at this time. 'Whether this offer is genuine or not I regard it as the most important move made since the Raid. It should certainly be treated as serious', he minuted:

> My own opinion is that the government of the S.A.R. are anxious to settle. Their financial difficulties, the strength of the South African League, their position with regard to the Dynamite Monopoly, the loss of

support from Germany, the altered position of England since Fashoda – all make in favour of a settlement – of course on their own terms. The terms offered will not do. It is no use for the financiers to undertake what they cannot perform and if the majority of the Uitlanders get no satisfaction, the agitation must go on. . . . Personally, I do not believe that the full franchise is of much importance. It is of no importance at all if it is to be delayed for five years and then given only to naturalised citizens or selected persons. What would be of immense practical importance to the majority of the Uitlanders, who all live in Jo'burg or the immediate neighbourhood, and could be granted by Kruger without any diminution of his power or abnegation of the National independence would be full municipal rights to Jo'burg. . . . If this were granted, all the pressing grievances of the ordinary Uitlander would be removed, the military strength and political power of the Boers would not be impaired, and the S.A. League and the hostile press would have no *raison d'etre*.[85]

Chamberlain's staff at the Colonial Office suggested that Kruger's government probably had 'an exaggerated idea of the political power of the capitalists' and assumed that the South African League and the press, both in Britain and South Africa, were under their control. They were also convinced that the inclusion of a vague offer to extend the franchise was merely an attempt to divert the Uitlanders from appealing to the British government; but only genuine reforms would remove Uitlander agitation 'however well the capitalists were satisfied', and on these they doubted if Kruger's government would ever 'make a concession of value'.[86] Chamberlain's declaration that he personally 'did not believe that the franchise was of much importance' seems at first surprising, but it has to be seen in the light of his enthusiasm for a 'municipal' solution for Johannesburg. He had first put forward this idea in February 1896 and he again spoke in favour of it in the House of Commons in March 1899. Its attractions were that it did not jeopardize either Kruger's government or the existing, qualified independence of the Transvaal; and under it the Uitlanders would obtain a fair measure of control over their own affairs *and yet remain British citizens*, who would still look to the British government for support and guidance and thereby enable that government to retain its hold over them.[87] It would, however, have left Kruger's republic 'unreconstructed', whereas a central purpose of Uitlander enfranchisement, in Milner's view, was to upset the Afrikaner oligarchy and bring about a transition to a reformed and more widely representative administration in which it was expected that Uitlander interests would soon predominate. It was for this reason that Milner had never warmed to the idea of turning Johannesburg into a largely self-governing 'municipality'; but all that he told Chamberlain was that he considered 'a genuine municipality' would be even harder to extract from Kruger's government than a modest franchise.[88] Milner had more confidence than Chamberlain did in the continued British loyalty of Uitlanders if they became citizens of a reformed Transvaal republic. Chamberlain's idea of a 'municipality' never won much support from the mine-magnates either, and it played no role in their negotiations. As everything came to revolve around the granting of an Uitlander franchise, it faded rapidly from view.

Both Rouliot and FitzPatrick were meanwhile keeping Wernher (in London) closely informed of the progress of the Great Deal negotiations. Rouliot took notes at every meeting and sent them to Wernher 'as a true resume of all what took place'. The Transvaal government's detailed proposals were also sent by telegraph – the lines being specially kept open on a Sunday for that purpose.[89] Rouliot – whose general attitude was far more conciliatory than that of FitzPatrick – felt that, on their present basis, the negotiations could not possibly succeed. The primary purpose of Kruger's government seemed to be to secure the agreement of the mining industry to the continuation of the dynamite monopoly, but Rouliot felt that would involve the industry in 'giving away solid facts and receiving only promises in return'. In addition, the mining industry was being asked publicly to disown the South African League – whose growing Uitlander following would then turn on the mine-magnates 'and we should succeed in making enemies of everybody'.[90] What they had to guard against, above all, in Rouliot's view, was division within the Uitlander community and between it and the mining industry: 'we must all pull together as it is only by presenting a united body that we shall ever be able to get anything'.[91] This made it essential for those representing the mining industry in the Great Deal negotiations to refuse to separate off and settle issues particular to mining operations from the more general Uitlander grievances and especially the franchise – which they insisted from the outset would require consultation with those affected by it, i.e. a body more representative of Uitlander opinion. *Only if* a franchise 'agreeable to the Uitlander population' was offered, would the mining industry be prepared to consider what Kruger's government had proposed with regard to dynamite and other mining issues.[92]

The senior partners of the leading mining companies on the Rand with headquarters in London also consulted both together and with the Colonial Office about the negotiations which were underway. On 9 March, Wernher saw Selborne and told him that he didn't expect them to come to anything. He also informed him that Kruger's government had just succeeded in obtaining a loan for £2 million through the good offices of the Netherlands Railway Company. Wernher then went on to claim that 'he and his friends could long ago have made their own terms' with Kruger's government but had always looked beyond their personal interests to the good government of the country and the welfare of the Uitlander population. Selborne said that he agreed with Wernher's sceptical view about the proposals and had no observations to give with regard to the specific concessions offered to the mining industry – which knew its own business best. As for the Uitlanders, no one could undertake to secure the requirement that all agitation should cease. It was caused by bad administration and only the reform of this could stop it. When Wernher asked what he meant by reform, Selborne repeated Chamberlain's long-held view about the granting of a *bona fide* municipality to Johannesburg, with control over its own police, education and administration. When Wernher pressed him about the franchise, Selborne said 'that that was going at once to the point of most resistance' and so perhaps Wernher and his friends might well refrain from putting that question to the forefront of the negotiations 'without any prejudice to their future attitude'.[93] When Beit also came to see him, on 15 March, Selborne, after consulting Chamberlain, repeated his view of the Great Deal proposals that 'the bargain seemed to me a disastrous one for the Uitlanders and pregnant with mischief for us'.[94]

After Wernher, Beit/H. Eckstein & Co., the next most powerful mining company on the Rand was Consolidated Goldfields. Its chairman, Lord Harris, went to see Chamberlain on 14 March 1899 and told him that his company was prepared to accept the Great Deal proposals unless the British government objected. Chamberlain at once responded:

> that Her Majesty's Government would not interfere but that public opinion would probably say that the financiers had sold their cause and their compatriots – and sold them cheap and would not in the long run get even the price they had accepted. It was however their business not ours . . . our policy was to get a municipality but we did not expect to succeed at present.[95]

On 16 March, senior representatives of the major mining companies on the Rand met in London to discuss the Great Deal proposals. This meeting was attended by three representatives from Consolidated Goldfields, Alfred Beit himself represented Wernher, Beit/H. Eckstein & Co., A.H. Marker represented A. Goerz & Co., and J. B. Robinson, S. Neumann, Solly Joel, and George Farrar were also present. During the course of this meeting the view consistently propounded by Rouliot and Wernher triumphed over that which Lord Harris had put to Chamberlain two days previously. Afterwards, a statement was issued welcoming a settlement of the dynamite issue but declaring that this would be unacceptable unless it were accompanied by the extension of the franchise.[96] In Johannesburg, Rouliot was gratified that this meant that the whole of the mining industry 'was in accord with the position which we have consistently taken up' but was convinced that the conditions attached to the present offer of the franchise would make it quite unacceptable to the majority of the Uitlanders. What was needed was a straightforward offer to pass a new franchise law giving full burgher rights, including the franchise, to all who wanted them and had been in residence in the Transvaal for seven years. Rouliot, however, was doubtful if Kruger's government would ever agree to this.[97]

It was Rouliot who wrote the detailed reply of the mining representatives to the government proposals – after consultation by cable with Wernher in London – and succeeded, not without difficulty, in getting all the mining representatives to sign it.[98] In this document (dated 27 March), a summary was given of what had happened, and the government's proposals with regard to the *bewaarplaatsen* and the appointment of a Financial Adviser were welcomed. The mining industry offered guarded support to the government if it required a loan. The signatories declared that they were not able to dictate to the press but would discourage any agitation on issues on which a settlement was reached. Whilst they would always repudiate any political organization dedicated to stirring up strife 'amongst the different nationalities inhabiting this State', they could not deprecate 'any legitimate representations which the community or any section of them may see fit to make in matters which concern them as inhabitants'. (This obviously applied to the Second Uitlander Petition which had just been delivered.) The subject of the control of the immigration of Indian and Coloured people into the Transvaal was governed by the London Convention and was clearly a matter for the British government. Total opposition to the granting of monopolies and concessions was expressed in connection with the dynamite issue, where the additional and unnecessary cost of £600,000 p.a. to the mining industry was emphasized. Nonetheless, the industry might be willing to make even such 'a great monetary sacrifice' in order to bring about a general settlement, providing the dynamite concession was not extended beyond its current contract, the price was reduced to 70 shillings a case, and the government was given 'the 5 shillings a case and the share of the profits to which it is entitled'. This matter would have to be referred to the Chamber of Mines. The reply ended with pleas for the government to assist the industry in the supply of labour for the mines and for the independence of the judiciary to be assured at all times.

One other subject was given prominent attention in the reply of the mining industry to the Transvaal government's Great Deal proposals: the franchise. This, it was declared, was 'the vital point upon which a permanent and peaceful settlement must hinge', but any scheme for it 'must first be laid before, and approved by, the unenfranchised [Uitlander] community'. Businesses such as the mining companies were not qualified to discuss this question on behalf of the Uitlanders generally. Means would have to be found to consult them, and their agreement on this question would have to be obtained *first*, 'before we recommend the sacrifices which we contemplate in order to ensure a general permanent and peaceful settlement'.[99] Thus, a political settlement of Uitlander grievances would be a prerequisite for a Great Deal between the Transvaal government and the mining industry.

Meanwhile, FitzPatrick had obtained official permission to begin the process of Uitlander consultation by calling a meeting, broadly representative of the Uitlander community, and putting to it the Great Deal proposals. This meeting took place at the Rand Club on the evening of 13 March where, after dinner, H. C. Hull (another member of the first Uitlander reform movement who had also had his political ban lifted) initiated proceedings by a toast to the Queen. FitzPatrick then gave a long speech which was not just a report of what had happened in the negotiations so far, but also a calculated bid by him for support from the wider Uitlander community for his own strategy.[100] This was first, to give the lie to the suspicion that the mining industry aimed to come to a settlement on its own account with Kruger's government, at the expense of the rest of the Uitlander population; secondly, to use the Great Deal negotiations to get the Transvaal government to 'admit the strength and reasonableness' of the combined grievances of the mining industry and the Uitlander population generally; and finally, to move towards 'laying the whole of the terms of this peace settlement before the Imperial Government and practically making them a party to it . . . this, it is my very strong opinion, we must, by hook or by crook, secure as a condition of any settlement which we may arrive at. It is the only security worth mentioning'.[101]

Like Milner, FitzPatrick aimed to draw the British government in to any final settlement. This was precisely what, in these negotiations

– which it regarded as concerned with internal, Transvaal matters – Kruger's government was determined to avoid. Whilst FitzPatrick acknowledged that 'in some ways, all of us would like to see a row' between the two governments, he accepted that if a means of reaching a peaceful settlement existed this should be pursued. Without the threatened intervention of the British government, FitzPatrick argued, there would be no readiness to reform. The admissions which Kruger's government had been forced to make about 'the intolerable state of affairs' in the Transvaal were 'strengthening the hands of the Imperial Government to get those reforms'.[102] Towards the end of his speech, FitzPatrick let slip another consideration which was in his mind: the economic revival underway on the Rand. At present there were two rows of mining companies at work on the reef, he observed, but these would soon become six. In bellicose language, he then suggested what a further surge in industrialization and immigration implied, as far as Kruger and his burghers were concerned: 'It means the absolute wiping out of these people. We have got to win and we will win as sure as God is above us.'[103]

FitzPatrick had used his speech to shift attention away from the specific economic and mining issues initially raised by the representatives of Kruger's government towards what Selborne had recognized as 'the point of most resistance': the franchise. This was because the franchise embodied not just the core of the Uitlander problem in the Transvaal but also the means for its solution. If the franchise could be obtained, it would enable the Uitlanders themselves to work through the Transvaal government to tackle all the other problems and these, FitzPatrick claimed, would then disappear 'like the mists before the morning sun'. But the conditions of that franchise were crucial and so was a redistribution of seats in line with population to go with it. Since the conditions so far outlined in the Great Deal discussions meant that it would be almost impossible in practice for many Uitlanders to obtain the vote, FitzPatrick announced in his speech that he and his colleagues were not going to agree to them. It was up to the Uitlanders themselves to draw up a statement for presentation to Kruger's government on this vital matter. Out of the meeting at the Rand Club, a consultative committee of nine people was formed, with FitzPatrick as its chairman, and this eventually produced a 'Memorandum re. Franchise' which was included by the mining industry's representatives along with their reply to Reitz and his government on 27 March.[104]

This Memorandum claimed to represent the views of 'a very large and influential section' of the Uitlander community and it criticized the franchise proposals, recently outlined by Kruger in a public speech at Heidelberg on 17 March, on five main grounds:

1. No allowance was made, in the residential requirements, for any period of residence already completed. The provision was therefore not for the present but for the future.

2. The fact that changes to the franchise law required the approval of two-thirds of the Transvaal burghers made any change unlikely. Even in the presidential election in 1898, less than two-thirds of the burghers on the register had voted.

3. The present form of the oath of allegiance would be regarded as unnecessarily humiliating by most non-Afrikaners, and had been rejected by the Orange Free State for precisely this reason.

4. The proposals required applicants for citizenship to renounce their existing citizenship without offering them any immediate replacement. A 'period of disqualification' would therefore occur, during which Uitlanders would have no citizenship and no guarantee that their prospective rights to Transvaal citizenship would not be 'legislated away as they were on the point of maturing', as had already happened as successive, increasingly restrictive franchise laws had been passed since 1890.

5. Extension of the franchise without some approach to an equitable redistribution of seats in the Volksraad was unacceptable and provoked doubts as to the *bona fides* of the government.

Finally, since most of the legislation 'designed to exclude for ever the great bulk of the Uitlander population' dated from 1890, it would be 'both possible and proper' for the Volksraad to annul it and restore the law to what it had been before that date.

These objections were not put forward as 'the irreducible minimum' but 'in good faith as indicating in our opinion the lines upon which it would be possible to work towards a settlement with a reasonable prospect of success'.[105]

All of these points were not without foundation, and many of them were to form the subject of further exchanges during the coming months. But what about the 'good faith' in which, it was claimed, they were being made the grounds for refusing the Great Deal proposals of Kruger's government? Here, there is every reason for concluding that it did not exist. From the outset, FitzPatrick had made clear to his confidants his 'private opinion' that 'nothing will result from the negotiations with the government'.[106] His purpose throughout had been to use them, first, to extract from the Transvaal government the acknowledgement that both mining and Uitlander grievances existed and required measures to rectify them; secondly, to re-establish on the Rand the solidarity between the mining industry and the general Uitlander population which had played so crucial a role in the reform movement in 1895. This meant not allowing the issues specific to the mining industry to be separated from the wider political issue of Uitlander enfranchisement; finally, he aimed to involve the British government in any overall settlement. Through the Great Deal negotiations and the simultaneous organization of a Second Uitlander Petition to the Queen – which was even more comprehensive in its coverage of Uitlander grievances than the first one had been – the objective was to present Chamberlain and the British government with evidence of grievances and an appeal for British intervention to rectify them which that government would be unable to resist.

FitzPatrick's final contribution was to ensure, through the deliberate leaking to the press of the mining industry's considered reply (of 27 March) to the government's proposals, together with the Memorandum about the Uitlander franchise, that the Great Deal discussions came to an abrupt end in a welter of bitter recriminations. FitzPatrick himself has left an account of how he once again played the link-man in the leak.[107] On 28 March, it was he who delivered both the mining representatives' reply and the Memorandum about the franchise to the State Secretary, F. W. Reitz. Then, ever reluctant to visit Pretoria without also calling on the British Agent, he went on to the latter's residence. There, he met not just Conyngham Greene, but also G. V. Fiddes (Milner's Imperial Secretary), who had just arrived from Cape Town, having been sent by Milner to spy out the land and report on the attitude of the Uitlanders on the Rand. FitzPatrick promptly showed him both the reply and the Memorandum – of which he had had some fifteen copies made, ready to distribute 'to all who have a right to it' – which Fiddes thought 'a wonderfully clever document'.[108] Conyngham Greene and Fiddes then urged FitzPatrick to make the details of the Great Deal negotiations public as soon as possible, arguing that this would refute the suggestion that the mining industry and the 'capitalists' were engaged in a deal to 'sell the Uitlander community for their own advantage'. It would also indicate their support for the more general grievances of the Uitlanders embodied in the Second Uitlander Petition, which had been delivered to Conyngham Greene on 24 March and been forwarded via Milner to London.[109]

Fiddes, who wrote the same day to Milner that FitzPatrick 'is in it heart and soul, & absolutely on *our* side', felt that 'the thing has come more suddenly than we expected; but it has come & we must either "go into it baldheaded" or drop the whole business – probably for ever . . . this is the turning point'.[110] He told FitzPatrick that Chamberlain was wholly sympathetic to their cause and was 'only waiting for a sufficiently strong and precise appeal from the Uit[lande]rs to enable him to overcome resistance in the Cabinet & in England'. It was therefore 'of vital importance that these negotiations sh[oul]d somehow or other become public property at a very early date'.

FitzPatrick responded by declaring:

> Mr. C. can push this line too far. He has now got an appeal from 22,000. If this isn't enough, he will never get another. We (the capitalists) can make our peace easily enough with the Govt., & we shall do it if this last effort isn't enough for Mr. C.[111]

But he needed little convincing about the advantages to be gained from the early publication of the documents he had just delivered to the Transvaal government. He feared, however, that he might be arrested (for breaking his pledge not to engage in politics) or have to 'clear out of the country', in addition to being accused of bad faith, if he leaked the documents himself. He therefore provided F. C. Falconer (a journalist who was the Pretoria correspondent of *The Cape Times*) with the money to bribe a Transvaal government official to obtain a copy, telling him: 'You do the work, but there's no reason why you should pay the expenses when it's our cause too.'[112] When the documents were published in the London *Times* on 3 April, and three days later in *The Cape Times* and other South African newspapers, Conyngham Greene felt that this was 'a splendid stroke and strengthens our position enormously'.[113] The Transvaal State Secretary (F.W. Reitz), however, wrote angrily of how this had caused him to doubt the good faith of those with whom he had been negotiating and to feel that 'the hand extended to the Industry in absolute good faith' had been 'slighted purposely and wilfully'.[114]

There is no doubt about the deep sense of betrayal felt by those who had initiated and conducted the Great Deal negotiations on behalf of the Transvaal government. Smuts wrote bitterly that conditions in the Transvaal were now worse than they had been for fifteen years – thanks to the attempt by himself and others to bring about a lasting reconciliation with the mining industry. He was convinced that it was because of the influence of the British government that the mine-magnates had taken up 'such an unexplicable attitude to our in every way acceptable proposals'.[115] Others believed that it was the other way round and that 'the heads of the mining industry had urged Mr Chamberlain to speak disparagingly of the Transvaal in order to bring about a collapse of the negotiations'.[116] Certainly, members of Kruger's administration felt, with some justification, that the mining industry and the British government had worked together to wreck the Great Deal discussions, and were incensed by the tone of Chamberlain's speech in the House of Commons on 20 March in which he accused Kruger's government of failing to keep its promises in the past and giving promises in the present which were 'entirely illusory'.[117] The British Consul in Swaziland happened to call on F. W. Reitz, in Pretoria, just after the latter had read what Chamberlain had said. He found him in a rage. Reitz said that Chamberlain was a man who was originally a screw-maker and, by deserting his party, had risen to the top of the tree and now adopted the tone of 'the mighty suzerain' addressing a weak state. He and Milner seemed to think that the members of the Transvaal government 'were a lot of Hottentots. . . . He [Reitz] had been keeping the peace for 23 years and would not provoke a row now; but if they wanted it, well, let them come'. Reitz was 'very hot' about the subject, reported the Consul, the virulence of his language indicating his strong antipathy towards Chamberlain and Milner.[118]

Thus, the attempt by the Transvaal government to reach a 'comprehensive settlement', through the Great Deal negotiations, ended in failure. Informal discussions with the mining industry continued in a desultory way, but Rouliot no longer believed that they would result in anything substantial.[119] In early May, at a private interview with Kruger, he urged the President to adopt some of the reforms which could so easily be granted 'without loss of dignity and without any peril to the independence of his country'. 'These measures', he observed, 'would satisfy those that feel [strongly] on the subject and would silence those that agitate merely for the purpose of agitation'.[120] Kruger listened attentively but then concluded the meeting abruptly, saying that he was going to lay his own programme before the Raad and this 'would give satisfaction to everybody'. Rouliot remained quite unconvinced and, after Kruger had gone, he was cornered by Reitz who declared that, just as the capitalists were behind the (reform) movement in 1895, so now they were trying to bring the Transvaal government 'into complications with England'. Rouliot challenged this directly, accusing Reitz of simply trying to shift responsibility away from the failings of his own government. 'If your government would act liberally, they would have everyone on their side', he said, 'but if you want to ignore facts, to ignore public feeling, attribute your own wrongs to other people, and, instead of remedying them, blame others and do nothing, then the situation is hopeless, you will never have peace, and you will be responsible for the consequences'.[121] Reitz had recently told Rouliot that, 'the Transvaal being a weak nation, they would have to give way a good deal . . . but that if one British soldier crosses the border, or one foot of their territory is touched, they will fight, and it will be a bitter and bloody struggle'.[122] Reporting these conversations to Wernher, in London, Rouliot observed that the Boers were preparing themselves for a war in which they reckoned on the support of their kinsfolk in the Orange Free State and the Cape Colony. 'From their point of view it would be purely suicidal, and from our side it would be a calamity that ought to be avoided by all possible means . . . everything possible that can be done ought to be done to avert this. But evidently the solution rests with the Boers.' He feared that they might well 'persist in their uncompromising attitude' and so determined to devote all his efforts to trying to 'induce them to give in before it is too late'.[123]

Wernher, too, as a leading mine-magnate, was firmly of the opinion that 'our salvation is with the government [of the Transvaal republic] to negotiate to obtain concessions etc. and gradually wriggle in a better position'.[124] If Kruger were 'really clever, he would make some concessions and the agitation would soon pause as nobody wants violent changes or measures'; what was needed was 'new negotiations to give reforms'.[125] Kruger could only improve his position by 'timely yielding' so 'one feels it ought to come. I have not the [s]lightest fear of war, which would be a great misfortune and to my mind uncalled for', he commented, 'what we should have is a rearrangement of the [London] Convention, with a clear definition of the relative positions and renewed guarantee of independence; unless that is done there will be always unrest which in the end could only be settled by war'.[126]

The failure of its attempt to placate the mining industry left the Transvaal government in a dangerously exposed position by April 1899. For this failure occurred at a time when the British government was asserting not just its suzerainty claim over the Transvaal but a right to intervene in the Transvaal's internal affairs which extended beyond the dynamite monopoly to the issues over which the Uitlander population was in mounting conflict with Kruger's government. Most ominously, the Great Deal negotiations had brought the mining industry and the Uitlander community together in a growing campaign for *political* change. These negotiations had compelled the

Transvaal government to acknowledge that Uitlander grievances existed and needed to be addressed. They had demonstrated the refusal of the mining industry to allow its particular grievances to be detached from those of the Uitlanders generally. Meanwhile, the South African League had been organizing a Second Uitlander Petition to the Queen. What the Transvaal government rightly feared was that this would pave the way for the direct intervention of the British government in support of the Uitlanders, whom many of Kruger's burghers had come to regard as a Trojan horse in their midst.

NOTES

1.   Milner to Fiddes, 23 December 1898, in C. Headlam, ed., *The Milner Papers* 2 vols (London, 1931/1933), 1, p. 299.
2.   Conyngham Greene to Milner, 22 July 1898, and Milner's reply of 17 August 1898, in ibid., pp. 236–7.
3.   Milner to Fiddes, 25 November 1898, in ibid., p. 299; Chamberlain to Salisbury, 30 November 1898, in J. L. Garvin and J. Amery, *Life of Joseph Chamberlain* 6 vols (London, 1932–69), 3, p. 380.
4.   Milner to Fiddes, 25 November 1898, in Headlam, ed., *The Milner Papers*, 1, p. 299.
5.   T. Pakenham, *The Boer War* (London, 1979), pp. 33–4.
6.   A. N. Porter, 'Sir Alfred Milner and the press 1897–1899', *HJ* XVI, 2 (1973) for details.
7.   Dr Samuel Evans to W. T. Stead, 7 July 1898, in ibid., pp. 330–1.
8.   P. FitzPatrick to J. Wernher, 6 April 1899, in A. H. Duminy and W. R. Guest, eds, *FitzPatrick, South African Politician: Selected Papers, 1888–1906* (Johannesburg, 1976), p. 202.
9.   Milner to Garrett, 17 July 1899, and Milner to Gell, 21 June 1899, both in Porter, 'Sir Alfred Milner', p. 337.
10. A. Duminy and B. Guest, *Interfering in Politics: A Biography of Sir Percy FitzPatrick* (Johannesburg, 1987), p. 80.
11. See J. A. Hobson, *The South African War: Its Causes and Effects* (London, 1900), especially Part II, pp. 206–19; Porter, 'Sir Alfred Milner'; Alan Jeeves, 'The Rand capitalists and Transvaal politics 1892–1899', Ph.D. thesis, Queens University, Kingston, Canada (1971), ch. VII.
12. J. A. Hobson, *The Psychology of Jingoism* (London, 1901).
13. An exception is Alan Jeeves, whose work first prompted me to study *The Standard and Diggers News* for these months. See Jeeves, 'The Rand capitalists' (unpublished Ph.D. thesis), especially Part III, ch. VI.
14. Wernher Beit to H. Eckstein, 17 December 1897, BRA, HE vol. 63; also *The Cape Times*, 3 June 1899, p. 4.

15. See, for examples, *The Standard and Diggers News*, 10 and 14 January 1899.
16. P. FitzPatrick to J. Wernher, 12 December 1898, printed in Duminy and Guest, eds, *FitzPatrick,* p. 171.
17. Rouliot to Wernher, 9 January 1899, BRA, HE 175. See also Jeeves, 'The Rand capitalists and the coming of the South African War, 1896–1899', *Canadian Historical Association Papers*, 1973, pp. 74–5.
18. *The Standard and Diggers News*, 31 March 1899.
19. *The Standard and Diggers News*, 5 April 1899.
20. *The Standard and Diggers News*, 26 April 1899.
21. *The Standard and Diggers News*, 28 April 1899.
22. See Conclusion, pp. 393–404 below; also Iain R. Smith, 'The origins of the South African War: a reappraisal', *SAHJ* 22 (1990), especially pp. 29–32.
23. As a senior member of the Colonial Office put it later: 'Before the war we used to think with dread of the Transvaal becoming a British Republic', Frederick Graham, 7 June 1904, cited in G. H. Le May, *British Supremacy in South Africa 1899–1907* (Oxford, 1965), p. 4.
24. The two key despatches are Chamberlain to British High Commissioner, 15 December 1898 and 13 July 1899, both in the Transvaal Archives, BA 13.
25. See P. FitzPatrick to J. Wernher, 30 January 1899, in Duminy and Guest, eds, *FitzPatrick*, p. 176.
26. See Ch. 5 p. 172.
27. Milner to Graham (CO), 18 December 1898, CO 417/247.
28. Milner to Selborne, 29 December 1898, SeP MS 11.
29. Milner to Selborne, 19 December 1898, SeP MS 11.
30. Judgement of 23 October 1893, enclosed in Chamberlain to British High Commissioner, 27 February 1897, Pretoria Archives HC 1/27 (also CO 27/2/97).
31. Full documentation in the Transvaal Archives, Pretoria, BA 9.
32. Chamberlain's minute cited in R. H. Wilde, *Joseph Chamberlain and the South African Republic 1895–99*, Archives Yearbook for South African History 1956 Part 1 (Pretoria, 1956), p. 73.
33. British despatch of 13 January 1899 in Transvaal Archives, BA 12, also printed in C.9317 (May 1899); Chamberlain to British Acting High Commissioner, 13 January 1899, CO 417/247; Acting High Commissioner to E. Fraser, 23 January 1899, Transvaal Archives, BA 12.
34. See P. FitzPatrick to J. Wernher, 30 January 1899, in Duminy and Guest, eds, *FitzPatrick*, pp. 175–6.
35. Ibid.
36. Chamber of Mines to the State Secretary, Pretoria, 2 February 1899, printed in the Chamber's Eleventh Annual Report (for the year 1899), 1900, pp. 3–5; Fraser to Acting British High Commissioner, 3 February 1899, Transvaal Archives, BA 20.
37. P. FitzPatrick to J. Wernher, 30 January, 6 and 25 February 1899, in Duminy and Guest, eds, *FitzPatrick*, pp. 172–80.

38. British Agent (Pretoria) to British High Commissioner, 20 May 1899, reporting a 'leaked' copy of the arrangement between Kruger's government and the dynamite company, Transvaal Archives, BA 20.

39. Chamber of Mines, Eleventh Annual Report (1900) for details; also J. S. Marais, *The Fall of Kruger's Republic* (Oxford, 1961), pp. 246–7.

40. Evidence of this is to be found not just in British government papers but also in the archives of Wernher Beit/H. Eckstein & Co., e.g. Eckstein to Wernher Beit (London), 19 December 1898, BRA, HE 131.

41. Marais, *The Fall of Kruger's Republic,* pp. 244–5.

42. See below, pp. 239–43.

43. See Marais, *The Fall of Kruger's Republic,* pp. 237–40, for a summary; I have also used evidence from the Transvaal Archives, BA 12 and BA 20.

44. *The Press,* Pretoria, 26 December 1898.

45. The full text of the Uitlander Petition is in the Transvaal Archives, BA 20; it was printed in *The Press* (Pretoria), 26 December 1898.

46. The extensive exchanges between Fraser, Evans and the Acting British High Commissioner on the matter during December 1898–January 1899 are in the Transvaal Archives, BA 20 and BA 12.

47. Fraser to Wybergh, 10 January 1899, Transvaal Archives, BA 20.

48. Exchanges between F. W. Reitz and E. Fraser enclosed in Fraser to Butler, 26 January 1899, Transvaal Archives, BA 20.

49. Marais, *The Fall of Kruger's Republic,* pp. 240–1.

50. Ibid., pp. 232–3; W. F. Butler, *An Autobiography* (London, 1911), pp. 398–400, 409–13.

51. Butler to E. Fraser, 4 January 1899, Transvaal Archives, BA 12; Butler to Colonial Office, 18 January 1899, CO 879/59.

52. See pp. 253–62 below.

53. Chamberlain to Milner, 30 December 1898, cited in A. N. Porter, *The Origins of the South African War, Joseph Chamberlain and the Diplomacy of Imperialism 1895–1899* (Manchester, 1980), p. 184.

54. Ibid., p. 185, citing Conyngham Greene to Graham and Selborne, 28 October, 1 and 6 November 1898, CO 417/255/24630.

55. Walrond to Fiddes, 12 and 16 January 1899, enclosed in Fiddes to Selborne, SeP MS 14.

56. Milner to Graham, 19 January 1899, CO 419/259.

57. Milner to Sir W. Hely Hutchinson, 23 February 1899, in Headlam, ed., *The Milner Papers,* 1, p. 303.

58. H. W. Just, minute of 30 January, CO 417/259.

59. See, for example, the speech by George Albu on 11 January 1899, reported in *The Star,* 12 January 1899, p. 4.

60. Fraser to Butler, 18 January 1899, Transvaal Archives, BA 20.

61. Fraser to Butler, 12 January 1899, Transvaal Archives, BA 20.

62. Milner to Selborne, 23 and 31 January 1899, in Headlam, ed., *The Milner Papers,* 1, pp. 301–2.

63. Chamberlain to Milner, 16 March 1898, in ibid., p. 228.

64. See Smuts to Leyds, 30 April 1899, in W. K. Hancock and J. van der Poel, eds, *Selections from the Smuts Papers* 7 vols (Cambridge, 1966–73), 1, pp. 227–8.

65. Milner to Fiddes, 3 January 1899, printed in E. Stokes, 'Milnerism', *HJ* V, 1 (1962), p. 54.

66. Manager of the Standard Bank to London headquarters, 12 April 1899, Standard Bank Archives 3/1/34.

67. Resolution of the Johannesburg Chamber of Commerce, 1 February 1899, Transvaal Archives, BA 20.

68. Address by the President of the Chamber of Mines (G. Rouliot), 26 January 1899, *Tenth Annual Report of the Chamber of Mines* (1899).

69. See Chapter 6, pp. 203–4 above.

70. Alan Jeeves, 'The Rand capitalists' (Ph.D. thesis), p. 404.

71. Milner to Colonial Office, 11 March 1899, CO 417/259.

72. Milner's diary for these weeks confirms this, but see also Milner to Conyngham Greene, 11 March 1899, and Milner to Fiddes, 1 April 1899, both in Headlam, ed., *The Milner Papers*, 1, pp. 325, 331.

73. Smuts to Merriman, 13 March 1899, and Smuts to Leyds, 30 April 1899, both in Hancock and van der Poel, eds, *Selections Smuts Papers*, 1, pp. 218, 227.

74. See especially Rouliot to Wernher, 6, 13, 20, 27 March and 10, 17 April 1899, BRA, HE 175, and Wernher's replies of 29 March and n.d. 1899, in HE 167.

75. Milner to Conyngham Greene, 11 March 1899, in Headlam, ed., *The Milner Papers*, 1, p. 325.

76. Speech by Kruger at Heidelberg, 17 March 1899, *The Standard and Diggers News*, 21 March 1899.

77. Marais, *The Fall of Kruger's Republic*, pp. 248–9; P. FitzPatrick, *The Transvaal from Within* (London, 1899), pp. 343–4. The proposals are summarized in Milner to Chamberlain, 4 March 1899, CO 417/259.

78. See Fiddes to Milner, 7 April 1899, reporting a conversation with F. Eckstein, in Headlam, ed., *The Milner Papers*, 1, p. 347.

79. FitzPatrick to Conyngham Greene, 3 March 1899, in ibid., p. 321; FitzPatrick to Wernher, 4 March 1899, in Duminy and Guest, eds, *FitzPatrick*, p. 184.

80. P. FitzPatrick, *South African Memories* (London, 1932), p. 171.

81. Ibid., p. 173.

82. Rouliot to Wernher, 6 March 1899, BRA, HE 175.

83. Conyngham Greene to Milner, 13 March 1899, and Milner's reply, 14 March 1899, in Headlam, ed., *The Milner Papers*, 1, pp. 326–7.

84. Milner to Conyngham Greene, 3 March 1899, in ibid., p. 322.

85. Chamberlain Minute 8 March 1899 on Milner to Chamberlain, 4 March 1899, CO 417/259/553.

86. Colonial Office Minutes, 9 March, on Milner's letter of 4 March 1899 and CO Memorandum (by Lambert), 13 March 1899, CO 417/259.

87. Speech on 20 March 1899, *Hansard*, Fourth Series, vol. lxviii, col. 1378; Marais, *The Fall of Kruger's Republic*, p. 251.

88. Milner to Sir W. Hely Hutchinson, 8 May 1899, in Headlam, ed., *The Milner Papers*, 1, p. 359.

89. Rouliot to Wernher, 13 March 1899, BRA, HE 175.

90. Ibid.
91. Rouliot to Wernher, 20 March 1899. BRA, HE 175.
92. Ibid.
93. Selborne Minute after meeting Wernher on 9 March 1899, CO 417/259/561.
94. Selborne to Chamberlain, 15 March 1899, in D. G. Boyce, ed., *The Crisis of British Power: The Imperial and Naval Papers of the Second Earl of Selborne, 1895–1910* (London, 1990), p. 71.
95. Chamberlain Minute, 14 March 1899, CO 417/259/629.
96. A. Duminy and W. Guest, *Interfering in Politics: A Biography of Sir Percy FitzPatrick* (Johannesburg, 1987), p. 67.
97. Rouliot to Wernher, 20 March 1899, BRA, HE 175.
98. Rouliot to Wernher, 27 March 1899, BRA, HE 175. The full text of the reply is printed in FitzPatrick, *The Transvaal from Within*, pp. 345–9. Those who signed it were: G. Rouliot, H. F. E. Pistorius, E. Birkenruth, J. M. Pierce, A. Brakhan, J. G. Hamilton and W. Dalrymple.
99. All quotations from Reply to the State Secretary (F. W. Reitz), 27 March 1899, printed in FitzPatrick, *The Transvaal from Within*, pp. 345–9.
100. Speech by P. FitzPatrick, 13 March 1899, in Duminy and Guest, eds, *FitzPatrick*, pp. 189–202.
101. Ibid., p. 199.
102. Ibid., p. 200.
103. Ibid., p. 202.
104. The Memorandum is printed in P FitzPatrick, *The Transvaal from Within*, pp. 350–1.
105. Summary and quotations from the 'Memorandum re. Franchise' cited above.
106. FitzPatrick to Selborne, 8 March 1899, SeP MS 18.
107. FitzPatrick, *South African Memories*, pp. 175–9.
108. Duminy and Guest, *Interfering in Politics*, p. 70; P. FitzPatrick to J. Wernher, 6 April 1899, in Duminy and Guest, eds, *FitzPatrick*, p. 203.
109. Duminy and Guest, *Interfering in Politics*, p. 70.
110. Fiddes to Milner, 28 March 1899, MP 13.
111. Ibid.
112. FitzPatrick, *South African Memories*, p. 178.
113. Conyngham Greene to Milner, 7 April 1899, MP 12.
114. F. W. Reitz to G. Rouliot and other representatives of the mining industry, 8 April 1899, printed in FitzPatrick, *The Transvaal from Within*, p. 354.
115. Smuts to Leyds, 30 April 1899, in Hancock and van der Poel, eds, *Selections Smuts Papers*, 1, pp. 227–8.
116. Conyngham Greene to Milner, 24 March 1899, Transvaal Archives, BA 20.
117. *Hansard*, Fourth Series, 20 March 1899, vol. lxviii, col. 1377.

118. Memorandum by the British Consul in Swaziland, 23 March 1899, enclosed with British Agent to British High Commissioner, 23 March 1899, Transvaal Archives, BA 20.
119. Rouliot to Wernher, 10 and 17 April 1899, BRA, HE 175.
120. Rouliot to Wernher, 8 May 1899, BRA, HE 175.
121. Ibid.
122. Rouliot to Wernher, 17 April 1899, BRA, HE 175.
123. Ibid.
124. Wernher to Rouliot, 23 March 1899, BRA, HE 167.
125. Wernher to Rouliot, 6 May 1899, BRA, HE 167.
126. Wernher to Rouliot, 13 May 1899, BRA, HE 167.

CHAPTER EIGHT

The Great Day of Reckoning

THE SECOND UITLANDER PETITION TO THE QUEEN

The organization of a Second Uitlander Petition to the Queen had been going on at the same time as the Great Deal negotiations and this had certainly been a consideration in the efforts of the Transvaal government to reach a separate settlement with the mining industry. Kruger himself had sought to take some of the wind out of the sails of this petition through the programme of reforms outlined by him in three major speeches, at Heidelberg (17 March), Rustenburg (25 March) and Johannesburg (1 April).[1] In these speeches, the President addressed four major issues, and conceded the need for reform in three of them. The appointment of a properly qualified person to oversee the financial administration of the state, including taxation, was uncontroversial and would be made as soon as a suitable person could be found. On *bewaarplaatsen*, the Volksraad had decided that these should be disposed of by public auction, but Kruger hoped to persuade it that such mines as held surface rights to *bewaarplaatsen* should be allowed to purchase the full mining rights to these areas after a proper valuation. On dynamite, Kruger repeated his view that the dynamite factory was part of the country's independence and made clear his determination to retain control of the factory (including the powder and ammunition parts of it) in the hands of the state. He pointed out that it would soon be able to supply the government with cartridges for all the new types of rifle.

On the key issue of the franchise, and reducing the period required to qualify for full burgher rights from the present requirement of fourteen years, Kruger spoke fully and remarkably frankly; and what he had to say varied little whether his audience consisted of already established Afrikaner burghers (as at Heidelberg or Rustenburg) or a largely Uitlander population (as at Johannesburg). Kruger declared that he would not be worthy to be Head of State if he did not protect the old burghers, but he conceded the need to do something for the new population (whom he referred to as 'aliens' and 'strangers'). The distinction he wished to draw, he said, was not between nationalities but between those who were loyal to the state and those who were not. When the law had been made, the burgher (i.e. adult male Afrikaner) population of the state had been about 12,000. The rapid influx of foreigners since the discovery of gold meant that he had 'had to protect the old burghers from being swamped'. The law had therefore had to be changed and a longer period of residence required before first naturalization and later full burgher rights could be obtained. Today, the burghers numbered 30,000–40,000. He therefore proposed to ask the Volksraad to reduce by five years the time required before full burgher rights could be gained by newcomers. This would result in a total of nine years being required (naturalization being possible after four years and full burgher rights after a further five).

At Rustenburg, Kruger said that he calculated that this would result in the Transvaal having 'about 70,000 burghers'.[2] In future, say in ten years' time, the period of residence required might be further reduced. It was true, he admitted, that the residential requirement in Europe and America was shorter (five years), but those countries were in a quite different situation. They had large, established populations, of millions, in comparison with which their newcomers were few. In the Transvaal, the situation was the reverse of this and so 'this could not be done, for this would open the door to all sorts of foreigners, who would thereby have the chance in less than one year to out-vote us'.[3] What could not, in the Transvaal, be done at once might be achieved by degrees; it was something which had to be regulated. His wish was to show the world that he was anxious to do something 'to meet the alien in this matter'. 'We must act honourably and justly', he told his Boer kinsfolk, 'but so that we do not injure ourselves'.[4] At Rustenburg, he assured them that his proposals 'would have to come before the Raad, and two-thirds of the burghers would have to signify their consent. [He hoped] they would do so . . . their independence would not be endangered thereby. They could protect themselves and, at the same time, show the world that they were anxious to meet the alien'.[5] At Heidelberg, Kruger emphasized that this reform to the franchise regulations 'would do no harm, and presented no dangers so far as the old burghers were concerned, especially as Johannesburg would not be able to return more than two members to the Volksraad'.[6] At no point did Kruger suggest that a redistribution of seats would accompany his franchise proposals.

The President's visit to Johannesburg on 1 April – a city he had avoided whenever possible – would seem to have been arranged at short notice and to have been, in part, an attempt to counter the effect of the Second Uitlander Petition, which had been delivered a week previously. There, before delivering a speech which largely repeated what he had already said at Heidelberg and Rustenburg, Kruger had first to listen to addresses, presented by the Chambers of Mines and Commerce, in which the franchise was emphasized 'as the question of chief importance for the Johannesburg community as a whole'. In his reply, Kruger pointed out that there were some, amongst that community, who were always making trouble and appealing to others instead of to himself, and they made things even more difficult. If everyone worked with the government in a friendly manner, and thus gained the confidence of the old burghers, they would get the franchise much sooner than otherwise.

> We don't allow bigamy in this country. When I speak of bigamy, I refer to the Government of this country and the Governments of England and other countries. If you want to live here, first divorce your other wife – then you can marry us. That is naturalisation. No man can serve two masters, and if he has two wives he will love one and despise the other. Therefore, if a man wants to make this country his home, let him first become naturalised. If he doesn't, let him remain a stranger. He will still be treated with all hospitality – provided he obeys the law – protected, helped to make money, to live comfortably, and to come and go as he pleased. [7]

Kruger made his Johannesburg speech after reports had appeared in the newspapers of Chamberlain's speech of 20 March, in which he had accused President Kruger of not keeping his promises. Clearly angry about a charge which he felt was totally unjustified, Kruger proceeded to defend his record since the Jameson Raid, and to blame 'the small section of the population who want to make trouble' for encouraging Chamberlain to say and believe such things. 'When they say that they are oppressed, and that they have grievances, what some of them mean is that they want to be out from under this Government and under another', Kruger declared. They wanted 'to fish in troubled waters. They do not want peace – they want trouble'. Whilst he, in his recent speeches, had outlined a programme of reforms, 'they frame memorials against us and send them to other countries'. This only made it more difficult for Kruger to gain the support of the old burghers for his reforms.

These speeches attracted much attention at the time, and they presented a programme of reforms which Kruger did seek to enact during the following months. Both on dynamite and the franchise, these speeches summarize views which Kruger had come to hold with striking consistency. He never accepted that the British government had any right to intervene over dynamite, which he regarded as a purely internal matter. As for the franchise, whilst Kruger accepted that some reform was necessary, this would never be permitted to run the risk of political control of the state moving out of Afrikaner hands. From this central commitment, the old President was never to waver. But, in the following months – in May, when he presented his proposed changes to the franchise law to the Volksraad, and most notably during the passage of a new franchise law through the Volksraad in July 1899 – Kruger certainly sought to keep the promises of reform which he had made during March. These reforms were therefore attempted, even though they were never to be regarded as sufficient by the British government. Milner dismissed the franchise proposals at once, virtually repeating to Chamberlain the objections already listed in the Uitlander Memorandum. Even if most of the Uitlander population naturalized and eventually succeeded in becoming full citizens of the Transvaal republic, he pointed out, 'they would still only return two members in a Raad of twenty-eight. . . . It is to this *impasse*', concluded Milner, 'that we owe the petition . . . the whole moral justification of which lies in the fact that the people who are calling to H.M. Government to help them would be ready enough to help themselves, if they were not absolutely debarred from every means of doing so'.[8]

The delivery of the Second Uitlander Petition at the same time as the breakdown of the Great Deal negotiations was no coincidence. The decision to close the list of signatures to the petition and to deliver it forthwith was also prompted by Chamberlain's speech on 20 March. After the failure of the first Uitlander petition, in the wake of the Edgar incident, the campaign for a second such petition had been well underway before Milner and Conyngham Greene returned to South Africa in February 1899. Neither of them, therefore, had much to do with its genesis; but both at once recognized its usefulness as part of the campaign to 'get things forrarder' in South Africa, and took care to see that both the form and the timing of its presentation ensured its maximum effect on the British government and public opinion. The leaders of the South African League, who were organizing the second petition, remained in constant touch with the British Agent in Pretoria to make sure that this time their efforts were successful. Both voluntary and paid canvassers were used to obtain the signatures of over 21,000 Uitlanders who were British subjects, and Conyngham Greene reported that the SAL leaders had 'bound themselves to be guided by me' and had agreed to limit their agitation to constitutional means in support of the reforms on which there was general agreement amongst the Uitlander population. Monypenny, the new editor of *The Star* in Johannesburg, said that as far as the SAL and its campaign were concerned, 'whilst he could not support them publicly in his paper, as a political Body, for fear of spoiling the game, he w[oul]d take care that their objects and efforts were supported'. 'This is, after all, what we want', observed Conyngham Greene to Milner.[9]

Conyngham Greene also orchestrated the timing of the delivery of the petition to his office, so that it coincided with the reply of the mining industry to the Transvaal government's Great Deal proposals. By 21 March, he knew, through FitzPatrick, that the latter was likely within the coming week. He therefore arranged to receive the Uitlander petition on Friday 24 March, in time for it to reach Milner by 27 March. On that same afternoon, *The Star* would publish a summary of its contents and Monypenny would cable *The Times* in London so that it could be first in the field in publishing the details.[10] In this way, the British government received a direct appeal from the Uitlanders to intervene on their behalf at the same time as the mining industry demonstrated its refusal to be separated from the Uitlander cause; and British public opinion had its attention clearly focused on the issue of Uitlander enfranchisement as the solution to the Transvaal problem. As Fiddes had intimated to Selborne: 'Unless H.M.G. see fit to recede all along the line, I am beginning to think that a crisis is nearer than would have seemed possible a few weeks ago.'[11]

The petition was presented by W. Wybergh (President of the South African League) along with 21,684 signatures and was forwarded to the British government by Milner on 28 March. It was a craftily constructed document, calculated to appeal to British public opinion and to maximize the likelihood that it would be taken up by the British government.[12] The petitioners began by justifying their appeal to the Queen on the grounds that they were British subjects who had no share in the government of the Transvaal, although they claimed to constitute an absolute majority of the European population and to contribute the most to the country's 'intellect, wealth and energy'.

Since the Transvaal government had failed to respond to previous remonstrances addressed to it about their grievances, the signatories now appealed directly to the Queen, asking for British protection, an enquiry into the grievances listed in the petition, and requesting that the British government's representative in South Africa should be authorized 'to take measures which will secure the speedy reform of the abuses complained of, and to obtain substantial guarantees from the Government of this State for a recognition of their rights as British subjects'. The petition itself made no direct mention of the franchise but emphasized the fact that most of its signatories were *British* subjects – since this gave them the right to appeal to their sovereign and formed the basis on which the British government could claim the right to intervene on their behalf.

Much emphasis was placed, in this second petition, on the grievances which had been listed in the first petition three months previously, and which, it was claimed, had now resulted in a 'well-nigh intolerable' situation in the Transvaal for the Uitlanders. The petitioners reminded the British government that, at the time of the Jameson Raid, the Uitlander population of Johannesburg had 'placed themselves unreservedly' in the hands of the British High Commissioner 'in the fullest confidence that he would see justice done to them'. The reforms promised at that time by President Kruger had not materialized. Instead, recent legislation had made the position of the Uitlanders 'even more irksome than before'. The promise to create an effective municipal government for Johannesburg had been subverted. The recommendations of the Transvaal Industrial Commission had been set aside. The independence of the High Court had been attacked through the dismissal of Chief Justice Kotze. Forts had been constructed overlooking Johannesburg and Pretoria, which threatened British subjects. The hostile attitude of the Transvaal government was exceeded by that of its police force, whose personnel constituted 'one of the standing menaces to the peace of Johannesburg'. The indignation aroused by Edgar's death had been accentuated by the light treatment of those responsible for it. The refusal of the first Uitlander petition had immediately been followed by the arrest of the leaders of the South African League, who had organized it, and the deliberate breaking-up of the meeting at the amphitheatre. It was claimed that efforts had been made to prevent British subjects petitioning their Queen; nonetheless, they had now succeeded in doing this.

In a speech in the House of Commons on 20 March 1899, Chamberlain had defended the government's policy of non-intervention in the Transvaal on behalf of the Uitlanders and their grievances on the grounds that the Uitlanders themselves had not yet asked the government to do so. Chamberlain said that therefore he did not feel 'at the moment that any case has arisen which would justify me in taking the very strong action' – action which might result in war – which some urged in support of Uitlander grievances.[13] On the Rand, Chamberlain's comments were regarded by the Uitlanders as a direct invitation to them to state their case and put it into the hands of the British government for settlement. They hoped that their petition would be taken up and acted on 'by a stiff despatch demanding reforms' and that, if these were not forthcoming, troops would be sent. Reporting this to Selborne, Fiddes (who was still spying out the land on the Rand) concluded that both Conyngham Greene and himself were 'absolutely convinced that you have now a good case for interference: that nothing more in the way of Uitlander action can now be looked for: and that if Her Majesty's Government do not see their way to act now, there will be no further opportunity – certainly not in the time of the present Government, or Sir Alfred, or Greene'. Further, unless the British government now took a firm stand, 'the capitalists' – who at present 'were friendly to us' and to the Uitlander cause – would make their peace with Kruger's government, if they concluded that nothing was going to come out of the present reform movement.[14] FitzPatrick had already said as much to Fiddes and Conyngham Greene during his visit to them on 28 March. Conyngham Greene wrote a lengthy despatch making exactly the same points on 4 April. Never, since he had first arrived in South Africa, he commented, had he observed so resolute an attitude:

> in all classes of the [Uitlander] community. All sections, from the capitalists downwards, want to see an end to the unrest which has prevailed since 1896. . . . All, I am assured, deprecate a resort to arms, but all believe that a resolute response on the part of H.M.G. to the appeal of the Uitlander community, and a publicly announced determination to enforce, if need be, a demand for fair reforms, would avert that danger and result in a general 'climb down' on the part of the Boer Govt. all along the line.[15]

The delivery of the Second Uitlander Petition gave the British government the justification which it needed to intervene directly in the Transvaal. It enabled Chamberlain to take the matter to the Cabinet and argue for the formulation of demands to be put to Kruger's government which were likely to result in an ultimatum and war if they were ignored. The taking up of the Second Uitlander

Petition by the British government was thus the crossing of the Rubicon in the development of British policy towards the Transvaal. Before 1896, the British Colonial Office had regarded Uitlander grievances as being 'fabricated to a large extent'. Since January 1896, however, they had been taken seriously; now they were to be used in an open and determined challenge to the Transvaal government. From this commitment stemmed all future steps along the path to war.[16] Yet between the delivery of the petition at the end of March, and the British Cabinet's considered response in May, there was to be over a month of intense lobbying and activity.

When FitzPatrick arrived in Cape Town on 31 March, Milner told him that he was 'immensely pleased' with what had been achieved and congratulated him on the 'consummate statesmanship' he had exhibited throughout the Great Deal negotiations. In demonstrating 'so strong an attitude' and 'securing cohesion and unanimity' between the mining industry and the Uitlander population, Milner declared that FitzPatrick and his colleagues had 'done far better than in his most hopeful moments he considered possible'.[17] Things had moved forward much more rapidly than he had expected, Milner said. Now, everything hinged upon how the Second Uitlander Petition was received in England. Much depended on the attitude of the press. What was needed now was a sustained press campaign which Milner looked to FitzPatrick to organize – since he himself could not do so. If Chamberlain got 'the idea that I want to rush him', declared Milner, 'the whole business would be dashed and done for'. In South Africa, Milner continued, 'I want to *do* something. I will take risks, big risks, but not silly ones'. He therefore looked to FitzPatrick 'to do the press' and get the mass of evidence in the Uitlander Petition before the House of Commons. Above all, FitzPatrick 'must *not* allow the petition to fizzle. That would be dreadful!'[18]

With extraordinary frankness, Milner then outlined what he expected to happen next. If Chamberlain dismissed the Uitlander Petition as a purely internal matter for the Transvaal government, Milner declared that he would resign at once. At the opposite extreme, the British government could decide to send an ultimatum, but this Milner considered unlikely. The third and most likely course was that Chamberlain would accept that the petitioners' claims were well-founded and warn Kruger's government that if it failed to address them, the British government would intervene. This would probably result in delay, which Kruger would use to try to split the Uitlanders into disunited factions. Milner felt that FitzPatrick had been 'most successful in holding the people together so far and must make a heroic effort to hold them together still'. It might take time, some months, to get the British government up to the mark but, concluded Milner, 'Remember, it is the chance of a lifetime'. In reporting this conversation to Wernher, FitzPatrick was careful to add that Milner 'is quite confident that Kruger will climb down when the Imperial Government show that they are in earnest'. Fiddes admitted to Selborne that he was not so sure. If Kruger's government made such a 'climb down' it would, he thought, be signing its own death-warrant.[19]

Milner and Conyngham Greene had sought to co-ordinate the publication of the exchanges which had taken place between the Transvaal government and the mining industry with the delivery of the Second Uitlander Petition to the Queen as a deliberate attempt to 'get things forrarder' in South Africa. Their objective was to demonstrate the solidarity of the mining interest with a reconstituted Uitlander reform movement, to present the British government with a direct appeal for intervention from the Uitlanders themselves, to arouse the interest of British public opinion in the Transvaal once more, and to focus attention on the franchise as the key issue which lay at the heart of the Uitlander problem in the Transvaal and also offered the best means for its solution.

Although Milner believed that it was 'too soon yet . . . to break the crockery', he believed that 'if the Uitlanders stick to their guns' this would make 'the issue perfectly clear both here and in England and ought certainly to direct attention to and excite interest in the question again'.[20] Already during March, Milner had embarked upon a sustained lobbying campaign with regard to Chamberlain and the British Colonial Office. He had presented the initiation of the Great Deal negotiations by Kruger's government as an attempt 'to burke the petition' of the Uitlanders to the Queen. He had pointed to the determination of those representing the mining industry in those negotiations 'not to separate themselves from the bulk of the Uitlander population and to make genuine political reform a *sine qua non*' of any agreement. He had sought to persuade Chamberlain 'that we are face to face with what is practically a revival of the Reform movement, which was temporarily extinguished by the Jameson Raid fiasco'.[21]

Now, he instructed Conyngham Greene:

The great point seems to be (1) to keep the future course of negotiations public and (2) to force the S.A.R. Govt. into some definite position – yes or no – about the franchise. . . . The other thing is to get the Uitlanders – as they cannot have a mass meeting – to express in any way they can – by a series of smaller meetings along the Rand, if they can be

261

organized – their approval of the scheme of reforms *outlined in the memorandum*. This would have a double effect. It would, so to speak, *canonize* that scheme as the Uitlanders' recognized programme, their Petition of Right – at present it is merely the opinion of a few individuals and it would keep up English interest and *rub the real issue well into the public mind*. . . . [22]

From March until the Bloemfontein Conference at the beginning of June, Milner master-minded what can only be described as a concerted campaign.

Kruger himself had focused attention on the issue of franchise reform in his speeches during March. Milner, however, dismissed Kruger's proposals as offering the Uitlander 'not a *right* at all . . . but merely a *prospect* which the caprice of the old burghers or the Government may render for ever delusive'.[23] Despite the absence of any direct reference to it in the Second Uitlander Petition, Milner now set out to make the franchise issue the central focus of his campaign. 'Political reform goes to the root of individual grievances', he emphasized to Chamberlain, 'and moreover it may become, if it is not today, a splendid battle cry, exciting sympathy throughout the Empire, and even in some foreign countries'.[24] As early as May 1897, Milner had expressed the view that 'there will be no ultimate peace without extension of the Franchise'.[25] By March 1899, he was insisting that this must also be accompanied by a redistribution of seats in the Volksraad. He now defined 'a genuine measure of enfranchisement' as one by which 'men having the necessary property qualifications, and say, 5 years' residence, should have the franchise at once, and the number of members for populous districts should be increased, if not strictly in proportion to population, yet more or less in such proportion'.[26] Milner also argued that 'a promiscuous wholesale enfranchisement 5 years hence is far less desirable than gradual enfranchisement beginning now'.[27] He believed that 'without a large influx of new blood into the body politic, swamping, or at least diluting the present oligarchy' there was no hope of any improvement in the situation. Nothing would come right by *mere* waiting, he wrote to Chamberlain. Kruger's government would only act under direct pressure from the British government and the time had now come for this to be applied.[28]

THE BRITISH GOVERNMENT TAKES UP THE FRANCHISE ISSUE

Under sustained bombardment from Milner and Conyngham Greene and their acolytes, and the carefully directed flow of information from South Africa which they largely controlled, Chamberlain and the Colonial Office shifted their ground during the month of April. Chamberlain's intention of sending Kruger a carefully compiled 'list of all his iniquities' was given a new focus and thrust by the decision to take a stand – not on technical infringements of the London Convention but on the issue which Chamberlain was now persuaded would have the most popular appeal: the 'splendid battle cry' of Uitlander grievances and the extension of the franchise as the means to remedy them.[29] Hitherto, Chamberlain had been reluctant to embark upon a course which he clearly saw might lead to a rebuff from the Transvaal government, an ultimatum from Britain, and the possibility of a war which he doubted British public opinion would support.[30] Yet now, he ignored the opinion of the one English member of the Volksraad, R. K. Loveday, who reported that 'unless it should be complicated by outside interference', the situation in the Transvaal 'looked more hopeful, in respect of internal reform . . . than at any time'.[31] He took soundings amongst his Colonial Office staff, and he prepared to take the matter to the Cabinet to obtain full government backing for 'a stiff despatch'.

The Colonial Office staff recognized in the arrival of the Second Uitlander Petition 'a new departure of a most serious kind' which could not be met 'with a disclaimer of our right to intervene'.[32] Milner had expressly stated his hope 'that nothing will be said by us which could possibly be construed into meaning that the internal affairs of the Transvaal are not our concern, and that, as long as the Convention is respected, we should under no circumstances be justified in interfering with them . . . I do not know how anybody can question our right to take up the position that, if the Govt. of the S.A.R. will not, after any amount of time given to it, redress the legitimate grievances of its inhabitants of British birth, we should compel such redress by force if necessary'. Further, Milner had said that he failed to see, 'so far as the local situation is concerned, what is ever going to make it easier than it is today to tell the Transvaal government that it must reform, and to offer to act as mediators between it and its discontented subjects with the full determination not to allow such proffered mediation to be refused'.[33]

Milner did not have everything quite his own way amongst

Chamberlain's staff in the Colonial Office. H. W. Just perceptively noted that 'there has been no appeal from the Cape or Natal that the position of affairs in South Africa is made intolerable through the misgovernment of the S.A.R.; there have only been petitions from the South African League. If public opinion is to play a part, it must be clear that the public opinion in S. Africa leads the way'. He also feared that Hofmeyr, representing the Cape Afrikaners, might bring a resolution before the Cape parliament deprecating any British intervention in the internal affairs of the South African Republic. The British public might well feel that, in restricting the franchise, 'the Boers are animated by the instinct of self-preservation, and cannot be expected to yield . . . without a great struggle'. Wingfield doubted if public opinion in South Africa would ever favour forcing reforms down the throat of the Transvaal government. Graham considered that 'we have first got to educate public opinion in this country' before Milner's policy of working things up to a crisis could be adopted.[34] Selborne, who had a direct hand in drafting the eventual British despatch and who had 'talked it round and over and all about' and 'tussled' with Chamberlain 'a good deal more than usual' over it, wrote to Milner that his chief concern was 'to avoid a despatch that wasn't going to be followed up'. He therefore hit on the idea of addressing it 'as a reply to the petitions and not as a remonstrance to the South African Republic Government' because, if 'you are not prepared to follow up your remonstrance for certain, if necessary, it is futile to pitch your abuse strongly'. Nevertheless, he assured Milner, that 'your little fatherly hints in your secret despatch have been absorbed', that he was 'drafting for the wider ground' and not restricting matters to the London Convention, and that the British government would not say that it would never interfere, 'but neither shall we threaten, this time: I propose, however, *encouraging the Uitlanders to continue constitutional agitation*'.[35] Selborne summarized to Lord Curzon how he saw the overall situation. 'You ought to know that the Transvaal carbuncle is ripening to pricking point', he wrote:

> We have settled with Germany. The British subjects in the Transvaal . . . have for the first time appealed to us. All the British in South Africa are vehemently on our side. Even European sympathy has abandoned Kruger. The opposition have surged up nearly abreast of us, not all, but very largely so, e.g. *Daily Chronicle, Daily News, Westminster Gazette* all now say that we can no longer leave things alone. The only hostile element which remains is our own Dutch [i.e. Afrikaner population in the Cape Colony and Natal who were British subjects], and because of them I should deplore a war. But a war will more probably not be necessary than be

necessary. The best thing that could happen would be that the pressure, led, directed and pointed by us, should become so strong that our Dutch would apply such pressure to Kruger and Company that he would give way. Then it would be pure gain. Whereas a war would leave a long bad raw. Consequently we do not mean to answer the petition by an ultimatum.

Instead, the Uitlander grievances listed in the petition would be examined, one by one, the whole situation exposed to public and international view, and the message indicated 'between the lines' to Kruger's government that the situation could not last and that 'This is your last chance'. 'We shall take our stand', Selborne concluded, 'not on the wretched [London] Convention, but on the duty and right of every civilised government to protect its subjects resident in foreign countries when they are oppressed, and our own special interest in everything South African as the Paramount Power there'.[36]

Chamberlain was well aware that an inadequate response to this petition by British subjects ran the risk of alienating Britain's key, long-term collaborators in the Transvaal. Conyngham Greene warned that 'The Uitlanders of Johannesburg are lacking now, as before, in cohesion, and it is impossible to hope to hold them, for an indefinite interval, together. This was the case at the Raid time. . . . The same influence is at work today . . . they are quite ready to wait any reasonable time – 2 or 3 months – for a result in the way of action by H.M.G.; but if this opportunity is passed by the Home Govt., and *no result* ensues, it will be a long day, if indeed it ever comes, when we need expect any combined movement again'.[37] Chamberlain decided to educate both public and political opinion in Britain about Uitlander grievances by publishing a Government Blue Book. Milner's secret despatches had 'too much vitriol' to be printed and so, in response to a request from Selborne for a full and frank statement suitable for informing public opinion about the true state of affairs in the Transvaal, Milner sat down and wrote his famous 'helots' despatch.

This emotive and revealing résumé was written at a time when Milner felt that events were moving towards 'the great day of reckoning' which he sought. Using rhetoric which was calculated to raise the temperature of the public debate, Milner traced the sequence of events since the Edgar incident which had resulted in the Uitlander Petition and emphasized the 'profound discontent of the unenfranchised population, who are a great majority of the white inhabitants of the State'. Like Kruger, Milner exaggerated the size of the Uitlander population – which certainly did not outnumber the *total* Afrikaner population of the Transvaal at this time, but may have outnumbered its adult male (i.e. burgher) population. The reform movement, Milner argued, was not artificial – 'the work of scheming capitalists or professional agitators' – but broadly supported and growing in force and extent. Whilst he acknowledged that many Uitlanders were only 'birds of passage' in the Transvaal and 'only want to make money and clear out', he stated that a growing number contemplated making it their permanent home and 'would make excellent citizens if they had the chance'. The Uitlanders had many well-founded grievances but these could gradually be removed if they only had a fair share of political power. This was what lay behind their demand for enfranchisement. The internal condition of the Transvaal was of vital interest to the British government, Milner declared, because South Africa was socially and economically one country, where the Boer and British populations were inextricably mixed and therefore needed to be treated alike in both the republics and the colonies. The constant friction in the Transvaal would only be remedied by striking at the root of the Uitlanders' grievances: their political impotence.

> What diplomatic protests will never accomplish, a fair measure of
> Uitlander representation would gradually but surely bring about. It seems
> a paradox but it is true that the only effective way of protecting our
> subjects is to help them to cease to be our subjects.

The admission of the Uitlanders to a fair share of political power would stabilize the Transvaal politically and also remove the suspicion and hostility towards the British government there. 'The spectacle of thousands of British subjects kept permanently in the position of helots, constantly chafing under undoubted grievances, and calling vainly to Her Majesty's Government for redress' steadily undermined Britain's influence and position throughout the Empire. Further, the growing armaments of the Transvaal, its alliance with the Orange Free State, and 'the doctrine of a Republic embracing all South Africa' were challenging 'the intention of Her Majesty's Government not to be ousted from its position in South Africa'. The best way to put a stop to 'this mischievous propaganda' and the best proof alike of Britain's power and justice, Milner argued, would be for the British government:

> to obtain for the Uitlanders in the Transvaal a fair share of the
> Government of the country which owes everything to their exertions. It
> could be made perfectly clear that this action was not directed against the
> existence of the Republic. Britain would be demanding the

re-establishment of rights which now exist in the Orange Free State, and which existed in the Transvaal itself at the time of and long after the withdrawal of British sovereignty. It would be no selfish demand, as other Uitlanders besides those of British birth would benefit by it. It would be . . . asking for nothing from others which we do not give ourselves.

The case for intervention, he concluded, was overwhelming.[38]

When this despatch was finally published, in June, it caused a sensation. As one of Milner's correspondents told him, 'it has forced you down into the arena, and cut off your retreat'. But as Milner replied, he had written it deliberately for publication, knowing that the government would not publish it 'without having made up their minds to support me'.[39]

The British Cabinet met on 2 May to consider a reply to the Uitlander Petition. For this meeting, Chamberlain circulated the petition itself and the draft of the despatch which he 'intended as a protest' to the Transvaal government but which he hoped avoided anything in the nature of an ultimatum. As Chamberlain explained:

> If we ignore altogether the prayer of the petitioners, it is certain that British influence in South Africa will be severely shaken. If we send an ultimatum to Kruger, it is possible, and in my opinion probable, that we shall get an offensive reply, and we shall have then to go to war, or to accept a humiliating check.[40]

The proposed despatch, therefore, whilst acknowledging and itemizing the Uitlanders' grievances, and surveying various alleged inadequacies and failures of the Transvaal government in some detail, confined itself to expressing the earnest hope that Kruger's government would now act to remedy a situation which the British government could no longer ignore. The tone of an ultimatum was carefully avoided. But the Cabinet, clearly recognizing that a Rubicon was about to be crossed, put off the decision about the final form of the reply for a week. During this time, Milner's 'helots' despatch, which was sent as a telegram, arrived (5 May). 'This is tremendously stiff, and if it is published it will make either an ultimatum *or* Sir A. Milner's recall necessary', Chamberlain commented.[41] Its publication was therefore withheld until June but it was meanwhile circulated amongst members of the Cabinet before their next meeting.

Milner sent a further persuasive telegram to Chamberlain (which arrived the day before the second meeting of the Cabinet) in which he said that meetings of working men and ordinary Uitlanders were taking place up and down the Rand at which the franchise was being demanded after five years' residence. 'We should be making a serious, and perhaps irretrievable mistake, if we did not take the present opportunity of definitely ranging ourselves on the side of the Uitlander Reformers in their struggle with the Transvaal Government', Milner argued, before going on to ask what had happened to the intervention of the British High Commissioner on the Uitlanders' behalf, which had certainly been contemplated, if not absolutely promised, at the time of the Jameson Raid.[42] Milner realized that, in intervening on behalf of the Uitlanders, the British government risked war. He now believed that Kruger's government would yield to 'nothing less than the fear of war, perhaps not even to that'. But this was a perpetual risk. Britain should choose the time to press matters 'and now, with agitation for the franchise under way, was the best time'.[43]

Chamberlain did not, apparently, place this latest telegram from Milner before the Cabinet. He did, however, make use of a further last-minute suggestion from Milner: that he should meet Kruger in a conference designed to arrive at a reform programme which both the Uitlanders and the British government could accept. In negotiations, Kruger could be forced 'either to accept specific reforms or else, by refusing them, to show . . . unmistakable obstinacy and justify us in taking stronger measures'.[44] Thus, Britain would not be sending a threatening despatch without at the same time showing the Transvaal government a way out.

Two senior members of the Cabinet had already recorded their unease with the new, confrontationist course which was now being suggested with regard to the Transvaal. Hicks Beach (Chancellor of the Exchequer) pointed out that the proposed despatch did not focus on alleged breaches of the London Convention but included 'complaints on matters of which we should never dream of complaining to a foreign government such as high taxation, excessive and corrupt expenditure, secret service, concessions and monopolies' and observed that 'the mining industry in Johannesburg gets on, in spite of them, pretty well!' He was uneasy about placing the Uitlander franchise issue in the foreground. The Transvaal 'is, after all, a Dutch state', he observed to Chamberlain, and

> there is one thing at the bottom of this matter which cannot be ignored, and with which I think it impossible not to have some sympathy. The Boers are, compared with us, the 'original inhabitants' – their title to 'their country', with practical independence in internal affairs, has been confirmed by us through the [London] Convention – they naturally don't want to be dispossessed by newcomers of a different race and different ideas. You recognise this in the last page of the despatch – I should like

to see its recognition *pervade* the despatch: and therefore would keep the franchise question a good deal in the background on this occasion.[45]

Balfour also was uneasy about the direction which was being taken under the powerful influence of Milner, and therefore wrote to emphasize certain aspects of the situation which Milner 'seems not sufficiently to have considered'. In an imaginative and perceptive memorandum, Balfour pointed out that the situation in the Transvaal was probably unprecedented, for there the Uitlander majority in the European population were 'alien in blood, different in language, superior in cultivation and wealth' to the Boer minority 'which constitutes the original national stock to whom the country politically belongs'. Where Britain might consider the admission of the Uitlanders to the franchise as a process of electoral reform, the Boers might regard it 'as a transfer of nationality'. Similarly, to ask that English be taught in the schools – since 'the majority of persons who have to be taught are English' and most of the money which paid for their teaching was contributed by Englishmen – seemed natural and proper; but this 'practically means, and must mean, that the national language will in no short time be eliminated and an alien language put in its place'. After listing the Uitlander grievances, Balfour asked whether 'in the case of any other State but the Transvaal, should we regard ourselves as justified in resorting to force to remedy them?' Britain's own record with the Transvaal was not entirely clean since the indemnity for the Raid had still not been paid. If the proposed despatch turned out to be 'the prelude to more vigorous action', Britain could expect the side of the case ignored by Milner to be 'very forcibly brought to our notice both here and at the Cape'. Balfour himself now put that other side of the case before the Cabinet with rare feeling:

> No doubt the Boers are engaged in fighting a hopeless cause. The South African Republic may last for ever, but it cannot for very long be a Boer Republic. In the nature of things, Boer supremacy means a condition of political equilibrium, which gets day by day more unstable. But I do not think that we can complain of the Boers not taking this view, nor (if they do take it) of their struggling to the last in favour of a lost cause. Were I a Boer, brought up in Boer traditions, nothing but necessity would induce me to adopt a constitution which would turn my country into an English Republic, or a system of education which would reduce my language to the *patois* of a small and helpless minority.[46]

After the first Cabinet meeting (2 May), Balfour wrote to Chamberlain to say that 'if the Transvaal were to be dealt with on ordinary principles, there does not seem to me to be anything like a *casus belli* established'. The proposed despatch was no more than 'a friendly remonstrance' to Kruger's government; but what if Kruger ignored it? 'If we are to insist at the point of a bayonet upon anything', Balfour argued, it should be for a comprehensive measure of municipal reform. This 'might be *fairly* insisted upon', although he recognized that it represented an interference in the Transvaal's internal affairs. When Chamberlain pointed out that such a measure would no longer satisfy the Uitlanders, Balfour concluded that 'they are rather unreasonable' and failed to press his objections further in the second Cabinet meeting on 9 May.[47]

At this decisive meeting, Chamberlain presented a revised draft of the proposed despatch in which the emphasis on 'financial grievances' was lessened and that on 'the personal disabilities of the Uitlanders and the inequality of their treatment as compared with the Boers' was increased. Carefully constructed and studiously moderate in tone, this despatch was unanimously approved by the Cabinet and sent off the following day (10 May).[48] As the Prime Minister revealed in a letter to the Queen, Uitlander grievances were accepted as an indisputable fact of long standing by the British government, which, after the petition, felt obliged to act to remedy them. The Uitlanders could not be abandoned, Salisbury declared, 'without grave injustice – nor without endangering Your Majesty's authority in the whole of South Africa. . . . We are most earnestly anxious to avoid any rupture with the Boers if it is possible. But they do not assist us to do so'.[49] Thus, the issue of Uitlander grievances became fatefully enmeshed with the preservation of British supremacy, authority and prestige in South Africa. Now taken up by a British government determined to obtain redress, the matter could not be relinquished without unacceptable loss of prestige and authority. Either Kruger's government would capitulate to British demands or there would eventually be an ultimatum and a resort to war.

Between the British and Transvaal governments there now existed not only the deepest mistrust but an unbridgeable gulf with regard to how they each viewed the situation. The British government had kept its reply to the Second Uitlander Petition studiously moderate because, whilst it recognized that war might result if Kruger's government failed to respond sufficiently, war was not intended or yet expected. Most of the Cabinet, hoping and believing that a negotiated settlement was still possible, seized eagerly upon the idea of a summit conference between Milner and Kruger at which the issues might be discussed 'in a conciliatory spirit' as a means towards achieving a peaceful settlement. It was also anticipated that W. P. Schreiner (the Cape Prime Minister), Hofmeyr and other leading Cape Afrikaners would use their influence on Kruger and his government to assist the British government towards this end by persuading him to make significant concessions.

Kruger's government, on the other hand, regarded the British government's despatch as an arrogant and presumptuous attempt to meddle and stir up trouble in the Transvaal. It considered that the issue of Uitlander grievances was being deliberately and artificially exaggerated to an absurd degree, and the British government's intervention in support of them was an unwarranted and unacceptable attempt to interfere and provoke a confrontation over what was an internal matter for the Transvaal. Britain's *right* to intervene as the 'paramount' power was denied, as was 'British supremacy' over South Africa. Successive efforts to negotiate away the mounting conflict between the two governments during the next few months were vitiated by the deep mutual mistrust. Under Milner's influence, the British government's room for manoeuvre became increasingly restricted as the issues became ever more narrowly focused on the Uitlander franchise, and this became fused with the concept of 'British supremacy'. As for the Transvaal government, its leading repre-sentatives became increasingly convinced that it was their country itself that the British were after, and that whatever concessions they made, the British would always find new grounds for a quarrel.

At the time of the British government's reply to the Second Uitlander Petition in May 1899, the gap of understanding and intent which had existed between Milner and Chamberlain for over a year remained. Chamberlain still hoped for a peaceful settlement but he had now been persuaded to make a stand. From that there could be no retreat. Unlike Milner, he still hoped for a compromise and believed there was a good chance that, once again, as in the past, Kruger would finally back down. He had therefore sought to avoid a threatening tone or anything approaching an ultimatum in the despatch, and looked to the possibility of a conference as a constructive way to achieve a peaceful, negotiated settlement. Milner did not. His attitude was increasingly belligerent and uncompromising. In his view, any concessions wrung out of Kruger's government would be grudging surrenders, yielded only under extreme duress. As ex-Chief Justice Kotze had said: 'If you want anything out of the old man, you must take him by the throat and then you'll get it: he's just a wily old Kaffir chief.'[50] Whether Kruger would ever go so far as to concede a franchise measure which would jeopardize the political control of himself and his oligarchy remained extremely doubtful. Milner's papers during these final months before the resort to war suggest a growing recognition by him of the likelihood that, rather than capitulate, Kruger would fight.

CONFERENCE AT BLOEMFONTEIN

The suggestion of a summit conference between Milner and Kruger originated not in Britain but in South Africa and not just with Milner himself but with Hofmeyr and the Cape Prime Minister, W. P. Schreiner. On 9 May, the day after Milner had telegraphed to Chamberlain with the suggestion of a conference, Milner had a long talk after dinner with Hofmeyr, 'who broached the idea of my meeting President Kruger at Bloemfontein'.[51] The next day, Schreiner presented Milner with an invitation from President Steyn to hold the meeting at the capital of the Orange Free State. Milner's initial reaction was non-committal and unenthusiastic. Whereas the British government welcomed the idea of a conference, and set some store by what it might achieve, Milner attributed it to 'the funk here on the part of the Afrikander party' and thought it was 'a very clever move' which had 'already produced one effect, viz. that of mollifying the British Press a bit and relaxing for the moment, unfortunately as I think, the screw upon the enemy'. He did not expect it to achieve much: he told Conyngham Greene, 'If I do go, it will be simply because the home Government do not wish to be accused of having refused any chance of arranging matters.' He therefore asked him to assure the Uitlander reformers on the Rand 'that I am not going to do anything which can weaken their positions or give their case away'. Milner at once pinpointed the issues which he had already decided would make or break any such meeting: full enfranchisement for the Uitlanders after five years' residence (which could be retrospective); modification of the oath of allegiance; at least seven seats at once for the Rand in the Volksraad.[52]

Chamberlain regretted that the proposal for a conference meant that the Blue Book (concerning Uitlander grievances and including Milner's 'helots' despatch of 4 May) and the British government's despatch of 10 May would have to be withheld for the present, since Kruger was likely to regard them as objectionable and use them as grounds for refusing to attend the conference. Chamberlain also feared that if the conference failed, this might encourage the Orange Free

State and the Cape Afrikaners to throw their 'moral support' behind
Kruger. But he saw the importance of 'exhausting this new line before
exerting pressure in any other way'. 'In view of momentous
consequences of an actual breach with the Transvaal, public opinion
will expect us to make every effort to avoid it', he told Milner.[53] It
cannot be said that Milner made any effort to avoid a breakdown in
relations with Kruger's government. Rather, in a revealing letter to
the Governor of Natal, he expressed his satisfaction 'that the
Government is in earnest this time' and would intervene in the
Transvaal 'if Kruger does not grant large reforms'. 'Perhaps it would
be best if Kruger hardened his heart and the smash came. But I don't
think we ought to aim at that', he declared. Nonetheless, Britain
should be prepared to fight rather than accept 'a piffling measure' of
reform. An immediate and *substantial share of political power for the
Uitlander* was what was needed. If this was achieved then it should be
accepted and worked fairly.

> The great thing now, in this intervening breathing space before the bomb
> bursts, is for us to stiffen the wobblers. I know perfectly well that as soon
> as it becomes evident that H.M.G. mean business, we shall have the usual
> outcry . . . that there is nothing to fight about, that a race war would
> be too awful, etc. *Once you convince the wobblers* . . . that the British
> Government is *resolute*, the whole force of the peace-at-any-price party
> will be directed to getting the Transvaal to give in. Sir H. de Villiers is
> decidedly on that tack already, and with a little more pushing, Schreiner
> will follow suit.[54]

Sir Henry de Villiers was the Chief Justice of the Cape Colony, the
cultivated and much-esteemed figure who had played an important
role in the peace settlement after the war of 1880–81 and had acted as
a mediator before with the Transvaal in 1897. During the remaining
months of peace he, together with other leading Cape political figures
such as Hofmeyr, Merriman and Schreiner, intensified their efforts to
persuade Kruger's government to make some of the concessions
without which they feared there would be a resort to war. Such a war
in South Africa would take on the character of a civil war, with Cape
Afrikaners (as British subjects) dragged in to fight their relatives and
kinsfolk in the Transvaal. The sustained efforts of these 'conciliators'
during the remaining months of peace, assisted by President Steyn and
Abraham Fischer of the Orange Free State, were only fully revealed
after the war was well underway. They form, nonetheless, a significant
sub-theme between April and September 1899.[55]

In March, after an interview with Milner, Merriman had told

Schreiner of his '*profound* apprehension and uneasiness . . . we are on the brink of a precipice'. Milner, he reported, was 'utterly out of sympathy with South Africa and . . . bitterly hostile and unsympathetic to the Transvaal. He is prepared to take the first opportunity to show his teeth in that quarter'. Full of apprehension for the future, Merriman felt it was up to the Cape government to try and prevent South Africa being 'plunged into a bloody and internecine conflict'.[56] In April, Schreiner had asked de Villiers to go to Pretoria to urge reforms and a possible conference on Kruger's government. When he returned on 4 May, de Villiers reported that although he had not seen Kruger himself, Reitz, Smuts and Schalk Burger had agreed 'to work for a liberal franchise and an inquiry into the dynamite monopoly. But on one condition. All the British demands must be presented fully and finally, once for all. . . . For the rest, they believed that good might come of a conference between the High Commissioner and the two Presidents'.[57]

Chamberlain had originally thought a conference might take place in Pretoria, but it was doubtful if either Kruger or Milner would welcome this – and there was the proximity of Johannesburg and the unhappy precedent of Lord Loch's visit in 1894 to bear in mind. President Steyn's invitation to hold the conference at Bloemfontein was therefore accepted by both the British and Transvaal governments – although Kruger stipulated that he would attend only on condition that the independence of the Transvaal republic was not called into question. A certain hardening of attitudes had occurred in the Transvaal after the breakdown of the Great Deal negotiations. On 10 May, Smuts reported to Hofmeyr that 'The President thinks, so far as I can gauge his feeling, that war is unavoidable or will soon become so – not because there is any cause, but because the enemy is brazen enough not to wait for a cause.' Smuts himself doubted whether Britain would resort to war without a justification which would satisfy 'the public opinion of the world'; 'even if the worst happens', he declared, 'I am quite calm and await the future with confidence'. His letter, however, reveals both a growing resolution in the face of the mounting challenge from Britain and the sort of inflamed nationalism which was to characterize *A Century of Wrong*, written with his assistance a few months later.[58] In defiant tones, Smuts declared:

> If England should venture into the ring with Afrikanerdom without a formally good excuse, her cause in South Africa would be finished. And then the sooner the better: as we for our part are quite prepared to meet her. Our people throughout South Africa must be baptized with the baptism of blood and fire before they can be admitted among the other

great peoples of the world. Of the outcome I have no doubt. Either we shall be exterminated or we shall fight our way out; and when I think of the great fighting qualities that our people possess, I cannot see why we should be exterminated.[59]

Hofmeyr at once poured cold water on Smuts's assumption that the whole of Afrikanerdom would rally to the Transvaal cause. 'Cherish no illusions about the Colony', he replied, 'you must not expect that Colonial Afrikaners will rush *en masse* to arms if hostilities break out – especially as most of them know nothing about the bearing of arms'.[60] Smuts, meanwhile, was also writing to Schreiner in defiant mood. If war came, he said, both of the republics would fight to the last:

With the O.F.S. we can bring more than 50,000 fighting men into the field and these will probably be reinforced from elsewhere: and to cope with such a defensive force, composed of such stuff as Boers are made of when fighting for home and country, England will require an offensive force of at least 150,000 to 200,000 men. Is England going to embark lightly on such an undertaking? Would she not by so doing expose herself in other parts of the world?[61]

President Kruger, meanwhile, introduced his proposals for an extension of the franchise (which he had outlined in his speeches in March) into the Volksraad on 23 May. These provided for naturalization after four years' residence and full burgher rights, including the franchise, after a further five years – nine years in all. He assured the Volksraad that his proposals would not result in the old burghers being overwhelmed by the newcomers' votes, but they would reward those who were friends of the republic and 'keep them on the side of the State'. Since the proposals had now to be put to constituents, there was little discussion of them, at this stage, in the Volksraad.[62] Kruger approached the Bloemfontein Conference expecting to negotiate and bargain on a whole number of issues but not prepared to be dictated to by Milner. The scanty evidence suggests that he was taken aback by Milner's insistence, from the outset, that there should be no consideration of other issues until an agreement on the franchise had been reached. Smuts, who accompanied Kruger but took no direct part in the meetings, felt that 'although it is for us a great humiliation to confer with Her Majesty's representative about our own affairs, it is and remains my earnest wish that all may come right'. Milner he found 'as sweet as honey but there is something in his very intelligent eyes that tells me that he is a very dangerous man'.[63]

Milner had persuaded Chamberlain to allow Conyngham Greene to give an interim reply to the Uitlanders that their petition was being given serious and sympathetic consideration by the British government but that, in view of the approaching conference at which these matters would be discussed, a full reply was being held over. When this was done on 24 May, the full text of the Second Uitlander Petition was then published. Meetings had been taking place up and down the Rand at which the idea of forming 'a sort of Uitlander Parliament' to give force and focus to the reform movement was developed. This was to emerge as the Uitlander Council in June, after the expiry, at the end of May, of the ban on political activity on those who were to form its leadership. FitzPatrick felt that the momentum of the Uitlander movement was being maintained, exactly as Milner had urged, with the help of a cooperative press. 'Monypenny seems to be quite excellent on *The Star*', he informed Wernher '*What* a comfort to have got him in the nick of time, and also Pakeman' (who was editor of the new mouthpiece of the Uitlander movement, *The Transvaal Leader*).[64] 'Pretoria is all war-talk, and in fact the whole country buzzes like a hive', he reported. Most satisfactory of all was 'to see, day by day, more evidence that the affair is out of the hands of the Rand population now and it seems clear . . . that the Imperial Government have and claim a concern on the settlement, quite apart from answering the petition'.[65] 'We adhere to the principle as fundamental that our only security is England and our only intermediary must be H.E. [Milner]', FitzPatrick commented; 'matters are now in the hands of the Imperial Government and out of ours. . . . The principals are the two Governments.'[66]

Rouliot also told Wernher of the widespread assumption, amongst all circles in the Transvaal, 'that there will soon be trouble'. With the cessation of negotiations between the mining industry and the government, matters had been taken out of their hands and were now in those of the British government. This, however, was ominous since 'it is not only the Transvaal question, considered independently, which is being considered, but the imperial question, that of British influence in South Africa'. The Transvaal would 'only be the pretext for interfering'. The spread of republican feeling and the existence of a Bond government in the Cape Colony had aroused fears of a future South African federation 'with Boer influence predominating', he commented. Realizing the danger of this from their point of view, the British government 'may be considering the means of establishing their supremacy now'.[67] As the Bloemfontein Conference approached, Rouliot reported that everybody looked to it to provide the basis for a settlement. He himself believed that Kruger's government would 'concede everything in the way of economic reforms and even some modifications to the franchise law, but they will not agree to anything which they fear would move the political power from out of their hands'.[68]

During May 1899, the press in South Africa embarked on a clamorous campaign of public information and opinion-formation about the issues which it was expected the conference would address. Extensive accounts were published covering the changes which had taken place in the Transvaal franchise laws during the preceding twenty years. Estimates were made of the numbers of Uitlanders likely to take up full citizenship and the franchise if these were made available to them on the basis of five or seven or nine years' residence. *The Cape Times* reminded its readers that there could be no dual citizenship: a British subject who became naturalized in the Transvaal ceased to be a British subject and thereafter lost the ability to appeal to the British government to act on his behalf. The purpose of the Uitlander franchise, it stated, was to alter 'the centre of gravity in the Transvaal government' so as to relieve the British government from the burden of further intervention. Although a redistribution of Volksraad seats to increase the representation of the Rand was essential, 'nobody has asked for anything more than an Uitlander minority in the Raad' and it argued that a quarter or a third of the total seats was all that was required.[69]

In the Transvaal, *The Star*, assisted by the new *Transvaal Leader*, championed the Uitlander cause. 'Liberalise the institutions of the Republic and all other questions will settle themselves', trumpeted *The Star*, with economic recovery and a gold-mining boom underway 'the reactionary policy of the Government is the one cloud on the horizon today'.[70] As the government mouthpiece, *The Standard and Diggers News* declared that the 'capitalist press' and 'the Chartered paper' (by which it meant *The Star*) were endeavouring to bring about a situation closely resembling that on the eve of the Jameson Raid. The 'turmoil-creators' were hiding behind the stalking-horse of Uitlander grievances in their efforts to draw the British government into forcible intervention in the affairs of the Transvaal. Yet it was surely 'ridiculous to suppose that England will use force to turn British subjects into Republicans', it declared.[71] 'Unwise attempts to force the pace in South Africa generally have the opposite effect to that confidently anticipated by advocates of pressure', it warned, before going on to appeal 'to ordinary working men' not to allow themselves to be used as 'the cats-paws of millionaires in England who were seeking to work up a crisis in order to increase their political control as well as their profits in the Transvaal.[72] On the eve of the Bloemfontein Conference, it published 'a timely literary offering at the altar of peace' by South Africa's most famous writer: Olive Schreiner. The demand for 'An English South-African's view of the situation' was so great that it had to be reprinted, three days later, and in June it appeared both in a Dutch translation and as a booklet in England.[73] Written in the characteristic, highly emotional style of Olive Schreiner's polemical writings, it attacked 'the capitalists', defended 'our old simple farmers or Boers', and appealed to 'the great, fierce, freedom-loving heart' of British public opinion for sympathy for the Transvaal with its immense problem.[74] Edmund Garrett, Milner's confidant and editor of *The Cape Times*, dismissed it as supporting 'the logic of a schoolgirl with the statistics of a romanticist, and wraps them both up in the lambent fire of a Hebrew prophetess'.[75] It is not known whether Milner – who admired *The Story of an African Farm* – ever read the copy of her view of the situation which she sent to accompany him on the train to Bloemfontein.

Milner approached the Bloemfontein Conference with no expectations that it would achieve anything, let alone a final settlement. As he intimated to Selborne beforehand, he intended 'to be *very stiff* about Uitlanders' grievances and put my demands on this subject high – though they may seem high to Kruger, they would be called very moderate in England – and get him to break off, if he does break off, on these, rather than on any one of the 101 other differences which, though they may afford better technical *casus belli*, do not really *mean so much* or excite so much interest'.[76] A few days before he left for Bloemfontein, Milner wrote again to say that he was still 'not hopeful of the result of the Conference'. 'One thing is certain', he commented, 'if we can't get reforms now by negotiations with so much in our favour, we shall never get them, and we must either be prepared to see Kruger carry out his policy of suppressing his English subjects, or compel him to desist from it. The latter means a greatly increased force and *may* mean war. The question has, therefore, got into a stage, when its *military aspect* is becoming of supreme importance.' If the Conference failed, the publication of the Blue Book and the delivery of the 10 May despatch should, he urged, be accompanied by military preparations. Additional troops – 10,000 to 30,000 – would be required; the importance of 'strengthening our position in Natal very much *before* the crash' and of doing something about the defence of Kimberley and Ladysmith were emphasized. The despatch of British troops was likely to cause 'a wild Bond outcry' in the Cape and perhaps necessitate the dismissal of the Cape ministry; Milner accepted that it was likely to provoke the Orange Free State into joining the Transvaal in an invasion of Natal and the northern districts of the Cape Colony. By this, however, the Boers would 'put themselves in the wrong and become the aggressors'. What Milner feared was a prolonged period when British forces would not yet be in a position to strike back. An initial Boer success 'of *some duration* would light a fire throughout South Africa', he predicted. Still, 'the people who are against us, are against us, and can't be won over *till after victory*', he concluded. 'My view has been and still is, in spite of all these alarms and excursions, that if we are perfectly determined we shall win without a fight or with a mere apology for one. It is a large period of suspense, or of enforced standing on the defensive which might lead to the big war.'[77] Milner went to Bloemfontein determined not on a compromise or a settlement but on a victory – by brow-beating Kruger into a capitulation, if possible; by war if necessary.

Milner had already succeeded in seizing the initiative from Chamberlain with regard to the arrangements for the Conference. Chamberlain had suggested that Schreiner should accompany the British High Commissioner, since he wanted peace and would use his influence towards achieving a settlement. If he were not present, and the Conference broke down, he might be inclined to attribute this to the obstinacy of Milner and the British government. Milner, who was determined to restrict the Conference to a direct exchange between himself and Kruger, dismissed the idea. Chamberlain accepted this but pointed out that the 'attitude of the Cape Prime Minister will have a most important influence on the ultimate decision of H.M.G.'.[78] He was, however, uneasy about Milner's response and commented that 'if Sir A. Milner is to keep in close sympathy with H.M.G., I think that he requires to be restrained rather than encouraged at this moment'.[79] Chamberlain's staff were more forthright. Graham commented that the tone of Milner's telegrams 'indicate that he has made up his mind that either he gets what he wants or there must be war', and suggested that he should be informed that, at present, British public opinion would not support threats or forcible measures.[80] Yet nothing was done to restrict Milner's freedom of action at the Conference nor to challenge his provocative claim that the opinion of Afrikaners in the Cape Colony and the Orange Free State could be ignored because, as he incorrectly assumed, Britons equalled or outnumbered the 'Dutch' in South Africa as a whole.

Chamberlain failed to give any formal instructions to Milner as to how he should proceed at the Conference, since he wished to leave him 'as free a hand as possible'. He agreed with Milner's own determination to 'lay all stress on the question of the franchise in first instance. Other reforms are less pressing and will come in time, if this can be arranged satisfactorily. . . . If fair terms of franchise are refused by President, it appears hardly worth while to bring forward other matters . . . and the whole situation must be reconsidered', he wrote. He urged Milner, however, not to lose sight of full municipal rights for the Rand and Johannesburg as 'a feasible solution if President [Kruger] fears that independence will be endangered by concession of general franchise'. The delicate subject of arbitration over the issues in dispute between the two governments was not to be introduced without further communication with Chamberlain himself. Otherwise, he left the details of the negotiations in Milner's hands.[81]

The form which the Conference was to take also made a head-on clash and a breakdown more likely. Milner insisted that the meetings should be between himself and Kruger alone (with interpreters), that no communications would be issued to the press until afterwards but that a full, verbatim record would then be published. This meant that Kruger and Milner would not just be talking to each other but addressing the public – both in Britain and South Africa – at the same time. It was part of Milner's campaign 'to keep the course of future negotiations public' and use them to educate public opinion.[82] In this exercise, the suave, experienced and articulate Milner had a distinct advantage over Kruger.[83] From the outset, Milner seized and retained the initiative. The published record shows Milner dominating the proceedings. His arguments are presented cogently and persuasively whilst Kruger is largely reduced to reacting to what Milner has to say.[84]

The Bloemfontein Conference opened on the afternoon of Wednesday 31 May and broke down the following Monday, 5 June. Whilst it was in session, the British Colonial Office received daily telegraphic summaries from Milner but it was scarcely in a position to control him. During the proceedings Kruger was able, on occasion, to take the discussion away from the issue of the Uitlander franchise, on which Milner was determined to concentrate; Milner reported to the Colonial Office that 'the old gentleman rambles fearfully'.[85] But the Conference failed essentially on the issue of the Uitlander franchise. Milner went to the Conference with a clearly defined objective on this but he was not prepared to bargain. Kruger conceded some ground – he offered to reduce the total minimum of nine years' residence, required by his proposals currently before the Volksraad, to seven years; to increase the number of seats for the Rand in the

Volksraad; and to reconsider the form of the oath of allegiance. But the gap between the two sides proved to be too great to be bridged.

Milner opened the proceedings by stating that there were many points at issue between the British and Transvaal governments but the treatment of the Uitlander population lay at the heart of the most serious of them. If the Transvaal government would take measures 'to content the reasonable people' amongst the Uitlanders, who formed the great majority, this would not only strengthen the independence of the republic but bring about 'a better state of feeling all round' which would enable most of the other issues to be settled.[86] Acknowledging that 'the citizens of the South African Republic are intensely jealous of British interference in their internal affairs', Milner pointed out that the British government had been petitioned by a vast number of Uitlanders, who were British subjects, and was bound to take up their case with the government concerned – wherever it was. If the Transvaal government would only treat the Uitlanders in a more liberal manner, this would not increase but enormously diminish British interference. If the Uitlanders were in a position to help themselves, they would not always be appealing to the British government. If agreement could be reached on the franchise question, 'this would render the raising of many other questions unnecessary'.

After indicating that he was ready to listen to friendly advice from Milner, even about the Transvaal's internal affairs, but was not prepared to be dictated to, Kruger elaborated on the peculiar difficulties facing the Transvaal government over the franchise issue. In other countries, the established populations were such that they could not be outvoted by newcomers; but in the Transvaal, if all those who had rushed in to the country to the gold-fields were given the vote 'equal to our burghers' and were able to vote in the Volksraad then, in a very short time, they could turn the laws 'topsy turvy, and do as they liked . . . and the burghers would be crushed out' and the independence of the country would fall. Kruger reminded Milner of his proposals, which were already before the Volksraad, gradually to extend the franchise and to reduce to five years the time required after naturalization. In time, 'we can, perhaps, go further', he said, and 'make our franchise shorter and shorter', but only when 'they cannot out-vote us'. A number of the Uitlanders who demanded the franchise did not want it, Kruger claimed, 'they use it as a pretext to egg on people with Her Majesty'. Further, they demanded the franchise without being ready to bear the burdens of full citizenship, which included serving on commando.

Milner agreed that to make a proposal to admit strangers to the franchise under conditions which would enable them to swamp the old burghers 'would be unreasonable'. But the present situation was that the Uitlanders did not have a single representative in the Volksraad of 28. Further, even if the time required to obtain full burgher rights and the franchise were reduced from the present fourteen years to nine years under the proposals at present before the Volksraad, applicants had to take an oath of allegiance (thereby losing their existing citizenship) and then wait twelve years (seven years under the new proposals) before becoming full citizens of the republic. This deterred people from attempting to obtain the franchise. It meant that the numerous foreigners in the Transvaal had no say in its government or in the making of the laws under which they had to live. Yet it was to their contribution, in commerce and industry, that the country owed its present wealth and position. They were treated as strangers. It would not be enough to let a few people in to the franchise and obviously the whole crowd could not be admitted; but this was not being asked for; what was needed was that a substantial number should be included and not excluded from the affairs of the state. 'I do not want to swamp the old population', Milner declared, 'but it is perfectly possible to give the new population an immediate voice in the legislation, and yet to leave the old burghers in such a position that they cannot possibly be swamped'. To this, Kruger replied: 'Our enfranchised burghers are probably about 30,000, and the newcomers may be from 60,000 to 70,000, and if we give them the franchise tomorrow we may as well give up the Republic.' Milner's proposal, he said, 'would be worse than annexation, and the burghers would not agree to it'. Milner protested against the view that Kruger was 'defending the independence of his country, and I wish to take it away' and said that 'the intense prejudice on the side of the present burghers, and their intense suspicion of us' was what made discussion so difficult. 'They think Her Majesty's Government wants to get their country back in one way or another. Her Majesty's Government does not' – or so Milner assured President Kruger.[87] Thereupon, the first day's proceedings closed with Kruger informing Milner that many of the 21,000 signatures on the Second Uitlander Petition were forgeries and that he had brought with him to Bloemfontein a petition, signed by 23,000 or 24,000 people, all of whom were 'strangers', which he presented on the second day. In what came to be called the 'counter-petition', the signatories declared their satisfaction with the Transvaal government and claimed that the Second Uitlander Petition had 'been caused by the Capitalists, not by the public' and that its purpose was 'detrimental to the whole public, including the Uitlanders'.[88]

The second day began with a protest from President Kruger about the build-up of British troops in the Cape and elsewhere. Was this 'a threat of the sword instead of a friendly conversation?', he asked. Milner denied that the British army in South Africa was being increased and claimed that the reports to the contrary were untrue. He too was continually receiving reports about the increased armaments in the South African Republic in recent years, but they must both put these alarms aside during the Conference. Kruger then asked Milner to outline the details of his proposal with regard to an extension of the franchise. Milner then proposed that the full franchise should be given to every foreigner who:

(a) had been resident in the Republic for five years;

(b) declared his intention to reside permanently there;

(c) took an oath to obey the laws, undertake all obligations of citizenship, and defend the independence of the country.

The franchise should be confined to persons of good character who possessed a certain amount of property or income. Since most of the new citizens resided in one district, the franchise should be accompanied by the creation of a number of new constituencies – which should be 'not so few as to leave the representatives of the Uitlanders in a contemptible minority'. Those fulfilling the requirements should be admitted to full citizenship immediately after taking the oath of allegiance.[89] Milner agreed that it would not be reasonable to give the franchise to all the Uitlanders at once.

Kruger at once objected that, under these proposals, the Uitlanders would at once become a majority of those enfranchised and his burghers would be swamped. If the Uitlanders 'once got the vote, and the majority came to the Volksraad saying that the number of members of the Raad should be in proportion to the number of electors, the Volksraad would be obliged to listen to it, and it would be all up with them', he declared. Milner denied this, saying he did not think that there would be a great in-rush of newcomers; a considerable number of the Uitlanders were birds of passage who did not want citizenship. As for the many Uitlanders 'who cry out for the franchise' but don't really want it, the best answer to them was to offer them the franchise and then, when they refused it, nobody would have anything more to say for them on the matter. He was *not* suggesting the franchise for everybody; a considerable level of property or income should be made a condition; but past residence should count; the repeated reference to 60,000 people was 'a bugbear'.

The Conference had reached a crucial point. During the afternoon of 1 June, however, it drifted off into a desultory and inconclusive discussion about other matters: the dynamite monopoly, Kruger's wish to see the incorporation of Swaziland into the Transvaal republic, the matter of the indemnity due from the British South Africa Company for the Jameson Raid, and the question of referring matters in dispute between the two governments to arbitration (which Kruger said he considered the most important of the four). Only on 2 June was there a return to what Milner considered 'the main question'. This was done by Kruger suggesting that it would be easier for him to gain the support of the Volksraad and his burghers if he could show them a *quid pro quo* for some concession on the franchise. 'I must tell them that something has been given in to me, if I give in to something.' Milner dismissed this at once as a 'sort of Kaffir bargain', insisting that if they could not reach agreement on the franchise proposals which Milner had put forward, then he would 'begin to feel rather hopeless about the outcome of the whole Conference'. Kruger then stated baldly that he could not agree to Milner's franchise proposals. An impasse had been reached. Before the Conference adjourned for lunch, Milner warned that if agreement was not possible on the franchise issue then 'nothing else is of any use'. He had come, he said, at a time of crisis, to see if by one big effort 'a great disaster, such as an open breach between the two governments' could be averted. When they reconvened, he would ask if President Kruger was willing to go into the franchise question. 'Possibly yes and possibly no', replied Kruger. 'If His Excellency doesn't want to go into any point but the franchise, it will not be my fault if we do not agree.'[90]

In the afternoon, Kruger turned up with 'a complete Reform Bill', worked out in detail, which Milner was convinced he had had in his pocket all along.[91] Milner saw at once that it did not provide for an immediate or early enfranchisement even for Uitlanders who had been resident in the Transvaal for many years; it also made no provision for an increase in the number of seats in the Volksraad for the Uitlander districts. Although he acknowledged it to be 'a great advance' on the existing law, Milner observed that it was full of restrictions and 'not calculated to lead to any considerable enfranchisement of Uitlanders'.[92] He agreed to take it away and study it in detail but he said that there seemed to be such a 'complete separation' between this and his own proposals that he could not see how he could recommend it. Meanwhile, he introduced – as Chamberlain had suggested he might – the municipal self-government idea for the Rand which Chamberlain had first outlined in his despatch of February 1896. Kruger rejected this completely, saying it was demanding 'the title deeds of the farm' and would never be agreed to.

When they met again, on Saturday 3 June, Kruger announced that he had forgotten to add a proposal for creating four electoral districts in place of the existing two for the Rand to his memorandum on franchise reform the previous day. Milner agreed that this was a vital point. He also repeated that, as far as an extension of the franchise to the Uitlanders was concerned, he was not considering the thousands of people who only wanted to stay in the Transvaal for a few years and then depart – their position was different. He was thinking 'only of people who want to make the country their home'; after resigning their previous citizenship and taking an oath of allegiance to the republic, these should at once be in a position of equality with the old burghers. Milner's objective was to achieve the immediate enfranchisement of a substantial number of Uitlanders. Kruger again emphasized

> that in England there are millions of burghers, and the number of
> burghers in the South African Republic is very small in comparison; that
> makes the difference. . . . If His Excellency would only see that
> difficulty and bear in mind how small our number of burghers is. They
> paid for that country by their blood, and they would be out-voted if your
> proposal was accepted.

Milner denied that they would be outvoted by his plan, but Kruger repeated his conviction that they would be. The Uitlanders, he continued,

> are always pursuing something; they are like naughty children, if you give
> them a finger they will take the whole hand, then an arm, then a head,
> and then they want the whole body, bit by bit. After I have given them
> the arm, they still go and try to get the same rights as my burghers in a
> short time.[93]

The Conference adjourned for the week-end and arranged to meet again on Monday morning, 5 June. Over the week-end, Milner learned that Kruger felt he had gone as far as he could and would not depart from his proposal of a seven-year retrospective franchise (naturalization after two years, full citizenship and franchise after a further five years), and this was confirmed in a memorandum from Kruger delivered on the Sunday afternoon. In this document, Kruger summarized his proposals, adding a readiness to suggest to the Volksraad that five seats instead of the present two should be made available for the Rand. He repeated that he could not agree to Milner's franchise proposals because they presented 'the great and threatening danger' of the old citizens being outvoted by the new.[94] Kruger had consulted the three advisers he had brought with him to Bloemfontein: Schalk Burger, A.D. Wolmarans and Smuts, and also President Steyn and Fischer of the Orange Free State. According to Steyn's testimony, he, Fischer and Smuts urged Kruger to accept the principle of a five years' retrospective franchise (which had been recommended by Chief Justice de Villiers), but both Schalk Burger and A. D. Wolmarans opposed this, and their influence was strengthened by a petition, signed by a substantial number of burghers, which arrived at Bloemfontein urging Kruger not to give way on the franchise.[95]

Milner now concluded that the Conference seemed likely to fail and that it was better not to prolong it, since 'my principal aim at the Conference was not to fight out the various points of difference between the Governments, but, by arriving at a settlement on the Uitlander question, which went to the root of many of those differences, to pave the way for the settlement of all'.[96] He therefore drew up a statement in which he declared that Kruger's final proposals were inadequate, that less than a quarter of the seats in the Volksraad seemed 'a scanty allowance' for the Uitlander population, and that his own aim of achieving the franchise and substantial representation for them had not been achieved. Milner emphasized that no small measure of reform would suffice any longer. He ended on a threatening note. The British government considered that the complaints embodied in the Second Uitlander Petition were well-founded and was 'only waiting for the result of this Conference before addressing the Government of the South African Republic on this subject'.

When the Conference met on Monday, 5 June, Kruger at once declared: 'I am not ready to hand over my country to strangers. There is nothing else now to be done.' Milner again reiterated that this was neither the intention nor the likely effect of anything he had proposed. In a final memorandum, Kruger reaffirmed his conviction that his own franchise proposals 'went as far as it was possible to go in the interests of my people and State'. He also indicated the importance he attached to the establishment of a procedure by which arbitration over issues in dispute between the two governments could take place and suggested that arbitration was possible by 'other than foreign powers'. As it was his 'earnest wish that this Conference should not be fruitless', Kruger therefore made a final attempt at a bargain:

> As, according to his own admission, my proposal about franchise is an important step in the right direction, I shall be prepared to lay my

proposal before the Volksraad and to recommend it, even though His Excellency does not fully agree with it. From his side, I shall then expect that His Excellency will lay before and recommend to Her Majesty's Government my request about arbitration on future matters of difference under the Convention.[97]

Kruger said that 'if there were anything like concessions' on Milner's part, he would be prepared to go on with the discussion. But Milner was not in the business of making concessions and so the Bloemfontein Conference ended in failure. Milner rejected any obligation with regard to arbitration, pointing out that there were clearly matters with regard to which arbitration was not possible, and methods – such as the involvement of a foreign government – which the British government would never permit. There were, however, a certain class of questions about which arbitration might be acceptable if a suitable method could be agreed; but this was something which could be dealt with quite separately from the Conference. This, he now declared, 'was absolutely at an end, and there is no obligation on either side arising out of it'.[98]

Milner had telegraphed to the Colonial Office, on 4 June, that the Conference was likely to fail and this had prompted Chamberlain to reply: 'I hope you will not break off hastily. Boers do not understand quick decisions but prefer to waste a lot of time over a bargain without coming to terms. I am by no means convinced that the President . . . has made his last offer, and you should be very patient and admit a good deal of haggling before you finally abandon the game.' Chamberlain went on to suggest possible lines for further negotiation which brought in other issues, as Kruger wished. 'Otherwise', he commented, 'we shall stand upon the franchise alone – and the legal claim for this is very weak'. He also offered to consider a formal assurance or guarantee about the Transvaal's independence which might set Kruger's mind at rest on this score.[99] But Chamberlain's telegram arrived too late. Milner had already exercised his free hand to bring the Conference to an abrupt end.

The Bloemfontein Conference was foredoomed to failure because Kruger went to it prepared to bargain and negotiate on a number of issues (including that of extending the franchise) whereas Milner was determined to make or break it on the issue which Selborne had accurately described as 'the point of most resistance' – an extension of the franchise to Uitlanders on terms which Kruger found unacceptable. On the franchise, as Abraham Fischer assured Hofmeyr, Kruger had in fact conceded more than anyone had expected.[100] He had offered it on a seven-year retrospective basis with five seats in the

Volksraad, which was an advance on the nine-year basis and four seats which he had outlined in March and proposed to the Volksraad in May. This represented a decisive shift away from the existing franchise law (dating from 1890) which required fourteen years' residence and provided for only two seats (out of a total for the Volksraad of 28) for the whole of the gold-fields area. What Milner had demanded at Bloemfontein was a straightforward retrospective franchise 'without pitfalls' based on a certain property qualification and five years' residence – valid retrospectively. Full and equal citizenship with the established burghers should be obtainable after naturalization through the taking of an amended oath of allegiance. He had looked towards there being at least seven seats for the Rand in the Volksraad; 'this would make 1/5 of it Uitlander members', he commented.[101]

What Milner sought was not a negotiated settlement but a capitulation; and since he did not expect that to occur, he had approached the Bloemfontein Conference convinced that it would fail. The faithful Fiddes accurately reflected this when he wrote: 'we didn't expect to score over this Conference: it was a cunning move of the other side; our one desire was to get through it with as little danger as possible: & I don't think we left much of our wool among the brambles'.[102] Chamberlain had been acutely aware that if the Conference failed 'we shall have exhausted conciliatory methods and the crisis . . . will be upon us'.[103] He was now annoyed by the abrupt way in which Milner had brought the Conference to an end. An ultimatum had been brought much nearer since the British government would now have to make demands on Kruger's government which, if not met, would have to be enforced.

As for Milner himself, he had already indicated to Selborne, before the Conference took place, that if it failed he expected events to take a military turn, for he believed that the best chance of a capitulation would be if Britain demonstrated her resolve by preparing to send troops to reinforce the inadequate British military presence in South Africa. Kruger would 'bluff up to the cannon's mouth' and then either capitulate – as he had done before – or fight. Milner did not shrink from the prospect of a war, since he was quite sure that it could only result in a British victory. He had gone to Bloemfontein because to have refused to do so 'would have been too likely to lead to an outcry both here and in England that we *wanted war*. Now I don't want war', he had told Selborne, 'but I admit I begin to think it may be the only way out. But, if so, we must seem to be forced into it'.[104] A week before the Bloemfontein Conference had taken place, he had already stated his own conviction:

(1) that absolute determination plus a large temporary increase of force will ensure a climb down. It is 20 to 1.

(2) that, if it didn't and there was a fight, it would be better to fight now than 5 or 10 years' hence, when the Transvaal, unless the Uitlanders can be taken in, in considerable numbers, will be stronger and more hostile than ever.[105]

NOTES

1. The texts of these speeches were printed in *The Standard and Diggers News*, 21 and 27 March and 3 April 1899.
2. Speech at Rustenburg, 25 March 1899, printed in *The Standard and Diggers News*, 27 March 1899.
3. Speech at Heidelberg, 17 March 1899.
4. Ibid.
5. Speech at Rustenburg, 25 March 1899.
6. Speech at Heidelberg, 17 March 1899.
7. *The Star*, 4 April 1899, p. 4.
8. Milner to Chamberlain, 11 April 1899, in C. Headlam, ed., *The Milner Papers* 2 vols (London 1931/1933), 1, pp. 334–5.
9. Conyngham Greene to Milner, 10 March 1899, in A. N. Porter, *The Origins of the South African War, Joseph Chamberlain and the Diplomacy of Imperialism 1895–1899* (Manchester, 1980), pp. 190–1.
10. Ibid., p. 191.
11. G. V. Fiddes to Selborne, 14 March 1899, SeP MS 14.
12. The text of the petition is in CO 417/260, pp. 14–36, and was printed in C.9345, 'Papers re. complaints of British subjects in the S.A.R.' (June 1899), pp. 185–9.
13. Chamberlain, Speech of 20 March 1899, *Hansard*, Fourth Series, vol. lxviii, col. 1376.
14. Fiddes to Selborne, 3 April 1899, in D. G. Boyce, ed., *The Crisis of British Power: The Imperial and Naval Papers of the Second Earl of Selborne, 1895–1910* (London, 1990), p. 74.
15. Conyngham Greene to British High Commissioner, 4 April 1899, Transvaal Archives, BA 20.
16. A. N. Porter, 'Lord Salisbury, Mr Chamberlain and South Africa 1895–99', *JICH* 1, 1 (1972), p. 17.
17. FitzPatrick to Wernher, 6 April 1899, in A. H. Duminy and W. R. Guest, eds, *FitzPatrick, South African Politician: Selected Papers, 1888–1906* (Johannesburg, 1976), pp. 202–6.
18. Ibid., p. 204.
19. Fiddes to Selborne, 3 April 1899, in Boyce, ed., *Crisis of British Power*, p. 74.
20. Milner to Fiddes, 1 April 1899, in Headlam, ed., *The Milner Papers*, 1, p. 331.

21. Milner to Chamberlain, 15 and 29 March 1899, CO 417/260/249.
22. Milner to Conyngham Greene, 15 April 1899, in Headlam, ed., *The Milner Papers*, 1, p. 332.
23. Milner to Chamberlain, 11 April 1899, in ibid., p.335
24. Milner to Chamberlain, 4 April 1899, JC 10/3/89.
25. Milner to Chamberlain, 25 May 1897, in Headlam, ed., *The Milner Papers*, 1, p. 65.
26. Milner to Conyngham Greene, 11 March 1899, in ibid., p. 325.
27. Milner to Chamberlain, 4 March 1899, CO 417/259.
28. Milner to Chamberlain, 4 April 1899, JC 10/3/89.
29. R. H. Wilde, *Joseph Chamberlain and South African Republic 1895–1899*, Archives Yearbook for South African History 1956 Part 1 (Pretoria, 1956), p. 91.
30. Chamberlain's notes for his Memorandum to the Cabinet, 29 April 1899, JC 10/3/89.
31. Wilde, *Joseph Chamberlain*, p. 96.
32. Ibid., pp. 96–7, quoting St. Just and Lambert.
33. Ibid., p. 98.
34. All quotations from the material in ibid., pp. 98–9.
35. Selborne to Milner, 20 April 1899, in Boyce, ed., *Crisis of British Power*, p. 7.
36. Selborne to Curzon, 7 May 1899, in ibid., pp. 78–9.
37. Conyngham Greene to Milner, 7 April 1899, in Headlam, ed., *The Milner Papers*, 1, p. 346.
38. Milner to Chamberlain, 4 May 1899, printed as No. 78 in C.9345 (June 1899) and in Headlam, ed., *The Milner Papers*, 1, pp. 349–53.
39. Exchange between Milner and Mr James Rendel, in Headlam, ed., *The Milner Papers*, 1, pp. 355–6.
40. Memorandum for the Cabinet, 28 April 1899, JC 10/3/89.
41. Chamberlain's minute on Milner to Chamberlain, 4 May 1899, CO 417/279.
42. Milner to Chamberlain, 8 May 1899. CO 417/260.
43. Ibid. See also Wilde, *Joseph Chamberlain*, pp. 102–3.
44. Wilde, *Joseph Chamberlain*, p. 103.
45. Hicks Beach to Chamberlain, 30 April 1899, JC 16/5/24.
46. Memorandum by Balfour, 1 May 1899, CAB 37/49/29, printed in E. Drus, 'Select documents from the Chamberlain Papers concerning Anglo-Transvaal relations 1896–1899', *BIHR* 27 (1954), pp. 173–5.
47. Balfour to Chamberlain, 6 May 1899, in Drus, 'Select documents', p. 175.
48. The full text is printed as No. 83, dated 10 May 1899, in C.9345, pp. 226–31.
49. Salisbury to the Queen, 9 May 1899, CAB 41/25/10, quoted in Porter, *Origins*, p. 207.
50. Fiddes to Selborne, 25 April 1899, in Boyce, *Crisis of British Power*, p. 78.
51. Details in the ScP, MSC 27, South African Library, Cape Town. Milner's quotation is from his diary, extract printed in Headlam, ed., *The Milner Papers*, 1, p. 360.

52. Milner to Conyngham Greene, 12 May 1899, in Headlam, ed., *The Milner Papers*, 1, p. 378.
53. Chamberlain to Milner, 12 May 1899, in J. L. Garvin and J. Amery, *Life of Joseph Chamberlain* 6 vols (London, 1932–69), 3, p. 401.
54. Milner to Sir W. Hely Hutchinson, 8 May 1899, in Headlam, ed., *The Milner Papers*, 1, pp. 358–9.
55. See chapter 9, pp. 300–5 below.
56. Merriman to Schreiner, 6 March 1899, in P. Lewsen, ed., *Selections from the Correspondence of J. X. Merriman, 1870–1890* 4 vols (Cape Town, 1966), 3, pp. 21–3.
57. E. Walker, *W.P. Schreiner: a South African* (Oxford, 1937), p. 141.
58. See Conclusion, n. 17 for the matter of the authorship of this work.
59. Smuts to Hofmeyr, 10 May 1899, in W. K. Hancock and J. van der Poel, eds, *Selections from the Smuts Papers* 7 vols (Cambridge, 1966–73), 1, pp. 233–4.
60. Hofmeyr to Smuts, 15 May 1899, in ibid., p. 237.
61. Smuts to Schreiner, May 1899, in Walker, *W.P. Schreiner*, p. 144.
62. Report of the Volksraad proceedings in *The Press*, 24 May 1899.
63. Smuts to his wife, 1 June 1899, in Hancock and van der Poel, eds, *Selections Smuts Papers*, 1, p. 242.
64. FitzPatrick to Wernher, 19 April 1899, in Duminy and Guest, eds, *FitzPatrick*, p. 208.
65. FitzPatrick to Walrond, 1 May 1899, in ibid., p. 209.
66. Ibid.; also FitzPatrick to Wernher, 8 May 1899, in ibid., p. 216.
67. Rouliot to Wernher, 24 April, 1 and 8 May 1899, BRA, HE 175.
68. Rouliot to Wernher, 29 May 1899, BRA, HE 175.
69. *The Cape Times*, 27 and 29 May 1899.
70. *The Star*, leader 15 March 1899.
71. *The Standard and Diggers News*, 25 and 26 April 1899.
72. *The Standard and Diggers News*, 28 April, 1 and 11 May 1899.
73. 'An Englishwoman's view of the situation', *The Standard and Diggers News*, 29 May and 1 June 1899.
74. Ibid. (pamphlet version), p. 66.
75. K. Schoeman, *Only an Anguish to Live Here: Olive Schreiner and the Anglo-Boer War* (Johannesburg, 1992), pp. 45–6.
76. Milner to Selborne, 17 May 1899, in Boyce, ed., *Crisis of British Power*, pp. 79–80.
77. Milner to Selborne, 24 May 1899, in ibid., pp. 80–3.
78. Chamberlain to Milner, 26 May 1899, in Garvin, *Life of Chamberlain*, 3, pp. 403–4.
79. Minute by Chamberlain on Milner to Chamberlain, 27 May 1899, CO 417/282.
80. Graham Minute on Milner to Chamberlain, 27 May 1899, in Wilde, *Joseph Chamberlain*, p. 107.
81. Chamberlain to Milner, 24 May 1899, in Garvin, *Life of Chamberlain*, 3, pp. 402–3.
82. Milner to Conyngham Greene, 15 April 1899, in Headlam, ed., *The Milner Papers*, 1, p. 332.

83. J. S. Marais, *The Fall of Kruger's Republic* (Oxford, 1961), p. 280.
84. The verbatim record of the Bloemfontein Conference was afterwards agreed and published in English and Dutch. The English version was published, together with Milner's full report of 14 June, in July 1899 as C.9404. Milner's own notes for the Conference are preserved in the MP 242.
85. Milner's telegraphic summary, 31 May 1899, in Garvin, *Life of Chamberlain*, 3, p. 405.
86. 'Correspondence relating to the Bloemfontein Conference 1899', C.9404, p. 14. All quotations in this section are from this verbatim account, page references as indicated.
87. C.9404, p. 23.
88. C.9404, pp. 44–5.
89. C.9404, p. 51.
90. C.9404, p. 37.
91. Milner's Report of the Conference to Chamberlain, 14 June 1899, printed in C.9404, p. 5.
92. C.9404, pp. 51–2.
93. C.9404, p. 41.
94. Full text of Kruger's memorandum, 4 June 1899, in C.9404, pp. 54–5.
95. N. J. van der Merwe, *Marthinus Theunis Steyn* 2 vols (Cape Town, 1921), 1, pp. 188–9.
96. Milner's Report to Chamberlain, 14 June 1899, C.9404, p. 8.
97. C.9404, p. 59.
98. C.9404, pp. 42–4.
99. Chamberlain to Milner, 5 June 1899, in Garvin, *Life of Chamberlain*, 3, p. 408; also Wilde, *Joseph Chamberlain*, pp. 110–11.
100. Fischer to Hofmeyr, 7 June 1899, HP MSC 8, Box 8c.
101. Milner to Chamberlain, 22 May 1899, in C.9345, p. 242.
102. Fiddes to Selborne, 27 June 1899, SeP MS 14.
103. Chamberlain to J. Sivewright (draft of letter of late May 1899 not sent), quoted in Wilde, *Joseph Chamberlain*, p. 106.
104. Milner to Selborne, 17 May 1899, in Boyce, ed., *Crisis of British Power*, p. 79.
105. Milner to Selborne, 24 May 1899, in ibid., p. 43.

CHAPTER NINE

British Supremacy

AFTER BLOEMFONTEIN

The failure of the Bloemfontein Conference made a resort to war much more likely. Kruger's government saw in Milner's intransigence there a direct reflection of the hostility towards the Transvaal which they had long assumed in Chamberlain. The dictatorial way in which Milner had rejected Kruger's attempts to achieve a negotiated settlement on a range of issues and had refused to deviate from his own franchise proposals confirmed their worst suspicions. Further negotiations became more difficult as what was regarded as the British government's aggressive stance evoked resistance. In the Orange Free State, the legislature passed a resolution expressing sympathy and support for the Transvaal President and his proposals and President Steyn despatched a large order for arms and ammunition. In the Transvaal, *The Standard and Diggers News* declared that the demands made by the British government could not possibly be conceded in their entirety without seriously compromising the country's independence.[1]

On his return to Pretoria, President Kruger at once discussed the outcome of the Bloemfontein discussions with the Volksraad and, on 9 June, a resolution was passed regretting Milner's refusal to agree to 'the extremely just proposals' which Kruger had made there. On 12 June, Kruger laid before the Volksraad the details of his government's proposed new franchise law, together with a provision for the increased representation of the Rand by three additional members. In his speech, Kruger conceded the need to do something for those foreigners who would form loyal citizens of the state, but dismissed the claims of those *rondlopers* (vagrants) who did not really want the franchise but wanted the country and 'were working towards a row'.[2]

The Volksraad then agreed to adjourn until 3 July to enable consultation with the burgher population to take place. At meetings at Boksburg and Germiston resolutions were passed declaring that as the number of burghers in the Transvaal was 40,000 and there were already 50,000 Uitlanders, this made it 'impossible to grant a general extension of the franchise for thereby the burghers would be swamped'.[3] At a gathering of over 4,000 burghers at the Paardekraal national monument on 17 June, Schalk Burger and A.D.W. Wolmarans made speeches defending Kruger's record at the Bloemfontein Conference and a resolution was passed supporting his proposals 'which are as liberal and far-reaching as they could possibly adopt with safety under present conditions'. The gathering was orderly but very determined, prayers were offered and God's help sought for the preservation of their independence. General Joubert made a speech which 'breathed patriotic devotion in every sentence'.[4]

Meanwhile, State Secretary Reitz returned to the matter of arbitration which Kruger had tried to raise at Bloemfontein. In a letter accompanying a fresh proposal on this matter on 9 June, Reitz pointed out that the lack of an arbitration procedure meant that 'as soon as a dispute arises between this Government and H.M.G., war is spoken of by the one party and thereby again the slumbering suspicions of the other party are awakened'. This would be greatly eased if an arbitration procedure, not involving foreign governments, could be agreed.[5] Milner at once argued that a 'redress of Uitlander grievances *must come first* . . . and nothing else can be considered till that matter is out of the way'; although he acknowledged the case 'for some sort of tribunal', preferably of a judicial kind. He told Chamberlain that he considered Reitz's proposal vague and 'absolutely unacceptable'.[6] The British government decided to respond cautiously but more positively. So long as any foreign element was excluded, Chamberlain informed Reitz, it might be possible to arrive at a procedure involving 'some judicial authority whose independence, impartiality, and capacity would be beyond and above all suspicion'.[7] The matter of arbitration, however, was enmeshed with the long-running dispute over suzerainty. This was why no foreign government could ever be accepted by Britain as an arbitrator over its relations with the Transvaal. At the Bloemfontein Conference, Kruger had at last accepted this. As the number and importance of the issues over which the two governments were in conflict increased, it became a pressing priority for Kruger's government to obtain some agreement on an arbitration procedure. At Bloemfontein, Kruger had sought and failed to achieve a 'trade-off' whereby the British government accepted an arbitration procedure in return for an extension of the franchise by the Transvaal government. Thereafter, the continued quest for an acceptable arbitration procedure remained a key consideration for Kruger's government right through to the final breakdown of negotiations in August.

Some pro-British observers felt that, with the Bloemfontein Conference, the British government had succeeded in asserting its right to intervene in the internal affairs of the Transvaal and that 'the thin end of the wedge has been inserted and the thick end will arrive sooner or later'. The need for franchise reform had been clearly acknowledged. If Kruger had accepted Milner's proposals at Bloemfontein, 'he would have ousted England from her position as Protector of the Uitlanders. As matters stand, he has confirmed England in that position'.[8] The publication of the official proceedings of the Bloemfontein Conference revealed to the Uitlanders the strong and sympathetic attitude of Milner to their cause. He was now openly espoused as their champion. A meeting attended by over 5,000 people on 10 June in the Wanderers' Hall in Johannesburg adopted his proposals as 'the irreducible minimum that could be accepted' of Uitlander demands and declared that 'they had appealed to Caesar and Caesar would see them through'.[9] At the same time, the formation of an Uitlander Council, to press for these demands, went ahead.

Percy FitzPatrick, with Milner's encouragement, had left for England at the beginning of June, there to work on British public opinion via contacts with the press and through the publication of his own account of the Uitlander reform movement, *The Transvaal from Within*. But he left behind him numerous suggestions for the continuation of the Uitlander campaign on the Rand.[10] On 16 June, the Secretary of the South African League in the Transvaal wrote to Milner to say that although his Bloemfontein proposals with regard to the franchise were gratefully acknowledged, a whole number of other grievances would not be removed simply by some Uitlanders becoming enfranchised and forming a minority in the Transvaal Volksraad; they would only be rectified 'by pressure from the Suzerain Power' being exerted at the same time. The issues included the redistribution of Volksraad seats (where it was suggested that twelve new seats should be created for the Uitlander area at once and that a procedure for automatic redistribution should be established for the future, since the Uitlander population of the Transvaal 'is bound to increase far out of proportion to that of the burghers'). Further recommendations were that the ability of the Volksraad to make changes to the constitution by resolutions (*besluiten*) should be removed; the civil service should be opened up to non-Afrikaners; the police force and the municipal administration should be reformed; the use of English should be allowed in both the Volksraad and the courts; the independence of the judiciary needed to be guaranteed; certain legislation restricting public meetings and the press should be abolished; and the fort overlooking Johannesburg should be demolished.[11] Both the South African League and the Uitlander Council continued to press the British government on these matters during the following months. Whilst it is certainly true that Milner, through his network of influence on the Rand and the dependence of the Uitlander organizations on him and access via him to the British government, utilized their petitions and grievances to further his policy with the Colonial Office, their demands soon exceeded his own. Indeed, between June and September 1899, Conyngham Greene found himself repeatedly trying to ride the tiger of Uitlander discontent and restrain its increasingly shrill and excessive demands.

Meanwhile, there was also a stiffening of resolve amongst the Boer population in the Transvaal and a determined effort to rally Afrikaner support throughout South Africa. 'The Republics are standing together', Smuts wired to Hofmeyr. 'Situation is very serious. The more so because the whole Afrikaner position is threatened by it. My fervent prayer is that England may see that Afrikaners are standing together as one man. That alone can bring her to a realization.'[12] With his usual insight, Smuts perceived that wider considerations than an Uitlander franchise were now impelling the British government towards war. Britain feared that her position and prestige in South Africa were being lost, he observed, that the 'Imperial Factor' was losing out and that everywhere those fighting for an 'independent South Africa' were gaining ground. He hoped that Cape Afrikaners would act circumspectly but put the demands of Afrikaner solidarity above everything else. He urged the Bond to pass a resolution in the Cape parliament declaring that Kruger's franchise proposals were reasonable and capable of further modification and expressing the opinion that the whole situation could be resolved in a peaceful way. The Cape parliament had 'a perfect right to pass a strong resolution in favour of peace and peaceful remedies', for the Cape Colony had a direct interest in the preservation of peace. Further, it might draw attention again to the resolution it had already passed in favour of arbitration for disputes under the London Convention. As for Milner, Smuts had formed a very unfavourable impression of him at Bloemfontein and was convinced that 'he was a very dangerous person and will become a second Bartle Frere. Either he is acting merely as the instrument of Chamberlain or he is by nature a haughty proconsul who is only concerned to make the idea of an "independent South Africa" give way to that of imperialism: in both cases I find him very dangerous'. Feeling in the two republics, he reported, was 'very strong and bitter' and convinced that Britain was determined 'to give Afrikanerdom the *coup de grace*', either by war or by threats.[13]

Schreiner's government in the Cape found itself in a difficult position. It was reluctant to express its criticism of Milner's handling of the situation too openly for fear of being dismissed and replaced by a totally compliant ministry under Sir Gordon Sprigg. After composing a protest Minute, it therefore decided not to present it formally. Instead, Schreiner asked Milner to convey to Chamberlain the view of the Cape government that Kruger's franchise proposals were a 'practical, reasonable, and a considerable step in the right direction' which might be improved on through further mediation, and 'that a state of things had not, in their opinion, arisen which would justify active interference in what were the internal affairs of the Transvaal'.[14] Milner at once indicated his own difference of opinion but agreed to convey Schreiner's message. Chamberlain, in reply, urged Schreiner and his colleagues to use their influence at Pretoria to induce Kruger's government to make the concessions necessary to relieve the British government from having to consider further interference.[15]

The possibility of an ultimatum had been considered by the British government in the wake of the failure at Bloemfontein. Milner had assumed that 'we now have a sufficient force of public opinion behind us to pursue a strong policy' but Chamberlain was increasingly doubtful about the possibility of using the franchise issue as the basis for an ultimatum. 'It seems difficult', he telegraphed, 'to treat as *casus belli* refusal by state to which we have given complete internal independence to grant particular form of franchise to aliens'; what about demanding the repeal of all legislation, passed since 1884, restricting 'the rights and privileges enjoyed by aliens'?[16] Milner replied that an ultimatum now would be premature and agreed that it would be difficult to base it on a refusal by Kruger's government to adopt a particular franchise scheme. 'I have always considered adequate franchise as alternative to demand for specific reforms', he commented, 'and I think there is still a chance, though a small one, of President adopting my minimum if he is sufficiently pushed'.[17]

Since Chamberlain was convinced that British public opinion was not yet ready to support a resort to war, and Milner knew that a rapid move to an ultimatum would alienate Cape Afrikaner opinion – whose support for British policy had always been emphasized as of great importance by the British government – both Chamberlain and Milner were ready to allow time for the Afrikaner leadership, both in the Cape and in the Orange Free State, to exert its influence on Kruger's government in an effort to persuade it that further concessions were essential if war was to be avoided. As Chamberlain put it to Milner, if the influence of these Afrikaner leaders provided the basis for a settlement:

> so much the better; if not, I shall send another despatch pressing urgently for franchise as proposed by you . . . and indicating plainly that if satisfactory reply is not given an ultimatum will follow. This carries out the policy of exhausting moral pressure before proceeding to extremities, which is demanded by public opinion here and absolutely necessary if more than party support is desired.[18]

The British Cabinet accordingly decided 'that they could not send an ultimatum yet but another stage or stages must intervene before public opinion would permit it'.[19] Lord Salisbury felt that 'the Govt. must go on, & apply steady & increasing pressure to Kruger, but there is no need to hurry, & that anything approaching an ultimatum should be delayed as long as possible'.[20] The Cabinet may have decided to modify the pace at which it contemplated moving immediately after the Bloemfontein Conference but, as Selborne emphasized to Milner:

> There is no idea of receding from the intervention which was commenced by your action at Bloemfontein and our reply to the [Uitlander] petition. . . . We have entered a lane, you have entered a lane, the Cabinet has entered a lane, the country has entered a lane, where no turning back is possible without humiliation or disaster. We must eventually force the door at the other end, by peaceful pressure if possible, but if necessary by war.[21]

Since it was accepted that substantial military reinforcements could only be sent to support an ultimatum, no immediate action was taken of a military kind. The Liberal leader, Campbell-Bannerman, declared publicly that there was nothing in the South African situation to justify even the preparation for war. Sir William Harcourt concluded privately 'that the real policy of the Government is to bluff Kruger and not to fight him'.[22]

In South Africa, Milner was determined to keep up the pressure. On 12 June, he made 'a strong speech' defending his policy of confining the discussion at Bloemfontein to the question of the Uitlander franchise and repeating that his franchise proposals would not have 'deluged the State with new citizens'. The obligations of citizenship, the length of residence required, the necessary property qualifications and other factors made him 'feel sure that the number of new citizens would not have been anything like so great as was supposed. And however numerous they might have been, the old burghers would have controlled, for a long time, the bulk of the constituencies'. 'They too', he observed, 'are increasing rapidly in number . . . moreover, it is not as if the Uitlanders were all of one kind or one mind. They are of various nationalities and represent different interests and opinions'. Kruger himself had produced a counter-petition, which supposedly showed that half the Uitlanders were on his side. Milner said he was convinced that Uitlander grievances, though sometimes stated in exaggerated language, were very real. The Transvaal was the only state in South Africa 'where inequality was the rule' amongst the European population. That had got to change. Perhaps the Transvaal government would see its way to passing a measure of reform more liberal than that proposed at Bloemfontein. 'If not', he warned, 'there may be other means of achieving the desired result'.[23]

Whilst he realized the 'necessity of not hurrying matters at home', Milner made clear to Chamberlain his own conviction that 'prolonged uncertainty here will cause many supporters to fall away'. Although further franchise concessions by Kruger's government should be discussed, anything 'which did not secure for Uitlanders at once a reasonable share of political power' must be refused. If agreement about the franchise proved impossible 'I think we must then at once pass from attitude of friendly suggestion to that of formal demand and specify in a single despatch the reforms etc. we are prepared to insist on in the interests of the Uitlanders. This Bill of Rights would have . . . to be embodied in a new Convention'. Kruger's government should be 'forced to accept or reject principles of settlement at once' and this demand should 'be accompanied by arrival of expeditionary force or advance portion of it in Natal'. Decisive action would secure all waverers and 'the most probable result would be a climb-down on part of S.A.R., and if not that a war which, however deplorable in itself, would at least enable us to put things on a sound basis for the future better than even the best-devised Convention can'.[24] The readiness to resort to war, which Milner had indicated to Selborne during May, had been intensified by the failure of the Bloemfontein Conference.

Meanwhile, a change of ministry in Natal early in June brought into power there a government committed to a policy of 'patience and conciliation' with regard to the Transvaal, which was not at all to

Milner's liking. On 17 June, this government declared that 'South Africa should not be exposed to war, by any act of her Majesty's Government, without their opinion having been heard'. It also committed itself to working with the governments of the Cape Colony and the Orange Free State to bring about a peaceful solution of the crisis.[25] The prospect of these governments cooperating to bring pressure to bear not just on Kruger but on himself, was intolerable to Milner, who told Chamberlain that such 'interference' was 'inadmissible and would ruin the whole game'.[26]

The publication of a British Blue Book and Chamberlain's Birmingham speech later in June helped to stiffen opinion in Natal and bring it back into a pro-British line and the Governor, Sir Walter Hely Hutchinson, was then able to assure Milner that the Natal press 'is sound and I will try to keep it right'.[27] During July mass meetings expressed 'profound confidence' in Milner's policy; two resolutions were passed in the Natal Legislative Council to this effect; and a petition to the Queen, signed by more than half of the European male population, urged that the situation in the Transvaal should be 'radically transformed'. On 26 July, Hely Hutchinson was able to inform Chamberlain that 'Her Majesty's Government can rely on practically unanimous support of an overwhelming majority of the whole population if war becomes necessary'. He warned, however, that 'nothing but a real and permanent settlement' would do because 'The present Transvaal oligarchy, if it be left, after this crisis, with power to injure, will undoubtedly revenge itself on Natal in one form or another for the attitude of uncompromising support of Her Majesty's Government which it has publicly adopted. Loyal and patriotic feeling has, at length, overcome the considerations of commercial prudence which have for so many years enabled the Transvaal to play Natal off against the Cape.'[28]

AFRIKANER MEDIATION AND THE NEW TRANSVAAL FRANCHISE LAW

Intense political activity was already underway in Afrikaner circles in South Africa. Schreiner and Hofmeyr were joined in their efforts to bring pressure to bear on Kruger's government by President Steyn and Abraham Fischer of the Orange Free State. Fischer shuttled between Bloemfontein, Pretoria and Cape Town as an intermediary. Milner met him in Cape Town and encouraged his efforts, making British cipher codes available to facilitate secret communications between the various parties. Hofmeyr's strategy, supported by Schreiner, was to rally the Cape Afrikaners behind a number of modest amendments to Kruger's franchise proposals which, if accepted by the Transvaal government, might go some way towards meeting the objections raised by Milner at Bloemfontein and spike the guns of the war party. In particular, provision for the speedy registration of Uitlanders who had been resident since before 1890 and the elimination of a prolonged period after naturalization (when those who had taken the oath of allegiance would be in the position of 'half burghers') were thought likely to win widespread support. Milner's franchise proposals had direct implications for the election of the President and the Commandant-General of the Transvaal and, on these grounds, had been dismissed by Smuts as nonsense, 'for then we should, at the next presidential election, have an English president with a Boer Volksraad, and you know that that would mean a civil war and the downfall of our people in this state'.[29] Hofmeyr hoped that a separate, ten-year residential requirement for those participating in the elections for these posts might both ensure that the posts themselves remained in burgher hands and persuade the present burgher population to support the other reforms. If this were to be achieved, he anticipated that many Uitlanders would also be won over, a deep impression would be made on 'the public opinion of the civilized world', and the Transvaal government would be placed 'in a better position in her other disputes with Chamberlain and a war will become as good as impossible'.[30]

Smuts replied that he was working 'day and night' and was not without hope that something might be achieved; but to Merriman he wrote in more reflective and pessimistic vein. 'The situation', he observed, 'is being forced from the outside in order, by an armed conflict to forestall or defeat the work of time'. The 'opponents of peace and gradual evolution' were adopting 'the tactics which succeeded in 1880'. Lying petitions, claiming to represent 'the true voice of the people', were being used 'as a final excuse for intervention'. 'All of a sudden, Sir Alfred Milner finds in a popular franchise the panacea for all our ailments and promptly suggests one which will result in the swamping of the old population in a couple of years.'

> I had thought that of late both our administration and legislation as affecting Uitlanders had been rapidly improving – and all at once I find that 'the case for intervention' has become overwhelming! I should say that the case for intervention is today weaker than it has been ever before. . . . Our people are gradually realizing that they are becoming a

301

great state and that with their rapidly developing importance come more onerous duties of careful administration and statesmanlike legislation. But then there must be no despatches with threats of intervention. I have great hope that within a few years all just causes of complaint of whatever kind will have disappeared altogether and it fills me with a savage indignation to think that the work of those who are spending their substance and life-blood for South Africa is to be undone in a moment by academic nobodies who fancy themselves great imperial statesmen.[31]

Smuts's anger can be directly attributed to the fact that he was writing shortly after the publication of the British Blue Book containing 243 pages of documentation about Uitlander grievances, Milner's 'helots' despatch of 4 May, and the British government's response of 10 May to the Second Uitlander Petition.[32] Held back because of the Bloemfontein Conference, this incendiary material was now released immediately after the despatch of 10 May had been delivered to Kruger's government. The purpose would seem to have been to keep up the pressure on the Transvaal government. The effect was devastating. Both in Britain and South Africa it was regarded as an extremely provocative act, the effect of which was to bring the prospect of war much closer. Milner's 'helots' despatch especially caused a sensation, as Milner had known and intended that it should. His close friend, Philip Gell, had warned him that it was probably 'best in the long run that your un-moderation should *not* be known unto all men. Your conciliatory *reputation* is an asset'.[33] Now, it was revealed for all to see that behind the supposedly 'friendly discussions' at Bloemfontein lay the mailed fist and bellicose attitude of the British High Commissioner. As Percy Molteno at once commented: 'Is it to be wondered at that the Conference failed when Sir Alfred Milner was the only man who did not want it, and who wished drastic measures instead ?'[34]

The Cape Prime Minister, Schreiner, was deeply shocked by Milner's despatch and its destructive effect 'coming at a time when we . . . are doing all we can to piece up the Conference china' and felt that this deliberate forcing of the pace by the British government jeopardized the efforts of himself and the others working for a peaceful resolution of the crisis.[35] What had been implied the previous year, at Graaff-Reinet, was now made quite plain. Schreiner and the Afrikaner Bond were outraged at the accusation of 'disloyalty' made against the Dutch-language press in Milner's despatch. The Cape Dutch press had been studiously moderate and restrained on Transvaal issues and Milner's accusations amounted to a gross misrepresentation.[37] Schreiner was convinced that, on the whole, the Cape Dutch population was 'loyal to the core' and he and Hofmeyr were demonstrably working with the British government to obtain a more liberal franchise for the Uitlanders in the Transvaal. Now he felt that he had been deceived by the British High Commissioner. For his part, Milner had for some time been convinced that a split between himself and Schreiner's ministry was 'bound to come sooner or later' and so relations between the two men became increasingly strained as peace and peace efforts were overtaken by the advent of war.[37]

Throughout South Africa, the publication of the material in the British Blue Book was regarded as a deliberate act of sabre-rattling. Further fuel was added to the flames when, at the precise moment when Fischer was in Pretoria (25–28 June) attempting to persuade the Transvaal government to accept further modifications to the franchise proposals and settle the dynamite question with the mining industry, Chamberlain made an openly provocative speech in Birmingham. Encouraged by Selborne to use the occasion to 'give public opinion a lead' and make it clear 'that the Cabinet mean business this time, once and for all', Chamberlain told a packed Town Hall that, having put their hands to the plough, the government would not now draw back; a critical turning- point in the history of the British Empire had been reached. 'We have tried waiting, patience and trusting to promises which were never kept. We can wait no more . . . having undertaken this business we will see it through.'[38] In Britain, Chamberlain's speech was widely acclaimed by both Queen and country, although its message was clearly that war might have to be waged. In South Africa, Merriman felt that 'all the old evil symptoms' which had led to war in 1880 were recurring, with 'the same light-hearted readiness to believe in force as the best remedy'. 'Here are we, with the knowledge of H.M. Government, doing our best to get Kruger to make reasonable modifications in his franchise proposals', he wrote, 'and Mr. Chamberlain deliberately sets himself to render our task impossible, with the view, I suppose, of creating a position that will enable him to use force'.[39]

Schreiner, who had dedicated himself to working for a peaceful settlement, now felt that the ground had been cut from under his feet. 'Can it be that no such settlement is desired?' he asked; 'the fundamental error which may yet embroil this subcontinent is the belief that when sufficient pressure is used Kruger will yield *everything*. The truth is that he and his burghers are very near the point at which, instead of moving forward under pressure, reflex action sets in'.[40] Fischer told Conyngham Greene that Chamberlain's speech 'had knocked the bottom out of his mission' and he could not help suspecting that it had been purposely delivered in order to upset the present negotiations and make a forcible issue inevitable. The Transvaal might be coaxed into making concessions, he warned, but could never be forced by threats.[41] An attempt by Milner to insist that any new franchise proposals by Kruger's government should first be submitted to the British government before being presented to the Volksraad met with the reply that the Transvaal government did not acknowledge the right of the British government to be consulted on what was an internal matter. Chamberlain then telegraphed to say, for the benefit of any other Afrikaner mediators negotiating with the Transvaal, that no franchise would be accepted which did not give the Uitlanders some genuine representation in the First Volksraad at once. 'Reforms postponed are of no value', he added.[42]

Hofmeyr followed Fischer to Pretoria at the beginning of July, where he addressed the Volksraad in secret session, warning its members that if the situation resulted in war nothing but moral support could be expected from the Cape. Hofmeyr made no effort to hide his disapproval of the way in which the Volksraad had just passed a resolution which, whilst allocating four new seats to the mining districts, added fifteen new seats to exclusively burgher areas. The combined influence of Hofmeyr, Fischer and Smuts soon resulted in the fifteen rural seats being rescinded but the four additional seats for the Rand remained. This would give a total of six seats to the Uitlanders in a Volksraad of 32. Hofmeyr also encouraged the Volksraad to amend further the franchise proposals before it along the lines advocated by Schreiner, Fischer and himself. After his departure, Smuts continued the effort and by 19 July had persuaded the Volksraad to accept most of the amendments proposed by the 'Cape friends'. The new franchise arrangements (which became law on 26 July) established a franchise, based on seven years' residence, which was so complicated that it required a lengthy memorandum from Smuts to explain it. Schreiner had already declared that his government regarded the new franchise arrangements as 'adequate, satisfactory, and such as should secure a peaceful settlement'.[43]

On his return to the Cape, Hofmeyr called a meeting of the Afrikaner Bond on 12 July at which motions were passed approving what had been achieved and calling for a peaceful resolution of the points at issue between Britain and the Transvaal. Hofmeyr feared, however, that the new franchise law would not be sufficient to secure a peaceful settlement 'if irritating guarantees and further concessions' kept on being demanded from Kruger's government.[44] When the details of the new franchise arrangements were discussed at a meeting with Milner, Milner remained firmly non–committal. Meanwhile, the Uitlander Council passed a resolution declaring that the new franchise measures were 'entirely inadequate and unacceptable'. *The Cape Times* (whose editor, Edmund Garrett, kept in close contact with Milner) declared that they 'do not afford any sufficient relief from the present difficulty' and represented a platform 'erected expressly as a refuge for those who seek by all manner of subterfuge and deceit the undermining of British influence in the [Cape] Colony, and the eventual elimination of the Imperial Factor altogether from South African affairs'. The efforts of Schreiner and the other Afrikaner mediators were dismissed as 'simply weaving ropes from sand'. *The Cape Times* reminded its readers that many other grievances against Kruger's government remained unaddressed, apart from the franchise, and it was now up to the British government 'to effect an adjustment of them, franchise or no franchise'.[45]

THE INADEQUACY OF THE FRANCHISE ISSUE

News of the new franchise measure arrived in Britain on 18 July and was greeted with widespread enthusiasm and relief. *The Times*, tipped off by the Colonial Office, announced that if the news was true, the crisis with the Transvaal was over.[46] Chamberlain at once telegraphed to Milner:

> If, as reported in the Press here, President S.A.R. has really given 7 years' retroactive franchise and 5 seats, I congratulate you on great victory. No one would dream of fighting over two years in qualification period and President S.A.R. will have been driven by successive steps to almost exact position taken by you [at Bloemfontein]. We ought to make most of this and accept it as basis of settlement.[47]

Lord Salisbury congratulated Chamberlain on 'a great diplomatic success' but added that it would be 'necessary to guard against backsliding'.[48]

Milner was aghast at Chamberlain's apparent readiness to settle for the new franchise (which he himself considered full of 'traps' and 'pitfalls' and quite unsatisfactory) and dismayed at the gulf which suddenly seemed to have opened up between himself and the British government. Chamberlain, he feared, seemed now '*to wish a patch-up*' peace with Kruger's government, 'not merely to wish to know that negotiation is being tried to the uttermost'.[49] The Uitlanders in

Johannesburg regarded the British response as a political Majuba. The Uitlander Council immediately telegraphed Chamberlain, imploring him not to depart from 'the five years' compromise' proposed by Milner at Bloemfontein and only 'accepted with great reluctance' by the Uitlander population.[50] Milner instructed the British Vice-Consul in Johannesburg to advise 'our friends' that the British government could not afford to deny that the new franchise law represented an advance without alienating British public opinion; but this did not mean 'that they are going to climb down'. The Uitlanders should moderate their tone as otherwise there was a danger of them being thought to be for 'War at any price'.[51]

Milner now set to work to bring Chamberlain and the British government 'back on the old right tack'.[52] He had already calculated that the new franchise law, whilst certainly a considerable advance even on Kruger's Bloemfontein proposals, would differ significantly from his own scheme (based on five years' residence) in its immediate effects. Milner pointed out that his own proposal 'would have admitted at once persons who came to the country during 1891, 1892, 1893, and portion of 1894. These were years of great immigration. These persons are now postponed for between 1 and 4 years, so that body of Uitlanders immediately admitted far smaller than that contemplated by me'.[53] The formalities involved in applying for enfranchisement were also likely to cause difficulty and delay. A large part of the Uitlander population in the Transvaal were transients and it would be difficult, in many cases, to obtain clear evidence of the length of residence already completed in the Transvaal. Further, evidence had also to be provided that an applicant for the franchise had obeyed the laws of the land and committed no crime against the independence of the state. If the applicant's field-cornet or *landdrost* could not vouch for him, he would have to obtain the sworn affidavits of 'two well-known, fully-enfranchised burghers'. For some Uitlanders, this would not be easy. Although the income qualification had been reduced (from £200 to £100 per annum), and the place of domicile had replaced the requirement for continuous residence, the required seven years' residence commenced not with arrival in the country but only from the time when notice was given of the intention to become naturalized. Since the Transvaal government wanted to know in advance how many 'aliens', already resident in the republic, intended to apply for the franchise it was decreed that any such applicants who did not give notice of their intention to apply for the franchise within six months of the enactment of the law, would lose the benefit of their previous period of residence.[54] These were just some of the complications in the new law. Milner knew about many of them in advance since, notwithstanding the Transvaal government's understandable reluctance to involve the British government officially, Smuts had discussed many of the details unofficially with the British Agent in Pretoria and Reitz had written that his government would 'always be ready to take into serious consideration any friendly counsels from Her Majesty's Government'.[55] This, however, was a very different thing from being required to make a formal submission to the British government for approval of the new franchise proposals before they became law. Throughout the discussions, it was evident that Kruger's government would resist any such direct intervention by Britain in what it regarded as a purely internal matter.

Milner, however, had become convinced that:

> no scheme adopted by [Transvaal] Government of its own accord will be calculated to carry out object we have in view. By one means or another administration will retain power to obstruct enfranchisement of obnoxious Uitlanders, whilst facilitating admission of its own friends or enfranchising them, though without regular qualification, under special clause. Arrangements as to new seats, as to registration, as to method of presidential election, all leave room for any amount of juggling to make measure a sham.[56]

Yet the very fact that the new law came closer to what Milner himself had stipulated at Bloemfontein made it difficult for the British government to reject it outright. If the new franchise measures were 'really substantial', Chamberlain observed:

> it will be practically impossible for us to find a *casus belli* in minor differences. I am sure in this case our policy is to accept them for what they pretend to be, and if they fail of their object or prove subsequently to have been made in bad faith our case will be stronger than it has ever been . . . .[57]

The passing of the new franchise law by the Transvaal government also made it less possible to convince British public opinion that, in the Uitlander franchise, lay the issue which might form not just a 'splendid battle cry' but an actual *casus belli*. Milner feared that, in its actual effects, the 'Franchise will thus be a fiasco while we shall have got no further about anything else. We could not accept that position without suffering diplomatic defeat at any rate in eyes of our supporters in South Africa'.[58] This point was also emphasized by Percy FitzPatrick, who had recently arrived in England. On 3 July, he told Selborne that the Uitlanders considered Milner's franchise proposals at

Bloemfontein had been too moderate, especially in allocating them only a fifth of the total seats in the Volksraad. He said 'that he was convinced Kruger would not yield an effective franchise till "he looked down the cannon's mouth", and that the policy of gaining time by a series of concessions which were no real concessions, was the avowed policy at Pretoria'. Kruger's government hoped thereby 'to split the present combination against them' of Uitlanders, Milner and the British government. FitzPatrick also emphasized Uitlander discontent with a policy of 'letting the franchise question cover everything' when there were other long-standing issues which the British government should settle 'now, once and for all' with the Transvaal.[59]

In the House of Commons on 20 July, Chamberlain temporized on the matter of the new franchise law.[60] He pointed to the conditions 'which might be so interpreted as to preclude those otherwise qualified from acquiring the franchise and might therefore be used to take away with one hand what has been given with the other'. He expressed the hope that, having accepted the principle of making the franchise more accessible to the Uitlanders, Kruger would be 'prepared to reconsider any detail of his schemes which can be shown to be a possible hindrance to the full accomplishment of the object in view'.[61] Encouraged by Milner, Chamberlain now moved towards insisting that the reality of the franchise reform should be established by a Joint Enquiry and that subsequently a further conference between Milner and Kruger should take place in Cape Town to settle the remaining issues between the two governments.

By July, neither Milner nor Chamberlain were prepared to settle with Kruger's government purely on the basis of a compromise over the Uitlander franchise. Before the Bloemfontein Conference, Chamberlain had urged Milner to 'lay all the stress on the question of the franchise in the first instance. Other reforms are less pressing and will come in time, if this can be arranged satisfactorily. . . . If fair terms on franchise are refused by President [Kruger], it appears hardly worth while to bring forward other matters . . . and the whole situation must be reconsidered'.[62] When the Conference looked like failing, Chamberlain was already having second thoughts and considered that it would be unwise for the British government to take its stand upon the franchise issue alone, as 'the legal claim for this is surely very weak'. The British position would be strengthened if the full schedule of its grievances were presented to Kruger's government, 'Edgar case, Aliens expulsion, High Court, Dynamite etc. etc. in order that we may have a formal refusal of redress in every case'.[63] But news of Chamberlain's change of mind reached Milner too late, after the

Conference had already broken down. Milner had deliberately focused on the franchise at the Bloemfontein Conference because he felt that with this 'we had got a clearish issue, whereas if we went on and on, as the other party seemed inclined to do, we might get a little more and a little more, each concession being *made to appear very big* and finally feel unable, after so many concessions, to break off, and yet find we had a perfectly hollow scheme'.[64] During the following weeks, Milner and Chamberlain had agreed that any franchise which did not at once secure for the Uitlanders a reasonable share of political power was unacceptable and that care would be needed to make sure that any franchise measure passed by the Transvaal Volksraad was 'not hampered by unreasonable conditions or liable to be defeated by subsequent legislation in an opposite direction'.[65] The difficulty of ensuring that these conditions were not only met but made foolproof for the future became increasingly apparent as successive franchise proposals and amendments replaced each other during the passage of the new franchise law through the Volksraad during July.

For over a year, Milner had consistently argued – both in official correspondence and in private conversation with people like Percy FitzPatrick – that once 'civil rights', including the franchise, were secured in the Transvaal for the Uitlanders, they would be in a position to use them to rectify their other grievances themselves, without repeated interventions by the British government in the future. Milner had always been more confident than Chamberlain that, once given access to the franchise, the Uitlanders would remain loyal to the British cause in South Africa. In May 1899, he had told the Governor of Natal, Sir Walter Hely Hutchinson, that if Kruger did grant 'large reforms . . . the Uitlanders must take them and work them *bona fide*. I have impressed this strongly upon them'.

Personally, I am not afraid that if the Uitlanders are admitted to political power by our aid – and it is *de toute evidence* that they would never have got it otherwise – they will turn and rend us. Possibly the Transvaal may never become part of our S. African Empire, though I think, with statesmanship on our side, it must come in time. But in any case I cannot see how a Transvaal, which is either Anglicized or, like the Cape Colony, neutralized by an Anglo-Dutch race fight *on equal lines*, can be the danger to us and the focus of disaffection in all our possessions which the Transvaal is today.[66]

If war were to be avoided, he had added, direct and straightforward negotiations with the Transvaal government would be needed 'as to the *amount of reform* which *we* can accept. They will naturally be unwilling to revolutionize their institutions on spec without knowing that we shall be satisfied at the end of it'. Yet this full and final list of British demands, the 'cumulative case' which Milner had originally argued should be presented at 'the great day of reckoning', had not been established at the Bloemfontein Conference, which had failed on the franchise issue alone. In the aftermath of that failure, Kruger's government had moved quickly some way towards meeting British demands on the franchise issue, and implementing what Kruger himself had promised in his speeches in March. During August it was to concede all that Milner had demanded on the franchise at Bloemfontein. In the interim, however, both Milner and Chamberlain had shifted their ground.

Only after the Bloemfontein Conference had the difficulty of estimating what the effect would be of any particular franchise measure amongst so diverse and unstable a population as that of the Uitlanders become fully apparent.[67] Nobody knew how many Uitlanders would accept the franchise, even if it were offered to them on the basis of the five years' residence (retrospective) envisaged by Milner at Bloemfontein. During the passage of the new franchise law through the Transvaal Volksraad Smuts had been asked if the change from nine to seven years would not double the number of new burghers who would be made eligible by the change. He had replied that he had no reliable statistics. Kruger had claimed that Milner's Bloemfontein proposal of five years 'had made the residential period too low . . . and to accept it would have been to swamp the burghers'. Kruger himself now supported a basis of seven years and assured the burghers that this 'would be quite safe, and there would be no fear for the independence of the state' whilst it would be 'at the same time fair, just and well-disposed towards the newcomers'.[68]

In fact there were no reliable census figures for the Transvaal and no one knew how many Uitlanders had entered or left in any given year. Thus, it was quite impossible to estimate how many Uitlanders would qualify – either on the five years' residence demanded by Milner or the seven years' basis of the new franchise law of July. Milner had repeatedly asserted that his franchise proposals were only intended for those Uitlanders who wanted to make the Transvaal their permanent home and he knew that this was likely to be a minority of the total Uitlander population.[69] Nonetheless, it was an increasing proportion of the Uitlanders and Milner had calculated that, under his proposals, they would control twelve constituencies in the Transvaal by 1901, and fifteen or sixteen by 1903. Meanwhile, a member of Chamberlain's staff at the Colonial Office in London produced an analysis on 20 July which suggested that, even under the most favourable assumptions, there would be only ten Uitlander-controlled constituencies by 1901 and, at most, thirteen by 1903. More important still, he predicted that nineteen constituencies out of the proposed new total of 35 would *always* remain under Afrikaner control, thus ensuring a continued Afrikaner predominance in the Volksraad.[70]

Growing doubts were also expressed about how many of those who would become eligible for the franchise would be prepared to renounce their British citizenship in order to take it up. Many would only relinquish British citizenship with reluctance since it could then only be regained after five years' residence in the British Isles.[71] The rate of Uitlander immigration into the Transvaal had fluctuated. The numbers who had arrived before 1890 were not so considerable as to cause a major stumbling block for Kruger's government. It was the numbers who had arrived since 1895, and were expected to arrive in the foreseeable future, who were the problem. At the beginning of July, Conyngham Greene had sought the assistance of Samuel Evans (a member of the Uitlander Council in Johannesburg) in the production of an estimate of how many Uitlanders would be likely to be enfranchised if something like Milner's Bloemfontein proposals were to be enacted. Milner himself had estimated that under his Bloemfontein proposals, based upon five years' residence (retrospective), 'something less than 15,000' might obtain the franchise, while on a seven years' basis (retrospective), the number was likely to be about 10,000. The number of established burghers who already enjoyed the franchise was estimated by the Transvaal Staats' Almanac for the year 1899 at 29,276.[72] The official population figures for the Transvaal were, however, dismissed as 'almost valueless' by Conyngham Greene, who estimated that the total European population of the Transvaal was about 300,000 (which was certainly an exaggeration). Of this population, 80,000 were accounted for by the Afrikaners – of whom about 30 per cent were estimated to have the vote. A rough and ready reckoning arrived at a maximum figure of 33,000 as the number of Uitlanders who might be eligible for the vote under Milner's scheme. This was admittedly theoretical, since in practice 'it is very likely that a large number of people entitled to the franchise would not take the trouble to secure it'. The figure was, however, considerably lower than that mentioned by President Kruger. Nonetheless, the most telling prediction was that within five years of a scheme such as Milner's coming into operation 'the new burghers would form something like two-thirds of the total number'.[73]

Since most of those who would become enfranchised were

concentrated in a very few districts and constituencies in and around the Rand, the redistribution of seats in the Volksraad was also a crucial matter. Until July 1899, the mining areas were represented by only two seats in a Volksraad of 28. Both at Bloemfontein and afterwards, Milner had indicated that he was quite prepared, for the moment, 'to depart from this principle of the absolute equality of new and old citizens with regard to their voting power . . . as the old population could not be expected to face with equanimity the prospect of being at once outnumbered'. So, 'for the present', he was ready to settle for 'a fixed number of seats – not so few as to leave the Uitlanders without substantial influence, and not so many as to swamp the old burghers'. To be precise, his initial aim was for the Rand to have seven seats in a Volksraad of 28.[74] Later, both Milner and Chamberlain settled on a fifth of the total number of seats in an expanded Volksraad.[75] During July, pressure was exerted by the Uitlander Council for an increase in the number of seats envisaged for the mining areas. It argued that the one-fifth of the total number of seats in the Volksraad envisaged by Milner and Chamberlain should only be regarded as a temporary measure and that 'the permanent basis of representation should bear some definite relation to the number of electors'.[76] In August, Milner admitted that, even at Bloemfontein, 'it never occurred to me to confine Uitlander representation to 7 or any particular number of seats. I only wanted to *start them with a certain number*'.[77] He told Chamberlain that he was determined to move towards 'a system of periodic redistribution according to numbers – which should, however, fix a somewhat larger number of voters for each member in the industrial than in the rural constituencies'.[78] These calculations and considerations suggest that the fears expressed by Kruger at Bloemfontein that the Uitlanders represented a potential Trojan horse in the Transvaal were well-founded. For, in the longer term, Milner was convinced that non-Afrikaner (mainly British) immigration into the Transvaal would not only continue but increase rapidly once 'the Augean Stable' there had been cleared. '*Thousands* of people would at once swarm into the Transvaal', Milner believed, 'and the balance of power, which even now would be clearly ours in S. Africa as a whole under a system of equal rights, would be rapidly and decisively turned against the Boer for ever'.[79]

Milner's 'grand design' for ensuring a future British predominance in the Transvaal and in South Africa was, however, fatally flawed. He was incorrect in thinking that the British population already outnumbered that of the Afrikaners in the Transvaal by 1899, or that it ever would do so in South Africa as a whole.[80] The campaign to establish in the Transvaal the equal rights for all Europeans which were already enjoyed elsewhere in South Africa was therefore not going to ensure British predominance there. As G.H.L. Le May has rightly observed: 'British supremacy and equal rights for white men need not necessarily mean the same thing: throughout South Africa, Afrikaners were in the majority.'[81]

For six weeks after the Bloemfontein Conference, Milner had felt compelled 'to play to the Secretary of State's lead' and had 'with a heavy heart, gone on with these franchise negotiations, feeling all the time that the South African Republic mean to give nothing real but to adroitly cheat us over them'.[82] Both Chamberlain and Selborne had made it clear to him that British public opinion was not ready to support a resort to war and the British Cabinet was not yet prepared to embark on military measures or present demands which might precipitate an ultimatum. The strategy which Milner had outlined to Selborne at the end of May therefore had to be put on one side in favour of a policy of making clear the determination of the British government to extract reforms, applying sustained pressure to Kruger's government, and allowing Afrikaner mediators to bring their influence to bear. Milner had wanted action from the British government: a strong despatch – insisting on a 'Bill of Rights' for the Uitlanders 'embodied in a new Convention' – backed up by military preparations and a clear indication that an ultimatum would follow if the demands of the British government were not met.[83] Instead, as his diary reveals, he had felt 'extreme discouragement' at the 'great change for the worse in the attitude of the Home Government', and feared that British public opinion was going to be 'bamboozled' by the further concessions being made 'at a very alarming rate' by the Transvaal Volksraad.[84] To a friend he wrote that although he had 'done all the man on the spot could do to recover the position . . . I have absolutely rallied all our forces on the spot . . . I have brought into the field *scores* who have long been sulking in their tents and vowed long ago never to trust G. Britain or any of her emissaries again', he feared that 'England may give us away – probably will – not from cowardice but from simple ignorance of the situation and the easy-going belief that you have only to be very kind and patient and magnanimous, and *give away your friends to please your enemies*, in order to make the latter love you for ever'.[85]

Milner's frustration had been increased by his awareness that 'the weeks as they pass work against us in every way'. Delay might be required in Britain, he told Selborne, but it imposed 'a deadly strain on us here', especially on holding the Uitlander movement together.

'British South Africa', which had been 'tuned to concert pitch' in June 'because they felt sure we meant business this time', was now beginning to waver. 'They say England has left us before. Is she going to weaken now? Where shall we be? . . . Delay thus weakens our support here, while it adds to the armaments of the enemy, who are still bringing in ammunition and may bring in more guns. And it brings us nearer the summer, when, with grass on the veld, the Boer, a mounted infantryman, is twice the man he is in winter, when he has to transport forage.' Milner had become ever more firmly convinced that if the British government 'really made up their minds to settle this business' this could never 'be satisfactorily done, after all that has happened, without an expedition'. 'Till the first shot is fired', he declared, 'I shall not believe in war, but rather that, with an army on the spot, they will submit to any terms', although he admitted to Selborne that this was uncertain.[86] Milner's appeal for action was accompanied by the statement that as 'the exponent of a strong policy' he did not expect to survive any backing-down by the British government. 'The only thing, if we have to go back to shilly-shally, is to let me resign or, if it is easier, simply to recall me.'[87]

Chamberlain had also become increasingly uneasy about resting British demands too narrowly upon the franchise issue. This may have served its turn 'to get things forrarder' in South Africa and as a 'splendid battle cry' to rally the support of British public opinion, but Chamberlain knew that if it came to a *casus belli*, grounds for this would have to be found elsewhere. British public opinion would not support a resort to war over the difference between a seven or a five years' franchise; and well-placed people, like Sir Edward Hamilton (of the Treasury), were convinced that 'the moral sense of the civilised world would be shocked at the mere notion of war on differences of opinion about the extension of the franchise to foreigners by a state over whose internal affairs we have no control'.[88] Breaches of the London Convention by Kruger's government had also been weakened as a potential *casus belli*, by July 1899, as a result of the British proposal for the establishment of a permanent court of arbitration at the Hague as part of the Disarmament Conference there.[89]

Like the rest of the British Cabinet, Chamberlain still believed that Kruger's government would make further concessions under pressure, as it had repeatedly done in the past. Faced with a resolute British government, backed up by British public opinion and clearly ready and able to bring the armed might of the greatest empire in the world to bear on South Africa, Kruger's government would back down rather than face a war which was certain to result in a British victory and the end of the republic. Both Chamberlain and other members of the Cabinet were becoming irritated by Milner's demand for 'some intimation that Her Majesty's Government realise the necessity of putting an end to the present state of things, and that if adequate franchise is unattainable, remedy must be sought by other means. This will give franchise a last chance, and pave the way to other action, if franchise fails'.[90] Chamberlain's staff at the Colonial Office feared that 'there is some danger of our being "rushed" by the party in S. Africa which, while its sympathies with the Uitlanders is genuine, has for its chief aim the wiping out of Majuba and the speedy annexation of the Transvaal', and that Milner was becoming 'too excited and impatient' and was being 'rapidly carried away' in this direction.[91] Selborne warned Milner privately of the effect he was having and Milner promised to 'take your hint most gravely to heart' and avoid any suggestion of excitement in his future communications.[92]

Chamberlain meanwhile set out to reassure Milner of his 'hearty and unflinching support' but warned him that 'opinion here is strongly opposed to war although the necessity of resorting to war in the last resort is gradually making its way among all classes'. If, however, the British government 'were driven to this extremity' it would be because they had 'been able to show that the question at issue is greater than any particular grievance or special act of oppression and that if we have to go further it will not be for the franchise, or Edgar or dynamite, but for the maintenance of our position in South Africa and the removal of the one great cause of race animosity in the country' – by which Chamberlain meant the system of Afrikaner domination in the Transvaal presided over by Kruger's government.[93] Milner, meanwhile, was telling Selborne that the situation was 'quite altered since Bloemfontein' and that the pro-British party in South Africa were praying for a 'thorough settlement this time [at] any cost'. The Transvaal government's new franchise measure, he declared, 'is plainly intended not to satisfy but to disarm us. It might serve as part of a general settlement but is not adequate by itself. Sooner or later H.M. Govt. must review situation as a whole and define its position on all questions in dispute. South Africa is now divided into two camps. Franchise and every other question have merged in one big issue: is British paramountcy to be vindicated or let slide?'[94]

BRITISH PARAMOUNTCY

By July 1899, Milner had lost any faith which he might originally have had in the ability of a negotiated franchise settlement to deliver the essentially political objective which both he and the British government were by now determined to achieve. This was to 'break the mould of Transvaal politics', to remove not only Kruger's government but the Afrikaner oligarchy which ruled the country, and to open up the Transvaal's institutions to what they assumed to be the beneficent effects of British influence. Whereas progressive Afrikaners, in the Cape Colony and elsewhere, sought a franchise measure in the Transvaal which would permit a limited and very gradual admission of Uitlanders, Milner had come to believe that this would simply ensure that they would become 'afrikanderized'. Where the Afrikaner mediators had sought a reformed and enlarged electorate in a 'still distinctly Afrikander i.e. non-British Republic', what Milner wanted was 'a liberal and wholesale admission of Uitlanders, which would immediately influence and in the long run wholly transform the character of the State, substituting real popular government, as in the Colonies, for a race oligarchy'. Milner had taken up the franchise issue not simply to achieve 'equal rights' for Uitlanders in a Transvaal republic still firmly under Afrikaner control, but as a means to break that control. This, he admitted to Sir Edward Grey, was why he attached 'such tremendous importance to the admission of Uitlanders to citizenship *in a certain way . . . and not in the way favoured by the Afrikander party*':

> What they want is to let in the Uitlanders in driblets, by favour, the Government practically selecting those who are friendly to the present system. What I want is to let them in gradually indeed, but in large numbers, as of right, so as to introduce into the State a powerful body, certain to transform the present system. They want to squeeze the new-comers into the existing mould. I want them to burst it.[95]

The vital point was to prevent the continuation of a political system which would 'enable the Government practically to admit its supporters and exclude its opponents'. If this could be achieved through negotiation, well and good. If not, Milner could not see any advantage, from a British point of view, in campaigning for the extension of citizenship and the franchise for Uitlanders. It would be better to 'fall back on the demand for certain safeguards for the Uitlanders, remaining Uitlanders i.e. resident foreigners outside the State'. This, however, would be 'a temporary makeshift, not a remedy', but Milner was convinced that

We must do something substantial to improve the position of our clients, or lose all reputation and political influence, even in what will remain nominally British South Africa. Such a result must, in my opinion, be avoided at any cost, even the cost of war, though I am fully alive to the risks, and should not except in the last resort contemplate it with anything but aversion. Meanwhile the increase in our forces here must not be regarded as involving war but rather as diminishing the chance of it. A *very expensive* precaution doubtless, but after all what is a million or two to Great Britain if it saves the situation in South Africa?[96]

Milner's objective was a transfer of power. This did not necessarily require the annexation of the Transvaal as a British colony. If there was a resort to war, annexation would certainly be a result which it would be difficult to achieve otherwise. But annexation itself was not the objective. It would simply be a more certain means to another end. That end was the removal of the 'illiberal system in the Transvaal' and its replacement by a political order 'similar to that of other S. African states'. Once this had occurred, Milner anticipated that 'the industrial population would increase with enormous rapidity and spread over many districts'. Most of this population coming into the Transvaal would be British and, since he believed that the British already accounted for at least half of the total European population in South Africa, this would ensure British predominance. 'Complete self-government in S. Africa', Milner believed, could then be conceded and even the British garrison there 'would soon be totally unnecessary, and a federated S. Africa could be left to work out its own destiny'.[97]

The failure of the Bloemfontein Conference and the nature of the new Transvaal franchise law passed in July had convinced Milner that Kruger's government would never agree to anything which would put at risk continued Afrikaner control of the state. No franchise measure could ever be effectively guaranteed and, given the flexible nature of the Transvaal's constitution, might easily be neutralized by a subsequent Volksraad resolution. Recent calculations suggested that, even under Milner's own proposals, Uitlanders were likely to remain an ineffective minority in the Transvaal Volksraad for some considerable time to come. The removal of Kruger's government and the breaking of the hold which the Afrikaner oligarchy had on the state showed no sign of coming about as a result of an internal take-over. By July 1899, Milner had little hope of obtaining his objectives by a peaceful settlement and was increasingly convinced that rather than surrender to a peaceful take-over of the government of his country, Kruger would fight. Milner was not at all daunted by the prospect of war and by July he certainly believed that, if the British government was determined to achieve its objectives, war should be risked rather than avoided. Since Milner assumed that a war would be short and would result in the removal of Kruger's government and the annexation of the Transvaal as a British colony, war would provide the opportunity for 'a clean slate' and the reconstruction of the Transvaal under British auspices. War would make possible something much more far-reaching than the establishment of a 'friendly' political order in the Transvaal. It would enable Britain to settle the whole South African problem once and for all. For war would justify not only the annexation of the Transvaal but, if the Orange Free State stood by her alliance with her sister republic, as she was expected to do, that of both republics. The whole of South Africa would thus be brought directly under British sovereignty and the ground would thereby be prepared for the final achievement of Britain's long-term goal of a South African federation ready to take its place, alongside Canada and Australia, as a source of strength rather than weakness within the British Empire.

Chamberlain and most of the British Cabinet, however, still seem to have believed that rather than fight a war which could only end in the downfall of the republic, Kruger would capitulate at the eleventh hour. This would be a perfectly acceptable solution from their point of view. A war, and nothing but a war, was certainly not their intention. The annexation, and nothing but the annexation of the Transvaal as a British colony, was not the British objective. On the contrary, a peaceful resolution of the crisis which resulted in British demands being met would be regarded as a fitting and successful conclusion to Chamberlain's diplomacy and to the British government's intervention on behalf of the Uitlanders. The Prime Minister was certainly determined to see that British demands were met but he did not yet believe that war was inevitable – or even likely – and hoped that it might be avoided and that Kruger's government would submit if pressure were to be maintained.[98] So uncertain were British public and parliamentary support for a resort to war that Sir Edward Hamilton felt that Chamberlain 'must be aware that a Boer war for which he was responsible might be his political death-warrant'.[99] As for the Cabinet, it too was acutely aware of the lack of support for a resort to war in the country at large, in Parliament and amongst some members of its own party. It was therefore reluctant to make military preparations, which would involve possibly needless expenditure and which were likely to jeopardize the chance of a peaceful settlement. As Sir Edward Grey informed Milner in mid-July: 'the state of public opinion in this country is so strongly against going to war, that it is not possible for the Government to go to that length upon the present issue respecting the franchise . . . war, in the absence of further provocation, is not practicable'.[100]

It was with these considerations in mind that Chamberlain had been drafting and redrafting a despatch to the Transvaal government in response to the new franchise law. This first major despatch since 10 May was considered by members of the Cabinet between 21 and 27 July.[101] In it the British government set out once more the background to the problem of the Uitlander franchise since 1881, welcomed the recent franchise proposals passed by the Volksraad and expressed the hope that these might prove to be the basis for a settlement of the issue. It stated that the objective of the British government was to secure for the Uitlanders:

> the immediate enjoyment of such a share of political power as will enable them, by the election of members from their own body, to exercise a real influence on legislation and administration, without, however, giving them the proportion of representation to which their numbers, taken alone, might entitle them, and which the President objected would enable them immediately to swamp the influence of the old burghers.

Since President Kruger had accepted the principle of extending the franchise, the British government hoped that now he 'will be prepared to reconsider any detail of his scheme which can be shown to be a possible hindrance to the full accomplishment of the object in view'. They hoped that 'many of the conditions now retained may be revised, and that the residential qualification may be further reduced'. Since the points which they still had to urge the Transvaal government to consider were of great importance, a further interchange of views between the two governments was suggested. First, a Joint Inquiry was proposed to consider the details and practical implications of the franchise law. If its recommendations were satisfactorily agreed by both governments then the new measure should be accepted by the Uitlanders. A further conference between Milner and Kruger was then suggested at which the other issues outstanding between the two governments could be discussed, and the matter of a Tribunal of Arbitration (excluding any foreign element) could be explored.

Chamberlain agreed with a member of his staff who minuted that 'A Conference between President Kruger and Sir Alfred Milner would strike the public eye and imagination and imply a climbdown on President Kruger's part from his attitude of *noli me tangere* on internal affairs'.[102] Salisbury and most other members of the Cabinet approved the draft, but Balfour, as in May, made some telling points with regard to its likely effects. He considered it unwise to include controversial commentary about the past – 'which may possibly be irritating and is at best superfluous' – in a despatch written for the purpose of expressing a positive response to the Transvaal government's latest franchise measure. He also doubted if it was prudent for the British government to commit itself to the proposal for a second conference between Milner and Kruger since if Kruger refused this, on the grounds that this represented an interference with an internal matter, the British government would have received a diplomatic rebuff 'which might do us harm in South Africa'.[103] Chamberlain considered that the despatch was firm but conciliatory. Yet it has about it the arrogant tone of a suzerain addressing a troublesome subject. The Transvaal government was certain to regard the tone of the despatch as insulting and its contents as a deliberate raising of the stakes between the two governments, and especially of the demands made by the British government. Selborne, who had been closely involved in the matter, reported to Milner that the Cabinet was 'all right', that Balfour was 'sound', and that in a conversation with the Prime Minister at Walmer, Salisbury had declared that he meant to secure full and effective compliance from Kruger's government of Milner's Bloemfontein demands 'as a minimum'.[104]

The despatch clearly indicated that the Transvaal government's new franchise measure would only be accepted by the British government (and the Uitlanders) if its provisions were agreed upon by *both* governments backed up by a Joint Inquiry. This was bound to be objected to by the Transvaal government since it marked a significant advance from 'friendly counsels' by the British government, to outright interference and a claim to an established role in the Transvaal's internal affairs. It amounted to a practical demonstration of British suzerainty and the Transvaal republic's limited sovereignty. This, it would seem, was precisely what Salisbury, Milner and Chamberlain had in mind. If the Transvaal government resisted the demand, Milner contended,

> we shall have a principle to contend for and not mere details. It makes all the difference, both to the security of Uitlanders and to our position in South Africa, whether a measure is shaped and secured by H.M. Government, or whether it is arranged, independently of us, by Government S.A.R. and Bond. Government S.A.R. practically deny that it is any business of ours and on that basis would have good ground for refusing to recognise our right to protest if they presently nullified

reforms, now granted, by other legislation. . . . To assert our power and retain confidence of loyalists are after all two main objects to keep in view.[105]

The British Cabinet had approved the text of the despatch of 27 July ahead of a major debate in both Houses of Parliament on 28 July. Since this was the last occasion when the South African situation was discussed in Parliament before the summer recess, what was said during the course of the nine-hour debate was awaited with acute interest both in Britain and South Africa and was copiously reported and commented upon in the newspapers. On the eve of the debate Balfour made a speech in which he underlined the determination of the British government to settle matters in South Africa by announcing that 'if endless patience, endless desire to prevent matters from coming to extremities, if all the resources of diplomacy' were ineffectual 'to untie the knot', other means would be found to do so.[106]

The debate itself established that the issue between the British and Transvaal governments was no longer confined to bringing about further improvements in the new franchise law. In the House of Lords, Selborne emphasized that the question was 'whether British influence in South Africa is really, in fact, predominant and not only so in theory' and repeated that, having set their hands to the plough, the British government would not turn back until 'the inequality of treatment between the two white races in the South African Republic is removed'; nor would any pledge be given which might limit the means at its disposal to achieve this result.[107] The Prime Minister warned that the Conventions governing relations between Britain and the Transvaal were 'mortal' and did not constitute 'an immovable landmark'. If their validity were to be challenged then he believed that 'they belong from that time to history'. If Britain had 'to make exertions' to secure justice and equal rights for her subjects in the Transvaal, she would then 'not reinstate a state of things which will bring back the old difficulties in all their formidable character at the next turn of the wheel'.[108] Meanwhile, the House of Commons had not forgotten Milner's 'helots' despatch of 4 May and was now in possession of further material in two new Blue Books, published during the previous ten days. In a robust debate, the Leader of the Opposition, Campbell-Bannerman, denied that there was any case for armed intervention or the threat of war over the franchise and the difference between seven years' and five years' residence in the Transvaal. He said that it was a strange idea that 'we should go to war in order to hurry our own fellow-citizens into another citizenship'.[109] Several speakers not only agreed with him but accused the government of being too much under the influence of the 'inflammatory' and 'violent' despatches from Sir Alfred Milner and the machinations of the South African League and the press. The British government was accused of attempting to 'bully the Transvaal government' and 'force a war'.

In his speech, Chamberlain surveyed the background to a problem which five times in fifteen years had led to a crisis and 'which had now been brought to a head' by certain developments in the Transvaal and by the receipt of the Second Uitlander Petition. That the grievances of the Uitlanders were genuine and serious, he declared, was now agreed – not just by the British government but by the Opposition, by progressive Afrikaner opinion and by world opinion. Attempts to ridicule or dismiss them as forced and exaggerated were 'not worthy of serious attention'. Since 1881, British subjects in the Transvaal had been consistently subordinated 'to the ruling race', in defiance of the equal treatment promised at the time of the Pretoria and London Conventions and operating elsewhere in South Africa. 'A race antagonism' between Boers and British, which had developed in the Transvaal, was spreading into the neighbouring states where it was becoming 'a constant menace to the peace and prosperity of the whole country' and was endangering 'our position as the paramount power in South Africa'. The problem was sometimes discussed, Chamberlain observed, as if it were a question of some petty reform – 'a matter of two years' difference in the qualification for the franchise' – but, he declared, 'It is nothing of the kind. It is the power and authority of the British Empire. It is the position of Great Britain in South Africa. It is the question of our predominance and how it is to be interpreted, and it is the question of peace throughout the whole of South Africa' which now made it 'absolutely necessary' that the issue 'should come to a head and be satisfactorily settled'.[110] Britain was intervening in 'what are admitted to be the internal affairs of the Transvaal' because she had the right of every civilized power to protect its own subjects; because she had special rights 'as suzerain Power'; because 'the Conventions have been broken both in the letter and in the spirit'; and because 'the promises upon which the Conventions themselves were based have not been kept'. The franchise was a means to an end and that end was to give the Uitlanders a substantial and immediate representation (he again mentioned a fifth of the seats) in the Volksraad which 'will enable them, not to swamp the burghers . . . but to put forward their views and their grievances, and . . . in the long run, to obtain satisfactory and sufficient redress'. The new Transvaal franchise measure was acknowledged as a great advance, but its probable results had to be carefully examined and this was the purpose behind the proposal for a Joint Inquiry. If it was found that an immediate and substantial Uitlander representation would not result from the new measure, then President Kruger would 'no doubt be willing to make such alterations in his latest proposals as will make them effective' in achieving this end. Having taken up the matter, the British government would not rest until it had seen it through to a satisfactory conclusion. In this the government was convinced that it had the support of the British people. No one dreamed of interfering with the independence of the Transvaal, Chamberlain claimed; 'on the contrary, we desire to strengthen its independence . . . by turning discontented aliens into loyal fellow-citizens of the present Dutch Republic. Our interest is to maintain the freedom and prosperity of the Transvaal Republic. We want to see it continuing in existence on similar lines to the Orange Free State, protected as to its outside relations and independent as to its internal affairs'. Britain did not seek to do any harm either to President Kruger or his country; 'rather, by the reforms which we insist upon, to help him to maintain his position and his authority, whilst at the same time securing justice to all the inhabitants of the country'.[111]

When Parliament broke up for the summer recess on 9 August, there was widespread expectation that the unity and resolution of the British government having been demonstrated, Kruger's government would make further concessions and there would be a peaceful resolution of the crisis. Sir Edward Hamilton considered that the parliamentary debate had made it quite clear that nobody in Britain wanted to go to war; nonetheless, he thought that 'some military demonstration' might possibly be needed 'before Kruger comes to terms'.[112] The Commander-in-Chief of the British Army, Lord Wolseley, thought that the best way to avoid war was to prepare for it and 'that the surest road to war was drift and . . . that we were getting unpleasantly near that danger'.[113] The Liberal Opposition in Britain found itself in some difficulty. Whilst disapproving of the 'violent and provocative language of the Colonial Secretary', they nonetheless felt that it was in the interests of South Africa and peace 'that the franchise should be extended in the Transvaal, and all grievances removed'. They had therefore not wished 'to do anything which would encourage the Transvaal Government to refuse to initiate reforms' which were themselves desirable. They had made clear their view that 'there was nothing in the case to justify war or preparations for war' but, James Bryce reported from England, they felt that the risk of war 'seems to have now quite passed away and there is a general sense of relief here'.[114]

In South Africa, Conyngham Greene reported that 'everyone' was delighted with the British parliamentary debate and the clear determination it revealed by the British government to bring to an end the 'excited conditions'.[115] In Johannesburg *The Star*, stalwart supporter of the Uitlander cause, observed that whilst Kruger's government had conceded much, 'those who thought that the limit of concessions had been reached had been proved repeatedly wrong' and argued for 'an end to the danger of a weak and unsatisfactory compromise', the establishment of Milner's Bloemfontein proposals as 'an irreducible minimum', and a determination 'to be content with nothing less than a complete and enduring settlement'.[116] *The Cape Times*, weather-vane of the 'pro-British' party, declared that the British government had given the Transvaal 'a stern warning' and made it clear that only fresh concessions could avert a conflict. 'Equal rights must now be granted to every white man north of the Vaal. One law alike for stranger and home-born' was its rallying cry. The British Prime Minister, it commented, had 'used language which cannot be too carefully pondered by everyone who wishes to see the Transvaal remain a republic'. With the prorogation of the British parliament, it observed, 'Mr Chamberlain and the Cabinet will have a free hand to deal with the South African situation'. There was, however, 'no danger of war providing the British government remains firm'.[117] *The Standard and Diggers News*, mouthpiece of Kruger's government, also feared that the advent of the parliamentary recess would give Chamberlain a free hand for his 'pushful programme' with regard to South Africa. It warned, however, that 'The Transvaal Government is not to be shaken by threats. If that is Mr Chamberlain's belief, he mistakes his man'. Kruger's government had done its duty and gone a long way to act with justice to meet the genuine grievances of 'the stranger within the gates . . . who had shown little loyalty to the Transvaal and a repeated inclination to appeal to the British government'. The new franchise law had been 'immediately dismissed as inadequate by the British party'. A 'peaceful, agricultural republic has been disturbed by the restless spirit of the century; attacked from without and within; abused, ridiculed, despised; its efforts at compromise rejected and treated with derision'. The Transvaal government, it warned, was likely to reject the British demand for a Joint Inquiry as 'a dangerous precedent of outside interference'. It would 'at all costs' stand for the principle of its independence. Both

Mr Chamberlain and the British government 'should pause before committing themselves to a war'.[118]

In May, the German Foreign Minister, Prince von Bülow, had assured the Kaiser that Britain had no *immediate* intention of taking action against the Transvaal, not least because they did not have 'anything like sufficient military forces in South Africa to attack the Transvaal with a prospect of success' and did not appear, so far, to be preparing to reinforce them.[119] At the end of July, the German ambassador in London, Count Hatzfeldt, reported that the speeches in the recent parliamentary debate had been designed to impress on President Kruger the unity and resolution of the British government and to keep up the pressure on him to make the concessions that were necessary. A recent confidential discussion with Lord Salisbury had made clear the latter's 'peaceful tendencies' and the general view was that the crisis between the British and Transvaal governments would not result in war. It was thought inconceivable that President Kruger might refuse the British demand for a Joint Inquiry on the franchise question, or the invitation to a further conference to settle other matters. Von Bülow was not so sure. It was clear, he observed, that the British government was now 'making demands on the South African Republic over and above the measure of the concessions already sanctioned by the Boers. It is not out of the question that, rather than endure this limitless pressure, President Kruger might finally prefer a war in which military superiority would at first be on the Boer side'. The parliamentary speeches were 'a further attempt at intimidation and part of the "game of bluff" . . . to force the Transvaal to grant further concessions'. The Kaiser, however, thought there would be war. President Kruger, he noted, regarded himself as the head of an independent state and denied Britain's right to interfere, let alone dictate in the internal affairs of his country. He would regard Britain's latest demands as an insult. Britain's claim to supremacy (or suzerainty) over the Transvaal would be challenged.[120]

WAR-CLOUDS GATHER OVER THE WITWATERSRAND

Meanwhile, the City of London did not believe that war was imminent. The Bank of England showed no major concern that its supplies of gold from the Rand might soon be interrupted by war and took no immediate steps to secure alternative sources of supply elsewhere.[121] South Africa had produced 27.55 per cent of the world's gold supply in 1898 and was now the world's leading gold-producing country. Now 1899 was proving to be a record year. The unproductive mines were being rapidly shut down whilst the yields of the deep levels were now accounting for the major part of the total output. The development of coal-mines meant that the country was now 'almost independent of foreign coal'. But both trade and activity on the Stock Exchange in Johannesburg had been severely hit and economic depression had intensified as political uncertainty took hold. The general economic down-turn in South Africa after the failure of the Bloemfontein Conference is well indicated in the archives of the Standard Bank and especially in the letters of its able General Manager, Lewis Michell.[122] Michell observed that mining companies were sending their securities out of the Transvaal; many customers were transferring their balances and bank accounts to the coast; the exodus from Johannesburg was assuming large dimensions. 'On the whole, the opinion is that war is almost inevitable', he reported.[123] He himself was convinced that Kruger 'is quite resolved that his "old burghers" shall alone administer the affairs of the republic . . . and no real intention exists of granting substantial reforms'. The result was disastrous for business. By July, trade in Johannesburg was paralysed, bank reserves were being reduced to a minimum, all safes were being removed to underground strong-rooms, and the bank had ordered iron shutters, strong doors, and sand-bags because 'if war occurs, Johannesburg would be vulnerable to internal disturbance before British troops can reach the town'.[124]

As General Manager of the premier bank in South Africa – 'which has many Dutch staff and clients and holds much Dutch money' – Michell was obliged to observe a policy 'of strict neutrality . . . and abstention from controversial politics'; but he had access to financial information which is of interest to historians. He noted that the government of the Orange Free State had ordered war material worth £53,000 by the end of June; when its government enquired about the possibility of a £1 million loan, Michell replied, at the beginning of October, that this was impossible 'since the result of its intervention in the growing crisis was likely to be its entire obliteration from the map of S. Africa'.[125] At the same time, the accounts of the Transvaal government revealed a mounting monthly excess of expenditure over revenue during 1899 at a time when its revenue was rising sharply. 'The considerably increased outgoings', he reported, 'have been devoted to fortifications, and purchases of munitions of war, foodstuffs etc. against a possible outbreak of hostilities'.[126] Meanwhile, private savings-bank withdrawals in the Transvaal during June were running at double the rate of those in May.[127] By August, many Uitlanders were out of work, some were destitute, and commercial relations with the Transvaal were virtually suspended. Michell reported that no revival was probable until the affairs of the republic were 'adjusted satisfactorily' under a new Convention. The situation left him with 'little doubt that the trend of events indicates war as the probable outcome'. Yet gold output from the Transvaal in 1899 was double that of 1895. Despite the war-clouds, it reached a record £1,700,000 in value for the month of July.[128]

In August, the Chamber of Mines reported that, despite the sharp down-turn in the commercial sector and the troubled times politically, the mining industry was still forging ahead; if only a peaceful resolution of the crisis could be achieved, even greater increases in output could be expected.[129] The archives of the mining companies reveal a situation in which the mine-magnates felt themselves to be acutely interested observers of a mounting drama between governments in which they were not key participants and for which they did not feel responsible. In May, Julius Wernher had thought it extremely unfair that the press actively blamed the capitalists, 'as we have done everything in our power to moderate the tone and work for rapprochement'; what was needed was a new Convention 'on a clear basis, with an expression guaranteeing the independence [of the Transvaal] and that would be the opportunity to settle the Uitlander question'.[130] 'My thesis', he wrote – in his idiosyncratic English – has always been

> that if the Boers wish to retain their independence, and a good many sweets besides for years to come, they have to make friends with the newcomer who has come to stay, and if there is contentment in the country it is absolutely safe and nobody will ever dream to attack it. If, on the other hand, the unrest continues, and the people remain ever dissatisfied, the interests of all, especially the neighbouring states, will suffer and, as feelings and pockets go together, there may be danger of war and an end to what is called now independence. . . . I never thought it my business to conquer the Transvaal for England when England was satisfied herself to give it up, but I hold strongly that the present position cannot last and that disaster must follow, political or financial.

Some kind of peaceful settlement was in the common interest, he declared, and everyone who tried to make the Boers see this was their friend and not their enemy.[131]

At the end of May, Rouliot, in Johannesburg, was convinced that

Kruger's government 'will concede everything in the way of economic reforms, and even some important modifications to the franchise law, but they will not agree to anything which they fear would move the political power from out of their hands'.[132] With the failure of the Bloemfontein Conference, Wernher felt that the situation had become 'very serious'. He did not believe that the British government had 'any designs on the independence of the Transvaal' but it was determined to extract an Uitlander franchise and other reforms. 'I know there is no evil intention here', he wrote to Rouliot, and the British government 'want to deal fairly and leave the country in independence, but it is felt that things cannot drift for ever and that unless the Transvaal falls in line a row must come, and that perhaps the present moment is not the worst'.[133] During July, a hardening of attitudes amongst the magnates is detectable as they became convinced that the prolonged crisis had now to be brought to an end and a final settlement made, even at the risk of war. Friedrich Eckstein wrote from Johannesburg of 'the strong feeling that an absolute settlement is necessary – no patchwork will satisfy the [Uitlander] community'.[134] Milner's close friend, Philip Gell, had meanwhile had a two-hour discussion with Wernher and some of the other 'capitalists' in England and wrote to tell Milner of his surprise

> considering their financial stake, to see how firm they were that the temporary risks and losses of a rupture were to be unswervingly faced. I put it to W[ernher] that the City and the foreign financial opinion would rat directly they felt the slump, inevitable during the progress of hostilities. He allowed for the weak-kneed, but assured me that the influential Houses would remain confident that you had acted for the best, and would not flinch because the markets went to pieces. . . . There is but one feeling. Let every resource of conciliation be exhausted. Let every guarantee for permanent local autonomy be offered – at this stage – if so a peaceful settlement may be assured. BUT – the suzerainty must be asserted *sans-phrase* and the situation must be terminated NOW.

Wernher, he added, 'does not expect much from the franchise, but regards it as a slow-working leaven and at any rate the minimum'. If it came to war, Wernher and his friends thought that the Transvaal should not be re-established as a republic, but as an autonomous colony with its own local institutions.[135]

The 'capitalists', however, were no monolithic block and in 1899, as in 1895, they were divided in their opinions – even within the firm of Wernher, Beit/H. Eckstein & Co. In July, Friedrich Eckstein – who saw Milner whenever he was in Cape Town – told Wernher that

Kruger's government would certainly give way further but 'only after England has sent out more troops and made a display of force'.[136] Rouliot was still 'convinced that it will be settled peacefully; the Boers have already gone far in the way of concessions if one remembers the first proposals of Kruger, which he said were the maximum of what they would concede'.[137] During August, however, when the extension of the dynamite monopoly was finally approved by the Volksraad and active military preparations increased the tension, Rouliot came to the conclusion that if Britain sent troops, war would become inevitable.[138] On 28 August, he wrote: 'Things do not look too bright at present. . . . The Boers repeat that they will not yield any further; we have therefore come to a deadlock, and I begin to fear that there will be no way out of it, and that it will lead to a row.'[139] Cecil Rhodes, meanwhile, told Beit that Kruger would 'bluff up to the last moment' and then 'give anything demanded' and that 'what would settle matter would be to ship at once first body of men'.[140]

By September, war seemed likely and the mining houses began to make their arrangements. One of the joint managers of Consolidated Goldfields, E.S. Birkenruth, fearing imminent arrest by the Transvaal government, left for Lourenco Marques; and Friedrich Eckstein moved to Cape Town, along with most of the deposits and much of the staff of Wernher, Beit/H. Eckstein & Co. Meanwhile, the editor of *The Transvaal Leader*, F. Pakeman, was arrested and, after being released on £500 bail, fled to Natal. A mood of panic developed amongst the leaders of the Uitlander population. W.F. Monypenny, the editor of *The Star*, hurriedly left the country – along with most of the members of the Uitlander Council and the South African League. A massive exodus of the Uitlander population from the Transvaal gathered pace towards the end of September. Packed into overcrowded trains, and latterly standing in open cattle-trucks, Uitlanders made for the coast at a rate of 1,000 or more each day. It has been estimated that 100,000 Europeans left the Transvaal between May and October 1899, and at least an equal number of Africans who were thrown out of work as most of the mines closed down.[141]

Kruger's government planned to keep a certain number of the mines working in the event of war. To this end, Article 140 of the Gold Law was hurriedly passed on 18 September, threatening mines which closed down their operations with governmental take-over. The government also made clear its intention to buy any gold produced and re-open the mint. The gold-mining companies, fearing that their gold stocks might be commandeered, hurriedly despatched them to Cape Town – although Kruger's government seized a final consignment (valued at £462,853) from Wernher, Beit/H. Eckstein & Co. from the Cape Town train in what was described as an act of piracy.[142] Shortages of coal, water and, above all, labour eventually forced many mines to close. By 7 October, 66 major mines had closed, along with two-thirds of the businesses in Johannesburg. A handful of mines continued in limited operation under the auspices of the Transvaal government after the war began.[143] Towards the end of September, when war seemed inevitable, Friedrich Eckstein wrote that he expected the Orange Free State to join the Transvaal in the struggle, 'from the imperial point of view, this is the best thing that can happen as it will thus make them to have a thorough cleaning up', he commented.[144] Wernher, meanwhile, assured Rouliot (who had also left Johannesburg for the coast) that 'the present situation is at last fast coming to an end'. It had lasted so long because of the reluctance of the British government to take action at a time when public support was uncertain. This, however, had changed and now that 'matters are understood, all admit that something must be done and nearly all agree that Chamberlain is not asking anything unfairly'. 'The fact that the military arrangements are far backward, proves that the thought of war was not seriously entertained here until quite recently', Wernher commented, adding that it seemed incredible that an empire ruling over half the world should be so ill-prepared.[145]

NOTES

1. *The Standard and Diggers News*, leader on 9 June 1899.
2. Speech to the Second Volksraad of 15 June 1899, printed in *Die Tweede Volksraad Notulen* for that date. A translation into English of Kruger's speech to the First Volksraad is enclosed in Conyngham Greene to Milner, 14 August 1899, Transvaal Archives, BA 21.
3. *The Standard and Diggers News*, 16 June 1899.
4. Full report in *The Standard and Diggers News*, 19 June 1899.
5. Reitz to Conyngham Greene, 9 June 1899, Transvaal Archives, BA 32.
6. Milner to Chamberlain, 14 June 1899, in C. Headlam, ed., *The Milner Papers* 2 vols (London, 1931/1933), 1, pp. 425, 435.
7. Chamberlain to State Secretary, 27 July 1899, in C.9518, p. 11.
8. Graham Bower to J. Rose Innes, 7 May and 2 July 1899, RIP MSC 21.
9. *The Cape Times*, 12 June 1899.
10. See A. H. Duminy and W. R. Guest, eds, *FitzPatrick, South African Politician: Selected Papers, 1888–1906* (Johannesburg, 1976) pp. 218–21.
11. Secretary of Transvaal Province of SAL to Milner, 16 June 1899, C.9415, pp. 32–4.

12. Smuts to Hofmeyr, 12 and 13 June 1899, in W. K. Hancock and J. van der Poel, eds, *Selections from the Smuts Papers* 7 vols (Cambridge, 1966–73), 1, pp. 244–5.

13. Smuts to Hofmeyr, 13 June 1899, in ibid., pp. 248–50.

14. Milner to Chamberlain, 11 and 15 June 1899, in Headlam, ed., *The Milner Papers*, 1, pp. 438–40; see also T. R. H. Davenport, *The Afrikaner Bond 1880–1911)* (Oxford, 1966), p. 194.

15. Chamberlain to Milner, 16 June 1899, in Headlam, ed., *The Milner Papers*, 1, p. 440.

16. R. H. Wilde, *Joseph Chamberlain and the South African Republic 1895–1899*, Archives Yearbook for South African History Part 1 (Pretoria, 1956) pp. 111, 113.

17. Milner to Chamberlain, 9 June 1899, in Headlam, ed., *The Milner Papers*, 1, p. 431.

18. Chamberlain to Milner, 3 July 1899, in J. L. Garvin and J. Amery, *Life of Joseph Chamberlain* 6 vols (London, 1932–69), 3, pp. 417–18.

19. Selborne to Milner, 25 June 1899, in D. G. Boyce, ed., *The Crisis of British Power: The Imperial and Naval Powers of the Second Earl of Selborne, 1895–1910* (London, 1990), p. 84.

20. Salisbury in conversation with G. E. Buckle, reported 13 June 1899, in A. N. Porter, *The Origins of the South African War, Joseph Chamberlain and the Diplomacy of Imperialism 1895–1899* (Manchester, 1980), p. 220.

21. Selborne to Milner, 25 June 1899, in Boyce, ed., *Crisis of British Power*, pp. 83–4.

22. Campbell-Bannerman, Speech, 17 June 1899, reported in *The Times*, 19 June 1899; Harcourt to J. Morley, 30 July 1899, in A. G. Gardiner, *The Life of Sir William Harcourt* 2 vols (London, 1923), 2, p. 499.

23. Speech reported in *The Cape Times*, 13 June 1899; also in C.9415, pp. 15–17.

24. Milner to Chamberlain, 22 June 1899, in Headlam, ed., *The Milner Papers*, 1, p. 444.

25. A. Duminy and Bill Guest, *Natal and Zululand from Earliest Times to 1910: A New History* (Pietermaritzburg, 1989), pp. 333–4.

26. J. S. Marais, *The Fall of Kruger's Republic* (Oxford, 1961), p. 294.

27. Ibid., p. 294.

28. Duminy and Guest, *Natal and Zululand*, p. 335, citing Hely Hutchinson to Chamberlain, 26 and 29 July 1899.

29. Smuts to Hofmeyr, 13 June 1899, in Hancock and van der Poel, eds, *Selections Smuts Papers*, 1, pp. 249–50.

30. Hofmeyr to Smuts, 17 June 1899, in ibid., pp. 254–6.

31. Smuts to Merriman, 18 June 1899, in ibid., pp. 257–8.

32. 'Papers re. complaints of British subjects in the South African Republic', C.9345, published on 14 June 1899.

33. Milner to Philip Gell, 22 May 1899, and Gell to Milner, 25 May 1899, GP, Transvaal Archives, copy FK 1619.

34. P. A. Molteno to J. C. Molteno, 16 June 1899, in V. Solomon, ed., *Selections from the Correspondence of Percy Alport Molteno* (Cape Town, 1981), pp. 85–6.

35. W. P. Schreiner to J. Ellis MP, 20 June 1899, ScP MSC 27 (Letter Book).
36. Davenport, *The Afrikaner Bond,* pp. 196–7.
37. E. van Heyningen, *The Relations between Sir Alfred Milner and W.P. Schreiner's Ministry, 1898–1900,* Archives Yearbook for South African History (Pretoria, 1978), p. 231.
38. Garvin, *Life of Chamberlain,* 3, pp. 415–16; Selborne to Milner, 25 June 1899, in Boyce, ed., *Crisis of British Power,* p. 84.
39. Merriman to J. Bryce, 20 and 28 June 1899, in P. Lewsen, ed., *Selections from the Correspondence of John X. Merriman* 4 vols (Cape Town, 1966–73), 3, pp. 71–2.
40. Schreiner to J. Ellis, 27 June 1899, ScP MSC 27, Letter Book for 1899.
41. Conyngham Greene to Milner, 29 June 1899, Transvaal Archives, BA 21.
42. Chamberlain to Milner, 30 June 1899, in Headlam, ed., *The Milner Papers,* 1, p. 450.
43. Van Heyningen, *Relations,* p. 239; E. Walker, *W. P. Schreiner: a South African* (Oxford, 1937), p. 166.
44. Hofmeyr to J. Sivewright, 19 July 1899, HP MSC 8, Box 86.
45. *The Cape Times,* 10 July 1899.
46. *The Times,* 19 July 1899.
47. Chamberlain to Milner, 18 July 1899, in Headlam, ed., *The Milner Papers,* 1, p. 468.
48. Salisbury to Chamberlain, 19 July 1899, JC 11/30/160.
49. Milner to Selborne, 12 July 1899, in Boyce, ed., *Crisis of British Power,* p. 90.
50. Telegram from Uitlander Council, 19 July 1899, in Headlam, ed., *The Milner Papers,* 1, p. 469.
51. Milner to British Vice-Consul, 21 July 1899, in ibid., p. 469.
52. The phrase is Selborne's in Selborne to Milner, 27 July 1899, in Boyce, ed., *Crisis of British Power,* p. 91.
53. Milner to Chamberlain, 13 July 1899, in Headlam, ed., *The Milner Papers,* 1, p. 459.
54. See Marais, *The Fall of Kruger's Republic,* pp. 300–2, for a detailed analysis.
55. Reitz to Conyngham Greene, 13 July 1899, C.9518, pp. 40–1.
56. Milner to Chamberlain, 17 July 1899, in Headlam, ed., *The Milner Papers,* 1, pp. 465–6.
57. Chamberlain to Milner, 7 July 1899, in Garvin, *Life of Chamberlain,* 3, p. 411.
58. Milner to Chamberlain, 17 July 1899, in Headlam, ed., *The Milner Papers,* 1, pp. 465–6.
59. Selborne to Chamberlain, 3 July 1899, in Boyce, ed., *Crisis of British Power,* pp. 88–9.
60. The two lengthy despatches of 19 and 26 July (printed in C.9518 (1899), pp. 45, 51) were preceded by a telegram of 19 July which Chamberlain utilized in his speech.
61. *Hansard,* 20 July 1899, Fourth Series, vol. lxxiv, cols 1350–1.

62. Chamberlain to Milner, 24 May 1899, in Headlam, ed., *The Milner Papers*, 1, p. 399.
63. Minute by Chamberlain, 5 June 1899, CO 417/262. See Chapter 8, p. 287 above.
64. Milner to Chamberlain, 14 June 1899, in Headlam, ed., *The Milner Papers*, 1, p. 424.
65. Milner to Chamberlain, 29 June 1899, in ibid., pp. 447–8.
66. Milner to Hely Hutchinson, 8 May 1899, in ibid., p. 359.
67. Wilde, *Joseph Chamberlain*, pp. 112–13.
68. Report in *The Cape Times*, 19 July 1899, of Volksraad debate of 18 July.
69. Milner to Chamberlain, 4 May 1899, in Headlam, ed., *The Milner Papers*, 1, p. 351.
70. Wilde, *Joseph Chamberlain*, p. 121, citing Minute by Just of 20 July 1899 in CO 417/263.
71. Ibid., p. 112.
72. Milner to Conyngham Greene, 29 June 1899, Transvaal Archives, BA 13.
73. Memorandum by Samuel Evans (a member of the Uitlander Council), 4 July 1899, enclosed in British Agent to Milner, 6 July 1899, Transvaal Archives, BA 21. The enquiry was prompted by a question in the British House of Commons at the end of June.
74. Milner to Chamberlain, 23 August 1899, JC 10/9/48.
75. Publicly stated by Chamberlain in the House of Commons debate on 28 July 1899, *Hansard*, vol. lxxv, col. 707.
76. Minute by Uitlander Council, 31 July 1899, enclosed in Conyngham Greene to Milner, 1 August 1899, in Transvaal Archives, BA 21.
77. Milner to Sir E. Grey, 7 August 1899, in Headlam, ed., *The Milner Papers*, 1, p. 478.
78. Milner to Chamberlain, 23 August 1899, JC 10/9/48.
79. Milner to Chamberlain, 14 June 1899, in Headlam, ed., *The Milner Papers*, 1, p. 425.
80. Milner to Chamberlain, 4 May 1899, in ibid., p. 350.
81. G. H. L. Le May, *British Supremacy in South Africa 1899–1907* (Oxford, 1965), p. 34.
82. Milner to Selborne, 12 July 1899, in Boyce, ed., *Crisis of British Power*, pp. 89–90.
83. Milner to Chamberlain, 22 June 1899, in Headlam, ed., *The Milner Papers*, 1, p. 444.
84. Milner Diary, 18, 19 and 23 July 1899, MP.
85. Milner to Mr Rendel, in Headlam, ed., *The Milner Papers,* 1, p. 473.
86. Milner to Selborne, 12 July 1899, in Boyce, ed., *Crisis of British Power*, pp. 89–90.
87. Ibid.
88. Sir Edward Hamilton, Diary, 9 June 1899, British Library Add. Mss. 48, 675.
89. Colonial Office Minute of May 1899, in Wilde, *Joseph Chamberlain*, p. 106.

90.   Milner to Chamberlain, 20 June 1899, JC 10/9/35.

91.   Comments by Graham and Wingfield, 23 June 1899, CO 417/262, 16194.

92.   Selborne to Milner, 27 June, and reply of 28 June 1899, SeP MS 11.

93.   Chamberlain to Milner, 7 July 1899, in Garvin, *Life of Chamberlain*, 3, p. 410; see also Chamberlain's speech on 28 July 1899, *Hansard*, vol. lxxv, cols 700–2.

94.   Milner to Selborne, 10 July 1899, in Headlam, ed., *The Milner Papers*, 1, pp. 456–7.

95.   Milner to Sir E. Grey, 7 August 1899, in ibid., pp. 477–8.

96.   Milner to Sir E. Grey, 7 August 1899, in ibid., pp. 477–9.

97.   Milner to Sir W. Hely Hutchinson, 15 June 1899, in ibid., p. 463.

98.   See, for example, the reports of conversations with him by Count Hatzfeldt, the German Ambassador in London, 30 July and 27 August 1899, in E. Dugdale, ed., *German Diplomatic Documents 1871–1914* 4 vols (New york, 1969), 3, pp. 89–90, 95–9. Also, A. N. Porter, 'Lord Salisbury, Mr Chamberlain and South Africa 1895–9', *JICH* 1 (1972), pp. 18–19.

99.   Sir Edward Hamilton, Diary, entry for 12 June 1899, British Library Add. Mss. 48,675.

100. Sir E. Grey to Milner, 13 July 1899, MP 16.

101. The full text of the despatch, dated 27 July 1899, is printed in C.9518 of 1899.

102. Minute of 22 July 1899, CO 417/264; Marais, *The Fall of Kruger's Republic*, p. 303.

103. Balfour to Chamberlain, 21 July 1899, cited in ibid., p. 304.

104. Selborne to Milner, 27 July 1899, in Boyce, ed., *Crisis of British Power*, pp. 91–2.

105. Milner to Chamberlain, 17 July 1899, in Headlam, ed., *The Milner Papers*, 1, p. 466.

106. *The Times*, 28 July 1899, p. 8.

107. *Hansard*, House of Lords, 28 July 1899, col. 652.

108. Ibid., cols 663–4.

109. *Hansard*, House of Commons, 28 July 1899, cols 694–6.

110. *Hansard*, House of Commons, 28 July 1899, cols 701–3.

111. All quotations from *Hansard*, 28 July 1899, vol. lxxv, cols 697–716.

112. Sir Edward Hamilton, Diary, 30 July 1899, British Library Add. Mss. 48, 675.

113. Ibid., 3 August 1899.

114. J. Bryce to J. X. Merriman, 20 July 1899, in Lewsen, ed., *Merriman*, 3, p. 74.

115. Conyngham Greene to British Vice-Consul (Johannesburg), 29 July 1899, Transvaal Archives, BA 22.

116. *The Star*, 19 and 22 July 1899.

117. *The Cape Times*, Leaders on 31 July and 9 August 1899.

118. *The Standard and Diggers News*, Leader of 11 August 1899.

119. Von Bülow to the Kaiser, 10 May 1899, in Dugdale, ed., *German Diplomatic Documents*, 3, p. 83.

120. Count Hatzfeldt to the German Foreign Office, 30 July 1899; von Bulow to the German Foreign Office, 31 July 1899, and the Kaiser's comments thereon, all in ibid., pp. 89–90.

121. Bank of England Archives, especially reports and tables re. gold supply of the Committee of Treasury. My own conclusion from this material agrees with that of J. J. Van Helten, 'British and European economic investment in the Transvaal with specific reference to the Witwatersrand gold fields and district 1886–1910', London Ph.D. thesis, 1981, and the same author's article, 'Empire and high finance: South Africa and the international Gold Standard 1890–1914', *JAH* 23 (1982), pp. 529–48. But see also Conclusion, pp. 411–12 below.

122. I am most grateful to the Archivist, Barbara Conradie, for her assistance during my research in this archive. A. Mabin and B. Conradie, eds, *The Confidence of the Whole Country: Standard Bank Reports on Economic Conditions in Southern Africa 1865–1902* (Johannesburg, 1987), is a most useful addition to the standard histories by G. T. Amphlett (Glasgow, 1914) and J. A. Henry (London, 1963). Some information in this paragraph is drawn from the Report for 8 August 1899, printed in Mabin and Conradie, eds, *The Confidence of the Whole Country*, pp. 465–74.

123. General Manager to London, 7, 14, 21, 28 June 1899, Standard Bank Archives, Johannesburg, 3/1/35.

124. General Manager to London, 28 June 1899, ibid.

125. Lewis Michell to London, 16 August and 4 October 1899, Standard Bank Archives, Johannesburg, 3/1/35.

126. Report for 8 August 1899, ibid.

127. General Manager to London, 28 June and 5 July 1899, ibid.

128. General Manager to London, 8 and 16 August 1899, ibid.

129. Speech by G. Rouliot at meeting on 17 August 1899, reported in *The Cape Times*, 18 August 1899; see also Eleventh Annual Report of the Chamber of Mines (for the year 1899), 1900.

130. Wernher to Rouliot, 6 May 1899, BRA, HE 167.

131. Wernher to Rouliot, undated but May–June 1899, BRA, HE 167.

132. Rouliot to Wernher, 29 May 1899, BRA, HE 175.

133. Wernher, Beit to Eckstein & Co., 16 June 1899, BRA, HE 66; Wernher to Rouliot, 16 June 1899, HE 167.

134. F. Eckstein to Wernher, Beit, 22 July 1899, BRA, HE 21.

135. P. Gell to Milner, 2 June 1899, GP.

136. F. Eckstein to J. Wernher, 8 July 1899, BRA, HE 121.

137. Rouliot to Wernher, 31 July 1899, BRA, HE 175.

138. Rouliot to Wernher, 21 August 1899, BRA, HE 175.

139. Rouliot to Wernher, 28 August 1899, BRA, HE 175.

140. C. J. Rhodes telegram to A. Beit, 23 August 1899, (copy) encl. in Wernher, Beit to W. Fisher, 26 August 1899, BRA, HE 67.

141. D. Cammack, *The Rand at War* (London, 1990), p. 41.

142. G. Rouliot, Address, Twelfth Annual Report of the Chamber of Mines (1902), p. 36. There is material on this incident in BRA, HE 67.

143. Ibid., pp. 48–9; also Cammack, *The Rand at War*, chs 3–4.
144. F. Eckstein to E. Evans, 21 September 1899, BRA, HE 130.
145. Wernher to Rouliot, 15 September 1899, BRA, HE 167.

CHAPTER TEN

Armageddon

THE MILITARY SITUATION

Nothing suggests more strongly that the British government was not deliberately planning a war against the Transvaal in 1899 than its repeated reluctance to engage in military preparations for one. The archives of the War Office reveal a situation in which the military men, led by Lord Wolseley, were at loggerheads with the politicians and failed to convince them either that war was likely or that the best chance of avoiding it was to prepare for it. The politicians succeeded in persuading themselves, until the end of August, that war could and would be avoided and that Kruger would eventually capitulate to British demands – as he had so often done in the past. They were therefore extremely reluctant to approve any expenditure on military preparations which might prove to be unnecessary. Even in September, when the British government finally faced the fact that an impasse had been reached and a resort to war was likely, its preparations were dilatory and based upon the assumption that what might occur was 'a small war', of short duration, the timing of which would remain under its control. Meanwhile, the military feared that the politicians would land them in a war in South Africa for which no adequate preparations had been made. So it proved. When war began in October, the humiliating series of British set-backs and defeats during the first three months caused many questions to be asked about the reasons for the manifest failure in military preparations on the British side. After the war, a Royal Commission investigated this further and the subject has continued to attract the attention of historians since.[1] All the research supports the same significant conclusion: as late as July 1899, the British government was not expecting a war against the Transvaal; nor was it planning 'a second Jameson Raid' to 'invade', 'occupy' and 'annex' the country as a British colony by military means.

When Milner had first been appointed as the new British High Commissioner to South Africa in April 1897, at the height of the crisis over the Aliens legislation, he had been dismayed to discover not only the obvious inadequacy of British forces in South Africa to meet a crisis but also the ability of the Treasury to obstruct repeated efforts to rectify the situation. Even at that stage in the confrontation between the British and Transvaal governments, Milner had stressed 'the absolute necessity of not playing these high games with no adequate force behind us'.[2] Milner had insisted that the British garrison needed to be increased to at least 10,000 men – if it was to be in a position to hold its own, in the event of war, until reinforcements could be sent out – but this had proved difficult to achieve. By December 1898, British forces in South Africa had been increased from 5,400 to 8,456 and equipped with more field guns. On the eve of the Bloemfontein Conference, Milner had emphasized the supreme importance of the military aspect of the situation and of the urgent necessity of further strengthening the British forces in South Africa. Just to defend Natal from attack might require 10,000 men, but if such an attack were initially successful, Milner estimated that 'we should require not 10,000 but 30,000 additional troops to reconquer our position in South Africa'. To the 'very serious' objection that the despatch to South Africa of such substantial numbers of British troops might provoke the Boers to move first 'and rush part of our territory', Milner replied that, if they did this they would 'put themselves in the wrong and become the aggressors'. What he wanted to ensure was that British troops were present in sufficient numbers to be able to retaliate at once and effectively; otherwise, 'a temporary success of theirs of some duration would light a fire throughout South Africa'.[3]

Milner had pleaded in vain. The Bloemfontein Conference came and went without any decision by the British Cabinet to reinforce its policy of putting increasing pressure on Kruger's government by the military backing which Milner argued was now essential to bring about a capitulation to British demands. By June 1899, a modest strengthening of the Natal garrison meant that there was now a total of 10,289 British troops in South Africa.[4] Meanwhile, the Intelligence Department of the British War Office estimated that if the Orange Free State stood by its treaty of mutual defence with the Transvaal, the two republics between them could raise a citizen army totalling 54,000 men, of which 34,000 (including 4,000 Afrikaners from the

Cape and Natal) would be available for an attack on the two English colonies whilst the remaining 20,000 would be deployed to maintain order within the republics. Yet it was assumed that the Cape Colony and Natal would only have to be defended against 'raiding parties' of 2,000–3,000 Boers on commando, rather than against a fully fledged invasion, and that it would only take one serious defeat to so demoralize the Boers that they would not 'make any further real stand'.[5] The fact was that the Boers were not regarded as a serious military adversary.

The reasons why the British government failed to prepare adequately for a war which appeared suddenly much more likely after June 1899 have been much investigated. Recent work has laid bare the division of opinion which existed not only within the British Cabinet but also between the War Office and the Commander-in-Chief of the British Army, Lord Wolseley. The parsimonious attitude of the Treasury towards military expenditure, and the influence within the Cabinet of the formidable Chancellor of the Exchequer (Michael Hicks Beach), have attracted particular attention.[6]

The 1890s had been a decade of rising imperial defence expenditure as Britain's world-wide trade and strategic interests came under increasing pressure from new European rivals. Since it was believed that Britain's position as a world power depended on her continued naval supremacy, favouritism had been shown towards the navy when it came to expenditure. Meanwhile, the army estimates continued to rise.[7] The enormous cost of the protracted Sudan campaign of 1897–8 had led Hicks Beach to warn the Prime Minister of the danger of trying to sustain 'a forward policy in too many places at once'.[8] 'Black Michael' was a strong and able Chancellor, who was greatly respected – even feared – in the Cabinet for his incisive mind and tongue. A traditionalist in financial policy, determined to exercise a strict control over government expenditure, he saw himself as a brake on the spending proclivities of his Cabinet colleagues, and especially of the Minister for War (Lord Lansdowne). When, after the failure of the Bloemfontein Conference, war-clouds again started to loom over the Transvaal, Hicks Beach was pessimistic, fearing that the crisis was becoming 'an exact reproduction of the state of affairs with Bartle Frere in 1879'.[9] He saw it as his role in the Cabinet to challenge and oppose any call for military expenditure which was not absolutely necessary.

The War Office, at this time, was presided over by the concientious but lightweight Lord Lansdowne. A member of one of the great patrician families, Lansdowne was a man of modest ability;

his housemaster at Eton had described him as 'talented without imagination, clear-headed but rather uncertain'. He had left the Liberal Party over Gladstone's Irish Land Act and, after being Governor-General of Canada and Viceroy of India, he was appointed as Minister of War in Salisbury's Cabinet in 1895.[10] In Cabinet, he was no match for either Hicks Beach or Chamberlain, both of whom treated him with scorn. Decisions about South Africa in 1899 were therefore affected by the presence of a strong and parsimonious Chancellor of the Exchequer and a weak and poorly regarded Secretary of State for War. The situation was further complicated by the state of things in the War Office itself. Regarded with contempt by most of the Cabinet – Chamberlain described it as 'rickety and useless' – riven by internal rivalries between Lord Wolseley's 'Africans' and Lord Roberts's 'Indians', the War Office in 1899 was neither a happy nor a very effective place. Having admired and worked closely with Lord Roberts in India, Lansdowne now had to work with his great rival, Lord Wolseley, as the Commander-in-Chief of the British army. Wolseley, for his part, found it difficult to accept being subordinate to a Minister whom he considered an amateur who meddled in army affairs. Relations between the two men were strained. As the South African crisis developed, their views about how to deal with it diverged. Wolseley had considerable South African experience and, like Milner, believed by June 1899 that a show of force was needed to demonstrate the resolution of the British government to the Transvaal; in his view the sooner a sizeable contingent of British troops was despatched to reinforce the manifestly inadequate South African garrison, the better. Lansdowne feared that the despatch of troops might sabotage the chances of a negotiated settlement and provoke the Boers into a pre-emptive strike against Natal before it was in a position to defend itself. He therefore favoured caution and procrastination until war seemed certain.

Lansdowne's reluctance to proceed with substantial military preparations reflected the general view within the British Cabinet, after the failure of the Bloemfontein Conference, that the British government should proceed with caution with regard to South Africa and 'keep out of war if possible'.[11] Whilst political pressure on Kruger's government was intensified, military action was limited to the quiet despatch of a handful of Special Service officers to strengthen the defences of the Cape Colony (amongst them was Colonel Baden-Powell, who was to make his name at Mafeking). Some rudimentary calculations were made in early July about what a war in South Africa might cost in terms of troops, transport and equipment, but these calculations were confined to the services and not even shared with the Treasury until five weeks later, since Lansdowne decided on 12 July that they did not need to be pursued further.[12] Strategic planning barely got beyond the assumption that, as the Orange Free State was likely to side with the Transvaal in the event of war (their mutual defence treaty had been renewed in 1897), advantage should be taken of the railway through the Orange Free State for any British military advance against the Transvaal.[13]

Three days after the Bloemfontein Conference ended in failure, Wolseley presented a memorandum to the Cabinet in which he argued that a war with the Transvaal would require at least 50,000 troops, in addition to the garrison already there, and was likely to last for 3–4 months. He asked the government to consider whether preparations should be begun at once for this contingency. He himself favoured the mobilization of a complete Army Corps on Salisbury Plain, under the general who would command it in South Africa, and argued that this would have the beneficial effect of demonstrating the resolution of the British government. He also pointed out that this could be done without calling out the reserves and would thus not necessitate consulting Parliament.[14] The Cabinet, however, rejected the idea of active military preparations. Nothing approaching an ultimatum was about to be presented to Kruger's government and British public opinion was not ready to support a resort to war. Nonetheless, during June, General Sir Redvers Buller was appointed as the commander of an expeditionary force, if one should be needed. On 3 July, Buller was told by the War Office that the despatch of 10,000 troops to South Africa was being contemplated and the following day, Lansdowne instructed Wolseley to investigate the associated transport, equipment and costs. By 7 July, Wolseley had declared his support for the immediate despatch of the 10,000 troops as being 'an open demonstration of a warlike policy, and also an efficacious method of strengthening our present military position there', but Buller had disagreed. Buller was reluctant to send troops from the main field force and suggested that it might be preferable to send the whole complement of troops only when war was inevitable. Meanwhile, defensive preparations should go ahead in the Cape and Natal.[15]

The successive amendments to the Transvaal franchise law, passed by the Volksraad during July, persuaded the British Cabinet to delay implementing the despatch of the additional 10,000 troops. Milner meanwhile emphasized the steady increase in the military strength of the Transvaal which had occurred since 1896 and argued that it was now such that 10,000 troops would be quite insufficient to contain it. He also questioned how the provisions of any franchise law could be effectively guaranteed in the future. Appalled at the possibility that the British government might be considering a 'patch-up' with Kruger's government, he pointed out that if the crisis were resolved without some measure of disarmament by the Transvaal, this would leave its government free to abrogate any treaty whenever it wished. The Transvaal's sustained programme of rearmament since the Jameson Raid meant that the British position was now so weak, in comparison, that 'for effective pressure in support of any demand' made by the British government, an army would have to be sent out from England. Since the cost of this would act as a severe deterrent, the Transvaal government would not pay the 'slightest regard to our representations hereafter' unless some measure of disarmament had meanwhile been imposed on it.[16] At the same time, the proposal for a Joint Inquiry into the new franchise law at once shifted attention away from the franchise issue itself to the even more problematic matter of the British government's claim to a role in the enactment of this law and thus to 'a practical demonstration of its suzerainty' over the Transvaal. As far as Kruger's government was concerned, doing something about an Uitlander franchise was one thing; compliance with the British government's insistence on its suzerainty and a measure of disarmament would be quite another matter.

Meanwhile, the strained relations between Milner and the Commander-in-Chief of British forces in South Africa, Sir William Butler, had reached breaking point. In June, Milner had warned Chamberlain that Butler's sympathies were 'all on the other side' and that if military measures were ever to be contemplated he would have to be replaced. Chamberlain had urged Milner 'to bear with him a little longer', as his recall would cause a commotion, but he promised that if it came to military measures, he would be superseded.[17] During the following month, Milner repeated his efforts to have Butler recalled and *The Cape Times* published a damning ('planted'?) article criticizing Butler for his 'peace at almost any price policy'.[18] Meanwhile, the War Office was becoming impatient with Butler's obsession with the efforts of the capitalists and Uitlanders to bring about a war and his reluctance to furnish the War Office with his plans should war occur. Milner thought that Butler was now 'penetrated with the great Rhodes and "capitalistic intrigues" myth' to a childish degree and said that he 'would do anything to get rid of him'.[19] At the beginning of August, Milner simply told Chamberlain that he and Butler could not 'stay here much longer together'. Butler 'conscientiously believes that we are in the wrong, that war would be wicked under the circumstances, and he cannot help shrinking from the contemplation of and preparations for it'. If things came to a pinch whilst he was still in charge, this would be disastrous; his replacement had become urgent and vital.[20] The War Office thereupon advised Butler to resign and offered him another post at home. This he accepted, leaving South Africa on 23 August 1899, to Milner's great relief.[21] His successor, a 'charming nonentity called Forestier-Walker', only arrived in September; but Lieutenant-General Sir George White was also sent out to take command of the British forces in Natal, where he arrived, in the nick of time, during the first week of October.[22]

Milner had used the situation in Natal in his efforts to stiffen the British government's resolve and persuade it not to waver in its demands upon the Transvaal government. By the end of July, the government of Natal had not only come round to a strongly pro-British position, it was asking for British reinforcements to be sent to assist in the colony's defence. Hitherto, the Natal government had opposed the stationing of British troops on its border with the Transvaal for fear of provoking the Transvaal government; now it asked for this to take place since it rightly feared that, in the event of war, it was likely to be attacked. Milner at once emphasized that this presented 'a good excuse . . . for greatly strengthening our position both for diplomatic and, in the last resort, for military purposes'. As the only colony in South Africa with a British majority in its European population, Natal was important. It was therefore essential to reassure its government and repay its loyalty. So Milner urged that a military force large enough to occupy the strategically important position of Laing's Nek, on the Transvaal border, be sent out 'as quietly as possible'.[23] Selborne wanted 5,000 troops to be sent and argued that this would be the cheapest way to conclude negotiations successfully. The Natal military authorities estimated that 5,600 men would be required to defend the colony. In the Cabinet, Lansdowne cautiously suggested 2,000 – 'to strengthen our own position, to reassure the colonists, and, above all, to strengthen our diplomacy during the new phase which is commencing' – and was supported by Hicks Beach, who was against anything but the most necessary expenditure. A force of 2,000 men was despatched to Natal during August. Wolseley welcomed this but believed that it was quite inadequate.[24] Sir George White was even more emphatic. On arriving in Natal to take up his command on 6 October, he wrote to his wife that 'we should have 20,000 more troops in South Africa than we have . . . the Cabinet have only themselves to thank if they have to reconquer South Africa from the sea'.[25]

The failure of Kruger's government to respond to the British proposal for a Joint Inquiry and a further conference with Milner led the British government to consider further what would be involved if military measures had to be taken. On 12 August, Lansdowne presented a memorandum which revealed that it would take *four months* to equip, mobilize and place in position an Army Corps of 50,000 men in South Africa. At an additional cost of £1 million, this could be reduced to three months. The Prime Minister did not consider it worth spending a million pounds simply to reduce the preparation time by a month and expressed the view that 'the wiser plan is not to incur any serious expenditure until it is quite clear that we *are* going to war', but feared 'the scandal which will certainly be created by the condition of our military preparations'.[26] Chamberlain was shocked by the time envisaged before British forces could be effective. His contempt for the War Office was reinforced. 'They are hopeless and it will be a mercy if they do not land us in a catastrophe', he commented to Selborne. Nonetheless, the hope that war might yet be avoided is clearly present in the decision of Chamberlain, Lansdowne and the Prime Minister not to press for 'the expenditure of a million which we cannot recover if we do not go to war'.[27] Only Balfour and Goschen urged Hicks Beach to sanction the money required for the military preparations, but Hicks Beach opposed this and so no positive decision was made.[28]

A day after Lansdowne's memorandum had revealed to the Cabinet 'the scandal' of the state of Britain's military unpreparedness, news arrived of a new political initiative by the Transvaal government which seemed to Chamberlain to promise 'another climb down on the part of Kruger' and justification for the course the Cabinet had taken.[29] This initiative had been made by J.C. Smuts, the Transvaal government's Attorney-General, in what was to prove a final set of proposals for a political settlement which he discussed with the British Agent in Pretoria, Conyngham Greene. Whilst these proposals were still being considered, Lord Wolseley presented a further memorandum in which he again urged the immediate strengthening of the British garrison in South Africa by 10,000 men at an estimated cost of £500,000. He warned the Cabinet that by not reinforcing the British military presence they were likely to save neither money nor the situation since only the despatch of a strong force would make Kruger concede and thereby prevent a war.[30] The hope that the Smuts initiative might yet result in a peaceful settlement persuaded

Chamberlain and the Cabinet yet again to delay embarking on active military measures 'which would involve heavy expenditure' and which they continued to hope would be unnecessary. Wolseley's recommendations were therefore again refused, Lansdowne informing him that the situation did not justify sending substantial military reinforcements to South Africa and nothing was to be done until the attempts to reach a negotiated settlement had been exhausted. If it came to military measures, he envisaged concentrating a British force in the Cape for an advance north through the Orange Free State, whilst reinforcements from India were deployed in Natal – where he considered the present garrison quite capable of looking after itself.[31] To the Prime Minister, Lansdowne expressed his fear that 'an ill-timed turn of the screw' by Britain might provoke the Boers and precipitate a war which he still clearly hoped to avoid.[32]

Wolseley's growing exasperation with what he regarded as the complete failure of the politicians to come to grips with the situation led him to reply to Lansdowne's rejection of his recommendations by reminding him that the present British military strength in South Africa was such that, if war came, 'we shall surrender the initiative to Kruger; and in no recent case that I can think of would . . . that initiative be more likely to seriously injure our national prestige'. To secure peace in South Africa it was necessary to have a show of force there.[33] Since July, Wolseley and Milner had been of one mind on the matter; the British government had been of another.

Wolseley was not without influence with people in high places. After a discussion with him on 3 August, Sir Edward Hamilton (who was the right-hand man of Hicks Beach at the Treasury) recorded Wolseley's opinion that 'Kruger intends to play the game of bluff for some little time longer – he has not yet put us to sufficient trouble and expense – and that he will then climb down'.[34] Hicks Beach, however, was more pessimistic and feared that Britain 'may have to prepare for the worst'. He therefore began to estimate the likely cost if Wolseley's recommendation of sending 50,000 troops to South Africa had eventually to be implemented. In mid-August, the War Office estimated that the cost of mobilizing and transporting 50,000 men and 10,000 animals to South Africa would be £5 million with charges of £600,000 per month.[35] Casting around for a suitable precedent for financing such a venture, Hicks Beach dismissed the Zulu and Afghan wars and settled on the Egyptian campaign of 1882. This proved to be a mistake with far-reaching implications as the cost of the war in South Africa escalated far beyond anything that had been anticipated. The Transvaal War of 1880–81 had cost Britain over £5 million. The

Abyssinian War had cost £9 million and the Zulu War £5 million. It was anticipated, in 1899, that a war in South Africa might cost £10 million. It eventually cost over £230 million. Britain paid for these wars out of current revenue from taxation and short-term loans and she had a consistent record of failure with regard to recouping her costs from the areas concerned. Despite tentative hopes beforehand that this time it would be different, the South African War of 1899–1902 proved true to the established pattern: the pursuit of a war indemnity from the Transvaal turned out to be a total chimera.[36] From the middle of August onwards, Hicks Beach was continuously paring down what he considered the extravagant estimates for a war in South Africa sent to him by the War Office. At the same time, he initially shared the hopes of the majority of the Cabinet, that the opportunity for a peaceful resolution of the conflict had unexpectedly occurred through the Smuts proposals, by which, he observed, 'Kruger had practically granted the Milner minimum'; the British government therefore 'ought to be able to come to terms with him – if only . . . that infernal *Times* does not make an arrangement impossible'.[37]

THE SMUTS PROPOSALS OF AUGUST 1899

The British despatch to the Transvaal government of 27 July was only delivered on 23 August, as it had been sent by sea; but the proposals it contained for a Joint Inquiry into the details of the recent franchise law and a further conference between Milner and President Kruger to settle other points at issue were communicated by telegraph. When the Transvaal government failed to respond, Chamberlain instructed Milner to 'press for an answer' and, if necessary, appoint a Commission of Inquiry unilaterally to investigate the franchise law. He hoped that Milner would be able to find a prominent Cape Afrikaner to act as one of the three commissioners whose report would form a useful basis if it came to an ultimatum.[38] If it came to an ultimatum, British demands would not be restricted to the franchise but would include everything else judged necessary to achieve a full and final settlement.[39] Chamberlain justified this on the principle of the Sibylline Books,[40] which he claimed had first been indicated by the Prime Minister in the House of Lords.[41] Thus, British terms for a settlement would increase if Kruger's government played for time and put Britain to the considerable expense of making substantial military preparations.

The failure of the Transvaal government to reply to the British proposals was not accidental but deliberate. It recognized a practical demonstration of British suzerainty and supremacy over the Transvaal when it saw one and knew that to accept a Joint Inquiry over its own recent franchise legislation would be to surrender legislative sovereignty over a vital internal matter. Yet a rejection was likely to precipitate an ultimatum and a resort to war. Well aware that a point of no return had been reached, Smuts telegraphed to a friend on 12 August, 'Answer still being earnestly considered. We realize profoundly the significance and consequences of it'.[42]

Kruger's government was under considerable pressure to accept the British demands. Both the Dutch and German governments warned Pretoria not to refuse them and Dr Leyds made it clear from Brussels that there would be no support for the Transvaal if a refusal were to be followed by war. The Transvaal government's agent in London, Montagu White, reported that the friends of the republic amongst British Liberals 'are one and all dead against our refusing the proposal(s)'.[43] Leading Cape Afrikaners took a similar view. They acknowledged that acceptance of the British demands would be humiliating but recognized that the alternative was likely to be an ultimatum followed by a resort to war which could only end in the total overthrow of the Transvaal's independence as a republic. Those who had worked for conciliation in June and July redoubled their efforts in August. Chief Justice de Villiers urged both his brother Melius, and Abraham Fischer in the Orange Free State, to join him in efforts to persuade Kruger to offer the Uitlanders a straightforward franchise based on five years' residence, and accept the British proposal for a Joint Inquiry. 'The British public is determined to see the matter through', he warned, 'and, if a contest is begun, will not rest until the Transvaal has completely submitted'.[44]

Such was the level of distrust with regard to British intentions, however, that Abraham Fischer – who had hitherto worked to bring about a peaceful settlement – now angrily exclaimed: 'Where are the demands to end?' All the concessions made so far in a conciliatory spirit by the Transvaal government, and going far towards meeting Milner's Bloemfontein demands, 'have been received with contempt', he observed. Now, he doubted the good faith of the British government, which seemed to have the deliberate intention 'with or without war' to supersede the London Convention and to humiliate not only the Transvaal but Afrikaners throughout South Africa by asserting a paramountcy claim which now seemed to be extended to include the Orange Free State as well. The British government could not expect the Afrikaner population 'quietly to submit' to this.[45]

On 5 August, de Villiers wrote to President Kruger, 'as your friend and well-wisher', urging him to do everything in his power to ward off a war which could only end 'in a destruction of your republic'. The question 'no longer is what right has the British Government to make its demands, but what concessions on your part will preserve the peace', he commented. 'I know the strong views which you hold as to your duty to preserve the independence of your republic, but a patriot should also be prudent and he should even be prepared to surrender a part of his independence if by that means alone he can prevent the loss of the whole'.[46] In his reply, Kruger asked him to imagine his own position as President:

I am sworn to uphold the independence of my country, and I have the very best of reasons for believing that Chamberlain and Milner are determined to rob me of that independence. Can you give me the assurance that if I yield all their present demands, others will not be sprung upon me which no self-respecting President could for a moment entertain? If we are to lose our independence, let it be taken from us by force, but do not ask me to be a consenting party. I have always been and still am willing to do everything reasonable to settle disputes amicably, but you must remember that there is a limit to our burghers' forbearance. They cannot understand what right the British Government has to interfere in our affairs when we have done nothing to endanger British rule in the British colonies or to interfere with the rights of British citizens in the Transvaal. On the contrary, British subjects have grown fat on the land, they are richer than our own people and we have done everything possible to protect them in their rights and liberty while many of them are doing everything possible to provoke us. The demand for the franchise is a pretence. They do not want the franchise under a republic, but they want to substitute the rule of the High Commissioner for that of the lawful President. . . . If you can prevail upon the High Commissioner to moderate his demands, or at all events to let us know everything that will be required of us, you may be the means of preserving the peace; and I, for my part, will do everything I honourably can towards the same object. Even now, negotiations are going on which, if the British Government would only be fair and just, may lead to a settlement of our disputes. It is our interest to keep the peace, but if our independence is to go, it must be taken from us by force.[47]

The negotiations which Kruger referred to were the ones initiated via his Attorney-General, J. C. Smuts, in an attempt to circumvent the British demand for a Joint Inquiry by making a new set of proposals for a comprehensive political settlement. By 12 August the Transvaal government had finally decided that the British demand for a Joint

Inquiry into the details of the recent franchise law passed by the Transvaal Volksraad could not be accepted, since this would give the British government the right to intervene in the internal affairs of the republic which had been consistently denied by Kruger's government. Now, Conyngham Greene was told that the Transvaal government would fight rather than agree to it, and Kruger telegraphed to President Steyn of the Orange Free State that compliance with the British request was impossible 'as it would be equivalent to a destruction of our independence'.[48] Steyn supported the stand taken by the Transvaal government but urged Kruger to offer a five years' retrospective franchise – along the lines demanded by Milner at the Bloemfontein Conference – in place of the Joint Inquiry. Reitz was instructed to notify the British government that its invitation to set up a Joint Inquiry could not be accepted; but to delay sending this notification pending the outcome of a fresh attempt at an overall settlement. This is what Smuts now tried and failed to achieve. Although there is every reason to believe in the *bona fides* of his efforts, the evidence also suggests that he was not hopeful of the outcome.[49] Smuts, like Kruger, had become convinced that the attitude of both Chamberlain and Milner 'was personally hostile to the S.A.R'.[50] He had also long believed that, far from being ready to reach a negotiated settlement on the franchise issue, 'the franchise has nothing to do with the situation' and, even if a franchise based on five years' residence were offered, 'England would still seek and find a cause for hostilities in other points of dispute'.[51]

In conversations with Conyngham Greene in Pretoria on three successive days (12–14 August), Smuts outlined fresh proposals on the franchise which conceded everything that Milner had demanded at the Bloemfontein Conference. The Uitlanders would be granted a five years' retrospective franchise and the Rand would be awarded eight new seats in the Volksraad. Together with the two existing seats for Johannesburg and Barberton, this would make a total of ten seats for the mining areas in a Volksraad of 36; in the future, a quarter of the total seats was guaranteed. Those newly enfranchized would have equal rights with the old burgher population with regard to the election of the Commandant-General and the President of the Transvaal. The details of the new franchise law would be discussed with the British Agent in Pretoria, who could be assisted by a legal adviser. The Transvaal government offered to support this measure and get the burghers to adopt it and believed that it might become law within about a fortnight.[52] These major concessions by the Transvaal government, on the franchise, were offered on three important conditions. Firstly, Britain was to agree to an arbitration procedure 'from which the foreign element is excluded', for the resolution of other points at issue between the two governments. It was also to agree

> that a precedent shall not be formed by their present intervention for similar action in the future, and that no future interference in the internal affairs of the [Transvaal] Republic will take place contrary to the [London] Convention. Further, that Her Majesty's Government will not insist further upon the assertion of suzerainty, the controversy on this subject being tacitly allowed to drop.[53]

The discussions between Smuts and Conyngham Greene on 12–13 August were of an informal, exploratory nature, but so much progress had been made by the evening of 13 August that the two men agreed to consult their respective governments about the proposals. Next morning (14 August), Smuts discussed the matter with the Executive Council – which expressed its readiness to proceed on the basis of a memorandum which Smuts had written and which he now initialled (to avoid any misunderstanding with regard to what was being proposed) and gave to Conyngham Greene to transmit via Milner to London. The purpose of this initial presentation was to test the readiness of the British government to consider the proposals and to accept them as a substitute for the Joint Inquiry. If the response was positive, they would then be presented formally. In forwarding the proposals, Conyngham Greene accompanied them with a second telegram in which he reported further on his conversations with Smuts. In it he said that he had told Smuts that 'the situation was most critical' and that 'the only chance' for his government was 'an immediate surrender to the Bloemfontein minimum'; that he would recommend acceptance of his proposals to the British government 'in return for waiving the proposal for a Joint Inquiry'. Further, whilst he had not 'in any way committed Her Majesty's Government to acceptance or refusal of proposal(s)' he had said that if they represented a *bona fide* attempt to settle the political rights of the Uitlanders, once and for all, the Transvaal government

> need not fear that we shall in the future either wish or have cause to interfere in their internal affairs. I have said as regards suzerainty that I feel sure Her Majesty's Government will not and cannot abandon the right which the preamble to the Convention of 1881 gives them, but that they will have no desire to hurt Boer susceptibilities by publicly reasserting it, so long as no reason to do so is given them by the Government of the South African Republic.[54]

There is no doubt that Conyngham Greene had led Smuts to believe that his proposals would be received favourably by the British government and would probably be accepted as a substitute for the Joint Inquiry. This was to lead to accusations of bad faith and 'misunderstandings' later. Smuts had also learned that the British government had hoped to use the Joint Inquiry to present Uitlander demands 'to go further than at Bloemfontein' and to win over public opinion to their side. Smuts concluded that the only way open for his government 'was to accept Bloemfontein proposals as alternative to prevent investigation and greater demands'. His suggestion that the details of these latest franchise proposals should be examined by Conyngham Greene, as the British Agent in Pretoria (together with a legal adviser), also avoided the inclusion of Milner, the British proposal for a further conference with whom Smuts hoped 'may now be allowed to lapse'.[55]

Not surprisingly, Milner did not take kindly to being upstaged by his subordinate in this way and regarded the Smuts proposals with profound distrust. He had found the day before this latest attempt at a negotiated settlement 'a depressing one, as the political outlook is once more one of unsatisfactory compromise'.[56] This was the outcome which he was now determined to resist. In forwarding Conyngham Greene's telegrams to London, Milner therefore criticized 'the extraordinary conduct of Greene' (who, he considered, had 'gone much too far'), expressed scepticism about Smuts's franchise offer, declared that 'nothing but confusion can result from this irregular method of negotiations' and urged Chamberlain to insist on a straight yes or no answer to Britain's Joint Inquiry and further conference proposal.[57] This latest 'manoeuvre' by Kruger's government, Milner claimed, 'shows their alarm. It also shows, however, their absolute determination not to admit our claim to have a voice in their affairs as the Paramount Power in South Africa. . . . They will collapse if we don't weaken, or rather if we go on steadily turning the screw'.[58]

In London, Chamberlain thought that Milner was being 'unnecessarily suspicious and pedantic' and insisted that 'the Boers should not be snubbed at this stage but rather encouraged to put their concessions on record'. Writing to the Prime Minister, he expressed his own initial impression that this latest offer amounted to a climb-down 'which, as far as I can see, is really complete this time'. 'I really am sanguine that the crisis is over', he added later.[59] Salisbury considered the news to be 'very satisfactory' and was critical of Milner. 'It looks as if he has been spoiling for the fight with some glee and does not like putting his clothes on again', he commented.[60]

Chamberlain's hopes that a settlement might still be reached are clearly indicated in his reply to Milner. If the proposals reported by Conyngham Greene were officially confirmed, he pointed out, 'they evidently constitute an immense concession and even a considerable advance on your Bloemfontein proposals'. The provision for the British Agent (together with a legal assistant appointed by Milner) to examine exactly how Smuts's franchise details would work in practice, offered an acceptable substitute for the Joint Inquiry – the purpose of which was 'to satisfy us that the Uitlanders would get substantial and immediate representation'. If this proved to be so, then Chamberlain initially saw 'no difficulty in answering' what he called 'the three requests made at the end of the proposals' by the Transvaal government. With regard to any future intervention in the internal affairs of the Transvaal, 'I should say that the fulfillment of the promises made and the just treatment of Uitlanders in the future will, H.M.G. hopes, render unnecessary any future intervention on their behalf'. As to suzerainty, it would be possible to 'say that, while retaining their own opinion, H.M.G. had no intention of pressing the controversy further at this time'. Finally, as to the establishment of an arbitration procedure, it could be agreed 'to discuss form and scope of Tribunal provided no foreigner or foreign influence is included'. Chamberlain emphasized his conciliatory stance by stressing that 'we need not jump down the throats' of the Transvaal government and should 'take care to avoid any reply that would discourage them from joining us'. This new phase in the situation had to be worked through 'and unless we can prove conclusively that it is dishonestly intended or altogether inadequate, it will be impossible to reject it'. Meanwhile, he warned Milner, 'you must avoid any language which would lead S.A.R. to think that we are determined to pick a quarrel'.[61]

Milner had wanted to take a stand on the Joint Inquiry – which he thought Kruger's government might accept 'after boggling . . . if not, I expect the row to come'.[62] He regretted that the British government had not stuck to this since, 'after weeks of wavering, we had at last made a reasonable and clear demand'. Now, the situation was again 'slipping out of the definite into the indefinite'.[63] Nonetheless, he dutifully informed the Transvaal government, in an ambiguously worded message, that its proposals would be considered if they were formally submitted. Kruger reassured Steyn that this meant that 'our compromise' was not being treated as a refusal of the Joint Inquiry and that the proposals would be treated on their merits by the British government.[64] The proposals were therefore formally presented on 19 August. On 21 August, however, the Transvaal government stiffened them by sending an official 'rider' stating that its proposals of 19 August were *expressly conditional* upon three guarantees being given by the British government: '(a) In future not to interfere in internal affairs of the South African Republic. (b) Not to insist further on its assertion of existence of suzerainty. (c) To agree to arbitration.'[65] The Smuts proposals were not to be understood as one-sided concessions on the franchise. This time, Kruger's government wanted something in return. Having circumvented the Joint Inquiry through the presentation of the Smuts proposals, it now wanted to use these to extract a guarantee from the British government not to interfere in the Transvaal's internal affairs in the future and not to persist in its claim to suzerainty. The question of an arbitration procedure was much less problematic. When President Kruger had sought an agreement on this in return for concessions on the franchise at the Bloemfontein Conference, Milner had dismissed this as an attempt at 'a Kaffir bargain'. But Chamberlain had since come to believe that agreement on an arbitration procedure from which a foreign element was excluded was both possible and advisable – not least because of British support for the arbitration principle at the recent Hague Conference.[66] The two other conditions went to the heart of the conflict between the British and Transvaal governments by 1899. Kruger clearly believed that the removal of British interference in the Transvaal's internal affairs was vital to the preservation of the republic, in view of the political power to be granted to the Uitlanders. Smuts recognized 'that the principal difficulty lies in the suzerainty' and told Conyngham Greene that if the British government could see its way to consider Boer susceptibilities in that matter, this would greatly improve the chances for reaching a negotiated settlement about everything else.[67]

Chamberlain's initial optimism that a settlement really was in sight, was soon replaced by caution. Although on the surface, the Smuts proposals appeared to promise 'a complete climb-down, on the part of Kruger', he warned Lansdowne, 'with our past experience we dare not assume that all is right until we have full confirmation and are sure that there are no hidden pitfalls on the way'. The new development justified further delay in military preparations, but if it came to nothing 'we should then have to deliver an ultimatum at once'.[68] By 24 August, he was clear that although the franchise proposals '*may* give us what we want . . . they are expressly made conditional on the acceptance of impossible terms as to suzerainty and future intervention – and an agreement as to Arbitration at which I expect we shall have difficulty in arriving. If the Boers want peace, they will give way on these points, but I am not clear that they do'.[69] The Prime Minister, too, was much less hopeful and cogently summarized the situation: 'At present, I understand the Boer's offer in effect to be – the Bloemfontein demands; *but* a renunciation of the Suzerainty in exchange. This does not seem a possible solution.'[70]

Lansdowne had to balance the possibility of a peaceful settlement arising out of the Smuts proposals with the need to have military preparations sufficiently underway to back up an ultimatum if they came to nothing. He still felt that Kruger would probably back down at the last moment, and he was therefore against sending out military reinforcements which might not only prove unnecessary but precipitate war by provoking the Transvaal into a pre-emptive strike against Natal. The concessions offered on the franchise certainly merited 'benevolent examination' but 'may prove to be illusory', he commented, and 'the conditions as to suzerainty and future non-intervention are obviously inadmissible, and, if literally persisted in, will render a peaceful solution, to my mind, impossible'.[71]

The *conditions* on which the Smuts proposals were made therefore doomed this final attempt at a settlement to failure, since there was never any possibility that the British government would accept the terms laid down in the 'rider' of 21 August. The exercise nonetheless provided the Transvaal government with a litmus test of whether the franchise was the key problem (which could be solved by concessions) or whether the real issue was that of British supremacy (on which Britain would make no compromise). It served to reveal that, as Smuts and Kruger had long assumed, the real issue was that of British supremacy and Transvaal subservience.

The British response served to confirm the view of Kruger's government that the more it offered concessions, the more the British government would accept these – without giving anything in return – and then go on to present fresh demands. Where the Transvaal government sought to negotiate a compromise settlement, the British government was set on a capitulation to British demands. As time went on, these demands would increase, by analogy with the Sibylline Books, as Hofmeyr reminded Smuts at the end of August – when he criticized Kruger's government for not having offered a straight-forward, seven years' retrospective franchise at the Bloemfontein Conference. By yielding 'in bits and pieces' since, Hofmeyr commented, 'all your concessions have acquired the appearance of being *extorted*'.[72] Yet the fact is that the British government had failed to present the full total of its demands together, despite Milner's earlier belief that it should do so and the plea by Chief Justice de Villiers that if Kruger's government 'knew the limit of the British demands there would be a much better chance of a general settlement'.[73] Kruger's government therefore faced a spiralling situation in which it felt that new demands were formulated as quickly as old ones were met. The British government's response to his latest proposals confirmed Smuts in his conviction that the issue between the British and Transvaal governments was 'not so much about the details of the [franchise] law as about possession of this land of gold'.[74] By the end of August, the sticking point had been reached. The British government had demonstrated that it would not 'simply let suzerainty go and bind herself not to interfere in our affairs again' and so Smuts saw 'no way out but a war which will finally break the neck of one or other of the contending parties'.[75]

Several developments in the week following the presentation of the Transvaal government's proposals, on 19 August, had caused the doubts of Smuts and his colleagues about British intentions to harden. First, there were the misunderstandings and accusations of bad faith which arose out of the second telegram which Conyngham Greene had sent on 14 August. This had reported further points, allegedly made in informal discussion between the two men, in addition to those embodied in the formal proposals. Amongst them were the right of elected representatives from the Rand to use English in the Volksraad and future provision for possible changes in the election procedures for the Commandant-General and President. Smuts had deliberately excluded these points from the formal proposals which had all been presented in the memorandum, initialled by him, and sent by Conyngham Greene as the first of his two telegrams on 14 August. On 24 August, Smuts was both surprised and angry to find that these additional points were being included by Chamberlain in what he took to be the full list of proposals, by the Transvaal government, for which 'a formal note' was now demanded.[76] Once again, Chamberlain appeared to be acting in an arrogant way, assuming more than had, in fact, been offered. The initial response from the Colonial Office, in a telegram shown to Smuts by Conyngham Greene, also failed to give any reassurance that the proposals would be accepted or even regarded favourably – whereas, encouraged by Conyngham Greene, Smuts and his government had been led to expect that their proposals would undoubtedly be accepted.[77] After consulting the State Secretary, Reitz, Smuts at once wrote to Greene pointing out the 'misunderstanding' and saying that he had never intended the details of their private conversations, as opposed to the formal proposals, to be conveyed to London. He accompanied this letter by a stiffly worded formal Note to be delivered to the British government. This stated that:

The terms of a settlement as contained in the formal note of this Government delivered 19 August were very carefully considered and I do not believe that there is the slightest chance that these terms will be altered or amplified. Your decision will therefore have to be arrived at on these terms as they stand.[78]

The noticeable hardening in the tone of this Note was also influenced by the fact that on 23 August the Transvaal government had finally received the full text of the important British despatch of 27 July which, through a blunder on the part of Conyngham Greene, was delivered without any indication that its contents had in any way been superseded by the Smuts proposals. Chamberlain's extraordinary decision to have the despatch delivered at this sensitive time probably stemmed from his need to publish it in a Blue Book, along with other recent material on South Africa, released on 25 August for the education of British public opinion.[79] He also seems to have been under the illusion that what he considered to be 'friendly proposals' in the British despatch of 27 July would be received as such in Pretoria. Yet, as Balfour had warned, much of the despatch was likely to be viewed as biased and irritating by Kruger's government, and the accusation of Transvaal bad faith which it contained was certain to be regarded as insulting. The despatch also indicated that there could be no question about British suzerainty over the Transvaal.[80] The effect on Kruger's government of receiving this communication at this time was bound to be wholly negative.

Chamberlain acted in ignorance of two other considerations which Conyngham Greene had reported but which Milner sent on by sea instead of by telegraph. Whether this was done deliberately, as a blocking tactic by Milner, or as a result of administrative error, remains unclear.[81] Conyngham Greene reported that Smuts had explained his government's refusal to enlarge upon the terms accompanying his proposals because of its suspicion that it was being drawn into making admissions which would afterwards be used against it, whilst the proposals themselves would be rejected. It also feared that it would have difficulty persuading the burghers and the Volksraad to agree to the five years' retrospective franchise unless it could show that it had received some major concession from the British government, especially regarding suzerainty, in return.[82] Had Chamberlain known of these considerations, perhaps he would have given more indication of British goodwill and readiness to negotiate than he did in his reply to Kruger's government on 28 August. But it is hard to see how there could have been any real concession by Britain on the issues on which this was being sought by Kruger's government. The delay therefore probably made little difference.

A further action by the British government at this delicate time contributed another negative indication of British intentions to the Transvaal government. On 19 August, a shipment of armaments and ammunition for the Transvaal, including a major consignment of cartridges for its new Mauser rifles, was stopped at the port of Delagoa Bay by Britain exerting its influence on the Portuguese government in Lisbon. The attempt by the British Foreign Office to block this shipment indefinitely only went awry through a garbled telegram at the end of the month; by the time this was sorted out, the arms and ammunition had been released and arrived safely in Pretoria; but the interference by the British government 'produced a great effect in South Africa'.[83]

Encouraged by his own past experience, Chamberlain had become convinced that Kruger's government only gave way under pressure and that the best chance for a final capitulation was to increase the pressure. He was also becoming impatient. On 24 August he minuted:

> It is clear that we will not go on negotiating for ever, and we must try to bring matters to a head. The next step in military preparations is so important and so costly that I hesitate to incur the expense . . . so long as there seems a fair chance of a satisfactory settlement. But I dread above all the continual whittling away of differences until we have no *casus belli* left, although the Boers may claim a partial diplomatic victory and be as disagreeable and intractable in the future as in the past.[84]

He was also, under Milner's influence, coming to appreciate the difficulties that Britain would face in ensuring that Kruger's government would observe, in the future, the conditions of any settlement extracted from him under duress. The experience of the Pretoria and London Conventions was not encouraging. Chamberlain developed this thought in a letter to the Prime Minister:

> I have no doubt that it is the fact that Kruger – who might have yielded gracefully at Bloemfontein and even later – will now only yield, if at all, to the fear of force and with the determination of repudiating his obligations whenever he thinks it safe to do so. The belief in this makes people anxious, in Natal especially, where they are open to attack and I can see clearly that they wish us to increase our terms and to take some security that all the conditions of a settlement shall be observed. I can think of only three ways in which this might be effected, viz., Occupation, Disarmament, or Federation, and neither (*sic*) could be secured except as the result of a successful war.[85]

On 26 August, Chamberlain made a public speech in which he again tried the effect on Kruger's government of threats unaccompanied by force. As in June, the speech was made in Birmingham, this time at a political rally in the grounds of his home, Highbury; and again it sent shock waves to South Africa. That morning, *The Times* had taunted him with putting his hand to the plough and then doing nothing. Now, in a 'short clanging speech', Chamberlain said:

> Mr Kruger procrastinates in his replies. He dribbles out reforms like water from a squeezed sponge and either accompanies his offers with conditions which he knows to be impossible or he refuses to allow us to make a satisfactory investigation of the nature and the character of those reforms. . . . The issues of peace and war are in the hands of President Kruger. . . . Will he speak the necessary words? The sands are running down in the glass. . . . The knot must be loosened . . . or else we shall have to find other ways of untying it. . . . If we are forced to make further preparations, and if this delay continues much longer, we shall not hold ourselves limited by what we have already offered [but go on to secure conditions] which once for all shall establish which is the Paramount Power in South Africa.[86]

The abrupt nature of Smuts's refusal to alter or amplify the terms offered by the Transvaal government, on 25 August, was regarded by Chamberlain as 'most significant. I fear the S.A.R. Govt. mean trouble', he commented, before finalizing the wording of the British government's reply and sending it on 28 August.[87]

It is a striking fact that the British Cabinet never met to consider the Smuts proposals or to decide the British response to them. The formulation of British policy, at this critical juncture, and the drafting of the important British Note of 28 August, lay essentially in the hands of Chamberlain and the Colonial Office, although the Prime Minister saw and softened the wording of the Note before it was sent. It was August. The Cabinet, like Parliament, was dispersed for the holidays. Chamberlain communicated with Lansdowne and the Prime Minister (but they did not meet) and Hicks Beach only read the text of Chamberlain's Note of 28 August after it had been sent. When he complained to the Prime Minister about this lack of Cabinet consultation, Lord Salisbury conceded that the failure to call a Cabinet meeting had been 'a very grave mistake' and agreed that a Cabinet meeting would be held before any decision was taken on the Transvaal's reply to the British Note.

In this Note, the Transvaal government's concessions on the franchise were accepted, with the hope that they would 'not be hampered by any conditions which would impair their effect' and with the proviso that the British Agent should investigate whether they would, in practice, confer 'immediate and substantial representation' on the Uitlanders. It was also suggested that the Transvaal government should await the British findings (and any consequent British 'suggestions') before submitting a fresh franchise law to the burghers and the Volksraad for ratification. But the two express conditions demanded by the Transvaal government, in return for its franchise concessions, were answered 'in equivocal language which amounted to rejection'.[88] In effect, Britain refused to abandon her claims either to suzerainty or to her right to intervene in the Transvaal's affairs. She expressed the *hope* that the Transvaal government would fulfil the promises it had made and treat the Uitlanders justly and thus 'render unnecessary any further intervention on their behalf'; but the British government reasserted its rights 'under the Conventions' (Chamberlain had insisted on the plural, i.e. that of 1881 as well as 1884) and gave no guarantee with regard to non-intervention in Transvaal affairs in the future.[89] The principle of establishing an arbitration procedure was agreed, and it was suggested that the details of this should be discussed at the further conference between President Kruger and Milner which Britain had already proposed and now suggested might take place in Cape Town. The final sting was in the tail, where Kruger's government was 'reminded' that yet further unspecified issues remained 'which will not be settled by the grant of political representation to the Uitlanders, and which are not proper subjects for reference to arbitration', but which would have to be 'settled concurrently with the questions now under discussion'. These, along with the arbitration question, could be considered at the conference in Cape Town. Thus, it was clearly indicated that yet further concessions would be required from Kruger's government before a settlement could be reached. This un-compromising response from the British government was accompanied by an instruction from Chamberlain to Conyngham Greene that, on delivering it to the Transvaal State Secretary, he was to inform him that if the reply was not 'prompt and satisfactory, and if it becomes necessary to despatch further troops, H.M. Government will feel justified in withdrawing previous suggestions for compromise and will formulate their own demands for a settlement not only of the Uitlander question but also of future relations between Great Britain and the Transvaal State'.[90]

Kruger's government responded to this peremptory demand on 2 September by withdrawing the Smuts proposals – since the conditions on which they had been offered had been refused – and reverting to the previous offer of a seven years' retrospective franchise and four additional seats for the Witwatersrand in the Volksraad. It prevaricated on the question of a Commission to investigate the working of this franchise, by asking how the British government 'propose that Commission should be constituted'. It remained non-committal towards the suggestion for a further conference in Cape Town. It repeated its already-expressed view about the 'non-existence' of British suzerainty.[91] The Transvaal government had decided it could go no further. 'It remains our ardent wish to follow a road which will lead to an honourable solution for both parties', Smuts wrote to a Cape friend, two days later, but 'rather than accept a humiliating solution this nation will again take up arms with all the danger attaching to that'.[92]

MANOEUVRING FOR POSITION

Chamberlain later liked to claim that his Note of 28 August had amounted to 'a qualified acceptance' of the Smuts proposals whereas Kruger's government understood it as a clear rejection of them. The gulf separating the two governments is here starkly revealed. Neither at the time of the Bloemfontein Conference nor during Smuts's final attempt at a peaceful resolution of the conflict, had Chamberlain acknowledged that a *negotiated* settlement would require the British government to give something in return. Yet, on both occasions, Kruger's government had clearly indicated that what it was seeking was a complete settlement, and not just a resolution of the franchise issue, and that some reciprocation from Britain would be necessary to achieve this. Step by step, Kruger's government had been brought to concede even more on the franchise issue than had been demanded from it in June. (Milner had insisted on a five years' retrospective franchise and seven seats; ten seats were now offered.) In the meantime, the British government had become convinced that the franchise was quite inadequate as a means to the larger end of strengthening the British hold over the Transvaal government. The franchise remained a useful rallying point for British public opinion; and, having finally offered a five years' retrospective franchise, Kruger's government would not now be allowed to settle for less. But the establishment of British supremacy over the Transvaal had come to require a good deal more. The Smuts proposals had brought Britain's purposes out into the open – as may well have been their intention. If an Uitlander franchise was the real concern, Britain would accept the proposals; but if the assertion of British suzerainty and supremacy was her aim, she would reject them. Reitz was quite clear that, if they were rejected, there would then be only 'a slender chance for peace'.[93] The Uitlander franchise was something over which concessions could be made. But all those in South Africa who had urged Kruger's government to make those concessions now recognized that over the assertion of British supremacy and suzerainty there could be no compromise. On that issue, the Transvaal would fight.

The British proposal for a Joint Commission (to investigate the working of the new franchise law passed by the Transvaal Volksraad during July) had stimulated some preparatory work, by the Colonial Office and its representatives in South Africa, during late July and early August. This had revealed, as the Colonial Office staff noted, that 'nobody knows what the population of the S.A.R. is or the relative number of Uitlanders to burghers' since the official figures where quite untrustworthy.[94] Milner estimated that a properly worked five years' franchise, along the lines of the Smuts proposals, might result in the enfranchisement of 'at least 15,000 new citizens' and would require 'a system of periodic redistribution according to numbers' of the seats in the Volksraad for the Uitlander areas. But he now argued strongly that even if a satisfactory agreement was reached on the franchise, and the Uitlanders could 'be left to fight their own battles', this would not provide a settlement of all the questions at issue between the British and Transvaal governments.[95]

Meanwhile, Chamberlain and the Colonial Office staff had become convinced that *any* franchise reform would be subject to administrative subterfuges, 'electioneering dodges, gerry-mandering of constituencies, and manipulation of ballot boxes' etc. which would weaken its effects; and even with ten seats in the Volksraad, 'the Uitlander members will be consistently talked down and outvoted on every question of reform by a majority of 2:1'. Conyngham Greene believed that they would be 'utterly swamped in the Volksraad' and that what was really needed was Uitlander representation on the Executive Council.[96] Yet the British government was now in thrall to the 'Bloemfontein terms' established by Milner, as far as the franchise was concerned; and, as late as 7 October, Selborne believed that if Kruger had been prepared to make a straightforward offer of these, 'we could not have rejected them!'[97] What the British government now sought was an opportunity to move away from the narrow issue of the franchise towards the presentation of its full demands 'for a radical and final settlement . . .

in a form that will practically be an ultimatum'.[98] Before the unexpected diversion brought about by the Smuts proposals, a refusal by Kruger to engage in a Joint Inquiry into the July franchise law had been expected to provide the opportunity which the British government was seeking. Selborne had already started to compile a full list of British demands on 12 August and Chamberlain had minuted that he intended to add things on the principle of the Sibylline Books.[99] This is what Milner wanted. He believed that it was now necessary 'to bring things quickly to a head'.[100]

Throughout the whole episode of the Smuts proposals, Milner had consistently urged Chamberlain to stick to a 'strong position' and not accept proposals which might lead to 'tying our hands for the future and from being debarred from proceeding at once with the discussion of other matters which it is impossible to drop'.[101] The republics expected the negotiations to break down and were already arming in earnest, he commented, and meanwhile the poor state of British military preparedness was so alarming that 'if there is further parley, respite thus gained should be utilised to reinforce the [Cape] Colony as well as Natal'.[102] On 23 August, Milner emphasized that in his opinion the problem was 'now a purely military one'.

> We have got the S.A.R. to go as far as they will go without not merely the threat but the actual application of force. I do not say war, for there is always the probability that, with an Army actually on their borders, they will submit to anything and everything, including disarmament. But to mere display of force at a distance they will pay no further heed. The question therefore is simply whether Great Britain is prepared to make that great effort which will finally settle the South African question.

Writing 'quite privately and frankly' to Chamberlain, Milner explained why he would deplore 'the loss of this opportunity of consolidating our position here'. 'If things remain as they are', he argued, 'the stronger cards will remain with the Afrikanders'. With their numbers and fighting power, and the sympathy of Cape Afrikaners, British 'paramountcy' would become an idle phrase. Britain would keep her naval base at Simonstown, but otherwise, Afrikanerdom would predominate. Whereas, he had no doubts about the after-effects of a war resulting in a British victory. 'With the Transvaal under real popular government, either as a Republic or a British Colony, the scale in South Africa would definitely and forever incline on the British side', he commented. 'With the artificial weight in the scale against us removed, the natural forces would make that position more and more impregnable every year.'[103] To Selborne, Milner declared that British suzerainty and 'our *right* to put things straight in the Transvaal' were now 'impossible without a war; or at least the verge of war – an army in South Africa'.[104] In language which testifies to the strain he was under, Milner wrote at the end of August:

> Please realise the strain here is really near breaking point *all round*. This is not screaming. I am terrified to say this officially, because of my fear of seeming to *hurry* you. But really, really, oh! excellent friend and staunch supporter, we have now had nearly 3 months of Raging Crisis and it is not too much to ask that things should now be brought to a head . . .

Amongst the Uitlanders, Milner reported, insolvencies were numerous. Trade was at a stand-still. Many people were out of work. The publication of the Blue Book on 25 August and Chamberlain's Highbury speech the following day meant that many of them 'had made up their minds for war, calmly, realising what it meant. They would welcome war even now, because of their confidence in the *thereafter*. But what they will not face is months more of drag . . .'. This would lead to a break-away movement before long unless hopes and promises were replaced by '*the actual beginning of that strong action*' by the British government which they had been led to expect. The Smuts proposals, after all that had happened, were manifestly inadequate to secure a real settlement. 'Is it necessary that I should tell you I *hope* the Transvaal will reject our last offer?' he asked. *Mere menace* would no longer suffice. Whilst the British government shrank from the plunge of a military expedition, 'involving *certainly* much money, *probably* some fighting and *possibly* heavy fighting', Milner declared his 'own absolute conviction it is worth those millions to settle for ever, as you would, the South African question'.[105]

On 8 September, Selborne was finally able to tell Milner what he wanted to hear:

> 10,000 more troops to go to South Africa, half, roughly from India and half from home. This is the decision of the Cabinet, just over, and which you will hear tonight or tomorrow morning. Also a telegram which may justly be called a penultimatum goes to you for Kruger forthwith.[106]

By 24 August, Chamberlain had finally decided that British resolve needed to be demonstrated by sending the reinforcements of 10,000 men to South Africa which both Milner and Wolseley had long been advocating. He had recently received Milner's long letter of 2 August, which had anxiously enquired 'whether any course of military action has been decided on, in case things get worse' and arguing that '*all real preparation*, everything that makes us more able to meet an emergency, should it arise, does much more good than harm. Mere menace and talk are easily seen through, but people are keenly impressed by anything that means business'.[107] Active military preparations were now discussed with the War Office, with Chamberlain expressing the optimistic belief that the 10,000 reinforcements 'would enable us to hold our own everywhere' until an Army Corps was ready to be sent if necessary. He wanted it made public that an Army Corps was also being prepared and he was keen to draw the initial reinforcements from India and the Mediterranean rather than from Britain itself because this would be cheaper and did not require parliamentary sanction.[108] Chamberlain emphasized his conviction that there now had to be 'a complete solution' in South Africa because it would require 50,000 troops to enforce British demands on the Transvaal and a large garrison could not be kept there indefinitely 'at a great expense to the British taxpayer, and involving the utter disorganization of our military system'.[109]

The military now confronted the politicians with the gap that existed between what the politicians suddenly wanted and what the military could provide. On 5 September, General Buller suggested that before the government decided on an ultimatum, the military should be in a position to enforce it. He therefore urged that any ultimatum should be delayed until reinforcements had arrived in Natal.[110] Wolseley, too, feared that the Cabinet 'may bring matters to a crisis too soon'. He therefore asked Lansdowne: 'Can we not stave off actual hostilities for five or six weeks to enable us to collect in Natal the military force I have all along recommended should be sent there?' Once this was in place he, like Chamberlain, was confident that a Boer invasion could be held and was prepared to 'stake his reputation' on this.[111] Hopes that Kruger would still capitulate to British demands at the last minute, combined with a serious underestimation of the Boers as a fighting force, resulted in the leisurely pace at which an Army Corps was gradually mobilized during September. Only on 23 September was Wolseley finally authorized to spend the £640,000 required for its transport – something which he believed should have been done in July. Wolseley poured out his frustration to General Ardagh:

> We have lost two months through the absolute folly of our Cabinet & the incapacity of its members to take in the requirements & the difficulties of war. . . . It is no wonder we never achieve much in war & have to struggle through obstacles created by the folly & war ignorance of civilian ministers & War Office clerks.[112]

On 2 September, Chamberlain at last informed Milner that he had asked the Prime Minister to call a Cabinet meeting 'to arrange for an ultimatum'. The majority of people in Britain had now recognized, he believed,

> that there is a greater issue than the franchise or the grievances of the Uitlanders at stake, and that our supremacy in S. Africa and our existence as a great Power in the world are involved in the result of our present controversy. Three months ago we could not – that is to say we should not have been allowed to – go to war on this issue; now although still most unwillingly and with a large minority against us – we shall be sufficiently supported.

The game had to be played out '*selon les regles*'; the franchise proposals had to be exhausted before 'we ask for more'. 'If and when we ask for more it means war, and therefore, before we do this, we must have a sufficient force in S. Africa to defend ourselves during the time that will be required to get the full fighting forces into the country.' Parliamentary sanction would have to be obtained. All this meant some delay. Meanwhile, what would Milner suggest should be included, when the time came 'to put forward fresh demands and to obtain, at the price of war, a final settlement?' At present, Chamberlain admitted, 'the technical *casus belli* is a very weak one'. He therefore proceeded to give his own provisional list of 'possible demands . . . all to be embodied in a new Convention' but doubted 'whether it would be good policy to put all of them forward before the war . . .'. The list was fairly comprehensive:

1. Explicit recognition of Suzerainty.
2. Foreign affairs to be conducted through H.M.G.
3. Acceptance of Judicial Committee of Privy Council, with Transvaal Judge added, to deal with all future questions of interpretation.
4. Franchise, etc., as in Cape Colony.
5. Municipal rights for gold Mining Districts.
6. All legislation since 1884 restricting rights and privileges of Uitlanders to be repealed.
7. Disarmament.
8. Indemnity for expenses incurred since refusal of Franchise proposals.
9. Federation of S. African Colonies and States.[113]

Milner preferred to 'ask directly what we really want':

1. Absolute equality of political status for all resident whites.
2. Recognition of British paramountcy, including not only control of foreign relations but ultimate right of interference even in internal affairs, when welfare of S. Africa is affected.

3. Disarmament measures, including dismantling of forts at Johannesburg and Pretoria, restriction on number of men and guns – these not to be increased without British permission.[114]

Milner urged that the situation now justified a move by the British government from the franchise issue 'to take up at once broader ground'. He feared that 'if there is a climb down, it will almost exceed the wit of man to prevent their cheating us' as 'the Pretoria gang' would remain in control of the Transvaal government for some time to come.[115] Both Milner and Chamberlain agreed that an ultimatum should be accompanied by the despatch of sufficient troops to secure the Cape Colony and Natal, although the main expeditionary force could follow later.

On 8 September, the Cabinet finally met. It had before it the reply of Kruger's government to Chamberlain's Note of 28 August, Milner's reports of the rapidly deteriorating situation amongst the Uitlanders, and two memoranda from Chamberlain arguing for the despatch of the 10,000 reinforcements. Reporting to Milner later in the day on this Cabinet meeting, Chamberlain said that its conclusions were 'arrived at after a satisfactory discussion which disclosed no difference of opinion on any important point'.[116] The decision was taken to send the 10,000 troops. It was also decided not to send an ultimatum yet but to give Kruger's government one last chance to back down. Some, perhaps even a majority of the Cabinet, still believed that he would do so – that he would 'bluff up to the cannon's mouth and then capitulate'. They hoped that war could be avoided. Others, including the Prime Minister and the Chancellor of the Exchequer, doubted this. Salisbury believed that war was likely but was determined to go at his own pace. The Cabinet was united in its policy of delaying things, if possible, until the reinforcements had arrived in South Africa. The military reasons for the diplomatic delaying tactics during the following weeks have to be constantly borne in mind.

The appearance of unity in the Cabinet veiled, but did not hide, criticism of the way Chamberlain had acted and Milner had brought his influence to bear. The Prime Minister, Balfour and Hicks Beach were acutely aware that the Cabinet's room for manoeuvre had been restricted by Chamberlain's recent actions – including the Note of 28 August. As in May and July, Balfour was critical of Chamberlain's provocative manner when dealing with Kruger's government; he felt that comparing President Kruger to a 'squeezed sponge' was not the language of diplomacy. He remained convinced, however, that Kruger would capitulate once troops were sent and therefore supported their despatch.[117] The Prime Minister had been asked by Chamberlain, on 2

September, 'whether our terms are at once to be raised, or whether we are in the first instance to confine our ultimatum to the franchise question?'[118] Now, Salisbury pointed out that he had never referred to the Sibylline Books in his speech in the House of Lords on 28 July and that he had never said anything in favour of increasing British demands so long as peace remained. He could see no advantage in doing this. It would not strengthen the British position 'and it would widely extend the impression of our bad faith, which, unfortunately, and most unjustly, prevails in many quarters abroad'. He was also against mixing up negotiations about arbitration and other questions – which 'are not specified, as the Boers justly complain' – with that of the franchise; this simply created distrust, in the present 'fever heat of opinion'.[119] Hicks Beach supported him, observing that the way in which the Colonial Office had increased the British demands in response to the Smuts proposals 'must surely tend to make the Boers think that their concessions – which, if honest, are an advance on Milner's own proposals at Bloemfontein – are useless, as their only effect is to make us ask for more'.[120]

Not for the first time, Salisbury was also critical of Milner's attitude and influence. After reading his letter of 2 August, he wrote to Lansdowne:

> Milner's letter suggests many reflections – but they may wait. His view is too heated, if you consider the intrinsic significance and importance of the things which are in controversy. But it recks little to think of that now. What he has done cannot be effaced. We have to act upon a moral field prepared for us by him and his jingo supporters. And therefore I see before us the necessity for considerable military effort – and all for people whom we despise, and for territory which will bring no profit and no power to England.[121]

Salisbury despised the Uitlanders and felt that Milner's recent letters revealed too much *'animus'* against Kruger's government.[122] British supremacy had to be upheld, but Salisbury showed no enthusiasm for a war which was likely to result in the British annexation of the Transvaal. Hicks Beach had already written to the Prime Minister expressing the hope that 'Milner & the Uitlanders will not be allowed to drag us into War'.[123] He thought that Milner 'had thrown himself blindly into the hands of the so-called "British" party in South Africa' and, despite being repeatedly instructed to proceed with patience, was in fact adding fuel to the flames. He regretted that Milner had ever been sent out to South Africa, as he had 'out-Chamberlained Chamberlain . . . [and] was not the man for the job'.[124] Hicks Beach had been a member of the British Cabinet at the time of the Transvaal

War in 1880–81 and, by August 1899, he again thought that war was likely. 'Does not this remind you of all that happened with Bartle Frere?' he asked Salisbury.[125] In advance of the Cabinet meeting, his Treasury staff had calculated that the £500,000 involved in the despatch of the 10,000 troops could easily be paid for out of surplus revenue; the fact that 5,700 of these troops were to be drawn from India made them both cheaper and more likely to arrive in Natal sooner than would have been the case if they had come from Britain.[126] Hicks Beach was relieved that the Cabinet was not yet calling for really large-scale expenditure on military preparations and therefore he made no difficulties with the War Office, where Lansdowne too was reluctant to proceed with anything but extreme caution for fear of jeopardizing a final chance for a peaceful settlement by overt preparations for a war.[127]

Chamberlain had prepared for the Cabinet meeting a draft despatch to be sent to Kruger's government and two memoranda for his colleagues. In the first memorandum (dated 5 September), Chamberlain stated that, after three months of negotiating in an attempt to reach 'an amicable settlement', the time had now come 'to bring matters to a head' and formulate demands for a final settlement. This should be accompanied by the despatch of troops.[128] In a lengthy second memorandum (dated 6 September), Chamberlain argued that what the Cabinet had to deal with was no longer the franchise question and other particular grievances but 'the general situation which has been created by the policy uniformly pursued by the South African Republic since 1881 and directed against any assertion of supremacy' by the British government and 'any claim to equality for British subjects'. What was now at stake, he claimed, was 'the position of Great Britain in South Africa – and with it the estimate formed of our power and influence in our Colonies and throughout the world. . . . The Dutch in South Africa', Chamberlain declared, 'desire, if it be possible, to get rid altogether of the connection with Great Britain, which to them is not a motherland, and to substitute a United States of South Africa which, they hope, would be mainly under Dutch influence'. The example of the Transvaal 'flouting, and flouting successfully, British control and interference' was affecting all South Africa. 'The contest for supremacy is between the Dutch and the English', he asserted. 'Everyone . . . sees that issue has been joined, and that it depends upon the action of the British government now whether the supremacy, which we have claimed so long and so seldom exerted, is to be finally established and recognized or forever abandoned'. This, he concluded, was 'the real question at stake. It has been simmering for years, and has now been brought to boiling point'.[129]

This important memorandum was written under the influence of a series of telegrams from Milner in which he urged a move towards a stand on the 'broad ground' and away from the franchise issue, because of the 'old difficulty of basing ultimatum on differences of detail on franchise only'. Milner argued that 'we should still keep admission of Uitlanders to citizenship in foreground of programme, but no longer be bound by Bloemfontein proposals . . . which, by themselves, are inadequate if rammed down throat of reluctant government able and evidently determined to prevent their working the gradual and peaceful revolution which I contemplated'.[130] Milner also played on British fears of a United States of South Africa under Afrikaner domination by emphasizing that 'if the Transvaal were to disappear from the map as an independent State or if it were to become an Uitlander Republic, the "Afrikander Nation" idea would be for ever doomed'.[131] In a final telegram on 7 September, which arrived before the Cabinet meeting on the following day, Milner ventured 'to sum up' and argued that the time had come for the British government to take up the broader ground and to 'quicken the pace', whereas the interest of Kruger's government was 'to confuse the issue and cause delay'. The next British communication therefore 'should be one rendering a direct answer necessary and precluding further quibbling and chaffering'.[132]

The draft despatch which Chamberlain had prepared to send to the Transvaal government was subjected to amendments by the Cabinet which meant that the result fell short of an ultimatum. In effect, it clarified but did not go much beyond what had been demanded on 28 August. It included, however, an unequivocal assertion of British supremacy. The British government, it pointed out, 'have absolutely repudiated' the Transvaal's claim to be 'a Sovereign International State', and would be 'unable to consider any proposal' which was made conditional on this view. This is what had made the Smuts proposals unacceptable. Britain was not now prepared to revert to earlier franchise proposals since, by presenting the Smuts proposals, Kruger's government 'have themselves recognized that their previous offer might be with advantage enlarged, and that the independence of the South African Republic would be thereby in no way impaired'. The British government would only be prepared to consider the Smuts proposals 'taken by themselves' – without conditions and subject to a Joint Inquiry – and still insisted on a further conference to consider other questions 'which are neither Uitlander grievances nor questions of interpretation'. If the Transvaal government's response was 'negative or inconclusive', the British government reserved 'the right to reconsider the situation *de novo*, and to formulate their own proposals for a final settlement'.[133] Selborne rightly described this as a 'penultimatum'. It interposed a 'last chance' at a negotiated settlement, on very clear terms, which some believed would call Kruger's bluff. Accompanied by the despatch of 10,000 troops and the announcement that a major expeditionary force was being prepared, it sent the unmistakable signal that the day of reckoning had finally arrived. It also bought the British government a little more time – not only for military purposes but also to grapple with what both Chamberlain and the Prime Minister recognized was an awkward task: the formulation of an ultimatum in which a public transition would have to be made from the franchise issue to the 'wider considerations' at stake in this South African conflict.

The despatch of 10,000 troops, with the clear warning of more to follow, caused intense excitement in South Africa. Far from precipitating a capitulation by Kruger's government to Britain's latest demands, however, it had the opposite effect. The Transvaal government knew that it faced an ultimatum and a resort to war but there is no evidence that it now hesitated in its determination to give way no further. On 31 August, Smuts wrote that 'the only thing that can bring an end to the situation is a definite answer that will show the British Government that we will not go further upon being threatened. They must then make peace or war'.[134] The diplomatic exchanges continued to run their course. Meanwhile, both sides prepared for war.

On 4 September, Smuts had sat down and drafted his plan of campaign. He began by observing:

> The relations between the South African Republic and England become day by day more strained; if at Bloemfontein last June there still was hope of a peaceful and, for both parties honourable solution, the last few months have taught that that hope is idle; that the enemy is quite determined that this country will either be conquered or be reduced by diplomatic means virtually to the position of a British colony. . . . All approaches from our side have been arrogantly rejected; our last proposal of a five-year franchise and a quarter representation for the Goldfields, under conditions which would make it an honourable solution for both parties, has also been refused – in spite of the fact that the British Government knew well that, by this refusal, she would weaken her own position before the world and also before her own public. . . . I come to the conclusion that our acceptance of a Joint Inquiry will only postpone, and in no way prevent, the end; humanly speaking a war between the Republics and England is certain.[135]

Smuts then went on to argue and outline the case for the Boers to take the offensive and invade Natal and the Cape Colony before the British troops arrived. He had no doubts that 'a long and bloody war' was now inevitable 'out of which our people will come, either as an exhausted remnant, hewers of wood and drawers of water for a hated race, or as victors, founders of a United South Africa . . . we should, within a few years, perhaps within one year, found an Afrikaner republic in South Africa stretching from Table Bay to the Zambesi'.[136]

The Transvaal government now replied to the latest British demands in a manner which indicated that the end of the road had been reached. It accused the British government of bad faith and Conyngham Greene of 'inducing' the Smuts proposals by suggesting that they (and their conditions) would be acceptable. It asserted that without the conditions, the five-year franchise proposal would never have been made and could not now be made. It also refused to agree to the right of elected members to use English in the Volksraad. The demand for a further conference was dismissed as 'premature' since it had not been made clear what were the precise questions to be discussed there. The readiness of the British government to establish a court of arbitration was welcomed. Finally, the hope was expressed that the British government 'would abandon the idea of making new proposals . . . and imposing new conditions' and would return to its own proposal for a Joint Commission to investigate the details of the already established seven-year franchise embodied in the law of July. This reply amounted to 'a solid negative thickly wrapped in woolly words'.[137] Its one striking feature – a declared readiness to accept, after all, a Joint Inquiry – was fatally compromised by being limited to the franchise law which the British government had already dismissed as inadequate.

With the arrival of this reply, on 17 September, the British government finally faced the fact that war was likely. In a conversation with Baron von Eckardstein of the German embassy, Chamberlain said that war was now unavoidable.[138] Salisbury wrote 'that we must prepare for war as the most probable alternative but . . . we should do nothing to precipitate an attack until our reinforcements arrive: which may be five weeks hence'.[139] The mobilization of an Army Corps at last went ahead, despite apprehensions that this might precipitate a Boer attack on Natal before the 10,000 reinforcements arrived. This had long been an acute concern of Milner's, although the Governor of Natal, Hely Hutchinson, did not believe – as late as 29 September – that the Boers 'would be so crack-brained as to strike the first blow at us'.[140] Hicks Beach rather hoped that they would. At one stroke, this would solve all the difficulties the British government faced in formulating an ultimatum and explaining to the British public why Britain was at war. Chamberlain remained remarkably optimistic to the end regarding a Boer pre-emptive strike at Natal. As late as 7 October, he declared:

> My own opinion is, as it has always been, that both Milner and the
> military authorities greatly exaggerate the risks and dangers of this
> campaign. I have never believed that the Boers would take the offensive
> at this stage – nor do I fear a British reverse if they do. . . . When all
> the reinforcements are landed, my own feeling is that we shall be quite a
> match for the Boers even without the army corps.[141]

At a Cabinet meeting on 22 September, the British government decided to play for time by sending an 'interim despatch' which stated that the refusal of Kruger's government to accept the terms outlined on 8 September made further discussion along those lines useless and the British government would now consider the situation afresh and formulate their own proposals for a final settlement.[142] This presaged an ultimatum which then failed to arrive.

THE ULTIMATUMS

'Cabinet unanimous and resolved to see matter through', Chamberlain assured Milner on 22 September. All the preparations for the expeditionary force would now proceed as quickly as possible. The Cabinet would meet again on 29 September to finalize the terms of an ultimatum and, if this were sent by sea mail, this would 'allow four weeks' interval for reinforcements which are now on the way to arrive'.[143] The troops from India were expected to reach South Africa during the second week of October.

Milner had abandoned any hopes he may once have had that Kruger would capitulate at the eleventh hour. He was now certain not only that war was coming but that the Orange Free State would side with the Transvaal and that the most pressing problem was 'how to get over the next 3 weeks, if, as now seems most probable, the Republics decide to have a dash at us'.[144] After protracted difficulties with Schreiner and the Cape government over measures for the defence of Mafeking and Kimberley, and much ill-feeling over a consignment of arms and ammunition which was allowed to proceed to the Orange Free State, Milner wanted assurance that Portugal would be prevented from supplying the Transvaal via Delagoa Bay. Salisbury (as Foreign Secretary as well as Prime Minister) had been working to ensure this since July and eventually succeeded by a secret Anglo–Portuguese treaty of 14 October.[145]

Whilst the British government wrestled with the awkward task of formulating an ultimatum, Milner came increasingly to believe that it might never be necessary to present it. Already, on 26 September, he felt that 'everything points to likelihood that the Boers will anticipate ultimatum by some action or declaration. . . . This being so, consideration of ultimatum becomes unnecessary'.[146] On 29 September, he commented:

> Personally I am still of opinion not to hurry in settling ultimatum, as events of next few days may supply us with a better one than anybody can compose. Ultimatum has always been great difficulty, as unless we widen issue, there is not sufficient cause for war, and if we do so, we are abused for shifting our ground and extending our demands.[147]

When the Cabinet pressed ahead with settling the terms for an ultimatum, Milner hoped that these would be kept secret for the present 'and will, if Boers commence hostilities, be witheld altogether. It will be great moral advantage to us, especially here, that conflict should be brought about by attack on us without the excuse which the ultimatum would give them'.[148] Chamberlain doubted whether the Boers really would take the offensive but was well aware of the immense political advantage to Britain if they did so; even those most sympathetic to the Boer cause in the Liberal Party, he commented, 'would not expect us to go on negotiating after an actual invasion of our territories'.[149] To Hicks Beach, he observed that if the Boers took the offensive, 'The Lord will have delivered them into our hands – at least so far as diplomacy is concerned'.[150]

When it came to deciding the terms of an ultimatum, the British government found itself in some difficulty. The Prime Minister stated:

> I want to get away from the franchise issue, which will be troublesome in debate – & to make the break on a proposal to revise or denounce the Convention of 1884 on the grounds that it has not been carried out as we were promised: and because it has been worked to benefit not the people of the Transvaal . . . but a very limited minority of them who are hostile to the rest. A proposal to revise it would, of course, be refused by the Boers; and it might then be formally denounced.[151]

Salisbury was here developing further what he had said in his speech on 28 July about the Conventions governing relations between Britain and the Transvaal being 'mortal' and not 'an immovable landmark'; and that if Britain had 'to make exertions' on behalf of the Uitlanders, she would not afterwards 'reinstate a state of things which will bring back the old difficulties'.[152] The Conventions of Pretoria and London had been made at a time when British supremacy in South Africa, and Transvaal weakness and subservience, were taken for granted. They had not been designed for the situation brought about as a result of the development of gold-mining on the Rand, and they had proved weak reeds when used by the British government in an attempt to maintain its precarious hold over the Transvaal government. What the British government wanted was to replace them by a new Convention which would clearly establish British supremacy over the Transvaal and buttress this by equality of rights for all Europeans within this state, as was already the case elsewhere in South Africa. Since the majority of the European population was already (though incorrectly) believed to be British, and was expected to become so by an increasing margin, this would secure British predominance. Of course, Kruger's government was not expected to accept such a proposal. Its refusal would therefore prompt a resort to war. But that war was expected to be short (over by Christmas), to cost about £10 million, and to result in a British victory. Britain could not demand the annexation of the Transvaal in an ultimatum; but that would be the result if Kruger's government declared war. If a British ultimatum were to be delivered, however, the British government would be bound by its terms, to a considerable extent, when peace came. The best of all possible worlds, from a British point of view, would be if Kruger's government issued an ultimatum first and then invaded Natal and the Cape Colony. This would not only enable the British government to suppress its own ultimatum (the terms of which would be kept strictly secret) but also to reap the immense political advantage, with British and world opinion, of being the party attacked.

On 29 September, at what turned out to be the last Cabinet meeting before the outbreak of war, the British government decided to press ahead with preparations for mobilizing the Army Corps, call out the Reserves on 7 October, and recall Parliament for 17 October. It also decided to delay any decision about delivering an ultimatum until the reinforcements already on their way had arrived in South Africa. A draft of the proposed terms of this ultimatum was discussed at this Cabinet meeting but its final form only emerged during the first week of October as it was pruned and amended in the light of ministerial comments. Although it was never delivered, it merits consideration since it followed the line suggested by the Prime

Minister. In summarizing the history of the relations between the two governments since 1881, it argued that Kruger's government had repeatedly failed to observe the conditions of the Conventions of Pretoria and London, broken its promises, discriminated against the Uitlander population, and sought 'to oust Her Majesty from the supremacy reserved to her' by those Conventions. It had also vastly increased its armaments 'for the purpose of strengthening the Republic against the Paramount State', and adopted a general policy 'which appears to have been mainly directed to get rid of the obligations by which their position as an independent State has been restricted'. In the light of this, the British government now proposed a new Convention, containing seven provisions:

1. The repeal of all legislation since 1881 which discriminated against the rights of Uitlanders. (In 1881, Uitlanders could obtain equal rights of citizenship after one year's residence.) A redistribution measure 'in some reasonable proportion to population' amongst the European population (although the 'general principle of equality' could be modified to prevent an immediate swamping of the old burghers by the new). The Uitlanders were to be allowed to use their own language in the legislature and the law courts.

2. Full municipal rights for the mining districts.

3. Guarantees for the independence of the Courts of Justice.

4. The removal of religious disabilities affecting non-Protestants.

5. A Tribunal of Arbitration excluding any foreign element.

6. The concession of most-favoured nation rights to Britain, not only in commercial matters, but in all matters affecting British interests or the position of British subjects, whether white or coloured.

7. The provisions of the Treaty with Portugal allowing the passage of arms through Portuguese territory to be surrendered, and an agreement to be arrived at with the British government for the reduction of the excessive armaments of the South African Republic.

If these conditions were agreed to, the British government was 'still prepared to give a guarantee against any attack upon the independence of the South African Republic, either from within any part of the British dominions or from the territory of a foreign State'. If Kruger's government refused, then the British government would 'take such other steps as may seem to be necessary to secure their objects'.[153]

Ministerial comments on this ultimatum are revealing. All agreed that a transition had to be made from a concentration on the franchise issue to the wider considerations. 'The object is to put our case before

375

the world, as well as before the Transvaal', Goschen commented, and 'to make what has been in our minds as our general policy, square with the past'. He feared, however, that the admission 'that the real issue is different and far wider than the points on which we have been negotiating, will lead to the exclamation from sceptical Europe etc. "We knew it! We said so! The British Government have meant all along much more than they confessed to!" The whole difficulty of the despatch is to make the *transition* as natural and as little open to attack as possible'.[154] Hicks Beach thought that 'the fewer our demands are in number, the fewer are the points on which we shall be open to attack'. The Boers had themselves admitted the inadequacy of the franchise law, by proposing a better one, and the strong point to emphasize was the establishment in the Transvaal of a political settlement 'with the equality of the white races as its basis'. If this principle was established, 'even the present independence of the Transvaal would do no real harm in practice', he commented, before adding: 'I see no reason for proposing anything now which would be taken as a revocation of independence. We can never govern from Downing Street any part of South Africa in which the whites are strong enough to defend themselves against the natives: so that equality of white races in the Transvaal would really secure all we can desire, viz. British predominance.'[155]

In a reply to Hicks Beach, Chamberlain agreed 'that we should ask as few things as possible, but they must cover a real settlement'. In a telling comment, he added: 'I agree we do not want in any case to make ourselves responsible for the Government of the Transvaal. It must be a Republic or a self-governing Colony – under the British flag in either case.'[156] What Chamberlain feared during these last days of peace was what Milner had feared for so long. In words which could have been Milner's, Chamberlain wrote:

> What I fear is some suggestion of compromise from them which will be totally inadequate to provide a permanent settlement but will nevertheless strengthen the hands of the Opposition at home and make many foolish people inclined to give more time and to patch up some sort of hollow agreement. Matters have come to such a pitch that unless there is a complete surrender on the part of the Boers, either as the result of agreement or of war, we shall never again be able to put forward any demands for redress of any grievances however great. The people of England will not provide an armament of fifty or sixty thousand men at an expense of five or more millions every time the Boers pass a Bill that we do not like, or extort money from the Uitlanders. Even outrages on British subjects, unless very serious, will not be redressed at such a cost.[157]

He was therefore apprehensive about the exchanges which Milner was having by letter with President Steyn of the Orange Free State. So were Hicks Beach and Selborne. Hicks Beach considered that it was 'essential now that the matter should be brought to a head as soon as possible', whilst Selborne wrote that 'the evil of becoming again entangled in endless negotiations' made him 'feel nervous whether we should ever . . . get to the war point again'.[158]

The Orange Free State had moved to support the stand taken up by its sister republic during the last week of September. In a speech on 21 September, at the beginning of a week of intense debate behind the closed doors of its Volksraad, President Steyn had declared that he and Abraham Fischer had 'used all possible influence with Pretoria' since the Bloemfontein Conference, urging the Transvaal government to 'concede as much as possible without damaging her independence'. This, Steyn argued, Kruger's government had done – despite the fact that 'every concession . . . was received by the other side with fresh demands' – until, in the end, Pretoria 'was required to make concessions which were unreasonable' and which Abraham Fischer described as 'palpably dishonest and insulting'.[159] Together with his Executive Council, President Steyn had decided that he could not advise Kruger's government to accept the latest British demands. Nothing had happened, in their view, to warrant a war – which would be 'a sin against mankind' – but if the Transvaal were attacked, the Orange Free State would be 'bound by everything that is near and dear' as well as by treaty to assist her.[160] A resolution to this effect was passed by the Bloemfontein Volksraad on 27 September. President Steyn also wrote directly to Milner appealing to him to withdraw British troops from the border areas and hold back the reinforcements which were about to arrive in South Africa.[161] Milner then engaged in a series of exchanges with Steyn, encouraging him to make proposals for a peaceful settlement and declaring that 'till the threatened act of aggression is committed, I shall not despair of peace'. His real purpose, however, as Chamberlain reassured Balfour, was to 'engage President Steyn in some sort of correspondence which may be drawn out till the reinforcements arrive'.[162] If the Orange Free State had declared its neutrality in the event of war, this would have obstructed the use of the railway through its territory for a British advance on the Transvaal. The Volksraad resolution now removed this difficulty. Balfour was greatly relieved, since he considered the Orange Free State as 'our "Achilles heel". The charge against us by our critics will be that we cannot tolerate the independence within our sphere of influence of free republics'. Chamberlain assured him that, if the government of the Orange Free State did not first take the offensive, Britain would 'send a definite summons to the O.F.S. once and for all to declare itself'.[163]

Meanwhile, the Transvaal's friends in the Cape Colony – led by Hofmeyr and Sir Henry de Villiers – continued in their efforts to persuade Kruger's government to make further concessions, on the franchise and a Joint Inquiry, to avoid war. In a message to Hofmeyr on 16 September, President Kruger finally registered the parting of the ways. 'Although we fully acknowledge and appreciate your good intentions', he wrote,

> we however regret that it is no longer possible for us to further accede to extravagant and impudent demands of British Government. . . . We are determined not to go any further than we have latterly done, and we are convinced that we cannot accept Secretary [of] State [for] Colonies' proposals regarding franchise after 5 years residence, now that all assurance for our independence embodied in our proposals has been taken away. . . . We are fully impressed with the very serious position in which we are placed, but with God before our eyes we cannot go further without endangering, if not totally destroying, our independence. The Government, Parliament and people are unanimous on this point.[164]

On 21 September, Schreiner and the Cape ministry appealed to the British government to approach Kruger's government in a 'spirit of magnanimous compromise' and, when this resulted in an unyielding reply, they petitioned the Queen. But the Cape parliament was divided and a counter-petition, signed by Sprigg and almost as many members, criticized the attempts which were being made to encourage Kruger's government 'to continue their resistance to the just demands of Her Majesty's Government'.[165] The fact was that the Cape conciliators – horrified at the prospect of being at war with their republican kinsfolk – continued to urge Kruger's government to give ground, on the mistaken assumption that yet further concessions on the franchise issue would avert war. When war broke out, Schreiner considered but decided against resignation and carried on with his declared policy: to keep the Cape Colony out of the war as far as possible, and the war out of the Cape Colony; and at all costs to try to prevent a wholesale Afrikaner uprising there.[166]

With the despatch of the 10,000 British troops to South Africa, and the clear indication of more to come, Kruger's government prepared for war. Until the British reinforcements arrived, the combined forces of the two republics would outnumber the British forces in South Africa by 4:1. The plan of campaign, sketched by Smuts on 4

September, depended on making the most of this brief initial time of maximum advantage by an offensive campaign. On 27 September, Kruger telegraphed to Steyn: 'Executive unanimous that commando order should be issued today. We beg you will also call out your burghers. As war is unavoidable we must act at once and strongly.'[167] Steyn hesitated whilst, without waiting for their allies, the Transvaal mobilized its commandos on the following day. On 29 September, Kruger again telegraphed: 'You still seem to think of peace but I consider it impossible. I am strongly of opinion that your burghers ought also to go to border to take positions. You think Chamberlain is leading us into a trap but if we wait longer our cause may be hopelessly lost and that would be our trap.'[168] Steyn still wanted to delay but finally, on 2 October, he gave in. The commandos of the Orange Free State were mobilized and Steyn stated, to those who advocated that his republic should declare its neutrality: 'I prefer to lose the independence of the Orange Free State honourably, rather than keep it in dishonour and disloyalty.'[169] Abraham Fischer had already written to Hofmeyr:

> Every reasonable concession has been granted and the British
> Government's requests complied with, and the only result of every
> concession has been trickery and increased demands. Further compliance
> would, I feel sure, only be an inducement for, and lead to further
> dishonourable and insulting treatment of the South African Republic. . . .
> We have honestly done our best, and can do no more: if we are to lose
> our independence – since that is palpably what is demanded – leave us, at
> all events, the consolation that we did not sacrifice it dishonourably.[170]

On 2 October, President Kruger told the Transvaal Volksraads, sitting together, that war was inevitable. By a *besluit* (resolution) of 29 September, all foreigners serving with the Boer commandos had been granted full burgher rights immediately. The Volksraads now adjourned *sine die*; President Steyn called out his commandos. On 30 September, Reitz had sent a message requesting to be informed by 2 October 'what decision, if any, had been taken by the British Cabinet'. 'This means that Boers, being ready to attack Natal, want to get our ultimatum out of us in order to reject it and go to war at once', observed Milner, and urged delay.[171] Accordingly, on 1 October, Conyngham Greene delivered a brief statement from the British government that its impending despatch was not yet ready.[172] Meanwhile, Reitz, who was a keen admirer of R. L. Stevenson's *Treasure Island*, had told L. S. Amery (*The Times* correspondent who had recently arrived in Pretoria) that Kruger's government was ready to tip 'the black spot to Long John Conyngham Greene'.[173] The two republics had finalized their joint ultimatum at the end of September. Due to Steyn's hesitation and the disorganized state of military transport and supplies for the commandos assembling on the Natal border, over a week elapsed before it was finally delivered to the British Agent in Pretoria at 5 p.m. on 9 October. During this time, the majority of the British reinforcements from India arrived at Durban and were hurried forward towards the border between Natal and the Transvaal.

The terms of the Boer ultimatum were quite uncompromising. At Steyn's insistence, what had begun as a short document had become much longer, but its terms were the same. The British government was required to give the Transvaal government assurances on four crucial points:

1. To agree to arbitration on 'all points of difference'.
2. British troops on the borders of the republic were to be instantly withdrawn.
3. All British reinforcements which had arrived since 1 June were to be withdrawn from South Africa.
4. All British troops 'which are now on the high seas shall not be landed in any port of South Africa'.

Unless the British government complied with these demands within 48 hours, the Transvaal would 'with great regret be compelled to regard the action as a formal declaration of war'.[174]

Chamberlain had minuted on 9 October his intention to telegraph the terms of the British ultimatum to South Africa on 11 October so that it could be delivered and then printed in a Blue Book being prepared for the re-assembly of Parliament on 17 October. He had also wondered if the Boers could be provoked into initiating hostilities by a massing of the recently arrived British reinforcements at Laing's Nek, on the Natal border.[175] At 6.15 a.m. on the morning of 10 October, however, he was awakened to read the ultimatum just received from Kruger's government. 'They have done it!' he exclaimed. By their joint declaration of war, the two republics removed the necessity for the British government to issue its ultimatum and handed it the political advantage. 'Accept my felicitations', Lansdowne wrote to Chamberlain, 'I don't think Kruger could have played your cards better than he has . . .'.[176] That evening, the British government replied, curtly stating that the conditions demanded by the Transvaal government were 'impossible to discuss'. On 11 October, President Steyn declared the support of the Orange Free State for 'our kith and kin' in the Transvaal, 'being well aware that when their independence ceases, our own existence as an independent nation will be meaningless, and that their fate, if they have to bow beneath an overwhelming Power, will also overtake us at no distant date'.[177] In the Transvaal, F. W. Reitz issued a manifesto appealing to 'all Afrikanders' to stand shoulder to shoulder and fight for 'a Free, United South Africa'.[178] President Kruger, who had celebrated his 74th birthday on 10 October, declared, in a statement to the *New York Herald*, that 'the Republics are determined, if they must belong to England, that a price will have to be paid which will stagger humanity'.[179] Late in the afternoon of 11 October, the first Boer commandos crossed the border into Natal and they were followed by others the following day. Amongst them was Deneys Reitz, the son of the Transvaal's State Secretary. 'There was not a man who did not believe that we were heading straight for the coast', he wrote, 'and it was as well that the future was hidden from us, and that we did not know how our strength and enthusiasm were to be frittered away in a meaningless siege, and in the holding of useless positions, when our salvation lay in rapid advance'.[180]

'War dates from today, I suppose', Milner wrote to his 'great stand by', Selborne, on 10 October:

> We have a bad time before us, and the Empire is about to support the greatest strain put upon it since the [Indian] Mutiny. Who can say, what may befall us before that Army Corps arrives? But we are all working in good heart, and having so long foreseen the possibility of this Armageddon, we mean to do our best in it, though it begins rather unfortunately for us. After all have not the great struggles of England mostly so begun?[181]

NOTES

1. *Royal Commission on the War in South Africa* (*RCWSA*), Cd. 1789–1791 (1903). For recent work, to which I am much indebted, see Thomas Pakenham, *The Boer War* (London, 1979), chs 7–8; W. Hamer, *The British Army and Civil–Military Relations 1885–1905* (Oxford, 1970); M. Yakutiel, 'Treasury control and the South African War 1899–1905', Oxford D.Phil. thesis, 1989; K. T. Surridge, 'British civil–military relations and the South African War 1899–1902', London Ph.D. thesis, 1994.

2. Milner to Selborne, 20 April 1897, in Headlam ed., *The Milner Papers* 2 vols (London, 1931/1933), 1, pp. 40–1.

3. Milner to Selborne, 24 May 1899, in D. G. Boyce, ed., *The Crisis of British Power: the Imperial and Naval Papers of the Second Earl of Selborne, 1895–1910* (London, 1990), pp. 81–2.

4. *RCWSA*, Cd. 1789, para. 22189.

5. *RCWSA*, evidence of Lord Wolseley; Pakenham, *The Boer War*, p. 77, citing unpublished secret 'Military Notes on the Dutch Republics', 1899, in the War Office Archives.

6. See Yakutiel, 'Treasury control'.

7. Hamer, *The British Army*, p. 218.

8. Yakutiel, 'Treasury control', ch. 1, p. 9.

9. A. G. Gardiner, *Life of Sir William Harcourt* 2 vols (London, 1923), 2, p. 498.

10. Pakenham, *The Boer War*, p. 72.

11. Sir Edward Hamilton, Diary, 20 June 1899.

12. Lansdowne Minute, 12 July 1899, WO 32/7847/8698, in Yakutiel, 'Treasury control', pp. 11–12.

13. Memoranda by Major Altham, 3 June and 8 August 1899, in Surridge, 'British civil–military relations', p. 70.

14. Wolseley memorandum of 8 June 1899, CAB 37/50/38, in ibid., p. 55.

15. Memorandum by Buller, 6 July, and comments by Wolseley, 7 July 1899, CAB 37/50/43; Surridge, 'British civil–military relations', p. 57.

16. Milner to Chamberlain, 16 July 1899, in Headlam ed., *The Milner Papers*, 1, p. 511.

17. Milner to Chamberlain, 25 June 1899, JC 10/9/37; Chamberlain's reply of same date, JC 10/9/36.

18. *The Cape Times*, 6 July 1899.

19. Milner to Selborne, 28 June 1899, in Boyce, ed., *Crisis of British Power*, p. 87.

20. Milner to Chamberlain, 2 and 9 August 1899, JC 10/9/44.

21. Sir William Butler, *Autobiography* (London, 1911), ch. 23.

22. Pakenham, *The Boer War*, pp. 96–9.

23. Milner to Chamberlain, 30 July 1899, in Headlam, ed., *The Milner Papers*, 1, p. 512.

24. Surridge, 'British civil–military relations', pp. 61–2.

25. Pakenham, *The Boer War*, p. 99.

26. Salisbury to Chamberlain, 16 August 1899, JC 5/67/115.

27. Chamberlain to Selborne, 14 August 1899, SeP 9/63.

28. Yakutiel, 'Treasury control', p. 18.

29. Chamberlain to Salisbury, 16 August 1899, Salisbury Papers HH 3M/E, cited in ibid., p. 20.

30. Wolseley memorandum, 17 August 1899, CAB 37/50/52.

31. Lansdowne to Wolseley, 20 August 1899, CAB 37/50/53.

32. Lansdowne to Salisbury, 26 August 1899, Lansdowne Papers L(5)49, in Yakutiel, 'Treasury control', p. 22.

33. Wolseley to Lansdowne, 24 August 1899, CAB 37/50/56; Surridge, 'British civil–military relations', p. 65.

34. Sir Edward Hamilton, Diary, 3 and 24 August 1899.

35. Hicks Beach to Hamilton, 15 August 1899, Hamilton Papers Add. MS. 48614; Marzials to Hamilton, 16 and 17 August 1899, in Yakutiel, 'Treasury control', p. 23.

36. Yakutiel, 'Treasury control', pp. 26, 276–7.

37. Sir Edward Hamilton, Diary, 18 August 1899.

38. Chamberlain to Milner, 8 and 14 August 1899, in R. H. Wilde, *Joseph Chamberlain and the South African Republic 1895–1899*, Archives Yearbook for South African History, 1956, Part 1 (Pretoria, 1956), pp. 128–9; Chamberlain to Selborne, 15 August, SeP MS 9.

39. Chamberlain to Milner, 31 July 1899, CO 217/464, 20110.

40. According to Livy, these three books of oracles – which were consulted by the Roman Senate in times of emergency – had originally been nine in number when they were first offered for sale to Tarquin by the Sibyl of Cumae. When Tarquin refused, she burned three of the books and then offered him the remaining six, at the same price, a year later. When he again refused, she burned three more and repeated her offer for the remaining three the following year. He then bought them for the original price.

41. Footnote by W. K. Hancock and J. van der Poel, eds, in *Selections from the Smuts Papers* 7 vols (Cambridge, 1966–73), 1, p. 308.

42. Smuts to Te Water, 12 August 1899, in ibid., p. 273.

43. J. L. Garvin and J. Amery, *Life of Joseph Chamberlain* 6 vols (London, 1932–69), 3, p. 430.

44. H. de Villiers to M. de Villiers and A. Fischer, 31 July 1899, in E. Walker, *Lord de Villiers and his Times* (London, 1925), pp. 343–5.

45. A. Fischer to J. Hofmeyr, 31 July 1899, HP MSC 8, Box 8c.

46. De Villiers to President Kruger, 5 August 1899, in Walker, *Lord de Villiers*, p. 346.

47. President Kruger to Sir H. de Villiers, August 1899, in ibid., pp. 346–7.

48. Headlam, ed., *The Milner Papers*, 1, p. 483; also Reitz to Conyngham Greene, 12 August 1899, C.9530.

49. Smuts to Hofmeyr, 22 August 1899, in Hancock and van der Poel, eds, *Selections Smuts Papers*, 1, pp. 300–2, and W. K. Hancock, *Smuts* 2 vols (Cambridge, 1962–8), 1, pp. 101–3; also J. S. Marais, *The Fall of Kruger's Republic* (Oxford, 1961), pp. 314–16, for a convincing rebuttal of Eric Walker's case against the *bona fides*.

50. Smuts's view reported in Conyngham Greene to Milner, 12 July 1899, Transvaal Archives, BA 21.

51. Smuts to W. J. Leyds, 30 April 1899, in Hancock and van der Poel, eds, *Selections Smuts Papers*, 1, p. 229.

52. Smuts, Report to the Transvaal government of 14 September 1899 of his conversations with Conyngham Greene, later published as a Transvaal Green Book (No. 10 of 1899) and, in English translation, as a British Blue Book (Cd. 43 of 1900) and in Hancock and van der Poel, eds, *Selections Smuts Papers*, 1, pp. 283–99. Conyngham Greene's account and telegrams are printed in C.9521 (September 1899) and in Headlam, ed., *The Milner Papers*, 1, pp. 488–93.

53. Conyngham Greene, first telegram reporting discussions, encl. in Milner to Chamberlain, 15 August 1899, printed in C.9521, p. 44.

54. Second telegram from Conyngham Greene, 14 August 1899, encl. in Milner to Chamberlain, 15 August 1899, C.9521, p. 45.

55. Smuts to Steyn, enclosed in Steyn to Hofmeyr, 14 August 1899, printed in T. R. H. Davenport, *The Afrikaner Bond (1880–1911)* (Oxford, 1966), p. 203.

56. Milner, Diary, 11 August 1899, MP.

57. Milner to Chamberlain, 15 August 1899, CO 417/264, 21624.

58. Milner to Chamberlain, 16 August 1899, in Headlam, ed., *The Milner Papers*, 1, p. 516.

59. Chamberlain to Salisbury, 16 and 18 August 1899, JC 11/30/164.

60. Salisbury to Chamberlain, 17 August 1899, JC 5/67/116.

61. Chamberlain to Milner, 16 August 1899, CO 417/264, 21624.

62. Milner to E. Garrett, 3 August 1899, MP vol. 182.

63. Milner to Conyngham Greene, 17 August 1899, Transvaal Archives, BA 22; Headlam, ed., *The Milner Papers*, 1, p. 491.

64. Milner's message of 17 August and Kruger's telegram of 18 August 1899, in Headlam, ed., *The Milner Papers*, 1, p. 490; also C.9521, p. 46.

65. The full text of this 'rider' of 21 August 1899 is printed in C.9521, p. 47.

66. Chamberlain to Milner, 7 July 1899, in Marais, *The Fall of Kruger's Republic*, p. 308.

67. British Agent to Milner, 20 August 1899, Transvaal Archives, BA 22.

68. Chamberlain to Lansdowne, 18 August 1899, JC 5/51/63.

69. Chamberlain to Lansdowne, 24 August 1899, JC 5/51/70.

70. Salisbury to Hicks Beach, 30 August 1899, in A. N. Porter, *The Origins of the South African War, Joseph Chamberlain and the Diplomacy of Imperialism 1895–1899* (Manchester, 1980), p. 237.

71. Lansdowne to Wolseley, 27 August 1899, CAB 37/50/57.

72. Hofmeyr to Smuts, 30 August 1899, in Hancock and van der Poel, eds, *Selections Smuts Papers*, 1, p. 307.

73. Walker, *Lord de Villiers*, p. 349.

74. Smuts to Hofmeyr, 22 August 1899, in Hancock and van der Poel, eds, *Selections Smuts Papers*, 1, p. 301.

75. Ibid.

76. Smuts's report of 14 September 1899, in ibid., p. 292.

77. Ibid., pp. 292–3.

78. Smuts to Conyngham Greene, 25 August 1899, in ibid., pp. 297–8.

79. Wilde, *Joseph Chamberlain*, p. 135; Porter, *Origins*, p. 238.

80. See Chapter 9, pp. 319–20 above.

81. Wilde, *Joseph Chamberlain*, p. 136; Pakenham, *The Boer War*, p. 86.

82. Conyngham Greene to Milner, 25 August 1899, CO 417/265, 24815.

83. Milner to CO, 25 August 1899, CO 417/265, 24059, 23398; also Wilde, *Joseph Chamberlain*, pp. 136–7.

84. Chamberlain Minute on Milner to Chamberlain, 20 August 1899, CO 417/265.

85. Chamberlain to Salisbury, 2 September 1899, JC 11/30/169.

86. Garvin, *Life of Chamberlain*, 3, pp. 438–9; Headlam, ed., *The Milner Papers*, 1, p. 493.

87. The successive drafts of this reply are in CO 417/265, 22937; the final text is printed as No. 43 in C.9521. See also Wilde, *Joseph Chamberlain*, p. 133.

88. The phrase is from Marais, *The Fall of Kruger's Republic*, p. 313, to which I am much indebted in this section.

89. The text of the British despatch is printed in C.9521, pp. 49–50.

90. Chamberlain to Milner, 28 August 1899, in Headlam, ed., *The Milner Papers*, 1, p. 493.

91. Official Note of 2 September 1899, printed as No. 49 in C.9521.

92. Smuts to Te Water, 4 September 1899, in Hancock and van der Poel, eds, *Selections Smuts Papers*, 1, p. 309.

93. Davenport, *The Afrikaner Bond*, p. 204, citing Reitz to Hofmeyr, 28 August 1899.

94. Minutes by CO staff, 10 August 1899, CO 417/265, 21248.

95. Milner to Chamberlain, 23 August 1899, JC 10/9/48 (a substantial extract is printed as No.51 in C.9521).

96. Conyngham Greene to Milner, 1 August 1899, CO 417/265, 23488; Minutes by Colonial Office staff on Uitlander Council memorandum, 25 August 1899, CO 417/265, 24815.

97. Selborne to Milner, 7 October 1899, in Boyce, ed., *The Crisis of British Power*, p. 95.

98. Chamberlain to Milner, 31 July 1899, CO 417/264, 20110.

99. Minutes by Selborne and Chamberlain, 12 August 1899, CO 417/264, 21248; Milner to Chamberlain, 2 August 1899, CO 417/264, 20239.

100. Milner to Chamberlain, 2 and 12 August 1899, CO 417/264, 20239, 21330.

101. Milner to Chamberlain, 22 August 1899, CO 417/265, 22484.

102. Milner to Chamberlain, 8 August 1899, CO 417/264, 21000.

103. Milner to Chamberlain, 23 August 1899, JC 10/9/48.

104. Milner to Selborne, 22 August 1899, in Headlam, ed., *The Milner Papers*, 1, p. 519.

105. Milner to Selborne, 30 August 1899, in Boyce, ed., *Crisis of British Power*, pp. 93–4.

106. Selborne to Milner, 8 September 1899, in ibid., p. 94.

107. Milner to Chamberlain, 2 August 1899, JC 10/9/40.

108. Chamberlain to Selborne, 24 August 1899, SeP MS 9; Chamberlain to Lansdowne, 24 August 1899, JC 5/51/70.

109. Chamberlain to Salisbury, 27 August 1899. SaP HH 3M/E; Memorandum of 6 September 1899, CAB 37/50/70.

110. Buller to Salisbury, 5 September 1899, JC 10/3/113.

111. Wolseley to Lansdowne, 5 September 1899, CAB 37/50/69; Lansdowne to Chamberlain, 9 September 1899, JC 5/51/80; Surridge, 'British civil–military relations', pp. 68–9.

112. Wolseley to Ardagh, 23 September 1899, in Surridge, 'British civil–military relations', p. 69.

113. Chamberlain to Milner, 2 September 1899, MP 8. (The long extract in Headlam, ed., *The Milner Papers*, 1, pp. 526–8, has important omissions.)
114. Milner to Chamberlain, 4 September 1899, CO 417/266, 23791.
115. Milner to Chamberlain, 6 and 7 September 1899, in Headlam, ed., *The Milner Papers*, 1, pp. 530–1.
116. Chamberlain to Milner, 8 September 1899, in ibid., 1, p. 533.
117. D. Judd, *Balfour and the British Empire* (London, 1968), pp. 169–70, citing Balfour to J. Bryce, 2 October 1899, Balfour Papers.
118. Chamberlain to Salisbury, 2 September 1899, JC 11/30/169.
119. Salisbury to Chamberlain, 6 September 1899, and Memorandum by Salisbury for the Cabinet, 5 September 1899, both in E. Drus, 'Select documents from the Chamberlain Papers concerning Anglo-Transvaal relations, 1896–1899', *BIHR* 27 (1954), pp. 179–80.
120. Hicks Beach to Salisbury, 31 August 1899, in ibid., p. 178.
121. Salisbury to Lansdowne, 30 August 1899, in Lord Newton, *Lord Lansdowne* (London, 1929), p. 157.
122. Salisbury to Chamberlain, 11 and 19 September 1899, JC 11/30/170 and JC 5/67/124.
123. Hicks Beach to Salisbury, 24 August 1899, quoted in Yakutiel, 'Treasury control', p. 34.
124. Sir Edward Hamilton, Diary, 18 August 1899, British Library Add. MSS 48, 675.
125. Lady V. Hicks Beach, *Life of Sir Michael Hicks Beach* 2 vols (London, 1932), 1, p. 106.
126. Sir Edward Hamilton, Diary, 7–9 September 1899.
127. Lansdowne to Chamberlain, 8 September 1899, JC 5/51/79.
128. Memorandum by Chamberlain, 5 September 1899, CAB 37/50/63.
129. Memorandum by Chamberlain, 6 September 1899, CAB 37/50/70.
130. Milner to Chamberlain, 2 September 1899, CO 417/266 No. 23550; also telegrams of 6 and 7 September 1899, in Headlam, ed., *The Milner Papers*, 1, pp. 530–1.
131. Milner to Chamberlain, 6 September 1899, in ibid., p. 531.
132. Milner to Chamberlain, 7 September 1899, CO 417/266 No. 24016.
133. Chamberlain's reply, 8 September 1899, printed as No. 52 in C.9521.
134. Copy of Smuts to A. Fischer, 31 August 1899, MP MS 242.
135. Memorandum by Smuts, 4 September 1899, in Hancock and van der Poel, eds, *Selections Smuts Papers*, 1, pp. 322–3.
136. Ibid., pp. 327–9.
137. Garvin, *Life of Chamberlain*, 3, p. 444; the full text of the reply is printed as No. 51 in C.9530.
138. Count Hatzfeldt to German Foreign Office, 20 September 1899, in E. T. S. Dugdale, ed., *German Diplomatic Documents 1871–1914* (New York, 1969), p. 101.
139. Salisbury to Chamberlain, 18 September 1899, JC 5/67/122.
140. Marais, *The Fall of Kruger's Republic*, p. 320, quoting Hely Hutchinson to Chamberlain, 29 September 1899.
141. Ibid., quoting Chamberlain to Hicks Beach, 7 October 1899.

142. British Note of 22 September 1899, printed in C.9530, pp. 16–17.
143. Chamberlain to Milner, 22 September 1899, in Headlam, ed., *The Milner Papers*, 1, p. 545.
144. Milner to Chamberlain, 27 September 1899, in ibid., p. 547.
145. Milner to Chamberlain, 24 September 1899, MP MS 229. For the Anglo-Portuguese negotiations see J. A. S. Grenville, *Lord Salisbury and Foreign Policy: The Close of the Nineteenth Century* (London, 1970 edn), pp. 260–3.
146. Milner to Chamberlain, 26 September 1899, in Headlam, ed., *The Milner Papers*, 1, pp. 545–6.
147. Milner to Chamberlain, 28 September 1899, JC 10/9/68.
148. Milner to Chamberlain, 30 September 1899, JC 10/9/69.
149. Chamberlain to Milner, 5 October 1899, in Headlam, ed., *The Milner Papers*, 1, p. 555.
150. Chamberlain to Hicks Beach, 27 September 1899, in Drus, 'Select documents', p. 321 188.
151. Salisbury to Chamberlain, 19 September 1899, JC 5/67/124.
152. See Chapter 9, p. above.
153. The full text of the British ultimatum is printed in Drus, 'Select documents', pp. 182–6. The earliest draft by Chamberlain, dated 22 September 1899, is in CAB 37/50/72.
154. Goschen to Chamberlain, 29 September 1899, printed in Drus, 'Select documents', pp. 186–7.
155. Hicks Beach to Chamberlain, 29 September 1899, printed in ibid., p. 187.
156. Chamberlain to Hicks Beach, 29 September 1899, printed in ibid., p. 188.
157. Chamberlain to Milner, 5 October 1899, JC 10/9/70.
158. Hicks Beach to Chamberlain, 4 October 1899, JC 16/5/26; Selborne to Milner, 7 October 1899, in Boyce, ed., *Crisis of British Power*, p. 95.
159. Fischer to Hofmeyr, 12 September 1899, HP; Steyn's speech was fully reported in *The Cape Times*, 22 September 1899.
160. Speech by President Steyn, 21 September 1899, reported in *The Standard and Diggers News*, 22 September 1899; see also *The Cape Times* for the same date.
161. Steyn to Milner, 27 September 1899, copy in HP.
162. Milner to Steyn, 5 October 1899, in Headlam, ed., *The Milner Papers*, 1, p. 553; Chamberlain to Balfour, 3 October 1899, JC 5/5/83.
163. Balfour to Chamberlain, 2 October 1899, and Chamberlain's reply, 3 October 1899, JC 5/5/83.
164. Kruger's message in Fischer to Hofmeyr, 16 September 1899, printed in Davenport, *The Afrikaner Bond*, pp. 205–6.
165. Davenport, *The Afrikaner Bond*, pp. 206–7.
166. E. Walker, *W. P. Schreiner* (Oxford, 1937), p. 198.
167. Garvin, *Life of Chamberlain*, 3, p. 466.
168. Ibid.
169. J. J. Oberholster and M. C. E. van Schoor, *President Steyn aan die woord* (Bloemfontein, 1954), pp. 81–2; F. Pretorius, *Kommandolewe tydens die Anglo-Boereoorlog 1899–1902* (Johannesburg, 1991), p. 13.

170. Fischer to Hofmeyr, 13 September 1899, HP.
171. Reitz message of 30 September 1899 and Milner's comment on it in Headlam, ed., *The Milner Papers*, 1, pp. 550–1.
172. Ibid.
173. L. S. Amery, *My Political Life* 3 vols (London, 1953–5), 1, p. 100.
174. The full text is printed as No. 53 in C.9530; it is likely that Smuts had a major part in its drafting, see Hancock, *Smuts*, 1, p. 106.
175. Chamberlain to Lansdowne, 7 October 1899, JC 5/51/88.
176. Garvin, *Life of Chamberlain*, 3, p. 472.
177. L. S. Amery, *The Times History of the War in South Africa* 5 vols (London, 1900), 1, p. 374.
178. Ibid., pp. 375–6.
179. Garvin, *Life of Chamberlain*, 3, p. 476.
180. Deneys Reitz, *Commando: A Boer Journal of the Boer War* (London, 1929), p. 26.
181. Milner to Selborne, 11 October 1899, in Boyce, ed., *Crisis of British Power*, pp. 95–6.

Myths and Realities about the Origins of the South African War

When Chamberlain faced the House of Commons on 19 October 1899 and was obliged to explain why Britain was at war in South Africa, he said that he had 'only recently and most reluctantly . . . come to the conclusion that war was always inevitable'. He claimed that he had striven to obtain a peaceful settlement with the Transvaal government but that 'there have been things which it was essential for us to demand and to obtain; and that these things President Kruger and his friends and advisers have always been determined not to grant'. The two major issues over which he said the country had gone to war were first, the determination of the British government to rectify the just grievances of the Uitlanders (many of whom were British subjects), and second, to secure British paramountcy over the Transvaal and over South Africa (which he defined as 'the two republics and the British colonies'). He challenged the Liberal opposition to disagree with either of these two objectives. He then went on to suggest that, since 1881, Kruger's republic had been patiently and persistently 'endeavouring to oust the Queen from her suzerainty, to throw off the last trace of subordination . . . and declare themselves to be a sovereign independent state'. The aim was not only to escape from subordination to Britain but to create a United South Africa entirely free of British imperial influence and control. To this end, a sustained programme of rearmament had lately turned the Transvaal into 'by far the most military state in Africa'. No British government, he argued, could have tolerated the continuation of this situation. In the last resort, a Liberal government also would have had to resort to war.[1]

Politicians who have played a vital part in bringing about a war usually like to regard that war as inevitable – for the more inevitable the war can be shown to be, the more readily can they justify it to their countrymen. Historians take a more sceptical view. Conflicts between governments do not turn into wars without the contributions of the politicians and decision-makers. Wars occur because of the breakdown of relations between governments. That is why I have followed the traditional path, in this book, of devoting much attention to the relations, and the eventual breakdown of relations, between the British and Transvaal governments between 1895 and 1899. In any explanation of this war, the aims, actions, perceptions, personalities, policies, calculations, expectations and illusions of governmental decision-makers are of obvious importance in explaining how and why and when the war began. The role of these individuals, however, needs to be understood in terms of the mounting conflict of interest between the governments of Britain and the Transvaal republic during the late nineteenth century. The arcane world of diplomatic exchanges took place not in a vacuum but amidst the changing position of Britain in the world, the emergence of new colonial rivals – especially Germany – in Africa, and the transforming effects of the mineral revolution on the Witwatersrand – which revolutionized the power and importance of the Transvaal at the same time as it weakened the hold of the British 'imperial factor'.

The South African War was not a war which blew up suddenly. It was long in the making, its roots went deep, it was not unexpected. Both sides made a conscious decision to resort to war; both prepared ultimatums. The fact that one of the then world's smallest states delivered an ultimatum to the government of the world's greatest imperial power astonished many people at the time. Given the grotesque disparity in the resources the two sides could draw on, the result of a war seemed so certain that a last-minute capitulation by Kruger's government to British demands had been widely expected. Britain may have provoked the war but, as Deneys Reitz observed, 'the Transvalers were also spoiling for a fight'. By September 1899, 'it was clear that the die was cast and that neither side was in a mood for further parleying'.[2] Wars are a means by which two states test their power, relative to each other, and they are sometimes avoided by the weaker party choosing to surrender to the demands of the stronger before, rather than after, a resort to arms. In 1899, the Transvaal government decided to fight rather than to capitulate; and the Orange Free State – with which Britain had no quarrel and which was outside the British empire – decided to fight too, in support of her ally, when she had everything to lose by doing so. Here is a case of a war which was declared against a Great Power by two small states which could not expect to win. For the Transvaal, the penalty for defeat must have appeared as little different from that of capitulating to British demands in order to avoid war: both were likely to involve the removal of Kruger's government and the end of the Transvaal's qualified independence as a republic. The possibility that the British government and people might weary of a protracted war and seek a peace settlement, as had happened in 1881, was not discounted. But a resort to war was regarded as the only honourable course and it was made with the clear support of the burgher population.

THE 'DOMINION OF AFRIKANERDOM'?

Chamberlain claimed that what Britain faced was a united South Africa, under Afrikaner republican auspices, if she failed to act to reassert her supremacy in the region. This anxiety had first been cogently expressed by Selborne in his Memorandum of 1896 and it had remained influential on British considerations thereafter. Chamberlain had reiterated it in his important memorandum for the Cabinet on 6 September 1899 and Lord Salisbury, on the eve of the war, wrote to Leonard Courtenay that he had come to believe that in the Transvaal, President Kruger 'was using the oppression of the Outlanders as a lever to extract from England a renunciation of suzerainty' and that in South Africa generally, there was 'an understanding among the leaders of Dutch opinion and that their aspiration is the restoration of South Africa to the Dutch race'.[3]

Was this British fear justified? As Courtenay replied to the Prime Minister, once it was suggested that there was an Afrikaner plan to 'regain' South Africa, 'a thousand innocent things will seem to fit in with this conspiracy. The most harmless suggestion becomes part of a plot'.[4] As war approached, the 'dominion of Afrikanerdom' idea was widely circulated in Britain in books and newspapers. Milner later denied the accusation, by James Molteno, that he had been 'determined to break the dominion of Afrikanerdom' but admitted that both he and the British government were committed to challenging the exclusiveness of 'the Dutch oligarchy' in the Transvaal. Certainly, he had written of the Afrikaner leadership in the two republics and the Cape Colony as an 'Afrikander triple alliance' which was 'solid and defiant in its opposition to our policy'; he was also obsessed with the idea that the Cape Afrikaner population would side with their republican kinsfolk in the event of a war.[5] Ethnic imperialists are particularly prone to projecting their own obsessions on to others and Milner and Chamberlain were certainly imperialists deeply imbued with ideas of 'racial solidarity'. British fears of Afrikaner solidarity, however, proved to be greatly exaggerated. The South African War was not characterized by great ethnic solidarity on the part of the diverse Afrikaner population of South Africa, amongst whom there existed substantial regional, historical and class divisions. Although several thousand Afrikaners in the frontier districts of the Cape Colony went over to the republican cause initially, most of the Cape Afrikaner population did not. The majority of them remained very critical of Kruger's government and were content to remain British subjects. Far from conspiring to bring about a United States of South Africa under Afrikaner domination, their leaders directed their pre-war efforts towards trying to persuade Kruger's government to meet Britain's demands and thus bring about a peaceful settlement. Chamberlain himself admitted this when, after the British occupation of Bloemfontein, captured correspondence revealed the efforts of the conciliators.[6]

Investigation by historians since has revealed no conspiracy between the two republics to impose an Afrikaner and republican dominion on the rest of South Africa or to achieve a United States of South Africa under Transvaal leadership. As James Rose Innes had observed, although some Cape Afrikaners might have 'a sort of academic preference for a Republic in the dim and distant future', this was merely a vague, 'pious opinion' of the few; the majority remained loyal citizens of the British Empire.[7] In the republics, the Afrikaners of the Orange Free State had developed a separate loyalty and identity and were certainly averse to the idea of putting themselves and their 'model republic' under Transvaal predominance and rule. The attempts by Smuts and others to rally all Afrikaners 'from the Zambesi to Simon's Bay' under the slogan 'Africa for the Africander' (which dates from 1880–81) was more a desperate bid for support for the Transvaal, in its hour of need, than a serious political programme in 1899.[8] When Balfour was asked directly, in the House of Commons, whether the British government had any evidence of Boer intentions to establish their supremacy over Natal and the Cape Colony, he had to admit that it did not.[9] The 'dominion of Afrikanerdom' was thus a convenient myth developed by the British to justify their aggression in 1899; but it was a myth which at least some of the decision-makers believed, at least to some extent. Myths do not have to be true to be effective and one of their functions can be to play upon people's fears. The importance of this particular myth is that it encouraged a resort to war by a British government anxious about the growing economic and military power of Kruger's republic, and the assumption by most of the British public, when war came, that it was 'the Boers' they were fighting. As Thucydides so memorably concluded, with regard to the origins of the Peloponnesian War: 'What made war inevitable was the growth of Athenian power and the fear this caused in Sparta.'[10]

HOBSON'S GHOST

When he came to look back on the war and its origins, Smuts reported:

> It was the rooted conviction of the Boers generally, a conviction which was I believe shared by their responsible leaders, that the war was at bottom a mine-owners' war, that it had its origin in the Jameson Raid – in the firm resolve of the mine-owners to get the political control of the Transvaal into their hands by fair means or foul, to shape the legislation and administration of the country along lines dictated by their economic interests, and to destroy the Boer Government which had stupidly proved obdurate to their threats no less than to their seductions. It was with the mine-owners not a desire to bring the Republic under the British flag; as was conclusively proved by the fact that the Rand financiers decided in 1895 to have a Republic of their own in the Transvaal and not to submit to Rhodes's desire to hoist the British flag in the country. . . . Neither in 1895 nor in 1899 was it a question of the British flag. As the Boers read the situation the one issue was whether the mine-owners had to govern the Transvaal in their own interest; the British flag was a minor phase of that fundamental issue.[11]

Smuts went on to argue that although the British Colonial Secretary had different objectives to the mine-owners, each used the other to attain their ends. It was 'a marriage of convenience', an 'unholy union' out of which the Jameson Raid was the stillborn issue. For Smuts, the Jameson Raid was 'the real declaration of war in the great Anglo-Boer conflict'. The 'four years of truce' which followed it were merely a time when 'the allied aggressors consolidated their alliance, found fresh tools for the execution of their South African and Transvaal policy and laid fresh schemes and beat the deafening tom-toms of Uitlander agitation, while the defenders on the other hand silently and grimly prepared for the inevitable'.[12]

Ever since it took place, the South African War has been regarded by many people as the classic example of an imperialist war in which specific economic interests and considerations accompanied, even determined, the resort to war in 1899 and the British conquest and annexation of the Transvaal the following year. This war, declared J. A. Hobson in 1900, was being fought 'in order to place a small international oligarchy of mine-owners and speculators in power at Pretoria'. It was 'a capitalists' war', provoked by and fought for the interests of capitalism. It had been brought about by 'a small confederacy of international financiers working through a kept press'. It was the mine-magnates who, 'owning the South African press and [Uitlander] political organisations', had 'engineered the agitation which has issued in this war . . . open-eyed and persistent, they have pursued their course, plunging South Africa into a temporary ruin in order that they may emerge victorious, a small confederacy of international mine-owners and speculators holding the treasures of South Africa in the hollow of their hands'.[13]

The view that the South African War was 'a mine-owners' war', fought by Britain with the encouragement of the mine-magnates to serve their interests through the overthrow of Kruger's government and its replacement by one more sympathetic to the needs of the mining industry, did not originate with Smuts or Hobson. Even before the war broke out, the idea that 'the mine-magnates' and 'the capitalists' were behind the mounting conflict with Kruger's government was widely articulated in the Transvaal in the editorial columns of *The Standard and Diggers News* during 1898–9.[14] Milner and Chamberlain both commented on and dismissed what Milner called 'the capitalist intrigues myth' at this time and acknowledged the mischievous influence that it might exert on public opinion.[15] Lord Salisbury reminded his colleagues 'that the one dangerous objection that is made to our policy is that we are doing work for the capitalists'.[16] On the outbreak of war, F. W. Reitz issued a powerful indictment of the British record in South Africa, *A Century of Wrong*, in which it was argued that it had now fallen to the Boers 'to begin the struggle against the new world tyranny of Capitalism . . . reinforced by the power of Jingoism'.[17] What Hobson did was to pick up this idea whilst he was in South Africa in 1899 as the correspondent for *The Manchester Guardian*. He then integrated it with his own emerging conclusions about late nineteenth-century European imperialism generally and served it up in an attractive and readable form to a wide audience – which has continued to respond to its potent appeal ever since. It is not too gross a simplification to say that the explanation so persuasively presented in Hobson's very influential book, *The South African War: Its Causes and Effects* (1900), has been the ghost in the machine of much historical writing about the origins of this war ever since.

In 1902, Hobson published a rather different and more widely known book, *Imperialism: a study*, about the economic factors at work in late nineteenth-century European overseas expansion generally. Many others, whose interest was in developments in Europe rather than in the non-European world, soon followed in Hobson's wake. When V. I. Lenin acknowledged his debt to Hobson's work, in the single most influential tract ever written on imperialism, there was a 'take-off' into self-sustaining theorizing and controversy in which each new contribution fed on the last one and provoked the next.[18] Cross-breeding between diverse theories about different things occurred on a promiscuous scale as the rapidly accumulating palimpsest of theories of economic imperialism went into perpetual orbit. The literature on this subject is now vast and confused.[19] The ideological agendas of historians have kept a misconceived debate alive. Marxists and neo-Marxists have been determined to salvage something from the wreckage of their theories. Anti-Marxists have sometimes seemed to imply that any admission that economic factors may have been involved is best avoided because it leads straight to economic determinism.

South Africa has always been popular as a test-case for theories of imperialism in general and for economic theories of imperialism in particular.[20] Two aspects of the South African case in 1899 have come in for particular attention: first, the role of the gold-mine owners and managers (the Randlords or capitalists) in the events leading up to the resort to war; secondly, the exceptional importance of South Africa to Britain and the British Empire at this time, not only because of its strategic position but also in terms of British investments and markets there and the British stake in the gold supply of the Transvaal. We need to consider each of these aspects in turn.

Hobson helped to popularize a view in which the Jameson Raid and the outbreak of war in 1899 have tended to be seen together. Like Smuts and many others at the time and since, he approached the causes of the war of 1899 with preconceptions formed out of what had already been revealed about the Jameson Raid and the conspiracy of Cecil Rhodes and a collection of capitalists and Uitlanders in 1895–6 to overthrow Kruger's government, by an Uitlander uprising on the Rand assisted from outside the Transvaal, and replace it with a government more progressive, reformist and sympathetic to the needs of the mining industry, the Uitlander population, and the political goal of a British-led federation of South Africa. As has been suggested in

Chapter 3, Hobson was right to sense that economic as well as political motives were at work in the conspiracy of Rhodes and his associates at the time of the Jameson Raid – even if it was the political ambitions of Cecil Rhodes rather than the economic interests of a very disunited mining industry which came to predominate in that sorry affair. But what about the situation after Rhodes had fallen from power, between 1896 and 1899, which resulted in war? Here, I would argue that the Siamese twins of the Jameson Raid and the resort to war in 1899 need separating.

Many people in South Africa, including Sir William Butler (Commander-in-Chief of the British garrison there 1898–9), believed that Cecil Rhodes was a major influence behind the events of 1899 as he had certainly been behind the Jameson Raid. Today, we know that they were wrong and that, whoever else was behind the resort to war in 1899, it was *not* Cecil Rhodes – who was a burnt-out case after 1898, politically; who believed that Kruger was a bully who bluffed and then gave way when confronted by superior power; and who repeatedly declared that war would not break out until it did so.[21] We also know that it was Milner, even more than Chamberlain, who was driving things towards either a capitulation by Kruger's government or a resort to war.[22] But what about the Randlords or capitalists? What can we now say about them? Where Hobson dealt in speculations and hypotheses, historians have been able to study the papers of the mine-magnates and the archives of governments and gold-mining companies. We know a great deal more than Hobson did about the relations between the mining industry on the Rand and Kruger's government during the 1890s. What conclusions can we now draw about the role and attitudes of the mining industry as war approached in 1899?

Over 30 years ago, J. S. Marais, in a classic work of historical scholarship, *The Fall of Kruger's Republic* (Oxford, 1961), effectively demolished the Hobson thesis (at least in the form asserted by J. A. Hobson himself) and came close to reversing it. Utilizing British government papers which had only recently become available to historians, he concluded that far from the mine-owners manipulating the British government during the approach to war in 1899, the British government and its agents manipulated them. Marais argued that, after the failure of their involvement in the Jameson Raid, the mine-magnates withdrew into the shell out of which some of them had ventured in 1895, and left the political initiative to the British government. As the crisis deepened, they re-emerged to add their weight to the reconstituted Uitlander reform movement, 'this time as instruments of British policy. They acted now as men under orders, relying on the superior political wisdom of the professional statesmen'.[23] The 'joint action' by the British government and the mining industry, in challenging Kruger's government over the dynamite monopoly in January 1899, brought the mine-magnates and the British government together. This was followed by the Great Deal negotiations in March in which, Marais suggested, the representatives of the mining industry were guided in their dealings with Kruger's government by the Colonial Office. Thereafter, the task of confronting Kruger's government with an accumulating list of demands for reform, which was by no means restricted to those of particular interest to the mining industry and included an Uitlander franchise, was left to the British government. The mine-magnates withdrew once more into the background and acquiesced in the British government's policy of extracting the reforms from Kruger's government or resorting to war.

Other historians have since extended and in certain important respects qualified the conclusions reached by J. S. Marais.[24] Marais has been criticized for suggesting a greater unity amongst the mine-magnates and Uitlanders in 1899 than subsequent research has revealed. His view that either of these two diverse groups of people acted simply as 'instruments of British policy', under the orders of the British Colonial Office, Milner or Conyngham Greene, must now be regarded as a simplification, even a distortion, of the truth. The mine-magnates pursued their own interests, irrespective of the rather different interests of the British government, and they were certainly not 'under orders'. The Uitlanders too had minds and wills of their own and the organizations which claimed to represent them (but had the active support of only an unstable minority) made demands on their behalf which far exceeded anything envisaged by Milner or Conyngham Greene. The efforts of Conyngham Greene to 'advise' and 'guide' them met with only limited success, especially after March 1899. To portray either him or Milner as puppet-masters pulling all the Uitlander strings is simplistic. What was achieved fell a good deal short of this, even with the assistance of Percy FitzPatrick. Certainly, the Uitlander leaders, whilst they recognized the vital importance of cultivating the imperial connection for their own purposes, did not regard themselves as being controlled by the British government or its agents in South Africa.

There has been a tendency to assume that the mine-magnates must have had a coherent political stance beyond a reaction to Transvaal policies and practices which adversely affected their businesses. Historians who have worked in their archives have emerged doubting if this assumption is true. Disunited in 1895, the mine-magnates were also disunited in 1899 and, in all sorts of respects, in competition with each other. Whoever ruled the Transvaal, they would establish and maintain a working relationship with the government, as they always had done and as capitalists usually do. Like cosmopolitan capitalists anywhere, they pursued their own interests in their own ways, whether these coincided with the rather different interests of the British government or not. They proved adept at keeping a foot in both camps as the conflict between the British and Transvaal governments mounted during 1899. Doubtful of British resolve, and half-expecting to be left to reach a settlement with Kruger's government on their own, as in 1896, they hedged their bets and continued their meetings with representatives of the Transvaal government and even President Kruger himself, long after the Great Deal negotiations had been broken off amidst mutual recriminations. War was likely to involve at least a temporary suspension of their mining operations with potentially huge losses and possibly serious damage to expensive equipment and mine-shafts through flooding or even sabotage. What they wanted was not a war but certain well-understood reforms in the Transvaal administration.

No convincing evidence has been found to support the idea that the British government acted at the behest of mine-magnates or capitalists with a stake in the Transvaal during the mounting crisis with Kruger's government. So this central tenet of 'the Hobson thesis' has had to be discarded as a plausible but incorrect hypothesis. Hobson himself was unable to demonstrate that the British government ever acted in this way. He arrived at his view of the war not by historical research but by a process of deduction. He asked who was likely to benefit most from the war. Since certain representatives of the mining industry had publicly declared that mining profits would increase by at least £2.5 million per year if the impositions of Kruger's government were to be removed, Hobson assumed that those who could expect to benefit most from the war must also have been behind the mounting crisis which had preceded it. But, as G. H. Le May has rightly emphasized, whatever the mine-magnates wanted, it was not they who took the crucial decisions in 1899. These were taken by the British government. The records of this government, and the private papers of members of Lord Salisbury's Cabinet, show that when they took their decisions with regard to the Transvaal in 1899, they were concerned not with the profits or conditions of the mining industry but with strengthening the political hold of Britain over the Transvaal and British supremacy over South Africa generally.[25]

Nor did the British government go to war 'to secure for the mines a cheap, adequate supply of labour' – another of J. A. Hobson's assertions which has reverberated down the century.[26] This idea also reflects Hobson's obsessive tendency to reduce everything to the interests of the mine-owners. His book was hurriedly put together out of articles written for newspapers. He did not have access to the personal papers and archives of the capitalists and mining companies he was writing about. His conviction that they were part of a 'conspiracy plot' behind the resort to war was central to his misguided attempt to reduce the origins of this war to their interests. What careful spade-work by historians in the archives has since revealed is that the problem of a shortage of cheap mine labour in the Transvaal was perennial; and the actions of governments and mining companies with regard to this issue both pre-dated and long outlasted the South African War. In fact, far from being 'totally obdurate' in this matter, Kruger's government had gone a considerable way towards assisting the gold-mining industry.[27] Although the mining companies remained unsatisfied, they were to remain so long after Kruger's government had been replaced by British colonial rule.

Hobson's assertion about the role of a 'kept press' in bringing about the war has proved to be one of his more fruitful insights into the situation in 1899. The research of Alan Jeeves into the English-language newspapers in the Transvaal during 1898–9 has shown the importance attached by Wernher, Beit/H. Eckstein & Co. to the influence of *The Star* and *The Transvaal Leader,* both of which were owned by them, through the Argus Company, and staffed by editors of their choosing. What I hope has emerged from my coverage of this issue is that a propaganda war was being fought in the Transvaal for the hearts and minds of the Uitlanders during this period, with *The Star* and *The Transvaal Leader* being used to counter-attack the campaign against the capitalists which had already been launched in 1898 in the columns of *The Standard and Diggers News,* a newspaper which was subsidized by Kruger's government and regarded as a government mouthpiece. Andrew Porter has revealed Milner's role in this propaganda war and his awareness of the need to cultivate British public opinion through the British press. Milner's readiness to use his network of contacts in both Britain and South Africa not only to win friends and influence people but to ensure that editors of the right outlook were in place in Johannesburg has to be seen as part of his contribution towards 'getting things forrarder in South Africa'.[28] In Britain, the 'new imperialism' and the 'new journalism' of the late nineteenth century worked on a 'new electorate' after 1884 to bring a new importance to public opinion in the considerations of British governments by the end of the century. The importance of winning public support for the government's policy in its mounting conflict with the Transvaal is repeatedly emphasized in the papers of members of Lord Salisbury's Cabinet. Hobson rightly detected the role which newspapers were already seen to play in forming this public opinion.

In the light of historical evidence, to which Hobson did not have access, including the records of the British and Transvaal governments and those of some of the gold-mining companies, we are now in a position to separate the wheat from the chaff in terms of his fertile legacy. Many of Hobson's acute observations about the situation in South Africa in 1899, based on personal experience there, have stood the test of later investigation by historians better than some of his obsessions, e.g. about capitalist conspiracy plots and Jews. The mining companies did not form the monolithic bloc which he imagined but were divided amongst themselves in 1899 as in 1895. Even over the presentation of their case to the Transvaal Industrial Commission (1897) or during the Great Deal negotiations (1899) it proved difficult to get them to pull together and maintain a common front in their attempts to persuade the Transvaal government to make reforms specific to the interests of the mining industry. The divisions between the mining companies enabled Kruger's government to operate a policy of divide and rule amongst them with considerable success, assisted by personal contacts with representatives of the mining companies who had long adjusted to a situation in which the regular giving of presents and receiving of favours served to lubricate the workings of business and government.[29] The Transvaal's pliable administration enabled the mining companies to use bribery to ease their way politically and support the candidates of their choice in both Volksraad and presidential elections. Some of the smaller mining firms refrained from criticizing Kruger's government, at least in public. The senior managers of the second-largest firm, Consolidated Goldfields, were determined that, after the debacle of the Jameson Raid, the firm should not be compromised again. They therefore took a strong line against any of their employees who engaged in active politics and were very reluctant to commit themselves to any action which might be regarded as hostile to Kruger's government as war approached in 1899. Even within the most important firm, Wernher, Beit/H. Eckstein & Co., there were important divisions of opinion. Lionel Phillips and Alfred Beit may have remained hostile towards Kruger's government after the Jameson Raid, but in 1899 neither were in South Africa and Beit was too ill to take an active part in the running of the firm.

Meanwhile Wernher, in London, although very critical of Kruger's government, maintained a cautious attitude – as befitted a true capitalist. In Johannesburg, Rouliot (who was the senior manager as well as the President of the Chamber of Mines) did not share the political views of the more junior Percy FitzPatrick and, unlike Friedrich Eckstein, only reluctantly reconciled himself to the fact that the wave of war was about to crash down on him in August 1899. Like Lewis Michell, the general manager of the Standard Bank, Rouliot feared that a war would be disastrous for his firm and for South Africa and hoped, until the last minute, that it could be avoided. Both clearly felt that they and their businesses were being overtaken by a war which was not of their making and which they were powerless to prevent.

The mine-magnates may not have wanted a war but their long-standing conflict with Kruger's government helped to bring it about. This conflict, as has been shown, long pre-dated the presence of Joseph Chamberlain at the British Colonial Office (1895) and the arrival of Milner as British High Commissioner in South Africa (1897). It had already contributed during 1894–5 to the plot to overthrow Kruger's government by means of a *coup d'état*. This conflict intensified during 1896–9, as the requirements of deep-level mining came to predominate on the Rand and the Transvaal government failed to implement the recommendations of its own Industrial Commission. Even smaller mining companies, such as A. Goerz and J. B. Robinson, which had previously been well disposed towards Kruger's government, became increasingly critical of it. Recent research has challenged the facile view of Kruger's government as that of a reactionary old autocrat, assisted by a corrupt oligarchy, which obstructed all change and treated the mining industry as the milch-cow of the state whilst increasing its operating costs through a perverse system of monopolies whose profits went less to swell state revenue than to fill private pockets abroad.[30] Corruption and inefficiency there certainly were in a rudimentary state administration lacking educated and skilled personnel and primarily geared to serving the needs of Afrikaner pastoral farmers. But it was not Kruger's objective to maximize the profits or accelerate the development of the mining industry. He regarded the system of concessions as a way of securing areas of the economy which he considered were of vital strategic importance to the country's independence (such as dynamite and railways); these also provided a valuable counterpoise to the burgeoning power of the Uitlander 'capitalists' and the mining companies on whose activities the Transvaal depended for most of its revenue. As Smuts had observed, on his first visit to the Transvaal in 1895, Kruger's government was reluctant to encourage changes which were already undermining the foundations of the republic.[31] Yet leading mining engineers, many of whom were Americans with wide experience of mining conditions elsewhere in the world, were extremely critical of the conditions which they encountered in the Transvaal in the late 1890s and emphasized the inefficiency of the government, 'the dynamite monopoly, the necessity of bribery, and the general inability of the Boers to understand capitalism, industrialization and progress'.[32] One of their number, William Hall, argued that major changes in the administrative structures of the Transvaal state and the attitudes of its officials were essential if gold-mining was to continue to develop. He pointed out that in the Transvaal there existed 'a great governmental problem outside of any particular complication made by the presence of a more or less troublesome Uitlander population' and said that the need for reforms had become acute as the long-term investment and costs associated with 'deep-level' mining had increased. The Transvaal, like any other rapidly developing country, he concluded, would have 'to remodel its fiscal system and administrative laws to meet the demands of its growing industries'.[33]

Historians too have pointed to the 'peculiar disjuncture' which existed between the enclave of gold-mining on the Rand and the form of the state in the Transvaal – with its inadequate administrative structures for the needs of a sophisticated mining industry and its concentration of political power in the hands of Afrikaner notables who represented a pre-industrial, agrarian society. Shula Marks has argued that by the late 1890s the mine-magnates were making demands on the South African Republic which it was unable as well as unwilling to meet and it was in this sense that they prepared the way not only for the war but for the reconstruction which followed it.[34] Kruger's government may have passed a whole series of reforms at an accelerating rate, between 1895 and 1899, but these were not enough. There were limits, she suggests, to what Kruger and his Volksraad could or would do, as their world changed rapidly around them. Kruger tried to use the opportunities opened up by the growing wealth of his country to secure and extend its independence and enrich his fellow-notables, whilst limiting the effects of rapid industrialization by controlling policy in key areas: cultivating alternative foreign allies; granting private concessions over things of strategic importance; developing an independent tariffs policy; building a railway to an independent port outside British control at Delagoa Bay; seeking to expand territorially to the north; appointing educated outsiders, like Smuts, to reform key areas of the administration; but excluding the Uitlanders from effective political power and ensuring that control of the state remained in Boer hands. The problem was that these policies brought Kruger's government into direct conflict with the governments of the other South African states, the mining industry, the Uitlander population, and the British government. In 1899 these mounting conflicts coalesced behind Britain's confrontationist policy and Kruger's government found itself faced with a formidable array of forces ranged against it both from within and without the republic. It lacked allies amongst those on whom the state depended. Only the loyal burghers, there and in the Orange Free State, would exert themselves in its defence. The long-standing internal conflicts within the Transvaal thus helped to bring about the downfall of Kruger's republic. There was also the fact that Milner's influence with the British government was greatly strengthened by the support given to him and his leadership in South Africa by the Uitlander organizations and by at least some of those managing the mining industry. By August 1899, the political crisis and uncertainty was affecting business and a resolution of the situation was widely regarded as essential. Many on the Rand believed that Kruger's government would fight rather than capitulate to Britain's demands. They therefore made preparations for a war which seemed increasingly likely.

In terms of the immediate origins of the war in 1899, it is a snare and a delusion to put the mine-magnates at the centre of the picture. At the heart of things was the determination of the British government to assert its control over the Transvaal government and to establish its supremacy over South Africa on a firmer basis. The conflict between the gold-mining industry and Kruger's government was a hardy perennial of the situation in the Transvaal. But British policy towards the Transvaal in 1899 was not dictated by the interests of the gold-mining industry. At the time of the Great Deal negotiations, in March 1899, there was some anxiety in British government circles that 'the capitalists' might part company with the Uitlander reform movement and make their own separate deal with Kruger's government. What Kruger's government sought from the mining industry and what it was prepared to concede in return soon put paid to any such settlement. The representatives of the mining industry did not need the British government to tell them of the danger of detaching the mining industry from the wider issues involving the Uitlander population generally – many of whom were their employees. Even more than in 1895, it was the coming together of important and influential sections of the mining industry with the Uitlander reform movement which, in 1899, confronted Kruger's government with a more formidable combination than it had ever faced before. The existence of this powerful local opposition within the Transvaal played its part in encouraging the British government to intervene in what it had previously acknowledged were the Transvaal's internal affairs, and insist on the reforms which it committed itself to obtaining in the wake of the Edgar incident and the Second Uitlander Petition to the Queen.

Hobson believed that the South African War was an unnecessary war, brought about by a small group of powerful and determined people in pursuit of their own, narrow interests and against the wider, general interest for which a resort to war was not only unnecessary but a disaster. Some historians, whilst rejecting Hobson's 'capitalist' conspiracy' explanation for the war, have nevertheless agreed with his conclusion that 'a war was neither inevitable nor necessary to modernize the republic'.[35] Noting the progress which had occurred since 1895 in the Transvaal, Hobson believed that 'the economic and other influences of the Rand had already acted as solvents of the old Boer conservatism'; a few more years and the death of Kruger himself, and a peaceful transformation would have occurred in the Transvaal which would have given Britain all that she wanted. What was as ill-judged as it was disastrous for South Africa, Hobson declared, was the adoption by the British government of 'the doctrine of force as the midwife of progress'.[36] For the war failed to pave the way for the establishment of that British supremacy in the Transvaal and in South Africa which both Milner and Chamberlain were seeking. Yet that forceful bid for British supremacy did more than anything else to fire the furnace of Afrikaner nationalism, which was to blaze its remarkable way to political dominance in South Africa for much of the twentieth century. What the British government did was to go to war in South Africa in 1899 'for a concept that was finished, for a cause that was lost, for a grand illusion'.[37]

A WAR TO SECURE THE INTERESTS OF BRITISH CAPITALISTS AND TRADERS?

Dispensing with a crude 'conspiracy plot' view of the role of the mine-magnates in the resort to war in 1899 has freed historians to assess afresh some of the other features of Hobson's analysis which he was right to emphasize. Hobson pointed to the underlying forces at work in South Africa itself which drew the British government into increasing intervention in its affairs in the wake of the transformations accompanying the discovery of first diamonds and then gold. These dramatic developments in South Africa occurred at the same time as changes in the relations between Europe and the non-European world were resulting in a European scramble for empire and dominance on a global scale. As part of this process virtually the whole of the African continent was partitioned and came under European colonial rule. There were 'pull' factors in Africa, as well as 'push' factors in Europe, which resulted in this extraordinary outburst of European empire-building.

Whilst Britain's strategic interest in Cape Town and the Cape sea-route to India and Australia remained a matter of continuing importance into the twentieth century, Britain's interest in South Africa had long since spread far beyond purely strategic considerations. The British government's increasingly determined stance over South Africa during the final third of the nineteenth century centred over the situation in the Transvaal, not over the Cape route or the Simonstown naval base – neither of which were under any threat.[38] Renewed British imperial intervention in South Africa had begun not with Carnarvon's annexation of the Transvaal and failed attempt at federation between 1877 and 1881 but a decade earlier, with the annexation of Basutoland (1868) and Griqualand West (1871).[39] Thereafter, the use of British troops to defeat the Pedi and the Zulu, the despatch of the Warren Expedition (1885), the readiness of successive British governments to annex more territory for the Crown, the Cape Colony and Natal, to grant a Charter to the British South Africa Company to 'open up' Rhodesia, and their determination to ensure that the coast came under British control, all testify to a growing British involvement in the region during the last third of the nineteenth century. The British military intervention against the Transvaal in 1899 was a logical culmination of Britain's increasing involvement in South Africa during the previous 30 years. It marked the culmination of the scramble for southern Africa which resulted in almost the entire region coming under British control by 1902.

This growing involvement was not just political; it had an important economic dimension to it. Investment in the Rand gold-mines stood at about £75 million by 1899, and although capital is cosmopolitan, and much of this investment was French and German in origin, more than half of it was British (estimates vary between 60 per cent and 80 per cent of the total). Similarly, on the eve of the war, two-thirds of South Africa's trade was carried out with Britain, and British exports were worth £15 million a year. For what was still the world's greatest financial and trading power, this was small beer in global terms, but it made South Africa by far the most important area of economic interest for Britain in Africa, where it accounted for two-thirds of that continent's total foreign trade and investment.[40] Within South Africa, it was the Transvaal which was the magnet for British investment and the most rapidly growing destination for British exports and it seemed certain to become even more important in the future. Yet British government records reveal no real anxiety about British economic interests in the Transvaal at this time. What the British government feared were the political consequences of the growing economic power and importance of the Transvaal for the rest of South Africa, not the present or future British economic stake in the Transvaal *per se*. This was not thought to be at risk, and it was certainly not considered necessary to go to war to safeguard it.

The Transvaal, in turn, was dependent on the City of London as the financial capital of the world in 1899. This dependency was not just in terms of the investment, long-term loans and credits required by the capital-intensive gold-mining industry and the coal-mines and railways developed in association with it. It extended into that whole network of financial, shipping, insurance, and technical services (including the refining and minting of South African gold) which London was uniquely well-equipped to provide. In 1898, a modest attempt by German financiers to divert a small amount of raw gold from the Rand to Germany, for refining and sale, only served to demonstrate how uncompetitive Berlin and Paris were in relation to the unrivalled services offered by London at this time.[41] The difficulties encountered by Kruger's government when it attempted to escape the London network and raise a modest loan of £2 million elsewhere similarly emphasized the Transvaal's economic dependency on Britain at precisely the time when Kruger was seeking to assert the country's independence from British overrule. By 1899, even Germany had proved a weak reed. Not only had the German government vacated the South African pitch politically, in Britain's favour, by the 1898 agreement, but German capitalists, like their French, Dutch and American counterparts, united in support of Britain's determination to impose far-reaching reforms on the Transvaal government during 1898–9, even to the point of war.[42] Internationally, South Africa was acknowledged as a predominantly British sphere of influence in which Britain's commitment to free trade allowed the capital investment and trade goods of other countries to play their part in the development of the region. This was indeed to continue to be the case after 1902.

Hard as some historians have looked, they have been unable to come up with any convincing evidence that the British government felt that its trade in South Africa was seriously threatened by outside rivals by 1899, or that this was a major consideration in the resort to war. The obvious contender, Germany, had not only been 'squared' politically, but German traders were as keen as British ones that the reforms which the British government was pursuing with Kruger's government should come about. As for the United States, its share of South African trade was growing but its capitalists and businessmen, like those of Germany and other countries, openly *supported* a British take-over of the Transvaal as likely to open up the country to the forces of progress, free trade and foreign investment. Kruger's government was regarded as an obstacle to economic progress and the establishment of good government. The Transvaal Boers were dismissed as an obstinate and backward lot of farmers who were obstructing the 'advancement of civilisation'. In the USA they were often compared with the slave-holding landowners of the ante-bellum South. By the late 1890s, the government of 'the richest spot on earth' by Kruger and his burghers was regarded as an anomaly which could not and should not last. It was assumed that political control of the Transvaal would inevitably pass out of their hands into those of the British – who would establish a strong and efficient administration, create better conditions for the expansion of trade and increased profits on investment, and unite the region into a more effective whole – to the great benefit and advancement of not just themselves but of the African population and of all those involved in the area generally.[43]

So, the British government did not go to war in 1899 to protect British trade or the profits of cosmopolitan capitalists in the Transvaal. Neither of these were felt to be under serious threat even if it was acknowledged that the capitalists did suffer from unnecessary impositions at the hands of an inefficient and corrupt government. The Transvaal was not the only part of the world where this occurred, as the rulers of the most extensive empire in world history well knew. Despite their justifiable complaints, the capitalists on the Rand not only made sizeable profits under Kruger's government but were also successful in attracting the large-scale private investment which was so essential to their operations. As Hobson himself admitted, these 'helots' wore their golden chains 'with insolent composure of demeanour' as they lived their lives of luxury 'in a land of simple-mannered, plain-living farmers'.[44]

A WAR FOR GOLD?

The inner citadel of Hobson's economic explanation of the war may have fallen when confronted by the evidence and assaults of historians, but active skirmishing is still going on to defend the outer ramparts. Andrew Porter's exhortation to historians to drop their preoccupation with gold, when writing about the origins of this war, has recently been dismissed as 'myopic'; what oil was to the Gulf War against Saddam Hussein in 1991, it has been suggested, gold was to the war against Kruger's republic in 1899.[45] Gold seems to have a mesmerizing and sadly reductionist effect on historians. This war, asserts one of South Africa's leading historians – without giving any evidence to support his contention – 'in the final analysis, hinged around gold and the future of the [Transvaal] Republic's enormously profitable mining industry'.[46] The British historian, Eric Hobsbawm, has also declared that 'whatever the ideology, the motive for the Boer War was gold'.[47] If the evidence of those who decided to resort to war is anything to go by, both are wrong.

Those who have claimed that the South African War was 'a war for gold' are legion; but one of the attractions of this 'catch-all' explanation is that it can mean very different things. When President Steyn declared that gold was 'the motive power' for Britain's 'shameful undertakings' in the Transvaal, the implication was that this was a war for loot and that the British government was driven by a determination to seize control of the gold-mines.[48] His resort to this most obvious of explanations is understandable, especially when one remembers how smartly the British had earlier outmanoeuvred the Orange Free State to ensure that the diamonds of Griqualand West came under British control. President Kruger and his burghers also believed that it was not just their political independence but the annexation of their territory that the British were after; and that it was not the government but the gold-fields of the Transvaal which formed the real object of British interest. When they had been defeated in the war and were entering into peace negotiations in May 1902, the State Secretary, F. W. Reitz, therefore proposed that Johannesburg and the Witwatersrand should be ceded to the British in return for the recognition of at least 'internal independence' for the Boers in the rest of the Transvaal.[49] Yet when Lord Salisbury spoke at the Lord Mayor of London's banquet on 9 November 1899, he stated that Britain's sole interest in the gold-mines of the Witwatersrand was that they should be worked under good government. 'But that is the limit of our interest', he declared. 'We seek no gold fields. We seek no territory. What we desire is equal rights for men of all races, and security for our fellow subjects and for the Empire. Those are the only objects that we seek.'[50] As *The Times* commented when reporting the speech the next day, Britain had not gone to war from any craving for gold-fields and it was 'the rigid truth' that Britain sought no territory, as such, in its conflict with Kruger's government. Since, however, it had become 'abundantly clear that no paper guarantees will bind the Boers' of the Transvaal, the annexation of this republic had become necessary if the objective of 'equal rights for all' Europeans was ever to be established there, as it already had been in the rest of South Africa. If Kruger's government had proved ready and willing to abide by a negotiated settlement embodying Britain's demands, it was implied, Britain would have had no need to annex the country.[51]

In successive British communications to Kruger's government during 1899 – including the final ultimatum which was never delivered – the control of the gold-fields and demands on the part of the gold-mining industry are strikingly absent. One conclusion which might be drawn from this is that this is only to be expected, that these objectives existed but were deliberately kept hidden. It might even be argued that we are here in the realm of 'unspoken assumptions'; that members of the British Cabinet never mentioned the British objective of control of the gold supply or the gold-fields, even to each other, because it was so obvious that it was taken for granted. The motive is assumed by the absence of any reference to it. This is not, however, the way that historical scholarship proceeds. The history which historians write stands or falls by the evidence which underpins it. The evidence about the decision-making on the British side, as war approached in 1899, points clearly to a different conclusion. It was the government, not the gold-mines of the Transvaal, which Salisbury's government felt that it must control.

The British demands were for political and constitutional reform in the Transvaal and a reduction of its armaments. In return, a guarantee was offered for the continued but limited independence established by the London Convention of 1884. If British demands were refused then, as Lord Salisbury had made quite clear, Britain would seek to replace the London Convention by something else. It was the view of the British government that the terms of the London Convention had been repeatedly 'ignored or evaded' by Kruger's government – to the growing detriment of Britain's interests and position in the Transvaal. A new Convention would therefore be sought or imposed which would enable the British 'to secure their objects' there.[52]

Would this necessitate the annexation of the Transvaal as a British colony? Because there *was* a resort to war and the Transvaal *was* annexed by Britain in 1900, there has been a tendency to assume that annexation was the British objective from the outset and to blur the distinction between the consequences of the war and its causes. To conclude that the annexation, and nothing but the annexation, of the Transvaal was the British objective is again to fly in the face of the evidence. In 1894, when the immense gold deposits of the Transvaal were already known, the British Colonial Secretary, Lord Ripon, had clearly set out the long-term British objective with regard to South Africa in terms of a federal Union of British colonies and Boer republics 'in which we, of course, should have the hegemony but no more'. He stated quite clearly that he would 'care little whether the Transvaal became a British Colony or remained the South African Republic within such a federation'.[53] As late as 23 August 1899, writing 'quite privately and frankly' to Chamberlain, Milner had stated his conclusion that force would now have to be used to 'finally settle the South African question'. But what he meant by this was not necessarily the annexation of the Transvaal but political reform and the establishment of an Uitlander franchise there to bring the country under 'real popular government *either as a Republic or a British Colony*'.[54] The reluctance of Lord Salisbury to fight a war 'for people whom we despise, and for territory which will bring no profit and no power to England'[55] has often been cited, but usually with a reluctance by historians to accept it at its face value. Yet the attitude of other senior members of the British government on the annexation issue, as has been shown, is absolutely consistent with that of the Prime Minister. As Hicks Beach, the Chancellor of the Exchequer, emphasized in September 1899, what Britain wanted was British *predominance* in the Transvaal, not necessarily responsibility for its government or a revocation of its qualified independence, and Chamberlain had agreed with him.[56] Britain had repeatedly offered to guarantee the independence of the Transvaal if Kruger's government would agree to British demands. Since these demands amounted to a peaceful take-over of the government from within, they were refused. But it was a take-over of the government, not the annexation of the territory over which it ruled, which the British government was really after. 'It is all one', wrote an American commentator at the time, 'to have your Government captured by a troop of horse, or to have your privileges taken away by alien voters'.[57] Exactly so, but it was the government which was the target.

The annexation of the Transvaal, it has often been implied, would enable Britain to 'possess' the gold-mines in some unspecified way which suggests their physical seizure or control. Behind this 'myth of possession' lies the mistaken idea that political control of the Transvaal would bring with it control over the gold deposits located there and the mining companies engaged in the process of gold extraction. The objectives of the British government certainly did *not* include the annexation of the gold-mines in the sense of owning or nationalizing them. The capital-intensive gold-mining industry on the Rand would remain in private hands whoever controlled the government of the country. As the product of nineteenth-century private enterprise on the grandest and most cosmopolitan scale, the gold-mines were far too dependent on private capital investment and technical expertise to be in other than private hands. As for access to South Africa's gold supply, the British government had no more need to *annex* the gold-rich territory of the Transvaal to secure this than it did to annex those areas of the Yukon, California or Australia where gold was also being mined at this time. Gold would continue to flow to London, as the bullion and financial capital of the world, and underpin the Gold Standard, whether the Transvaal remained a republic or became a British colony. Yet it is still argued that anxiety over continued and unrestricted access to the Transvaal's gold supply underlay whatever other considerations the British government had in mind when it resorted to war in 1899.[58]

To deny that control of the gold supply from the Transvaal was an objective in the considerations of the British government in its resort to war in 1899, it has recently been said, is 'to stretch credulity'.[59] It is time this credulity was stretched and nailed firmly in place. My own research in the Bank of England and British government archives supports the conclusions clearly articulated by J. J. Van Helten over a decade ago.[60] In 1914, the British government did act to secure South African gold supplies (and deny them to Germany) for the duration of the First World War; but this was done as part of an Empire-wide policy and with South African agreement (since it served South African as well as British interests).[61] It was also done at a different time and in the context of a totally different situation to that of 1899, so there is no case for simply extrapolating back from one case to the other. As war approached between Britain and the Transvaal in 1899, there is no evidence that anxiety over the gold supply to London was ever a consideration – let alone a major consideration – in the minds of members of the British government, the Treasury, or the Bank of England.[62]

The war in 1899 was expected to be short and its outcome certain; and the Bank of England simply used its traditional 'gold devices' to attract such additional gold as it needed during the course of what turned out to be a much bigger and longer war than had been anticipated. Transvaal gold had, in any case, formed only a small proportion of the low level of gold reserves which was such a deliberate feature of Bank of England policy during the 1890s and early 1900s. A brief rise in the Bank Rate to 6 per cent for three months, in conjunction with the other 'gold devices', proved quite sufficient to provide Britain with the gold it required from alternative sources when the war brought about a cessation of Transvaal supplies. Germany and France proved more important than Australia, in this regard, between 1899 and 1902. This was also a time when the absence of any apparent shortage of gold on the London bullion market is suggested by the fact that the price paid for gold *actually declined*. The Bank Rate soon returned to 3–4 per cent for the rest of the war and, after the war was over and Transvaal gold was once more available in large quantities, the Bank of England's gold reserves still remained low. These indicators suggest what the Bank of England archives reveal: that London experienced no difficulty in attracting such gold as it required during the South African War by using traditional methods; and that the Bank of England policy of maintaining only low gold reserves was a practice which both pre-dated and outlived the South African War and had little to do with the state of things in the Transvaal.[63] This is, of course, testimony to the still awesome strength of the British economy and the fact that sterling operated as an international currency on equal terms with gold at this time. Many countries held a large part of their reserves in sterling (as 'London Reserves') rather than in gold, and also settled their trade accounts in sterling, with gold only being used and transferred as a balancing item. Recent research on the British Treasury during the South African War confirms what has already been established for the period immediately before the war began.[64] Neither Treasury minutes nor Bank of England correspondence suggest that Britain's low reserves of gold were regarded as a problem, or that a solution to this non-problem might be sought outside the operation of the traditional 'devices' through obtaining control over the Transvaal gold-mines or the Transvaal state. The British government was not anxious at this time about the gold supply from South Africa or the effect that an interruption of it might have on the gold reserves in the Bank of England or on London's hegemonic position in the international financial system in the hey-day of the Gold Standard. To suggest otherwise is to fly in the face of such evidence as has already been unearthed from the most relevant archives and to counter historical research with plausible surmise about what seems to be a red herring.

MILNER'S CHARIOT WHEELS

The roles played by Milner and Chamberlain in the resort to war in October 1899 have never ceased to attract the attention of historians. G. H. Le May and Thomas Pakenham are amongst those who, having written on the subject since J. S. Marais did so in 1961, have been accused of reducing the causes of the war to the actions and inter-actions of these two powerful individuals. Both of them described the war as 'Lord Milner's war' and ascribed the predominant part in bringing it about to this single individual.[65]

This view has a long pedigree which goes back to the writings of W. T. Stead and Liberal critics of British policy, both in Britain and South Africa, at the time when the war began. As respectively British High Commissioner in South Africa and Colonial Secretary in London, these two exceptionally able and dominant individuals occupied key positions which made them, in combination, a powerful influence on British policy-making. This means that their roles must indeed form a part of any explanation of the resort to war in 1899. But it will not do to reduce the origins, even the immediate origins, of this war to the process by which Milner brought Chamberlain and Chamberlain brought the British Cabinet to accept that the only solution to Britain's South African problem was a war. This is not to deny the ability of dominating individuals in powerful positions to affect the course of history – our present century is full of examples of them doing so – but it is to assert that an approach to the war which revolves purely around the Milner–Chamberlain axis is inadequate. Milner's role as the representative and key informant of the British government in South Africa after 1897 was clearly important, but the war was not his single-handed achievement. Nor did 'pushful Joe' Chamberlain lead the British Cabinet by the nose. The evidence marshalled by Andrew Porter demolishes the myth that Chamberlain bulldozed an ageing Lord Salisbury and a reluctant British Cabinet into a policy of confrontation which they were reluctant to endorse. The Cabinet and Prime Minister not only supported the policy of the Colonial Secretary, but on more than one occasion they prompted a policy of confrontation with the Transvaal government. The possibility that war might result was faced repeatedly from 1895, at the time of the Drifts Crisis, and was clearly acknowledged by the British government from May 1899, when it finally committed itself to direct intervention in the internal affairs of the Transvaal in order to extract an Uitlander franchise and other reforms from Kruger's government. From this commitment stemmed all the steps which followed on the way to war. The possibility of using military force may not have resulted in effective preparations, but it was in no way ruled out.[66]

Milner considered that a readiness to resort to war by the British government made war less likely. Most members of the British Cabinet seem to have believed, as late as August 1899, that war would be avoided and Kruger would capitulate to British demands – as he had repeatedly done before – if he were confronted with the threat of sufficient force. As for Milner, historians have been less than unanimous in the conclusions which they have drawn from the voluminous and well-thumbed papers which he left behind. Some have cast him in a conspiratorial role and claimed that he deliberately planned the war and the British annexation of the Transvaal from a date which many have based on the letter which he wrote to Chamberlain on 23 February 1898.[67] Others have felt less certain that Milner ever worked for a war, and nothing but a war, before the Bloemfontein Conference in June 1899. Certainly, from February 1898 Milner worked towards a 'great day of reckoning' when the Transvaal government would either have to capitulate to British demands or go to war and his papers reveal no compunction about a possible resort to force. Initially, he liked to declare that he was quite confident that Kruger would climb down when the imperial government showed that they were in earnest. As late as 10 July 1899, he told his closest ally, Lord Selborne, that 'it is quite impossible to say whether we're going to have Armageddon or not'.[68] But after the Bloemfontein Conference, Milner believed that war with the Transvaal was likely, even desirable, and certainly preferable to a 'patch-up' peace. Chamberlain was prepared for war but hoped that it might still be avoided, at the last minute, when Kruger's government realized that Britain was prepared to fight.

Ever since Headlam's carefully selected two volumes of *The Milner Papers* were published in the 1930s, there has been a tendency for historians to put Milner at the centre of their explanations of the war and to depict him as successfully manipulating the various parties to the conflict, and especially the Uitlanders and the mine-magnates in the Transvaal, in order to bring it about. Having succeeded in strapping them to the wheels of his war chariot, Milner is then portrayed as riding into a war (which was thus chiefly of his making) and following this with a peace and a post-war reconstruction of

South Africa which were also largely fashioned by him. Whatever Milner's intentions, this is certainly to exaggerate his achievements. Milner may have helped to stir the pot, but he did not supply the ingredients.[69] These long pre-dated his arrival and many of them proved intractable and difficult to manipulate even when he attempted to do so. To portray Milner as some sort of puppet-master simplifies the truth and suffers from the inadequacy of all explanations of the war which seek to attribute sole responsibility for it to particular individuals. It represents what E. H. Carr has called 'a primitive stage of historical consciousness'.[70] Whatever Milner may have wanted, the decisions were made by governments in London and Pretoria and not by him. On many occasions, as we have seen, Chamberlain repudiated a line of policy which Milner wished to adopt. After the 'helots' despatch and other similar communications, the Prime Minister and other members of the British Cabinet distrusted Milner's judgement even whilst they acknowledged that they had 'to act upon a moral field prepared for us by him and his jingo supporters'.[71] They may have disliked some of the means employed by Chamberlain and Milner, but they united behind the end and were 'prepared to face war sooner than not get out of Kruger terms that will secure good government at Johannesburg and make the Boers feel that we are and must be the paramount power in South Africa'.[72]

Milner hated South Africa and it was not just his personal ambition but his imperialism which had taken him there. He was convinced that, at the end of the nineteenth century, South Africa was the test-case for the future of the British Empire. Chamberlain too was a convinced imperialist who believed that the consolidation of the British Empire was vital to Britain's survival as a great power in the twentieth century. South Africa acted as an arena in which the imperialism of these two dominant individuals was put to the test. Like Chamberlain, Milner regarded the situation there in terms of rival imperialisms, Boer versus British, which could only be resolved by the predominance of one or the other of them. Milner's aim in South Africa came to be not a settlement, and certainly not a 'patch-up' with Kruger's government, but a transfer of power in the Transvaal. The Uitlander franchise was a means to achieve this larger end of British predominance within the Transvaal and British supremacy in South Africa. During 1899, Milner played a key role first in focusing attention on the franchise issue and then in emphasizing its inadequacy. By July 1899, he concluded that the differences between the various franchise proposals were of 'diminishing interest' amongst the Uitlanders. 'What men really want to know', he declared, 'is whether Great Britain is going to prove herself in fact what she has so often claimed in name, the "Paramount Power" in South Africa'.[73] When there was a resort to war, Milner was quite ready to acknowledge his own role in bringing this about. 'I precipitated the crisis, which was inevitable, before it was too late', he told Lord Roberts. 'It is not a very agreeable, and in many eyes, not very creditable piece of business to have been largely instrumental in bringing about a big war.'[74]

Chamberlain, too, was quite unrepentant. In a secret letter to Milner in December 1899, he reflected:

> It was all very well for you and me to know, as we did, what a tremendous issue was behind such questions as Franchise and Alien Immigration, but the public did not. They could not see that the things that we were contending for were worth a big war, nor were they particularly pleased with the clients on whose behalf we appeared to be acting. There was too much 'money-bags' about the whole business to be agreeable to any of us. Fortunately, as the argument developed, and especially owing to the diplomatic mistakes made by Kruger, the country became alive to the intolerable position into which we were settling. Even some of our strongest opponents are at last awake to the intentions of the Transvaal Government and, bad as this war is, and heavy as are the sacrifices which it entails, they see that if we had gone on in the old rut for a year or two longer, nothing could have saved South Africa to the British Crown.[75]

As Colonial Secretary, Chamberlain had many other considerations to bear in mind when dealing with South Africa and, like other members of the Cabinet, he believed up to the last minute that Kruger might well capitulate rather than fight. Milner was more single-minded and more scheming. As he lost any faith he might originally have had that Kruger's government would ever agree to a settlement which would meet Britain's demands, and that the British government would be able to enforce it, he showed no compunction in facing a resort to war. The failure of Britain's efforts to control the Transvaal by informal means opened the way to the advocates of force.[76] Not only Milner and Chamberlain but Lord Salisbury and the other members of his government were also convinced, by 1899, that Britain must intervene directly if South Africa were to be welded into a British dominion. The power and importance of the Transvaal made it essential to include it in the wider federation or union which had been the British objective for over 30 years. In 1899, Chamberlain believed 'that the Transvaal may be expected in the course of a year or so to have a large British majority' and Milner was certain that once 'equal rights' were established for the European population there, 'the scale in S. Africa would definitely and forever incline on the British side'.[77] British supremacy in the Transvaal would therefore be underpinned by British immigration and predominance. On this grand illusion it was anticipated that a post-war reconstruction of the Transvaal would be built and 'the great game . . . for the mastery of South Africa' between the British and the Boers would be won.[78]

UITLANDER GRIEVANCES: TROJAN HORSE OR STALKING-HORSE?

Uitlander grievances against Kruger's government were a long-standing feature of the situation in the Transvaal throughout the 1890s. But the question is, why did they play such a prominent part in the immediate origins of the war? Grievances over the inflated cost of living, the private and state monopolies, the high rates of taxation, the poor provision of schools, the corruption in the administration and the high-handed actions of the police, were present throughout the 1890s. Relations between Boers and Uitlanders were made worse by the repeated raising of the citizenship and franchise requirements by the Volksraad, by its refusal to consider Uitlander petitions, and most of all by the failed Uitlander uprising on the Rand in connection with the Jameson Raid in January 1896. But the franchise issue was only of concern to a small minority and Uitlander grievances generally had proved insufficient to sustain an effective reform movement before 1899. What happened to change this?

As in 1895, a vital contribution was made in 1899 by the support of at least some of the mining companies. This gave the Uitlander reform movement a new effectiveness, leadership, financial backing and access to the newspapers owned by the Argus Group – with their ability to mobilize support and form opinion amongst the Uitlander population generally. The role of certain individuals, such as Percy FitzPatrick and Samuel Evans – both of them employees of Wernher, Beit/H. Eckstein & Co. – was certainly important. The grievances already existed, they were a genuine product of Transvaal circumstances, but the backing which the reconstituted Uitlander reform movement obtained from the mining industry, before and after the Great Deal negotiations, played a significant part in transforming not only its effectiveness but its importance in the eyes of the British government. The growing frustration of the Uitlanders at the failure of

Kruger's government to rectify their grievances led them to direct their efforts towards involving the British government on their behalf. The initiative came originally from the Uitlanders in the Transvaal, *not* from the British government (or its agents) which, until 1899, repeatedly resisted Uitlander efforts to embroil them in what they acknowledged were the internal affairs of the Transvaal. This changed in the wake of the Edgar incident and the two Uitlander petitions to the Queen.

What changed, with regard to Uitlander grievances in 1899, was that the British government took them up in a new and determined way. Why did it do so? A simple answer, which has all the attractions of another 'conspiracy plot' explanation, is that it did so as a result of the machinations of Milner and the British Agent in Pretoria, Conyngham Greene, who set out to use Uitlander grievances, Uitlander organizations, and especially the Uitlander franchise issue, as the basis on which to rally the support of British public opinion for a confrontationist policy with Kruger's government. Once committed, the British government would not be able to withdraw. Either the franchise would be granted and the grievances rectified or there would be a resort to war.

There is no doubt that, in 1899, Milner deliberately set out to focus attention on Uitlander grievances in general and on the issue of an Uitlander franchise in particular as part of his campaign 'to get things forrarder' in South Africa. But it was Chamberlain who had first taken up these issues, on behalf of the British government, in 1896. Milner helped the return to them in a more determined way in 1899. He wanted to get away from the interminable wrangling over the terms of what he called 'these wretched treaties' (the London Convention of 1884 and the Swaziland Convention of 1894). With his sharp eye for the main chance, Milner saw that these were unlikely ever to provide an opportunity for confronting Kruger's government on a matter which would arouse the support of a reluctant British public opinion. What Milner wanted was to concentrate attention on 'the big facts, all of them internal Transvaal questions with which *in theory* [i.e. legally] we have nothing to do'.[79] If it came to a fight, then he thought that fight should be fought on 'equal rights for all white men' in the Transvaal, as elsewhere in South Africa.[80] Milner's influence played a major part in swinging the British government behind this 'splendid battle cry'. Yet Chamberlain and the Colonial Office were well aware that the British case for intervening on this issue was weak; but they were even more aware that it was even weaker without it. As the final crisis mounted, it was the Uitlander franchise which came to occupy the most prominent place in the British government's demands on Kruger's government.

The attractions of making a stand on this issue were many. It had moral and popular appeal, since the treatment of the Uitlanders in the Transvaal was unequal and exceptional by the standards operating with regard to Europeans in the rest of South Africa. It united the fractious Uitlanders and rallied the support of public opinion, both in Britain and abroad. The successive concessions made on the franchise by Kruger's government during 1899 testified to the fact that even the Transvaal government admitted its legitimacy. An Uitlander franchise also appeared to offer the best means for enabling the Uitlanders to rectify their own grievances in the future without perpetually involving the British government. British government papers point emphatically to the conclusion that Salisbury, Chamberlain and the British Cabinet were convinced, by 1899, that Uitlander grievances were genuine and required action, and that the franchise offered the best means by which the various grievances of the Uitlanders might be rectified, the government of the Transvaal improved, the need for perpetual nagging by the British government removed, and British paramountcy and control could be reasserted over a Transvaal increasingly set on a course of complete, republican independence.

The Uitlander franchise, in other words, offered the best means to a larger end and that end was not just the alleviation of Uitlander grievances. The franchise, as Kruger well saw, formed the stalking-horse behind which the 'deep down thing' of British supremacy over the Transvaal was being advanced. The extreme reluctance of Kruger's government to enfranchise the Uitlanders stemmed from its not unreasonable belief that the majority of this amorphous population – whom Kruger never ceased to refer to as 'strangers' and 'aliens' – were present in the Transvaal on a different basis to the Boer burghers. Their sudden influx represented an immediate or potential Trojan horse. As Kruger repeatedly pointed out to Milner at the Bloemfontein Conference, 'to grant the franchise to any large number of aliens would immediately result in the outvoting of the old burghers'.[81] Kruger's fears may have been exaggerated, since it is very doubtful if more than a small minority of the Uitlanders would have been willing to exchange their existing citizenship for that of the Transvaal, but Milner's reassurances were certainly disingenuous. Kruger was not deceived. It was not just an Uitlander franchise but the take-over of his government that the British were after: through a peaceful internal take-over if possible, by the application of external force if necessary. What the British wanted was a transfer of power.

On this issue, Kruger and his burghers would fight.

In England, the Liberal leader, Henry Campbell-Bannerman, had also come to this conclusion. As he observed shrewdly to Harcourt on the day before war broke out:

> If you ask me my own opinion, I hold this 'franchise' movement as the biggest hypocrisy in the whole fraud. It was designed in order that:
> a) Kruger, seeing the real drift of it, might refuse it, and supply a direct ground of quarrel;
> b) If he accepted it, it would mean that not being able to get in by the front door they would get the area gate opened and get possession in this way of the country;
> c) The innocent Briton would be gulled by the flavour of legality and of civilised progress in the word 'franchise' . . . the Outlander does not care about it and would not use it if he might.[82]

So, the Uitlander franchise was always a means to a larger end, and that end was British supremacy in the Transvaal and in South Africa. This larger end comes more prominently into view during July 1899 in both the private and the public statements of the British government and its agents. On 10 July, Milner observed: 'Franchise and every other question have merged in one big issue: is British paramountcy to be vindicated or let slide?'[83] This was the issue which Chamberlain emphasized in his final speech to the House of Commons on 28 July, before it broke up for the summer recess. This was what was at stake in South Africa, he told the Cabinet in September, as it prepared to go to war with the Transvaal.[84]

At the end of 1895 an Uitlander uprising on the Rand, assisted from outside the Transvaal by Jameson and his Raiders, was to have been the pretext for a direct intervention by the British government in the Transvaal as a result of which Kruger's government would have been removed. The British High Commissioner, Sir Hercules Robinson, was expected to arrive from Cape Town and issue a Proclamation ordering submission to his arbitration and the formation of a new Constituent Assembly, 'to be elected by every adult white male in the country', many of whom were Uitlanders.[85] The failure of the uprising and Jameson's fiasco put paid to any such reform. But Chamberlain took up the gauntlet of Uitlander grievances in January 1896, in the wake of this debacle, and the British government continued thereafter to champion them. They did this long before Milner arrived on the scene and they did it because the Uitlanders represented Britain's best hope of bringing about a peaceful revolution in the Transvaal, where they formed Britain's obvious allies and collaborators (or 'clients' as Chamberlain preferred to call them).

Chamberlain might point out to Kruger that Uitlander unrest would only cease when their grievances were rectified. Kruger was well aware of the potential fifth column which the Uitlanders represented. Between 1896 and 1899, Chamberlain continued to press Kruger's government for the redress of Uitlander grievances but achieved very little. Milner's initial conclusion was that 'the remedy may be found in time in an English party in the Transvaal getting the franchise. . . . *But the Boer oligarchy of the Transvaal is going to die hard.* And it is not going to precipitate its own demise by provoking us too much'.[86]

As Milner was to learn after 1902, the Uitlanders were a fickle lot who could not be counted upon to support the British cause – even though the majority of them were British. In 1899, however, he was more optimistic than Chamberlain was that they would not 'turn and rend us' after Britain had championed their interests.[87] Since it was assumed that the long-term future of the Transvaal lay in the Uitlanders' burgeoning numbers and unreliable hands, it was regarded as essential to retain their loyalty and maintain their confidence in Britain's determination to stand by her supremacy in South Africa. Chamberlain, like Salisbury, disliked and distrusted the Uitlanders and was irritated by their demands, but he was tied to them and to championing their cause. If Britain refused to act on their second petition to the Queen, it was feared that they would come to terms with the republic and leave Britain without a leg to stand on in the Transvaal. Lord Salisbury was rather more sanguine and believed that the Uitlanders 'must come to us – because they have no one else to go to'.[88] Meanwhile, the accelerating power and importance of the Transvaal convinced him that the British government had to exert itself and restore its weakening hold over what was clearly going to be the hub of the entire region. The last best chance to do this, without a resort to war, seemed to be to compel Kruger's government to give the Uitlanders a franchise.

Thus, the British government was more concerned in 1899 with strengthening Britain's hold over the Transvaal and British supremacy in South Africa than with the rights of the Uitlanders. But Uitlander rights and an Uitlander franchise offered a means to the larger end which gradually won the support of public opinion and became central to the *casus belli*. Between July and September 1899, the Transvaal government made successive moves to meet the British demand on the Uitlander franchise: first by passing the new franchise law in July and then by the Smuts proposals in August which, on this issue, would have conceded all that Milner had demanded at the Bloemfontein Conference in June. Meanwhile, however, the level of distrust was such that the British government doubted whether even if a settlement was reached on this matter with Kruger's government, it would be implemented in good faith. The franchise proposals of Kruger's government amounted to the granting of a privilege to certain Uitlanders on conditions which were designed to ensure that power remained in the hands of Kruger and his burghers. As Milner put it: 'they want to squeeze the new-comers into the existing mould. I want them to burst it'.[89] What the British government was after was a transfer of power in the Transvaal: by a peaceful internal take-over if possible, by war if necessary.

Only after the war had begun did the British government decide to annex the Transvaal. This had not been the original objective. What Britain needed in 1899 was a 'friendly' and subservient government in the Transvaal, *not* sovereignty over Transvaal territory. What Britain sought and failed to get from Kruger's government was influence over the *polity* of the Transvaal, not necessarily the establishment of a British colony there. Thus, the evidence is strong that some sort of a self-governing Transvaal would have been acceptable to the British, just as the Orange Free State was, *providing* that it was under a 'friendly' government which could be relied upon to cooperate in the larger British imperial project for a federation or union of South Africa, along Canadian lines, in which British supremacy and British interests would prevail. It was because Kruger was hostile and determined to oppose these objectives that Britain went to war to replace him by a government which would assist rather than obstruct the achievement of British aims. That it was these essentially *political* objectives which predominated is also suggested by asking the question: what did Britain do with the gold-mines and the Transvaal after she had conquered and annexed the country, as a result of the war, in 1900? The answer is that the gold-mines remained in the same private hands and, although the monopolies were abolished and the Uitlanders obtained the 'equal rights' long established for Europeans elsewhere in South Africa, gold-mining was subjected to even higher taxation under the post-war administration than it had been under Kruger's government. As for the Transvaal, Britain put it back under Boer self-government in 1907 and then encouraged the emergence of a Union of South Africa, in 1910, which was Boer-led and Boer-dominated. What happened was that Britain followed the course which had already been set in Canada, Australia and New Zealand, and was to follow elsewhere during the twentieth-century exercise in decolonization. Britain transferred power in South Africa to the dominant ruling elite, which they had come to view as the best means for the preservation of British interests, including economic interests, in the area. British rule may have come to an end but British interests were maintained and gold-mining boomed in the unified, if Boer-controlled, dominion which had been brought into existence within the British Empire–Commonwealth, where it remained until 1961 and to which it returned in 1994.

Why then did Kruger's republic go to war with Britain in October 1899, when it had everything to lose by fighting? The short answer is that it fought for its internal independence and against a future in which Kruger and his burghers feared that control over the Transvaal's internal affairs would pass out of Boer hands. The growing pressure of British imperialism provoked a response in the form of a narrow and assertive nationalism. The ruling white Afrikaner minority in the Transvaal feared the prospect of being swamped by another white, mainly English-speaking minority, with very different values and backed up by the world's then greatest power. Since Kruger's republic had recovered its qualified independence from Britain in 1881 after fighting and winning a war against British forces, its government had jealously sought to preserve its Afrikaner identity and extend its independence amidst the transforming effects of the mineral revolution on the Rand. Its Afrikaner ruling minority had no wish to admit to equality foreigners who did not share their language, history, religion, culture or way of life, and did not have the same interest in preserving Afrikaner group power and control over a land which they had always regarded as full of potential enemies. The South African Republic ended by fighting and losing a war in an attempt to protect itself from such a change.

NOTES

1. Speech on 19 October 1899, *Hansard*, Fourth Series, vol. lxxvii, cols 264, pp. 270–5.
2. Deneys Reitz, *Commando: A Boer Journal of the Boer War* (London, 1929), pp. 17–18.
3. Salisbury to Leonard Courtenay, 5 October 1899, in G. P. Gooch, *Life of Lord Courtenay* (London, 1920), pp. 377–8.
4. G. H. Le May, *British Supremacy in South Africa 1899–1907* (Oxford, 1965), p. 33.
5. Milner to Chamberlain, 30 November 1899, in C. Headlam, ed., *The Milner Papers* 2 vols (London, 1931/1933), 2, p. 23; also 22 September 1899, in ibid., 1, p. 542.

6. Le May, *British Supremacy*, p. 33.
7. J. Rose Innes to R. W. Rose Innes, 22 March 1897, in Harrison M. Wright, ed., *Sir James Rose Innes: Selected Correspondence* (Cape Town, 1972), p. 201. This view is reinforced by the recent work of Professor M. Tamarkin on Rhodes and the Cape Afrikaners.
8. In F. W. Reitz, *A Century of Wrong* (London, 1900), p. 98.
9. *Hansard*, Fourth Series, 1 February 1900, vol. lxxviii, col. 257.
10. Thucydides, *History of the Peloponnesian War* (London, 1954 edn), p. 25.
11. 'Memoirs of the Boer War', unfinished MS written by Smuts between 1903 and 1906 and printed in W. K. Hancock and J. van der Poel, eds, *Selections from the Smuts Papers* 7 vols (Cambridge, 1966–73), 1, p. 623.
12. Ibid., p. 624.
13. J. A. Hobson, *The War in South Africa: Its Causes and Effects* (London, 1900), pp. 197, 229, 240.
14. See Chapter 7, pp. 215–17 above.
15. Milner to Selborne, 28 June 1899, in D. G. Boyce, ed., *The Crisis of British Power: The Imperial and Naval Papers of the Second Earl of Selborne, 1895–1910* (London, 1990), p. 87.
16. Salisbury to Chamberlain, 9 October 1899, JC 5/67/129.
17. Reitz, *A Century of Wrong*, p. 98. In a new Introduction to an Afrikaans version, *'n Eeu van Onreg* (Cape Town and Pretoria, 1985), Professor D. J. van Zyl convincingly argues that although the book was issued under F. W. Reitz's name, its authors were J. C. Smuts and J. de V. Roos.
18. V. I. Lenin, *Imperialism: The Highest Stage of Capitalism* (1916).
19. Eric Stokes, 'Late nineteenth century colonial expansion and the attack on the theory of economic imperialism: a case of mistaken identity?', *HJ* XII (1969); B. Porter, 'Imperialism and the scramble', *JICH* 9 (1980); N. Etherington, *Theories of Imperialism: War, Conquest and Capital* (London, 1984).
20. See N. Etherington, 'Theories of imperialism in southern Africa revisited', *African Affairs* 81 (1982).
21. R. Rotberg, *The Founder: Cecil Rhodes and the Pursuit of Power* (Oxford, 1988), pp. 619–20.
22. Smuts, like most others at the time, blamed Chamberlain until the publication of C. Headlam's first volume of selections from *The Milner Papers* (London, 1931) caused him to change his mind.
23. J. S. Marais, *The Fall of Kruger's Republic* (Oxford, 1961), p. 324.
24. The works of Alan Jeeves, R. V. Kubicek, J. J. Van Helten, A. N. Porter, Thomas Pakenham and Richard Mendelsohn, cited in the bibliography, are especially relevant here.
25. Le May, *British Supremacy*, p. 30.
26. Hobson, *The War in South Africa*, p. 231. This aspect attracted particular attention during the 1970s. See Dennis Bransky, 'The causes of the Boer War: towards a new synthesis', unpublished paper, Oxford, 1974.
27. See especially A. Jeeves, *Migrant Labour in South Africa's Mining Economy 1890–1921* (Johannesburg, 1985), and P. Harries, 'Capital, state and labour on the 19th century Witwatersrand: a reassessment', *SAHJ* 18 (1986).

28. See especially Chapter 6 of Alan Jeeves, 'The Rand capitalists in Transvaal politics 1892–1899', Ph.D. thesis, Queen's University, Kingston, Ontario, Canada, 1971; A. N. Porter, 'Sir Alfred Milner and the Press, 1897–1899', *HJ* xvi, 2 (1973).

29. See R. Mendelsohn, *Sammy Marks, 'The Uncrowned King of the Transvaal'* (Cape Town, 1991).

30. I am much indebted to the work of Alan Jeeves in this section and especially to his unpublished Ph.D. thesis cited in n. 28 above.

31. See Chapter 2, p. 49 above.

32. T. J. Noer, *Briton, Boer and Yankee: the U.S.A. and South Africa 1879–1914* (Kent State University Press, 1978), p. 32.

33. *Transvaal Industrial Commission* (Johannesburg, 1897), evidence given by Mr William Hall, pp. 413–14.

34. A. Jeeves, 'Aftermath of rebellion: the Randlords and Kruger's Republic after the Jameson Raid', *SAHJ* 10 (1978), p. 112; Shula Marks, Chapter 8 in R. Oliver and G. N. Sanderson, eds, *The Cambridge History of Africa* (Cambridge, 1985), vol.6, pp. 470–9; also the same author's 'Scrambling for South Africa', *JAH* 23 (1982), p. 108.

35. J. and R. Simons, *Class and Colour in South Africa 1850–1950* (Harmondsworth, 1969), p. 62.

36. Hobson, *The War in South Africa,* pp. 5–6.

37. R. Robinson and J. A. Gallagher, *Africa and the Victorians* (London, 1961), p. 461.

38. I am here in agreement with P. Cain and A. G. Hopkins, *British Imperialism: Innovation and Expansion 1688–1914* 2 vols (London, 1993) 1, p. 380. Like them, I am indebted to the work of R. L. Cope, 'Strategic and socio-economic explanations for Carnarvon's South African Confederation policy: the historiography and the evidence', *History in Africa* 13 (1986). This has provided a valuable corrective to the over-emphasis on 'the sea-route to India' in the interpretation of Robinson and Gallagher, *Africa and the Victorians.*

39. For a fine synthesis by Shula Marks see Chapters 7 and 8 in Oliver and Sanderson, eds, *The Cambridge History of Africa,* 6.

40. Cain and Hopkins, *British Imperialism*, pp. 373–4. More detailed information is to be found in the tables in J. J. Van Helten, 'British and European economic investment in the Transvaal, with specific reference to the Witwatersrand gold fields and district 1886–1910', London Ph.D. thesis, 1981, pp. 336–8.

41. J. J. Van Helten, 'Empire and high finance: South Africa and the International Gold Standard 1890–1914', *JAH* 23 (1982), p. 541.

42. For the attitude of Germany and German capitalists I owe a great deal to discussions with Harald Rosenbach and his recent research in German archives for his book *Das Deutsche Reich, Grossbritannien und der Transvaal (1896–1902)* (Göttingen, 1993). I have also had a cursory look at contemporary French and German newspapers. There are nuggets of information about the Dutch position in W. J. Leyds, *Tweede Verzameling Correspondentie 1899–1900* (Dordrecht, 1934). American attitudes are well

delineated in Noer, *Briton, Boer and Yankee*, and R. B. Mulanax, *The Boer War in American Politics and Diplomacy* (University Press of America, 1994); J. J. Van Helten, 'German capital, the Netherlands Railway Company and the political economy of the Transvaal 1886–1900', *JAH* 29 (1978), is a most useful article, and there is further data in his 'British and European investment in the Transvaal'. R. V. Kubicek, *Economic Imperialism in Theory and Practice: The Case of South African Gold Mining Finance 1886–1914* (Durham, NC, 1979); R. V. Turrell, 'Finance . . . the governor of the imperial engine', *JSAS* 13 (1987); and Cain and Hopkins, *British Imperialism*, pp. 370–80, also contain useful material.

43. See Noer, *Briton, Boer and Yankee*; also Mulanax, *The Boer War in American Politics.*

44. Hobson, *The War in South Africa*, p. 61.

45. A. N. Porter, *The Origins of the South African War: Joseph Chamberlain and the Diplomacy of Imperialism 1895–1899* (Manchester, 1980), and idem, 'The South African War (1899–1902): context and motive reconsidered', *JAH* 31 (1990), pp. 43–57. For the criticism see S. Marks and S. Trapido, 'Lord Milner and the South African State reconsidered', in M. Twaddle, ed., *Imperialism, the State and the Third World* (London, 1992), p. 86.

46. C. van Onselen, *Studies in the Social and Economic History of the Witwatersrand 1886–1914: New Babylon* (London, 1982), p. 14.

47. E. Hobsbawm, *The Age of Empire* (London, 1987), p. 66.

48. See President Steyn's manifesto, on the outbreak of the war, printed in L. S. Amery, *The Times History of the War in South Africa* 7 vols (London, 1900–9), 1, p. 375.

49. See J. D. Kestell and D. E. Van Velden, *The Peace Negotiations . . . which terminated in the Peace concluded at Vereeniging on 31 May 1902* (London, 1912), p. 73.

50. Speech reported fully in *The Times*, 10 November 1899.

51. Ibid.

52. All quotations from the text of the final British ultimatum, dated 9 October 1899 and printed in E. Drus, 'Select documents from the Chamberlain Papers concerning Anglo-Transvaal relations 1896–99', *BIHR* 27 (1954), pp. 182–6.

53. Lord Ripon to Lord Rosebery, 5 September 1894, RP 43516. See Chapter 3 p. 71 above.

54. Milner to Chamberlain, 23 August 1899, JC 10/9/48, italics mine.

55. Salisbury to Lansdowne, 30 August 1899, in Robinson and Gallagher, *Africa and the Victorians,* p. 454.

56. See Chapter 10 p. 376 above.

57. Quoted in Le May, *British Supremacy*, p. 21.

58. There is now a considerable literature on this still continuing debate. Amongst the most directly relevant contributions are S. Marks and S. Trapido, 'Lord Milner and the South African State', *History Workshop* 8 (1979), and the same authors' 'Lord Milner and the South African State reconsidered'; J. J. Van Helten, 'Empire and high finance', pp. 529–48;

Russell Ally, 'The Bank of England and South Africa's gold 1886–1926', Cambridge Ph.D. thesis, 1990, published in revised form as *Gold and Empire: the Bank of England and South Africa's Gold Producers 1886–1926* (Johannesburg, 1994); also his unpublished paper 'Great Britain, gold and South Africa – an examination of the influence gold had in shaping Britain's policy towards South Africa 1886–1914', Institute of Commonwealth Studies, London, 25 May 1989; Marc Yakutiel, 'Treasury control and the South African War 1899–1905', Oxford D.Phil. thesis, 1989; A. N. Porter, 'The South African War (1899–1902): context and motive reconsidered', *JAH* 31 (1900), pp. 43–57.

59. Marks and Trapido, 'Lord Milner and the South African State reconsidered', p. 86.

60. J. J. Van Helten, 'Empire and high finance', pp. 529–48.

61. See Ally, *Gold and Empire*, ch. 2; also his article, 'The South African pound comes of age: Sterling, the Bank of England and South Africa's monetary policy 1914–1925', *JICH* 22, 1 (1993), pp. 109–26.

62. For the Treasury see Yakutiel, 'Treasury control'.

63. This section was improved by a discussion with Professor Alec G. Ford, whose book on *The Gold Standard 1880–1914, Britain and Argentina* (Oxford, 1962) is a standard authority on the subject. In addition to my own research in the Bank of England and British government papers, I have also drawn heavily on the work of J. J. Van Helten, especially his article, 'Empire and high finance', and his unpublished Ph.D. thesis, 'British and European economic investment in the Transvaal', particularly pp. 81–2, 336–8, 370.

64. This paragraph is indebted to much discussion with Marc Yakutiel and his research for his Oxford D.Phil. thesis 'Treasury control'.

65. Le May, *British Supremacy*, ch. 1; T. Pakenham, *The Boer War* (London, 1979), Part 1; critique by Marks and Trapido, 'Lord Milner and the South African State'.

66. See A. N. Porter, 'Lord Salisbury, Mr Chamberlain and South Africa 1895–1899', *JICH* 1, 1 (1972), p. 17.

67. Printed in Headlam, ed., *The Milner Papers*, 1, pp. 220–4.

68. Milner to Selborne, 10 July 1899, SeP MS 11.

69. Cain and Hopkins, *British Imperialism*, p. 379.

70. E. H. Carr, *What is History?* (London, 1961), p. 45.

71. Salisbury to Lansdowne, 30 August 1899, in Lord Newton, *Lord Lansdowne* (London, 1929), p. 157.

72. Sir Edward Hamilton, Diary, 6 October 1899, British Library Add. MSS 48675.

73. Milner to Chamberlain, 5 July 1899, cited in Porter, *Origins*, p. 230.

74. Milner to Lord Roberts, 6 June 1900, quoted in Pakenham, *The Boer War*, p. 113.

75. Chamberlain to Milner, 6 December 1899, JC 10/9/74.

76. Cain and Hopkins, *British Imperialism*, p. 379.

77. Chamberlain to Milner, 6 December 1899, JC 10/9/74; Milner to Chamberlain, 23 August 1899, JC 10/9/48.

78. The quotation is from Milner to Chamberlain, 6 July 1898, printed in Headlam, ed., *The Milner Papers*, 1, p. 267.
79. Milner to Selborne, 9 May 1898, D. G. Boyce, ed., *The Collapse of British Power*, in ibid., p. 59.
80. Milner to Hely Hutchinson, 22 April 1899, in ibid., p. 398.
81. Verbatim record of the Bloemfontein Conference enclosed in Milner to Chamberlain, 14 June 1899, and printed in C.9404, p. 2.
82. Campbell-Bannerman to Harcourt, 10 October 1899, in A. G. Gardiner, *The Life of Sir William Harcourt* 2 vols (London, 1923), 2, p. 504.
83. Milner to Selborne, 10 July 1899, in Headlam, ed., *The Milner Papers*, 1, pp. 456–7.
84. Memorandum for the Cabinet by Chamberlain, 6 September 1899, CAB 37/50/70, p. 2.
85. See Chapter 3 p. 88 above.
86. Milner to Sir Clinton Dawkins, 25 August 1897, in Headlam, ed., *The Milner Papers*, 1, p. 87.
87. Milner to Hely Hutchinson, 8 May 1899, in ibid., p. 359.
88. Salisbury to Chamberlain, 19 September 1899, JC 5/67/124.
89. Milner to Sir Edward Grey, 7 August 1899, in Headlam, ed., *The Milner Papers*, 1, p. 478.

Bibliography

Note : Not all of the works listed in the notes are cited here.

A: MANUSCRIPT SOURCES

LONDON
Public Record Office, Kew
Colonial Office
CO 417 (1894–1902) South Africa Correspondence
CO 537 (1895–9)   Further Correspondence
CO 879 (1894–1900) Confidential Print series

Foreign Office
FO 2   (1895–9)   Africa General Correspondence
FO 63   (1895–9)   Portugal
FO 64   (1895–9)   Germany
FO 881 (1896–9)   Confidential Prints

War Office
WO 32, WO 33 and WO 108   Misc. Papers on the South African War
WO 132   Buller Papers

Cabinet Records
CAB 37 (1894–9)   General Papers
CAB 38 (1894–1902) Committee of Defence
CAB 41 (1896–9)   Prime Minister's Letters to the Queen

Bank of England Archives
Committee of Treasury Papers
Policy Files, Gold (1889–1905)
Weekly Data on Gold and Silver Bullion Imports (1897–1905)

British Library
Diary of Sir Edward Hamilton
Ripon Papers

Society of Friends Library
Report of Arthur Guy Enock, 1899

OXFORD
Bodleian Library
Milner Papers
Selborne Papers

Rhodes House Library
Graham Bower Papers
Cecil J. Rhodes Papers
Records of the Central Mining & Investment Corporation 1890–1900

CAMBRIDGE
University Library
J. C. Smuts Papers (microfilm)

BIRMINGHAM
University Library
Joseph Chamberlain Papers

PRETORIA
Government Archives
BA 12–34 British Agent's Papers
South African Republic Government Green Books 1895–9
Minutes (*Notulen*) of The First Volksraad (1898–9)
J. C. Smuts Papers
W. J. Leyds Papers
Philip Gell Papers (photocopies)

JOHANNESBURG
Barlow Rand Archives
Papers of Wernher, Beit/H. Eckstein & Co.

Standard Bank of South Africa Archives
General Manager's Letters 1898–9
General Correspondence 1896–1900

Economic Reports
Half-yearly Reports 1897–9

Chamber of Mines Archives
Letterbooks 1897–9
Annual Reports 1895–1902
Evidence and Report of the Mining Industry to the Industrial
   Commission of Enquiry, 1897

CAPE TOWN
South African Library
J. Hofmeyr Papers
W. P. Schreiner Papers
Sir Henry de Villiers Papers
Sir James Rose Innes Papers
P. A. Molteno Papers
John X. Merriman Papers

Cape Archives
British High Commissioner/Governor of the Cape Colony Papers
   1897–9
Lewis Michell Papers

Jagger Library, University of Cape Town
Louis Esselen Papers
Olive Schreiner Papers

GRAHAMSTOWN
National English Language Museum
Sir Percy FitzPatrick Papers

Cory Library, Rhodes University
Gold Fields of South Africa Documents

B: PRINTED DOCUMENTARY COLLECTIONS

Boyce, D. G., ed., *The Crisis of British Power: The Imperial and Naval Papers of the Second Earl of Selborne, 1895–1910*. London 1990.
Boyd, C. W., ed., *Mr. Chamberlain's Speeches*. 2 vols, London 1914.
Buckle, G. E., ed., *The Letters of Queen Victoria*. Third Series, 3 vols, London 1932.

Comaroff, J. L., ed., *The Boer War Diary of Sol. T. Plaatje: an African at Mafeking*. London 1973.

Dugdale, E. T. S., ed., *German Diplomatic Documents 1871–1914*. 4 vols, New York edn, 1969.

Duminy, A. H. and Guest, W. R., eds, *FitzPatrick, South African Politician: Selected Papers, 1888–1906*. Johannesburg 1976.

Eybers, G. W., ed., *Select Constitutional Documents illustrating South African History, 1795–1910*. London 1918.

Fraser, M., ed., *Johannesburg Pioneer Journals 1888–1909*. Cape Town 1985.

Fraser, M. and Jeeves, A., eds, *All That Glittered: Selected Correspondence of Lionel Phillips, 1890–1924*. Cape Town 1977.

Hancock, W. K. and van der Poel, J., eds, *Selections from the Smuts Papers*. 7 vols, Cambridge 1966–73.

Headlam, C., ed., *The Milner Papers*. 2 vols, London 1931/1933.

Kestell, J. D. and Van Velden, D. E., eds, *The Peace Negotiations . . . which terminated in the Peace concluded at Vereeniging on 31 May 1902*. London 1912.

Lewsen, P., ed., *Selections from the Correspondence of J. X. Merriman, 1870–1890*. 4 vols, Cape Town 1960–9.

Leyds, W. J., *Eenige Correspondentie uit 1899*. Amsterdam 1938.

Leyds, W. J., *Tweede Verzameling (Correspondentie 1900–1902)*. 2 vols, The Hague 1930.

Mabin, A. and Conradie, B., eds, *The Confidence of the Whole Country: Standard Bank Reports on Economic Conditions in Southern Africa 1865–1902*. Johannesburg 1987.

van Reenen, R., ed., *Emily Hobhouse: Boer War Letters*. Cape Town 1984.

Rive, R., ed., *Olive Schreiner, Letters 1871–1899*. Cape Town 1987.

Shaw, G., ed., *The Garrett Papers*. Cape Town 1984.

Solomon, V., ed., *Selections from the Correspondence of Percy Alport Molteno, 1892–1914*. Cape Town 1981.

du Toit, A. and Giliomee, H., eds, *Afrikaner Political Thought: Analysis and Documents 1780–1850*. Los Angeles 1983.

Vindex (pseudonym of Verschoyle, J.), *Cecil Rhodes: His Political Life and Speeches 1881–1900*. London 1900.

Wright, H. M., ed., *Sir James Rose Innes, Selected Correspondence, 1884–1902*. Cape Town 1972.

C: OFFICIAL PRINTED DOCUMENTS

British Parliamentary Papers
1895–6 LIX (C. 7933), 'Correspondence re. the Jameson Raid'
1896 LIX (C. 8063) 'Further Correspondence re. the Jameson Raid'
1897 LXII (C. 8423) 'Further Correspondence re. the affairs of the S.A.R.'
1898 LX (C. 8721) 'Further Correspondence re. the S.A.R.'
1899 LXIV (C. 9093) 'S.A.R. : report on trade, commerce and goldmining'
1899 LXIV (C. 9317) 'Correspondence re. the explosives monopoly in the S.A.R.'
1899 LXIV (C. 9345) 'Papers re. complaints of British subjects in the S.A.R.'
1899 LXIV (C. 9404) 'Correspondence re. the Bloemfontein Conference'
1899 LXIV (C. 9415) 'Further Correspondence re. proposed political reforms in the S.A.R.'
1899 LXIV (C. 9518) 'Further Correspondence re. proposed political reforms in the S.A.R.'
1899 LXIV (C. 9521) 'Further Correspondence re. political affairs in the S.A.R.'
1899 LXIV (C. 9530) 'Further Correspondence re. political affairs in the S.A.R.'
1899 LXIV (C. 9507) 'Correspondence re. the status of the S.A.R.'

Royal Commission on the War in South Africa, Report, Minutes of Evidence and Appendices. Cd. 1789–1792 (XL, XLI, XLII of 1904).
Hansard, Fourth Series, Parliamentary Debates

D: NEWSPAPERS

The Times
The Cape Times
The Star
The Standard and Diggers News

E: UNPUBLISHED THESES AND PAPERS

Ally, R., 'The Bank of England and South Africa's gold, c. 1886–1926', Ph.D. thesis, Cambridge University, 1990.

Ally, R., 'Great Britain, gold and South Africa – an examination of the influence gold had in shaping Britain's policy towards South Africa 1886–1914', paper given at the Institute of Commonwealth Studies, London, 25 May 1989.

Bitensky, M. F., 'The South African League: British imperialist organisation in South Africa 1896–1899', M.A. thesis, Witwatersrand University, 1950.

Bransky, D., 'The causes of the Boer War: towards a new synthesis', unpublished paper, Oxford University, 1974.

Cammack, D., 'Class, politics and war: a socio-economic study of the Uitlanders of the Witwatersrand 1897–1902', Ph.D. thesis, University of California (Irvine), 1983.

Cuthbertson, G. C., 'The non-conformist conscience and the South African War, 1899–1902', D.Litt. and Phil., University of South Africa, 1986.

Duminy, A. H., 'The political career of Sir Percy FitzPatrick, 1895–1906', Ph.D. thesis, Natal University, 1973.

Etheredge, D. A., 'The early history of the Chamber of Mines, Johannesburg, 1887–1897', M.A. thesis, Witwatersrand University, 1949.

Van Helten, J. J., 'British and European economic investment in the Transvaal with specific reference to the Witwatersrand goldfields and district 1886–1910', Ph.D. thesis, London University, 1981.

Van Helten, J. J., 'Milner and the mind of imperialism', paper given at the Institute of Commonwealth Studies, London, November 1978.

Jeeves, A., 'The Rand capitalists and Transvaal politics 1892–1899', Ph.D. thesis, Queen's University, Kingston, Canada, 1971.

Mawby, A., 'The political behaviour of the British population of the Transvaal 1902–1907', Ph.D. thesis, Witwatersrand University, 1969.

Mendelsohn, R., 'The Cape and the Drifts Crisis of 1895', History Honours dissertation, University of Cape Town, 1971.

Surridge, K. T., 'British civil–military relations and the South African War 1899–1902', Ph.D. thesis, London University, 1994.

Wilburn, K., 'The climax of railway competition in South Africa 1887–1899', D.Phil. thesis, Oxford University, 1982.

Yakutiel, M., 'Treasury control and the South African War 1899–1905', D.Phil. thesis, Oxford University, 1989.

F: ARTICLES

Atmore, A. and Marks, S., 'The imperial factor in South Africa in the nineteenth century: towards a reassessment', *JICH* 3, 1 (1974): 105–39.

Blainey, G., 'Lost causes of the Jameson Raid', *Econ. Hist. Rev.* 18 (1965): 350–66.

Blake, R., 'The Jameson Raid and the Missing Telegrams', in Lloyd-Jones, H., ed., *History and Imagination: Essays for H. R. Trevor-Roper* (London, 1981): 326–39.

Butler, J., 'Sir Alfred Milner on British policy in South Africa in 1897', *Boston University Papers on Africa* 1 (Boston, 1964): 243–70.

Butler, J., 'The German factor in Anglo-Transvaal relations', in Gifford, P. and Louis, W. R., eds, *Britain and Germany in Africa* (New Haven, 1967): 179–214.

Cain, P. J., 'J. A. Hobson, financial capitalism and imperialism in late Victorian and Edwardian England', *JICH* 13, 3 (1985): 1–27.

Cain, P. J. and Hopkins, A. G., 'The political economy of British expansion overseas', *Econ. Hist. Rev.*, 2nd series, 33, 4 (1980): 463–90.

Cain, P. J. and Hopkins, A. G., 'Gentlemanly capitalism and British expansion overseas', Parts 1 and 2, *Econ. Hist. Rev.*, 2nd series, 39 (1986): 501–25, and 40 (1987): 1–26.

Cammack, D., 'The politics of discontent: the grievances of the Uitlander refugees, 1899–1902', *JSAS* 8 (1982): 243–70.

Cammack, D., 'The Johannesburg republic: the re-shaping of Rand society, 1900–1901', *SAHJ* 18 (1986): 47–72.

Cassis, Y., 'The banking community of London, 1890–1914', *JICH* 13, 3 (1985): 109–26.

Cope, R. L., 'Shepstone, the Zulu and the annexation of the Transvaal', *SAHJ* 4 (1972): 45–63.

Cope, R. L., 'Strategic and socio-economic explanations for Carnarvon's South African Confederation policy: the historiography and the evidence', *History in Africa* 13 (1986): 13–34.

Dachs, A. J., 'Rhodes's grasp for Bechuanaland, 1889–1896', *Rhodesian History* 2 (1971): 1–9.

Denoon, D., ' "Capitalist influence" and the Transvaal government during the Crown Colony period, 1900–1906', *HJ* 11, 2 (1968): 301–31.

Denoon, D., 'Capital and capitalists in the Transvaal in the 1890s and 1900s', *HJ* 23, 1 (1980): 111–32.

Denoon, D., 'The Transvaal labour crisis, 1901–6', *JAH* 7 (1967): 481–9.

Drus, E., 'A report on the papers of Joseph Chamberlain relating to the Jameson Raid and the Inquiry', *BIHR* 25 (1952): 33–62.

Drus, E., 'The question of imperial complicity in the Jameson Raid', *EHR* 68 (1953): 582–93.

Drus, E., 'Select documents from the Chamberlain papers concerning Anglo-Transvaal relations, 1896–99', *BIHR* 27 (1954): 156–89.

Drus, E., 'Chamberlain and the Boers', *JAH* 4 (1963): 144–5.

Etherington, N., 'Theories of imperialism in Southern Africa revisited', *African Affairs* 81 (1982): 385–407.

Etherington, N., 'Labour supply and the genesis of South African Confederation in the 1870s', *JAH* 20 (1979): 235–53.

Fieldhouse, D. K., ' "Imperialism" – an historiographical revision', *Econ. Hist. Rev.*, 2nd series, 14, 2 (1961–2): 187– 209.

Galbraith, J. S., 'The "turbulent frontier" as a factor in British expansion', *CSSH* 11 (1959–60):150–68.

Galbraith, J. S., 'The British South Africa Company and the Jameson Raid', *JBS* 10, 1 (1970): 145–61.

Galbraith, J. S., 'Cecil Rhodes and his "Cosmic Dreams": a reassessment', *JICH* 1, 2 (1973): 173–89.

Galbraith, J. S., 'The pamphlet campaign on the Boer War', *JMH* 24, 2 (1952): 111–26.

Gallagher, J. A. and Robinson, R. E., 'The imperialism of free trade', *Econ. Hist. Rev.*, 2nd series, 6 (1953–4): 1–15.

Garson, N. G., 'British imperialism and the coming of the Anglo-Boer War', *SAJE* 30, 2 (1962): 140–53.

Giliomee, H., 'The beginnings of Afrikaner nationalism 1870–1915', *SAHJ* 19 (1987): 115–42.

Harcourt, F., 'Disraeli's imperialism, 1866–1868: a question of timing', *HJ* 23, 1 (1980): 87–109.

Harries, P., 'Capital, state, and labour on the 19th century Witwatersrand: a reassessment', *SAHJ* 18 (1986): 25–45.

Van Helten, J. J., 'German capital, the Netherlands Railway Company and the political economy of the Transvaal 1886–1900', *JAH* 19 (1978): 369–90.

Van Helten, J. J., 'Empire and high finance: South Africa and the International Gold Standard 1890–1914', *JAH* 23 (1982): 529–48.

Hobson, J. A., 'Capitalism and Imperialism in South Africa', *The Contemporary Review* 77 (1900): 1–17.

Holli, M. G., 'Joseph Chamberlain and the Jameson Raid: a bibliographical survey', *JBS* 3, 2 (1964): 152–66.

Hopkins, A. G., 'The Victorians and Africa: a reconsideration of the occupation of Egypt, 1882', *JAH* 27 (1986): 363–91.

Howard, M., 'Empire, race and war in pre-1914 Britain', in idem, *The Lessons of History* (Oxford, 1993), pp. 63–80.

Jeeves, A., 'Aftermath of rebellion – the Randlords and Kruger's republic after the Jameson Raid', *SAHJ* 10 (1978): 102–16.

Jeeves, A., 'The Rand capitalists and the coming of the South African War, 1896–1899', *Canadian Historical Association Papers* 1973 (Ottawa, 1974): 61–83.

Jeeves, A., 'The control of migratory labour in the South African gold mines in the era of Kruger and Milner', *JSAS* 2, 2 (1975): 3–29.

Kruger, D. W., 'The British imperial factor in South Africa, 1870–1910', in Gann, L. H. and Duignan, P., eds, *Colonialism in Africa, 1870–1960* (Cambridge, 1969), 1, pp. 325–51.

Kubicek, R. V., 'The Randlords in 1895: a reassessment', *JBS* 11, 2 (1972): 84–103.

Kubicek, R. V., 'Finance capital and South African gold-mining, 1886–1914', *JICH* 3, 3 (1975): 386–95.

Landes, D., 'Some thoughts on the nature of economic imperialism', *JEH* 21 (1961): 496–512.

Legassick, M., 'The frontier tradition in South African historiography', in Marks, S. and Atmore, A., eds, *Economy and Society in Pre-Industrial South Africa* (London, 1980), pp. 44–79.

Lonsdale, J., 'The European scramble and conquest in African history', in *Cambridge History of Africa* 6 (Cambridge, 1985), pp. 680–766.

Louis, W. R., 'Great Britain and German Expansion in Africa 1884–1919', in Gifford, P. and Louis, W. R., eds, *Britain and Germany in Africa* (New Haven, 1967), pp. 3–46.

Madden, A. F., 'Changing attitudes and widening responsibilities, 1895–1914', *Cambridge History of the British Empire* 3 (Cambridge, 1959), pp. 339–405.

Marks, S., Chapter 7 ('Southern Africa, 1867–1886') and Chapter 8 ('Southern and Central Africa, 1886–1910'), in Oliver, R. and Sanderson, G. N., eds, *The Cambridge History of Africa* 6 (Cambridge, 1985).

Marks, S., 'Scrambling for South Africa', *JAH* 23 (1982): 97–113.

Marks, S. and Trapido, S., 'Lord Milner and the South African state', *History Workshop* 8 (1979): 50–80.

Marks, S. and Trapido, S., 'Lord Milner and the South African state reconsidered', in Twaddle, M., ed., *Imperialism, the State and the Third World* (London, 1992), pp. 80–94.

Mawby, A., 'Capital, government and politics in the Transvaal, 1900–1907: a revision and a reversion', *HJ* 17, 2 (1974): 387–415.

Mendelsohn, R., 'Blainey and the Jameson Raid: the debate renewed', *JSAS* 6, 2 (1980): 157–70.

van Onselen, C., 'Reactions to rinderpest in South Africa 1896–7', *JAH* 13 (1972): 473–88.

Ovendale, R., 'Profits or patriotism: Natal, the Transvaal, and the coming of the second Anglo-Boer War', *JICH* 8 (1980): 209–34.

Phimister, I., 'Rhodes, Rhodesia and the Rand', *JSAS* 1, 1 (1974): 74–90.

Pogge von Strandmann, H., 'Domestic origins of Germany's colonial expansion under Bismarck', *PP* 42 (1969): 140–59.

Porter, A. N., 'Lord Salisbury, Mr Chamberlain and South Africa, 1895–9', *JICH* 1, 1 (1972): 3–26.

Porter, A. N., 'Sir Alfred Milner and the Press, 1897–1899', *HJ* 16, 2 (1973): 323–39.

Porter, A. N., 'Joseph Chamberlain: a radical reappraised?', *JICH* 6, 3 (1978): 330–6.

Porter, A. N., 'Lord Salisbury, foreign policy and domestic finance, 1860–1900', in Blake, R. and Cecil, H., eds, *Salisbury. The Man and his Policies* (London, 1987), pp. 148–84.

Porter, A. N., 'The South African War (1899–1902): context and motive reconsidered', *JAH* 31 (1990): 31–57.

Porter, A. N., ' "Gentlemanly capitalism" and empire: the British experience since 1750?', *JICH* 18 (1990): 265–95.

Porter, B., 'Imperialism and the scramble', *JICH* 9 (1980): 76–81.

Richardson, P. and Van Helten, J. J. 'The development of the South African gold-mining industry, 1895–1918', *Econ. Hist. Rev.*, 2nd series, 37, 3 (1984): 319–40.

Richardson, P. and Van Helten, J. J., 'Labour in the South African gold-mining industry 1886–1914', in Marks, S. and Rathbone, R., eds, *Industrialisation and Social Change in South Africa 1870–1930* (London, 1982), pp. 77–98.

Robinson, R. E., 'Imperial problems in British politics', *Cambridge History of The British Empire* 3 (Cambridge, 1959).

Robinson, R. E., 'Non-European foundations of European imperialism: sketch for a theory of collaboration', in Owen, R. and Sutcliffe, B., eds, *Studies in the Theory of Imperialism* (London, 1972) pp. 117–40.

Robinson, R. E. and Gallagher, J. A., 'The partition of Africa', in *The New Cambridge Modern History* 11 (Cambridge, 1962), pp. 593–640.

Sanderson, G. N., 'The European partition of Africa: coincidence or conjuncture?', *JICH* 3, 1 (1974): 1–54.

Smith, I. R., 'The origins of the South African War (1899–1902): a re-appraisal', *SAHJ* 22 (1990): 24–60.

Stokes, E. T. 'Milnerism', *HJ* 5, 1 (1962): 47–60.

Stokes, E. T. 'Late nineteenth-century colonial expansion and the attack on the theory of economic imperialism: a case of mistaken identity', *HJ* 12, 2 (1969): 285–301.

Thompson, L., 'The origins of the South African War', *JAH* 3 (1962): 148–50.

Trapido, S., 'Reflections on land, office and wealth in the South African Republic, 1850–1900', in Marks, S. and Atmore, A., eds, *Economy and Society in Pre-Industrial South Africa* (London, 1980), pp. 350–68.

Trapido, S., 'South Africa in a comparative study of industrialisation', *JDS* 7, 3 (1971): 309–20.

Trebilcock, C., 'War and the failure of industrial mobilisation: 1899 and 1914', in Winter, J. M., ed., *War and Economic Development* (Cambridge, 1975), pp. 139–64.

Turner, H. A., 'Bismarck's imperialist venture: anti-British in origin?', in Gifford, P. and Louis, W. R., eds, *Britain and Germany in Africa* (New Haven, 1967), pp. 47–82.

Turrell, R. V., ' "Finance . . . the Governor of the Imperial Engine": Hobson and the case of Rothschild and Rhodes', *JSAS* 13, 3 (1987): 417–32.

Turrell, R. V. and Van Helten, J. J., 'The Rothschilds, the exploration company and mining finance', *Business History* 27, 2 (1986): 181–205.

Walker, E., 'Lord Milner and South Africa', *Proceedings of the British Academy* 28 (1942): 155–78.

Wehler, H-U., 'Bismarck's imperialism 1862–1890', *PP* 48 (1970): 119–55.

G: BOOKS

Ally, R., *Gold and Empire: The Bank of England and South Africa's Gold Producers 1886–1926.* Johannesburg 1994.

Amery, L. S., ed., *The Times History of the War in South Africa.* 7 vols, London 1900–9.

Amery, L. S., *My Political Life.* 3 vols, London 1953–5.

Arthur, G., *Life of Lord Kitchener.* 3 vols, London 1920.

Barnett, C., *Britain and her Army 1509–1920.* London 1970.

Beinart, W., *Twentieth Century South Africa.* Oxford 1994.

Beloff, M., *Britain's Liberal Empire 1897–1921.* 2nd edn, London 1987.

Benyon, J., *Proconsul and Paramountcy in South Africa.* Pietermaritzburg 1980.

Blake, R. and Cecil, H., eds, *Salisbury: The Man and his Policies*. London 1987.

Bond, B., *Victorian Military Campaigns*. London 1967.

Breytenbach, J. H., *Die geskiedenis van die Tweede Vryheidsoorlog in Suid-Afrika, 1899–1902*. 5 vols, Pretoria 1969–83.

Breytenbach, J. H., *Die Tweede Vryheidsoorlog*. 2 vols, Cape Town 1948–9.

Bryce, J., *Impressions of South Africa*. London 1897.

Buchan, J., *Memory Hold the Door*. London 1940.

Butler, J., *The Liberal Party and the Jameson Raid*. Oxford 1968.

Butler, W. F., *An Autobiography*. London 1911.

Cain, P. J. and Hopkins, A. G., *British Imperialism 1688–1990*. 2 vols, London 1993.

Cammack, D., *The Rand at War 1899–1902*. London 1990.

Cartwright, A. P., *The Corner House. The Early History of Johannesburg*. Cape Town 1965.

Cecil, Lady G., *Life of Robert, Marquis of Salisbury*. 4 vols, London 1931–2.

Cook, E. T., *The Rights and Wrongs of the Transvaal War*. London 1902.

Crankshaw, E., *The Forsaken Idea: A Study of Viscount Milner*. London 1952.

Darby, P., *Three Faces of Imperialism: British and American Approaches to Asia and Africa 1870–1970*. New Haven 1987.

Davenport, T. R. H., *The Afrikaner Bond (1880–1911)*. Oxford 1966.

Davenport, T. R. H., *South Africa: A Modern History*. 4th edn, London 1991.

Davey, A., *The British Pro-Boers*. London 1978.

Davis, L. E. and Huttenback, R. A., *Mammon and the Pursuit of Empire: The Economics of British Imperialism*. Cambridge 1988.

Delius, P., *'The Land Belongs To Us': The Pedi Polity, the Boers and the British in the Nineteenth Century Transvaal*. London 1983.

Denoon, D. A., *A Grand Illusion. The Failure of Imperial Policy in the Transvaal Colony during the Period of Reconstruction 1900–1905*. London 1973.

Denoon, D. A., *Southern Africa since 1800*. London 1984.

Denoon, D. A., *Settler Capitalism*. Oxford 1983.

Doyle, Sir A. Conan, *The Great Boer War*. London 1902.

Dugdale, B., *Arthur James Balfour*. 2 vols, London 1936.

Duminy, A. H., *Sir Alfred Milner and the Outbreak of the Anglo-Boer War*. Durban 1976.

Duminy, A. H., *The Capitalists and the Outbreak of the Anglo-Boer War*. Durban 1977.

Duminy, A. H. and Guest, W., *Interfering in Politics: A Biography of Sir Percy FitzPatrick*. Johannesburg 1987.

Duminy, A. H. and Guest, W., *Natal and Zululand from Earliest Times to 1910: A New History*. Pietermaritzburg 1989.

Eldridge, C. C., *British Imperialism in the Ninetenth Century*. London 1984.

Elphick, R. and Giliomee, H., eds, *The Shaping of South African Society 1652–1840*. Cape Town 1989.

Etherington, N., *Theories of Imperialism: War, Conquest and Capital*. London 1984.

Farwell, B., *The Great Boer War*. New York 1977.

Fieldhouse, D. K., *Economics and Empire 1830–1914*. London 1973.

Fieldhouse, D. K., *The Colonial Empires: A Comparative Survey from the Eighteenth Century*. London 1965/1982.

FitzPatrick, J. P., *The Transvaal from Within*. London 1899.

FitzPatrick, J. P., *Lord Milner and His Work*. Cape Town 1925.

FitzPatrick, J. P., *South African Memories*. London 1932; new edn Johannesburg, 1977.

Flint, J., *Cecil Rhodes*. London 1976.

Ford, A. G., *The Gold Standard 1880–1914, Britain and Argentina*. Oxford 1962.

Fraser, P., *Joseph Chamberlain: Radicalism and the Empire*. London 1966.

Fredrickson, G. M., *White Supremacy: A Comparative Study in American and South African History*. Oxford 1981.

French, D., *The British Way in Warfare 1688–2000*. London 1990.

Fuller, J. F. C., *The Last of the Gentlemen's Wars*. London 1937.

Galbraith, J. S., *Crown and Charter: The Early History of the British South Africa Company*. Berkeley CA, 1974.

Garson, *The Swaziland Question and the Road to the Sea 1887–1895*. Archives Yearbook for South African History 1957 Part 2, Pretoria 1957.

Garvin, J. L. and Amery, J., *Life of Joseph Chamberlain*. 6 vols, London 1932–69.

Gollin, A. M., *Proconsul in Politics: Milner*. London 1964.

Goodfellow, C. F., *Great Britain and South African Confederation 1870–1881*. Cape Town 1966.

Gordon, C. T., *The Growth of Boer Opposition to Kruger (1890–1895)*. Cape Town 1970.

Grenville, J. A. S., *Lord Salisbury and Foreign Policy: the Close of the Nineteenth Century*. London 1964.

Grundlingh, A. M., *Die 'hendsoppers' en 'joiners'. Die rasionaal en verkynsel van verraad*. Pretoria 1979.

Halperin, V., *Lord Milner and the Empire*. London 1952.

Hamer, W., *The British Army. Civil–Military Relations 1885–1905*. Oxford 1970.

Hammond, J. H., *Autobiography of John Hays Hammond*. New York 1935.

Hancock, W. K., *Smuts*. 2 vols, Cambridge 1962–8.

Hannah, W. H., *Bobs: Kipling's General*. London 1972.

Hatch, F. H. and Chalmers, J. A., *The Gold Mines of the Rand*. London 1895.

Heyningen, E. van, *The Relations between Sir Alfred Milner and W. P. Schreiner's Ministry 1898–1900*. Archives Yearbook for South African History 76, Pretoria 1978.

Hicks Beach, Lady V., *Life of Sir Michael Hicks Beach*. 2 vols, London 1932.

Hobsbawm, E., *The Age of Empire*. London 1987.

Hobson, J. A., *The War in South Africa: Its Causes and Effects*. London 1900.

Hobson, J. A., *The Psychology of Jingoism*. London 1901.

Hobson, J. A., *Imperialism: A Study*. London 1902.

Hyam, R., *Britain's Imperial Century 1815–1914*. London 1976.

Ingham, K., *Jan Christian Smuts*. London 1986.

Jaarsveld, F. A. van, *The Awakening of Afrikaner Nationalism 1868–81*. Cape Town 1961.

James, L., *The Savage Wars: British Campaigns in Africa 1870–1920*. London 1985.

Jeeves, A. H., *Migrant Labour in South Africa's Mining Economy 1890–1920*. Johannesburg 1985.

Judd, D., *Balfour and the British Empire*. London 1968.

Judd, D., *Radical Joe: A Life of Joseph Chamberlain*. London 1977.

Kennedy, E. E., *Waiting for the Boom*. Cape Town 1985.

Kiewiet, C. W. de, *A History of South Africa Social and Economic*. Oxford 1941.

Kiewiet, C. W. de, *The Imperial Factor in South Africa*. Cambridge 1937.

Krikler, J., *Revolution from Above, Rebellion from Below: The Agrarian Transvaal at the Turn of the Century*. Oxford 1993.

Kruger, D. W., *Paul Kruger*. 2 vols, Johannesburg 1961–3.

Kruger, R., *Goodbye Dolly Gray: The Story of the Boer War*. London 1959.

Kruger, S. J. P., *The Memoirs of Paul Kruger as told by himself*. 2 vols, London 1902.

Kubicek, R. V., *Economic Imperialism in Theory and Practice: The Case of South African Gold-Mining Finance 1886–1914*. Durham NC 1979.

Kubicek, R. V., *The Administration of Imperialism: Joseph Chamberlain at the Colonial Office*. Durham NC 1969.

Lang, J., *Bullion Johannesburg: Men, Mines and the Challenge of Conflict*. Johannesburg 1986.

Le May, G. H. L., *British Supremacy in South Africa 1899–1907*. Oxford 1965.

Lehmann, J., *The First Boer War*. London 1972.

Lewsen, P., *John X. Merriman: Paradoxical South African Statesman*. New Haven 1982.

Longford, E., *Jameson's Raid*. 2nd edn, London, 1982.

Lovell, R. I., *The Struggle for South Africa 1875–1899: A Study in Economic Imperialism*. New York 1934.

MacKenzie, J. M., *Propaganda and Empire: The Manipulation of British Public Opinion 1880–1960*. Manchester 1984.

MacKenzie, J. M., ed., *Popular Imperialism and the Military 1850–1950*. Manchester 1992.

Macnab, R., *Gold Their Touchstone: A History of Consolidated Goldfields*. Johannesburg 1987.

Magnus, P., *Kitchener. Portrait of an Imperialist*. London 1968.

Malan, S. F., *Politieke Strominge onder die Vrystaatse Afrikaners 1854–1899*. Durban 1982.

Mansergh, N., *The Commonwealth Experience*. 2 vols, Cambridge 1982.

Marais, J. S., *The Fall of Kruger's Republic*. Oxford 1961.

Marlowe, J., *Milner: Apostle of Empire*. London 1976.

Maurice, Sir F. and Grant, M. H., *Official History of the War in South Africa*. 4 vols text, 4 vols maps, London 1906–10.

Maurice, F. and Arthur, G., *The Life of Lord Wolseley*. London 1924.

Maylam, P., *A History of the African People of South Africa*. London 1986.

Maylam, P., *Rhodes, the Tswana and the British*. London 1980.

Mendelsohn, R., *Sammy Marks, 'The Uncrowned King of the Transvaal'*. Cape Town 1991.

Muller, C. F. J., *Die oorsprong van die Groot Trek*. Cape Town 1974.

Muller, C. F. J., *Die Britse owerheid en die Groot Trek*. 4th edn, Cape Town and Pretoria 1977.

Nasson, B., *Abraham Esau's War: A Black South African War in the Cape, 1899–1902*. Cambridge 1991.

Newton, Lord, *Lord Lansdowne: A Biography*. London 1929.

Niekerk, L. E. van, *Kruger se regterhand. 'n Biografie van dr. W. J. Leyds*. Pretoria 1985.

Niekerk, L. E. van, *Dr. W. J. Leyds as Gesant van die Zuid-Afrikaansche Republiek*. Archives Yearbook for South African History, Pretoria 1980.

Nimocks, W., *Milner's Young Men: the 'Kindergarten' in Edwardian Imperial Affairs*. London 1970.

Onselen, C. van, *Studies in the Social and Economic History of the Witwatersrand 1886–1914*. 2 vols, London 1982.

Pakenham, T., *The Boer War*. London 1979.

Phillips, Sir L., *Some Reminiscences*. London 1924/new edn (M. Fraser ed.) Johannesburg 1986.

Poel, J. van der, *The Jameson Raid*. Oxford 1951.

Poel, J. van der, *Railways and Customs Policies in South Africa 1885–1910*. London 1933.

Porter, A. N. *The Origins of the South African War: Joseph Chamberlain and the Diplomacy of Imperialism 1895–1899*. Manchester 1980.

Porter, A. N. and Holland, R. F., eds, *Money, Finance and Empire 1790–1960*. London 1986.

Porter, B., *Critics of Empire: British Radical Attitudes to Colonialism in Africa 1895–1914*. London 1968.

Porter, B., *The Lion's Share: A Short History of British Imperialism*. 2nd edn, London 1984.

Pretorius, F., *The Anglo-Boer War, 1899–1902*. Cape Town 1985.

Pretorius, F., *Kommandolewe tydens die Anglo-Boereoorlog, 1899–1902*. Cape Town and Johannesburg 1991.

Price, R., *An Imperial War and the British Working Class: Working-Class Attitudes and Reactions to the Boer War 1899–1902*. London 1972.

Pyrah, G., *Imperial Policy and South Africa 1902–1910*. Oxford 1955.

Reitz, D., *Commando: A Boer Journal of the Boer War*. London 1929.

Reitz, F. W. et al., *A Century of Wrong*. London 1899.

Rhoodie, D., *Conspirators in Conflict: The Johannesburg Reform Committee and its Role in the Conspiracy against the South African Republic*. Cape Town 1967.

Robinson, R. E. and Gallagher, J. A., *Africa and the Victorians: The Official Mind of Imperialism*. London 1961/81.

Rotberg, R., *The Founder: Cecil Rhodes and the Pursuit of Power*. Oxford 1989.

Saunders, C., *The Making of the South African Past*. Cape Town 1988.

Saunders, C., *The Annexation of the Transkeian Territories*. Archives Yearbook for South African History 1976, Pretoria 1978.

Scholtz, G. D., *Die oorsake van die Tweede Vryheidsoorlog, 1899–1902*. 2 vols, Johannesburg 1948–50.

Scholtz, G. D., *Die Tweede Vryheidsoorlog, 1899–1902*. Johannesburg 1960.

Schreuder, D. M., *Gladstone and Kruger: Liberal Government and Colonial 'Home Rule' 1880–1885*. London 1969.

Schreuder, D. M., *The Scramble for Southern Africa, 1877–1895*. Cambridge 1980.

Searle, G. R., *The Quest for National Efficiency. A Study in British Politics and Political Thought 1899–1914*. Oxford 1971.

Semmel, B., *Imperialism and Social Reform. English Social–Imperial Thought 1895–1914*. London 1960.

Shannon, R., *The Crisis of Imperialism 1865–1915*. London 1976.

Smith, M. van Wyk, *Drummer Hodge. The Poetry of the Anglo-Boer War*. Oxford 1978.

Spiers, E. M., *The Late Victorian Army 1868–1902*. Manchester 1992.

Spies, S. B., *Methods of Barbarism*. Cape Town and Pretoria 1977.

Spies, S. B., ed., *A Soldier in South Africa: The Experiences of Eustace Abadie 1899–1902*. Johannesburg 1989.

Spies, S. B., *The Origins of the Anglo-Boer War*. London 1972.

Spies, S. B. and Cameron, T., eds, *An Illustrated History of South Africa*. Johannesburg 1986.

Streak, M., *Lord Milner's Immigration Policy for the Transvaal, 1897–1905*. Johannesburg 1969.

Thompson, L., *A History of South Africa*. New Haven 1990.

Thompson, L. and Wilson, M., *The Oxford History of South Africa*. 2 vols, Oxford 1969–71.

Turrell, R. V., *Capital and Labour on the Kimberley Diamond Fields, 1871–1890*. Cambridge 1987.

Walker, E., *The Great Trek*. 5th edn, London 1956.

Walker, E., *A History of South Africa*. 3rd edn, London 1957.

Walker, E., *Cambridge History of the British Empire: South Africa* (vol. 8). 2nd edn, Cambridge 1963.

Walker, E., *Lord de Villiers and his times*. London 1925.

Walker, E., *W. P. Schreiner: A South African*. Oxford 1937.

Warwick, P., ed., *The South African War: The Anglo-Boer War 1899–1902*. London 1980.

Warwick, P., *Black People and the South African War 1899–1902*. Cambridge 1983.

Webber, H. O'K., *The Grip of Gold*. London 1936.

Wheatcroft, G., *The Randlords*. London 1985.

Wilde, R. H., *Joseph Chamberlain and the South African Republic 1895–1899*. Archives Yearbook for South African History 1956 Part 1, Pretoria 1956.

Wilkinson, H. S., *British Policy in South Africa*. London 1899.

Wilkinson, H. S., *Lessons of the War*. London 1900.

Williams, R., *Defending the Empire. The Conservative Party and British Defence Policy 1899–1915*. New Haven 1991.

Worden, N., *The Making of Modern South Africa*. Oxford 1994.

Worden, N., *Slavery in Dutch South Africa*. Cambridge 1985.

Worger, N., *South Africa's City of Diamonds: Mine Workers and Monopoly Capitalism in Kimberley, 1867–1895*. New Haven 1987.

Worsfold, B., *Lord Milner's Work in South Africa*. London 1906.

Younghusband, F. E., *South Africa Today*. London 1899.

Index